MW01503164

THE FABRIC OF PEACE IN AFRICA

HENRY RICHMOND SLACK

EX LIBRIS

THE FABRIC OF PEACE IN AFRICA
Looking beyond the State

Pamela Aall and Chester A. Crocker, Editors
Foreword by Kofi Annan

Centre for International
Governance Innovation

© 2017 Centre for International Governance Innovation

ALL RIGHTS RESERVED. No part of this publication may be reproduced, stored in a retrieval system or transmitted by any means, electronic, mechanical, photocopying, recording or otherwise, without the prior written permission of the publisher, application for which should be addressed to the Centre for International Governance Innovation, 67 Erb Street West, Waterloo, Ontario, Canada N2L 6C2 or publications@cigionline.org.

ISBN 978-1-928096-36-8 (cloth)
ISBN 978-1-928096-35-1 (paper)
ISBN 978-1-928096-41-2 (ePUB)
ISBN 978-1-928096-42-9 (ePDF)

Library and Archives Canada Cataloguing in Publication

   The fabric of peace in Africa : looking beyond the state / foreword by Kofi Annan ; edited by Pamela Aall and Chester A. Crocker.

Includes bibliographical references.
Issued in print and electronic formats.
ISBN 978-1-928096-36-8 (hardcover).--ISBN 978-1-928096-35-1 (softcover).--
ISBN 978-1-928096-41-2 (HTML).--ISBN 978-1-928096-42-9 (PDF)

   1. Peace-building--Africa. 2. Conflict management--Africa. 3. Social institutions--Africa. I. Aall, Pamela R., author, editor II. Crocker, Chester, A., author, editor III. Centre for International Governance Innovation, issuing body

JZ5584.A35F33 2017   327.1'72096   C2017-900004-7
                                                 C2017-900005-5

The opinions expressed in this publication are those of the authors and do not necessarily reflect the views of the Centre for International Governance Innovation or its Board of Directors.

Published by the Centre for International Governance Innovation.

Printed and bound in Canada.

Cover design by Melodie Wakefield.

Centre for International Governance Innovation and CIGI are registered trademarks.

**Centre for International
Governance Innovation**

Centre for International Governance Innovation
67 Erb Street West
Waterloo, ON Canada N2L 6C2

www.cigionline.org

Contents

Foreword

Kofi Annan

Those of us who have worked on conflict know the dangers of a breakdown of the social compact between state and society: instability, ethnic or religious discrimination, and a descent into violence. In extreme cases, governments become the agents of gross human rights abuses to their citizenry, as in Cambodia, Rwanda, Darfur and Syria. In the 1990s and 2000s, the United Nations led the international community to recognize that when a government is unable or fails to provide security for its citizens, the international community has a responsibility to act. We moved the concept of security beyond the state to embrace individuals, peoples and groups.

These developments are universal and they have direct relevance to the peace and security of Africa. The African continent has made important progress — political and economic — in recent decades, but some countries remain in the throes of violent conflict, while others are prone to relapses. As a result, Africa continues to host a majority of

UN blue helmets. What has changed, however, is that African states themselves are playing a bigger role in their own collective security. The African Union has developed an impressive set of institutions to prevent, manage and resolve conflict, including early warning capacity.

These African solutions must also reach beyond the state. Soon after stepping down as UN Secretary-General, I worked to help organize a multi-stakeholder effort in the Kenyan electoral crisis of 2007-2008. It is not an exaggeration to recognize that the strength of Kenyan civil society institutions helped to bring the country back from the brink.

This brings me to this book. *The Fabric of Peace in Africa: Looking beyond the State* addresses the societal environment of conflict and the potential contribution to managing conflict of a wide range of social groups and institutions. These studies, edited and framed by scholar-practitioners Chester A. Crocker and Pamela Aall, bring together leading African and external experts who make a significant contribution to our understanding of the challenges and possibilities of African efforts to build sustainable peace and security. This volume shines a light on the role that individuals, groups and social institutions play in peace and conflict.

The authors in this book delve into topics ranging from religion and education policy to migration and youth engagement in order to understand how these groups and organizations affect social attitudes and proclivities toward violence and peace. It is clear from this examination that all those institutions that respond to conflict — the United Nations, the African Union, the sub-regional organizations and non-government organizations — need to reach out beyond the state in order to build a firm foundation for peace. The book is a rewarding mosaic that looks at Africa's conflict challenges from the inside as well as the outside, and helps us understand the complexities of building peace and building equitable, accountable and inclusive societies.

January 2017

Acknowledgements

In this book, as in its predecessor, *Minding the Gap: African Conflict Management in a Time of Change*, we have to start by thanking the authors both for their wisdom and their commitment to the project. Through their contributions, they have furthered our understanding of the link between conflict and its larger social environment. Individually and collectively, they have been wonderful partners in this venture. We also thank the Centre of International Governance Innovation (CIGI) for its critical role in making this project possible. President Rohinton Medora and Fen Hampson, director of the Global Security & Politics Program, gave the leadership, wise counsel and full support needed to allow this project to grow and thrive. Research Fellow Simon Palamar played many roles — herding his two Washington-based editors, advocating for the project both at CIGI and in the wider community, managing the authors and giving critical research help to the project. Brenda Woods, Linda Nilsson and Kaili Hilkewich made sure that the project ran smoothly and effectively, and in the right direction. With Simon and his CIGI colleague Anne Blayney, senior conference planner, they made the authors' meeting in Waterloo, Ontario, in June 2016 into an exceptional opportunity for the authors to meet and exchange ideas. Special thanks to Publisher Carol Bonnett and her team, particularly Editor Sharon McCartney, for bringing their excellent skills and judgment to the manuscript, and to the rest of the CIGI staff whose hard work has made this project a pleasure.

We are very grateful for the guidance, cautions and creative ideas from our core group of advisers: Johnnie Carson, Payton Knopf, George Moose and David Smock, as well as authors Princeton Lyman, Elizabeth Murray, Susan Stigant and Bill Zartman. We also benefited greatly from advice and support of Jakkie Cilliers of the Institute for Security Studies in Pretoria, Alan Doss of the Kofi Annan Foundation, Lauren Van Metre for her thoughts on resilience, Andrew McPherson for research, as well as many others whose work has helped shape our thinking.

Finally, we would like to recognize Callisto Madavo, who passed away as this book was going to press. Dr. Madavo, a colleague of Chet's at Georgetown University and former vice president at the World Bank, supported fully the idea that lay behind this book project — that the wider social environment was key to bringing peace to troubled countries. He was persuasive in defining the role that the private sector could play and his chapter is a strong expression of a constructive and inclusive approach to resolving conflict. He will be missed by his many friends and colleagues.

Abbreviations and Acronyms

ACCORD	African Centre for the Constructive Resolution of Disputes	AU	African Union
		AUPSC	AU Peace and Security Council
ACHPR	African Commission on Human and Peoples' Rights	BBC	British Broadcasting Corporation
ACtHPR	African Court on Human and Peoples' Rights	CAR	Central African Republic
ADR	alternative dispute resolution	CAT	Convention against Torture
AFDB	African Development Bank	CBMs	confidence-building measures
AFISMA	International Support Mission in Mali	CBOs	community-based organizations
AFRICOM	United States Africa Command	CBS	Central Bureau of Statistics
		CIGI	Centre for International Governance Innovation
AMISOM	African Union Mission in Somalia	CJTF-HOA	Combined Joint Task Force – Horn of Africa
ANC	African National Congress		
APSA	African Peace and Security Architecture	CNDD-FDD	National Council for the Defense of Democracy – Forces for the Defense of Democracy
AQIM	al-Qaeda in the Islamic Maghreb		
ASF	African Standby Force	COI	Commission of Inquiry

COMESA	Common Market for Eastern and Southern Africa	FAB	Forces Armées Burundaises
CPA	Comprehensive Peace Agreement (Sudan)	FARDC	Armed Forces of the Democratic Republic of the Congo
CSIS	Canadian Security Intelligence Service	FDI	foreign direct investment
CSOs	civil society organizations	FDLR	Democratic Force for the Liberation of Rwanda
CURRASW	Curriculum Assessment and Examinations	FGS	Federal Government of Somalia
CVE	countering violent extremism	FRELIMO	Mozambique Liberation Front
DAC	Development Assistance Committee (OECD)	GBV	gender-based violence
DDPD	Doha Document for Peace in Darfur	GIZ	Deutsche Gesellschaft für Internationale Zusammenarbeit
DDR	disarmament, demobilization and reintegration	GNU	Government for National Unity
DFID	Department for International Development	HD Centre	The Centre for Humanitarian Dialogue
DHS	Demographic and Health Surveys	HDI	Human Development Index
DKRI	Dandal Kura Radio International	ICC	International Criminal Court
DPA	Darfur Political Agreement	ICCPR	International Covenant on Civil and Political Rights
DPKO	Department for Peacekeeping Operations (UN)	ICG	International Crisis Group
DPP	Darfur Political Process	ICGLR	International Conference on the Great Lakes Region
DRC	Democratic Republic of Congo	ICRC	International Committee of the Red Cross
DW	Deutsche Welle	ICTR	International Criminal Tribunal for Rwanda
EAC	East African Community		
EACJ	East African Court of Justice	ICU	Islamic Court Union
ECCAS	Economic Community of Central African States	IGAD	Intergovernmental Authority on Development
ECOMIB	ECOWAS mission in Guinea-Bissau	IFFs	illicit financial flows
ECOMIL	ECOWAS mission in Liberia	IFIs	international financial institutions
ECOWAS	Economic Community of West African States	IPCC	Intergovernmental Panel on Climate Change
EFA	Education for All	iPRS	interim Poverty Reduction Strategy
EUFOR	European Union Force		

ISIS	Islamic State of Iraq and al-Sham		MSN	Mediation Support Network
KCSE	Kenya Certificate of Secondary Education		MUJAO	Movement for Unity and Jihad in West Africa
KMF	Knowledge Management Framework for Mediation Processes		NATO	North Atlantic Treaty Organization
KNEC	Kenya National Examinations Council		NCA	National Constituent Assembly
LGA	local government area		NEPAD	New Partnership for Africa's Development
LNP	Liberian National Police		NGO	non-governmental organization
LRA	Lord's Resistance Army		OAU	Organization of African Unity
LURD	Liberians United for Reconstruction and Development		OECD	Organisation for Economic Co-operation and Development
LVB	Lake Victoria basin			
M23	March 23 rebellion		PEAP	Panel of Eminent African Personalities
MENA	Middle East and North Africa		PoW	Panel of the Wise
MICOPAX	Mission for the Consolidation of Peace in Central Africa		PRS	Poverty Reduction Strategy
MINUSCA	UN Multidimensional Integrated Stabilization Mission in the CAR		PSGs	peace- and state-building goals
			R2P	responsibility to protect
MISCA	International Support Mission to the CAR		RCD	Rally for Congolese Democracy
MLC	Movement for the Liberation of the Congo		RECs	Regional Economic Communities
MNJTF	Multinational Joint Task Force		RENAMO	Mozambican National Resistance
MNLA	National Movement for the Liberation of the Azawad		RFI	Radio-France Internationale
			RNP	Rwanda National Police
MODEL	Model for Democracy in Liberia		ROs	Recognized Organizations
MONUC	United Nations Organization Mission in the DRC		RTNC	Radio-Télévision nationale congolaise
MONUSCO	United Nations Organization Stabilization Mission in the DRC		SABC	South African Broadcasting Corporation
MRC	Mombasa Republican Council		SADC	Southern African Development Community
			SAF	Sudan Armed Forces
MRSB	Mara River sub-basin		SALW	small arms and light weapons

SAP	South African Police
SAPS	South African Police Service
SATRC	South African Truth and Reconciliation Commission
SMS	short message service
SOCOM	Special Operations Command
SOEs	state-owned enterprises
SPLA	Sudanese People's Liberation Army
SPLM	Sudanese People's Liberation Movement
SPLM-N	Sudanese People's Liberation Movement – North
SRSGs	Special Representatives of the Secretary-General
SSD	security sector development
SSPS	South Sudan Police Service
SSR	security sector reform
SST	security sector transformation
SWAPO	South-West African People's Organization
TAWA	Tonj Area Women's Association
UCDP/PRIO	Uppsala Conflict Data Program/International Peace Research Institute Oslo
UGTT	Tunisian General Labour Union
UN DESA	UN Department of Economic and Social Affairs
UNAMID	UN-AU Mission in Darfur
UNCST	Uganda National Council for Science and Technology
UNDP	United Nations Development Programme
UNECA	United Nations Economic Commission for Africa
UNEP	United Nations Environment Programme
UNESCO	United Nations Educational, Scientific and Cultural Organization
UNMIL	UN Mission in Liberia
UNMISS	UN Mission in the Republic of South Sudan
UNSC	United Nations Security Council
UNSOA	UN Support Office to AMISOM
UNSOM	UN Assistance Mission in Somalia
USAID	United States Agency for International Development
USIP	United States Institute of Peace
VMT	Verification and Monitoring Team
VOA	Voice of America

Part One
Introduction

1

The Social Environment and Conflict in Africa

Pamela Aall and Chester A. Crocker

The prevailing discourse about Africa in the peace and conflict realm paints a picture of a conflict-ridden continent, with the worst refugee and internal migration problem in the world. The discourse emphasizes that it is an extremely poor region, prone to barely containable epidemics, damaged by its colonial history and increasingly threatened by Islamic extremism. And indeed, Africa has seen dozens of conflicts over the past two decades concerning a variety of issues — land, resources, political power, profits, security, religion and identity. Often at the core of these conflicts are profound disagreements over the basic vision of what the nation is, struggles over state-society relations and contests over who gets to rule.

However, there is another side to the story. Some of these conflicts — for instance, Sierra Leone, Liberia, Côte d'Ivoire, Rwanda, Angola, Namibia and South Africa — have come to an end. In other cases, early

action has prevented conflict from spreading. In 2008 in Kenya, for instance, a determined mediation effort by former UN Secretary-General Kofi Annan stopped the post-election violence before it became widespread. Other countries are relatively peaceful. According to the *2015 Global Peace Index* of the Institute for Economics and Peace, eight African countries rank in the top 60 most peaceful countries: Mauritius (25), Botswana (31), Namibia (48), Senegal (49), Malawi (51), Ghana (54), Zambia (55) and Sierra Leone (59) (Institute of Economics and Peace 2015).

Responding to conflicts requires concerted action to manage crises of inter-communal violence, political discord and humanitarian consequences of prolonged fighting. There is also, however, a need to rebuild communities, societies and states torn apart by the conflict and to address the long-term social and economic impact of the conflict. Important questions are how well African states and societies cope with these dual challenges and what role the international community plays in building up or undercutting conflict management capacity. Just as important, however, is the question of what accounts for the difference between societies that experience conflict and societies that manage to resist falling into conflict or resolve conflicts once they have broken out. It may be clear that the answer is both multi-dimensional and context-specific, and involves enlightened leadership, a stable neighbourhood, a degree of economic stability, legitimate governance and, at times, help from the international community. What is not so clear is how to achieve these ends.

In order to answer these questions, the Centre for International Governance Innovation (CIGI) undertook a multi-year review of African conflict management capacity. The first part of the project examined how African institutions and partners in the international community cope with traditional security threats — power challenges, economic struggles, the inability of weak states to assert control and provide security over their territory, terrorism, arms flows and religious extremism. *Minding the Gap: African Conflict Management in a Time of Change*, published in March 2016, marked the culmination of this first phase. *Minding the Gap* focused on the two principal instruments for managing these challenges: coercive or semi-coercive strategies (such as peacekeeping, peace enforcement, armed intervention and sanctions) and political strategies (such as mediation, negotiation, facilitation, high-level groups, summits, commissions and other political instruments). In so doing, it looked at state-based and regional organizational capacity, as well as the contributions of civil society and international partners (Aall and Crocker 2016).

This book grows out of the second part of the project and examines societal actors, norms and institutions in Africa that shape social attitudes toward peace and conflict. Understanding the role played by the wider society presents a number of challenges, not least because "wider society" is a flexible concept and can include any number of political, economic, social, religious, educational and cultural institutions

and groups. Some of these groups exist within the organized civil society space or, like elders, religious leaders and traditional authorities, have recognized roles in society. Others are less defined but potentially powerful collectivities (for example, youth, women or migrants). Some of these entities are official institutions (for example, schools and universities) that play key roles in shaping social attitudes; others, such as the news media, may reflect official views or offer an alternative to those views. Other official institutions — the courts and the police — exist in that borderland where individuals meet official authorities and develop opinions about their effectiveness and legitimacy. We use the term the "social environment" of conflict to refer to this open-ended universe of peoples, institutions and resources that have some potential to help societies become resilient in the face of risks of conflict onset or recurrence.

The ability to manage conflict is only partly a function of political leadership, good peacekeeping practice, effective mediation and the provision of sufficient official capabilities. The capacity also resides in the relationship between state and society, and among different identity and interest groups within a society. It lies in the teaching of civics and history, in the quality of professional associations, in ideas encouraged by traditional and social media, in the habits inculcated by old and new legal norms, in inter-religious behaviours, and in the arts and cultural events. These social relationships and attitudes can either knit together a society or tear it apart. Lost in the traditional approach to understanding conflict management is the contribution to peace and stability that may come from the groups and social institutions that inhabit the conflict zone. Looking at a number of these institutions and groups — including organized civil society, religion, education, the security sector, legal norms and traditions, private enterprise, the media, women's groups and youth groups — this book explores the impact of political, economic and demographic stresses on societal stability in Africa, as well as approaches to building conflict management capacity in the social environment of conflict.

Four Links between Society and Conflict

The link between conflict and various individuals, social groups and social institutions has been the subject of much scholarly and practitioner-oriented research, especially since the explosion of internal conflict in the 1990s. Analysis of the role that society plays in conflict typically focus on one of three characterizations: social groups and institutions as drivers of conflict, victims of conflict, or fixers of conflict. We identify a fourth characterization by examining the overall role that these institutions, groups and societal characteristics play in building or weakening a society's capacity to resist the outbreak of conflict or to recover from conflict once it has broken out.

Social Groups and Institutions as Drivers of Conflict

One view of the intersection between conflict and society emphasizes the role that social groups and institutions play as drivers of conflict. Much of this work revolves around individual and group attitudes and motivations, especially in determining why conflict becomes violent. Morton Deutsch, Herbert Kelman, Dean Pruitt, Louis Kriesberg and others have opened a broad avenue to understanding why people fight (Deutsch 1973, Kelman 1990; Pruitt 2005; Kriesberg 2007). They emphasize the psychological and social processes that lead to fighting, such as competition, isolation or mutually incompatible goals. Others have analyzed the motivations of terrorists and violent extremists, stressing that terrorists are often acting rationally within their own environments (Post 2007; Crenshaw 2000). Clark McCauley and Sophia Moskalenko (2008) identify 12 mechanisms or avenues toward political radicalization, including personal victimization and political grievance at the individual level. At the group level, the mechanisms include extreme cohesion within the group or, conversely, extreme competition to dominate the thoughts and actions of the group.

Stephen Stedman's (1997) studies of spoilers provide a typology of political/military actors that can and may undermine peace processes. He makes the point that while some of them are insiders, others are outsiders and both may be leaders or followers. Recognizing the role of followers is important for understanding the relationship between spoilers and the wider public, because followers often provide the link to a broader community of players that have a stake in the outcome. Ted Robert Gurr (1970) examined the gap between a person's expectations about what he or she deserves and the reality of what they get. When expectations are higher than reality, it can lead to frustration, and if prolonged and deeply felt, can result in aggression against others. The same dynamic operates in social groups. Groups that feel relative deprivation vis-à-vis other groups may resort to violence out of a general frustration.

Frances Stewart and Graham Brown (2007) have also explored the effect of relative deprivation — or horizontal political, social and economic inequalities — and its link to conflict. They find that the extent to which the basic needs of certain groups in society are systematically denied and discriminated against by those in power can lay the seeds for conflict, especially if there is no legitimate way to channel those grievances through the political process.

There have also been examinations in both the scholarly and practitioner worlds of how social institutions can contribute to conflict. Some have looked at the effect of schools, curriculum and teaching on creating or preserving positive or negative impressions of other groups. These analysts point out the critical influence of these institutions on the formation of attitudes and behaviour (Korostelina, Lässig and Ihrig 2013; Williams 2014; Smith 2011).

During the Bosnian conflict, for instance, each of the three ethnic groups actively used the education system to promote adverse images of the others. After the conflict was over, the international community tried to reform the education system in Bosnia by pushing for a system of joint education.

A 2010 report on the state of Bosnian schools pointed out that after 15 years, Muslim and Catholic students were still learning in segregated classrooms. They attended the same school but used separate entrances (Magill 2010; Reed 2014). The conflict, while officially over, was perpetuated by the education system. The growing hostility between Christian and Muslim communities in Africa may be similarly fostered in education systems around the continent. Educational resources may also become the object of conflict when competing political or social groups argue over their allocation.

The Bosnian example illustrates how difficult it is to develop a response to groups and institutions that act as perpetuators or drivers of conflict. Changing social institutions such as schools not only involves bringing change to institutions that transmit core values of a society, but also generally involves engaging ministries of education. In those cases in which the government has been a party to the conflict, government ministries often reflect the same hostilities and suspicion of the other side as the political leaders. While there have been attempts at inoculating societies from radicalization through programs aimed at countering violent extremism (CVE), the growing number of recruits to ISIS (Islamic State of Iraq and al-Sham) and other radical groups indicates that scholars and practitioners have not yet fully understood how to prevent extremism or de-radicalize individuals and groups that have embraced an extremist agenda.

Social Groups and Institutions as Victims of Conflict

Another approach to looking at society and conflict explores conflict's harmful effect on social groups and institutions. Conflict has always resulted in civilian casualties and suffering. However, the tactics of today's combatants places special emphasis on this element. In 2014, for instance, Boko Haram — the extremist Islamic rebel group operating in northeast Nigeria — kidnapped 250 students from a girls' school in Chibok in Borno State. A year later, Al-Shabaab staged a gruesome attack on Garissa University in Kenya. Schools have become targets for groups spreading terror in the new conflict environment, just as have other places important to community life, such as churches, mosques, synagogues, temples, markets, shopping malls, train stations, major thoroughfares, restaurants and places of entertainment. Journalists, too, find themselves at risk in a number of conflict zones. According to the Committee to Protect Journalists (2016), hundreds of journalists have been killed in combat over the past 25 years, and many more have been murdered or killed on dangerous assignments in the same period. The prevalence of sexual violence in conflict situations, kidnapping and forced conscription of children, and massive refugee crises have highlighted the plight of individuals in today's conflicts.

The human rights field has long focused on the deleterious effect that conflict has on individuals. In the 1990s, this perspective entered into the security field as well. A common tactic in the brutal civil wars of the 1990s was to target civilian non-combatants as part of the war campaign. In these wars, it was apparent that governments could not protect their civilian populations. Worse still, in a number of conflicts (Rwanda, Burundi, Sudan, the Democratic Republic of Congo), the government or government troops were the source of the threat to civilian life and safety. These experiences introduced changes in the conception of security from the safety of the state to the safety of the individual. In addition, many held that in circumstances where the state itself was the problem, the international respect for national sovereignty had to yield to the protection of human lives. In other words, the international community had a responsibility to protect individuals against the predations of the state (International Commission on Intervention and State Sovereignty 2001).

A number of scholars and practitioners helped to develop the concept of human security (United Nations Development Programme 1994;

Hampson 2001; Commission on Human Security 2003; Owen 2013). A common element among these works was the focus on the individual and the protection of the integrity of that individual. Beyond that, however, there was disagreement over whether the concept should be applied broadly to cover all threats to individuals (disease and natural disaster as well as conflict), or more narrowly to encompass only the threats to individuals from conflict (Owen 2004). In addition, some analysts criticized the whole concept for its lack of clarity and definition (Paris 2001; Newman 2010).

Despite its shortcomings, an international endorsement of the human security concept came rather rapidly. Using the narrower concept of threats to individuals from conflict, the International Commission on Intervention and State Sovereignty developed its recommendations on the responsibility to protect (referred to as R2P) in 2001 and, four years later, 191 heads of states endorsed this principle at the 2005 World Summit of the United Nations (UN) General Assembly (International Commission on Intervention and State Sovereignty 2001, UN General Assembly 2005). This endorsement, however, has not led to consistent policy, principally because the international community has not agreed on implementation. As a result, cases of clear violation of human security have met with insufficient international reaction to make a difference.

Social Groups and Institutions as Fixers of Conflict

Until the 1990s, there was limited space for civil society organizations in the conflict resolution sphere. The end of the Cold War, however, provided an opening for new voices and new actors. The internal conflicts of the late 1980s and the 1990s — for instance in Mozambique and Rwanda — drove conflicts deep into society. Governments did not have the skills or experience to deal with the social or ethnic violence that resulted from these civil conflicts. The United Nations and its

specialized agencies also were overstretched and unprepared to deal with multiple civil wars, and in need of support from other actors. The private, non-governmental sector stepped into this gap to help meet the demands these new conflicts brought about.

In the 1990s, research on the non-governmental organization (NGO) community tended to focus on international NGOs and their impact on peace and conflict (Stephenson 2005; Perito 2007).[1] Over the past 15 years, both practitioners and academics have increasingly turned their attention toward the civil societies within conflict states (Paffenholz and Spurk 2006; Paffenholz 2010).[2] However, even in those early years, scholars such as John Paul Lederach (1997) pointed to the role that "insider partials" — peacemakers from within the conflict environment — play in effecting reconciliation. In another study, Herbert Kelman (1990) developed a model of problem-solving workshops that brought together influential individuals who represented different camps in a conflict.

---

1   While NGOs had been a growing presence in the international sphere since the mid-nineteenth century, their growth exploded after World War II. There were only about 3,000 international NGOs in 1945, but there were over 13,000 in 1990 and nearly 40,000 by 2006.

2   Definitions of civil society abound. A useful one is found in "Civil Society, Civic Engagement and Peacebuilding" by Thania Paffenholz and Christoph Spurk (2006):
 • "Civil society is the sector of voluntary action within institutional forms that are distinct from those of the state, family and market, keeping in mind that in practice the boundaries between these sectors are often complex and blurred;
 • It consists of a large and diverse set of voluntary organizations, often competing with each other and oriented to specific interests. It comprises non-state actors and associations that are not purely driven by private or economic interests, are autonomously organized, and interact in the public sphere; and
 • Civil society is independent from the state, but it is oriented toward and interacts closely with the state and the political sphere."

In sectarian conflicts, the practice of interfaith dialogues has engaged religious leadership and laity in efforts to bring peace (Abu-Nimer, Welty and Khoury 2007; Wuye and Ashafa 1999). Other forms of dialogue, including national dialogues, have involved individuals, social groups and institutions in conflict resolution processes in a way that builds social cohesion (Ramsbotham 2010). Pressure on the United Nations and national governments to increase the inclusion of women in peace processes reflects this growing understanding that women's perspectives — which, as a result of their roles, often reflect grassroots concerns — are essential to achieving a sustainable peace.

Through its focus on the need to move beyond political actors and the "guys with guns" to engage civil society and social groups in peace building, the conflict resolution field has moved closer to the field of economic and social development (Hughes et al. 2014).[3] The challenge for both fields is to understand how best to develop capacity in local actors. Here, it is important to note the difficulty in a conflict situation of identifying the local organizations that have the legitimacy and credibility to act as peacemakers. As Sharath Srinivasan (2016) points out, Western donors often focus on those civil society institutions that have mastered the intricacies of developing proposals

and producing reports to be read by Western partners. These, however, are not necessarily the organizations that are the most effective in engaging and representing their communities or the wider society.

Social Groups and Institutions as Sources of Social Cohesion and Resilience

In addition to these three views of the societal environment, one can also look at the ability of social groups and institutions to resist or overcome conflict. This fourth view looks at the intersection between conflict and groups or institutions that affect social attitudes and build social cohesion and resilience.

Resilience is a term with a long pedigree but little agreement on its meaning. Some have used the term resilience to capture the characteristics that allow a society to resist or recover from conflict. In their review of works on resilience (for a Rockefeller Foundation project on building resilience in poor and vulnerable communities in the face of climate change), Patrick Martin-Breen and J. Marty Anderies (2011) identify three principal definitions of the concept of resilience. The first definition, and the one most commonly identified with the term, emphasizes the ability to return to the *status quo ante*, "… to withstand a large disturbance without, in the end, changing, disintegrating, or becoming permanently damaged…" (ibid., 5-6). For this definition, for instance, resilience resembles a physical property found in material like rubber that can absorb energy in the form of pressure or blows and return to its original shape.

The second definition recognizes that change will be part of the outcome no matter how well an entity can "withstand a large disturbance." Nonetheless, the entity is able to adapt and keep functioning, delivering services and carrying out its mission. This definition, which focuses on systems, holds that "resilience…can be defined as maintaining system function in the event of a disturbance" (ibid., 7). Resilience in this case might describe a

---

3   The New Deal for Engagement in Fragile States, endorsed by the Fourth High Level Forum on Aid Effectiveness held in Busan, Korea, in 2011, changed the formula for development. Instead of avoiding the political obstacles that can hinder social and economic development, the New Deal put forward goals that touched the heart of the relationship between state and society — inclusive politics, citizen security and access to justice. The New Deal also included voices from the recipient countries: the g7+ (a group of endorsing countries that includes among others Afghanistan, Central African Republic, Democratic Republic of Congo, Liberia, South Sudan, Sierra Leone and Timor-Leste) have volunteered to implement the New Deal, including the governance principles. This model is very different from the traditional development approaches that stressed foreign aid and individual development projects.

psychological capability to absorb hardships and continue on. In this sense, a society or country may be resilient in the face of hardship.

The first definition emphasizes the ability to preserve. The second definition brings in the ability to adapt. A third definition — resilience in complex adaptive systems — includes the ability to innovate, to "withstand, recover from, and reorganize in response to crises" (ibid., 7). Here, resilience may be a result of specific governmental or societal action that institutions have taken to prepare for different outcomes. Together, these three definitions suggest that resilience incorporates an innate ability to preserve core functioning with flexibility in the face of change, and a willingness to learn from experience and to innovate.

Our focus in this book is on resilience in the face of conflict, on the ability to resist and recover from violent disruptions of peaceful social order. Resilience in the sphere of conflict management shares many of the characteristics of the definition above, particularly in the ability to both endure and adapt. However, given the political nature of conflict, resilience to conflict also incorporates a political element — the interaction between a government and the social institutions and groups in the wider society. Lauren Van Metre (2014) has identified three key components of a society resilient to conflict: a sense of shared meaning and solidarity among society members; appropriate distribution of resources, services and rights; and inclusive forms of governance. Building on her work, we will focus on three elements of resilience: social cohesion; a sense of fairness and equity; and an ability to participate in decision making.

Research and understanding on how to build and support a resilient society is still in its early stages. It is also important to recognize that resilience is a relatively neutral property in terms of the goals of the resilient institution. Governments can be resilient — at least for a period of time — whether or not they embrace accountability and transparency or introduce democratic practices.

The resilience of a number of African elected leaders who have imposed constitutional changes in order to stay in office is a case in point. And, at times, the ability to endure and adapt inhibits the demand for change, as may be the case in Zimbabwe. These examples illustrate the point that resilience can sometimes promote social unrest and violence.

The Shape of the Book

In order to understand this complex social terrain, this book brings together an impressive set of guides from Africa, Europe and North America. Each author brings years of research and analysis on African conflict management to the task. As a whole, they have produced a volume that reaches far beyond conventional analyses of the sources of conflict and the means to address them. The overarching questions that these authors explore are what constitutes social cohesion and resilience in the face of conflict; what are the threats to cohesion and resilience, how can the positive elements be fostered and by whom?

The first several chapters in the book examine deeply the major stresses that contribute to conflict in the African setting: stresses over governance, identity, economic differences and environmental change. By so doing, these chapters help to deepen understanding of the nature and complex interactions involved in social conflicts. Pierre Englebert points out that while social conflict may be associated with ethnic or religious divisions within a state, it is often intensified by battles over the vision of the state and over control of the power and resources. He argues that the "plural softness" — that is, the state's inability or lack of desire to privilege one ethnic group over all others — that characterizes many African states, serves to reduce the possibilities of revolt against a sitting government. Eghosa Osaghae's chapter on the ethnic conflicts involving Fulani herdsmen in Nigeria, however, shows the difficulties of maintaining a sense of *balance* among ethnicities when dealing with groups whose identities are nomadic and not bound by borders.

Arnim Langer and Leila Demarest add further depth to understanding the link between the outbreak of violent conflict and the unequal distribution of economic, social and political opportunities and status among groups. They point out that in situations of horizontal inequalities, violence may be initiated by the more deprived and excluded groups. On the other hand, it may be a tool of the more privileged groups that wish to preserve their standing and advantages. Or, it may arise out of other circumstances. In the case of Boko Haram, the presence of marginalized and unemployed youth in northern Nigeria provided an endless flow of recruits to its cause. Violence does not arise from inherent ethnic, cultural or religious differences, but from group marginalization and the absence of fair treatment and equal opportunity. The chapter by Donald Anthony Mwiturubani shows how climate change can produce stress and potential conflict at different levels of society. This is a cause for concern for areas experiencing drought and other climate-induced challenges, but it also indicates that resilience is important at the level of family, community, state and region, and should be supported at each of these points.

The next section of the book looks at several institutions that lie in the borderland between state and society and play important roles in forming social attitudes toward peace and conflict. It is clear from these chapters that many governments in Africa have failed to establish institutions or policies that promote tolerance and social cohesion. Sometime this failure is the result of unintended consequences. Charles Olungah's chapter examines the result of expanding the number of higher education institutions in Kenya in order to educate increasing numbers of people. He notes, however, that the new institutions are tribally based and serve to reinforce ethnic and tribal differences and unequal access, rather than build a national or regional identity. Other failures are the result of attempts at reform that were not well conceived, were cast too narrowly, or were based on wrong assumptions, as Mariama Awumbila's chapter on urban migrants clearly shows.

The chapter on rule of law and the role of justice by Allan Ngari and Raeesah Cassim Cachalia, on the other hand, focuses on the weakness of government institutions that deal with justice in many African states and the consequent lack of respect for the rule of law. They argue that the reform of legal systems needs to be a central part of post-conflict reconstruction, but warn that this period carries danger for strengthening legal systems. Following this theme, Mathurin Houngnikpo's chapter on security sector reform looks at the experience in six countries, noting that leadership motivations and uses of the security sector explain the key differences, and concludes that reform needs to involve a whole-of-government approach in order to be effective.

In the pursuit of elements that strengthen the ability to knot together fractures, the book then turns to the complicated issue of inclusion in peace processes and post-conflict governance. Alex de Waal's chapter sets the stage, developing a framework for understanding different concentric circles of inclusion in peace negotiations, from armed belligerents to civil society. Rejecting the argument that increasing participation is inefficient in a peace process, he argues that the increased legitimacy of an inclusive process can make it more efficient. The chapters that follow — Gilles Yabi on civil society, Callisto Madavo on the business sector, Akinyi Walender on women, and Marc Sommers on youth — give powerful illustrations of the potential of these groups to play a constructive role for peace and the systematic ways that both national governments and international actors exclude them from peace processes, political negotiations and in some cases from playing a part in society in general.

The last section of the book focuses on current approaches to strengthening resilience and social cohesion. I William Zartman examines the under-explored area of indigenous methods of conflict resolution in African societies and notes that these methods emphasize restoration over retribution, with the desired objective to re-establish the status quo and "proper functioning of social relations." The modern era may have eroded these approaches and delegitimized the customary authorities that exercised them, but it has not erased them completely. National dialogues in post-transition or post-conflict situations have received both national and international support as effective ways of increasing participation and resolving conflicts. Susan Stigant and Elizabeth Murray examine the record of these dialogues in Africa and conclude that dialogue processes can increase the sense of participation in the process of envisioning the future, but only if political authorities are willing to listen. Lacking political support, they are window-dressing exercises, giving the central authorities the appearance of popular support rather than a real mandate.

Alex Thurston's chapter notes that religion is only one factor in the complex conflicts on the continent. He is skeptical of the major approaches to resolving conflicts with a religious character: entrenching conservative religious leaders in positions of power, inter-religious dialogues and strategies to counter violent extremism. Instead, he echoes some of Pierre Englebert's conclusions about plural softness, and suggests that the growing fragmentation within the religious communities in Africa provides opportunities for engagement, encouraging different points of view and increasing democracy, accountability and conflict resolution within and perhaps between religious communities.

The David Smith and Stephanie Wolters chapter on media in Africa notes that as the principal source of news, radio can help to build social cohesion in post-conflict communities. However, as long as governments — and international aid groups — overlook smaller, less dominant communities, they will not be able to reach those groups on the marginalized end of the horizontal inequality spectrum. Unless broadcasters make efforts to reach these communities through their programming, radio broadcasts may serve to widen long-standing fractures rather than bridge them.

Why are some regions more resilient than others in resisting and recovering from conflict? Alexandre Marc, Neelam Verjee and Stephen Mogaka consider this question by looking at the history and current status of west Africa, a region in Africa that has seen the outbreak of civil conflict decrease markedly since 2000. Reasons for this trend seem to lie in the increasing democratization of the region, and the opening up of a more inclusive political space. Responsive regional organizations and the growth of civil society have also contributed to increasing ability to arrive at political or legal solutions for contested issues.

Finally, Princeton Lyman reminds us of the critical importance of leadership in building up resilience, but he also sets a challenge to civil society organizations to act. He underscores the point that resilience does not mean acceptance or quiescence in the face of conflict. It means building the ability to preserve core functions while allowing changes that will make society more inclusive, tolerant and cohesive. In order to strengthen the fabric of peace in Africa, you need to look beyond the state to understand how various actors in the larger social environment help to weave the tapestry.

Works Cited

Aall, Pamela and Chester A. Crocker, eds. 2016. *Minding the Gap: African Conflict Management in a Time of Change*. Waterloo, ON: CIGI.

Abu-Nimer, Mohammed, Emily Welty and Amal Khoury. 2007. *Unity in Diversity: Interfaith Dialogue in the Middle East*. Washington, DC: United States Institute of Peace (USIP) Press.

Committee to Protect Journalists. 2016. www.cpj. org/killed/.

Crenshaw, Martha. 2000. "The Psychology of Terrorism: An Agenda for the 21st Century." *Political Psychology* 21 (2): 405–420.

Deutsch, Morton. 1973. *The Resolution of Conflict*. New Haven, CT: Yale University Press.

Gurr, Ted Robert. 1970. *Why Men Rebel*. Princeton, NJ: Princeton University Press.

Hampson, Fen Osler. 2001. *Madness in the Multitude: Human Security and World Disorder*. Oxford, UK: Oxford University Press.

Hughes, Jacob, Ted Hooley, Siafa Hage and George Ingram. 2014. "The New Deal for Fragile States." Global Views Policy Paper 2014–02. Washington, DC: The Brookings Institution.

Institute of Economics and Peace. 2015. *Global Peace Index Ranking 2015*. http://economicsandpeace.org/wp-content/uploads/2015/06/Global-Peace-Index-Report-2015_0.pdf.

International Commission on Intervention and State Sovereignty. 2001. *The Responsibility to Protect: Report of the International Commission on Intervention and State Sovereignty*. Ottawa, ON: International Development Research Centre.

Kelman, Herbert C. 1990. "Interactive Problem-solving: A Social-psychological Approach to Conflict Resolution." In *Conflict: Readings in Management and Resolution*, edited by John Burton and Frank Dukes. London, UK: Palgrave Macmillan.

Korostelina, Karina and Simone Lässig with Stefan Ihrig, eds. 2013. *History Education and Post-conflict Reconciliation: Reconsidering Joint Textbook Projects*. London and New York: Routledge.

Kriesberg, Louis. 2007. *Constructive Conflicts: From Escalation to Resolution*. Oxford, UK: Rowman & Littlefield.

Lederach, John Paul. 1997. *Building Peace: Sustainable Reconciliation in Divided Societies*. Washington, DC: USIP Press.

Magill, Clare. 2010. "Education and Fragility in Bosnia and Herzegovina," EEIP Research Paper, UNESCO. http://unesdoc.unesco.org/images/0019/001910/191060e.pdf.

Martin-Breen, Patrick and J. Marty Anderies. 2011. "Resilience: A Literature Review." The Bellagio Initiative Background Paper. The Institute for Development Studies, The Resource Alliance and the Rockefeller Foundation. http://opendocs.ids.ac.uk/opendocs/bitstream/handle/123456789/3692/Bellagio-Rockefeller%20bp.pdf?sequence=1.

McCauley, Clark and Sophia Moskalenko. 2008. "Mechanisms of Political Radicalization: Pathways Toward Terrorism." *Terrorism and Political Violence* 20 (3): 415–33.

Newman, Edward. 2010. "Critical Human Security Studies," *Review of International Studies* 36 (1): 77–94.

Owen, Taylor. 2004. "Challenges and Opportunities for Defining and Measuring Human Security." United Nations Disarmament Research, *Human Rights, Human Security and Disarmament, UNIDIR Disarmament Forum 3*. www.isn.ethz.ch/Digital-Library/Publications/Detail/?ots783=0c54e3b3-1e9c-be1e-2c24-a6a8c7060233&lng=en&id=47968.

Owen, Taylor, ed. 2013. *Human Security*. London, UK: Sage Publishing.

Paffenholz, Thania and Christoph Spurk. 2006. "Civil Society, Civic Engagement and Peacebuilding." Social Development Papers No. 36. Washington: Conflict Prevention and Reconstruction (CPR) Unit in the Social Development Department of the Sustainable Development Network of the World Bank.

Paffenholz, Thania, ed. 2010. *Civil Society & Peacebuilding: A Critical Assessment*. London, UK: Lynne Rienner Publishers.

Paris, Roland. 2001. "Human Security: Paradigm Shift or Hot Air?" *International Security* 26 (2): 87–102.

Perito, Robert, ed. 2007. *Guide to Participants in Peace, Stability and Relief Operations*. Washington DC: USIP Press.

Post, Jerrold M. 2007. *The Mind of the Terrorist: The Psychology of Terrorism from the IRA to al-Qaeda*. London, UK: Palgrave Macmillan.

Pruitt, Dean G. 2005. "Whither Ripeness Theory?" Working Paper No. 25. Fairfax, VA: Institute for Conflict Analysis and Resolution, George Mason University. http://scar.gmu.edu/wp_25_pruitt.pdf.

Ramsbotham, Oliver, 2010. *Transforming Violent Conflict: Radical Disagreement, Dialogue and Survival*. London and New York: Routledge.

Reed, Susan E. 2014. "Bosnia's Segregated Schools," *The Boston Globe*, May 18. www.bostonglobe.com/ideas/2014/05/17/bosnia-segregated-schools/P9Z30b1IZRTQz1C0d6jNTJ/story.html.

Smith, Alan. 2011. "Education and Conflict: Think Piece Prepared for the Education for All Global Monitoring Report 2011 on The Hidden Crisis: Armed Conflict and Education." UNESCO, 2011/ED/EFA/MRT/PI/44.

Srinivasan, Sharath. 2016. "Civil Society as Counter-power: Rethinking International Support toward Tackling Conflict and Fostering Non-violent Politics in Africa." In *Minding the Gap: African Conflict Management in a Time of Change*, edited by Pamela Aall and Chester A. Crocker. Waterloo, ON: CIGI.

Stedman, Stephen J. 1997. "Spoiler Problems in Peace Processes." *International Security* 22 (2): 5–53.

Stephenson, C. 2005. "Nongovernmental Organizations (NGOs)." In *Beyond Intractability*, edited by Guy Burgess and Heidi Burgess. Boulder, CO: University of Colorado Conflict Research Consortium. www.beyondintractability.org/essay/role-ngo.

Stewart, Frances and Graham Brown. 2007. "Motivations for Conflict: Groups and Individuals." In *Leashing the Dogs of War: Conflict Management in a Divided World*, edited by Chester A. Crocker, Fen Osler Hampson and Pamela Aall. Washington, DC: USIP Press.

United Nations Development Programme. 1994. *Human Development Report*. Oxford and New York: Oxford University Press.

UN General Assembly. 2005. *2005 World Summit Outcome*. A/RES/60/1, October 24.

Van Metre, Lauren. 2014. "Resilience as a Peacebuilding Practice: To Realism from Idealism" *US Institute of Peace Insights*. www.usip.org/insights-newsletter/resilience-peacebuilding-practice-realism-idealism.

Williams, James H., ed. 2014. *(Re)Constructing Memory: School Textbooks and the Imagination of the Nation*. Rotterdam, Boston, Taipei: Sense Publishers.

Wuye, James Movel and Muhammad Nurayn Ashafa. 1999. *The Pastor and the Imam: Responding to Conflict*. Lagos, Nigeria: Ibrash Publications.

Part Two
Social Tension and Conflict

2

State Capture and State Building as Stress Factors in African Conflicts

Pierre Englebert

Introduction: The State and Patterns of Conflict in Africa

The capacity of African societies to resist and recover from conflict is partly a function of the nature of the underlying tensions that led to, or threaten, conflict in the first place. Prime among these are tensions over the nature and control of the state. After more than 50 years of independence for most countries, the African state remains first and foremost a material resource, one that dwarfs many other economic opportunities. With many African economies still plagued with relatively small private markets and industry (despite more than a decade of sustained growth), African states continue to provide access to significant "rents" for those who can control them. These rents derive from the state's ownership of land and natural resources, from its centrality to flows of official development assistance (and, increasingly, foreign

direct investments), and from its capacity to tax and otherwise extract resources from its citizens. The poorer and less diversified their economies, the more important these rents.

Yet, at the same time as African states remain a disproportionate resource for rent seekers, many also continue to struggle with developing sufficient capacity to project power effectively and control their territories and populations. The African state-building project has Sisyphus qualities. Across the continent, it is largely unfinished, in places a work in progress, elsewhere little more than a chimera.

African politics, and particularly conflict, is largely structured around this double helix. Both the bountiful nature of the state for those who control it and its enduring difficulties in fully establishing itself and developing effective universal governance lie at the core of African states' problems in resisting, and recovering from, conflict.

Conflict is both a permanent feature of African politics and one whose contours have significantly evolved. While the 1980s saw considerable conflict in southern Africa (largely a by-product of the Cold War), that region is now largely pacified and displays relatively high levels of functional governance (Zimbabwe notwithstanding). The other regions, where conflict has endured (mainly the Horn of Africa) or where it has developed (Sahelian and central Africa), embody the two dimensions discussed in this chapter. The Horn, where violent conflict truly is a permanent feature of politics, has dealt more than other regions with repeated problems of state "ownership" and exclusion. In west and central Africa, in contrast, more fundamental problems of projection of authority have dominated. Yet, the Horn also has problems of state building (witness South Sudan) and west and central Africa problems of state capture (witness Côte d'Ivoire or the Democratic Republic of Congo [DRC]).

This chapter addresses these two dimensions of control and capacity, state capture and state building, as factors that can both favour or inhibit conflict in Africa. It further subdivides each in two additional themes. With respect to stresses over control of the state, the chapter first highlights how the use of the African state as a resource might have plagued its development potential, but has also acted as a pacifier, keeping disparate societies together, united in rent-seeking. Despite long-run contradictions, the maintenance of common property in the state has been a factor of resistance to conflict. It is when some groups seek to monopolize these rents that conflict has erupted.

Related, but conceptually distinct, is the issue of legitimacy of incumbents. Irrespective of the extent to which incumbents "consume" the state (Bayart 1993), conflict can be avoided if their behaviour in office follows implicit norms of legitimacy. These are intrinsically difficult to observe or measure, but can conceptually be derived from a range of factors, from respect for constitutional rules (Fomunyoh 2016) to honouring redistributive obligations (Schatzberg 2001; Platteau 2014). When incumbents stray from

these legitimacy foundations, whether by usurping the spirit of the law while displaying respect for its letter or by "eating" too much of the state by themselves, the capacity of the latter to resist conflict falters.

The theme of state building and conflict also calls for two distinct analytical angles for, ironically, both the lack of sufficient state building and ongoing efforts at state building are fundamental drivers of conflict. Many African states suffer from stalled state-building agendas: weak resources, vast territories and peripheral populations conspire to undermine national integration. The spread of Islamic armed militancy has compounded the problem, challenging states whose ineptitude had so far been concealed by a benign security environment.

Yet, paradoxically, state-building strategies also trigger significant stresses on the fabric of politics and rarely, if ever, take place without conflict. State building in resource-poor environments is exhausting to the state and heavy with opportunity costs. It produces resistance, which might lead weak states to adopt hybrid strategies that undermine their long-term capacity.

After discussing these four dimensions of control and capacity, and the manner in which they affect resistance to and recovery from conflict, the chapter concludes with a brief discussion of the extent to which mitigating conflict-inducing stresses might require greater flexibility on the part of outside interveners in working with non-state actors.

Problems of State Control and Capture

Challenges to the "Plural Softness" of the State

The exogenous origins of Africa's post-colonial states are well documented, and their drawbacks are abundantly lamented (see, for example, Davidson 1992; Jackson 1990; Jackson and Rosberg 1982; Englebert, Tarango and Carter

2002; Michalopoulos and Papaioannou 2011). While there is little doubt that this exogeneity has hampered Africa's development, weakened its states and often laid the groundwork for conflict-inducing communal grievances, some of its more positive effects have not always been fully appreciated. Particularly, there are dimensions of African states' disconnection with their societies and local history that have promoted their peaceful reproduction.

One such dimension is what Benyamin Neuberger (1991) has referred to as the "plural softness" of the African state — that is, its unwillingness or incapacity to fully enforce itself upon its minorities. This is not to deny that African states, their apparatus and resources frequently get appropriated or captured by certain groups. What it suggests, however, is that African states remain neutral in the process: communities that are squeezed out of power at any given time generally retain equal rights, compared to incumbents, to claim access to the benefits of sovereignty at some other time. In other words, the modal post-colonial African state and its resources are available to all. It is common property.

This characteristic of African states, which derives largely from their superimposed colonial origins, facilitates compliance and reduces incentives to revolt, as political exclusion is understood as mere deferment. It stands in contrast to most other regions of the world where the state is most often associated with the dominant project of specific groups. That these groups often name the state after themselves illustrates their claim to monopolistic ownership: Croatia, Serbia, Afghanistan (and all other "stans" or "land of…"), Russia, Vietnam, Mongolia and Slovakia are but a few examples. In Africa, titular groups are rare: the Tswana of Botswana, Swazi of Swaziland and Sotho of Lesotho — all three small relatively homogeneous former British protectorates — constitute the exceptions, with the Somalis of Somalia, where clan divisions prevail, however, undermining effective ownership of the state. Elsewhere on

the continent, the frequent topographical nature of countries' names (for example, Central African Republic, South Africa, Western Sahara), their references to geographical or natural features (for example, Cameroon, Côte d'Ivoire, Niger) or their invocation of largely unrelated pre-colonial systems (for example, Ghana, Mali), evoke the state's neutrality and plural softness.

While often largely unstated, this plural softness is an essential condition for the peaceful reproduction of many African states. Should ruling groups depart from it and seek to redefine the state in exclusionary terms, conflict ensues almost without fail. For example, Sudan's long conflict with its southern populations illustrates the consequences of violation of plural softness by incumbents. The self-identification of the Khartoum regime as Arab in the 1960s and Islamic from the early 1980s onward, and its subsequent attempts at Arabicizing and Islamicizing the rest of the country, hijacked the state, giving it a non-negotiable identity that effectively excluded southerners, who are black and largely Christian, from any meaningful sharing of state power and resources, denying Sudan's plural softness. Although the conflict eventually resulted in the complete secession of the South in 2011, the goals of the southerners equivocated through the years between separatism and attempts at turning Sudan back into a more conventionally neutral African state. The conflict began almost at independence, as northerners quickly moved to Arabicize the state. It abated in 1973 when a power-sharing agreement was established, and then flared up again in the early 1980s, after the Khartoum government undermined the autonomy of the South and pushed for an Islamic agenda. The 2006 Comprehensive Peace Agreement envisioned secession as one possible option, but both parties also committed to working together toward successful integration, and southern leader John Garang reportedly had mixed feelings about independence. For the southern elite, it seems that the goal was participation in statehood, whether a new one or the existing Sudanese one. When the latter option proved lastingly unavailable, the breakup ensued (see Crossley 2004; Garang 1992; Johnson 2003; and Prunier and Gisselquist 2003).

Similarly, under Siad Barre, power in Somalia was dominated by the southern Darrod and Hawiye clans who pushed the northern Issaq from positions of authority and commerce. In 1981, Issaq exiles in London set up the Somali National Movement and started an insurrection from Ethiopian territory that led to the separation of Somaliland in 1991 (Bryden 2004; Shinn 2002). And in Côte d'Ivoire, the adoption of the exclusive *Ivoirité* ideology by the successive Bédié, Guey and Gbagbo regimes, starting in 1996, effectively promoted an Akan ethno-national foundation to Ivorian identity (Banégas and Losch 2002) and led to the "retribalization" of Ivorian society (Akindès 2003), which all but excluded Muslim and "Dioula" populations from the north, and led to the war of 2003–2011 under the impulse of the northern Forces Nouvelles fighting for their reinsertion in the state. (That the head of Forces Nouvelles, Guillaume Soro, a former student activist, is now speaker of the National Assembly, speaks volumes about their goal of partaking in the state.)

Ethiopia presents a final example of the conflict consequences of reneging on, or ignoring, plural softness in Africa. Not coincidentally, Ethiopia is Africa's only non-post-colonial state and has historically been the hegemonic project of Amharic people. It was the systematic attempts of the Ethiopian regime to impose direct Amharic control over Eritrea that led to the latter's 30-year war of secession, which ended with the separation of the two countries in 1991 (Iyob 1995). Since its takeover the same year, the Tigrinya-dominated Tigre People's Liberation Front, which is the core group in the ruling Ethiopian People's Revolutionary Democratic Front, has pursued a similar, albeit more nuanced, policy of cultural imposition over other groups, such as the Oromos and Ogadenis, despite the adoption of a federal constitution in 1995 that gave titular groups in

regions "proprietary rights" over their territory (Clapham 2006, 29) and recognized the right of "nations, nationalities, and peoples" to secede.[1] In practice, however, the Tigrinya still dominate the state apparatus, even regionally, through clientelistic and co-opted local leaders. As a result, both groups saw a resurgence of conflict from 1996, with their rebellions demanding "equal-citizenship rights" (Keller 2005, 119).

These cases illustrate the extent to which attempts to undermine the cultural, religious or ethno-linguistic neutrality of the African state promote conflict or undermine resistance to it. The cases of the long-lasting wars of Ethiopia and Sudan (see Figure 1) also demonstrate how such neutrality-violating policies undermine the possibilities for recovery from conflict. Note, in this respect, that the only time the Sudan conflict abated between its inception in the late 1950s and its resolution through secession in 2011, was over the period 1973–1983, when Khartoum temporarily suspended its Arabic and Islamic hegemonic drives, making it possible for southerners to participate in national and local governance for a time.

Yet, the plural softness of the African state is a mixed blessing. While it allows a degree of resistance to conflict (despite stereotypes, *most* African states are at peace *most* of the time), it does so in a manner that promotes the instrumentalization of the state to the extent that it magnifies its nature as a material resource to be shared rather than as a tool of public policy. Such instrumentalization produces state weakness in the long run and further potential for conflict. This is an important contradiction well worth pondering in the context of long-run resistance to, and recovery from, conflict. Plural softness might well imply a trade-off with long-run empirical

---

1   Oromos and Ogadenis were initially forcefully integrated into Ethiopia throughout the colonial era, as military conquests of the emperor or as a result of acquisition from European colonial powers in the region.

statehood. It might promote the relatively peaceful reproduction of African states, but at the possible cost of their effectiveness and capacity. As a result, African states might remain more vulnerable to assaults against their existence than states in most other regions, as suggested by the deployment of terror groups in the Sahel region.

Stresses from Contested Legitimacy

Complete ownership of the state by a subnational group is rather unusual in African politics; more common is the attempt by a specific elite or group of incumbents to outlast their legal or political welcome in office. Christopher Fomunyoh (2016) rightly highlights the increased currency of electoral legitimacy in African politics and the diminishing legitimacy returns of time in office. The region might still have some of the longest-lasting heads of state in the world, but their rule stands on increasingly shaky political grounds. *A contrario*, regimes where attempts at constitutional manipulation have been pushed back might, subsequently, derive considerable benefits from such precedents in terms of democratic consolidation. Olusegun Obasanjo's failure to change the Nigerian constitution to allow himself a third term in office in 2006 maintained the promise of regional alternation and the continued buy-in of northern elites, and might have paved the way for the stunning electoral defeat of incumbent Goodluck Jonathan in 2015. Similarly, although popular mobilization was unable to stop Senegal's Abdoulaye Wade from engineering a self-serving constitutional change to give himself a third term in 2012, the very same mobilization, inspired by principles of political legitimacy derived from constitutional and electoral norms (and manifested through grassroots mobilization), successfully robbed him of his expected victory to produce another precedent-setting alternation in office.

However, cases where constitutions or electoral outcomes are grossly sidestepped, or where rules are changed once in office, continue to dominate across the continent. That they do so at the cost of increasing political tensions suggests shifting norms of legitimacy and highlights the potential for violent conflict that such reckless strategies of power imply. Laurent Gbagbo's cynical, overt and televised reneging of the presidential election's results in 2010, despite having soundly lost to his opponent Alassane Ouattara, unleashed a wave of violence — much of it of his own making — that cost more than 3,000 lives in four months. That 10 years earlier he had slipped into the presidency after equally flawed elections without a similar outcry suggests normative changes have unfolded on the continent in the meantime. Yet instances of violence, such as those that happened in 2010-2011, have potentially long-lasting impact on the subsequent capacity of the state to fend off further conflict. They may have precedent value in norm creation, but they also weaken the state, create a sore group of political "losers," and bias the subsequent administration of justice in favour of victors, which can in turn erode the perceived legitimacy of state institutions.

The DRC seems headed in a similarly dangerous direction. Incumbent Joseph Kabila, whose constitutional two terms in office expired in December 2016, was unable during his legal term to legally engineer a modification of the constitution, but allowed elections to slip past their due dates into a high-risk constitutional limbo, which he hopes will give him time to further consolidate his rule. In a testimony to rising democratic norms in a country better known for patronage politics, resistance has been stiff. Still, all evidence suggests that the regime is not giving up and is ready to resort to increasingly unconstitutional means to stay in power. Repression of opponents has been on the rise since early 2015, while the regime refuses to allocate resources to electoral preparations and has resorted instead to "dialogues" that have little purpose short of seeking legitimacy for shirking the constitution. Increased resistance to such strategies suggests that constitutional norms might already be more deeply ingrained than the regime realizes. Yet the potential for conflict, in a nation still at war with itself in part of its territory, is enormous. Specifically, the manipulation of state institutions to the benefit of the incumbent undermines their value as genuine tools of collective action and risks hollowing the state of its already limited capacity to peacefully regulate social life.

Burkina Faso stands as a warning to Congolese rulers. Blaise Compaoré was following the letter of his constitution when he sought to have Parliament amend, with the proper majority and following proper procedures, one of his provisions to allow him to stay in office and run for yet another election in October 2014. But he was giving short shrift to its spirit, unaware maybe of the frustration of urban populations with the manipulation of democratic norms by the regime. Parliament, having been only too willing to surrender its constitutional duties, was set on fire. With demonstrators marching toward the presidency, Compaoré tergiversated, then fled. Rapid switches in allegiance from important members of the armed forces and the presidential guard prevented the violence from spreading, and allowed for a relatively peaceful and successful transition.

The abruptness of such transitions, however, when a group of outsiders inherit the tools of statehood without the acquiescence of departing elites, can damage the capacity of the state to prevent conflict. In this case, engaged in a political standoff with the former security apparatus of the Compaoré regime — largely embodied in the presidential guard — the new elites have struggled to control and secure the state, with the consequence that they remain vulnerable to threats and fell victim to one of them with the terrorist attack on the Splendid Hotel in Ouagadougou in January 2016.

While Compaoré failed to stay in power and Kabila has yet to be successful, the continent has known a large number of more ambiguous cases, where incumbents have successfully altered rules, sometimes with genuine popular support, but not without possibly deleterious consequences. Both Cameroon and Uganda removed limitations to presidential terms of office several years ago, before the issue became salient among donors, and largely got away with it. In Cameroon, the price of the manoeuvre might have been a greater need for patronage to placate potential dissidents. A recent study in *Jeune Afrique* (Olivier 2016) showed the steadily rising size of Cameroonian governments, from 36 ministers at the time Paul Biya took office in 1982 to 63 since 2011 (with 34 distinct governments in as many years in power). While these elites are busy redistributing state resources among themselves, state capacity erodes, as illustrated by the regime's increasing difficulty to control its northern regions, where violence is rampant.

Uganda's Yoweri Museveni, once a champion of Africa's renaissance, also removed term-limit rules years ago, and has now been in power for 30 years. While he has, at times, benefited from genuine legitimacy, increased corruption, regime sclerosis and continuous meddling in conflict in the DRC have taken their toll. Each election is the occasion for violence, as Ugandans realize possibilities for alternation in power are fictitious, and Museveni increasingly needs to lock up his electoral opponents throughout presidential campaigns to stifle their momentum. The costs to Uganda are great. A regime once known for its proactive stance on HIV/AIDS is letting the disease creep back in (Kajubi 2016), and once-upbeat development prospects have remained hampered by the weak governance that comes with personal rule.

Burundi, Congo-Brazzaville and Rwanda are the most recent cases of tinkering with constitutional and electoral legitimacy. In Burundi, Pierre Nkurunziza's forcing himself onto his people despite earlier parliamentary rejection of his manoeuvrings has resulted in widespread violence since 2015, and the loss of almost all previous post-conflict progress. Most worrisome is the regime's tendency to resort to ethnic polarization to shore up its power and victimize opponents. Mass violence is a significant risk, as is the possibility of Rwanda being dragged into the conflict. Things have, so far, been more peaceful in both Congo-Brazzaville, where Denis Sassou-Nguesso managed to have the constitution changed and himself re-elected in a matter of a mere few months in 2015 and 2016, and in Rwanda, where Paul Kagame officially relented to popular pressure to remain in office. At least Kagame has a development and post-conflict governance record to show for his time in office. In both cases, however, the failure to institutionalize the regime beyond the person of the president carries the seeds of future weakness and raises the odds of eventual conflict, as suggested by the skirmishes that rocked the region south of Brazzaville in March 2016 following Sassou's presidential victory.

Constitutional legitimacy is no doubt on the rise across the continent, but patronage remains an essential foundation of African political legitimacy. Most current African regimes are best characterized as relying on hybrid patrimonial and legal legitimacy. Redistribution is an essential feature of patronage (Platteau 2014). Its normative side evokes the obligation of taking care of one another, particularly the responsibility of the patron to take care of his clients, like a father his family (Schatzberg 2001). In many countries, the commodity boom of the past decade has fostered this redistributive obligation. But the limits of such legitimacy have been tested since the boom began abating in 2014. For some regimes, irrespective of commodity prices, it is the greed of incumbents that has undermined patrimonial legitimacy. Eating excessively might be tolerated, provided others eat too. Eating alone is proscribed. The wealth of the families of Denis Sassou-Nguesso of Congo-Brazzaville or Teodoro Obiang Nguema of Equatorial Guinea, both of whom are the objects of legal proceedings in France for ill-acquired wealth, suggests the fragility of their regimes with respect to the redistributive obligation. Similarly,

Zimbabwe's Robert Mugabe, in power for 36 years, has probably lost much of his patrimonial legitimacy with his country's continuous economic decline, as witnessed by rising protests over unpaid public service salaries in 2016. And if the "Panama Papers" are any indication, the DRC's Kabila and his family are showing a voracious and exclusive appetite that might further weaken their regime (Sharife 2016; Kavanagh, Wilson and Wild 2016).[2]

Problems of State Building

Pre-Westphalian Challenges: State Authority, Territory and Periphery

Weak policy and institutional capacity is another fundamental challenge to the ability of African states to resist and recover from conflict, particularly their frequent lack of sufficient territorial reach, difficulties in projecting power across space and the subsequent tendency to neglect peripheral groups. African troubles with the projection of state authority have been identified since the path-breaking work of Jeffrey Herbst (2000). In many cases, these difficulties betray a failure to reach the Westphalian status of nation-states defined by control over territory and exclusionary sovereignty.[3]

Figure 1 illustrates the extent of the problem. Based on travel advisories issued by the French Foreign Affairs Ministry, it shows the degree to which multiple African states are unable to project power across their territories, identifying 34 percent of Africa's continental mass as beyond

---

2   The Panama Papers are millions of documents from Panama law firm Mossack Fonseca, which were leaked in 2015 and reveal ownership of more than 200,000 offshore companies.

3   Note, however, that Westphalia remains an ideal type for many states around the world, and might be in the process of being superseded by "post-Westphalian" developments (see Pavel and Engelke 2015).

Figure 1: Effective Territorial Reach of African States

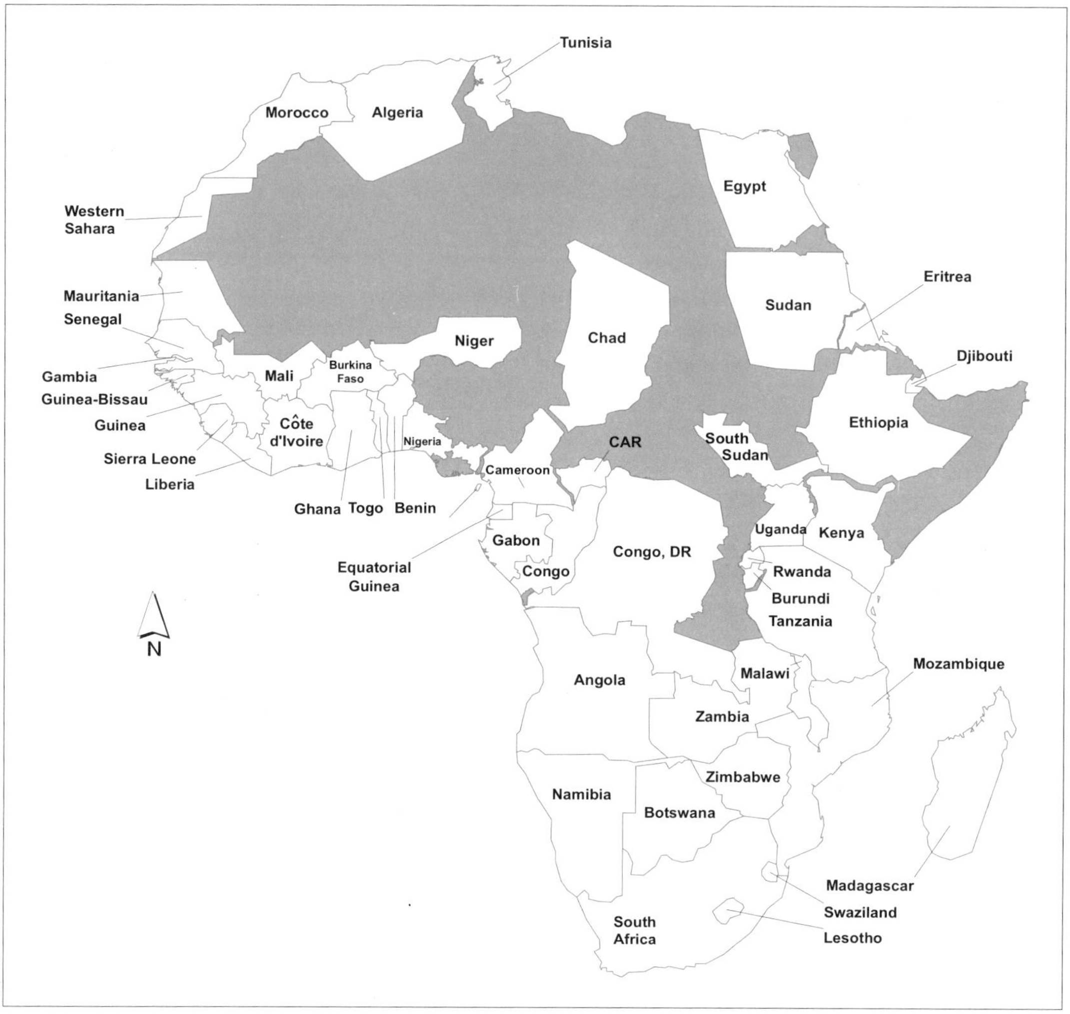

Source: Author (reprinted with permission from Foreign Affairs).

state control (Englebert 2015).[4] There is little doubt that this failure is in part a function of size. Jeffrey Herbst highlighted the diseconomies of scale of

African statehood as early as 2000. Having a vast territory when one is incapable to broadcast power and infrastructure across it is a factor of weakness.

As Figure 2 illustrates, the percentage of a country's territory beyond state control is closely related to its overall area (with a correlation of 0.54). The weakness of the centre-periphery connection is a hallmark of African statehood, resulting as it does from the joint effects of pre-colonial power consolidation based on loose bonds of personal loyalty and colonial control unhindered by the necessity of creating territorial buffers to domestic

---

4   The map shows in grey areas where the French government advises its citizens to avoid travel at all costs for security reasons. Obviously, factors affecting the security of French nationals in Africa differ from those affecting the security of locals. A Tuareg Malian, for example, might not find as much risk travelling through northern Mali as a French citizen. Nonetheless, the advisories provide a proxy for effective state control over territory, albeit a possibly biased one.

Figure 2: Country Size and Lack of Territorial Control

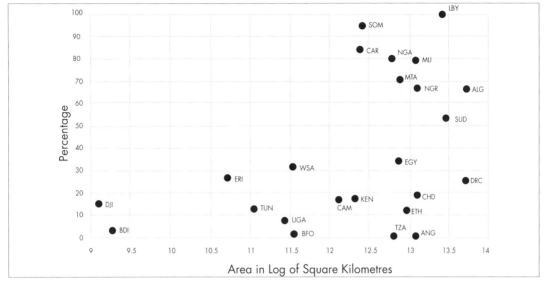

Source: Author.

Note: countries sitting at zero percent: BEN; BOT; CGO; CIV; EGU; GAB; GHA; GUI; GUB; LES; LIB; MAD; MWI; MOR; MOZ; NAM; RWA; SEN; SLE; SAF; SSU; SWA; TOG; ZAM; ZIM.

Country abbreviations: ALG = Algeria; ANG = Angola; BEN = Benin; BOT = Botswana; BFO = Burkina Faso; BDI = Burundi; AMC = Cameroon; CAR = Central African Republic; CHD = Chad; CGO = Congo; DRC = Congo, DRC; CIV = Côte d'Ivoire; DJI = Djibouti; EGY = Egypt; EGU = Equatorial Guinea; ERI = Eritrea; ETH = Ethiopia; GAB = Gabon; GHA = Ghana; GUI = Guinea; GUB = Guinea-Bissau; KEN = Kenya; LES = Lesotho; LIB = Liberia; LBY = Libya; MAD = Madagascar; MWI = Malawi; MLI = Mali; MTA = Mauritania; MOR = Morocco; MOZ = Mozambique; NAM = Namibia; NGR = Niger; NGA = Nigeria; RWA = Rwanda; SEN = Senegal; SLE = Sierra Leone; SOM = Somalia; SAF = South Africa; SSU = South Sudan; SUD = Sudan; SWA = Swaziland; TZA = Tanzania; TOG = Togo; TUN = Tunisia; UGA = Uganda; WSA = Western Sahara; ZAM = Zambia; ZIM = Zimbabwe.

state formation (Herbst 2000, 41). Despite the high-salience cases of Eritrea and South Sudan, however, surprisingly few of Africa's conflicts are of a secessionist nature (Englebert 2009). This is partly related to constraining rules of recognition that limit the effective supply of sovereignty for would-be separatist actors, and increase the relative returns of strategies predicated upon maintaining national unity.

Yet size matters to the extent that by limiting the territorial reach of the state, it reduces opportunity costs to peripheral violence and facilitates mobilization (Fearon and Laitin 2003). Before they took over Bangui in 2013, the Central African rebels of Séléka had been active for years, with considerable impunity, in the east and northeast margins of the country, where many non-state

authorities coexist (Lombard 2015). Similarly, the continued presence of almost 70 armed groups of various sizes in eastern DRC (Stearns and Vogel 2015) would not be possible if the Kivu provinces were not so far from the capital Kinshasa and bordering on Burundi, Rwanda and Uganda, which provide convenient rear-bases and supply routes. That local conflict endures despite the deployment of the vast majority of MONUSCO (United Nations Organization Stabilization Mission in the DRC) troops in the region, as well as many battalions of the Congolese armed forces, suggests the burden of space and terrain on conflict prevention and avoidance.

Deficits of state building and national integration underwrite these conflicts even when they do not provide direct causes for them. These same deficits have recently favoured the rise of Islamic insurgencies. It is worth noting that lack of territorial control, as illustrated in Figure 3, also correlates at 0.55 with the prevalence of Islam. To some extent, Islamic ideology can provide support for radical challenges of the post-colonial African state, and its appeal is magnified when these states have fallen short in delivering the benefits of modernity, as most have. The existence of pre-colonial emirates and caliphates in some of these countries provides attractive narrative and alternative visions of statehood for these movements and their supporters. But it bears asserting that it is the initial failure of the post-colonial state to live up to its own expectations that provides the opening for such challenges.

Nigeria's Boko Haram is now the best known of African Islamist insurgencies. The appeal of political Islam in Nigeria became apparent with the adoption of sharia by 13 northern states in 1999, after Olusegun Obasanjo, a born-again Christian southerner, assumed the presidency. However, the lack of serious religious commitment by the corrupt northern governors led younger and more radical Muslims to create Boko Haram around 2004 (first called "Taliban"), which is opposed to all things Western and, as such, to the Nigerian state too. While sharia adoption was an elite political move aimed at weakening the new president, Boko Haram is more of a grassroots militant effort. Its goals include the dissolution of Nigeria as it exists now and the rise of an Islamic state (it pledged allegiance to the Islamic State of Iraq and al-Sham, or ISIS, in 2015). *Africa Research Bulletin* (2012) notes that Boko Haram wants "to restore the Islamic state that once existed [in northern Nigeria] and was 'destroyed' by British colonialists."

More so even than Boko Haram in Nigeria, the rise of Al-Shabaab in Somalia is a response to state failure. Al-Shabaab arose in 2004-2005, first as the Islamic Court Union (ICU), following some 15 years without a central government. In the absence of the state, local neighbourhoods had developed clan courts to maintain some degree of law and order.

A couple of more radical courts used Mujahedeen police and united in 2005 to coordinate justice and police, leading to the creation of the ICU. They came to power in 2006, and later ruled as Al-Shabaab until the Ethiopian invasion of 2006. Since then, Al-Shabaab has continued to control significant rural areas of the country, empowered by the failure of the Transitional Federal Government to extend its control beyond a few street blocks of Mogadishu (Menkhaus 2014).

Zanzibar and coastal Kenya offer similar cases, albeit at much lower levels of violence. Yet the region's pre-colonial political history as an Islamic state carries the same type of narrative as in northern Nigeria. Zanzibar and the strip of coastal mainland it controlled in today's Tanzania and Kenya was part of the Sultanate of Oman until 1856, when it became its own sultanate under British patronage. In 1890, both the islands and the coastal strip became a British protectorate. The Tanganyika part of the strip was subsequently purchased by the Germans and merged with Tanganyika, while the Kenyan part remained a distinct British protectorate (as opposed to Kenya, which was a colony) until 1961. However, the sultan was quickly eliminated from Tanzanian politics during the Zanzibar Revolution of 1964, which reinforced pro-union political actors on the island for decades to come.

Here too, the influence of Islamism has been rising. An Islamic group called the Association for Islamic Mobilization and Propagation has demanded a referendum to leave the union because of its secular status, and its activities have involved small riots and the burning of churches. In Kenya, the grievances of coastal communities, some but not all Arab and Muslims, have found a voice since 2005 in the Mombasa Republican Council (MRC). The sultanate provides a convenient historical narrative, which connects loosely with Muslim rule. The Kenyan government has taken the MRC threat seriously and has cracked down on its militants after cases of violence linked to the MRC increased in 2013.

All of these examples illustrate deficits of state and nation building, the corresponding difficulties of African post-colonial states to absorb, subsume or reconcile pre-existing political identities, and the ensuing generation of conflict-inducing grievances. Obstacles to integration derived from socio-cultural diversity and territorial size have limited the capacity of many states to effectively expand their hegemony and have made them vulnerable to challenges as recently embodied by Islamist insurgencies.

Stresses from State Building in States with Limited Viability

Ironically, state building itself can be a factor prompting state weakness and generating both significant stresses and reduced capacity to deal with them on the part of the state. Some African states have such dire resource bases that their attempts to project power across their territories can exhaust their limited abilities and trigger existential crises.

This issue of country size is worth revisiting in this respect, as the imbalance it often creates between territory and resources in low-income countries makes state building much more of a challenge than it might be elsewhere. Just as we think of countries' development in terms of per capita GDP, we can think of this imbalance by assessing the relationship between their GDP and their surface area. Based on 188 countries for which data is available, the average country produces about US$31 million per km^2. (This average is somewhat biased by tiny rich city-states such as Monaco, Macao, Singapore or Bahrain — however, removing the five smallest countries still yields an average of US$5.7 million.) In contrast, the Central African Republic's GDP per km^2 is US$2,469; Mauritania's US$4,034; Niger's US$5,846; and Mali's US$8,823. As a matter of fact, 16 of the 20 "poorest" countries in the world per km^2 are in Africa.[5] Attempting to build and

project statehood with such limited resources for such vast territories can easily backfire and bring about state failure and conflict.

Mali, which literally fell apart in 2012 under the combined assaults of mutineering soldiers, quasi-separatist insurgents and Islamist invaders, is a case in point. Mali had never ceased to state build since its inception in 1960. Although it had been French Soudan as a colony, it chose the name Mali at independence to echo the state-building achievement of a thirteenth-century empire. But it did not seek to build on this legacy beyond labelling, and instead attempted to create a republic on the French model, with a heavy dose of socialism. That the country lacked all the prerequisites for such an exercise did not cool the ardours of its first president, Modibo Keita, or his successors. Keita kicked out the remaining French troops in 1961, abandoned the CFA franc (pegged to the French franc and backed by the French Treasury) in 1962 to create his own Malian franc, waged a military campaign of submission to the state against northern Tuareg autonomists in 1963, and imposed socialist economic policies that demanded a level of state effectiveness and bureaucratic capacity far above what he had at his disposal. His successor, Moussa Traoré, walked back some of Keita's most extreme policies, but the basic agenda of building an interventionist imitation of France in the desert endured.

It comes as no surprise that state building failed in Mali. It never had any of the prerequisites for Westphalian statehood. The notion that a weak post-colonial state with hardly any revenue, an immense territory reaching deep into the Sahara desert, a largely illiterate population and significant ethno-linguistic diversity could establish the kind of authority and societal penetration that its elites had in mind seems delusional in hindsight.

Mali's transition to democracy in 1992 actually made things worse with respect to state building. It raised the demands on the state in terms of governance performance, called for more

---

5   Author's calculations based on data from World Development Indicators (current US dollars GDP divided by surface area in km^2).

institutions, and brought about decentralization and its own multiplication of governing agencies. More important, it significantly raised popular expectations in terms of services and employment, and made the regime less able to ignore or resist them than its authoritarian predecessor. School enrolments, for example, increased dramatically, but education quality collapsed and Mali's skin-deep economy was unable to absorb them.

Contemporary governance demands on weak states are overwhelming. Expectations, promoted by donor conditionality, include rule of law, defined and enforced property rights, control of corruption, bureaucratic quality, enforcement of contracts, decentralization, public sector reform, security sector reform, tax reform (including the increasingly frequent introduction of administratively burdensome value added taxes) and more (see Thomas 2015). For Mali, the demands of contemporary liberal governance are at least as burdening to the state as its earlier socialist ambitions. With a paltry GDP of $12 billion and limited revenues from the export of some gold, cotton and livestock, the Malian state is simply unable to sustain itself, much less to consolidate and project its power. Altogether, the Malian state barely generates $116 per inhabitant in state revenue with which to perform all of the tasks of modern governance, not to mention fighting off Islamist terrorist and insurgents. (See Figure 3 for a comparison with the revenues of more developed states.) State building of the contemporary Westphalian variety might simply not be possible in Mali.

The argument here is not so much that Mali is poor, but that countries with limited resources and prohibitive territories, such as Mali, are likely to exhaust themselves when attempting to state build. This is a potentially important insight as the international agenda remains uncritically focused on state reconstruction in places like Mali.

Figure 3: Comparing Tax Revenues as a Measure of Extractive Capabilities

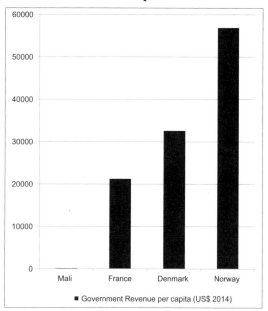

Source: Author, with data from Thomas (2015, 79) and ICTD (n.d.).

In some countries, the state has adapted to its material limitations by resorting to state building on the cheap. This is the case with the reliance of many African countries on customary authorities as state agents, essentially reproducing the post-colonial state on the foundations of pre-colonial politics. While expedient, the resulting institutional hybridity might undermine overall capacity. For example, the legal and institutional pluralism it produces can weaken the effectiveness of state presence and policies. The conflict in eastern Congo is related to this problem to a significant extent. Violence in eastern Congo is often thought of in terms of a mix of ethnic polarization, foreign invasions and access to mineral resources. While these dimensions are far from irrelevant, the prevailing confusion over property rights of land in the area, and the role of chiefs in allocating it, is at least as important a factor. Ambiguities such as legal pluralism result in part from the incomplete penetration of the state in the region, incomplete because it is focused more on commanding and extracting than on organizing collective action and facilitating life in common, a pattern inherited from colonial rule.

The African state-building conundrum is worth noting. For large and poor African countries, state building is a self-defeating strategy more likely to produce breakdown than effective statehood. Yet, the alternative patchwork strategy of hybrid governance only takes them so far, reproducing states in their very weakness and institutional balkanization.

Policy Implications

African states make for relatively good providers of patronage and relatively poor organizers of collective action. Their material appeal to political actors and their weak capabilities conspire to make them prone to conflict. Ironically, those that avoid conflict might do so by generously redistributing the state's resources and refraining from aggressive state building. Yet, such strategies seem only to postpone the problem by facilitating the resilience of states but not their construction, leaving them vulnerable to challenges and the violent expression of grievances.

The international state-reconstruction agenda squarely confronts the logic of redistribution and governance on the cheap. It never gives up on failed states. It props up the post-colonial project everywhere it has crumbled. But neither does it acknowledge the low odds that its efforts, hardly successful to begin with, can endure after its thousands of staff and military personnel, and its billions of dollars, have left. Must Humpty Dumpty always be put back together? What will make the CAR, Mali or Somalia more sustainable the next time around?

Conversely, can one give up on nation building? At a time of widespread Islamist threat, the alternative is hardly palatable. Falling well short of policy recommendations, this chapter concludes with a short reflection on how to dislodge some African states from the equilibrium trap of resource redistribution, weak legitimacy and state failure.

To the extent that donors drive most of the state-reconstruction agenda in Africa, could they show greater flexibility in the institutions they work with? Currently, supporting states at all costs largely exonerate the latter from their responsibilities for successful state building. How about giving non-state actors that are able to provide some public goods, starting with local security, a degree of recognition, which might in turn stimulate institutional competition and maybe a salutary state reaction? It might indeed be time to think of state building in Africa not entirely along post-colonial lines. For sure, many African post-colonial states might provide adequate foundations for statehood — but not all. There might be other options, based on alternative political narratives and institutions.

Some might be pre-colonial. Customary chiefs, who are often co-opted in the service of post-colonial states, could be granted greater administrative and political autonomy, provided they retain local legitimacy. Some state-like customary entities such as Buganda in Uganda or Barotseland in Zambia deserve a chance at decentralized rule, if not federalism.

Other options might be religion-based. Western aversion for Islamic violence should not blind policy makers to the popularity and legitimacy of certain forms of religious governance in Africa. Many Africans harbour genuine local grievances about the state and aspirations for a different order, for which, in parts of west and east Africa, Islam is a beacon. The apparent retreat from liberal values by some groups is part and parcel of broader efforts by populations to free themselves from imposed arbitrary structures that have failed at delivering the supposed benefits of those liberal values, mostly prosperity and liberty. In this respect, it is hard to conceive of a lasting and workable political dispensation in Mali that would not involve some form of participation from organizations like the High Islamic Council. And, once Boko Haram is militarily defeated — or as a political counterpart to defeating it — the Nigerian state will have to come to terms with the political grievances and aspirations of its Muslim populations.

Other options still might capitalize upon new grassroots initiatives such as the anticorruption movements *Y'en A Mare* in Senegal and *Balai Citoyen* in Burkina Faso, or on the actions of local political entrepreneurs if they have shown their capacity to deliver public goods. Either way, donors interested in promoting genuine resistance to conflict in Africa will want to find ways to work with the non-violent actors who represent alternative values that have appeal and legitimacy in view of the limited effective benefits of Western statehood in some of Africa.

Works Cited

Africa Research Bulletin. 2012. Political and Economic Series, 19318A.

Akindès, Francis. 2003. "Côte d'Ivoire: Socio-Political Crises, 'Ivoirité,' and the Course of History." *African Sociological Review* 7 (2): 11–28.

Banégas, Richard and Bruno Losch. 2002. "La Côte d'Ivoire au bord de l'implosion." *Politique Africaine* 87: 139–161.

Bayart, Jean-François. 1993. *The State in Africa: The Politics of the Belly.* London, UK: Longman.

Bryden, Matt. 2004. "State-within-a-Failed-State: Somaliland and the Challenge of International Recognition." In *States within States: Incipient Political Entities in the Post-Cold War Era,* edited by Paul Kingston and Ian Spears, 167–192. New York, NY: Palgrave Macmillan.

Clapham Christopher. 2006. "Ethiopia." In *Big African States,* edited by Christopher Clapham, Jeffrey Herbst and Greg Mills, 17–38. Johannesburg, South Africa: Wits University Press.

Crossley, Ken. 2004. "Why Not to State-Build New Sudan." In *States within States: Incipient Political Entities in the Post-Cold War Era,* edited by Paul Kingston and Ian Spears, 135–151. New York, NY: Palgrave Macmillan.

Davidson, Basil. 1992. *The Black Man's Burden: Africa and the Curse of the Nation-State.* New York, NY: Random House.

Englebert, Pierre. 2009. *Africa: Unity, Sovereignty and Sorrow.* Boulder, CO: Lynne Rienner Publishers.

———. 2015. "The 'Real' Map of Africa: Redrawing Colonial Borders," *Foreign Affairs,* November 8. www.foreignaffairs.com/articles/2015-11-08/real-map-africa.

Englebert, Pierre, Stacy Tarango and Matthew Carter. 2002. "Dismemberment and Suffocation: A Contribution to the Debate on African Boundaries." *Comparative Political Studies* 35 (10): 1093–1118.

Fearon, James and David Laitin. 2003. "Ethnicity, Insurgency, and Civil War." *American Political Science Review* 97: 75–90.

Fomunyoh, Chritopher. 2016. "Crises of Political Legitimacy." In *Minding the Gap: African Conflict Management in a Time of* Change, edited by Pamela Aall and Chester A. Crocker, 33–48. Waterloo, ON: CIGI.

Garang, John. 1992. *The Call for Democracy in Sudan.* New York, NY: Kegan Paul International.

Herbst, Jeffrey. 2000. *States and Power in Africa.* Princeton, NJ: Princeton University Press.

International Centre for Tax and Development (ICTD). n.d. "The ICTD Government Revenue Dataset." www.ictd.ac/datasets/the-ictd-government-revenue-dataset.

Iyob, Ruth. 1995. *The Eritrean Struggle for Independence: Domination, Resistance, Nationalism, 1941–1993.* Cambridge, UK: Cambridge University Press.

Jackson, Robert. 1990. *Quasi-States: Sovereignty, International Relations and the Third World.* Cambridge, UK: Cambridge University Press.

Jackson, Robert and Carl Rosberg. 1982. "Why Africa's Weak States Persist: The Empirical and the Juridical in Statehood." *World Politics* 35 (1): 1–24.

Johnson, Douglas. 2003. *The Root Causes of Sudan's Civil Wars.* Bloomington, IN: Indiana University Press.

Kajubi, Phoebe. 2016. "HIV/AIDS Epidemic in Uganda: Response, Progress and Challenges." Presentation at Pomona College, African Politics Lab, March 10.

Kavanagh, Michael J., Tom Wilson and Franz Wild. 2016. "Congo President's Twin Has Indirect Stake in Vodacom Unit." *Bloomberg*, April 5. www.bloomberg.com/news/articles/2016-04-05/congo-president-s-twin-sister-has-indirect-stake-in-vodacom-unit.

Keller, Edmond. 2005. "Making and Remaking State and Nation in Ethiopia." In *Borders, Nationalism, and the African States*, edited by Ricardo René Laremont, 87–134. Boulder, CO: Lynne Rienner Publishers.

Lombard, Louisa. 2015. "The Autonomous Zone Conundrum: Armed Conservation and Rebellion in North-Eastern CAR." In *Making Sense of the Central African Republic*, edited by Tatiana Carayannis and Louisa Lombard, 142–165. London, UK: Zed Books.

Menkhaus, Ken. 2014. "State Failure, State-building, and Prospects for a 'Functional Failed State' in Somalia." *The Annals of the American Academy of Political and Social Science* 656 (1): 154–172.

Michalopoulos, Steios and Elias Papaioannou. 2011. "The Long-Run Effects of the Scramble for Africa." National Bureau of Economic Research Working Paper No. 17620.

Neuberger, Benyamin. 1991. "Irredentism and Politic sin Africa." In *Irredentism and International Politics*, edited by Naomi Chazan, 97–110. Boulder, CO: Lynne Rienner Publishers.

Olivier, Mathieu. 2016. "Infographies—Cameroun: Paul Biya, le président aux 299 ministres." *Jeune Afrique,* April 18. www.jeuneafrique.com/318915/politique/infographies-cameroun-paul-biya-299-ministres/.

Pavel, Barry and Peter Engelke. 2015. "Dynamic Stability: US Strategy for a World in Transition." Atlantic Council Strategy Paper No. 1.

Platteau, Jean-Philippe. 2014. "Redistributive Pressures in Sub-Saharan Africa: Causes, Consequences, and Coping Strategies." In *Africa's Development in Historical Perspective*, edited by Emmanuel Akyeampong, Robert H. Bates, Nathan Nunn and James Robinson. Cambridge, UK: Cambridge University Press.

Prunier, Gérard and Rachel Gisselquist. 2003. "The Sudan: A Successfully Failed State." In *State Failure and State Weakness in a Time of Terror*, edited by Robert Rotberg, 101–127. Cambridge, MA: World Peace Foundation.

Schatzberg, Michael. 2001. *Political Legitimacy in Middle Africa: Father, Family, Food.* Bloomington, IN: Indiana University Press.

Sharife, Khadija. 2016. "Panama Papers: The DRC's Gold Standard." *Times Live*, April 4. www.timeslive.co.za/africa/2016/04/04/Panama-Papers-The-DRC%E2%80%99s-Gold-Standard.

Shinn, David. 2002. "Somaliland: The Little Country that Could." CSIS Africa Notes No. 9.

Stearns, Jason, and Christof Vogel. 2015. "The Landscape of Armed Groups in Eastern Congo." New York, NY: Center on International Cooperation Congo Research Group, December.

Thomas, M. A. 2015. *Govern Like Us: US Expectations of Poor Countries.* New York, NY: Columbia University Press.

3

Violent Group Mobilization and Conflicts in Africa: Understanding When and How Horizontal Inequalities Lead to Violence

Arnim Langer and Leila Demarest

Despite a noticeable surge in conflicts in recent years, the total number of internal armed conflicts in the world has significantly fallen since the beginning of the 1990s. The number of ongoing conflicts in Africa has continued to hover around 12 to 13 in the same period (see Figure 1). As noted by Frances Stewart and Graham Brown (2007), an important trend has been the steady increase of the proportion of violent conflicts in which people of different identity groups are confronting each other. Indeed, as Stewart and Brown (ibid., 221) show, "the proportion of conflicts attributable to ethnic violence" has increased progressively from 15 percent in 1953 to nearly 60 percent in 2005. In recent years, the identity basis of conflicts has continued to become increasingly explicit in

most violent conflicts (Brown and Langer 2010). To further substantiate this point in the African context, it is worth pointing out that in the three most recent civil wars in Africa — that is, the civil wars in South Sudan, the Central African Republic (CAR) and Mali — the violence has clearly occurred across ethnic or religious lines.[1]

---

1   In particular, in Mali, the resurgence of the long-standing Tuareg rebellion in the beginning of 2012 led to the de facto control of the north of the country by militant Islamist groups and a *coup d'état* against President Amadou Toumani Touré. In the CAR, the overthrow of the government by rebels from the north in 2013 resulted in widespread violence between Muslims and Christians, while in South Sudan, the power struggle between President Salva Kiir and Vice President Riek Machar has led to extreme ethnic violence between the Dinka and Nuer groups.

Figure 1: Ongoing Internal Armed Conflicts in the World (UCDP/PRIO)[*]

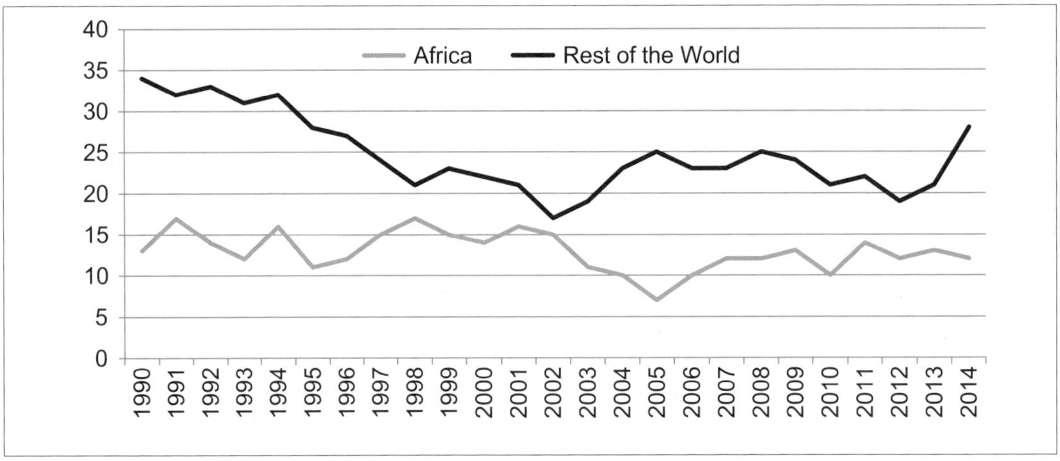

Source: The authors, based on data from UCDP.

[*] The Uppsala Conflict Data Program/International Peace Research Institute Oslo (UCDP/PRIO) armed conflict dataset includes conflicts that have led to at least 25 battle-related deaths in a given calendar year. We have included internal armed conflicts and internationalized internal armed conflicts in which the state government is an actor in the conflict.

While many factors and circumstances have been linked to the outbreak of violent conflicts, arguably the most widely studied variable for explaining the emergence of violent conflicts has been the presence of inequalities. Although qualitative investigations often stress the role of inequality, quantitative investigations into the relationship between inequality and conflict have often led to contradicting results (Nagel 1974; Lichbach 1989). Christopher Cramer (2003, 397) noted in this respect that "the role of economic inequality in...the political economy of violent conflict has remained elusive." However, around the same time that Cramer came to his sobering conclusion about the state of our knowledge concerning the inequality-conflict nexus, the academic debate on this important relationship was rekindled by the introduction of the concept of "horizontal inequality," defined by Stewart as political and economic inequalities between culturally defined or ethnic groups (see Stewart 2000; 2002). Horizontal inequalities are hypothesized to make countries more vulnerable to conflict because the prevailing socio-economic and political inequalities are likely to arouse severe frustrations and grievances among relatively

disadvantaged ethnic groups, which, in turn, may induce group mobilization along ethnic lines and possibly violent conflict (see Stewart 2008; Langer and Stewart 2014; Cederman, Weidmann and Gleditsch 2011). Thus, the relationship between horizontal inequalities and violent conflict is theoretically underpinned by a grievance-based discourse (see Stewart, 2008; Cederman, Weidmann and Gleditsch 2011). In this chapter, we will critically review the relationship between the presence of horizontal inequalities and the outbreak of violent conflicts, and discuss a range of possible policy options in order to address these inequalities.[2]

The chapter will proceed as follows. In the next section, we will discuss the origins of the concept and review the theoretical and empirical linkages

---

2   This review will draw heavily on the earlier works by Arnim Langer on this topic, either done alone or in collaboration with other researchers. We will particularly draw on Langer (2005), Stewart, Brown and Langer (2008), Brown and Langer (2010), and Langer and Stewart (2014). We are grateful to Graham Brown and Frances Stewart for allowing us to draw on these publications.

between the presence of horizontal inequalities and the emergence of violent conflicts in multi-ethnic societies. Then we will analyze to what extent the presence of horizontal inequalities has contributed to the emergence of violence in two African countries — the Boko Haram insurgency in Nigeria and the civil war in the CAR. We will subsequently discuss a range of policy interventions and measures that could be undertaken to address and mitigate prevailing horizontal inequalities in Africa and beyond. The final section provides a conclusion and identifies several avenues for future research on the relationship between horizontal inequalities and different forms of political mobilization and violent conflict.

Horizontal Inequalities and Violent Conflict: A Critical Review

In 2000, Oxford-based development economist Frances Stewart introduced the concept of "horizontal inequalities" and its hypothesized relationship with violent group mobilization (Brown and Langer 2010). The concept of horizontal inequality differs from "the normal definition of inequality [which Stewart termed 'vertical inequality'] which lines individuals or households up vertically and measures inequality over the range of individuals" rather than between culturally defined or ethnic groups (Stewart 2002, 3). It is further important to note that horizontal inequality is a multi-dimensional concept with social, economic, political and cultural status dimensions. These different dimensions, in turn, include a range of items:

- *Economic horizontal inequalities* include inequalities in ownership of assets — financial, natural resource-based, human and social — and of incomes and employment opportunities that depend on these assets and general economic conditions;

- *Social horizontal inequalities* include access to a range of services — education, health and housing — and inequalities in health and educational outcomes;

- *Political horizontal inequalities* consist of inequalities in the group distribution of political opportunities and power, including control over the presidency, the cabinet, parliamentary assemblies, the army, police and regional and local government. Political horizontal inequalities include inequalities in people's capabilities to participate politically and voice their needs; and

- *Cultural status horizontal inequalities* refer to differences in recognition and (de facto) hierarchical status of different groups' cultural norms, customs and practices (Langer and Stewart 2014, 105).[3]

The horizontal inequality hypothesis is often seen as a redevelopment of the theory of relative deprivation. Ted Gurr (1974) first developed this theory in his well-known book *Why Men Rebel*. Gurr argued that men engage in political violence when "their value capabilities are not compatible with their value expectations" (ibid.) or, in other words, men engage in political violence if they do not receive what they perceive to be entitled to and hence experience relative deprivation. While the theory was originally aimed at explaining individuals' motivations and incentives for joining a rebellion, Gurr (1993) later adapted his theory and extended his logic of relative deprivation to the mobilization of minority groups.

In contrast to the relative deprivation theory, the theory of horizontal inequality explicitly hypothesizes that if there are sharp inequalities between different groups in society, these inequalities may directly lead to violent conflict because the relatively disadvantaged groups will feel aggrieved about their inferior positions.

---

3   The concept of cultural status inequalities has been more fully developed in Langer and Brown (2008).

However, the relatively advantaged groups may also mobilize along ethnic lines, in order to maintain or safeguard their relatively advantaged position in society (Stewart 2008). Indeed, there are also cases in which relatively rich groups have mobilized against relatively poorer ones (for example, in South Africa and Burundi). This latter point also distinguishes the theory of horizontal inequality from the theory of relative deprivation. It has further been established that countries where different dimensions of horizontal inequalities are consistent (in other words, the same ethnic groups are politically excluded and socio-economically disadvantaged) are more at risk of having violent conflict (see, for example, Østby 2008). Arnim Langer (2005) has theorized in this respect that the risk of violent conflict increases in these situations because both the political "elites" and "masses" of the relatively deprived groups have a strong incentive to mobilize along ethnic lines in order to improve their positions.

The emphasis on grievances as a cause of conflict in the horizontal inequality theory does not preclude that other factors can be important in bringing about violent conflict. The feasibility or opportunity approach to conflict, for example, forms another major school of thought on violent conflict (see, for example, Tilly 1978; Collier 2001; Collier and Hoeffler 2002; Fearon and Laitin 2003). This approach does not focus on people's motivations for joining a rebellion or supporting an insurgency, but focuses on the factors that induce or constrain the organization of an armed rebellion against the state. Commonly investigated factors include the presence of mountainous terrain, which allows rebels to hide from government troops, as well as weak state military capacity. Importantly, ethnic identity has also been investigated from a feasibility perspective. Ethnic diversity has, for example, been found to have a negative effect on civil war onset, which has been theorized as indicating collective action constraints (Collier and Hoeffler 2002; Fearon

and Laitin 2003). Greater diversity in terms of ethnicity would hamper the organization of armed rebellion. Ethnic polarization, on the other hand, or the presence of two dominant groups, has been found to increase the chances of the onset of civil war (Collier and Hoeffler 2002; Garcia-Montalvo and Reynal-Querol 2004). It is important to note, however, that measurement difficulties jeopardize the conclusiveness of these findings (Hegre and Sambanis 2006).

In the past five years, a growing body of both qualitative and quantitative empirical research has found evidence in support of the hypothesis that the presence of horizontal inequalities increases the risk of violent conflict. In-depth case studies and qualitative comparative research has been conducted on a range of countries and regions, including, for example, Sudan (Cobham 2005), Côte d'Ivoire (Langer 2005), Nigeria (Ukiwo 2008) and Indonesia, the Philippines and Malaysia (Brown 2008). Due to a serious lack of internationally comparable data on political and socio-economic horizontal inequalities, quantitative analyses of the relationship between horizontal inequalities and violent conflict onset have remained relatively scarce.[4] Some notable exceptions in this respect are as follow: Gudrun Østby's (2008) analysis of the link between socio-economic horizontal inequalities (approximated

---

4   In recent years, a number of important new global datasets have become available that provide internationally comparable data on the evolution of political horizontal inequalities and, therefore, allow for more rigorous testing of the relationship between horizontal inequalities and violent conflict. The most notable data project in this respect is the GROW[up] data portal, which integrates a number of datasets on ethnic groups and intrastate conflict from various sources into a single relational database. The data are collected jointly by the International Conflict Research group at ETH Zurich, the University of Essex, PRIO and the University of Uppsala. For more information on the GROW[up] data portal, please visit: http://growup.ethz.ch/pfe/.

on the basis of data taken from the Demographic and Health Surveys [DHS] Program, funded by the US Agency for International Development) and the risk of violent conflict in 36 developing countries in the period 1986–2004; Luca Mancini's (2008) analysis of inter-district inequalities and the risk of communal conflicts in Indonesia in the period 1997–2003; S. Mansoob Murshed and Scott Gates' (2005) study of the impact of economic horizontal inequalities on explaining geographical differences in conflict intensity in Nepal; Lars-Erik Cederman, Andreas Wimmer and Brian Min's (2010) analysis of the impact of political horizontal inequalities (measured by different ethnic groups' access to executive political power) and the risk of armed conflicts; and, especially, Cederman, Nils B. Weidmann and Kristian Skrede Gleditsch's (2011) global study of ethno-nationalist civil war. The latter study is particularly noteworthy because it is the first global analysis of the linkages between horizontal inequalities and violent conflict. The authors find not only that both political and economic horizontal inequalities increase the risk of ethnic conflict, but also that both advanced and backward ethnic groups (proxied by wealth deviations vis-à-vis the national average) are more likely to be involved in conflict than groups whose wealth lies closer to the national average.

In the following section, we demonstrate the continued relevance of the horizontal inequality framework for analyzing and understanding the emergence of violent conflicts in Africa. In particular, we analyze how the presence of horizontal inequalities has contributed to the emergence of the Boko Haram insurgency in Nigeria as well as the civil war in the CAR. For both case studies, we provide an overview of the main political events that led to the emergence of the violent conflicts, trace the root causes of the conflicts and analyze the extent and evolution of the prevailing horizontal inequalities.

Horizontal Inequalities and Violent Conflict in Africa: Insights from Two African Case Studies

The Boko Haram Insurgency in Northern Nigeria

The outbreak of the Boko Haram crisis in Nigeria is commonly traced to the July 2009 attacks in several northeastern states and the subsequent military reaction by Nigeria's armed forces in August of that year (Higazi 2013, 2015; Mohammed 2015; Raufu Mustapha 2014). However, the origins of the Boko Haram movement go back to at least 2003, when a group of about 200 young men called the "Nigerian Taliban" withdrew from the Borno State capital of Maiduguri and went to rural Kanama in Yobe State to establish an Islamic community. They came into conflict with local authorities, and a series of deadly attacks were launched in Yobe and Borno states. The intervention of the Nigerian military quelled the uprising in 2004. It is not exactly clear to what extent Mohammed Yusuf, the late leader of Boko Haram, was involved in this uprising, but many of his followers appeared to have been part of the Nigerian Taliban movement before joining the Boko Haram movement. In the wake of the uprising in 2004, Yusuf left for Saudi Arabia and only returned in 2005. On his return, Yusuf established his base in Maiduguri and recruited members for a radical Islamist movement. The 2009 crisis was triggered by a violent incident between the police and the members of Yusuf's movement, in which several of his followers were killed. In the military's counterattack, Yusuf was arrested and he was subsequently executed on July 30, 2009. The movement went underground until October 2010, at which stage the movement attacked the Bauchi prison. It was at this time that the movement, now led by Abubakar Shekau, started operating under the name

Table 1: Horizontal Inequalities between the North and the South in Nigeria in 2008 (standard errors in brackets)

Indicator	South	North	North (BH)*	Christian	Muslim	Kanuri
Education in single years	9.08 (0.037)	3.10 (0.035)	2.19 (0.057)	8.83 (0.036)	2.91 (0.041)	1.09 (0.110)
Illiteracy rate	20% (0.3)	71% (0.3)	80% (0.6)	22% (0.3)	72% (0.4)	92% (1.0)
Household electricity rate	68% (0.4)	33% (0.4)	27% (0.6)	59% (0.4)	41% (0.4)	22% (1.5)
Distance to health facility is problematic	31% (0.4)	42% (0.4)	44% (0.7)	35% (0.4)	37% (0.4)	60% (1.8)
Proportion of poorest households	5.41% (0.2)	34.19% (3.4)	46.46% (0.7)	12.01% (0.2)	31.77% (0.4)	55.62% (1.7)

Source: The authors, based on data from DHS IV 2008 Nigeria, available at http://dhsprogram.com.

* North BH refers to the five northern states in which Boko Haram is most active.

"*Jama'at ahl al-sunna li'l-da'wa wa'l-jihad*" (people committed to the propagation of the prophet's teachings and jihad).

Since 2010, Boko Haram has conducted guerrilla warfare with the proclaimed goal of carving out an independent Islamic state in the north of Nigeria. In 2014, the rebels conquered substantial territories in Borno and Adamawa states, but they were later pushed back by Nigerian troops supported by forces from Chad, Cameroon and Niger, just ahead of the March 2015 presidential elections. Under the regime of newly elected President Muhammadu Buhari, the struggle against Boko Haram has continued. It is worth noting that the violent conflict in Nigeria is characterized by severe human rights abuses and atrocities, which have been committed by both sides. (See, for example, Human Rights Watch 2016a.)

An important factor behind the Boko Haram insurgency is often argued to have been the development of radical Islamist doctrines in the north of Nigeria, a view that is, to some extent, supported by the fact that sharia law has been introduced in 12 northern states since 2000 (Higazi 2015; Mohammed 2015; Onuoha 2012; Raufu Mustapha 2014). Yet despite the

movement's radical Islamism, the explicit targeting of Christians did not occur until 2010 (Pérouse de Montclos 2015). Moreover, because Boko Haram has also brutally killed numerous Muslims, it does not enjoy support among the general Muslim population in Nigeria. The Boko Haram insurgency has also been linked to the repressive strategies used by the Nigerian state (Mohammed 2015; Pérouse de Montclos 2015). Between 2005 and 2009, members of Mohammed Yusuf's movement often became victims of police violence, arbitrary arrests and extrajudicial killings. The execution of Yusuf in 2009 is often argued to have been a major catalyst for accelerating the violent radicalization of the movement. Another crucial factor behind the Boko Haram insurgency has been the relative socio-economic deprivation and marginalization of the northern regions in Nigeria (Agbiboa 2013; Onuoha 2012; Raufu Mustapha 2014). Indeed, the success and expansion of the Boko Haram movement was crucially dependent on its ability to recruit from a vast pool of marginalized, unemployed youths, who were very susceptible to their extremist ideology and violent radicalization. Notwithstanding the multicausal complexity at the heart of the Boko Haram crisis, we now further explore how the socio-economic deprivation and relative disadvantage of the north vis-à-vis the south of Nigeria has contributed to the emergence of the Boko Haram movement.

The wealth difference between the north and the south of Nigeria is a legacy of British colonial rule (Cheeseman 2015; Suberu 2001). While the north was administered via indirect rule through Hausa-Fulani emirs, British modernization efforts were essentially limited to the economically more relevant south. Since independence, the north-south divide has led to political as well as violent conflict. For instance, the power struggles between Nigeria's three dominant ethnic groups, the Hausa-Fulani in the north, the Yoruba in the south and the Igbo in the east, directly contributed to the Biafra War, which took place from 1967 to 1970 and resulted in 500,000 to 2,000,000 casualties. The relative difference in wealth and inequality between the north and the south have persisted throughout the post-colonial period. Table 1 shows the severe socio-economic north-south disparities in Nigeria in 2008. The data are drawn from the fourth wave of Nigeria's Demographic and Health Survey (DHS), which was conducted in 2008 just before the Boko Haram uprising. The DHS surveys are administered to women between 15 and 49 years of age, and focus on issues of economic affluence, health and family planning. The total sample size was 33,385 respondents, with about 1,000 respondents for each state in Nigeria. This allows for reliable comparisons between different regions of the country.

Five indicators from the DHS data were selected to illustrate the sharp socio-economic inequalities that exist in Nigeria across regions and religions. The first indicator is the number of years of education (with standard errors in brackets). As clearly shown in the table, women in the south have much higher levels of education than those in the north. It is further noticeable that women in the five northern states in which Boko Haram is the most active — that is, Borno, Adamawa, Gombe, Yobe and Bauchi states — have by far the lowest number of years of education. The difference between the north and the south is also found when comparing Christians and Muslims, which may at least, in part, explain why religion has

become such a salient mobilizing factor in Nigeria. Finally, we also investigate the relative position of the Kanuri ethnic group, given that Boko Haram is said to have recruited disproportionately from this particular ethnic group (Higazi 2015). Clearly, this is an extremely disadvantaged group, performing much worse than both Muslims in general and the northeastern regions. The same picture emerges when exploring the proportion of women who cannot read, the proportion of households that have electricity and the proportion of women who report that the distance to a health facility is a problem when seeking help in case of illness. Based on the DHS wealth classification index, 5.4 percent of respondents in the south belonged to the poorest households, while 34.2 percent of respondents in the north belonged to the poorest households. Similar results were found for the Christian-Muslim divide.

The grievances and discontent among many northern people about their seriously disadvantaged position vis-à-vis the south clearly contributed toward creating a fertile mobilization ground for the Boko Haram insurgency. The lack of initiative and progress in reducing the existing horizontal inequalities and improving the socio-economic situation in the north clearly made matters worse in this respect. Indeed, despite the clear potential for causing serious grievances, tensions and possibly violent conflict, since independence, very little has been done in Nigeria to redress or mitigate the prevailing regional, religious and ethnic socio-economic differences and inequalities; not even the northern political elites (who have had their share of political power throughout the post-colonial period) have seriously attempted to implement policies aimed at reducing the prevailing horizontal inequalities. Unfortunately, the loss of lives, the massive displacement and the extensive destruction of infrastructure (including health clinics and schools) caused by the Boko Haram insurgency have directly contributed to a situation in which the relative socio-economic position of the north vis-à-vis the south is likely to have worsened considerably since 2009.

The Emergence of Civil War in the CAR

The CAR gained independence from France in 1960 as one of the poorest countries in the world — a feature that has not changed over time. Its political history is rife with political instability and violence (Berg 2008; Mayneri 2014). The recent episode of violence stems from a rebellion in the northeast of the country directed against the incumbent President François Bozizé. The Séléka rebel alliance grouped together different rebel actors that were unsatisfied with the implementation of earlier peace agreements with the government in 2007 and 2008.

In 2012, the Séléka rebels decided to try to capture the capital of Bangui and overthrow the Bozizé regime. The Economic Community of Central African States was, nonetheless, able to broker a new peace agreement between the rebels and the Bozizé government, which was signed in January 2013. However, Bozizé's apparent unwillingness to respect the power-sharing part of the peace deal triggered a Séléka-led coup in March 2013. A new government of national unity was appointed, with Michel Djotodia as president. Although the Séléka rebel forces were subsequently disbanded, violence in the CAR surged from the second half of 2013 onward (Human Rights Watch 2014; 2016b). The violence had now been transformed into a communal conflict between Christians and Muslims. Marauding ex-Séléka rebels, predominantly recruited from the Muslim east of the country as well as from neighbouring countries, continued to kill and plunder after the *coup d'état* and targeted predominantly Christian villages. This led to a counter-reaction by Christian self-defence groups, the anti-balaka (anti-machete), which grew out of vigilante organizations. Mutual distrust and social envy because of Muslim control over commerce in the west further exacerbated tensions between Christians and Muslims, and ultimately led to a spiral of inter-religious violence (International Crisis Group 2015). This resulted in the de facto partitioning of the country, with Muslims fleeing persecution in the west, talks of a partition in the east and recurrent fighting in the middle (ibid.). On the political level, the Séléka coalition splintered after the resignation of President Djotodia in January 2014. After an interim period, Faustin-Archange Touadéra became president in March 2016. Different armed groups have continued to operate throughout the territory.

In 2014, the CAR ranked third on the Fragile States Index, with the first place taken by South Sudan and the second place by Somalia.[5] In the same year, the CAR was ranked 187 (out of 188) on the UN Development Programme's (UNDP's) Human Development Index (UNDP 2015). During the period of colonization under France, the country was governed from the capital of Bangui with only a limited public administration (Berg 2008). Since independence, the state has not made substantial efforts to expand its reach and vast territories remain out of government control. Lacking investment and public infrastructures, most of the population remains impoverished. Furthermore, the general security situation has remained dire. Multiple armed groups operate throughout the country. (See, for example, International Crisis Group 2015; Mayneri 2014; Spittaels and Hilgert 2009.) Many rebel movements continue to prey on local populations after disbandment has failed to bring progress. Some groups have established de facto control over a territory. Foreign rebel groups, such as Uganda's Lord Resistance Army, as well as criminal gangs from Cameroon, Chad and Sudan, have also operated throughout the CAR. Indeed, the CAR is a textbook case of the "bad neighbours" argument in explaining failed states. (See, for example, Collier 2007.) The persistent violence and criminality in the country has led to the establishment of self-defence groups from which some of the anti-balaka groups have grown (International Crisis Group 2015).

---

5   More information about the Fund for Peace's Fragile States Index can be found at http://fsi.fundforpeace.org.

Table 2: Horizontal Inequalities in the CAR in 1994-1995 (standard errors in brackets)

Indicator	South	North	Christian	Muslim
Education in single years	2.91 (0.062)	1.14 (0.041)	2.28 (0.044)	1.24 (0.117)
Illiteracy rate	60% (0.9)	83% (0.7)	68% (0.7)	82% (1.7)
Household electricity rate	8% (0.5)	1% (0.2)	4% (0.3)	15% (1.6)

Source: The authors, based on data from DHS III, 1994-1995, CAR, available at http://dhsprogram.com.

Some observers note that inter-religious violence is a new feature of conflict in the CAR (see, for example, Kane 2014), where previously, the Christian majority seemed to coexist peacefully with the country's Muslim minority (Zacka 2013). However, signs of the politicization of religion were already present, as churches had become a strong instrument of neo-patrimonial rule (International Crisis Group 2015). Moreover, for a long time, CAR authorities distrusted Islamic organizations and opposed their legal registration until 1984. Muslim festivals were also not recognized as official holidays. According to Andrea C. Mayneri (2014), the Christian-Muslim divide is rooted in a deeper historical division between autochthones and Muslim migrants from the east and northeast.

Given the security climate in the CAR over the past decades, socio-economic data are scarce. Only one DHS survey, DHS III, which was completed in 1995, is available. Not all items included in DHS IV, which was used earlier in this chapter for the case of Nigeria, are included in the DHS III survey. (See Table 2.) The total number of respondents was 5,884. In Table 2, comparisons between the north and the south,[6] and between Muslims and Christians, are presented. Muslims form a 10 percent minority in the sample, but are equally represented in the north and the south. The results, first of all, give credence to the view that the relative impoverishment of the north compared to the south has formed a motivational factor in the Séléka rebellion. This also coincided with Bozizé's disregard for the 2007-2008 peace agreements, which had promised political

inclusivity. The indicators for inter-religious horizontal inequalities are not that consistent. While Muslims fare worse in terms of education and literacy levels, they have more frequent access to electricity in the household. Although not all inequality indicators run in the same direction, it appears nonetheless that the prevailing socio-economic regional and religious disparities have contributed to the emergence of violent conflict in the CAR.

Tackling Horizontal Inequalities

While it is important to address and mitigate horizontal inequalities in countries where they are severe in order to decrease the risk of violent conflict, reducing horizontal inequalities may also be "desirable from the perspective of well-being, justice and efficiency" (Langer and Stewart 2014, 112). Moreover, Langer and Stewart argue that policies aimed at reducing horizontal inequalities should "be a part of development policies more generally, both as a conflict preventative measure and because they will contribute to more just and inclusive societies" (ibid., 113). However, in the current international development practice, relatively little attention is paid to the management and reduction of horizontal inequalities. Indeed, the international donors' prime concerns "are poverty reduction and the promotion of economic growth — neither agenda includes considerations of horizontal inequalities" (ibid.). Even post-conflict countries appear to see the reduction of socio-economic horizontal inequalities as a secondary policy objective at best. While post-conflict countries often recognize

---

6   "Régions sanitaires" 4, 5 and 6 were taken to represent the north of the country.

horizontal inequalities as a contributing factor to the emergence of their country's violent conflict and may even proclaim the need and intention to develop and implement policies and measures to address these inequalities, in practice, very few post-conflict countries have actually introduced comprehensive policies and measures to correct the prevailing horizontal inequalities (Langer, Stewart and Venugopal 2011). The latter observation is all the more intriguing given that there are a range of policy interventions and options that could be used to manage horizontal inequalities.

In tackling horizontal inequalities, policy makers can use direct, indirect or integrationist approaches (Stewart, Brown and Langer 2008). Table 3 shows examples of policies and measures for each of these approaches. Direct approaches target relatively disadvantaged groups directly and aim to advance their status by implementing, for example, a fixed share of seats in Parliament or government, minority language recognition or quotas for

the allocation of jobs, and access to education and assets. Indirect policies are policies "that are universally applicable without differentiating according to group identity, but as a result of their design they can reduce horizontal inequalities" (Langer and Stewart 2014). Measures include progressive taxation, anti-discrimination policies and regional decentralization. Finally, integrationist approaches focus on the identity dimension of horizontal inequalities. Integrationist policies aim to reduce the salience of ethnic identities and instead promote a national identity. Examples of integrationist policies include the promotion of cross-group economic and social activities and the introduction of civic citizenship education in the school system.

Introducing policies aimed at reducing horizontal inequalities is not self-evident, however, and may have adverse and unintended consequences, even if the policies themselves are well intended and justifiable. For instance, the effects of ethnic

Table 3: Approaches to Reducing Horizontal Inequalities (HIs)

		Policy Approach		
		Direct HI-reducing	Indirect HI-reducing	Integrationist
Dimension	Political	Group quotas; seat reservations; list proportional representation	Design of voting system to require power-sharing across groups (e.g., two-thirds voting requirements in assembly); design of boundaries and seat numbers to ensure adequate representation of all groups; human rights legislation and enforcement	Geographical voting spread requirements; ban on ethnic/religious political parties (national party stipulations)
	Socio-economic	Quotas for employment or education; special investment or credit programs for particular groups	Anti-discrimination legislation; progressive taxation; regional development programs; sectoral support programs (e.g., Stabex)	Incentives for cross-group economic activities; requirement that schools are multicultural; promotion of multicultural civic institutions
	Cultural Status	Minority language recognition and education; symbolic recognition (e.g., public holidays, attendance at state functions)	Freedom of religious observance; no state religion	Civic citizenship education; promotion of an overarching national identity

Source: Stewart, Brown and Langer (2008).

power-sharing have been strongly scrutinized, as these types of institutions can lead to the entrenchment of ethnic identities with political competition revolving mainly around ethnicity (Brown, Langer and Stewart 2012) . This can also hamper the creation of cross-cutting political ties. A case that is often cited in this respect is Bosnia, in which the Dayton Agreement is seen to have consolidated ethnic group divisions. (See, for example, Woodward 2012.) Ethnic power-sharing institutions may break down and lead to political tensions in the long term, especially if the system is said to need revision because of differential population growth (for example, in Lebanon). Similar dynamics can arise with affirmative action policies. While affirmative action may be welcomed and seen as justified by members of relatively disadvantaged groups, relatively privileged or advantaged groups may still perceive these policies and measures as unfair, especially if these policies are maintained for long periods of time (Brown and Langer 2015). In short, policies and measures aimed at reducing horizontal inequalities are usually politically sensitive and may result in political tensions and/or the perpetuation of salient ethnic identities. This should not mean, however, that policies toward horizontal inequalities should not be implemented, but rather that they should be carefully designed and evaluated.

In order to design effective policies toward horizontal inequalities, access to reliable data is also crucial. As we have seen in the case of the CAR, data collection is not always feasible. Furthermore, not all countries allow the collection of ethnically segregated data (for example, Rwanda and Nigeria). In recent years, it has also been recognized that the focus on objective indicators of inequality, such as education levels and access to electricity, in much of the horizontal inequality literature can be problematic, as objective indicators do not necessarily correspond to people's subjective perceptions on their social status (Langer and Mikami 2013; Langer and Smedts 2013). Yet, data on how people compare their ethnic group's position relative to other groups is even scarcer

than objective socio-economic data. Nonetheless, the subjective dimension is important to consider in policy making, especially when designing and evaluating integrationist policies toward horizonal inequalities.

Some Conclusions and Future Directions of Research

In this chapter, we have reviewed the relationship between horizontal inequalities and the outbreak of violent conflicts. In the past 10 years, an increasing body of literature has shown that the presence of severe horizontal inequalities, in particular where the political and socio-economic dimensions overlap or are consistent (hence, the same group is politically excluded and socio-economically disadvantaged), significantly increases the risk of violent conflict. Moreover, as noted by Langer and Stewart (2014, 115), "while socioeconomic horizontal inequalities generate generally fertile ground for conflict to emerge and cultural status inequalities act to bind groups together, political horizontal inequalities provide incentives for leaders to mobilize people for rebellion." The two cases that were analyzed in this chapter — the Boko Haram insurgency in northern Nigeria and the emergence of civil war in the CAR — provided further evidence for the continued relevance and importance of horizontal inequalities as a factor contributing to the emergence of violent conflicts and civil war in Africa. However, while the presence of horizontal inequalities may lead to serious grievances and discontent among members of the disadvantaged group or groups, thereby creating a fertile ground for group mobilization, it is equally true that there are a range of other factors that may decide whether violence will ultimately occur or not, including, for example, the ethno-political geography and demography of a country, the history of inter-group relations, the nature and actions of the state, the presence of natural resources and the involvement (or the lack thereof) of the international community.

Despite the fact that horizontal inequalities are increasingly being recognized as an important cause of conflict, "for the most part, especially among the international community, too little attention is paid to the issue of horizontal inequalities, and the policies that are implemented in practice often accentuate them" (ibid., 115). And, even in countries emerging from violent conflict, consideration for horizontal inequalities does not seem to be given much priority (Langer, Stewart and Venugopal 2011). In this respect, it is important to note that post-conflict countries and many developing countries in general usually face a range of daunting challenges, besides reducing or mitigating the existing horizontal inequalities (ibid.). Moreover, the international community usually prioritizes poverty reduction and economic growth, and tends to neglect or completely ignore issues of horizontal inequalities. The first avenue for future research is directly linked to this observation and requires more research to be done on how considerations for horizontal inequalities can be integrated into the dominant poverty reduction and economic growth agendas. It is particularly important to study and analyze what kind of trade-offs may, at times, be necessary between these different policy agendas (Langer and Stewart 2014).

The second subject that requires research has to do with the drivers of horizontal inequalities. Horizontal inequalities have been shown to be very persistent and can sometimes last decades or even centuries. While some research has been done on the question of why horizontal inequalities are so persistent and hard to tackle (see Stewart, Brown and Langer 2008), more research is clearly needed on the drivers of horizontal inequalities as well as on the question of which policies are most effective in overcoming these persistent inequalities.

The third significant area for future research deals with the determinants of the perceptions of horizontal inequalities. While some work has recently emerged on this key issue (see, in particular, Langer and Smedts 2013), overall, there has been extremely little research conducted on the relationship between objective and subjective or perceived horizontal inequalities. More research is therefore greatly needed on the question of how objective horizontal inequalities are perceived by members of both relatively advantaged and disadvantaged groups, and more generally on the question of what drives people's perceptions of the prevailing inequalities (Langer and Stewart 2014). This is all the more important because, to a large extent, the social and political consequences of horizontal inequalities are crucially dependent on the way these inequalities are perceived by different groups within society.

Works Cited

Agbiboa, Daniel E. 2013. "Why Boko Haram Exists: The Relative Deprivation Perspective." *African Conflict and Peacebuilding Review* 3 (1): 144–157.

Berg, Patrick. 2008. *The Dynamics of Conflict in the Tri-Border Region of the Sudan, Chad and the Central African Republic*. Friedrich Ebert Foundation, Country Conflict-Analysis Studies.

Brown, Graham K. 2008. "Horizontal Inequalities and Separatism in Southeast Asia: A Comparative Perspective." In *Horizontal Inequalities and Conflict: Understanding Group Violence in Multiethnic Societies*, edited by Frances Stewart, 252–281. Houndmills, UK: Palgrave Macmillan.

Brown, Graham and Arnim Langer. 2010. "Horizontal Inequalities and Conflict: A Critical Review and Research Agenda." *Conflict, Security & Development* 10 (1): 27–55.

———. 2015. "Does Affirmative Action Work? Lessons from around the World." *Foreign Affairs* 94 (20): 49–56.

Brown, Graham, Arnim Langer and Frances Stewart, eds. 2012. *Affirmative Action in Plural Societies: International Experiences*. Houndmills, UK: Palgrave Macmillan.

Cederman, Lars-Erik, Andreas Wimmer and Brian Min. 2010. "Why Do Ethnic Groups Rebel? New Data and Analysis." *World Politics* 62 (1): 87–119.

Cederman, Lars-Erik, Nils B. Weidmann and Kristian Skrede Gleditsch. 2011. "Horizontal Inequalities and Ethnonationalist Civil War: A Global Comparison." *American Political Science Review* 105 (3): 478–495.

Cheeseman, Nic. 2015. *Democracy in Africa: Successes, Failures, and the Struggle for Political Reform*. New York, NY: Cambridge University Press.

Cobham, Alex. 2005. "Causes of Conflict in Sudan: Testing The Black Book." *European Journal of Development Research* 17 (3): 462–480.

Collier, Paul. 2001. "Economic Causes of Civil War and Their Implications for Policy." In *Turbulent Peace: The Challenges of Managing International Conflict*, edited by Chester A. Crocker, Fen Osler Hampson and Pamela Aall, 134–162. Washington, DC: United States Institute for Peace Press.

———. 2007. *The Bottom Billion: Why the Poorest Countries are Failing and What Can Be Done About It*. Oxford, UK: Oxford University Press.

Collier, Paul and Anke Hoeffler. 2002. "Greed and Grievance in Civil War." Centre for the Study of African Economies Working Paper Series No. 2002-01.

Cramer, Christopher. 2003. "Does Inequality Cause Conflict?" *Journal of International Development* 15: 397–412.

Fearon, James D. and David D. Laitin. 2003. "Ethnicity, Insurgency, and Civil War." *American Political Science Review* 97 (1): 75–90.

Garcia-Montalvo, José G. and Marta Reynal-Querol. 2004. "Ethnic Polarization, Potential Conflict, and Civil Wars." Universitat Pompeu Fabra Economics and Business Working Paper No. 770.

Gurr, Ted Robert. 1974. *Why Men Rebel*. Princeton, NJ: Princeton University Press.

———. 1993. *Minorities at Risk: A Global View of Ethnopolitical Conflicts*. Washington, DC: United States Institute of Peace Press.

Hegre, Håvard and Nicholas Sambanis. 2006. "Sensitivity Analysis of Empirical Results on Civil War Onset." *Journal of Conflict Resolution* 50 (4): 508–535.

Higazi, Adam. 2013. "Les origines et la transformation de l'insurrection de Boko Haram dans le nord du Nigeria." *Politique Africaine* 2013/2 (130): 137–164.

———. 2015. "Mobilisation Into and Against Boko Haram in North-East Nigeria." In *Collective Mobilisations in Africa/Mobilisations collectives en Afrique: Enough is enough!/Ça suffit!* edited by Kadya Tall, Marie-Emmanuelle Pommerolle and Michel Cahen, 305–358. Leiden, Netherlands: Brill.

Human Rights Watch. 2014. *World Report: Central African Republic.* www.hrw.org/world-report/2014/country-chapters/central-african-republic.

———. 2016a. *World Report: Nigeria.* www.hrw.org/world-report/2016/country-chapters/nigeria.

———. 2016b. *World Report: Central African Republic.* www.hrw.org/world-report/2016/country-chapters/central-african-republic.

International Crisis Group. 2015. "Central African Republic: The Roots of Violence." Africa Report No. 230. September 21.

Kane, Mouhamadou. 2014. "Interreligious Violence in the Central African Republic." *African Security Review* 23 (3): 312–317.

Langer, Arnim. 2005. "Horizontal Inequalities and Violent Group Mobilisation in Côte d'Ivoire." *Oxford Development Studies* 33 (1): 25–45.

Langer, Arnim and Graham Brown. 2008. "Cultural Status Inequalities: An Important Dimension of Group Mobilization." In *Horizontal Inequalities and Conflict: Understanding Group Violence in Multiethnic Societies,* edited by Frances Stewart, 41–53. Houndmills, UK: Palgrave Macmillan.

Langer, Arnim and Satoru Mikami. 2013. "The Relationship between Objective and Subjective Horizontal Inequalities: Evidence from Five African Countries." In *Preventing Violent Conflict in Africa: Inequalities, Perceptions and Institutions,* edited by Sakiko Fukuda-Parr, Frances Stewart and Yoichi Mine, 208–250. Houndmills, UK: Palgrave Macmillan.

Langer, Arnim and Kristien Smedts. 2013. "Seeing is Not Believing: Perceptions of Horizontal Inequalities in Africa." Leuven University Centre for Research on Peace and Development Working Paper No. 16.

Langer, Arnim and Frances Stewart. 2014. "Horizontal Inequalities and Violent Conflict: Conceptual and Empirical Linkages." In *Routledge Handbook of Civil Wars,* edited by Edward Newman and Karl DeRouen Jr., 104–119. Abingdon, UK: Routledge.

Langer, Arnim, Frances Stewart and Rajesh Venugopal, eds. 2011. *Horizontal Inequalities and Post-Conflict Development: Laying the Foundations for Durable Peace.* Houndmills, UK: Palgrave Macmillan.

Lichbach, Mark Irving. 1989. "An Evaluation of 'Does Economic Inequality Breed Political Conflict?' Studies." *World Politics* 41 (4): 431–470.

Mancini, Luca. 2008. "Horizontal Inequality and Communal Violence: Evidence from Indonesian Districts." In *Horizontal Inequalities and Conflict: Understanding Group Violence in Multiethnic Societies,* edited by Frances Stewart, 106–135. Houndmills, UK: Palgrave Macmillan.

Mayneri, Andrea C. 2014. "La Centrafrique, de la rébellion séléka aux groupes anti-balaka (2012-2014): usages de la violence, schème persécutif et traitement médiatique du conflit." *Politique Africaine* 2014/2 (134): 179–193.

Mohammed, Kyari. 2015. "The Message and Methods of Boko Haram." In *Boko Haram: Islamism, Politics, Security, & the State in Nigeria,* edited by Marc-Antoine Pérouse de Montclos, 9–32. Los Angeles, CA: Tsehai Publishers.

Murshed, S. Mansoob and Scott Gates. 2005. "Spatial-Horizontal Inequality and the Maoist Insurgency in Nepal." *Review of Development Economics* 9 (1): 121–134.

Nagel, Jack. 1974. "Inequality and Discontent: A Nonlinear Hypothesis." *World Politics* 26 (4): 453–472.

Onuoha, Freedom C. 2012. "The Audacity of the Boko Haram: Background, Analysis and Emerging Trend." *Security Journal* 25 (2): 134–151.

Østby, Gudrun. 2008. "Polarization, Horizontal Inequalities and Violent Civil Conflict." *Journal of Peace Research* 45 (2): 143–162.

Pérouse de Montclos, Marc-Antoine. 2015. "Boko Haram and Politics: From Insurgency to Terrorism." In *Boko Haram: Islamism, Politics, Security and the State in Nigeria*, edited by Marc-Antoine Pérouse de Montclos, 135–157. Los Angeles, CA: Tsehai Publishers.

Raufu Mustapha, Abdul. 2014. "Understanding Boko Haram." In *Sects and Social Disorder: Muslim Identities and Conflict in Northern Nigeria*, edited by Abdul Raufu Mustapha, 147–198. Woodbridge, UK: James Currey.

Spittaels, Steven and Filip Hilgert. 2009. *Mapping Conflict Motives: Central African Republic.* International Peace Information Services. www.geneva-academy.ch/RULAC/pdf_state/IPIS-CAR-mappingconflictmotives.pdf.

Stewart, Frances. 2000. "The Root Causes of Humanitarian Emergencies." In *War, Hunger and Displacement: The Origins of Humanitarian Emergencies, Volume 1: Analysis*, edited by E. Wayne Nafziger, Frances Stewart and Raimo Väyrynen. Oxford, UK: Oxford University Press.

———. 2002. "Horizontal Inequalities: A Neglected Dimension of Development." Queen Elizabeth House, University of Oxford, Working Paper No. 81.

———. ed. 2008. *Horizontal Inequalities and Conflict: Understanding Group Violence in Multiethnic Societies.* Houndmills, UK: Palgrave Macmillan.

Stewart, Frances and Graham Brown. 2007. "Motivations for Conflict: Groups and Individuals." In *Leashing the Dogs of War: Conflict Management in a Divided World*, edited by Chester A. Crocker, Fen Osler Hampson and Pamela R. Aall, 219–244. Washington, DC: United States Institute of Peace Press.

Stewart, Frances, Graham Brown and Arnim Langer. 2008. "Policies towards Horizontal Inequalities." In *Horizontal Inequalities and Conflict: Understanding Group Violence in Multiethnic Societies*, edited by Frances Stewart, 301–325. Houndmills, UK: Palgrave Macmillan.

Suberu, Rotimi. 2001. *Federalism and Ethnic Conflict in Nigeria.* Washington, DC: United States Institute of Peace Press.

Tilly, Charles. 1978. *From Mobilization to Revolution.* Reading, MA: Addison-Wesley.

Ukiwo, Ukoha. 2008. "Horizontal Inequalities and Ethnic Violence: Evidence from Calabar and Warri, Nigeria." In *Horizontal Inequalities and Conflict: Understanding Group Violence in Multiethnic Societies*, edited by Frances Stewart, 190–204. Houndmills, UK: Palgrave Macmillan.

UNDP. 2015. *Human Development Report.* New York, NY: UNDP.

Woodward, Susan L. 2012. "The Bosnian Paradox: On the Causes of Post-War Inequality and Barriers to Its Recognition and Reduction." In *Horizontal Inequalities and Post-Conflict Development*, edited by Arnim Langer, Frances Stewart and Rajesh Venugopal. Houndmills, UK: Palgrave Macmillan.

Zacka, Jimi P. 2013. "Centrafrique: Chrétiens et Musulmans, pouvons-nous reapprendre à vivre ensemble?" Al Wihda, December 22. www.alwihdainfo.com/Centrafrique-Chretiens-et-musulmans-pouvons-nous-reapprendre-a-vivre-ensemble_a9096.html.

4

Conflicts without Borders: Fulani Herdsmen and Deadly Ethnic Riots in Nigeria

Eghosa E. Osaghae

Nigeria has been in the throes of complex identity-based conflicts since the 1990s. Although some of the conflicts such as the one under focus in this chapter can be regarded as new, spontaneous and fleeting, belonging to the category of what Donald Horowitz (2001) characterizes as "deadly ethnic riots," which tend to be episodic rather than ubiquitous, involve widespread hostility and brutal killings, and produce memories that linger and shape group relations afterward, nevertheless, they are products of historically embedded cleavages and triggers that make divided societies continuously open to conflicts. Issues of contested citizenship, resource inequalities, uneven development and political exclusion and marginalization, which have been accentuated by shocks of resource boom and doom, upsurges in global terrorism and conflicts, violent electoral politics and the like, have been crucial factors in this regard. But this is only one part of what makes the recent conflicts protracted, deadly and more difficult to manage.

The recurrent nature, strategies and scale of destruction make the forms of conflict unusual, unconventional and new, with Boko Haram, Niger Delta minorities' militancy and the ethnic riots of Fulani herdsman being prototypical. The guerilla, terrorist and militant strategies employed by the warring groups — sophisticated firearms, kidnapping, robbery, rape, suicide bombing, unprecedented scales of killing and destruction, random targeting, clandestine operations and large areas attacked, and cross-boundary mobility fuelled by forces of globalization — defied conventional wisdom on conflict management, and posed new challenges the already weak and overstressed state had difficulty coping with. More specific characteristics of the conflicts expose their complexity and elusiveness. First, they involved multiple identities, whose mutually reinforcing connections made the conflicts more politically consequential and divisive. Of particular note is the recursive intersection among ethnic, religious and regional identities (Zacharias and Zenn 2016), which has been conducive to ethnic malleability and reconstructions. Second, the non-elite and underclass social backgrounds of the major actors, as well as the spontaneous and dispersed nature of conflicts that involved one ethnic group conflicting with members of several other ethnic groups at once, challenge conventional wisdoms that hinge on elite mobilization, inter-group hostilities and ethnic battles to capture state power and resources. Although these factors are generally crucial in identity-based conflicts in Africa, the analysis undertaken in this chapter suggests that pressures of material reproduction and survival were at the core of the spontaneous ethnic riots. One implication this has for managing riot conflicts is that the actual conflict actors and protagonists have to be involved in the search for solutions. This requires a deviation from the usual elite-directed, top-down frameworks in which the so-called interests of actual protagonists are intermediated by self-appointed leaders. These emerging complexities are amply exemplified by the case of the Fulani herdsmen discussed in this chapter.

Also, there has been a great deal of conflict mobility — that is, the tendency of conflicts to permeate or "travel" across conflict zones and state boundaries (de Bruijn and Osaghae 2011; de Bruijn and van Dijk 2012; Lake and Rothchild 1998). Indeed, the dimensions, technologies and impact of conflict mobility within and across states have increased tremendously. Major facilitators include protocols on free trade and movements of persons and goods across national boundaries, migrations, internal displacements and refugee flows, arms proliferation,

globalization of anti-state and terrorist ideologies, radicalization, organizations and activities (such as al-Qaeda in the Maghreb), information and communication technologies (social media), and activities of diaspora communities. The diffusion and similarities of strategies such as kidnapping, child soldiers, rape, robberies, extensive use of militias and sophisticated weapons, human rights justification, organization of conflict groups into cells and networks including diaspora units, and suicide bombing are some of the manifestations of conflict mobility that also involve learning, imitation, adoption and even training. The Arab Spring and the rise of militant and terrorist activities in north Africa, Somalia and the Middle East in particular, and global terrorism in general, have been linked with the rise of terrorism in Nigeria, Mali, Cameroon and other places in west and central Africa. As a result of conflict mobility, very few conflicts today can be regarded as truly local, particularistic or isolated; every conflict has the actuality or potential to spread and trigger or affect conflicts elsewhere. The notion of conflict mobility is very relevant to the conflicts involving the Fulani in Nigeria because of the dispersal of members of the group across several countries, the nomadic culture of the group that underlies movements and migrations across boundaries, the employment of mobility as a productive strategy, and the traditional practice of "flight" or retreat from one conflict zone to another (Wilson-Fall 2000). In fact, one of the factors that complicated the recent Fulani conflicts in Nigeria was the fact that the herdsmen that attacked local communities included alien Fulani from Chad, Niger, Mali and Mauritania. According to the Nigerian minister of agriculture, this was inevitable: "For pastoralists from neighbouring West African countries, access to grazing rights in other countries in the ECOWAS [Economic Community of West African States] zone including Nigeria is guaranteed by the ECOWAS Transhumance Protocol of 1998 and ECOWAS Protocol on free movement of goods and services in West Africa" (*The Nation* 2016d). This also explains the increased incidence of conflicts between herdsmen and farmers in Ghana, Burkina Faso and other parts of west Africa.

Third, and as a result of the foregoing, recent and ongoing deadly conflicts in Nigeria have tended to be national or countrywide in scope and impact. Even where they have involved two or a few groups, or the issues have been local, the intensity and scale of destruction, loss of lives and displacement of human populations, as well as their interconnectedness with larger issues of state legitimacy and potential to escalate and spread rapidly, have attracted the intervention of state and global actors. The evidence suggests not only an increase in the incidence of identity-based conflicts, but also an increase in complexity and scale of destruction that renders manageability more difficult. The case of the Fulani herdsmen, the *Bororo*, whose deadly riots in various parts of Nigeria precipitated a rash of conflicts that were at once regional, religious, ethnic and communal, is analyzed against this backdrop. The conflicts not only threatened the legitimacy and survival of the fragile Nigerian state, but involved another crucial dimension, the cross-national character of Fulani identity. From this character, it follows that attempts at managing or resolving Fulani-related conflicts have, of necessity, to involve crucial external considerations of what to do with Fulani from other countries.

What was the nature of the Fulani deadly riots that erupted in Nigeria beginning from the early 2000s? Which identities were involved and how were they mobilized? What were the sources and triggers of the riots, and how did the riots precipitate a national question-type crisis? What solutions have been proposed or deployed, and what are the chances of success? These are some of the crucial questions to be tackled in this chapter. The chapter begins with a conceptual location of the Fulani attacks in terms of Horowitz's deadly ethnic riots, followed by an examination of the intricacies of Fulani identity and ethnicity, and the Nigerian episode. The final section presents

the conclusions from the Nigerian episode within the larger framework of identity-based conflicts of the conflict mobility genre, and how they can be managed or resolved.

The Nature of Deadly Ethnic Riots

Since the end of the Cold War, identity-based conflicts have increased in intensity and destructive propensity. From Rwanda to Kosovo, Bosnia, Darfur, Croatia and Congo, the scale of violence, massacres and genocide was incredible. The unravelling of hegemonic state structures presented the ostensible enabling environment for resurrections of old conflicts and new contestations for supremacy, but the vicious character of the conflicts challenged scholars of ethnicity to search for new frameworks of analysis. How and why would groups attack each other with so much sadism and in such a sporadic, yet organized, manner?

One of the more insightful frameworks for understanding such conflicts, and the one that I consider appropriate for analyzing the conflicts involving Fulani herdsmen in Nigeria is that of deadly ethnic riots formulated by Donald Horowitz. Horowitz (2001, 1) defines a deadly ethnic riot as "an intense, sudden, though not necessarily unplanned, lethal attack by civilian members of one ethnic group on civilian members of another ethnic group…The deadly ethnic riot is a passionate but highly patterned event…an episode triggered by events — precipitants — that are regarded as sufficient to warrant violence." The fact that the riots are sudden and episodic does not of course mean that they are ahistorical and unrelated to previous conflicts and enmities, a point that Horowitz acknowledges. Even in their sporadic forms, ethnic riots are not isolated or single riots. They tend to occur in sets or sequences that may be weeks, months, even years apart, but with the same initiators and victims.

The most extended of riots, which take place at different times and places, belong to the category of "recurrent riots." This is an apt description of the violent activities of Fulani herdsmen in Nigeria who randomly attacked members of different ethnic groups and communities across the country. However, an important distinction should be made here. Horowitz's focus is more on discriminate violence bordering on "ethnic terrorism" in which riot initiators target members of one or a few ethnic groups for extermination, if possible. In the Fulani case, the attacks on the Jukun of Taraba state and other communities in Benue, Plateau and Kaduna states, which have long histories of conflicts with Fulani "settlers," had this character. In fact, a Nigerian lawyer and human rights activist, Femi Falana, filed a case of genocide and ethnic cleansing against the Fulani herdsmen for the atrocious massacres of Jukun people of southern and central Taraba state in the ECOWAS Court of Justice in April 2016. Allegations of ethnic cleansing were also made by victims in Benue, Kaduna and Plateau states. By contrast, attacks on communities in other parts of the country, especially in the south, were too random to suggest that particular ethnic groups were targeted. Ethnic and religious — in-group out-group — differentiation was fundamental in the attacks, of course (attacks on churches, for instance, gave the riots a religious slant), but all non-Fulani communities that stood in the way of grazing access were fair game for attack. And, although they took place in different places and at different times, the attacks followed a similar pattern: they were either offensive or defensive-retaliatory against cattle rustlers or communities that opposed free-range cattle grazing; the attackers used AK-47 and other high-calibre assault weapons; and the attacks took place mostly at night and involved massive destruction of lives and property.

Horowitz adopts a psychoanalytical approach to explaining riots, which emphasizes group solidarity and the roles of fear, insecurity, rumour, the calculus of passion and conditions and precipitants that are conducive to disorder and provocation, which are often underlying and proximate concomitants of deadly ethnic riots. However, we consider these to be necessary, not sufficient, factors for ethnic riots, which are approached here as outcomes of the desperation for economic or material reproduction and survival. We take the position of Stefan Wolff's (2006) rational choice explanation for ethnic conflict, which holds that ethnic violence is deliberate rather than spontaneous: it is the result "of deliberate choices of people to pursue certain goals with violent means. Often they see this as the only choice in conditions that are beyond their control" (ibid., 90). David A. Lake and Donald Rothchild (1998) analyze such choices in terms of "strategic interactions" between and within groups. For Wolff (2006, 74), the deliberate choices are forced by security dilemmas, one of which may arise from "changes in access to, or control over, economic resources." The origins — or triggers — of the attacks by Fulani herdsmen, as we shall see, lie in the security dilemma propelled by diminishing spaces of and access to cattle grazing, following the adverse effects of climate change (desertification, disease), and prolonged conflicts and terrorist attacks in the northern parts of Nigeria and the Sahel region as a whole, which forced migrations in large numbers to the southern parts of the country (and Ghana, Cameroon and the Central African Republic as well). The situation presented violence as the only option for people whose source of livelihood — cattle breeding — was receding and directly threatened.

Ethnic riots have another important attribute that differentiates them from normal ethnic conflicts: the difficulty of identifying actual participants, even when the identities of rioters are known. In the case of rioting herdsmen in Nigeria, the riots evoked ambiguities and contestations over the actual identity of the rioters. While the victims claimed they were Fulani, some Fulani and sympathetic northern leaders rejected the equation of the amorphous herdsmen with Fulani, even while defending the herdsmen. Because riots are mostly clandestine, spontaneous and unorganized, "it is possible to learn more about the victims of violence than about those who victimize them" (Horowitz 2001, 224). "What the evidence shows is that most riots seem to be unorganized, partially organized and partially spontaneous, or organized by ephemeral leadership that springs up to respond to events as they happen, often suddenly. Most riots, in other words consist of angry violence. Even where riots are reasonably well organized, as in the case of party-organized riots, their main objective is to further ethnic polarization in an already polarized environment or to take advantage of a hostile mood" (ibid., 225).

Horowitz's conclusion that the absence of evidence pointing to the role of organizations does not necessarily mean the absence of any organizational involvement provides a lead for analysis of how identities were mobilized, but there can be no denying the fact that the phenomenon of ethnic riots challenges conventional wisdom on ethnogenesis. Explanations that allude to elite leadership and organizational impetuses for politicizing ethnic identity and mobilizing action, provide only partial and sometimes conspiratorial perspectives of ethnic riots. This is so because the riots are perpetrated by bands of local people (in the Fulani case nomads) propelled by "angry violence." Fulani leaders and interest groups such as the Gan Allah Fulani Association, Jamu Nate Fulbe Association and Miyetti Allah Cow Breeders Association of Nigeria have either absolved their kinsmen from instigating the riots or defended their actions, and this has led to accusations that the *Hardo* (Fulani chiefs) and Miyetti Allah "sponsor" the attacks. The role of the chiefs who head the dispersed groups and, therefore, are critical to group actions, may be important, but in the absence of any known central body of chiefs, the connections are at best speculative. However, bands of pastoralists from within and outside Nigeria, especially those who share grazing routes

and migration patterns, have been known to take concerted action based on cultural practices when threatened by other groups. The best known of such practices is the "sending of kola nuts" to leaders of proximate bands and camps as an invitation for support in times of conflict or, in this case, in the deadly attacks.

Fulani Identity in Perspective

The Fulani (also called Fula, Fulbe or Peul by the French) are one of the most widely dispersed peoples in Africa. The vast majority of them are spread across west Africa (Nigeria, Guinea, Mali, Niger, Chad, Burkina Faso, Mauritania, Senegal and Gambia), and significant populations are found in the northern parts of central Africa (Cameroon, Central African Republic), Sudan and Egypt.

The dispersal of Fulani identity and ethnic politics, including cultural variations and peculiarities induced by differences in colonial experience, contemporary state politics, political economy and inter-group relations within the different states, makes the definition, space and boundaries of Fulani identity a little tricky. If we define Fulani as those who speak the Fulbe or Fulfude language, for example, what do we make of the wide varieties between the language spoken in Guinea and that in the Adamawa region of Nigeria and Cameroon, or even of the fact that many Fulani in Nigeria speak Hausa, the perceived language of political power (never mind that a few puritans insist on maintaining separate Fulani identity in this regard)? Territoriality, another popular ethnic diacritic in Africa, is also problematic in relation to the Fulani. Territoriality means that an ethnic group has a homeland or an area over which its members claim (exclusive) ownership (Harneit-Sievers 2006). Such claims become the basis for in-group out-group differentiations in access to land and resources, power structures and allocation of resources and privileges by higher political authorities, which separate so-called indigenes[1] from non-indigenes, create ethnic hierarchies and can foment conflict.

As a predominantly pastoral nomadic people whose main preoccupation is cattle herding, the Fulani are traditionally itinerant. Indeed, the major intra-group cleavage separates the nomadic Fulani cattle herders (*Bororo* or *Fulbe ladde*) from the settled or town Fulani, each traditionally led by different leaders. The settled Fulani have ethnic homelands, simply meaning places where they have settled over time, which in Nigeria are spread across present-day Sokoto, Kebbi, Katsina, Kano, Adamawa, Bauchi and Gombe states, as well as the Benue River Valley, Garoua, Chamba and Mambilla Plateau, which house the so-called Benue Fulani. The core of Fulani homeland is made up of areas that belonged to the Sokoto caliphate or fell under caliphate rule and influence in the aftermath of the jihad of 1804. Claims to other homelands, such as those in the Benue region and "conquered" territories such as Ilorin and Kano, which have Fulani traditional rulers, are tenuous and disputed by indigenous groups who regard the Fulani as settlers. The nomadic Fulani, on their part, are peoples without borders. The Fulani have no history of attempts at territorial unification, although in the recent past, global and diaspora Fulani organizations have emphasized the unity of the group and sought to protect the interests of Fulani in the various countries where they exist. Notwithstanding the problematic diacritic, the Fulani constitute a distinct ethnic group within the countries in which they live and across the countries. They are bound together by a common ancestry, the Fula (Fulfude) language, common religion, cultural elements and practices, common physical and racial traits, and pastoralism. Of all the ethnic markers, however, cattle herding is

regarded as the most intrinsic to Fulani identity and social reproduction: "The Fulbe origin as a people is tied in with their role as keepers of cattle. In Fulbe ideology and mythology, they came into existence as caretakers of cattle, and the future existence of Fulbe culture and identity is intimately related to the continued association of Fulbe people with their animals" (Wilson-Fall 2000, 49).

More important, the Fulani have — and are perceived by members of other groups to have — a sense of collective uniqueness, solidarity and common destiny, which provides the basis for collective action in relations with other groups and the state.

A good proportion of Fulani are urbanized and live in the modern sector, but the vast majority are nomadic rural pastoralists (an estimated 65 percent of all Fulani are nomadic). It is the nomadic character of the group that has shaped its history of migration and relations with other groups. Since the sixteenth century, nomadic groups of cattle breeders have traversed the Sahel grasslands stretching from present-day Senegal to Sudan in search of grazing lands, and have established grazing routes and sites over the years, with scant regard to cross-national boundaries (the porosity of the boundaries has made this possible) or ethnic boundaries within the countries. In recent times, the adverse effects of climate change, notably drought and desertification, which have been increasing since the 1990s, drastically reducing water supply, pasture and land available for herding on the one hand, and the protracted conflicts and terrorist activities in the Sahel (Mali, Burkina Faso, Niger, Mauritania, northern Nigeria and Chad) on the other, have forced migrations by herdsmen further into the more arable southern parts of west Africa.

This pattern of grazing-induced migrations has made the Fulani an ethnic group without borders, both within and across countries. It has also brought them into conflict with host communities, especially local farmers whose farmlands, crops

---

1 Harneit-Sievers (2006, 1), however, makes the important point that "To be an indigene does require residence; it usually means to be identified, by birth or link of ancestry, with a particular *community of origin*" (emphasis original).

and water supply are most directly affected. In a sense, the Fulani have been some of the earliest harbingers of conflict mobility. These factors have cumulatively produced a Fulani identity that is tied to nomadic herding (in addition to language, cultural and religious similarities), and strengthened intra-group cohesion as Fulani wherever they may be, and irrespective of national identities (Nigerian, Nigerien, Burkina Faso, Malian, Chadian, Mauritanian), have a duty to defend the interests of their risk-prone kin. It is for this reason that the differentiation made between Nigerian and foreign Fulani herdsmen in the deadly riots in Nigeria is not really helpful.

Let us turn to the Fulani in Nigeria. The first point of note is the group's pre-eminent Islamic and political status following the jihad of Usman dan Fodio in 1804, which brought many parts of the north, including the powerful Hausa states, under the suzerainty of the Sokoto caliphate, and the divide-and-rule policies of British colonizers that further privileged Sokoto and the Fulani in the country's political hierarchy. The Fulani are a dominant political force in the north and the country as a whole, with the Sultan of Sokoto, *sarkin musulumi (*spiritual leader) of all Muslim faithful in Nigeria (Muslims constitute an estimated 50 percent of the country's population) and president of the National Supreme Council for Islamic Affairs, as the rallying point. The Fulani have further strengthened their political influence through ethnic fusion and coalition with the Hausa, the dominant ethnic group in northern Nigeria, through intermarriage, religious, socio-cultural and political integration, elite collaboration and adoption of the more widely spoken Hausa language. This synthesis, which Wendy Wilson-Fall (2000) describes as one of the traditional conflict management mechanisms pursued by the Fulani elite in west Africa, has produced the Hausa-Fulani ethnic group, which has been the most powerful political group in the north and the whole of Nigeria since independence. The perception of Hausa-Fulani political domination has shaped relations with

members of other ethnic groups in the country, and was a major factor in the perceived audacity and impunity of the herdsmen in the ethnic riots under focus, especially with Muhammadu Buhari, a Fulani, as president. However, while Fulani and Hausa elite have strategically acted to strengthen this perception, using Islam as a major cementing force, the Fulani have maintained a distinct identity in many areas, especially nomadic lifestyles and herding. (The Hausa are by contrast settled land-owning and agrarian peoples.) In effect, the Fulani constitute a minority ethnic group that has used its Muslim suzerainty established since the conquest of the larger Hausa group in the 1804 jihad and strategic fusion with the Hausa elite to wield great political influence in Nigeria. The non-elite Fulani obviously benefit from this power contrivance (the perceived "protection" of rioting herdsmen by the federal government suggests this is so), but have maintained their Fulani identity through nomadic lifestyle, herding and use of Fulfude language. (Most nomadic Fulani speak Hausa as a second language in contradistinction to the elite Fulani who freely speak Hausa.)

But who exactly are the Fulani in Nigeria, and to what extent were the attacks ethnic? These questions became very significant with the outbreak of the riots when many Fulani and northern leaders rejected the equation of Fulani with herdsmen — they argued that while it was true that the Fulani were predominantly nomadic pastoralists, not all cattle breeders and farmers, the so-called herdsmen, were Fulani. For example, the leader of the Northern Senators Forum, Senator Abdullahi Adamu, argued that the categorization of all herdsmen as Fulani was wrong because there were also Yoruba and Igbo cattle farmers who, in the context, were regarded as Fulani. Similarly, the Northern Governors Forum, Jama'atu Nasril Islam, a coalition of several Islamic groups in Nigeria, and the Sultan of Sokoto, Alhaji Mohammed Sa'ad Abubakar III, criticized those who blamed the Fulani herdsmen for the attacks perpetrated against farmers in Benue, Enugu and other states across the country, describing the widespread insinuation as "absurd" and "unfortunate," and an insult to the Fulani. For the governors, it was wrong to politicize and ethnicize what were essentially economic conflicts between "herdsmen" and "farmers." Some commentators and federal government officials also absolved the Fulani and blamed some of the attacks on "fifth columnists" and alien Fulani from neighbouring countries such as Chad, Mali, Niger and Cameroon. According to Sultan Abubakar, the killer herdsmen who he described as "terrorists" were "foreigners" coming into Nigeria to cause a breach of the peace; by contrast, Nigerian Fulani herdsmen "are peace-loving and law-abiding" (*The Nation* 2016f). There were even those who speculated that the so-called herdsmen were Boko Haram operatives and that the attacks were part of the new terrorist strategies of the insurgents (there was very little evidence to support this speculation, especially as Boko Haram activities remained restricted to the northeast region of the country).

However, members of communities that were attacked by herdsmen claimed they were Fulani because they "looked alike," "were Muslim," "were cattle herders," and "spoke the language" (Hausa, which most people know, or Fulfude, which many do not know?). Although these identifying features were adequate but not sufficient to prove that the herdsmen were Fulani, local or alien, what was important for members of the out-groups was the age-long common interest that underlaid their actions: safeguarding their cattle and pastoral livelihood. One way to resolve the identity issue is to go back to the long histories of migrations, grazing routes and conflicts between nomads and host communities, especially in the Benue Valley area that has been a popular site of grazing and Fulani settlement, and other locations in present-day Benue, Taraba, Plateau, Nasarawa and Kaduna states. The histories pitched the Fulani against local communities, and the attacks of the 2000s were simply a (more desperate and deadly) continuation of the age-long conflicts over grazing and settlement rights.

In other parts of the country, including the south, cattle breeding and pastoral migrations have long been associated with the Fulani, and Fulani settlements and camps, which serve as migration centres, have existed in some communities for several years. For example, Okada, Udo and Okhomu communities of Edo state, which were sites of recent riots, have had Fulani camps since the late 1960s. Similarly, Adada-Nkpologu-Adani-Iggah and Agwu-Nkani-Abakaliki areas of Enugu state, which also came under attack, have had Fulani settlements for a long time. Also, the fact that the attacks on other parts of the country took their bearings from the attacks on the Middle Belt[2] communities (the attack on Ukpabi Nimbo in southeastern Nigeria in April 2016 was launched from the Middle Belt fringes of Kogi state), reinforces the belief that the warring herdsmen were Fulani. On balance, therefore, the question of the identity of the ethnic rioters is fairly well settled on the part of the victim communities, many of which have had contacts with the herdsmen for a long time. Furthermore, in circumstances of disputed identities, scholars of ethnicity place a premium on how members of the conflicting group — in this case Fulani — define themselves and why they would sacrifice for collective interests (Rajchman 1995; Horowitz 2001).

The Fulani themselves, through associations such as the Miyeti Allah Cattle Breeders Association, a well-known umbrella association of Fulani pastoralists that was founded in 1972 and has branches in most parts of the country, Gan Allah Fulani Association and Jamu Nate Fulbe Association affirmed the Fulani identity of the herdsmen, and insisted on their right to engage in legitimate economic activity in any part of the country in terms of the constitutionally guaranteed

---

2   The Middle Belt is a geographical area in northern Nigeria where the bulk of northern ethnic minorities (mostly non-Hausa/Fulani, non-Muslim) are located.

freedom of movement to all citizens.[3] Others justified the attacks on the grounds that they were provoked by the killing and stealing of Fulani cattle, which deprived members of the group of their heritage and livelihood. As for the non-Nigerian Fulani who were believed to be involved in the attacks, all that need be said is that they have historically been part of the Fulani grazing migrations. To the extent that their Nigerian kin share with them a sense of common destiny and collective survival, and do not have a history of discriminating against them in the pursuit of economic survival, the fact of being alien should not be overemphasized. As Aluh Moses Odeh, national leader of the All Middle Belt Forum pointed out, "the argument that the perpetrators are foreigners is false. They are Fulani herdsmen who move their cows about" (*The Nation* 2016a). This fits with our characterization of the Fulani, especially the nomadic Fulani as an ethnic group without borders. At a more underlying conceptual level, the fluidity and ambiguity of Fulani identity provides a classical illustration of the situationality of ethnic identities, the tendency of identities to be constructed (even invented) and deconstructed in conflict situations. The occasion of the ethnic riots presented the Fulani an opportunity for "reconfirming" their distinctly Fulani identity.

Fulani Herdsmen and the Deadly Ethnic Riots in Nigeria

Since 2010 violent conflicts have erupted between armed herdsmen believed to be nomadic Fulani and members of mostly farming communities all over the country. The conflicts have been triggered by disputes over access — and rights — to stock routes, grazing fields and water for cattle. Host communities are angered by the destruction of crops and farmlands, and the pollution of waters and what some claim are attempts by the Fulani herdsmen to dispossess them of their lands. This has been the case in the Benue Valley areas of present-day Benue, Plateau, Nasarawa, Taraba, Adamawa and (southern) Kaduna states where indigene/non-indigene conflicts have been somewhat endemic. However, southward seasonal migrations by herdsmen (including alien herdsmen) from the Sahel to rainforest regions during the dry season (November–March) in search of grazing fields also have a long history. Indeed, "traditional" grazing routes and Fulani settlements and camps have been established in many communities over the years. Furthermore, relations between herdsmen and host communities have been generally peaceful, and the odd dispute and conflicts were resolved through meetings of leaders of the groups, payment of fines and so on. This partly explains the stability of migration patterns and routes, although it should be noted that there has been very little integration between the Fulani and host communities through intermarriage for instance; the Fulani have maintained their (separate) identities of ethnicity, language, faith, livelihood methods and land-use patterns peculiar to their Sahel belt, which have kept them apart from host communities.

The situation has changed rapidly in the last decade, especially since 2010. Conflicts between Fulani herdsmen and grazing communities have increased in scope and intensity all over the country, leading to vicious attacks, rape, killings and massive destruction by gangs of herdsmen. The herdsmen also perpetrated violent crimes of armed robbery and kidnapping. For some time, the attacks, which led to displacements and dispossession of land in some cases, were concentrated in the Jos area and other parts of Plateau state, and later spread to Benue, Nasarawa, Taraba, (southern) Kaduna, Zamfara, Adamawa, Kwara and Kogi states. These areas had long histories of disputes and conflicts with Fulani herdsmen, but still, the scale of violence

---

3   According to Ardo Ahmadu Suleiman, chairman of the northwest zone of the association, the Fulani have "been living peacefully with tribes across the country for ages. Therefore, for anyone to say he wants to ban Fulani from entering their land is uncalled for" (*The Guardian* 2016).

Attacks on Benue State Communities (2013–2016)

April 23, 2013

Ten farmers killed in an attack on Mbasenge community in Guma local government area (LGA).

May 7, 2013

Forty-seven mourners gunned down in Agatu.

May 14, 2013

Over 200 herdsmen surrounded Ekwo-Okpanchenyi, Agatu LGA, killing 40 locals.

July 5, 2013

Twenty people killed in a conflict between Tiv farmers and herdsmen at Nzorov, Guma LGA.

July 28, 2013

Herdsmen invade two villages in Agatu LGA, killing eight villagers.

November 7, 2013

Seven killed in Ikpele and Okpopolo communities; over 6,000 displaced.

November 9, 2013

Thirty-six locals killed and seven villages overrun in Agatu.

November 20, 2013

Twenty-two killed in attack on communities in Guma LGA.

January 20, 2014

Attack on Adeke village left three dead.

February 24, 2014

Attack on a Tiv community left eight dead.

March 10, 2014

Former governor Suswam's convoy attacked by herdsmen at Umenger.

March 12, 2014

Twenty-eight killed during a raid on Ukpam village in Guma LGA.

March 23, 2014

Twenty-five killed and over 50 injured in Gbajimba, Guma LGA.

Twenty-two killed when suspected herdsmen attack Suswan's village in Logo LGA.

April 15, 2014

Twelve killed in Obagaji, Headquarters of Agatu LGA.

September 10, 2014

Herdsmen attacked five villages in Ogbadibo LGA.

March 15, 2015

Over 90 killed in Egba village in Agatu.

March 24, 2015

One hundred killed in an attack by herdsmen in villages and refugee camps.

February 8, 2016

Ten killed and over 300 displaced in Buruku LGA.

February 29, 2016

Over 500 killed and 7000 displaced in Agatu LGA.

March 9, 2016

Eight killed in Logo LGA.

March 13, 2016

Six, including an All Progressives Congress youth leader, killed in Tarkaa LGA.

Data source: The Nation (2016c).

and killings was unprecedented. The 2015 Global Terrorism Index classifies the herdsmen as Fulani militants and ranks their attack on Galadima as the tenth-deadliest in the world in 2014, with 200 fatalities (Institute for Economics & Peace 2015). Some of the other horrendous attacks took place in Barkin Ladi local government area of Plateau state and Agatu and Guma local government areas of Benue state, which were constantly raided by the herdsmen between 2013 and 2016 (see above). Communities in Taraba and Nasarawa states and southern Kaduna also suffered heavy casualties.

The trajectory and implications of the riots changed when the killing herdsmen moved further and further into the southern parts of the country. Again, Fulani migrations and herding activities in the south, whose rainforest vegetation provides greener pasture for cattle, especially during the dry season, were not new. From time to time there were conflicts with local communities over grazing access and destruction of farmlands by cattle (the Oke Ogun communities of Oyo State have a long history of such conflicts), but these were not widespread, as the hosts and foreigner herdsmen lived in relative harmony. But things changed dramatically when the herdsmen extended their new all-year grazing migration and deadly ethnic riots to southern communities. The abduction of Chief Olu Falae, a prominent Yoruba leader from his farm in Akure by herdsmen in 2015, portended the new phase of conflict. This was followed by several more abductions and robberies by herdsmen who waylaid people on the highways, raped and killed many of their victims. As in the north, the core of the onslaught remained the attacks on agrarian communities, which quickly spread to virtually all states in the south, including unlikely riverine ocean-lying states such as Bayelsa, Rivers and Lagos. The height of the violence came in March 2016, with the attack on the Igbo Ukpabi Nimbo community of Enugu state in which more than 40 people were killed. This attack and others in Ekiti, Delta, Edo,

Oyo and Ondo States finally triggered a rash of hostilities and conflict.

Against the backdrop of the tensions already generated by Boko Haram terrorism, which had strong links with global Muslim fundamentalism and terrorism, separatist agitations by Igbo-Biafra ethno-nationalists and Niger Delta militants, unfulfilled demands and expectations by several aggrieved groups, diminishing resources and declining state capacity to provide basic public goods and services, the Fulani wars led to a resurgence of the traditional, mutually reinforcing cleavages of Nigerian politics: ethnicity, religion and regionalism. The character and patterns of attacks and conflicts made this somewhat inevitable: the attackers were mostly Muslim; the communities attacked were mostly non-Muslim (churches were main targets in some cases); and those who defended, even justified, the riots of the herdsmen were mostly Muslim northern political and religious leaders, thereby giving the conflicts a north (Muslim)–south (Christian) coloration. We have already referred to the perspectives of northern leaders who not only absolved the Fulani, but seemed to equate the vehement counter-mobilization by southern and Middle Belt leaders as attacks on the (Muslim) north, which further raised the stakes of conflict.

Indeed, various southern and Middle Belt ethno-nationalist and militia groups, notably the Yoruba Agbekoya Farmers Association, Igbo Movement for the Actualization of the Sovereign State of Biafra and Independent Peoples of Biafra, Conference of Autochthonous Ethnic Communities Development Associations, and the All Middle Belt Forum threatened to launch retaliatory attacks on herdsmen and ban them from their territories. The governor of Ekiti state, Yoruba southwest, advised farming communities in the state to spray poisonous herbicides on their farmlands to keep the herdsmen at bay. Ekiti state subsequently passed a law in August 2016 prohibiting grazing by cattle, sheep and goats at night and outside designated lands reserved for that purpose in various parts of the state, and making it a crime for pastoralists to carry offensive weapons (the law designated armed pastoralists terrorists). Reactions to the passage of the Ekiti law mirrored the political divides already referred to: "While spokespersons of states that had experienced loss of many lives: Ekiti, Benue, Plateau, Enugu, Anambra, Abia, Kaduna, and sociocultural organizations such as Afenifere, Afenifere Renewal Group [both Yoruba south-west] and Ohaneze Ndigbo [Igbo south-east] hailed the law, the Arewa Consultative Forum [North] warned of dangers inherent in a state law that may contravene rights of citizens to movement in any part of the federation. Anti-grazing spokespersons are already warning that the constitution recognizes the rights of citizens rather than the rights of cattle" (*The Nation* 2016e).

Most of the "proxy" wars between the north and south over the deadly activities of the herdsmen were fought on the pages of newspapers and in social media, with the southern dailies, notably *Nigerian Tribune*, *The Nation*, *The Guardian*, *This Day* and *Daily Telegraph*, pushing anti-herding editorials and opinions in their larger political and religious connotations, and the major northern dailies, *Daily Trust*, *Leadership* and *New Nigerian*, defending the activities of the Fulani herdsmen and their intricate associations with core Hausa-Fulani/Muslim/northern interests.

Proposals on how to manage and resolve the conflicts elicited further tension and division along the lines of the regional (north-south), religious and ethnic divisions. By far the most controversial were the proposed bills tabled at the federal House of Representatives in March 2016 to establish the National Grazing Route and Reserve Commission, and to create a department of cattle ranches under the federal ministry of agriculture and other appropriate agencies. The grazing bill proposed the establishment of national grazing reserves and stock routes on land at the disposal of the federal government or acquired by the proposed commission through purchase, assignment and payment of compensation to communities. The proposed commission was also to take over control and management of existing grazing reserves on agreed terms with the states concerned. Again, reactions to the bills followed the north-south divide, with the greatest support coming from the Fulani and northern Muslim leaders, and greatest opposition from the south and northern Middle Belt where land ownership and access issues with herdsmen had raged on for a long time. Some of the arguments advanced in support of the bills were that cattle were a national resource and heritage — like crude oil — whose breeding and protection ought to be provided for in all parts of the country; that the Nigerian constitution and ECOWAS protocol provided for the free movement of persons and goods; that traditional reserves, stock routes and ranches already existed; and that the proposals would minimize Fulani migration and clashes with communities.

Those opposed to grazing reserves, on the other hand, argued that the proposal amounted to dispossessing non-pastoral peoples of their land rights; that it would further extend "Fulani conquest"; that grazing zones should be restricted to parts of the north where they are historically located; and that herdsmen are private business people who, like commercial farmers and other entrepreneurs, should purchase or lease land themselves. According to Abiola Ajimobi, governor of Oyo State, "Those clamouring for creation of grazing zones across the country should have a rethink. It is against the land use act;[4] it is against the law of natural justice to seize people's land to cater for other people's cattle. Grazing zones could be created for those who are traditional cattle breeders in their areas. I am not against that. But you cannot come here and tell me you want to occupy our land for grazing zones…It won't happen" (*The Nation* 2016b).

---

4   The Land Use Act vests ownership of all land within the territory of a state in the governor of the state.

The proposals in the bill were not entirely new — in fact, at the time the bill on cattle ranches was being proposed in 2016, the federal government was already importing quick-yielding grazing feeds from Brazil for ranches and had acquired 65,000 ha of land in 13 states for the establishment of ranches (*The Guardian* 2016). Years of seasonal migration by herdsmen from northern Nigeria and the Sahel had created reasonably well established grazing and stock routes in several parts of the country, including the south. Also, the idea of establishing grazing reserves and cattle ranches was not new in the country. The old northern regional government designated 415 grazing reserves that spread across the present 19 states, although fewer than 150 saw the light of the day because of corrupt acts of land stealing and misappropriation. With the assistance of the World Bank, six grazing reserves were established in 1976 covering a total land area of 115,000 ha spread across the northern states of Borno, Bauchi, Adamawa and Kaduna, and between 1987 and 1995, the federal government established two Ndama cattle[5] ranches in Adada in Enugu state and another one in Fashola in Oyo State. Since 2011, the Miyetti Allah Cattle Breeders Association of Nigeria has consistently demanded the creation of grazing reserves and stock routes from presidential candidates and political parties. Some states' governments, notably those of Cross River, Benue, Plateau and Kaduna, have planned to or have actually established commercial cattle ranches.

So why did the bill on grazing reserves generate such rancour and tension? One reason was, of course, the unprecedented scale and impunity of the deadly ethnic riots. Second was the dark cloud of insecurity that pervaded the country, especially following Boko Haram terrorism. Third, and perhaps most important, was that the riots provoked old, recurrent and unresolved issues of state legitimacy and true federalism. As long as issues of grazing reserves and stock routes were restricted to the north, and especially parts of the region where cattle breeding was the major source of livelihood, the problems were tolerable and within limits as one of the diversity elements that made the federal solution imperative in Nigeria. But once the herdsmen crossed "traditional" boundaries, and grazing and stock routes became national issues with the federal government taking the lead, old fears of unequal citizenship, domination and oppression were resurrected. For the ethnic minority communities of the Middle Belt in particular, the activities of Fulani herdsmen marked a new phase in the politics of subjugation and domination that has hallmarked northern regional politics (Dudley 1968). One key indicator here was the perceived partisan role of the federal government, which has responsibility for safety and security, and control of police, military and security agencies. Leaders of the various communities that were attacked by the herdsmen accused the federal government of complicity for failing to take decisive action to protect the victims of the attacks and bring the aggressors to justice. The responses by the police, military and security forces were generally reactive and sluggish, even when, as in the Agatu and Ukpabi Nimbo attacks, there were allegedly intelligence reports of impending attacks.

These were the main grounds on which a civil society group, the Socioeconomic Rights and Accountability Project, filed a suit against the federal government and its agencies at the ECOWAS Court of Justice in May 2016: "failure to exercise due diligence and to take steps to prevent attacks, killings, raping and maiming of hundreds of Nigerians…and destruction of property and other serious human rights violations and abuses by…herdsmen and other unknown perpetrators, and to conduct prompt, impartial, thorough and transparent investigations and to hold those responsible to account…" (*The Nation* 2016b). The fact that several top government officials, including President Muhammadu Buhari, were

---

5   Ndama cattle is a species that is resistant to Tryponosomosis, a sleeping sickness caused by the tsetse fly, which was imported from Senegal.

Fulani and patrons of global and local Fulani associations (President Buhari was formerly patron of the Miyetta Allah Association), was commonly cited as an explanation for federal indolence — or protection — as the official government position, as articulated by the minister of state for agriculture, was that the killing herdsmen were mostly "foreigners" and not necessarily Fulani. The president later ordered the police and security agencies to go after the killer herdsmen, but the perception that the federal government was not neutral and acted too late in the day remained strong.

The immediate and the remote factors that precipitated the deadly ethnic riots revolve mostly around the imperatives of material reproduction and survival on the part of the Fulani herdsmen. The immediate factors or triggers were, first, the devastating effects of climate change manifest in famine, increased desertification and cross-border animal disease, all of which decimated food, grazing lands and water in much of the Sahel region. In particular, the Lake Chad basin, which had provided pasture for ages, shrank by over 90 percent from 25,000 to less than 2,500 square kilometres in a period of 50 years, displacing an estimated 60 million herds and 30 million people, most of them pastoralists. The devastations forced unprecedented numbers of herdsmen and cattle to move southward from northern Nigeria and the Sahel region (Chad, Niger, Mauritania, Burkina Faso, Mali) to the rainforest zones in search of greener pasture (similar movements took place in Ghana, Burkina Faso and Cameroon). Second, conflicts and terrorist activities across the Sahel and, in particular, Boko Haram terrorism in northeastern Nigeria, forced migrations from zones of insecurity to more secure zones. In all of this, the key factor was the desperation to survive, which was tied to the livelihood of cattle breeding. In the absence of policies guaranteeing access to grazing and protection by the state, the herdsmen had little or no option to taking up arms in the defence and furtherance of their interests.

The recourse to self-defence was somewhat inevitable, but was made more pronounced by the stiff opposition of the landowners, which gained momentum as the riots spread from one part of the country to the other. Indeed, Fulani leaders argued that the attacks were mostly retaliatory, provoked by cattle rustling and killings, and attacks on herdsmen. It is claimed, for example, that over 60,000 cattle were rustled or killed in Agatu, Apa, Gwer West and Guma local government areas of Benue state in 2013; 350 cows were stolen in Wamba local government area of Nasarawa state in March 2014; and between March and April 2014, more than 500 herdsmen and 3,000 cows were killed in Jos South, Riyom, Barkin Ladi, Wase, Langtan South local government areas of Plateau state (see the *Daily Trust*, *National Mirror* and *Premium Times* articles from March to April 2014). In all cases, the herdsmen retaliated with vicious attacks. This validates Wolff's (2006, 90) argument that ethnic conflicts "are the result of deliberate choices of people to pursue certain goals with violent means. Often, they see this as their only choice in conditions that are beyond their control."

The remote and facilitative factors consist mainly of state fragility variables (Osaghae 2007). The key variables include the inability of the state to effectively secure its territory and monopoly of the legitimate use of force within it, and protect lives and property (manifest in porous borders, weak police, military and security agencies, arms proliferation, ethnic militias, local vigilantes and self-defence); contested legitimacy (manifest in disorderliness, anti–status quo ethno-nationalist and religious mobilizations); economic incapacitation (evident in diminishing resources, deprivations, poverty, unemployment, infrastructural decay and inability to deliver public goods and social services); poor governance (exclusionary politics, marginalization, non-accountability, flawed and unstable policies, weak institutions, lack of access to justice and poor conflict management); and unresolved grievances over resource distribution, access and equity.

For these reasons, fragile states experience perennial conflicts and crises that justify the recourse to extra-systemic strategies by aggrieved groups. The relative ease and success with which ethnic and religious groups and militias mobilized against other groups and the state (the Niger Delta militants, Shiites and Boko Haram terrorists are good examples), and the prevalent milieu of chaos and violence, encouraged the impunity of the attacks by the herdsmen. With specific reference to Fulani herdsmen, Wilson-Fall (2000, 63-64) has pointed to the absence of formalized "management and oversight of state policy on the protection and assurance of grazing, pasture, and water rights for pastoralists" in the states of the Sahel including Nigeria. "In fact," she states further, "most governments in the region have been quite conservative about voicing clear policies about transhumance as a production strategy, and the question remains whether pastoralists have any formal land tenure rights in the context of the modern state. This has caused anxiety and conflict…" According to Ian Scoones (1994, 4), "Without a recognition of the problems of pastoral areas and support for development needs, problems of insecurity are likely to increase."

Trends in Kenya, Swaziland, Lesotho and South Africa, where cattle rustling is a major issue, support this contention. The rise of self-defence vigilante groups indicate that groups in conflict have had to rely on themselves rather than the state (and which, ironically, the military and police sometimes had to rely on to suppress insurrections) was also part of the weak state-induced developments. The other facilitative factors were those of globalization; they ranged from the learning and adoption of militia tactics from riots and terrorist activities in other parts of the world and, more specifically, in west Africa, where Fulani herdsmen also ran riot (Ghana and Cameroon easily come to mind) in search of grazing fields, to arms proliferation and trade, the ECOWAS protocol on free movement of persons and goods, social media (gamji.com was a major site for Fulani activities) and diaspora communities.

The key factor, of course, remained the desperation to survive and to sustain transhumance political economy and livelihoods, with the external variables of global trends serving to reinforce the violent and terrorist tendencies of the riots. The pattern was the same in Ghana and Cameroon, where several farming and non-Muslim communities were ravaged by rioting herdsmen, but the situation in those countries (as well as in Burkina Faso and Mali) did not assume the dangerous levels reached in Nigeria, where a mix of Boko Haram terrorism, oil-based Niger Delta conflicts, unresolved ethno-regional and religious tensions, and increased deprivations and poverty made an escalation of the deadly Fulani riots inevitable.

Managing the Riots

The deadly ethnic riots of Fulani herdsmen belonged to the category of sporadic and recurrent riots. Our analysis shows that the riots have a historical continuity whose ebbs and flows have been determined by the extent to which the herdsmen have enjoyed regular and peaceful interactions with host communities, which was the case when migrations were seasonal and negotiated, leading to the establishment of Fulani camps and settlements; and by periodic shocks that have made material reproduction and survival more desperate. In the case of the riots under review, the adverse effects of climate change that threatened pastoral life in the Sahel region and Boko Haram terrorism and chronic conflicts, which pushed unprecedented numbers of Fulani herdsmen and their families from within and outside Nigeria into the greener pastures and relatively safer parts of the country, were the key shocks. To these must be added the policy and governance failures of the weak state, which made it unable to cope with the admittedly unusual, unconventional and new forms of conflict, of which Boko Haram, Niger Delta minorities militancy and the ethnic riots of Fulani herdsman were prototypical. The guerilla, terrorist and militant strategies employed by the warring groups — the sophisticated firearms, kidnapping, robbery, rape, suicide bombing, unprecedented scales of killing and destruction, clandestine operations and large areas attacked, and cross-boundary mobility, which was fuelled by forces of globalization, made the conflicts difficult to engage. Then there were also the intricate linkages of the conflicts with larger and more troubling issues of state legitimacy to contend with.

The complexity of the conflicts, especially their recurrent nature, which makes them likely to erupt from time to time (and far less likely to be resolved once and for all), the ambiguity of the identities involved, and the spontaneous character of the vicious attacks, makes them less amenable to conventional state responses of "defeating the enemy" and restoring or maintaining law and order, as the evidence of dealing with Boko Haram and Niger Delta militants clearly shows. The case of the Fulani riots was further complicated by the nomadic and cross-national nature of Fulani identity, which meant that wholly within-state engagement would, at best, be partial; a regional approach that addresses Fulani movements across state boundaries would also be necessary. The management or resolution of the Fulani riots of necessity entails two related dimensions: within state and across state. At the within-state level, Nigeria's federal system, which presupposes a multi-centre system of government, presents a structural advantage for dealing with dispersed conflicts such as the Fulani riots. This is because, as Yolamu Barongo (1989) rightly argues, unlike uni-centre systems in which only the central government is able to deal with conflicts, the multi-centre nature of federalism allows the deflection of conflicts away from the centre so that the central government does not get involved in every conflict. (See also Suberu 2001.) But that

can only be the case if the constituent units have the jurisdiction (over police, safety and security, for example) and resources to address conflicts.

Unfortunately, state governments in Nigeria have neither the jurisdiction nor resources to deal with conflicts. The federal government has exclusive control over police and security agencies, and state governments accordingly depend on the federal authorities to address conflicts, even of the most routine and remote type in their domains. This deficit played a major part in the escalation of the Fulani riots, as state governments (and local governments as well) were helpless, and the federal government had a delayed response. The innate capacity of federalism to function as a system of conflict management has to be re-activated in Nigeria by restoring the powers that previously belonged to the constituent units but were taken over by the federal government under military rule (Osaghae 1997; 2004; 2005).

We have seen how the proposal to establish grazing reserves and stock routes, which seems appropriate to the extent that it has historical antecedents, provoked further tension. This was partly because, as many of those opposed to it pointed out, the proposal implied further loss of state (and communal) power — especially over land ownership — and it attempted to foist a one-size-fits-all solution without regard to cultural differences, which negated core federal principles. It is, however, noteworthy that stakeholders' meetings of Fulani leaders and herdsmen, farmers, host communities, police, security agencies and civil society were convened at state, local government and community levels to seek participatory solutions to the various local riots. The only snag was that the "elusive" herdsmen who were in the thick of the conflicts did not participate in the meetings and it was not certain that the Fulani spokespersons (mostly settled cattle breeders under the aegis of groups such as the Miyetti Allah Cattle Breeders Association and Jamu Nate Fulbe Association of Nigeria, not herders) who claimed to represent them, were legitimate representatives — the meetings did not halt the deadly attacks even after agreements had been reached to stop hostilities. This validates the point about the riots being non-elite/underclass-directed, the implication being that elite-driven top-down solutions are too self-interest-begotten to suffice. Following from this, one missing link in the various efforts at engaging the Fulani riots was the perspective of the rioters themselves. The objectives of the proposal on cattle grazing reserves and stock routes, for example, included the inducement of the herdsmen to abandon their transhumant or nomadic lifestyle in favour of becoming settled cattle breeders. It is very unlikely that this was what the herdsmen from and outside of Nigeria wanted, because "Unlike a ranching system, pastoralists traditionally do not 'own' or 'inherit' land in the sense that settled farming communities do. Independence of spirit is necessary to the often lonely and isolated life of a herder who may spend weeks alone or with one or two others while pasturing cattle far from the family camp or village" (Wilson-Fall 2000, 61). In any case, previous grazing reserves and ranches did not transform them in any significant manner. Even the nomadic education project, which the federal government established in the 1980s to encourage young Fulani to become educated and settled, has not yielded the desired results. The point cannot be overemphasized that attempts at resolving identity-based conflicts should involve the perspectives of the main actors, in this case the herdsmen. A crucial part of the process of resolving the deadly riots in Nigeria, therefore, is to identify the actual Fulani herdsmen.

Within-state containment or management of the ethnic riots cannot work in isolation of across-state engagements because of the dispersal of Fulani identity across several countries and the fact that their nomadic migrations have historically had scant regard for state boundaries in the Sahel and west African regions. Fulani herdsmen from Chad, Niger, Mali, Cameroon and Mauritania have moved into Nigerian territory in search of grazing lands and water, just as Nigerian Fulani have also moved in and out of the country in search of pasture. The fact that some of the rioting herdsmen were said to be alien could not, therefore, have come as a surprise — the situation was similar in Ghana and Cameroon, where deadly ethnic riots that mostly involved "alien" Fulani herdsmen also erupted. Closing the Nigerian borders to these aliens is one of the possible ways of addressing the problem, but not only does this detract from the fact that Fulani pastoralists are peoples without borders, it also violates the ECOWAS Transhumance Protocol that guarantees the grazing rights of pastoralists across state boundaries and ECOWAS protocol on free movement of persons and goods around west Africa. What is required is for countries in the Sahel and west Africa that have Fulani (and) herdsmen to work out concerted efforts to deal with a *common* problem under the aegis of regional bodies such as ECOWAS and the African Union, and with the support of international development partners. (It is significant that litigations over the ethnic riots from aggrieved groups in Nigeria have been taken to the ECOWAS Court of Justice.) Individual states can then take their bearing from the concerted framework to deal with local peculiarities. One path-setting initiative in this regard is that of the African Union, which has created the Pan-African Agency of the Great Green Wall to address the adverse consequences of desertification and prolonged droughts by reviving the Sahara and Sahel to regenerate livelihood. Participating states need to sign the Great Green Wall Project agreement, which promotes concerted action. With 43 percent of its total land mass spread across 11 of 36 states ravaged by desertification in Nigeria, and with the deadly riots by herdsmen, Nigeria was one of the first countries to embrace the project, and this resulted in the establishment of a National Agency for the Great Green Wall. Another practical point of convergence is the resuscitation of the famished Lake Chad basin, which, for a long time, provided a hub for cattle breeding for herdsmen from Chad, Cameroon, Nigeria, Niger, Mali and other parts of west Africa.

Works Cited

Barongo, Yolamu. 1989. "Ethnic Pluralism and Political Centralization: The Basis of Political Conflict." In *Conflict Resolution in Uganda*, edited by K. Rupesinghe. Oslo, Norway: International Peace Research Institute.

de Bruijn, Mirjam, and Eghosa E. Osaghae. 2011. "Conflict Mobility and the Search for Peace in Africa." In *Politics, Land and Conflict Management in Africa: Studies in Memory of Gerti Hesseling*, edited by J. Abbink and M. de Bruijn. Leiden, Netherlands: Brill.

de Bruijn, Mirjam and Rijk van Dijk, eds. 2012. *The Social Life of Connectivity in Africa*. New York, NY: Palgrave Macmillan.

Dudley, Billy J. 1968. *Parties and Politics in Northern Nigeria*. London, UK: Franck Cass.

Falaju, Joke. 2016. "Miyetti Allah Asks Government to Develop Grazing Reserves before Ranches." *The Guardian*, June 9.

Harneit-Sievers, Axel. 2006. *Constructions of Belonging: Igbo Communities and the Nigerian State in the Twentieth Century*. Rochester, NY: Rochester University Press.

Horowitz, Donald L. 2001. *The Deadly Ethnic Riot*. Berkeley, CA: University of California Press.

Institute for Economics & Peace. 2015. *Global Terrorism Index*. http://economicsandpeace. org/wp content/uploads/2015/11/Global Terrorism-Index-2015.pdf.

Lake, David A. and Donald Rothchild, eds. 1998. *The International Spread of Ethnic Conflict: Fear, Diffusion and Escalation*. Princeton, NJ: Princeton University Press.

The Nation. 2016a. "Killer Herdsmen Furore: Enugu Governor Raises Judicial Panel." *The Nation*, April 30.

———. 2016b. "Curbing Herdsmen's Menace." *The Nation*, May 3.

———. 2016c. "The Herdsmen's Killing Fields." *The Nation*, May 3.

———. 2016d. "Why We Can't Stop Influx of Non-Nigerian Herdsmen — FG." *The Nation*, June 11.

———. 2016e. "Fayose's Grazing Law." Editorial. *The Nation*, September 7.

———. 2016f. "Gun-carrying Herdsmen Are Foreign Terrorists says Sultan." *The Nation*, September 13.

Osaghae, Eghosa E. 1997. "The Federal Solution in Comparative Perspective." *Politeia* 16 (1).

———. 2004. "Federalism and the Management of Diversity in Africa." *Identity, Culture and Politics* 5 (1–2).

———. 2005. "State, Constitutionalism and the Management of Ethnicity in Africa." *Asian and African Studies* 4 (1–2).

———. 2007. "Fragile States." *Development in Practice* 17 (4–5).

Pieri, Zacharias P. and Jacob Zenn. 2016. "The Boko Haram Paradox: Ethnicity, Religion and Historical Memory in Pursuit of a Caliphate." *African Security* 9 (1).

Rajchman, John. 1995. *The Identity in Question*. New York, NY: Psychology Press.

Scoones, Ian. ed. 1994. *Living with Uncertainty: New Directions in Pastoral Development in Africa*. London, UK: Intermediate Technology Publications.

Suberu, Rotimi. 2001. *Federalism and Ethnic Conflicts in Nigeria*. Washington, DC: United States Institute of Peace Press.

Wilson-Fall, Wendy. 2000. "Conflict Prevention among the Fulbe." In *Traditional Cures for Modern Conflicts: African Conflict "Medicine."* edited by I. William Zartman. Boulder, CO: Lynne Rienner.

Wolff, Stephan. 2006. *Ethnic Conflict: A Global Perspective*. Oxford, UK: Oxford University Press.

5

Climate Change and Access to Water Resources in the Lake Victoria Basin

Donald Anthony Mwiturubani
Postscript by Simon Palamar

The Intergovernmental Panel on Climate Change (IPCC) has concluded that climate change and variability have the potential to impact negatively on water availability, and access to and demand for water in most countries, but particularly in Africa (IPCC 2007). Climate change is expected to alter and hence bring changes to the hydrological cycle, temperature balance and rainfall pattern. This has wide-ranging implications since water is one of the most important of all natural resources for socio-economic, cultural, political and environmental development. It is a commonly used resource and therefore a fundamental economic asset for sustainable development. Water is required in an adequate and sustainable supply for domestic, farming (livestock and agriculture) and industrial use, and other environmental functions on all spatial and temporal scales. It is estimated that globally, 70 percent of water withdrawn is used for irrigated agriculture, 20 percent for industry and the remaining 10 percent for other uses, including domestic use (Organisation for Economic Co-operation and Development [OECD] Development Assistance Committee [DAC] 2009).

Although water is a renewable resource through the hydrological cycle, it is likely to be significantly affected by climate change and variability primarily because the main source of water is rainfall — a component of climate. Rainfall change and variability in the arid and semi-arid zones, such as in the Lake Victoria basin (LVB), will result in the uneven distribution of water resources over time and space, and this may have a significant negative impact on access to and utilization of water resources (Yin and Nicholson 1998). Consequently, climate change and variability are expected to increase the vulnerability of socio-economic activities through hydrological extremes such as prolonged droughts and extensive floods. It is in this context that this chapter examines the effects of rainfall changes and variations in access to and utilization of water resources and the resulting conflicts regarding their use in the LVB, with particular focus on the Mara River sub-basin (MRSB) within the LVB. The chapter begins by describing the state of the LVB, which is followed by an examination of the emerging evidence of rainfall changes and variations in East Africa, and then a consideration of the impact of rainfall changes and variations on the availability of water for different uses. It then proceeds with an assessment of the effects of water scarcity on economic development, followed by a consideration of the likely water-use conflicts, their causes and effects. Finally, there are concluding remarks and recommendations to enhance adaptation to, and mitigation of, the impacts of climate change and variation.

Lake Victoria Basin: An Overview

Geographically, the LVB includes Tanzania, Uganda, Kenya, Burundi and Rwanda. The latter two countries are part of the LVB catchment area, as a number of tributaries originate in these countries (United Nations Economic Commission for Africa 1999). The LVB occupies an area of approximately 240,000 km², of which about 69,000 km² are the lake itself. The largest part of the LVB lics in Tanzania (44 percent), followed by Kenya (21.5 percent), Uganda (15.9 percent), Rwanda (11.4 percent) and Burundi (7.2 percent) (United Nations Environment Programme [UNEP] 2006). Lake Victoria, which is the main water source in the region, is the largest freshwater body in Africa and second in the world after Lake Superior in North America (Wikipedia n.d.). Water from Lake Victoria is a transboundary resource shared among Kenya, Tanzania and Uganda. The inflows to the lake from major and small tributaries contribute about 13 percent of the water entering the lake annually, while the remaining 87 percent comes from rainfall (Phoon, Shamseldin and

Vairavamoorthy 2004). The White Nile is the only outflow from the lake at Jinja in Uganda (Pearce 2006).

Most parts of the LVB can be characterized as semi-arid, with the exception of some areas close to the lake that have a relatively high rainfall of between 1,200 and 1,500 mm per year (Yin and Nicholson 1998). The LVB is estimated to host a human population of about 30 million. These people engage in various activities in support of their livelihoods, including agriculture, fishing, quarrying and mining, hydroelectric power generation and trade (UNEP 2006). Agriculture, however, is the dominant economic activity in the LVB, supporting more than 80 percent of the population, of which 60 percent practise rain-dependent agriculture, which generates from 30 to 40 percent of the basin states' GDP (World Bank 1997). Lake Victoria also supports freshwater fishing, with estimated annual fish yields of about 500,000 tonnes, which contributes significantly to both local consumption and export earnings in the region (UNEP 2006).

Although the LVB is known to have a diversity of both terrestrial and aquatic life, it has undergone enormous environmental changes in the last 40 years (Odada et al. 2004). Climate change — the decrease of rainfall in particular — and land degradation, together with rapid human population increase, have been repeatedly recognized as among the major contributors of rapidly evolving changes in the LVB that seriously threaten its ecosystem functions, overall biodiversity and the livelihoods of the basin's population (Verschuren et al. 2002). Water levels in the lake are said to have been decreasing over time, with climate change, land degradation and the overutilization of water from the lake for hydroelectric generation being cited as the main causes (Munaabi 2006). Overutilization of water for hydroelectric power generation and other socio-economic activities are likely to cause tension between the countries sharing the lake, and this may result in water-use conflicts.

The main river of the MRSB, a sub-basin within the LVB, the Mara River, originates in southwest

Kenya on the steep slopes of the Mau escarpment, at an elevation of approximately 3,000 m above sea level (Krhoda 2001). It then flows for a distance of about 350 km into Tanzania to Lake Victoria, situated 1,100 m above sea level (United Republic of Tanzania 1976). The entire basin covers an area of 13,750 km², of which 4,812.5 km² (35 percent) lies in Tanzania and the remaining 8,937.5 km² (65 percent) in Kenya. The Mara River is the main water source in the upper and middle parts of the MRSB, while both the Mara River and Lake Victoria serve as main water sources in the lower part. The main water uses in the MRSB include domestic and livestock farming, wildlife maintenance and irrigation for agriculture. Large-scale irrigation is practised on the Kenyan side, in the upper part of this basin.

Climate Change Indicators

East Africa's climate has changed dramatically in the last century or so, as it has throughout the world. Lawrence M. Kiage and Kam-biu Liu (2006) used information from paleo-environmental records of the past 50,000 years, based on the level of Lake Victoria and ice-core records among other indicators, to show that there have been major climate and vegetation changes in East Africa, with warmer and cooler periods, and wetter and drier conditions. However, Phillip W. Mote and Georg Kaser (2007) and Françoise Gasse (2008) investigated ice cores from Kilimanjaro and concluded that the diminished snows and glaciers of the mountain are not due to climate change, but to rainfall changes and variability — mainly decreased rainfall on the mountain. They relate the decrease in rainfall to deforestation around the mountain. Thus, although Mote, Kaser and Gasse blame human activities as the main cause of deforestation, they fail to give explicit reasons for these activities, which may well be associated with the impacts of climate change. For example, local communities may clear forests in search of water for livestock because of the decrease of water flows downstream. Similarly, the incidence of forest fire

tends to increase during the prolonged droughts (dry seasons). In turn, deforestation may expose the land and make an area vulnerable to the negative effects of climate change.

In the LVB, water scarcity and its negative impact on socio-economic development are attributed to the changes and variations in rainfall, which is the main source of both surface and subsurface water in the region. The IPCC (2001) and Mike Hulmes et al. (2001) have shown that Africa has experienced an increase in temperature of .05°C per decade in the twentieth century. On the other hand it is predicted that East Africa's temperature will increase by between 0.2°C per decade (low scenario) and more than 0.5°C per decade (high scenario) in the twenty-first century. According to the IPCC, the warmer temperatures in East Africa may lead to a five to 20 percent increase in rainfall for December to February (wet months), and a five to 10 percent decrease in rainfall from June to August (dry months). Rainfall changes and variations are not expected to be constant, but rather more sporadic and unpredictable, resulting in periods of prolonged droughts and periods of high rainfall leading to floods.

East Africa has undergone periods of both prolonged drought and of high rainfall — rainfall changes and variations. From 1983 to 2005, for example, East Africa has experienced prolonged droughts in 1983-1984, 1991-1992, 1995-1996, 2004-2005 and the La Niña-related drought of 1999-2001, all of which led to famine in the region (Nganga 2006). Similarly, the El Niño-related floods of 1997-1998 were considered to be evidence of the impact of climate change (ibid.).

Furthermore, the analysis of total annual rainfall for 21 meteorological stations in selected regions of Tanzania reveal that there is a trend toward decreasing rainfall for more than 13 stations, and a trend toward increasing rainfall for only seven, while one station has recorded a constant pattern (United Republic of Tanzania 2007). Moreover, it was noted that at most of the stations variability in rainfall cycles was common. Similarly, an analysis of information and data published by the Sokoine University of Agriculture (SUA) shows rainfall variability over both time and space in Tanzania. According to SUA's analysis, the Lake Victoria zone as represented by Bukoba and the southern zone represented by Mbeya show a positive trend for both long and short rainy seasons, while the central region represented by Dodoma and the northern region represented by Arusha show a negative trend (Sokoine University of Agriculture 2008). The data reveal that areas close to Lake Victoria, such as Bukoba, receive relatively high rainfall compared with areas far away from the lake.

In the MRSB, available data from five rain-gauge stations in Tanzania indicate significant changes and variation in rainfall between 1970 and 1989, as indicated in Figure 1 (Anthony 2007).

Rainfall variations are well correlated with the average annual water discharge in the Mara River, the main river in the MRSB, in the same period (1970–1990). This ranges from 0 to 57 m³/sec with the mean annual discharge of 28.4 m³/sec as indicated in Figure 2 (ibid.).

Since the main water catchment area for the Mara River is in the Mau forest complex in Kenya,

making the MRSB a transboundary entity, the same rainfall trends may have been evident for the whole MRSB. However, other factors such as modified land use and land cover may have contributed to the changes in the river's flow (Mutie et al. 2005). These variations in the flow of the Mara River significantly affect water availability and hence determine access to water and utilization systems, which, if not properly coordinated, may result in water-use conflicts.

Biodiversity Degradation and Climate Change

One of the factors influencing rainfall distribution in arid and semi-arid climates is the type of land use and land cover. Change in land use and land cover, in particular, the decrease of forests, may alter rainfall runoff and runoff infiltration processes. In East Africa, forested land is said to have decreased extensively in the last three decades or so, at the rate of between one and four percent, with a two percent reduction in forests in Kenya, one percent in Tanzania and four percent in Uganda (Society for International Development 2006). The main

Figure 1: Annual Rainfall Variations at Five Rain Gauge Stations in the MRSB (1970–1989)

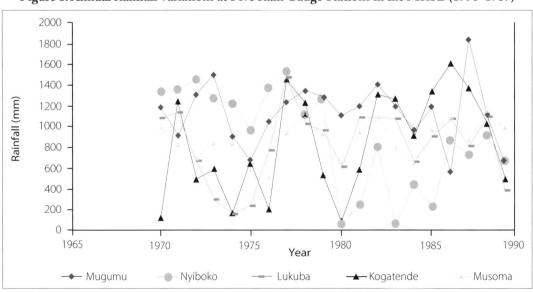

Source: Author.

Figure 2: Average Annual Discharge at MRSB (1970–1990)

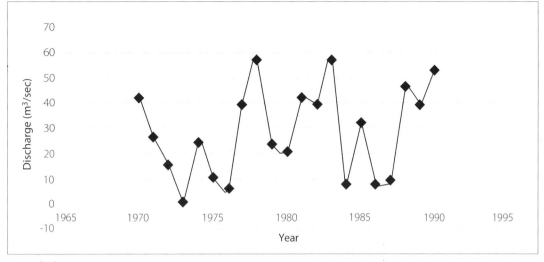

Source: Author.

reasons for deforestation include clearing forests and woodlands for agriculture and settlement, mining, wild fires, charcoal production and the overexploitation of wood resources for commercial purposes. All these activities contribute to the increase of carbon dioxide (CO_2) in the atmosphere as carbon sinks are progressively reduced.

In the MRSB, comparisons of land use and cover between the 1960s and 1996 using land-use and land-cover maps indicate the major changes to forests and wetlands. Analyses of these maps, for example, indicate the decrease of wetlands on the Tanzanian side of the MRSB by 13 percent within three decades, from 1966 to 1996.[1] The decrease in wetland areas is mainly associated with the decrease in rainfall. This has resulted either in the dramatic decrease or drying up of water in the swampy areas because of the decline and variability

of river flows that feed wetlands. Similarly, an analysis of land-use and land-cover maps on the Kenyan side of the MRSB reveals a 2.3 percent reduction in forests, while about 30 percent of the basin was opened up for agriculture between 1986 and 2000 (Mutie et al. 2005, 237). The findings for the Kenyan side of the MRSB, however, show that wetlands have increased by 7.5 percent in the same period as opposed to the decrease on the Tanzanian side of the MRSB. This difference in the status of the wetlands in Kenya and Tanzania in the MRSB may be due to increased large-scale irrigation on the Kenyan side, hence more water retention in the agricultural land. It may, in fact, reflect a misleading interpretation of Landsat images in which water retention in the agricultural land is interpreted as wetlands development.

The decrease or removal of vegetation from the earth's surface tends to increase surface runoff and consequently reduces the infiltration capacity of the water, although this may depend on other factors such as the nature of the landscape. Furthermore, the increase of surface runoff may increase soil erosion and hence the amount of eroded material that is transported and deposited in the rivers and streams. This, in turn, results in the decrease of the water storage capacity of the

---

1   Two land-use and land-cover maps, one for 1963 (United Republic of Tanganyika 1963) and the other for 1996 (United Republic of Tanzania 1996), were analyzed to determine the rate of change of key natural resources: forests and wetlands. Although these changes are not associated with climate change, it is believed that the reduction in forests has a negative impact on rainfall occurrence and intensity. The change may also increase the incidence of droughts and floods.

rivers and streams, and consequently natural water sources may become seasonal, flowing only during the rainy season. In the MRSB the changes in the seasonal variability of the Mara River's flow is thought to have been exacerbated by land-use and land-cover change over time and the consequent reduction in rainfall in the catchment areas (Ndiiri 2005; Mutie et al. 2005). Mugini Jacob (2005), on the other hand, reports that the decrease in the Mara River flows is a result of changes to most tributaries from permanent to seasonal water sources. The decrease of forest cover therefore is expected to affect water resources availability negatively — mainly through reduced storage — and hence result in water scarcity in the region.

Impact of Climate Change on Socio-Economic Activities

Rainfall changes and variations significantly affect water's availability for socio-economic activities, including water for domestic use, crop and livestock production, and hydroelectric power generation, in particular in arid and semi-arid areas in developing countries. Decreased rainfall, for example, is likely to reduce the water available for crops and livestock, the key economic activities of most rural populations in developing countries where rain-fed agriculture is dominant. Globally, however, the potential for food production is projected to increase with increases in local average temperatures ranging from 1°C to 3°C. Above this temperature range, however, food production is projected to decrease. At lower latitudes, especially in seasonally dry and tropical regions, crop productivity is projected to decrease even with small local temperature increases (1°C to 2°C), which will increase the risk of hunger (IPCC 2007).

In the LVB, where more than 60 percent of the population depends on rain-fed agriculture for its livelihood, a dramatic decline in the rainfall in the region will have a significant effect on food security. The projected decline in rainfall of between 50 and 150 mm per season, and variations and deviations of rainfall from the normal, are expected to reduce food production in the region (WWF 2006). The reduction in rainfall may compel people to encroach on marginal lands such as water catchment areas, wetlands and mountain ecosystems for cultivation and the grazing of livestock. In the MRSB in Tanzania, as noted above, 13 percent of the wetlands (for example, the Kubigena wetlands), were converted into agricultural land in the past three decades (Anthony 2007, 198–208). In the MRSB in Kenya, on the other hand, about 30 percent of the basin, of which 2.3 percent is forest land, was opened up for agriculture less than two decades ago (Mutie et al. 2005). Recently, a similar occurrence has been observed in the Usangu wetlands in southern Tanzania, where crop cultivators and livestock keepers encroached on the wetlands owing to the persistent drought in most parts of the country between 1999 and 2001 (Mfugale 2007). According to Martin Parry et al. (1999), regional predictions suggest that 10 percent of grain production in East Africa may be lost by 2080 because of climatic changes and variations manifested in the increase of temperature and decline of rainfall. However, the impact of climatic change on crop production varies considerably between regions and countries, and between types of agricultural production. With regard to Tanzania, for example, Mark J. Mwandosya, Buruhani Salam Nyenzi and Matthew Laban Luhanga (1998) argue that climate change and variations will have more impact on maize production than on root crops. The impact of climate change on food production is also likely to be more pronounced in the central part of the country than in other zones in Tanzania. However, it must also be borne in mind that forecasters do not always predict the changes and variations of rainfall over time and space absolutely correctly. Similar observations have been made by K. T. Ingram, M. C. Roncoli and P. H. Kirshen (2002), namely that climate change and the failure to forecast the changes and variability correctly have negatively affected agricultural production in Burkina Faso.

However, the relationship between rainfall changes and variability on the one hand, and socio-economic activities on the other, is even more complex and interwoven. As noted above, some economic activities such as crop and livestock husbandry, charcoal making and mining contribute to the changes in land use and land cover, especially the decline in forest cover. Deforestation affects the occurrence of rainfall as it interferes with the hydrological cycle and consequently increases CO_2 in the atmosphere as carbon sinks are progressively reduced. Crop production may involve the clearing of forests to obtain new land for cultivation in response to greater demand for food, owing to the increase in the human population and decrease in food production because of reduced rainfall. On the other hand, traditionally livestock has been grazed on the open grassland and bush country, hence livestock keepers tend to clear forests to extend their pastures. Furthermore, forests may be cleared as a strategy to eradicate tsetse flies, which threaten livestock. This cleared land is eventually used for settlements, crop cultivation or as pasture.

The relationship between economic activities, such as crop and livestock husbandry and charcoal production and water resources changes, and variations in the MRSB therefore relates to the ways these activities alter natural vegetation cover, runoff and infiltration, and reduce the capacity of water sources to hold water after the rainy season. As a result, water scarcity is particularly likely to occur during the dry season owing to, among other factors, siltation that reduces the depth of water sources and hence reduces their storage capacity. Deforestation therefore increases the likelihood of both hydrological and agricultural drought, which results in water scarcity and food insecurity for areas that depend mostly on rain for their agriculture. "Agricultural drought" refers to the condition in which the water in the soil (soil moisture) is insufficient for crop growing. "Hydrological drought" refers to the condition where rainfall, as the main source of water, is

extremely low, to the extent that there is not enough water to meet the different demands for it.

Water resources are highly sensitive to climate change and variations. Thus, the changes in the global climate as a result of increased greenhouse gases such as CO_2, nitrous compounds and methane are expected to affect the availability of water in most parts of the world, Africa in particular. The IPCC (2007, 444) indicates that the vulnerability of water resources to climate change is a result of overdependence on rainfall as the main source of water. A reduction in water supply to meet different socio-economic, political and environmental needs is likely to result in resource-use conflicts among and between different users and uses of water resources.

Climate Change and Conflicts over Water Access and Use

Climate change and variation are expected to reduce water supply for different uses. As water becomes scarce, competition in accessing and using water sources will intensify. As a result, conflicts (here referred to as a dispute about social, economic, political and territorial-related issues) are more likely to occur as a struggle to utilize this scarce resource increases. Water-use conflicts occur when one water source is used for more than one use by different users and the uses are not complementary. Conflicts over water access and use may also arise from the uneven distribution of available water between uses and users (OECD DAC 2005). As such, we can identify several levels and types of water-use conflict.

Conflicts at the Household Level

At the family level, water-use conflicts relate to the gendered division of labour in which men and women, youths and adults have different roles. For instance, in the MRSB, men are responsible for taking care of livestock and farming, while women are responsible for household chores and farming. Here the men wanting to utilize some water sources for livestock may be opposed to the women's uses, thus creating water-use conflicts. Furthermore, because of a water shortage, some family activities that require water may not be performed. Depending on which group wields the greater power — men or women, youth or adults, girls or boys — conflict is more likely to occur between these groups in the use of the available water for gender-specific activities. For instance, because of water scarcity, women walk up to 10 km and back to collect water daily. Collected water is used for domestic chores such as cooking, washing utensils and personal hygiene for children. In some instances, men may request some water for a shower, but when the women refuse to part with their water, given the long distance they walk to collect it, conflict may arise between spouses, in particular because the patriarchal system gives men the right of decision making in the family.

Conflicts at Village Level

During the rainy season, when water is plentiful, members of one village can access water sources at another nearby village. However, as water becomes scarce owing to prolonged drought, villages may prohibit members of another village from using water sources located within their jurisdiction. This kind of restriction on water access and use has sometimes resulted in inter-village fighting, especially where members of the two villages are from different ethnic groups. Water access and use conflict at this level involves mainly livestock keepers who take their livestock for water to a nearby village. In some instances, livestock owners migrate with their livestock to areas with permanent water sources, a practice that puts more pressure on the resource. Conflicts arise when the local community feels that the immigrants are impinging on their resources.

Conflict between Local People and Government Institutions

As noted, the impact of climate change may result in people encroaching on marginal lands and protected areas in search of water and pasture. Access to protected areas such as game reserves and national parks and their natural resources is prohibited. However, owing to the scarcity of resources — especially water resources — local people do encroach on protected areas for crop production and livestock keeping. This creates conflict not only between the institutions that manage these protected areas and the encroachers, but also between humans and wildlife. In 2004, for example, more than 800 families were forcibly evicted from the buffer zone of the Serengeti National Park. These families were alleged to have invaded the area in search of pasture and water because of the persistent drought in their villages. Most parts of the Serengeti National Park lie within the MRSB. A similar example is the eviction of livestock keepers and crop cultivators from the Usangu Game Reserve in southern Tanzania (Mfugale 2007; Malsh 2006). Livestock keepers in the Usangu sub-basin were immigrants from different parts of Tanzania that had been affected by water scarcity owing to prolonged drought. In Kenya, there are water-use conflicts between local people living near the Yala swamp and the regional government authorities that granted a 25-year lease for rice cultivation to Dominion Farms Ltd. The company is accused of blocking access to the swamp for more than 200 fishermen (Waititu 2009).

Conflict between Livelihood Systems

Water-access and water-use conflict may be caused by competition between groups of people practising different economic activities, such as livestock keepers and crop cultivators. In some places, livestock keepers tend to encroach and use land and water meant for crop production.

Similarly, crop cultivators may utilize pastoral land, thereby reducing the pasture for the livestock. Water-access and water-use conflicts at this level are more pronounced during the dry season, when water is very scarce, than during the wet season. This type of water-use conflict is also manifested between upstream and downstream users of water, regardless of whether they practise the same or different economic activities. Users of the Mara River in Tanzania blame the users in Kenya for withdrawing great quantities of water for large irrigation schemes, thus leaving insufficient water to flow downstream. Downstream users of the Mara River also blame upstream users for polluting the water in the river, claiming that the brown water in the river is a result of cultivation along the river banks. This, however, as Annabel Waititu noted, is caused by the loss of forest in the Mau complex, the main source of water for the Mara River (ibid.). Since the Mara River is a transboundary water source, water-use conflicts between downstream and upstream water users on the Mara River, although they affect individuals, can be viewed as an interstate (Tanzania and Kenya) conflict.

Interstate Conflict

As water becomes scarce owing to prolonged drought, increased temperature and the decrease of rainfall, competition for this vital resource will intensify. Competition for shared transboundary water resources between nations may occur and lead to conflict regarding access to and utilization of the resource. In the LVB, there are several shared transboundary water sources, including the lake and its tributaries, such as the Mara River. The Mara River, for example, is a transboundary water source shared between Tanzania and Kenya. The river originates from the Mau forest complex in Kenya and flows through large-scale irrigated agriculture in Kenya to open savannah grassland in the Masai Mara National Park in Kenya and

Serengeti National Park in Tanzania. These national parks are renowned protected areas in the region. The Mara River further flows through small-scale agricultural land (used for crops and livestock husbandry) in Tanzania before discharging into Lake Victoria. Therefore, water from the Mara River is utilized for domestic consumption, livestock farming, irrigated agriculture, wildlife and environmental maintenance. The likely conflicts regarding access to and use of water from the Mara River will be between upstream users in Kenya and downstream users in Tanzania, and between the wildlife and human populations, which may also spark conflicts between Kenya and Tanzania. An inadequate water supply in the Mara River is caused by two main factors, which impact on each other: climate change, and land use and land cover. Climate change leads to a decrease in rainfall and rise in temperature, hence an increase in evaporation. On the other hand, a change in land use and land cover, such as the deforestation in the Mau forest complex caused by the expansion of agriculture and encroachment on the forests by livestock keepers, alters runoff and infiltration processes, thus interfering in the hydrologic cycle. Inappropriate land use and land cover can result in land degradation as a result of poor planning and ineffective water resource management systems along the Mara River in both Kenya and Tanzania.

Conclusion and Recommendations

Climate change and variability have the potential to impact negatively on water availability, access to and demand for water in most countries, in Africa in particular. Climate change is likely to result in water scarcity, which will consequently result in stiff competition with regard to access and use. As competition for access to and use of water resources for different uses and users intensifies, water-use conflicts are likely to occur. This chapter examines the impact of climate change with specific focus on the effect of rainfall change and variability on water resource availability, access to and use in the LVB. It is argued that the LVB in particular, and East Africa in general, is experiencing dramatic rainfall changes and variations over time and space, resulting in a decrease of river flows and drying up of many other natural water sources. It is further argued that, owing to the decrease of the water supply for domestic use, livestock and crop production, hydropower production and industrial use, water-use conflicts may occur at different levels such as in the family, among villages, between ethnic groups, government institutions and local people, between different livelihood systems and between countries. This calls for the formulation and implementation of national policies and other legal frameworks that are geared toward addressing issues of climate change, and in particular the adaptation to and mitigation of climate change impacts. It further calls for stakeholder dialogue to improve both customary and formal governance systems with regard to natural resources utilization and management.

Since water resources touch every sector of the economy, it is important to improve water management in order to reduce the degradation of water sources and enhance equitable access to and utilization of the resource, thus reducing or alleviating sources of conflict pertaining to water access and utilization. It is therefore recommended that policy makers and planners integrate climate impact adaptation and mitigation measures in the formulation of policies and planning for development projects. It is further recommended that sector-specific policies that relate to the hydrology of water resources, such as forestry, agriculture and mining, be reviewed to include issues of climatic change and variations and their effects.

It is also necessary that countries that share transboundary natural resources such as water share information on meteorological, hydrological and socio-economic activities, and the way they are practiced in order to maximize the potential of the transboundary resources by minimizing tensions and conflicts that may otherwise result.

Acknowledgement

This chapter was first published in *Climate Change and Natural Resources Conflicts in Africa*, ISS Monograph 170, published by the Institute for Security Studies (ISS), Pretoria, in June 2010, and reprinted here with the permission of ISS.

Postscript

Climate Change and Violent Conflict: The Emerging Science

Simon Palamar

Does climate change cause violent conflict? Do warming global temperatures affect the ability of societies to resist falling into political discord or their ability to recover after the fact?

These are hard questions to definitively answer. Climate change is literally and figuratively a massive phenomenon. While there is little doubt in the scientific community that human activity is making the world a warmer place, pinpointing exactly what effects a global increase in temperatures will have on the weather and climate of any one part of the world is difficult. More difficult still is predicting how human societies will respond to increased rainfall, droughts, a change in the jet stream, more frequent storms or some of the other possible consequences of climate change. While it may seem like common sense to assume that climate change will be associated with increases in violent conflict, a prominent commentary on a large body of scientific studies looking for such a relationship concluded "that research to date has failed to converge on a specific and direct association between climate and violent conflict"(Buhaug et al. 2014, 396).

However, simply because research has failed to draw a specific and direct line between a warming planet and violent conflict does not mean there are no conditional relationships between the two phenomena.

Some recent research on climate change and violence is pointing to what types of societies may be more vulnerable to climate change-induced conflict than others. Carl-Friedrich Schleussner, Jonathan F. Donges, Reik V. Donner and Hans Joachim Schellenhuber (2016) offer evidence that specific types of climate-related events such as heat waves and droughts are significantly associated with the outbreak of armed violence in ethnically fractionalized societies.[1] Their analysis also finds that climatological events that cause large-scale economic damage (that is, equal to one percent of GDP) are associated with outbreaks of violence in countries with high income inequality.

When Schleussner et al. look at climate events in other samples of countries, the story changes. While climate events that cause large-scale economic damage are associated with societies that have high income inequality, climatological events (regardless of the magnitude of economic damage) are significantly associated with the onset of violence in the world's 50 most ethnically fractionalized countries. In other words, while severe weather alone may not be associated with violence, severe weather in the presence of ethnic politics is.

---

1   Schleussner et al. test for a significant relationship between other kinds of climate-related events (such as meteorological events including heavy snowfall, cyclones and other violent storms, and hydrological events such as floods) and violent conflict using samples of countries based on other measures of social stratification such as Gini coefficients, perceived corruption levels, literacy rates, a history of violence, the size of the agricultural sector or absolute poverty rates, to name a few. The temporal relationship between climate events and the outbreak of violent conflict was strongest and most robust when observing climatological events (for example, droughts and heat waves) in highly ethnically fractionalized societies.

We can think about Schleussner et al.'s analytical model in the following general and informal way:

Climate change → increases likelihood of heat wave or drought → effects of heat waves and droughts (for example, damage to the agricultural economy) → moderated or multiplied by existing ethnic cleavages → violent conflict.

For students of multivariate statistical analysis, Schleussner et al.'s thinking is evocative of a classic interaction term: a decrease in rainfall on its own might not increase the risk of violence, but a decrease in rainfall in the presence of ethnic cleavages does.

Schleussner et al.'s analysis further suggests that all sorts of climate-related natural disasters (for example, rainstorms, snowstorms, typhoons and hurricanes, floods, landslides, droughts, heatwaves and cold snaps), in the presence of high levels of ethnic fractionalization, are robustly related to the start of violent conflict within the same month.

So, while there may be no single simple relationship between climate change and violent conflict (for example, as temperatures increase, so does violence) it is possible that some of climate change's specific direct effects — such as extreme weather events — can, in turn, have secondary effects that exacerbate existing tensions depending on the social, political and economic conditions on the ground. Not all climate change effects are equal, and some societies are better at managing them than others. In other words, climate change affects politics and causes violence indirectly.

If certain types of societies are more likely to experience violence because of climate change, then having this knowledge gives policy makers, business people and civil society leaders a tool to identify the places that are most vulnerable to climate-induced violence. Schleussner et al. correctly point out that some of the world's most ethnically fractionalized countries are in Africa. Forewarned is forearmed, after all, and the emerging science of violence and climate change offers some clear advice about how to think about adapting to a warming world. For governments and development non-governmental organizations, this may mean concentrating resources and efforts to change policy on countries and regions that are vulnerable to the effects of climate change, not just because of their geography, but because of their ethnic, political and economic characteristics.

Thus, while slowing or preventing a major warming of the global climate appears to be an increasingly difficult goal, the research on the relationship between climate change and armed violence does give some reason to be cautious about concluding the worst. When and if climate change "causes" violence, it is moderated by human decision makers. Ethnic fractionalization, for example, can be moderated (or exacerbated) by political leaders. Income inequality can be addressed via economic reforms and by direct government-led redistribution. Public policy can mitigate or exacerbate the likelihood that climate change will help cause conflict. When crafting research and policy agendas, scholars and governments, rather than relying on the covering assumption that climate change will inevitably contribute to more violence and discord, should instead focus on how pre-existing social and economic conditions might make conflict more or less likely. While climate change is coming — if it is not already here — it does not lead us inexorably toward conflict.

Works Cited

Anthony, D. 2007. "Traditional Environmental Management Systems Related to Changes and Variations of Water Resources in Semi-arid Tanzania: A Case of the Mara River Basin." Ph.D. dissertation, University of Dar es Salaam.

Buhaug, H., J. Nordkvelle, T. Bernauer, T. Böhmelt, M. Brzoska, J. W. Busby, A. Ciccone, H. Fjelde, E. Gartzke, N. P. Gleditsch, J. A. Goldstone, H. Hegre, H. Holtermann, V. Koubi, J. S. A. Link, P. M. Link, P. Lujala, J. O'Loughlin, C. Raleigh, J. Scheffran, J. Schilling, T. G. Smith, O. M. Theisen, R. S. J. Tol, H. Urdal and N. von Uexkull. 2014. "One Effect to Rule Them All? A Comment on Climate and Conflict." *Climatic Change* 127 (3): 391–397.

Gasse, Françoise. 2008. "Kilimanjaro's Secrets Revealed." *Science* 298: 548–549.

Hulme, Mike, Ruth Doherty, Todd Ngara, Mark New and David Lister. 2001. "African Climate Change: 1900–2100." *Climate Research* 17: 145–168.

Ingram, K. T., M. C. Roncoli and P. H. Kirshen. 2002. "Opportunities and Constraints for Farmers of West Africa to Use Seasonal Precipitation Forecasts with Burkina Faso as a Case Study." *Agricultural Systems* 74: 331–49.

IPCC. 2007. "Impacts, Adaptation and Vulnerability." Contributions of Working Group II to the Fourth Assessment Report. Cambridge, UK: Cambridge University Press.

Jacob, Mugini. 2005. "Mara River Water Level Comes Down." *Daily News*, December 17.

Kiage, Lawrence M. and Kam-bin Liu. 2006. "Late Quaternary Paleo-environmental Changes in East Africa: A Review of Multiproxy Evidence from Palynology, Lake Sediments and Associated Records." *Progress in Physical Geography* 30 (5): 633–58.

Krhoda, G. O. 2001. "The Hydrology of the Mara River: Preliminary Phase, Project Development and Stakeholder Analysis." Nairobi: World Wildlife Fund, East Africa Regional Programme Office.

Malsh, M. 2006. "Conservation Myths, Political Realities and the Proliferation of Protected Areas." Paper presented at African Environment Lectures, Oxford University, November 24.

Mfugale, Deodatus. 2007. "Usangu Game Reserve to Become Part of Ruaha National Park." *The Guardian*, July 11.

Mote, Phillip W. and Georg Kaser. 2007. "The Shrinking Glaciers of Kilimanjaro: Can Global Warming Be Blamed?" *American Scientist* 95.

Munaabi, G. 2006. "Decreasing Levels of Lake Victoria Worry East African Countries." www.ugpulse.com/articles/daily/homepage.asp.

Mutie, S. M., B. Mati, H. Gadain et al. 2005. "Land Cover Change Effects on Flow Regime of Mara River." Proceedings of the 2nd International Information Systems for Crisis Response and Management Conference, Brussels, April. www.iscram.org/dmdocuments.

Mwandosya, Mark J., Buruhani Salum Nyenzi and Matthew Laban Luhanga. 1998. *The Assessment of Vulnerability and Adaptation to Climate Change Impacts in Tanzania.* Dar es Salaam: The Centre for Energy, Environment, Science and Technology.

Ndiiri, J. A. 2005. "Assessing the Applicability of Hydrological Models under Changing Flow Regimes in the Mara River Basin." M.Sc. thesis, University of Dar es Salaam.

Nganga, J. K. 2006. "Climate Change Impacts, Vulnerability and Adaptation Assessment in East Africa." Paper presented at the United Nations Framework Convention on Climate Change African Regional Workshop on Adaptation in Accra, Ghana, September 21–23.

Odada, Eric O., Daniel O. Olago, Kassim Kulindwa and Shem Owandiga. 2004. "Mitigation of Environmental Problems in Lake Victoria, East Africa: Causal Chain and Policy Options Analyses." *AMBIO: A Journal of the Human Environment* 33 (1-2): 13–23.

OECD DAC. 2005. "Water and Violent Conflict." Issues Brief, Mainstreaming Conflict Prevention. www.oecd.org.

Parry, Martin, Cynthia Rosenzweig, Ana Iglesias, Günther Fischer and Matthew Livermore. "Climate Change and World Food Security: A New Assessment." *Global Environmental Change* 9 (1999): S51–S67.

Pearce, Fred. 2006. "Uganda Pulls Plug on Lake Victoria." *New Scientist*, February 8. www.newscientist.com/article/mg18925384-100-uganda-pulls-plug-on-lake-victoria/.

Phoon, Syin Yi, Asaad Y. Shamseldin and Kala Vairavamoorthy. 2004. "Assessing Impacts of Climate Change on Lake Victoria Basin, Africa." Paper presented at the 30th WEDC International Conference, Vientiane, Lao. http://wedc.lboro.ac.uk/resources/conference/30/Phoon.pdf.

Schleussner, Carl-Friedrich, Jonathan F. Donges, Reik V. Donner, and Hans Joachim Schellnhuber. 2016. "Armed-conflict Risks Enhanced by Climate-related Disasters in Ethnically Fractionalized Countries." *Proceedings of the National Academy of Sciences* 113 (33): 9216–21.

Society for International Development. 2006. *The State of East African Report 2006: Trends, Tensions and Contradictions; The Leadership Challenge.* Dar es Salaam. April. www.sidint.org/publications.

SUA. 2008. "Proposal for a Programme on Climate Change Impacts, Adaptation and Mitigation in Tanzania." Sokoine University, Morogoro, Tanzania.

United Nations Economic Commission for Africa. 1999. *Global Environment Outlook 2000.* London: Earthscan.

UNEP. 2006. *Lake Victoria Basin Environment Outlook: Environment for Development.* http://start.org/download/publications/lake-victoria.pdf.

United Republic of Tanganyika. 1963. *Land Use/Cover of Tanganyika.* Dar es Salaam: Survey Division, Ministry of Lands, Forests and Wildlife.

United Republic of Tanzania. 1976. *Study for the Development of the Mara River Valley.* Preliminary report of the pre-feasibility study in three sections, prepared by experts from the Yugoslavia Regional Commissioner's Office, Mara Region.

———. 1996. *Land Use/Cover of Tanzania.* Dar es Salaam: Ministry of Natural Resources and Tourism.

———. 2007. *National Adaptation Programme of Action (NAPA).* Vice President's Office, Dar es Salaam, Division of Environment.

Verschuren, Dirk, Thomas C. Johnson, Hedy J. Kling, David N. Edgington, Peter R. Leavitt, Erik T. Brown, Michael R. Talbot and Robert E. Hecky. 2002. "History and Timing of Human Impact on Lake Victoria, East Africa." *Proceedings of the Royal Society of London Series B-Biological Sciences* 269 (1488): 289–94.

Yin, Xungang and Sharon E. Nicholson. 1998. "The Water Balance of Lake Victoria." *Journal of Hydrological Sciences* 5 (43): 789–811.

Waititu, Annabel. 2009. "Global Warming and Conflicts over Water in Eastern Africa." Paper presented at Alliance Sud conference, "Water: Source of Conflicts," March 6. www.alliancesud.ch/it/politica/clima/copy_of_downloads/conflitti-aw.pdf.

Wikipedia. Lake Victoria. https://en.wikipedia.org/wiki/Lake_Victoria.

World Bank. 1997. *World Development Report 1997.* Washington, DC: World Bank.

WWF. 2006. "Climate Change Impacts on East Africa: A Review of the Scientific Literature." Gland, Switzerland: World Wide Fund for Nature.

Part Three
Tension between State and Society

6

Rule of Law and the Role of Justice in Managing Conflict

Allan Ngari and Raeesah Cassim Cachalia

The rule of law, described as a principle of governance in which all entities in a state are accountable to the law (UN Secretary-General 2004), has gradually emerged as a key objective in crisis management. The rule of law is an essential part of the United Nation's approach to peace and security, as enshrined in the UN Charter (UN 1945) and practised by the UN Security Council. It is also linked to stability, law and order in conflict and post-conflict states.

It is imperative for the prevention of conflict and for long-term consolidation of peace, security and development that a state's governance system be based on the rule of law. African states are not exempt from this requirement of good governance. Justice and the rule of law are mutually reinforcing tools that assist states fraught with civil war and mass violence to overcome their difficult circumstances and, in some instances, have the potential to mitigate or prevent conflict.

To achieve long-term goals of peace, security and development, every state emerging out of conflict must ensure a system of rule of law and justice for serious violations of human rights, for violations of the laws and customs of war and for international crimes. A state whose governance system is based on the rule of law is less likely to have a recurrence of violence or conflict. A stable state based on good governance structures, where the rule of law is respected by both state and non-state actors, is the bedrock that ensures access to justice by its citizens. The respect for the rule of law in a state is therefore directly proportional to the access its citizens have to justice.

In Africa, there is a limited respect for the rule of law. Consequently, there are significant challenges regarding access to justice for citizens of African states. Although the number of democracies is increasing within the 55-state continent, many of these are very young, fledgling democracies. Some

African states such as Somalia remain plagued by weak governance systems that barely support credible justice mechanisms. Other states emerging out of conflict, such as the Central African Republic (CAR) and South Sudan, are having great difficulty in ensuring their justice mechanisms have the capacity and ability to operate effectively. Still others, such as the Democratic Republic of Congo (DRC), Burundi and Côte d'Ivoire, seem to be reneging on positive steps and peace agreements or relapsing into periods of protracted armed conflict or violence between state and non-state actors.

Access to justice within society is one of the core components of the rule of law, ensuring an avenue for protection and accountability against the arbitrary use of power as well as equal application of the law. A number of challenges exist regarding access to justice in parts of Africa. In some instances, there is a lack of understanding or awareness of the available justice mechanisms within a state and how they operate. In others, there may be a fear of a state's legal system, particularly in authoritarian contexts, where the judiciary is seen as being an extension of the executive, at the service of the ruling elite. Corruption also poses a further threat to the respect for the rule of law in African states that are not engaged in conflict. This vice has so permeated governance structures in these African states that justice sometimes belongs to those who can pay for an outcome to a dispute.

This chapter seeks to explore the nexus between the rule of law and justice, and the management of conflict and its aftermath. Justice may assume many different forms and necessarily involves achieving a sense of fairness, accountability and redress. Increasingly, the notion of justice extends beyond bringing perpetrators of crimes to account to include reparations for victims. In the context of this chapter, access to justice particularly refers to access to courts and legal recourse or protection. A general lack of sufficient legal norms in African states is identified as a significant cause of inappropriate or ineffective responses to conflict. Where legal norms exist, they are poorly formulated or difficult to implement because of a lack of political or financial will and other capacity challenges faced by African states. A discussion on the norms that govern national, subregional and continental judicial mechanisms is therefore important. Access to justice from the perspective of a human rights and international crimes framework is also discussed.

The chapter addresses the role of the international community in the context of the work of intergovernmental and international bodies such as the United Nations and the International Criminal Court (ICC), and as related to the preventive tool of the responsibility to protect (R2P), as well as national and continental transitional justice frameworks. The chapter concludes with recommendations on how to ensure the respect for the rule of law and the role of justice in addressing violations of the rights of African citizens.

Lack of Norms and Institutional Apparatus to Prevent and Address Armed Conflict

The law-making process in African states, in particular as it applies to the laws that relate to addressing gross violations of human rights, serious international crimes and violations of the laws and customs of armed conflict, forms the bedrock on which states can prevent conflict and, where conflict occurs, address it and its aftermath.

Law-making processes in the African continent are as diverse as there are states on the continent. Each state has adopted its own procedures for making laws and regulations. While it is not possible to discuss the law-making process in each of the 55 African states, it is possible to discern some common features in the various processes. In particular, most common law jurisdictions in Africa apply a dualist framework, which is not bound by international law, but African states that follow a civil law tradition generally have a monist constitutional framework, which allows international law to be applied in national courts without further interpretation.

Exceptions to this general rule do exist, but, on the whole, application of international treaties and norms and their interpretation by national courts come either directly from the provisions of the ratified treaty or are derived from national law.

For purposes of this chapter, the focus is on how international law and norms are domesticated in African states. Most African states' legal systems have either a civil or common law tradition. In some states, other legal traditions such as customary law and religious law apply, but most legal systems follow civil or common law. Both common and civil law traditions emphasize statutory law as a source of law. In all African states, the constitution is the *grundnorm* (a concept in Hans Kelsen's pure theory of law that denotes the basic norm, order or rule that forms an underlying basis for a legal system) from which all other laws derive their validation. The hierarchy of laws of the land is stipulated in most constitutions. The application of international treaties and norms into a state's laws is therefore also subordinate to the country's constitution.

Monist African States and the Application of International Law Norms

Monist African states view international and national law as a part of a single conception of law. This means that the courts of monist African states do not require that an international norm be adopted by the legislature of the state before applying the international law to a given situation (Dugard 2005, 47). This is, however, subject to the state having ratified or acceded to the international treaty from which the court derives the application of a norm to that state. In francophone Africa, which has adopted a civil law tradition, the application of the monist theory is modelled on article 55 of the 1958 Constitution of France (France 1958). As seen in the constitutions of Benin (article 147), Burkina Faso (article 151), Burundi (article 292), Cameroon (article 45), the CAR (article 69), Chad (article 222), Congo-Brazzaville (article 185), Côte d'Ivoire (article 87), the DRC (article 215), Guinea (article 79),

Mali (article 116), Mauritania (article 80), Niger (article 132), Rwanda (article 190), Senegal (article 91) and Togo (article 140), the law provides in relevant part: "Treaties or agreements duly ratified or approved shall, upon publication, prevail over Acts of Parliament, subject, with respect to each agreement or treaty, to its application by the other party" (ibid., article 55).

In this regard, international norms ratified by a monist African state are superior to the national laws enacted by the state. The only requirement for the application of international law in such a monist state is the act of publication of the ratified or acceded treaty. Amsatou Sow Sidibé (2003, 54) says, "Publication determines the date of entry into force and creates a presumption of awareness of the treaty towards everyone." The reciprocity aspect is, however, derogated for international human rights norms; for example, the application of article 3(1) of the Convention on the Rights of the Child (UN General Assembly 1989) is self-executing, as held by the French Cassation appeal in *X v. Y and Anor*.[1] This practice is, however, not uniform. Some courts of monist African states have not applied international norms directly, as in the case of the Senegalese Court of Cassation, which held that the relevant provisions of the Convention against Torture (CAT) (UN General Assembly 1984) were not self-executing and, therefore, implementation legislation was required in Senegal before Hissène Habré could be prosecuted for charges of torture. Interestingly, in this case, the UN Committee against Torture also found in *Guengueng v. Senegal*[2] that the provision to prosecute as provided in the CAT was not self-executing.

It is clear that for monist African states, the application of international law norms begins upon ratification and publication of the international

---

1 *X v. Y and Anor* (2005), Information Bulletin of the Court of Cassation No. 626 of 1 October 2005, No. 810 (France Appeal).

2 *Guengueng v. Senegal* (2006), CAT/C/36/D/181/2001 (UN Committee against Torture).

treaty. While the enforcement of these international law norms is not uniform, it does not negate the fact that monist African states that have ratified and published international treaties that relate to international human rights, humanitarian and criminal laws have the legislative framework to prevent conflict and address its aftermath. The judicial cultures of these states, however, indicate a dualist approach despite constitutional provisions that provide direct application. A further challenge, as discussed later in this chapter, is access to justice to remedy violations of human rights as represented by international treaties and law in the aftermath of conflict.

Dualist African States and the Application of International Law Norms

Unlike monist states, dualist states view national and international laws as separate legal systems. The dualist theory provides that unless a state has domesticated an international treaty that it has ratified or acceded to, the norms in that treaty cannot be enforced in the courts of that state. All African states that are former British colonies have a common law legal tradition and, accordingly, a dualist approach in the relationship between international and national laws.

Some dualist African states have, however, taken a monist approach, where the constitution or the courts provide for the direct application of international treaties. The 2002 decision of the Supreme Court of Namibia in *Government of the Republic of Namibia v. Mwilima*,[3] held that article 14(3)(d) of the International Covenant on Civil and Political Rights (ICCPR) (UN General Assembly 1966) took precedence over the provisions of the Legal Aid Act of Namibia (Namibia 1990), even where there was not a statute to domesticate the ICCPR in Namibia. Section 231(4) of the constitution of South Africa (South Africa 1966) and section 238(4) of

the constitution of Swaziland (Swaziland 2005) provide that the courts of those states can apply a self-executing provision of an international treaty, even when the treaty has not been domesticated into national law.

Although the practice is not uniform for dualist African states enacting domestic laws to give effect to international treaties, where the domestication is properly achieved, international treaty norms form a bedrock from which individuals and the state can address conflict-related violations of those treaties. As with monist African states, there is scant evidence that these norms are applied by the courts of dualist African states, even in the presence of national laws.

The Role of the Legislature in Preventing and Addressing Conflict

Other than applying international treaties to the laws of African states, as provided by monist and dualist theories, the national legislatures of African states also provide opportunities to make national laws to prevent and address conflict. Laws are made on the basis of policy, which represents the hopes and aspirations of government. Once the policy has been adopted by government, the process of law-making can then commence. As with international treaty making, the law-making process in African states is a lengthy process that involves negotiation and debate; a law must receive a majority vote in Parliament before the act obtains executive sanction and finally achieves publication.

Over the past five decades, all African states have been or are in some form of transition — from colonialism, apartheid or authoritarianism to democracy and the respect for the rule of law (Ngari 2016, 49). With most African states emerging from some form of conflict or still embroiled in conflict, few, if any, African states have national laws that adequately address the aftermath of conflict. Nor do they have national policies or legislation aimed at preventing or managing conflict. Of all African states, Uganda is the only country that currently

---

3   *Government of the Republic of Namibia v. Mwilima* (2002), SA 29/01 (Namibia).

has a transitional justice policy that would pave the way for national laws to address accountability, seek the truth, provide reparations and prevent a recurrence of conflict in that country. The African Union (AU) has also embarked on a continental transitional justice policy framework, with the aim of providing African states with the framework to deal with the past and prevent further conflict.

It is therefore incumbent on national legislatures to draw policies and laws that can address conflict in the state. Technical assistance and the capacity building of national actors to develop the necessary responses are crucial to addressing conflict in the continent. The cross-border nature of African conflicts also brings to the fore the need for regional responses.

Although African states are described in this chapter as being in a post-conflict or transitioning phase, it is important to note that these states and their national legislatures must be also be concerned with preventing conflict in the future.

The Role of Investigation, Prosecution and Judicial Authorities

Factors such as corruption, socio-economic imbalances and weak governance often contribute to conflict within a society. Strong and impartial investigative, prosecutorial and judicial authorities have the ability to mitigate such conflict and foster an environment of stability as well as respect for the rule of law within state institutions and society at large, which in turn will lower a society's propensity for conflict.

Investigative bodies play an important role in promoting access to justice within a state. Ensuring that investigations into human rights abuses are carried out impartially, efficiently and thoroughly is key to building public confidence in a country's justice system. This is because the strength of a prosecution and subsequent judicial decisions relies upon the findings of investigative authorities. In states with a civil law tradition, notably Côte d'Ivoire, Mali, the DRC and the CAR, judges

may play an investigative role as well. The reality is that the effective functioning of investigative authorities, in many instances, is hampered by a number of factors. These include an inadequate legal framework to inform investigative procedures, undue political influence or interference with investigative bodies by other spheres of government (such as organs within the executive), a lack of resources to conduct investigations and inadequate technical skills or insufficient expertise on the part of investigative officials.

Prosecuting authorities also play a crucial role in ensuring access to justice. Where strong prosecutions are secured for human rights violations, that contributes to public confidence in the legal system. Effective prosecutions are dependent on a number of factors, such as the strength of evidence provided by investigating authorities, the level of skills or experience they have in dealing with certain types of cases and the impartiality of prosecutorial officials.

In conflict situations particularly, the capacity of national authorities to thoroughly investigate and prosecute crimes may be limited by instability within the state. The outbreak and progression of violent conflict in Libya illustrates the challenges that conflict brings to justice regimes within a state. In March 2011, the North Atlantic Treaty Organization initiated a military intervention into Libya, ostensibly on humanitarian grounds. Although the intervention was noted as a success by some for its ability to dismantle the Gadhafi regime within a relatively short space of time, it opened the state up to anarchy and further constrained already frail justice mechanisms and the rule of law. Caught between armed conflict and a volatile transition, competing Libyan authorities have struggled to maintain order and to ensure accountability for common crimes and for human rights abuses, in particular.

In response, sectors of the international community have made efforts toward improving access to justice for citizens or, at least, revealing the extent of abuses within the country. Various non-governmental organizations (NGOs) have conducted on-the-ground investigations into abuses by various parties to the conflict. Despite progress made by various bodies, in advocacy and awareness raising, there are often limitations on translating such findings into action. Fostering accountability for such abuses often depends on the state. Civil society organizations are generally limited to making recommendations or playing an advisory role rather than taking action, and, therefore, national courts or international tribunals have the greatest potential to address conflict and its aftermath from a human rights perspective. Domestic judicial authorities hold primary legitimacy (in the sense of being regarded as being more effective and more accessible) over regional or international organs, as well as the authority to have their rulings enforced.

Situations of violent conflict can seriously hamper judicial processes in many ways. A report compiled by the United Nations High Commissioner for Human Rights detailed the situation in Libya in 2014 and 2015, when prosecutors and judges were subjected to intimidation and violence, including court bombings, assaults and even abductions (UN 2016). Such attacks, carried out by various armed groups, were at times accompanied by demands that certain prosecutions be dropped or suspects be released from detention. As a result, courts shut down in certain locations and limited operations in others. This breakdown in the justice system has meant that victims are left without avenues for protection or recourse. It is crucial that provision be made for the protection of judicial and prosecutorial officials as well as substantive and procedural guarantees to protect victims and witnesses. In a different vein, there are reports of massively flawed processes whereby detainees are made to confess to crimes under visible duress. Similar concerns exist regarding suspects who are detained and serving prison sentences without having been brought to trial or who have been convicted in flawed trials. It is in these instances that international bodies may play a valuable role, as is discussed later in this chapter.

The role of access to justice and its potential to prevent or limit conflict within a society is often underestimated. Many cases of instability in Africa can be linked to problems related to access to justice and the rule of law. The Arab Spring uprisings that were sparked in 2011 demonstrate the ways in which deficiencies in a state's justice system can lead to varying degrees of conflict and violent extremism. The various revolutions, as they were termed, embodied the desires of citizens in the Middle East and North Africa (MENA) region to see not only political change and economic progress but also greater justice and accountability within society. Decades of autocratic rule in Egypt, Libya and Tunisia came to be marked by gross human rights violations, including torture, repression of political dissent, forced disappearances and restrictions on freedom of speech and expression, all for which citizens had little recourse to justice. While the majority suffered these injustices, kleptocratic systems flourished. Closed groups of ruling elites amassed wealth in the midst of ailing economies affecting the bulk of the population. Regimes were opaque and unaccountable to their citizens. These factors ultimately led to unrest and, at times, conflict within the region.

The Egyptian government is, at the time of writing, battling a mounting insurgency along with the rapid expansion of terrorism in the Sinai Peninsula. Indicators point to a number of factors at the root of the violence. These include the economic marginalization of the Sinai population over many years, the neglect of the province and the resultant lack of development attributed to the government.

Discontent in the Sinai has further festered as a result of heavy-handed and arbitrary military responses to extremist threats within the region and the lack of access to justice for those residing in the province. Between 2013 and 2015, the homes of approximately 3000 Sinai residents were marked for demolition by the government to create a buffer zone between the Sinai and neighbouring

Gaza for security purposes. In some instances, residents were given 48 hours' notice to vacate their homes and were given no opportunities for consultation before the demolition and no avenues for legal recourse thereafter (Human Rights Watch 2015). Besides incidents such as these, the government has been accused of carrying out extrajudicial executions of suspected terrorists in the region. Such excesses have become apparent within Egypt's justice system as well. A number of mass trials (together with mass convictions and sentencings) have taken place since 2013, as have trials rife with legal and procedural irregularities (Cachalia 2015).

Collectively, these attitudes and incidents have fostered the notion that Egypt's armed forces, law enforcement agencies and judiciary are tools of the ruling class. This has led to a breakdown in the rule of law as well as of citizens' trust in the law. The prevailing situation has bred divisiveness between the government and the population and has been linked to the rise of extremism in the country. Without a sense of justice and the rule of law, the potential for conflict rises significantly. Citizens are left without recourse to institutions or national processes to address injustices suffered and have little hope that disputes can be resolved peacefully. It is in such instances that the people, youth in particular, may turn to violence as a last resort (Cachalia, Ndungu and Salifu 2016).

Access to Justice through Human Rights, International Crimes and Transitional Justice Frameworks

Introduction

The following section addresses three different frameworks on the African continent that seek to deal with the aftermath of conflict and which are aimed at preventing conflict by securing society against the recurrence of conflict. The human rights and international crimes frameworks are purely legal, while the transitional justice framework is broader and incorporates other disciplines to provide a holistic response to post-conflict societies.

The three frameworks have differing objectives. The human rights framework looks to the regime to protect individual rights of African citizens against abuse by the state and non-state actors. The international crimes framework seeks individual accountability and, in the case of the Protocol on Amendments to the Protocol on the Statute of the African Court of Justice and Human Rights (the Malabo Protocol) (AU 2014), corporate liability for international crimes and redress for victims of these crimes. The transitional justice objective is to deal holistically with the past using a range of mechanisms.

These frameworks find their origins in national laws as well as in the continental body of member states, the AU and regional entities such as the Economic Community of West African States (ECOWAS), the East African Community (EAC), the Southern African Development Community (SADC) and the International Conference of the Great Lakes Region (ICGLR), among others.

Many African states belong to more than one regional integration arrangement apart from the AU. This phenomenon, though advantageous in numerous ways, especially in economic and trade relations between states, creates a multiplicity of obligations on states that belong to more than one arrangement. With limited resources, the effect is that many states are unable or unwilling to comply with all of their obligations. At the same time, a lack of resources for regional integration arrangements makes enforcement of state obligations difficult.

Human Rights Framework

Citizens' rights and access to justice can be strengthened at a number of different levels, with the state being but one role player in such efforts. Recent history has shown the value of regional and global efforts toward the provision of justice, although these endeavours have been more successful in redressing injustices suffered during conflict than in preventing the outbreak of conflict. The United Nation's International Criminal Tribunal for Rwanda (ICTR) is one example of the role that the international community may play in securing justice for victims. It is necessary to recognize other mechanisms that have been put in place to increase access to justice across Africa, at continental and regional levels.

The African Commission on Human and Peoples' Rights was established in 1987 to promote and protect human rights as envisioned in the African Charter on Human and Peoples' Rights (Organization of African Unity [OAU] 1981). According to the African Charter, the commission may hear complaints from states, organizations and individuals regarding violations of rights embodied in the African Charter. The subsequent action of the commission comes in the form of recommendations to state parties in question or to the AU Assembly. One major challenge with this mechanism, as well as with the African Court on Human and Peoples' Rights (ACtHPR), however, is that it requires complainants to exhaust domestic remedies before bringing a matter forward. This may result in many complaints failing the admissibility requirements contained in article 56 of the African Charter or in recourse being significantly delayed, as held by the commission in its 2002 decision in *Modise v. Botswana*.[4] A further challenge that needs to be met centres around state compliance with the commission's decisions, because these are not legally binding and cannot be enforced, although the commission has tried to mitigate the effects of this by putting forth material recommendations in its decisions (Van der Linde and Louw 2001).

The ACtHPR is a further mechanism put in place by the AU. According to article 2 of the Protocol to the African Charter on the Establishment

of the ACtHPR (OAU 1998), the court's role is complementary to that of the commission and also aims to protect and promote human rights on the continent. Based on its findings, the court is entitled to make whatever orders it deems necessary to redress violations, including the payment of compensation as provided for in article 27 of the protocol. In theory, states that are parties to the protocol are bound to execute the judgments handed down by the court, within the time periods stipulated by the court as provided for in article 30 of the protocol.

The court, similar to the commission, has certain limitations. Access to the court is provided to the commission, state parties involved in a case and African intergovernmental organizations. Access may be granted to NGOs and individuals, subject to the controversial provisions of article 34(6) of the protocol, which holds that for the court to receive petitions for hearings, state parties should have accepted and made a declaration accepting the court's granting of access to NGOs or individuals. Article 34(6) is often viewed as an impediment to access to justice for NGOs and individuals, who are in a less empowered position than states or governmental organizations. To date, only six states — Burkina Faso, Malawi, Mali, Tanzania, Ghana and Côte d'Ivoire — have made article 34(6) declarations, limiting what the court is able to do to protect human rights and obtain redress for violations. Rwanda withdrew its declaration in 2016. The framework has thus come under criticism for not offering automatic access to the court to those who are most in need of access to justice and its remedies (Southern African Litigation Centre 2014). There have been numerous cases in which individuals and NGOs were unable to access the court because of article 34(6), regardless of the merits of such cases or the severity of the violations in question (Ssenyonjo 2013, 18). This has led to questions about how realistic it is to expect states to make a declaration on article 34(6) and, in the process, open themselves up to possible claims and actions, as

---

4   *Modise v. Botswana* (2000), Comm No 97/93 (ACtHPR).

well as the argument that the court is inaccessible to the very people it is meant to protect (ibid., 22).

Substantial efforts have also been made at regional levels toward promoting access to justice for citizens regionally in the form of the ECOWAS Community Court of Justice, the SADC Tribunal and the East African Court of Justice (EACJ).

The ECOWAS Community Court (ECC), which is governed by the 1991 Protocol on the Community Court of Justice (ECOWAS 1991), was conferred with the jurisdiction to adjudicate on matters of human rights relatively recently, in 2005. The ECC is open to all ECOWAS member states and serves to adjudicate on issues of human rights including interstate disputes. The ECC is set apart from the African Commission or or the ACtHPR and other regional tribunals by a number of factors, a pertinent one being that one need not have exhausted domestic remedies before approaching the ECC. The ECC has secured broader jurisdiction than other similar fora and also offers direct access to individuals bringing forth human rights violations. As such, it has proven to be a viable avenue for seeking recourse for human rights violations.

Part of the strength of the ECC lies in its evolution and growth over time and the reforms instituted during the ECC's initial stages, which addressed the gaps that became evident in the functioning of the ECC. While compliance with rulings is undoubtedly problematic — for instance, Gambia has failed to comply with the notable *Manneh*[5] and *Saidykhan*[6] (2010) rulings — the ECC has significantly increased access to justice for those within the region. Moreover, measures have been taken to increase state compliance with judgments handed down by the ECC. The legitimacy that the ECC holds means that, at times, pressure has also been exerted by the United Nations and the larger

international community regarding compliance with its judgments. Changing perceptions of state sovereignty and increasing pressure from the international community on states to heed international human rights standards are likely contributors to changes within the ECC, which saw the ECC resist calls to limit its authority. In addition, unlike the EAC and SADC, the ECOWAS heads of state have not been roused against the court when decisions have been made against an individual state.

The ECC has, at times, experienced opposition from states, including challenges to its jurisdiction and calls for its authority to be limited (Alter, Helfer and McAllister 2013, 747). After two cases in which the ECC found Gambia guilty of torture and the enforced disappearances of journalists, Gambia not only attempted to circumvent and resist the rulings by asking the ECC to dismiss the claims as an infringement on Gambia's sovereignty, it also called for the revision of the ECC's governing protocol so that its jurisdiction would be limited in cases deemed to be domestic affairs that should be free of interference. On occasions such as these, collective efforts by NGOs, lawyers operating in west Africa and the media, as well as by the ECOWAS committee of legal experts, have ensured that access to justice, and the intended functions of the ECC, were not impeded by such opposition. This has undoubtedly strengthened the ECC's legitimacy and sent out signals against state impunity. In the long run, such efforts may go a long way to achieving greater respect for the rule of law in the region (ibid.).

Other regional mechanisms have not been as successful as the ECC. In the early 1990s, the SADC established a tribunal that, after a significant delay, began its work in 2005. The SADC tribunal was initiated with the purpose of overseeing the compliance with the treaty of the SADC by the 15 SADC member states and to adjudicate disputes between those member states. The tribunal also had the authority to hear cases concerning human rights violations and, after

---

5   *Manneh v. The Gambia* (2008) ECW/CCJ/JUD/03/08 (ECC).

6   *Saidykhan v. The Gambia* (2010), EWS/CCJ/JUD/08/10 (ECC).

its inception, ruled on several controversial cases in the region. One of these rulings eventually led to the suspension of the tribunal. This raised questions as to whether SADC member states were ready for the types of commitments affirmed in the SADC treaty or even ready to begin building toward greater human rights observance in the region.

In 2008, the SADC tribunal ruled on a case concerning the expropriation of land without compensation by the state of Zimbabwe. In the case of *Mike Campbell (Pvt) Ltd. v. Republic of Zimbabwe,*[7] the tribunal ruled in favour of the applicant and found Zimbabwe in breach of the principles set out by the SADC treaty concerning human rights, the rule of law and non-discrimination. Zimbabwe dismissed the ruling and announced that it was withdrawing from the tribunal's jurisdiction. Zimbabwe's non-compliance was later raised as a concern by the tribunal before the SADC Summit. In addition to disregarding the ruling, Zimbabwe proceeded to lobby other SADC member states to support its position. It argued that the tribunal's ruling amounted to interference in Zimbabwe's domestic affairs. SADC member states, with the exception of Botswana, refused to take a stance against Zimbabwe and, at the 34th SADC Summit, convened in 2010, it was announced that the heads of state had suspended the tribunal for six months to review the mandate and functions of the body. Subsequently, the terms of tribunal officials were not renewed and no new officials were appointed (Erasmus 2015); with no mechanisms in the SADC treaty or the protocol on the tribunal to protect against such suspension, the body was rendered defunct. The president of Zimbabwe, Robert Mugabe, declared that the suspension of the tribunal meant the ruling against Zimbabwe was nullified. The SADC member states later decided that a new protocol was to be added to the treaty to revise the role and jurisdiction of the

tribunal. At the SADC Summit in 2014, the new protocol was adopted and signed, but it has yet to be ratified by all member states, leaving the SADC tribunal inoperative for the time being. Once effective, the new protocol will entail significant changes for the tribunal: only states will have access to the tribunal, and the jurisdiction of the body will be limited to interstate disputes, effectively leaving no mechanism in place to deal with claims of human rights violations by individuals or groups (ibid.). Those seeking recourse will have to do so through domestic legal systems, which are often perceived as frail and biased when it comes to abuses by states in particular.

The short history of the SADC tribunal highlights the challenges for access to justice in a highly politicized landscape where countries are likely to place political interests and allegiances above human rights and governance. What the saga demonstrates is that states are still largely unwilling to limit their sovereignty and cede authority over domestic affairs to supranational bodies. Pressure from the international community, slowly shifting global norms on the weight of human rights issues and dependence on development aid from foreign donors mean that certain states will endeavour to institute democratic reforms and conform to international governance standards. However, where states openly condone the behaviour of other regional states that are clearly defying international law, their actual commitment to strengthening democracy and the rule of law is questionable (Nathan 2013).

Another important factor that this brings to light is that instruments in themselves do not establish compliance with human rights obligations. Collective commitment and cooperation on the part of states are essential for such fora to yield results; together with this, a shift is required toward the notion that regional or international courts, tribunals and so on derive authority from the law, itself, rather than from state permissiveness. The decision to suspend the SADC tribunal ran completely contrary to the spirit of the treaty that

---

7   *Mike Campbell (Pvt) Ltd v. Republic of Zimbabwe,* [2008] SADCT 2.

created and endowed the tribunal with a human rights mandate. It is never easy to reach such a decision in treaty law. What happened was a consensus of convenience by heads of state who seemed propelled by considerations other than the equal protection of the law on SADC citizens, amounting to rule by people instead of rule by law.

Moreover, there is a lack of uniform approaches in dealing with states that refuse to conform to expected obligations under various regional and international treaties and instruments.

Civil society organizations in the southern Africa region have taken steps to voice dissatisfaction with the suspension of the tribunal and its new proposed mandate. They have tried to increase awareness of the implications of the proposed diminished mandate and have encouraged citizens in the SADC region to petition their governments against ratifying the new protocol (South African Litigation Centre 2015). Whether these efforts will yield the desired results is debatable. The International Commission of Jurists (ICJ) also added its voice to the debate, criticizing SADC states for what amounted to a limitation on access to justice for citizens in the SADC region (ICJ 2012). In the southern Africa region, such limits give rise to the possibility that citizens will take matters into their own hands where relief cannot be sought through national or regional court systems (Mavhinga 2016). A further consequence is general distrust of and dissatisfaction with the government, which may result in political discord as well as the breakdown of state-citizen relations. In some instances, such discord may lead to conflict, whether sporadic, low-intensity conflict or protracted violence on a large scale.

The EACJ, established in 2001, is primarily tasked with interpreting and enforcing the Treaty for the Establishment of the EAC (EAC 1999). Beyond economic development and integration, the treaty emphasizes certain principles meant to guide member states within the region. These include adhering to good governance, the promotion of democracy and the rule of law. Article 6(d) of

the treaty also highlights the importance of social justice and the protection of human rights in the region and uses the African Charter as a guide to achieving these goals. The EACJ does not have the jurisdiction to hear complaints of human rights violations. In May 2005, a draft protocol was issued with a view to extending the jurisdiction of the court to include human rights claims. The draft has yet to be approved.

The EACJ has, at times, also been the subject of political interference by states. The case of *Nyong'o v. Kenya (AG)*[8] is significant in this regard. The EACJ found Kenya in contravention of EAC treaty provisions with the election of Kenyan members for the East African Legislative Assembly. The EACJ ruled in favour of the applicant and ordered Kenya to undertake the election process once more, this time in compliance with the EAC treaty. Soon after the ruling, Kenya initiated processes to limit the reach of the EACJ. Besides this, there have been instances in which Kenya has challenged the jurisdiction of the EACJ when claims were raised against the state (Wandia 2012). Although these efforts have not all been successful, they do provide insight into the reluctance of states to cede power to regional authorities.

In spite of the many challenges surrounding regional courts and tribunals, these bodies have played a significant role in fostering greater respect for the rule of law and human rights across the continent. Though the ideal of protection against abuses and recourse in cases of violations has not been realized yet, it could be argued that states are now more open to accountability than before. Though these structures may not necessarily have the power to prevent conflict in all cases, it could be argued that they have the ability to prevent the escalation of conflict, particularly between states and citizens. When citizens are equipped with a sense of justice and are aware of available avenues

---

8   *Nyong'o v. Kenya (AG)* (2006) Reference No. 1 of 2006 (EACJ).

for recourse, they are less likely to resort to violent means to be heard or to achieve their aims. It is therefore important that there exists a growing awareness among citizens that avenues for seeking justice are not limited to domestic legal systems. This awareness, together with pressure from the international community, could further compel states to abide by international norms of justice and the rule of law. Moreover, considering the resource challenges faced by the African Commission as well as the ACtHPR, regional bodies provide good supplementary mechanisms for access to justice.

It should be noted, however, that a number of African states fall outside the scope of the regional organizations mentioned. The north Africa region, for instance, has no supranational regional body through which citizens may have their grievances heard. Although its states fall within the ambit of the Arab League, the organization strictly limits its role to that of mediator between state affairs and in its charter expressly espouses principles of non-interference. The strong emphasis on state sovereignty in the Arab League charter indicates its lack of commitment to addressing serious violations of human rights and a reluctance to elevate the status of rule of law in its member states. This is unfortunate given that the MENA region has some of the lowest freedom and human rights compliance ratings in the world (Freedom House 2015). The Arab League established the Arab Human Rights Committee in 2009 to monitor compliance with the Arab Charter on Human Rights (League of Arab States 1994). However, only 14 of the 22 Arab League states are parties to the charter, and the charter provides no mechanism for hearing individual complaints but is instead limited to the review of reports provided by states every three years. Also problematic is the lack of transparency, as the state reports are not made public and can therefore not be independently verified or challenged.

To understand the challenges of access to justice and the rule of law in the MENA region, one needs to take into account the authoritarian histories of its regimes and understand the deficiencies in the justice systems of these states, which were geared more toward the protection of the status quo and state authority than the promotion of civilian rights. It may be argued that the international community has not played an effective role in the region. Scant measures have been taken against states in cases of non-compliance or even severe transgression of international law, thus leaving states within the MENA region with little reason or incentive to initiate genuine reforms that would see increased access to justice in the region. The non-response of states to the Rabaa massacre carried out in 2013 by the Egyptian government, during which 800 to 1000 people were killed during the course of a day, illustrates the extent of the problem. The August massacre was preceded by the overthrow of Egypt's first-ever democratically elected government a month earlier. The AU initiated what would be a year-long suspension of Egypt following the 2013 coup. Although many states (most notably the United States) offered verbal condemnation of the two events, no further action was taken against Egypt, and financial and military aid to the government responsible soon followed. This undoubtedly sent the message that the state could act in whichever way it deemed fit, without consequences. Perhaps more concerning were those regional states, most notably Bahrain, Jordan and Saudi Arabia, that went as far as voicing support for the government and its actions during this period.

Central Africa's regional integration body is the Economic Community of Central African States (ECCAS). Article 16 of the ECCAS treaty establishes the Court of Justice (ECCAS 1983). The primary focus of the ECCAS is economic integration. In this case, there are no direct provisions in the ECCAS treaty granting human rights protection. There is therefore no judicial enforcement available on human rights issues at the ECCAS Court of Justice.

The Intergovernmental Authority on Development (IGAD), operational in the east and the Horn of

Africa, is meant to enhance regional cooperation within an economic and developmental context. One of the IGAD's core objectives is the promotion of peace and stability throughout the region by establishing mechanisms to prevent and resolve both interstate and intrastate disputes within the region. The body has plans to establish an international arbitration centre to support this objective. The focus, however, will be on the resolution of business disputes.

The ICGLR was established against the backdrop of instability on the continent and mass atrocities such as those that took place during the Rwandan genocide in 1994. The body aims to promote and protect human rights, stability and good governance between its 12 member states. In 2004, the ICGLR adopted the Dar-es-Salam Declaration reiterating its vision to secure peace and stability within the region (ICGLR 2004). The declaration includes plans to establish mechanisms to aid in the realization of these goals. Although these have yet to become a reality, such mechanisms may further open the way for access to justice on the continent.

International Crimes Framework

At the end of World War II, the international community of nations resolved "to save succeeding generations from the scourge of war… reaffirm faith in human rights…and establish conditions under which justice and respect for the obligations arising from treaties and other sources of international law can be maintained" (UN 1948, Preamble). The statutes of the International Military Tribunal for Nürnberg of 1945 (Charter of the International Military Tribunal 1945) and the International Military Tribunal for the Far East of 1946 (International Military Tribunal for the Far East Charter 1946) represent the first treaties in the international crimes framework post-1945. The Nürnberg principles developed by the UN International Law Commission (UN International Law Commission 1950) represent the foundation of assertions that international law imposes a duty on individuals to account for

international crimes, such as war crimes, crimes against humanity and the crime of aggression even if national laws do not specifically provide for this responsibility. The Convention on the Prevention and Punishment of the Crime of Genocide of 1948 (UN General Assembly 1948) represented the consensus of the international community that genocide is a crime under international crimes. Under international law, the core international crimes are war crimes, crimes against humanity, genocide and the crime of aggression.

In June 2014, the AU Assembly of Heads of State and Government adopted the Malabo Protocol (AU 2014). The protocol extends the jurisdiction of the African Court of Justice and Human Rights, which has yet to be established, to include an international crimes jurisdiction.

The Malabo Protocol, which has not entered into force, is a continental criminal court that has jurisdiction over the core international crimes and an additional 10 transnational and organized crimes. While there are no ratifications at the time of writing, there are nine signatories to the Malabo Protocol: Benin, Chad, Congo, Ghana, Guinea-Bissau, Kenya, Mauritania, Sierra Leone and São Tomé and Príncipe. The Malabo Protocol is seen as Africa's response to the ICC focus on the African continent and as an attempt to scuttle that process and provide what is known as "African solutions to African problems." The regional courts in Africa — the ECOWAS Community Court of Justice, the EACJ and the defunct SADC tribunal — do not have international crimes jurisdiction, although there were proponents for this as a result of anti-ICC sentiments. The politicization of the ICC intervention will be discussed later in this chapter.

Out of 55 African states, there are currently 34 African states parties to the Rome Statute of the ICC (UN Diplomatic Conference 1998), which gives the ICC jurisdiction for international crimes committed in these countries. The ICC, however, remains a court of last resort, with primacy of jurisdiction over international crimes resting with national criminal justice systems. Of the 34 African states, a few have domesticated the Rome Statute, thereby allowing national courts the legislative framework to bring to justice perpetrators of international crimes.

It is important to note that unless individuals are effectively and efficiently held to account for international crimes in any state, there is a likelihood that violence will recur in the future. It is therefore important that the legal framework in the African continent is implemented both to deal with the past and to act as a preventative tool for serious human rights violations in conflict.

Transitional Justice Framework

Transitional justice seeks to address legacies of large-scale past abuses and includes mechanisms such as truth telling, criminal trials, reparations, memorialization and institutional reform. The anticipated outcome of these mechanisms is the creation of a platform where national healing, cohesion and reconciliation can begin. Such mechanisms are intended not only to redress past injustices but also to manage and prevent further conflict in future.

The relationship between reconciliation and transitional justice is interdependent. Reconciliation is perceived as one of the pillars of transitional justice, with truth seeking, justice, reparations and guarantees for non-recurrence. Reconciliation is also the product of transitional justice interventions in a given society. Ultimately, the core of the reconciliation process is the institutionalization of a process of transitional justice (Murithi 2009, 136). The rule of law and democracy are essential foundations for independent and accountable government. These foundations assist states in preventing conflict and, where it happens, in addressing the past.

Truth Seeking

Truth commissions are a common institution formed by states emerging from conflict or authoritarian rule. Conversations about "the truth" should be promoted. States that employ truth-seeking mechanisms in the continent include the DRC, Kenya and South Africa, among others.

While hailed as a model for truth commissions, the South African Truth and Reconciliation Commission (SATRC) did not heal all the wounds left behind by apartheid in South Africa. Archbishop Desmond Tutu, who chaired the SATRC, was quick to point this out. He noted that the process contributed to the reconciliation process in that country but that more work was required beyond the life of the SATRC to reconcile that nation.

Truth commissions must be seen as initiators of dialogues within fragmented societies. Their objective is to provide safe spaces for genuine remorse and for creating narratives for a collective truth that does not suppress the contributions of certain communities to nation building. They should be able to grant amnesty where appropriate within the ambit of internationally accepted standards and provide platforms for a continued healing process (Assefa 2001, 57). It should be noted, however, that international law has set standards for the parameters of amnesties granted by truth commissions or through related post-conflict processes. Amnesties for international crimes are not permitted. This position has meant that some truth commissions are almost stillborn, notably those in Kenya, Côte d'Ivoire, Burundi and the DRC. In each of these countries, truth commissions have been either established by legislation or peace accords, but have never really served their objectives. In Kenya, the Truth, Justice and Reconciliation Commission (TJRC) was fraught with legitimacy challenges to its leadership, its resource allocation from the national budget and its actual work. In the end, the TJRC report was never adopted by the necessary powers that would allow implementation of its recommendations to proceed. In Côte d'Ivoire, the Commission Dialogue Vérité et Réconciliation has suffered a fate similar to that in the Kenyan process. The body suffers from a lack of legitimacy in its leadership, as the leaders themselves are accused of committing human rights violations.

The work of the commission remains very vague to date. Burundi took 14 years to set up its Truth and Reconciliation Commission. Legislation was adopted in 2014, but the body has not yet been operationalized as a result of the deteriorating political situation. Moreover, the leadership was not chosen in a consultative manner, as envisioned by the 2000 Arusha peace accords, which has created further challenges.

Justice

Formal Justice

The retributive theory of justice has punishment for past crimes and the deterrence of future crimes as its objectives. In this sense, retribution could be said to be both a preventative and management tool in conflict situations. Depending on how they are managed, international and locally owned justice processes may foster or impede national reconciliation in conflict and post-conflict states. It is possible for international criminal trials to contribute to political reconciliation by fostering the social conditions required for the rule of law.

Cultivating respect for the rule of law is a constitutive part of the process of political reconciliation. International criminal trials can contribute to reconciliation by cultivating legal decency and good judgment among officials and encouraging faith in law among citizens (Murphy 2010, 224).

Following the genocide and other systematic, widespread and flagrant violations of international humanitarian law committed in Rwanda in 1994, the UN Security Council Resolution 955 of 1994 created the ICTR with the objective that it "would contribute to the process of national reconciliation and to the restoration and maintenance of peace" (UN Security Council 1994).

International criminal trials can influence prospects for conflict prevention and management in African states through exposure, contrasting a country's past practices with the structured respect for due process of law practised at international criminal tribunals or courts. In this educative role, international criminal trials can shape the way a state in transition adheres to the rule of law in accordance with internationally accepted standards. Some useful practices that states could adopt include providing national witness protection regimes, as in South Africa and Kenya, and including substantive and procedural rights of victims of international crimes in national criminal proceedings. To the extent that such practices are followed, international criminal trials provide a model for how national criminal proceedings should be conducted.

Traditional Justice

In Africa, disputes are also solved within the community context. Communal or informal justice has a place in addressing community conflicts. The use of this mechanism in response to mass atrocities or large-scale conflict, however, has its limitations. For example, while the *gacaca* system was instrumental in assisting Rwanda to address the genocide in 1994, it was specific to a community that spoke one language and had a common cultural background that was homogenous in its application of traditional justice as traditionally practised throughout Rwanda. The situation is not the same in other African post-conflict states. In Uganda, for example, the *mato oput* mechanism of traditional justice was and remains an integral part of dispute resolution among the Acholi people in the north. This traditional justice method, which entails carrying out certain rituals culminated by compensation to the families of victims, is, however, not applicable to other ethnic groups in the northern region and would not on its own satisfactorily address the atrocities occasioned on the residents of northern Uganda who come from various ethnic groups with varied traditional justice practices. Transitional justice practitioners in northern Uganda, reacting to the use of traditional justice in post-conflict situations, seem to agree that there is a place for traditional justice mechanisms when they are well understood by the people of a community and where they are complementary to the formal justice process. Yet the consensus is that traditional justice is unlikely on its own to satisfy the justice needs of a multi-ethnic community in conflict and suffering mass atrocity (Ogora 2009, 11).

Although traditional methods of providing justice still play an important role in Africa, particularly in rural or remote areas where conventional national courts do not necessarily or easily operate, they need to be treated with circumspection. The framework and value systems in which traditional or community courts function may, in some instances, contradict a country's constitutional principles and may, likewise, be out of touch with international laws as well. Such fora may be well placed to adjudicate on community matters; however, they may not be appropriate avenues for recourse in cases of human rights violations. An examination of tribal courts operating in Morocco's highlands illustrates the shortfalls of such systems. For example, the election of tribal leaders is not necessarily based on competence but rather tribal affiliation and is, further, not based on community-wide consensus but rather agreement between the "elders" of the community. Punishments, including ostracizing offenders, may be arbitrary, and community customs dictate that an *amghar* or tribal leader's decisions may not be questioned. Further concerns exist regarding women's rights, which may not necessarily have progressed or be recognized under such fora in rural areas, especially considering these tribunals are often called upon to adjudicate on matters of divorce and inheritance with decisions that may be particularly prejudicial to women. Thus, although in some cases traditional courts may serve as mechanisms to close gaps in access to justice and provide quick recourse, their significant limitations need to be taken into account. It is advisable that national authorities exercise some oversight of such bodies to ensure their compliance with national laws.

Reparations and Guaranties for Non-recurrence

Reparations refer to the obligation of a wrongdoing party to redress the damage caused to an injured party and may take the form of restitution, compensation, rehabilitation, satisfaction and guarantees of non-repetition (McClain and Ngari 2011, 3). The nexus between reparations and guarantees for non-recurrence to reconciliation is the recognition that for any society whose members have experienced harm as a result of mass violence or violations of human rights, there is an urgent need to redress the harm thus caused, to capacitate the members of society to participate meaningfully in the healing process of a nation, and to avert the risk of reprisals and a recurring cycle of violence.

A reparations policy is needed in African post-conflict states to redress past injustices. A carefully developed, managed and implemented reparations program has the potential to legitimize other processes under the truth-seeking and justice rubrics and, ultimately, the respect for the rule of law. Reparations have the function of confirming the events of the past; they both provide victims with the capacity to cope with the harm they have suffered and also contribute to the deterrence of future crimes. Such reparations policies must be developed in a consultative process, involving all stakeholders in a given state and relating to a specific conflict. The implementation of the policies must equally be consultative to ensure that the complexities of the conflict, including the fluid roles that characterize individuals in a conflict setting, from victim to perpetrator, are considered. In this regard, policy makers may be guided by international standards of what reparation programs should entail. Of course, there is no reparations program in one country that could be wholly replicated in another country.

The Role of the International Community in Preventing and Addressing Conflict in Africa

Examining the role of the international community in preventing and addressing conflict in Africa is important to this discourse. In cases in which states are the root of the problem, there are a number of avenues through which the international community may act. Pressure may be exerted on states through sanctions, diplomatic pressure or aid restrictions. Additionally, military support to states with long-term, documented records of human rights abuses should be reconsidered. Further, there is available a broad range of interventions, including peacekeeping operations, military and humanitarian interventions and international trials. In this discussion, we restrict ourselves to the R2P and consider the ICC interventions in Africa and their subsequent politicization as an impediment to addressing serious crimes of international concern in Africa.

R2P

The R2P connotes a global political commitment by the international community to intervene in a situation in which international crimes of genocide, war crimes and crimes against humanity occur. Its aim is to find the appropriate ways in which the international community can react to mass atrocity and international crimes in violent conflict and, at the same time, to address systematic abuses of human rights in periods of peace or violent conflict (Heindrich 2016, 217).

As a whole, the R2P doctrine is based on lifting the veil of the sovereignty of states, where the state has failed to protect its citizens from gross violations of human rights and serious international crimes. The R2P doctrine covers a wide range of measures, including, specifically, a preventive arm that encompasses a variety of tools. Alleged perpetrators are subject to targeted sanctions, threats of international criminal prosecution, Security Council resolutions that name or warn individuals and the breaking of diplomatic or economic ties.

In Africa, military interventions, in particular, have been met with mixed reactions. As was alluded to in the discussion on Libya above, such interventions are fraught with challenges. Decisions to intervene are highly politicized, with humanitarian considerations being just one of many factors. History has also shown the detrimental aftermath of military interventions, in the loss of civilian lives, the decimation of a country's infrastructure, the creation of political vacuums leading to total prolonged anarchy and the collapse of state economies as well as setbacks to arms control or non-proliferation efforts in Africa. The selective and varied involvement and actions of the international community is also problematic. For example, in the most recent past, we have seen the slow-to-act international community response to the violence that broke out in Burundi in 2015 following President Pierre Nkurunziza's announcement that he would be running for a third term as head of state.

While there has been significant progress in the use of sanctions from when entire states such as Zimbabwe were slapped by sanctions, the effect of which was felt mostly by the very victims of the authoritarian regime, to targeted sanctions, the sanctions regime itself has come under severe criticism. The less effective recommendations of the report of the Security Council sanctions committee of South Sudan include international travel bans for senior military personnel and senior commanders of the dissident forces, although a significant majority of these individuals neither travel across international borders nor possess passports. Another sanction was that these same individuals would have their assets frozen and not be allowed to operate bank accounts; yet South

Sudan at the time of the conflict and possibly to date has an illicit financial market, with no links whatsoever to the formal banking system, that is used by the very individuals targeted by this sanction to mobilize funds and perform other financial transactions.

Ultimately, to meet the objectives of preventing and managing conflict, the preventive tool of the R2P doctrine requires a more context-specific application.

The Politicization of the ICC Interventions in Africa

The Rome Statute was adopted in June 1998; to date, African states form the largest block of states parties to the Rome Statute (UN Diplomatic Conference 1998). The focus of the work of the ICC has predominantly been the African continent. There are 10 situations before the court, nine of which involve African states; these include six self-referrals from Uganda, the CAR (I) and (II), Côte d'Ivoire, Mali and the DRC. There are eight ongoing preliminary examinations, three of which involve African states. While African states have dominated the work of the ICC, this attention is not unwarranted. Governed by the principle of complementarity, the ICC remains a court of last resort and states retain the primacy of jurisdiction for war crimes, crimes against humanity and genocide that occur in their territory. As discussed earlier in this chapter, African states have limited or no legislation to address these international crimes. Where the legislation exists, there is little or no political will to investigate, prosecute and try international crimes. The ICC therefore intervenes when a situation is within its jurisdiction and the state is unwilling or unable to genuinely institute proceedings relating to international crimes.

The tension between the AU, its member states and the ICC remains a thorn in the flesh of advancing international criminal justice in Africa and effectively inhibits access to justice and respect for the rule of law to address crimes of mass atrocity. These tensions are based on the concerns of the AU and its member states regarding the work of the ICC, especially the Office of the Prosecutor of the ICC's focus on investigating and prosecuting sitting African heads of state. As a result, the international criminal justice project beyond the ICC has suffered a significant blow, with calls for mass withdrawals from the Rome Statute by African states parties. The effect of these withdrawals would be to significantly reduce opportunities to address international crimes committed in Africa — a regrettable situation that would destroy efforts in the fight against impunity for international crimes.

Conclusion

A number of states on the African continent find themselves under the strain of conflict and instability. Adding to these pressures is the mounting challenge that violent extremism has posed in recent years. Although the rule of law and access to justice at national, regional and continental levels are still problematic, significant progress has been made toward the promotion of rights and securing redress for victims.

As a starting point, it is imperative that states possess adequate legal frameworks that make provision for the rule of law and access to justice. This may entail minor revisions to legislation or the complete overhaul of legislative systems, as in Libya, for instance. States should also be encouraged to respect international conventions and laws and to domesticate certain laws to facilitate the prosecution of international crimes when necessary.

Good governance and respect for human rights obligations by states are key to preventing the outbreak of violence. As in the Arab Spring uprisings, iron-fisted approaches to governance are no longer effective means to containing civilian discontent. Government repression and the limitation of rights only serve to heighten a society's inclination toward violent conflict or extremism. Effective avenues for access to justice serve to strengthen confidence in the law and enable societies to resolve conflicts constructively.

Isolated, short-term, non-contextual strategies to prevent and manage conflict end up undermining efforts to ensure respect for the rule of law in African states. While conflict continues to threaten peace and security in African states, it is clear from the discussions in this chapter that a number of context-specific mechanisms and strategies need to be employed in a complementary fashion to prevent and manage conflict in African states. In turn, institutions with a mandate to deliver on justice will be strengthened, as will the rule of law.

Works Cited

Alter, Karen J., Laurence R. Helfer and Jacqueline R. McAllister. 2013. "A New International Human Rights Court for West Africa: The ECOWAS Community Court of Justice." *The American Journal of International Law* 107: 737–779.

Assefa, Hizkias. 2001. "Reconciliation." In *Peacebuilding: A Field Guide*, edited by Luc Reychler and Thania Paffenholz, 336–42. Boulder, CO: Lynne Rienner Publishers.

AU. 2014. *Protocol on Amendments to the Protocol on the Statute of the African Court of Justice and Human Rights.* June 27.

Cachalia, Raeesah Cassim. 2015. "Has Egypt's Judiciary Become the New Theatre of the Absurd?" Institute for Security Studies. www.issafrica.org/iss-today/has-egypts-judiciary-become-the-new-theatre-of-the-absurd.

Cachalia, Raeesah Cassim, Irene Ndungu and Uyo Salifa. 2016. "The Dynamics of Youth Radicalization in Africa: Reviewing the Current Evidence." Institute for Security Studies. https://issafrica.org/research/papers/the-dynamics-of-youth-radicalisation-in-africa-reviewing-the-current-evidence.

Charter of the International Military Tribunal. 1945 [*Charter of the Nuremberg Tribunal*]. 82 U.N.T.S. 279, 59 Stat. 1544, 3 Bevans 1238. August 8.

Dugard, John. 2005. *International Law: A South African Perspective.* Cape Town, South Africa: Juta and Company.

EAC Secretariat. 1999. *Treaty for the Establishment of the East African Community.* November 30. Arusha, Tanzania.

ECCAS. 1983. *Treaty Establishing the Economic Community of Central African States.* October 18. Libreville, Gabon.

ECOWAS. 1991. *Protocol A/P.1/7/91 on the Community Court of Justice.* July 6.

Erasmus, Gerhard. 2015. "The New Protocol for the SADC Tribunal: Jurisdictional Changes and Implications for SADC Community Law." Tralac Working Paper No. US15WP01/2015.

France. 1958. *Constitution of the Republic of France of 4 October 1958.* JO, 5 October 1958, 9151.

Freedom House. 2015. "Discarding Democracy: Return to the Iron Fist — Freedom in the World 2015." https://freedomhouse.org/sites/default/files/01152015_FIW_2015_final.pdf.

Heindrich, Dorota. 2016. "Responsibility to Protect: An (In)Effective Tool for Mass Atrocity Crimes Prevention." In *The Legacy of Crimes and Crises: Transitional Justice, Domestic Change and the Role of the International Community,* edited by Klaus Bachmann, 217–236. Oxford, UK: Peter Lang.

Human Rights Watch. 2015. "Egypt: Thousands Evicted in Sinai Demolitions: In Insurgent Fight, Border Families Left to Fend for Themselves." September 22. Beirut, Lebanon: Human Rights Watch. www.hrw.org/news/2015/09/22/egypt-thousands-evicted-sinai-demolitions.

ICGLR. 2004. *Dar-es-Salaam Declaration on Peace, Security, Democracy and Development in the Great Lakes Region.* November 20.

ICJ. 2012. "ICJ Disappointed by Decision Taken on SADC Tribunal." International Commission of Jurists Joint Statement. August 22.

International Law Commission. 1950. "Principles of International Law Recognized in the Charter of the Nürnberg Tribunal and in the Judgment of the Tribunal, with Commentaries." *Yearbook of the International Law Commission, 1950* II: 374–378.

International Military Tribunal for the Far East Charter. 1946. T.I.A.S. 1589. January 19.

League of Arab States. 1994. *Arab Charter on Human Rights.* September 15.

Mahvinga, Dewa. 2016. "Zimbabwe Returns to its Ugly Past." September 12. Johannesburg, South Africa: Human Rights Watch. www.hrw.org/news/2016/09/12/zimbabwe-returns-its-ugly-past.

McClain, Lindsay and Allan Ngari. 2011. *Pay Us So We Can Forget: Reparations for Victims and Affected Communities in Northern Uganda.* Policy Brief. Gulu, Uganda: Justice and Reconciliation Project. http://justiceandreconciliation.com/UlngO/2011/09/pay-us-so-we-can-forget-reparations-for-victims-and-affected-communities-in-northern-uganda-policy-brief-no-2/.

Murithi, Timothy. 2009. *The Ethics of Peacebuilding.* Edinburgh, UK: Edinburgh University Press.

Murphy, Colleen. 2010. "Political Reconciliation and International Criminal Trials." In *International Criminal Law and Philosophy,* edited by Larry May and Zachary Hoskins, 224–244. New York, NY: Cambridge University Press.

Namibia. 1990. *Legal Aid Act.* No. 29 of 1990.

Nathan, Laurie. 2013. "The Disbanding of the SADC Tribunal: A Cautionary Tale." *Human Rights Quarterly* 35: 870–892.

Ngari, Allan. 2016. "Dealing with the Legacy of Mass Atrocities in the Great Lakes." In *The Legacy of Crimes and Crises: Transitional Justice, Domestic Change and the Role of the International Community,* edited by Klaus Bachmann, 49–70. Oxford, UK: Peter Lang.

OAU. 1981. *African Charter on Human and Peoples' Rights.* CAB/LEG/67/3 rev. 5, 21 ILM 58. June 27.

OAU. 1998. *Protocol to the African Charter on Human and People's Rights on the Establishment of an ACtHPR.* OAU/LEG/MIN/AFCHPR/PROT.1 rev. 2. June 10.

Ogora, Lino Owor. 2009. "Moving Forward: Traditional Justice and Victim Participation in Northern Uganda." Cape Town, South Africa: Institute for Justice and Reconciliation.

South Africa. 1996. *Constitution of the Republic of South Africa.* Act No. 108 of 1996.

Southern Africa Litigation Centre. 2014. *Justice for All: Realizing the Promise of the Protocol Establishing the African Court on Human and Peoples' Rights*. Johannesburg, South Africa: Southern Africa Litigation Centre.

———. 2015. "Radio Today Podcast on the SADC Tribunal." October 21. www.southernafricalitigationcentre.org/2015/10/21/radio-today-podcast-on-the-sadc-tribunal/.

Sow Sidibé, Amsatou. 2003. "Communication introductive generale." In *Actes du colloque international sur l'application du droit international dans l'ordre juridique interne des Etats africains francophones*. 54.

Ssenyonjo, Manisuli. 2013. "Direct Access to the African Court on Human and Peoples' Rights by Individuals and Non Governmental Organizations: An Overview of the Emerging Jurisprudence of the African Court 2008–2012." *International Human Rights Law Review* 2: 17–56.

Swaziland. 2005. *Constitution of the Kingdom of Swaziland Act*. Act No. 001 of 2005.

UN. 1945. *Charter of the United Nations*. 1 UNTS XVI. October 24.

———. 2016. *Investigation by the Office of the United Nations High Commissioner for Human Rights on Libya: Report of the Office of the United Nations High Commissioner for Human Rights*. A/HRC/31/47. February 15.

UN Diplomatic Conference of Plenipotentiaries on the Establishment of an International Criminal Court (UN Diplomatic Conference). 1998. *Rome Statute of the International Criminal Court*. A/CONF. 183/9. July 17.

UN General Assembly. 1948. *Convention on the Prevention and Punishment of the Crime of Genocide*. 78 UNTS 277. December 9.

———. 1966. *International Covenant on Civil and Political Rights*. 999 UNTS 171. December 19.

———. 1984. *Convention Against Torture and Other Cruel, Inhuman or Degrading Treatment or Punishment*. 1465 UNTS 85. December 10.

———. 1989. *Convention on the Rights of the Child*. 1577 UNTS 3, 28 ILM 1456. November 20.

UN International Law Commission. 1950. *Principles of International Law Recognized in the Charter of the Nurnberg Tribunal and in the Judgment of the Tribunal*. A/1316. July 29.

UN Secretary-General. 2004. *The Rule of Law and Transitional Justice in Conflict and Post-Conflict Societies*. S/2004/616. August 23.

UN Security Council. 1994. *Security Council Resolution 955 (1994) (Establishment of the International Criminal Tribunal for Rwanda)*. S/RES/955. November 8.

Van der Linde, Morné and Lirette Louw. 2001. "Considering the Interpretation and Implementation of Article 24 of the African Charter on Human and Peoples' Rights in Light of the SERAC Communication." *African Human Rights Law Journal* 3 (1): 167–187.

Wandia, Mary. 2012. "Stop Manipulating and Bullying the EA Court to Serve Interests of Regional Elites." *The East African*, May 12.

7

Repressing or Protecting?
The Security Sector and Society in Africa

Mathurin C. Houngnikpo

onflict, which is inherent in all societies, arises when two or more groups believe that their interests are incompatible. "Conflict" is not, however, interchangeable with "violence." Peaceful resolution of conflict is possible when individuals and groups trust their governing structures, society and institutions to manage incompatible interests (Haider 2009, 2). It is only when this trust and relevant conflict management capacities are lacking that conflicting parties resort to the use of force to secure their goals. For years, the African state has been seen as increasingly incapable of providing for the general welfare and incapable of asserting its claim to be the moral arbiter of its citizens' lives (Houngnikpo 1999). Such developments support earlier claims of the state's withering competence

that focused on its inability to protect its citizens. In fact, for quite a while the prevailing narrative on Africa has been that it is a continent awash with violent conflict. Indeed, Africa does suffer from a multitude of conflicts — from border skirmishes to civil wars to terrorist attacks.[1]

Arguably, conflict is one of the most intractable problems of contemporary Africa. Millions of people have been killed, and millions more have become refugees or have been internally displaced. Economic and social infrastructure has been

---

1   *Minding the Gap: African Conflict Management in a Time of Change* (Aall and Crocker 2016) scrutinizes the source of conflicts in Africa and assesses African management capacity in the face of these conflicts.

destroyed, security compromised and development reversed. Conflict in Africa is manifested in a variety of forms and in differing intensities at different times and places (Aall 2015). Conflict makes life tenuous and living unbearable for large numbers of Africans. It impedes the development of the continent and keeps African societies from realizing their potential. It undermines confidence in leaders and destroys hope for the future. It precludes the partnerships that could bring investment and development, while also undercutting other desirable international relationships.

Unfortunately, the sources of African conflict, like its manifestations, are varied and sometimes obscure (Aall and Crocker 2016). Conflict within states generally is the symptom of deeper socio-economic and political problems. Often it is the result of competition for scarce advantage, whether economic opportunity or political or social power. The fact that much of the conflict in Africa has been internal rather than external should give room for reflection on its causes. In any case, once it has ignited, conflict is like a cancer that destroys already fragile social relationships and institutions, generating new reasons for continued violence (Shah 2014). This inevitability highlights the importance not only of mechanisms to prevent conflict from occurring in the first place, but also of the mechanisms to control, limit or extinguish it when it does occur. However, such mechanisms may be of only limited use unless the root causes of conflict are identified and attenuated. This is why Africa's security problems are not easily separated from the problems of poverty, inequitable access to wealth and opportunity, and inept or irresponsible leadership and governance.

Although conflicts in Africa are diverse and complex, there have been a number of cases of successful conflict management and resolution (Aall 2015, 1). However, the role, if any, of the security sector in the success or failure of conflict resolution in Africa remains untested.

The "security sector," according to the United Nations (UN) Secretary-General,

> is a broad term often used to describe the structures, institutions and personnel responsible for the management, provision and oversight of security in a country. It is generally accepted that the security sector includes defence, law enforcement, corrections, intelligence services and institutions responsible for border management, customs and civil emergencies. Elements of the judicial sector responsible for the adjudication of cases of alleged criminal conduct and misuse of force are, in many instances, also included. Furthermore, the security sector includes actors that play a role in managing and overseeing the design and implementation of security, such as ministries, legislative bodies and civil society groups. Other non-state actors that could be considered part of the security sector include customary or informal authorities and private security services (UN 2008, paragraph 14).

While most African countries are in the process of political transition, both the nature and the process of transition, and the role of the security sector in it, are determined by a range of factors that make generalizations difficult. However, the security sector remains a key player in any genuine transition, whether from single-party politics to more pluralistic systems, from military to civilian government, or from war to peace. Any genuine democratic governance requires an enabling security sector (Houngnikpo 2012). More specifically, for democracy to have its true meaning, the military, the police, the gendarmerie and the justice system must become allies of the citizens they are tasked with protecting. For several decades, military intervention has been a key feature of African politics. The might and rise of the African military are well captured in Patrick McGowan's study (2003), which reveals that between 1956 and 2001, there have been 80 successful *coups d'état*, 108 failed coup attempts and 139 reported coup plots in Sub-Saharan Africa.

Because of its track record on the continent, the military has long been perceived not only as the enemy of the state, but also of the people. Indeed, decades of use and abuse of the armed forces in the political realm have negatively affected civil-military relations on the continent, and emerging democracies' failure to address the army's insertion in the democratic process will harm the transition process (Houngnikpo 2010). The security sector and, more specifically, the military, the police and the gendarmerie, are urged to play a key role in conflict resolution in particular and in democratic governance in general. The new paradigm should lead to a unity of purpose, effort and action, because the ultimate goal that both civilian and military leaders pursue should be the overall well-being of the population. Human security "introduced changes in the conception of security from the safety of the state to the safety of the individual" (chapter 1 of this book).

To defeat the whole range of transnational threats such as violent extremism/terrorism and trafficking, the population has to be involved. This is too big a task to be handled by the military alone. More than before, citizens' vigilance and collaboration is required. Citizens can enhance efforts and focus resources to ensure swift and direct methods of information exchange among police agencies of different jurisdictions, both domestically as well as across national borders (Deflem 2013). According to Helmoed Heitman (2011), combatting irregular forces has become a common feature of the contemporary African security landscape. However, the security sector in most African countries is ill-prepared to conduct effective counter-insurgency operations. Long overdue is a realignment of force structures to address these threats while building security sector professionalism to gain the trust of local

populations. Because of the nature of emerging menaces, what is required is an overhaul of the security sector. Yet this cannot be achieved in isolation, but must be embedded in a broader process of political reform and improved public sector governance (Ball, Bouta and van de Goor 2003, 24). It must also extend to an evaluation of what constitutes security, whose security it is, and the role of the security apparatus in achieving it. In a post-conflict environment especially, preventing societies from falling back into violent conflict requires building up domestic capacity to provide security in an accountable manner (Bryden 2007).

Whether it takes the form of a reform or a transformation, a security sector overhaul should create national forces that seek to advance their institutional interests in competition with other state bodies, and to contribute to the formulation of defence and security policies on the basis of their functional expertise (Foster 2005). These forces should serve as special government agencies, tasked with *implementing*, rather than *formulating*, policies (Chuter 2006). Besides the semantic definitional difference, what matters in this play of words is the new attitude expected of the security and defence forces. Security sector reform (SSR) involves enhancing the capacity of existing institutions that already function with a certain degree of efficacy. It is undertaken by countries whose security institutions are able to meet most of their security challenges. On the other hand, security sector transformation (SST) involves conducting a complete overhaul of existing institutions or establishing institutions for the very first time. SST is necessary in countries emerging from conflict or countries that are finally in a position to address long-standing and pervasive security challenges

But frankly speaking, most African countries seem to be emerging from everlasting conflict caused by poor governance. Besides, they have been unable to make their colonial European "Armies of

Africans"[2] into "African armies." For the colonial powers to extract economic benefits from their newly acquired territory, they needed to install a repressive state apparatus. Colonization was often imposed by force of arms, or through intimidation based on the threat of force. The colonial order established by conquest was typically a military order that coerced the colonized peoples into a state of submission (Solomon 1999, 28). Unfortunately, the post-colonial state has failed to dismantle the colonial security apparatus. Rather, it used it to perpetuate the neo-colonial diktat on dissenting voices. African security organizations have consequently become forces of insecurity for both the state and its citizens, rather than a means of guaranteeing individual and collective security. Boubacar N'Diaye (2009) argues eloquently that in nearly all aspects of security sector management, francophone African states remained prisoners of French African security policies, many facets of which did not conform to sound security sector governance principles or convey these to African (political or military) leaders. He furthermore maintains that the evidence indicates that francophone Africa's security establishments, the armies in particular, were conceived as overseas appendices and instruments of French security policies both before and after the adjustments made necessary by the major changes in the 1990s (ibid.).

For all practical intents and purposes, what is called for in contemporary Africa is a transformation of the security sector, a complete reconstruction, to align the citizens' interest with that of the security sector and to create an environment conducive to more harmonious relations between the people and its protective forces. In fact, according to Neil Cooper and Michael Pugh (2002, 8), the term "security sector reform" may be inappropriate. A more appropriate label would be "security sector transformation" because the shortfalls in security

sector governance in countries targeted for action are so substantial that nothing short of a transformation in the relationship between civil authorities, civil society and the security sector is required. SSR needs, rather, to be couched within a broader transformative approach. As a prerequisite, the exit strategies that hobble the development of effective policy in post-conflict societies need to be replaced by engagement strategies that conceive of peace building as a long-term process (ibid., 51). Specifically, SST aims to rebalance economic structures and the socio-political environment so as to reduce the incentives for militarization and encourage a more nuanced approach to the varied security needs of societies. SST encompasses reform, but also addresses the broader political economy of conflicts; it engages with a wider set of actors, issues and security concerns; and it questions the role that developed states' security policies play in fostering instability (ibid., 52).

Although because of the nature of their respective missions the challenges facing the police and the gendarmerie are more acute than those confronting the military, these actors of the security sector should ultimately side with the people. While redressing the shortcomings of defending territorial integrity seems easier for reforming the armed forces, dealing with the complexity of the provision of internal security and justice is proving more challenging for African countries. The police, the gendarmerie and the justice system are all facing uphill battles in reforming themselves in order to reclaim their proper roles within society. Because old habits die hard, the new behaviour expected of police and the gendarmerie is taking much longer to become established (Downie 2013). Until nepotism, corruption, extortion and other improper and unethical attitudes are dealt with, Africans will continue to be exposed to the arbitrary abuses and whims of the security sector actors. The right to justice is also at risk in Africa because of weaknesses in the judicial system such as a shortage of lawyers, especially legal aid lawyers,

---

2   *Army of Africa* was an unofficial but commonly used term for those parts of the French Army recruited from Africa to fight foreign wars.

and a lack of financial and material resources. Overcrowding and degrading prison conditions are the results of a lack of legal assistance provided to poorer members of the community and delays in criminal justice procedures (Anderson 2006).

In a nutshell, democratic governance of security institutions, the key to peaceful conflict resolution in Africa, lies at the very heart of SSR, as experience suggests that civilian oversight and control over the security sector does not necessarily equate to "democratic control" let alone "democratic governance" (Chuter 2006; Bryden 2007). If effective delivery of security as a public good is the desired end state, a related question is not only how to secure, but also whom to secure (that is, all citizens). Democratic security sector governance (that is, the will to protect not some, but all citizens, regardless of ethnicity, class and gender or other social divisions) has to be the ultimate goal of SSR (UN 2011, 10).

This chapter seeks to explore the relationships between major security providers (the police, the gendarmerie and the military) and the community in which they operate with the hypothesis that quite often conflicts stem from the behaviour of those who are supposed to guarantee security to the population. Having explored the constant search for peaceful resolution of conflict through human history, and after a careful examination of the record of the SSR in some countries, the chapter will determine whether the security sector is strengthening or instead weakening social cohesion in fractured societies. In a nutshell, this chapter examines the extent to which capacity-building interventions in SSR can lead to improved outcomes in accountability, responsiveness and capacity to deliver in security institutions and agencies in Africa. It further seeks to explore the factors enabling or hindering these improvements (Denney and Valters 2015) and the relationship between organizational capacity-building interventions and the longer term outcomes of increased stability and reductions in outbreaks of conflict.

The Search for Peaceful Conflict Resolution

The search for peaceful resolution of conflict is as old as humanity. The affairs of primitive society were marked by chronic raiding and feuding between groups. Conflict exists as the interactions and altercations between different parties that include emotions, perceptions and behaviours. It is an inevitable part of human existence, and is often associated with feelings of frustration and anger. While the evidence suggests that humans seem hardwired to come into conflict with one another, often violently, it is also clear that they have the capacity to resolve fights. Throughout history, various mechanisms have been used to protect society. A liberal democratic state, for instance, fulfills its protective role within the political community by instituting a rule of law enforced by punishment (Bowman 2005, 6). To retain its authority, the state must protect its citizens from foreign threats, not least of all by means of an effective security sector establishment. Ironically, in Africa, the security sector itself is quite often the very threat citizens need protection from. While it is important that the military be strong enough to protect the state, the armed forces cannot be left uncontrolled by the state. Freed from state restraints, the security sector might pursue the objects of its own passions and pose an internal threat to sovereign power. Neither should the security sector be entirely dominated by the state, because it might then be forced to follow civilian authorities' passions, which might sap its strength and consequently weaken security (Chuter 2006).

One way to overcome such a dilemma is to reorganize the entire security sector by taking into account the new concept of security: human security. Security concerns perceptions of both individual and collective well-being and of the assurance of "core values" central to the self-definition of communities. While it is the state that, in the Weberian tradition,[3] holds the right to maintain and exercise coercive force to keep order and to settle disputes, national agencies or bureaucracies such as the military, the police and the gendarmerie can take violent action on behalf of the state or the people.

For several centuries, security has been defined as politico-military threats within the strict realm of the security apparatus. Nowadays, human security has emerged as a response to today's challenges. Policies and institutions must respond to growing insecurities in stronger and more integrated ways. The state continues to have the primary responsibility for security, evidently. But as security challenges become more complex and various new actors attempt to play a role, a paradigm shift is required. The focus must broaden from the state or regime security to the security of the citizens — to human security.

As the Commission on Human Security (2003) puts it, the concept of human security — which combines elements of national security, economic development and basic human rights with the objective of protecting people from the fear of violence — is particularly relevant in Africa. While protecting the state and its citizens from external aggression remains a consideration, the most serious threats facing countries on the African continent at the beginning of the twenty-first century tend to be those that either derive from internal causes or are transnational and collective in nature.

Human security means protecting vital freedoms. It means protecting people from critical and pervasive threats and situations, building on their strengths and aspirations. It also means creating systems that give people the building blocks of survival, dignity and livelihood. Human security connects different types of freedoms — freedom

from want, freedom from fear and freedom to take action on one's own behalf (ibid., 1). To do this, human security offers two general strategies: protection and empowerment. Protection shields people from dangers. It requires concerted effort to develop norms, processes and institutions that systematically address insecurities. Empowerment enables people to develop their potential and become full participants in decision making. Protection and empowerment are mutually reinforcing, and both are required in most situations (ibid.).

Taking a wider view of security, however, should not lead to a diminished role for security forces, or to their neglect, since weak and underfunded security establishments can be — and often have been — a significant source of insecurity. Professional, effective and efficient militaries, able to perform their legitimate and constitutionally defined functions, are an essential element of national security strategies. In many countries, and especially those that have known military rule, the military and other security forces are distrusted and civil-military relations are unhealthy (Houngnikpo 2012). Moreover, a lack of transparency leads to public misunderstanding of security issues and defence policy. Restructuring and right-sizing the different forces do not follow the same path. Reorganizing the military seems more possible, while bringing the police back to its law enforcement function and the judiciary to its justice provision remains a daunting task for many African countries.

One of the most critical security institutions of the state is the police, especially in nations emerging from conflict (Downie 2013, 1). Naturally, a nation's military has an important role to play in dealing with external threats and establishing basic security in the immediate aftermath of conflict. But the institution of the police is best suited for handling internal security and addressing the safety needs of the public. A citizen views a police officer as the symbolic representation of state authority and accepts or denies the state through interaction with the police (ibid.).

---

3   To Max Weber (1965), a state is a political organization with a centralized government that maintains a monopoly over the legitimate use of force within a certain territory.

Unfortunately, many Africans, according to Richard Downie (ibid.), have very negative perceptions of the police, viewing the police as ineffective, unprofessional, corrupt and even predatory. Its primary interest seems to be to protect the regime instead of serving the public. Due to a lack of resources and equipment, the African police, for the most part, remains one of the most dysfunctional and underperforming state institutions. To make matters worse, police corruption and unprofessionalism erode people's faith in the criminal justice system. Little wonder that reforming the police and the justice system seems more complicated. Until such structural challenges as political interference, lack of funding and human rights abuses are removed, reforming or transforming the police and justice sectors remains fraught with huge difficulties.

The Security Sector Governance: Reform or Transformation?

The Commission on Human Security (2003) maintains that the inability of African security organizations to provide a safe and secure environment for economic and political development arises to a large degree out of poor governance — both of the state in general and of the security sector in particular. In broad terms, the security sector comprises all those institutions responsible for protecting the state and communities within it (Chuter 2006; Bryden 2007). Although the focus is more narrowly on the military, the gendarmerie, police, paramilitary and intelligence services, and the civilian structures responsible for their oversight and control, it is important to remember that these institutions are part of a broader picture.

The role of the state and its security forces directly affect the opportunities for sustainable development and ensuring peoples' physical security. An effective, credible and accountable security sector also provides a safe and secure environment

in which to entrench other programming initiatives, including poverty-reducing development. There is a growing consensus that security needs should be approached both from the perspective of protecting individuals and communities from violence and with an awareness of how much defence spending can crowd out development expenditure (Houngnikpo 1999). Too often, the military is used to sustain governments in power and is inappropriately involved in internal security. Police forces are often underfunded and unable to guarantee security, thus giving rise to coercion and corruption (Downie 2013).

While the purpose of the security community's actions is to provide a safe and secure environment for people to go about their daily lives, without broader human development, insecurity can re-emerge and quickly spread throughout a region.[4] In the African context, it is most constructive to speak of a peace-building approach to human security. As noted earlier, the best way to reach that goal remains contentious: while some advocate SSR, others call for a SST.

Reform versus Transformation

In both the literature and the official discourse on improving security sector governance (Ball and Fayemi 2004; Boshoff 2008; Cawthra 2005; McFate 2008), the process of changing the security sector is described as "SSR." However, reform processes tend to be incremental and relatively ineffective in dealing with significant institutional weaknesses. Reforms may change the superficial appearance of an organization without fundamentally altering its character, culture or the de facto balance of power within the organization, as the many attempts at restructuring post-coup armed forces in Africa and Latin America have repeatedly shown. As Bello (2016) puts it, "Latin America's armed forces have accepted democracy but remain a law unto themselves."

---

4   This point is substantiated by Narayan et al. (2000) in *Voices of the Poor: Crying Out for Change.*

What is more, the term "reform" has negative political connotations in democratically inclined communities in the developing world, especially in Africa. Politically, it is often associated with the implementation of policy decisions by the executive from above without any attempt to secure the broader participation of and consultation with legislative or non-state actors. Many of the reform strategies adopted in Africa have been undertaken to legitimize unpopular regimes and have failed to alter the existing balance of power within the state or between the state and society to any meaningful extent (Bryden 2007). Reform, according to Banlaoi (2006), involves piecemeal changes to the security sector, often limited to doctrinal changes, operational effectiveness and cost-cutting drives, occurring as by-products of other state reform initiatives and often without buy-in from critical stakeholders and thus subject to reversal depending on the power structure in the state.

Transformation, in contrast, entails a more profound intent on behalf of elected governments to ensure that the practices of the security organizations are consistent with the democracies that they serve. Countries with serious governance deficits may require a fundamental transformation of relations between the civil authorities and civil society on the one hand and the security organizations on the other hand. Transformation seeks to dismantle dysfunctional security governance. However, such transformations should occur within a framework of democratic oversight and control.

As a concept, SST, in Banlaoi's (ibid.) view presents a paradigm shift in security sector governance. It recognizes the blurring of lines between internal and external security challenges. It identifies the current and evolving role played by military and non-military players as well as government and non-government stakeholders in addressing the multifaceted security challenges faced by the nation (ibid.). The concept of security transformation primarily seeks to understand underlying conditions for the emergence of these security challenges and builds capacity to strengthen national and local leadership "in dealing with new security demands and to establish effective processes and structures commensurate with the new challenges" (ibid.).

To achieve professional security institutions that meet the needs of citizens, society and the state and which operate within the rule of law and under effective democratic control, African governments would need to reform their security sector governance. The roles played by the state and its security forces have a direct impact on the opportunities for sustainable development and peoples' physical security. Security sector rebuilding must account for the overall security context and address the fundamentals as well as the specifics. Effective management, transparency and accountability of the security sector is just as necessary as with any other part of the public sector.

The Future of Security Sector Reform, edited by Mark Sedra (2010), provides an understanding of the complexities of reforming and transforming the security and justice architecture of the state. Written by leading international practitioners in the SSR field, the book offers valuable insight into what has worked and what has not, and lessons that can be drawn in development, security and state building for the future. Among the key lessons is that security itself needs to be secure so that security forces do not become the source of insecurity. While several African countries have embarked on SSR experimentation, not all of them have been successful in generating atmospheres conducive to peace and stability.

In *Security Sector Transformation in Africa*, edited by Alan Bryden and Funmi Olanisakin (2013), contributors clarify the relationship between SST and SSR, and provide insight on the challenges and opportunities for an operational SST agenda in Africa. Africa needs a holistic change to its security sector, aimed at a transformation that alters the power relations within the sector in the direction of civil and constitutional control. It needs to transform institutional culture, promote professionalism, improve resource utilization and operational effectiveness (on the side of the security forces), and improve policy management (on the side of the civil authorities), in tandem with increased accountability and respect for human rights and international law and with input from a range of stakeholders and role players (Banlaoi 2006).

Arguably, SST is considered vital to the success of internal armed conflict resolution and peace processes in Africa. It is regarded as an effective antidote to armed violence, criminality, insurgency and terrorism. SST is also crucial to fostering structural stability so that communities can live in a safe and secure environment necessary for the enjoyment of human life. SST aims to ensure state security without compromising human security. It endeavours to build the capacity of the security sector in order for the state to fulfil its role in advancing human security of its citizens (ibid.).

Securing the Security Sector: Protection Shield versus Repression Sword

While Africa's security landscape features an array of unconventional threats, weak management of the security sector remains a source of continuing fragility and capacity shortcomings in many countries (Malan 2005). Clearly, our understanding of security has evolved over the past 20 years. No longer is war the only security threat that nations face. Nor, for that matter, is war what it once was. Evidence suggests that, at least at the local level, the military is unlikely to be the principal guarantor of security (Downie 2013). The people's needs should essentially determine what constitutes security for them. In fact, what I call the "security trinity" must rest on three pillars: securing the state in order to protect a regime that ultimately provides a safe environment for the citizens. Under these circumstances, conflict, when it does occur, is likely to be nipped in the

bud, because the means for peaceful resolution prevail over contentious ones (Malan 2005). Although it is generally acknowledged that conflicts can be prevented, or at least mitigated, in practice this requires great sophistication in diagnosing conflict-prone situations. This is where the security sector can have a key role. It can be part of the early warning arrangement to facilitate timely and efficient response to conflict and crisis situations. However, the security sector in general and the military in particular need to be overhauled.

The reformed African military should be socially responsible. It should be a reflection of society, with a balanced ethnic composition. It should be an affordable military — one that can be fielded and maintained without draining or diverting vital national resources from other key strategic aims such as education, public health and safety, infrastructure, environmental protection, and research and development (Foster 2005, 94). The military should earn enough prestige to be respected by society. Its members should demonstrate moral superiority without arrogance. It should enjoy enough professional autonomy to perform without alienating itself from society. It should abide by national, regional and international instruments of human rights. It should engage in, and be expected to engage in, responsible dissent without crossing the line into disobedience. It should be part of the overall system of checks and balances (ibid., 96).

In the end, the success of any SSR or SST hinges on whether citizens are protected against violence, fear and basic needs. There are two categories of countries that went through or are still in the process of SSR or SST. Some have clearly made important strides in improving the security environment in which their populations live while others continue to struggle to generate an environment conducive to peace and prosperity. Although they are still works in progress, SSR efforts in South Africa, Liberia and Rwanda have made enough positive change to allow hope for better future. Ongoing challenges facing SSR in Burundi, the Democratic Republic of Congo (DRC) and South Sudan, however, continue to raise considerable concerns for peace, security and development in these nations.

The Security Sector as a Protection Shield: South Africa, Liberia and Rwanda

Over the past few years an important focus of peace and conflict research, and also of security studies, has been on the relationships between large-scale violent conflict, the performance of states and global security. State fragility is seen to engender violent conflict, which leads to state failure or even collapse. As states have a dual role, namely providing security and order for their citizens (internal role) and serving as the building blocks of the international system (external role), state fragility not only affects the citizens of the state and society in question, but also neighbouring states and the international community at large. Regions of state fragility are perceived as providing breeding grounds and safe havens for transnational terrorism, weapons proliferation and organized crime. The issue of fragile states is seen as being at the core of a variety of today's most pressing security problems (Boege et al. 2008, 2).

A state's capacity to provide security to its citizens remains the bedrock upon which its legitimacy and credibility rest. Legitimacy is a crucial aspect of all power relations. Without legitimacy, power is exerted through coercion; with legitimacy, power can be exerted through voluntary or quasi-voluntary compliance. Legitimacy lies at the core of state-citizen relationships and thus of the whole state-building agenda (McCullough 2015). Unfortunately, many African countries claim legitimacy without the corollary variable, which is to have effective control over one's territory and to provide adequate security for the populations. This essential mission is proving challenging for most, although South Africa's progress since the

end of apartheid is remarkable. Yet police services continue to face uphill battles.

South Africa

With the transition from apartheid to democratic rule in 1994 came a massive restructuring of the state security service providers. The reforms in the transitional period focused on creating state security structures that represented national racial and gender demographics. The reforms also created systems of democratic control, accountability and professionalism to ensure that the security services could no longer be used as a tool of oppression and a symbol of elite control. The 1996 white paper on national defence (South Africa 1996) was developed using an inclusive process and focused on democratic control and establishing a human security approach to domestic security.

A key primary criticism, however, has been the lack of an overarching national security policy, which lack still hampers the coherence of the state security architecture. Criticisms have also been levelled at the country's intelligence agency, with observers arguing that the intelligence mandate is too broad and ill defined (Cawthra 2005). Private security has become pronounced in recent years, and the total number of private security offices has overtaken the number of uniformed police. Although the industry is reasonably well regulated, there are flaws and omissions in oversight and monitoring. This is especially pertinent because in some areas, private security has replaced the public police entirely.

As the democratic state has matured and the ideals of accountability, transparency and security service delivery have become institutionalized, it has become possible for researchers and academics to focus not on the SSR programs but on the outcomes of the change initiatives. According to Gavin Cawthra (ibid.), South Africa has consciously and fairly successfully sought to apply best democratic practices to the governance of security. While an ambitious, extensive and systematic process of reform has been carried out, progress has, however, been uneven and fragmentary, and organizational and perhaps political fault lines have emerged. Although military reform has been a clear success, policing remains in the spotlight after a series of incidents that were seen to have highlighted police brutality and corruption (Watson 2013).

South African Police Service (SAPS) was officially established in January 1995, bringing together the apartheid-era South African Police and the police services of the former homelands. It was a difficult birth, combining a number of police forces with different training standards, approaches and attitudes to human rights, racism, discrimination and the use of force. Not only did SAPS need to develop a homogenous approach but it also had to become an accountable, transparent institution that moved away from the brutality and repression the police forces were reputed for. However, demands to scale up recruitment and political appointments, combined with pressure to tackle rising levels of violent crime, have resulted in a police *force* rather than a police *service*. Levels of violent crime have been declining but allegations of police brutality and investigations into police behaviour have not followed suit. According to David Smith (2013), reports of police brutality in South Africa have soared by 313 percent in a decade, yet only one in 100 cases against officers results in a conviction. A series of high-profile cases, including the shooting of striking mineworkers at Marikana and the killing of a Mozambican taxi driver dragged behind a van, have left the reputation of the service in tatters. Cases of police brutality leaped from 416 during 2001-2002 to 1,722 cases by 2011-2012.

Two decades after the peaceful transition from apartheid to democracy, state and society in South Africa are still in a state of transition. The vision of a "better quality of life for all the country's citizens" proclaimed by the African National Congress has so far become a reality for only a minority of people. The transition into a respectable democratic police organization faces challenges (Pruitt 2010, 116). Although a new black middle class is beginning to develop, large swathes of the population feel excluded from the progress. Poverty and growing inequality could pose a threat to social peace. Violence and crime are already impeding the country's economic and social development (Gould 2014). Under Nelson Mandela's successors, South Africa has become a slow-growing, often cranky, one-party-dominant state that only partially succeeds in providing the basic education and health services, housing, electrical power and human security that its 55 million citizens demand and expect. Courageous, intelligent, bold and principled political leadership is required if South Africa is going to build upon Mandela's legacy and successfully address the major problems that engulf the nation and restore South Africa to primacy in Africa (Rotberg 2014).

Liberia

Liberia's security institutions continue to face the daunting task of ensuring the country's political stability and reviving their deeply degraded image. Although significant SSR gains have been made in the past several years, these have all been accomplished while the United Nations Mission in Liberia (UNMIL) exercised its role as the country's main guarantor of peace. Liberia's national security institutions are increasingly able to cope with some of this work. But the country's security sector is still not currently able to function without considerable external support (International Crisis Group 2011). Moreover, Liberian democracy remains fragile, with a polarized politics tinged by corruption, nepotism and impunity and an economy still closed to many Liberians.

Liberia's civil war has become one of the defining features of its modern history. Following decades of misrule, Liberia spent 15 years engaged in two bloody civil wars that killed more than 200,000 people and displaced another million (Human Rights Watch 2013). Fighting came to an end in

2003 with the signing of a Comprehensive Peace Agreement (CPA), which called for an immediate ceasefire, the disarmament of all combatants, the formation of a transitional government and creation of a truth and reconciliation commission (International Crisis Group 2011). The CPA also called for the complete restructuring of the country's two main security institutions: the Liberian National Police (LNP) and the Armed Forces of Liberia. By the end of the war, both institutions were widely viewed as sources of insecurity and misery for Liberians across the country, owing to 14 years of predatory behaviour and a general blurring of the distinction between security and politics.

Initial SSR efforts began in 2004. At that time, UNMIL moved in to reform the LNP, even as early planning was made to disband, demobilize and reconstitute the army. SSR programs overall have had mixed results. The complete disbanding and rebuilding of the former Liberian army has been generally successful, while efforts to reform the police and other major security actors have faced greater challenges. The bold approach adopted to reform the army was made possible largely thanks to a strong national consensus and the presence of a large international UN presence. The same factors, however, have not enabled such bold action in restructuring Liberia's other security institutions (International Crisis Group 2009).

A key challenge inherent in decentralizing Liberia's national security architecture is that many national laws actually enshrine centralization, which leaves the security institutions vulnerable to abuse by the executive (SSR Resource Centre 2015). In a 2015 report, Margarita Yakovenko maintains that the main factors driving the change in security have been a plurality of local actors providing security, the presence of UNMIL, a relatively stable political reform, and donor financing. When compared to other factors, SSR has been a small but significant factor to improving Liberia's security environment.

However, Francisca Zanker (2015) maintains that despite a decade of police reform, the effectiveness of the Liberia National Police is still limited. Corruption, perceptions of insecurity, lack of resources and overlapping institutions are major challenges that still need to be dealt with. In the same vein, IRIN (2013) confirms that a decade of efforts to reform the LNP has resulted in an increasingly professional police force, yet abusive behaviour, a culture of impunity and endemic corruption continue to erode the force's credibility. SSR programs in Liberia overall have been unprecedented in ambition and scope but with mixed results. Army reform, entailing complete disbanding of existing forces, has made significant progress despite a lack of proper oversight of private military companies and of consensus on strategic objectives. But police and other security reforms are much less satisfactory (International Crisis Group 2009). In his assessment, Downie (2013, 5) maintains that the LNP has a long way to go ·before Liberians can be confident in its ability to provide effective, professional policing services.

Rwanda

Officially, SSR began in Rwanda when the Arusha Peace Agreement took effect in 1993. Those priorities changed dramatically, however, following the genocide that took place in 1994. Much of Rwanda's security reforms post-genocide have focused on the prosecution of individuals responsible for the genocide, and ensuring that genocide is never repeated. Specifically, with external support the Government of Rwanda has sought to enhance the capacity of its justice system to build the rule of law and meet the demand for prosecution, to train and professionalize its new police force, and to demobilize thousands of soldiers and reintegrate them into Rwandan society (SSR Resource Centre 2015).

While Rwanda is still dependent on external support for its SSRs, it has retained a great deal of local ownership over those reforms. This is largely a result of ongoing tension between the Rwandan government and the international community, which is still held responsible for failing to prevent the genocide. Many of the reforms have improved the capacity of the Rwandan security sector; however, significant challenges remain. With the Gacaca courts officially closed, the capacity of the court system is being tested, as it is responsible for continuing the prosecution of those responsible for the genocide. As well, significant security concerns such as small arms trafficking, border skirmishes with Hutu rebels in neighbouring countries, and the ongoing situation in the DRC continue to exert pressure on the Rwanda National Police and the armed forces.

This positive outlook should, however, be tempered, because some consider Rwanda an authoritarian state (Smith 2012; Sundaram 2016), describing a political system that emphasizes the authority of the state or, more accurately, the authority of its ruler or ruling party (with centralized, repressive and opaque power structures). Political power is concentrated in a strong man who maintains control by means of coercive resources such as the military, police and special units, and through personal or ethnic networks. And the police force is accountable to the president, enforcing decisions taken by the political elite to which it is accountable (Hills 2007). If indeed Kagame's Rwanda is an authoritarian state where democracy and human rights are trampled upon and dissenters are hunted down (Smith 2012), any progress made on the SSR front is likely to recede sooner rather than later. In fact, Anjam Sundaram's (2016) book compares Rwanda to a theatre in which everyone knows the script and must perform their part, because the punishment for "forgetting" one's lines is harsh. In such a theatre, genuine security and defence reform is unlikely to last.

According to Deutsche Gesellschaft für Internationale Zusammenarbeit (GIZ), the transitional government formed after the genocide introduced numerous reforms that managed to stabilize the country. Elections have taken place since 2003. More than half of Rwanda's members of Parliament are women. Although resource-poor, Rwanda is projected to meet most of the Millennium Development Goals. Notable successes are being achieved in the fields of health care, food security and primary education thanks to its zero tolerance strategy in the fight against corruption. Callisto Madavo may be right in stating that "Rwanda represents a post-conflict recovery marked by remarkable economic growth resting on the Asian model of a developmental state leading the formation of a competitive advantage." (See chapter 12). From a human security perspective, Rwanda has, overall, made the best out of its SSR program even if police reform is lagging a bit behind. The same cannot be said of its neighbours Burundi and the DRC.

The Security Sector as a Repression Sword: Burundi, the DRC and South Sudan

Any security sector activity that seeks to change and implement policy, process and procedure, or that builds capacity to increase accountability, transparency, sustainability and alignment with fundamental standards of human rights, qualifies as SSR — as long as broader SSR objectives, sustainable development and the governance dimensions are not neglected. SSR is a highly political process, shifting and reshuffling power relationships in government, the security sector and society. If pursued as intended — shifting power over providing society's security from the few to the many — SSR puts security institutions in the service of an empowered society. It is thus part and parcel of democratization efforts and the strengthening of good governance in transition societies. Burundi, the DRC and South Sudan are three countries that are supposed to be moving into the post-conflict category. Unfortunately, these countries continue to face tremendous overall development challenges, and the security sector, despite some reforms, is actually contributing to the chaos as opposed to improving the security environment.

Burundi

After a 12-year-long civil war and ongoing development and governance challenges, Burundi is still facing a very unstable security environment. Early hopes that genuine SSR was going to generate a political and security environment conducive to sustainable development vanished quite rapidly. Such optimistic scholars as Nicole Ball (2014) reported that progress made by Burundi's Security Sector Development (SSD) program in advancing democratic security sector governance was noteworthy given that there have been relatively few successful SSR cases from which to draw. Political will for security sector reform was expanded over time by supporting tangible priorities of the Burundian security sector that established the trust enabling broader engagement on governance issues. But Ball did note some early warning signs likely to derail the process: "The armed forces have subsequently made important strides in becoming ethnically integrated and professional. Nonetheless, serious challenges remain. The political rules of the game in Burundi are still not fully agreed upon. The political elite remains divided. The ruling party has yet to fully embrace democratic norms and continues to use the police for political ends. Moreover, for many Burundians, a large rift persists between the security sector and society at large" (ibid., 1).

Through its SSD program, sponsored by the Dutch government, Burundi established a new army and police force, into which many demobilized combatants from former armed groups were integrated. Today, Burundi has a distinctly oversized army and police force alongside weak government institutions. However, the government faces the challenge of carrying out important reforms while providing security

as a service to its citizens so that social tensions are resolved without recourse to violence. In fact, President Pierre Nkurunziza's third term and its subsequent consequences on the country have only exacerbated a political and security environment already deteriorated, putting at risk any progress noted in terms of human security. According to Ball (ibid.), the relative success of the SSD program — and particularly its governance pillar — depended heavily on its ability to address politically sensitive issues. SSD's eight-year time frame provided the time to adapt the program to evolving circumstances, facilitate increasing Burundian ownership of the reform process and realize the incremental gains from which substantive change was possible.

Following independence in 1962, there was a gradual monopolization of the army (Forces Armées Burundaises) by Burundi's Tutsi ethnic minority. This resulted in the domination of the country's institutions and elite by Tutsi nationals and the violent repression of the majority Hutu civilian population. In June 1993, Hutu presidential candidate Melchior Ndadaye won Burundi's first pluralistic election on a platform of reforming the security sector. These reforms threatened some privileged actors and triggered the assassination of President Ndadaye by elements of the army in October 1993, sparking a civil war that lasted until August 2000.

Two events can be associated with the beginning of the SSR process in Burundi. The first is the 2000 signing of the Arusha Peace Agreement, which identified SSR as indispensable for a sustainable peace. The second is the August 2003 election of the candidate of the National Council for the Defense of Democracy–Forces for the Defense of Democracy, a coalition that became the primary driver of SSR. The SSR process has focused mainly on the reorganization of the armed forces to ensure greater ethnic balance in the institution (SSR Resource Centre 2015). In addition, since 2005, Burundi has had a democratically elected government, representing the longest period in the country's history that a democratic regime has held power. The progress made faces significant challenges, however, in establishing effective public institutions and dealing with the legacy of ethnically charged civil war. Any progress made in the past few years is being tested as stability remains elusive.

Nicole Ball (2014) credits the success of the SSD program to the weight placed on governance, extensive involvement of local actors, careful attention to the politics involved in security reforms and the program's emphasis on gradually changing societal expectations of the security sector. In a similar vein, GIZ maintains that as a result of various measures taken, the security institutions of Burundi are becoming increasingly capable of planning and implementing their own policy, strategic and infrastructure projects, independently, transparently and efficiently. Unfortunately, instead of contributing to the greater institutional professionalism of the security forces in Burundi, thereby guaranteeing security as a service to citizens, SSR reforms, as recent events have shown, remain shallow and incomplete.

Since the attacks on military installations in the capital on December 11, 2015, the regime is further cracking down on the few dissenting voices that have not fled the country, and its Imbonerakure[5] militia is taking an ever more prominent position in the fracturing security forces. With no plan but to stay in power as long as possible, the regime and its hardline supporters are increasingly turning to an ethnic rhetoric that unjustifiably paints all opposition as a plot by the minority Tutsi community (International Crisis Group 2016).

From a human security perspective, available evidence indicates a pattern of violence and

counterviolence in the country with many dozens dead. It is also evident that security forces are playing key roles in these murders. Aside from the need to clarify the scale of casualties and respective responsibilities, there is clear risk of a cycle of violence setting in, with killings driven by revenge and fear — a pattern Burundians are all too familiar with. A climate of impunity has been established, which can only lay the ground for more violations and atrocities. Under such circumstances, since the country seems to be back to square one, it is difficult to credit SSR in Burundi with genuine success.

Democratic Republic of Congo

Having expressed its concerns regarding the adverse impact of the conflict on the human rights situation in the DRC, particularly in the eastern parts of the country, and the continuing violations of human rights and international humanitarian law committed throughout the territory, the UN Security Council established in 1999 the United Nations Organization Mission in the DRC (MONUC) (UN Resolution 1279). Among other assignments, MONUC was tasked with building a stable environment and protecting civilians, consolidating democracy, safeguarding human rights and, above all, contributing to SSR. Its mandate evolved to include overseeing the withdrawal of foreign armed forces and assuming greater responsibility for elements of internal security, including protection of the transitional government. In 2010, MONUC became, under Chapter VII of the Charter of the United Nations, MONUSCO (the United Nations Organization Stabilization Mission in the DRC), and was given a clearer mandate: to use "all necessary means to carry out its mandate relating, among other things, to the protection of civilians, humanitarian personnel and human rights defenders under imminent threat of physical violence and to support the government of the DRC in its stabilization and peace consolidation efforts" (UN Resolution 1925).

---

5   The Imbonerakure (Kirundi word for "those who can see far enough") is the youth wing of the Burundi ruling party; it has been accused of beatings and injuries, extrajudicial killings and banditry as well as political killings.

After years of security challenges it had become obvious in 2010 that activities of both legitimate and illegal armed groups were causing tremendous suffering among the civilian population. Calls for reforming the security sector were consequently made in order to bring some accountability to security governance in the country. The most pressing task was to curtail the power of armed groups de facto dividing the country into three strongholds. Sadly, a combination of divergent interests of national elites, neighbours and the international community made SSR in the DRC an "impossible mission." From inception, SSR was obstructed because various stakeholders in the crisis saw the process as a roadblock to their selfish ambitions. A 2012 report by 13 leading international and Congolese civil society groups (Open Society Foundation [OSF]), *The Democratic Republic of Congo: Taking a Stand on Security Sector Reform* (OSF 2012), argued that the lack of political will to reform the security sector in the DRC risks not only billions of dollars of international aid but also the very stability of the country. It argued that the army has not only failed to provide security but that it actively preys upon the population, and is one of the major perpetrators of human rights violations in the country. The report concluded that the main reason for the failure of army reform in the DRC was a lack of political will from the Congolese government, notably those elements which have benefited from endemic corruption.

More than 17 years later, with a budget of US$1.5 billion per year, and employing 20,000 uniformed staff, the UN peacekeeping force (MONUSCO), the largest mission in the organization's history, continues to struggle for credibility. According to the 2012 report: "Rather than articulating a vision for Congolese security and marshaling assistance to achieve it, the government has instead encouraged divisions among the international community and allowed corrupt networks within the security services to flourish, stealing the resources intended to pay basic salaries or profiting from exploitation of natural resources. Unless this is changed, sustainable reform will be impossible. The investment made by Congo's partners could be wasted, and Congo's people will continue to suffer" (ibid., 3).

Amid criticism of MONUSCO, there are aspects of the UN operations that deserve credit. During the capture of Goma by M23 rebels, MONUSCO set up a Force Intervention Brigade (FIB), a highly robust, mobile and versatile force, to tackle various armed groups operating in the eastern DRC (Vogel 2014). Between July and November 2012, the FIB engaged by various means, including artillery, aerial attacks and snipers, alongside the Armed Forces of the DRC (FARDC) national army units that were leading the pushback against the DRC's then strongest armed militia group. The offensive led to an unexpectedly quick win on the side of FARDC/FIB. The primary reason for this was the use of well-trained and disciplined FARDC units (mostly Unités de Reaction Rapide) that benefited from functioning supply chains for equipment, logistics and food in conjunction with massive FIB support (ibid.).

Against this background, taking stock of progress and assessing SSR in the DRC since 1999 becomes a sobering exercise. Failure, if any, lies in the very nature of political stakes within and around the DRC and not necessarily with MONUSCO. Establishing an effective security sector is the first and fundamental step to meeting all other objectives, from ending the humanitarian crisis, preventing human rights abuses and encouraging investment and growth, to stopping the trade in conflict minerals and preventing regional tensions from escalating. It is widely acknowledged that adequate security is a development, economic and geostrategic imperative. Yet insecurity remains the DRC's Achilles heel (ibid., 8). Several years of assistance of all kinds have yielded very little in terms of provision of human security to Congolese populations. And, if history is any guide, postponing elections, or *glissement du calendrier électoral,* is likely to worsen the security situation in the country.

South Sudan

Despite or because of its youth, South Sudan, which gained its independence from Sudan in July 2011 after decades of civil war, remains essentially a fragile state. Just a few months after independence in December 2013, armed conflict broke out, claiming thousands of lives and displacing around two million people. This ongoing conflict has reversed much of the development progress achieved by this young country. The lack of infrastructure, low level of education and high costs of goods and services pose particular challenges to the local economy (GIZ 2015). The government has an ambitious agenda: it must establish essential administrative structures, support human capacity and skills building, and develop regulatory and legal frameworks, while also ensuring that the general public has access to basic services such as education and health care.

As daunting and critical a challenge as economic reform is, SSR poses an equally great, if not greater, test for South Sudan and its regional and international partners. For more than a generation, South Sudanese society has been dominated by armed groups — by the mythos of the Sudan People's Liberation Army (SPLA), by the perception that conflict brings rewards, and by the status of the SPLA as South Sudan's single largest employer. In the wake of a devastating conflict, it is imperative that thousands of men under arms be able to transition from the armies of both sides into peaceful and productive citizens (US House of Representatives 2016). Unfortunately, ongoing bouts of obstructionism by the government and the opposition, both of which are dedicated to a military solution, have prevented genuine SSR.

Since 2005, South Sudan has embarked on a widespread SSR process. South Sudan's SSR approach is, however, overly focused on the reform of police and defence sectors, and the reform of justice and penal sectors seems neglected. Key priorities have included improving police training and performance, improving oversight of the SPLA, demobilization or integration of former combatants into the army, justice sector reform and the provision of basic security (SSR Resource Centre 2015). Yet a whole set of parameters prevent SSR from becoming reality on the ground. Ongoing tensions with its northern neighbour Sudan, internal infighting and foreign manipulation have all effectively brought South Sudan to a standstill in the security realm. SSR in South Sudan naturally concerns how people perceive their level of personal security and how they feel about a security sector mandated to protect them against local security threats (Fick 2010). Unfortunately, both the armed forces (SPLA) and the police (South Sudan Police Service, or SSPS) tasked with maintaining civilian security have been ineffective. In fact, the police constitute a constant threat to the South Sudanese people.

Built from scratch at the end of the civil war in 2005, the police service gradually began assuming its responsibilities. Unfortunately, because of a lack of capacity and other failings, the SSPS is perceived by the people of South Sudan as a bloated institution, made up (at least partly) of army rejects, struggling with internal divisions and with making the transition from guerilla movement to professional force (LeRiche 2015). Numerous challenges prevent the SSPS from fulfilling its mandate effectively. It does not possess adequate means of communication and therefore often receives information about dangers when it is too late. It is not only the lack of infrastructure and equipment that makes the work of the police more difficult; poor and even non-existent training exacerbates the problem. The people do not feel adequately protected and often resort to alternative methods of protecting themselves or taking the law into their own hands (ibid.).

Overall, South Sudan is likely to see more frustrating delays, political disagreements and posturing regarding the way forward and especially SSR objectives. Although the South Sudanese people have made it clear that they consider justice and reconciliation vital aspects of the transitional agenda, political and ethnic grievances will slow down any reconciliation process likely to boost SSR. SSR considerations were at the heart of previous failures and constitute the key to future success. While politicians haggle over power-sharing equations, commanders in the field worry what will happen to their men and their own rank and status. Some are faring comparatively well in war and others see little opportunity in laying down their arms (SSR Resource Centre 2015). As the number of active fighters grows, the challenges to any SSR agenda and to the security provisions of a peace agreement also grow.

According to Conrad Schetter (quoted in Bonn International Centre for Conversion 2013), the security apparatus in South Sudan is similar to a patronage system that serves to maintain the power and to enrich political elites. He further notes that current events in South Sudan were a disturbing reminder of how difficult it is to get the logic of war out of the minds of its actors. The capacity to manage conflict — beyond being a function of political leadership, good peacekeeping practice, effective mediation and the provision of sufficient official capabilities — also resides in the relationship between state and society, and among different identity and interest groups within a society (see chapter 1 of this volume). It is only fair, at this complex and fluid stage of South Sudan's history, to speculate that security forces in Africa's newest country are far from providing the shield their populations deserve.

In response to the ongoing crisis, Majak D'Agoot (2016) calls for a need to confront the dominant "gun class," which inhibits genuine political dialogue and consensus building. As far as Kate Almquist-Knopf and Princeton Lyman (2016) are concerned, South Sudan should simply be put on life support or under a temporary external administration to adequately address fundamental drivers of the conflict. In its first investigative report, entitled *War Crimes Shouldn't Pay: Stopping the Looting and Destruction of South Sudan*, The Sentry[6] (2016) documented the assets and wealth of top officials in both government and opposition. The report also described the international network of collaborators, from banks to lawyers to international war profiteers, that allows violent South Sudanese kleptocrats to move money with ease and enjoy the spoils of war. In reality, both President Kiir and his former vice president Machar have manipulated and exploited ethnic divisions, and competed not for the best interest of their country, but rather for control over state assets and the country's abundant natural resources. Under such circumstances, it is not farfetched to argue that SSR was not meant to succeed in South Sudan.

Conclusion

The security landscape in Africa is increasingly dynamic, presenting defence and security policy makers and professionals with a complex set of challenges. Despite shouldering a larger share of the conflict burden, in absolute terms, Africa has become a bit quieter. However, the slow transition away from traditional conflicts has yet to bring genuine peace to the continent. Instead, new intrastate conflicts driven by social divisions, demographic shifts and environmental changes have proliferated while new transnational threats pose regional and continental challenges that increasingly stem from violent non-state actors rather than neighbouring states. Given the direct and indirect costs of violence and armed aggression to African nations and peoples, it is unsurprising that more research is focusing on prevention, mitigation and resolution of conflict. Some call for revisiting traditional conflict resolution methods (see chapter 15 of this volume). Other means of anticipating conflict include examining

---

6   The Sentry is an initiative of the Washington-based The Enough Project that seeks to disrupt and ultimately dismantle the networks of perpetrators, facilitators and enablers who fund and profit from Africa's deadliest conflicts (see https://thesentry.org/).

the behaviour of security forces. For decades, unprofessional forces have committed their loyalty to a regime and its leader, quite often to the detriment of the people.

For peaceful conflict resolution to have a meaning in Africa, it must first begin with a peaceful, secure environment where security forces play a positive, rather than a negative, role. Lack of good security governance has alienated the people from their governments and led to problems of security. To alter their security environment, some countries, especially the so-called post-conflict nations, have embarked on SSR or SST even while admitting that, quite often, insecurity stems from poor governance of the security sector, a lack of peace-building efforts and weakness in the rule of law. SST is an important process for the promotion of justice, peace and overall national development (Banlaoi 2006).

Decades of poor management have forced most countries to reassess their security systems. For practical reasons, most are going through a combined process of security sector reform and transformation. Many diverse human security issues facing African countries, such as public health, education, food and water availability, and the environment, can have an impact on how much security institutions change. There is a growing realization that only a whole-of-society approach to SSR is likely to strike the right balance between achieving human security and conventional security goals. Using that approach, SSR is meant to reduce security deficits (inefficient and ineffective provision of security or even provision of insecurity) as well as democratic deficits that result from dysfunctional security sectors (such as lack of oversight over the security sector). While states must be adequately protected against aggression and internal subversion, the lives of ordinary people must not be crippled by state repression, violent conflict or rampant criminality.

The military is too often used to sustain governments in power and is inappropriately involved in internal security. Police forces are generally underfunded and unable to guarantee security, thus giving rise to coercion and corruption. A badly managed security sector not only generates insecurity, but also hampers development, discourages investment and helps to perpetuate poverty. That is why countries such as South Africa, Liberia, Rwanda, Burundi, the DRC and South Sudan have all experimented with SSR. The jury is still out on their performance overall. Although there is enough evidence in the literature to credit SSR with some degree of success in the first three countries, the process in the last three remains fraught with tremendous challenges. While not entirely out of the woods yet, the populations of South Africa, Liberia and Rwanda have seen some improvement in their security sectors. *A contrario*, citizens of Burundi, the DRC and South Sudan continue to face daily abuses by the very forces tasked with protecting them.

Ultimately, sound governance of the security sector is crucial not only for the success of democratic consolidation and sustainable economic and social development but also for effective conflict resolution (Ball, Bouta and van de Goor 2003, 30). It is also essential for the quality of security, that is, creating a safe and secure environment for the state and its entire population. If people and states are not secure from the fear of random, capricious, systemic or unsanctioned violence at the local, national, regional and international levels, development will not be sustainable in Africa. This means that states must be adequately protected against aggression and internal subversion and that the lives of individuals must not be crippled by state repression, violent conflict or rampant criminality. Governments and security bodies must adhere to the principles of democratic governance, closely linked to human rights and the rule of law, in order to anticipate, prevent and peacefully resolve African conflicts.

Works Cited

Aall, Pamela. 2015. *Conflict in Africa: Diagnosis and Response*. CIGI Papers No. 71, June 1, 2015, 1–8.

Aall, Pamela and Chester A. Crocker, eds. 2016. *Minding the Gap: African Conflict Management in a Time of Change*. Waterloo, ON: CIGI.

Almquist-Knopf, Kate and Princeton Lyman. 2016. "Spotlight: To Save South Sudan, Put It on Life Support." Africa Center for Strategic Studies, July 20.

Anderson, Hillery. 2006. "Justice Delayed in Malawi's Criminal Justice System Paralegals vs. Lawyers." *International Journal of Criminal Justice Sciences* 1 (1): 1–11.

Ball, Nicole. 2005. "Strengthening Democratic Governance of the Security Sector in Conflict-Affected Countries." *Public Administration and Development* 25: 25–38.

———. 2014. "Lessons from Burundi's Security Sector Reform Process." Africa Center for Strategic Studies Africa Security Brief No. 29, 1–8.

Ball, Nicole and Kayode Fayemi, eds. 2004. *Security Sector Governance in Africa: A Handbook*. Lagos: Centre for Democracy and Development. www.gsdrc.org/docs/open/gfn-ssr-securitysectorgovernanceinafrica-ahandbook.pdf.

Ball, Nicole, Tsjeard Bouta and Luc van de Goor. 2003. *Enhancing Democratic Governance of the Security Sector: An Institutional Assessment Framework*. The Hague, Netherlands: Clingendael Institute for the Ministry of Foreign Affairs. www.clingendael.nl/sites/default/files/20030800_cru_paper_ball.pdf.

Banlaoi, Rommel C. 2006. "Security Sector Governance in the Philippines." Presentation to the international workshop on Challenges of Security Sector Governance organized by the Friedrich Ebert-Stiftung, Institute of Defence and Strategic Studies and Geneva Centre for the Democratic Control of the Armed Forces at Hotel Plaza Parkroyal, Singapore, February 14-15.

Bello. 2016. "Of Soldiers and Citizens." *The Economist*, March 19. www.economist.com/news/americas/21695083-latin-americas-armed-forces-have-accepted-democracy-remain-law-unto-themselves-soldiers.

Boege, Volker, Anne Brown, Kevin Clements and Anna Nolan. 2008. "On Hybrid Political Orders and Emerging States: State Formation in the Context of 'Fragility.'" *Berghof Handbook Dialogue* 8: 1–21.

Bonn International Centre for Conversion. 2013. "Security Sector Reform in South Sudan Has Failed — at Least for the Moment." Bonn International Centre for Conversion press release, December 20. www.bicc.de/press/press-releases/press/news/security-sector-reform-in-south-sudan-has-failed-at-least-for-the-moment-394/.

Boshoff, Henri. 2008. "Security Sector Reform in the Democratic Republic of Congo: The Status of Military Reform." *African Security Review* 17 (2): 62–65.

Bowman, Anthony. 2005. "A Descriptive Study of Manuscripts and Reviewers for the Armed Forces & Society Journal." Master's thesis, Texas State University.

Bryden, Alan. 2007. *Security Governance in Post Conflict Peacebuilding*. Münster, Germany: Lit Verlag.

Bryden, Alan, Boubacar N'Diaye and Funmi Olonisakin. 2005. "Security Sector Governance in West Africa: Turning Principles to Practice." Geneva Centre for the Democratic Control of Armed Forces Policy Paper No. 8.

Bryden, Alan and Funmi Olanisakin. 2013. *Security Sector Transformation in Africa*. Münster, Germany: Lit Verlag.

Cawthra, Gavin. 2005. "Security Governance in South Africa." *African Security Review* 14 (3): 95–105.

Chuter, David. 2006. "Understanding Security Sector Reform." *Journal of Security Sector Management* 4 (2): 1–22.

Commission on Human Security. 2003. *Human Security Now.* New York, NY: Commission on Human Security. www. un.org/humansecurity/sites/www.un.org. humansecurity/files/chs_final_report_-_ english.pdf.

Cooper, Neil and Michael Pugh. 2002. "Security-Sector Transformation in Post-Conflict Societies." Draft paper, International Studies Centre, University of Plymouth.

D'Agoot, Majak. 2016. "Spotlight: South Sudan's Stability Hinges on Controlling the 'Gun Class.'" Video interview. Africa Center for Strategic Studies, July 26. http:// africacenter.org/spotlight/south-sudan-stability-hinges-controlling-gun-class/.

Deflem, Mathieu. 2013. "Policing Terrorism after Boston." *FrontLine Security* 8 (2). http://security.frontline.online/article/ 2013/2/2415-Policing-Terrorism-After-Boston.

Denney, Lisa and Craig Valters. 2015. *Evidence Synthesis: Security Sector Reform and Organisational Capacity Building.* London, UK: Department for International Development.

GIZ. 2015. "South Sudan." www.giz.de/en/ worldwide/313.html.

Downie, Richard. 2013. *Building Police Institutions in Fragile States: Case Studies from Africa.* Washington, DC: Africa Center for Strategic Studies.

Fick, Maggie. 2010. "Prioritize Security Sector Reform in South Sudan." *Enough* (blog), April 14. www.enoughproject.org/blogs/ prioritize-security-sector-reform-south-sudan.

Fortin, Jacey. 2016. "Riek Machar, South Sudan Opposition Leader, Returns as Part of Peace Deal." *The New York Times,* April 26. www.nytimes.com/2016/04/27/ world/africa/riek-machar-south-sudan-opposition-leader-returns-as-part-of-peace-deal.html?_r=0.

Foster, Gregory D. 2005. "Civil-Military Relations: The Postmodern Democratic Challenge." *World Affairs* 167 (3): 91–100.

Gould, Chandra. 2014. "Why Is Crime and Violence So High in South Africa?" *Mail and Guardian,* September 19. http://mg.co. za/article/2014-09-19-why-is-crime-and-violence-so-high-in-south-africa/.

Haider, Huma. 2009. *Conflict: Topic Guide.* Birmingham, UK: University of Birmingham Governance and Social Development Resource Centre. http:// reliefweb.int/sites/reliefweb.int/files/ resources/CON69.pdf.

Hatcher, Jessica and Alex Perry. 2012. "Defining Peacekeeping Downward: The U.N. Debacle in Eastern Congo." *Time Magazine,* November 26.

Heitman, Helmoed. 2011. "Optimizing Africa's Security Force Structures." Africa Center for Strategic Studies Security Brief No. 13, 1–7.

Hills, Alice. 2007. "Police Commissioners, Presidents and the Governance of Security." *Journal of Modern African Studies* 45 (3): 403–23.

Houngnikpo, Mathurin C. 1999. "Peaceful Democracies on Trial in Africa." *Peace Research: The Canadian Journal of Peace Studies* 31 (4): 33–43.

———. 2000. "The Military and Democratization in Africa: A Comparative Study of Benin and Togo." *Journal of Political and Military Sociology* 29 (2): 210–229.

———. 2010. *Guarding the Guardians: Civil-Military Relations and Democratic Governance in Africa.* Farnham, UK: Ashgate Publishers.

———. 2012. "Africa's Militaries: A Missing Link in Democratic Transitions." Africa Center for Strategic Studies Africa Security Brief No. 17, 1–7.

Human Rights Watch. 2013. "No Money, No Justice: Police Corruption and Abuse in Liberia." August 22. www.hrw.org/report/2013/08/22/no-money-no-justice/police-corruption-and-abuse-liberia.

International Crisis Group. 2006. "SSR in the Congo." Africa Report No. 104, February 13.

———. 2009. "Liberia: Uneven Progress in Security Sector Reform." Africa Report No. 148, January 9.

———. 2011. "Liberia: How Sustainable Is the Recovery?" Africa Report No. 117, August 19.

———. 2016. "Burundi: Time for Tough Messages." Africa Statement, February 24. www.crisisgroup.org/africa/central-africa/burundi/burundi-time-tough-messages.

IRIN. 2013. "Despite Reforms, Corruption Rife among Liberian Police." *IRIN*, October. www.irinnews.org/report/98924/despite-reforms-corruption-rife-among-liberian-police.

Kilson, Martin. 1976. "Politics of the African Military." *Armed Forces and Society* 2 (2): 333–336.

LeRiche, Matthew. 2015. "Security Sector Reform in South Sudan and Prospects for Peace." SSR Resource Centre, July 3. www.ssrresourcecentre.org/2015/07/03/security-sector-reform-in-south-sudan-and-prospects-for-peace/.

Malan, Mark. 2005. "Conflict Prevention in Africa: Theoretical Construct or Plan of Action?" Kofi Annan International Peacekeeping Training Centre Paper No. 3.

McCullough, Aoife. 2015. *The Legitimacy of States and Armed Non-state Actors: Topic Guide.* Birmingham, UK: University of Birmingham Governance and Social Development Resource Centre.

McFate, Sean. 2008. *Securing the Future: A Primer on Security Sector Reform in Conflict Countries.* United States Institute of Peace Special Report No. 209.

McGowan, Patrick J. 2003. "African Military Coups D'état: 1956–2001: Frequency, Trends and Distribution." *Journal of Modern African Studies* 41 (3): 339–370.

Narayan, Deepa, Robert Chambers, Meera K. Shah and Patti Petesch. 2000. *Voices of the Poor: Crying Out for Change.* New York, NY: Oxford University Press for the World Bank.

N'Diaye, Boubacar. 2009. "Francophone Africa and Security Sector Transformation: Plus Ça Change." *African Security* 2 (1): 1–28.

OSF. 2012. *The Democratic Republic of Congo: Taking a Stand on Security Sector Reform.* OSF Report, April 16. https://www.opensocietyfoundations.org/sites/default/files/drc-ssr-report-20120416-1.pdf.

Pruitt, William R. 2010. "The Progress of Democratic Policing in Post-Apartheid South Africa." *African Journal of Criminology & Justice Studies* 4 (1): 116–140.

Rotberg, Robert I., ed. 2014. *Governance and Innovation in Africa: South Africa after Nelson Mandela.* Waterloo, ON: CIGI.

Sedra, Mark. 2010. *The Future of Security Sector Reform.* Waterloo, ON: CIGI.

Shah, Anup. 2014. "Conflicts in Africa." www.globalissues.org/issue/83/conflicts-in-africa.

Smith, Chris. 2001. "Security-Sector Reform: Development Breakthrough or Institutional Engineering?" *Conflict, Security & Development* 1 (1): 5–20.

Smith, David. 2012. "Paul Kagame's Rwanda: African Success Story or Authoritarian State?" *The Guardian,* October 10. www.theguardian.com/world/2012/oct/10/paul-kagame-rwanda-success-authoritarian.

———. 2013. "South Africa Reports of Police Brutality More than Tripled in the Last Decade." *The Guardian,* August 22. www.theguardian.com/world/2013/aug/22/south-africa-police-brutality-increase.

Solomon, Hussein. 1999. "Overcoming the Achilles Heel of the African Renaissance: The Legacy of the Colonial State." *Conflict Trends,* April: 28-29.

South Africa. Department of Defence. 1996. *Defence in a Democracy: White Paper on National Defence for the Republic of South Africa.* www.dod.mil.za/documents/WhitePaperonDef/whitepaper%20on%20defence1996.pdf.

SSR Resource Centre. 2015. "Country Snapshot: South Sudan." www.ssrresourcecentre.org/countries/South Sudan/.

———. 2015. "Country Snapshot: Liberia." www.ssrresourcecentre.org/countries/ssr-country-snapshot-liberia/.

———. 2015. "Country Snapshot: Rwanda." www.ssrresourcecentre.org/countries/rwanda/.

———. 2015. "Country Snapshot: Burundi." www.ssrresourcecentre.org/countries/burundi/.

Sundaram, Anjam. 2016. *Bad News: Last Journalists in a Dictatorship.* New York: Doubleday.

The Sentry. 2016. *War Crimes Shouldn't Pay: Stopping the Looting and Destruction in South Sudan.* Washington, DC: The Sentry.

UN. 1999. S/RES/1279. November 30.

———. 2008. *Securing Peace and Development: The Role of the United Nations in Supporting Security Sector Reform. Report of the Secretary-General.* A/62/659-S/2008/39. January 23.

———. 2010. UN S/RES/1925. May 28.

———. 2011. High-Level Forum on African Perspectives on SSR. New York, NY: SSR Unit.

US House of Representatives. 2016. *Testimony of the Special Envoy to Sudan and South Sudan to the House Foreign Affairs Subcommittee on Africa, Global Health, Global Human Rights, and International Organizations,* 114th Cong. (April 27) (statement of Donald Booth, Special Envoy to Sudan and South Sudan).

Vogel, Christoph. 2014. "DR Congo — How Successful Has the UN's Intervention Brigade Been?" *African Arguments,* July 14. https://africajournalismtheworld.com/2014/07/14/dr-congo-how-successful-has-the-uns-intervention-brigade-been/.

Watson, Charlotte. 2013. "Policing in South Africa: A State in Crisis." *South Africa,* March 21. www.ssrresourcecentre.org/2013/03/21/policing-in-south-africa-a-state-of-crisis/.

Weber, Max. 1965. *Politics as a Vocation.* Minneapolis, MN: Fortress Press.

Yakovenko, Margarita. 2015. *Progress in Small Steps: Security against the Odds in Liberia.* London, UK: Overseas Development Institute.

Zanker, Francisca. 2015. "A Decade of Police Reform in Liberia: Perceptions, Challenges and Ways Ahead." Centre for Security Governance SSR 2.0 Brief No. 4, September. http://secgovcentre.org/wp-content/uploads/2016/11/SSR-2.0-Brief-4-Zanker.pdf.

8

(Re) Thinking the Relationship between Education and Conflict in Africa: Between Benevolence and Negative Force

Charles Owuor Olungah

"Education is the most powerful weapon which you can use to change the world." — Nelson Mandela

Mandela's analogy is critical and describes the most respected role of education. Looked at from a multiplicity of lenses, however, the comment may imply both latent and manifest functions of education. Traditionally, before colonialism, education practices in Africa consisted of groups of elders teaching aspects of life and rituals that would help girls and boys in adulthood. The teachings included artistic performances, ceremonies, games, festival, dancing, singing and drawing. Boys and girls were taught separately to prepare each sex for adult roles and each community member participated in the transition from childhood to adulthood. The traditional teachings were meant to make the young members of the community full members with knowledge of the communal secrets and to enable them to appreciate their culture. This was based on gerontocracy, and the elders were the final authorities in all issues.

Then came colonialism, which changed many indigenous education systems. Schooling was no longer just about rituals and rites of passage. School now meant earning an education that would allow Africans to compete in the wider global market. The education systems inherited from the colonial powers were designed for formal sector and public administration. All across the African continent, there is evidence that education serves as a gateway to lucrative employment in the public sector and as one of the surest means out of poverty. However, literature also shows that education is the place where elite interests are most prevalent and, through unequal distribution of educational resources, as will be shown in the case of Kenya, where they have maintained their privileged position.

There is no shortage of literature showing that education has often been promoted as a weapon for socio-economic transformation of human beings; it has been viewed as the best available mechanism for lifting people out of poverty, as a route to dialogue and national cohesion, and as no "after-thought" but an entitlement innate to human rights.[1] However, what has rarely been asked about this "weapon" is why it is only portrayed as countering conflict, rather than aggravating conflict. Alan Smith and Tony Vaux (2003) take a balanced view, proceeding on the path that education can be part of the problem, as well as part of the solution. They propose that policies and practices at all levels within the education system need to be analyzed in terms of their potential to aggravate or ameliorate conflict. Whichever side of the divide one stands on, the fact is that the relationship between education and conflict remains fluid and contested.

Debate on the relationship between education and conflict has been a focus in a number of international instruments, notably, the Universal Declaration of Human Rights (UNGA 1948), the Geneva Convention Relative to the Protection of Civilian Persons in Time of War (ICRC 1949),[2] the UN Convention Relating to the Status of Refugees

(UNGA 1951), the UN Declaration of the Rights of the Child (UNGA 1959), the Convention against Discrimination in Education (UNESCO 1962), the International Covenant on Economic, Social and Cultural Rights (UNGA 1966), the Convention on the Elimination of All Forms of Discrimination against Women (UNGA 1979) and, more important, the UN Convention on the Rights of the Child (UNGA 1989).[3] The bottom line is that education is a fundamental human entitlement that should be provided even in the most difficult situations, including those in which there is conflict or other structural inhibitions.

Besides reviewing literature on the role of education as both a social stabilizer as well as destabilizer, this chapter discusses specific issues currently present in Africa that make education a location of conflict or increase its destabilizing potential. Among the issues examined are the role of education in feeding ethnic and social divisions, the politicized nature of the distribution of educational institutions, the quality of delivery and an examinations system that encourages rote learning. Unless the education system encourages fairness and justice to the entire population of a country, it will remain a site of division and fragility.

Education as a Resource and Societal Stabilizer

The common theme in describing the positive effects of education is that schooling, irrespective of its dimensions, reduces the intensity of conflicts in Africa, and the channels of transmission vary

---

1 Article 26 of the Universal Declaration of Human Rights (UNGA 1948) states that education is a fundamental human right that develops values, self-confidence, problem-solving abilities and critical thinking.

2 Article 50 of the Geneva Convention (ICRC 1949) states: "The Occupying Power shall, with the cooperation of the national and local authorities, facilitate the proper working of all institutions devoted to the care and education of children."

3 Article 28 of the UN Convention on the Rights of the Child (UNGA 1989) assures the child's right to education, specifying that primary education is compulsory and available free to all. Article 29 states that the aims of education include "respect for human rights and fundamental freedoms" and "the preparation of the child for responsible life in a free society in the spirit of understanding, peace, tolerance, equality of sexes, and friendship among all peoples, ethnic, national and religious groups and persons of indigenous origin."

according to the education dimension considered (Agbor 2013). The World Bank (2002) sees education as a powerful weapon for peace in reducing the likelihood of violent societal conflict, enhancing social cohesion, reducing inequalities and improving mutual understanding and respect for diversity. This position is shared by Andrew M. Francis (2009), who opines that education significantly decreases the likelihood of militarized conflict between nations, suggesting that human capital promotion helps increase peace around the world.

Clive Harber (2004) notes that the dominant discourse in international debates on education and development is that education is of significant benefit both to the individual and society. This can be an economic benefit, within the meaning of human capital theory, according to which education increases the employment skills, productivity and earning power of individuals and hence contributes to economic growth. Harber further observes that, according to modernization theory, education can be a social benefit in the form of the development of more "modern" social attitudes toward, for example, science, gender equality and the desire to achieve. Education is further seen to contribute politically by developing the values and behaviour required for a political culture that will help sustain a democratic political system.

Education has been seen as an indispensable key to, though not a sufficient condition for, personal and social improvement. It can help ensure a safer, healthier, more prosperous and environmentally sound world, while simultaneously contributing to social, economic and cultural progress. Education, whether formal or informal, has been seen as a lifelong process that enhances the capacity of individuals to exploit and manage their environment and dominate it for the benefit of themselves and society at large. Accordingly, you can produce a useful citizen only if he or she is educated enough to be aware of his or her environment and is capable of dominating it (Ohanyido 2012).

According to functionalists, the benefits of education include the teaching of knowledge and skills, cultural transmission of values, social integration, gatekeeping and mainstreaming. Schools facilitate social integration by moulding students into a more cohesive unit and helping socialize them into mainstream culture. In the functionalists' view, this forging of national identity is meant to stabilize the political system. Kendra Dupuy (2008) contends that within a given context, education can help produce the benefits of inclusive and constructive integration of individuals and communities socially, politically and economically, which can contribute to conflict prevention and long-term peace building.

The social stabilizing theorists, Daron Asemoglu and James A. Robinson (2001) among them, contend that resource transfer or redistribution from the so-called elites to the disadvantaged represents an attempt at purchasing social stability, which is a necessary condition for sustainable economic growth. In this view, educating the poor is a way of raising their opportunity cost of conflict, suggesting that human capital transfer and conflict are inversely related.

The second variant of the social stability hypothesis argues that education lowers conflict by changing the time preferences of individuals from the short run to the long run, implying that less educated people have a higher time preference for current, as opposed to future consumptions, and consequently are more likely to engage in criminality and violence as a way of satisfying their immediate needs (Becker 1996). Yet another variant suggests that class conflict will be eliminated as a result of the transfer of human capital from the elite to the poor, because of the complementarity between physical and human capital (Galor and Moav 2004).

In essence, contemporary debates treat education largely as inherently benevolent and representing a "force for good" in situations of conflict, without acknowledging that education can have negative consequences (Walker-Keleher 2006, 1). This view is reflected in the report "Education for All: Is the World on Track?" (UNESCO 2002),[4] which describes education as one of the best means of preventing conflict: "Education is increasingly seen as one means to reduce and overcome the effect of violence. It can help prevent emergencies from occurring and can bring a sense of normalcy and stability into an otherwise chaotic situation" (ibid.). This standpoint is blind to the fact that education by design or default could become a platform to foment divisions that give rise to conflict. This "evil divide" of education, albeit alive in the intellectual discourse, is rarely discussed.[5]

Education as a Social Destabilizer or Source of Conflict

Although education is seen as a positive factor in human relations, recent studies have indicated that it has the potential to create division and violent tensions in society if not well implemented and if instituted without peace education.

Social destabilization theorists argue that education increases the likelihood of societal conflicts. According to Jack Hirschleifer (1995) and Robert Bates, Avner Greif and Smita Singh (2007), education potentially raises the likelihood of conflict through two ways: by enhancing the fighting technology of belligerent parties and by increasing the number of non-contestants in a conflict (in this model, more knowledge acquired from schooling means a better technology of

fighting and an increasing number of unemployed graduates implies an increased number of potential belligerents).

Reflecting another tradition that is more relevant in Africa, with ethnicity and sectarianism taking centre stage, Davies (2003) observes that education potentially compromises social peace by raising socio-economic inequalities and individualism. Traditional African communities were extended in nature and people gave support to each other. The individualism resulting from the elite form of education creates inter-communal as well as intra-communal tensions.

Further, Smith and Vaux (2003) note that by exacerbating ethnic diversity, education ignites ethno-political conflicts, and Kenneth D. Bush and Diana Saltarelli (2000) see the mismatch between education and jobs as the primary mechanism through which education compromises social peace. In *Two Faces of Education in Ethnic Conflict*, Bush and Saltarelli (ibid.) observe that education is more than service delivery since it extends to the domain of socialization and identity development through transmission of knowledge, skills, values and attitudes across generations.

Bush and Saltarelli assert that education can also gravitate toward conflict when used wrongly, in the following seven different ways:

- the uneven distribution of education as a means of creating or preserving privilege;

- education as a weapon of cultural repression;

- denial of education as a weapon of war;

- education as a means of manipulating history for political ends;

- education serving to diminish self-worth and encourage hate;

- segregated education as a means of ensuring inequality, inferiority and stereotypes; and

- the role of textbooks in impoverishing children's imagination and inhibiting constructive conflict resolution.

4   The Dakar Framework for Action (UNESCO 2000, paragraph 28) notes that "The significant growth of tensions, conflict and war, both within nations and between nations and peoples, is a cause of great concern. Education has a key role to play in preventing conflict in the future and building lasting peace and stability."

5   In analyzing education in post-conflict settings, Lynn Davies (2003) notes that the link between conflict and education is a grossly under-analyzed area. This is not surprising, as it is an uncomfortable notion for policy makers and curriculum developers.

Examples exist of education being used as a weapon in cultural repression of minorities, by using education to suppress their language and cultural values. Segregated education, such as the apartheid system in South Africa, served to maintain inequality between groups within society. Evidence shows that unequal access to education divided along religious, ethnic or linguistic lines can exacerbate grievances and tensions among different groups in society, and that has become one of the main factors associated with the increasing risk of violence and conflict.

Further, the manipulation of history and textbooks for political purposes, particularly where government defines the "national story," has also been a way in which education is misused to perpetuate the skewed interests of the elites.[6] Education has also been used to inculcate attitudes of superiority, for example, in the way that other peoples or nations are described and the characteristics that are ascribed to them. Marie Smyth et al. (2004, 32), in affirming this position, noted that for a substantial number of children, their first conscious exposure to sectarianism or issues related to troubles such as discrimination took place within the school environment.

Harber (2004, 38) further argues that the dominant model of schooling worldwide is authoritarian and that this authoritarianism provides the context for school's role in the reproduction and perpetuation of violence. Some authors blame the inherently violent nature of certain types of educational curricula for promoting intolerance and extremism (Davies 2003; Sommers 2002).

In terms of gender relations, Robert W. Connell (2000) notes that the dominant masculinity in many countries is characterized by toughness, misogyny, homophobia, confrontational sport and use of violence and fighting. Schools act to reproduce gender relations and they are in most cases sites for gender-based violence. Homophobia is still rife, as recently witnessed in South Africa, and the sexual abuse of girls by fellow students and by teachers is commonplace.

Davies (2003) calls out one important way in which schools prepare for war: through competitions and the examination system. This system instills fear and anxiety from an early age. Failure can lead to frustration and low self-esteem, predisposing students to violence or tension. Corruption and cheating in examinations can become part of the breakdown of trust and responsibility that ought to characterize peaceful societies. Individual competition deskills and devalues the cooperative efforts that ought to characterize more harmonious societies (ibid.). The greed for success is fuelled by obsessions with standards and winners in education. There are thus myriad ways in which a culture of testing can militate against the promotion of peace, as is seen in the case of Kenya. According to James Porter (1999), what is disturbing is that quality education that endures is ignored in the race for supremacy in educational achievement, as measured by the grades and the demands of a market in which certificates count for much more than people's demonstrable capabilities.

To explore this topic, this chapter narrows the role of education in conflict to specific aspects and focuses on Kenya. The aspects include the role of education in enhancing ethnicity and social division, the politicized nature of the distribution of educational institutions and, finally, the examinations system as a key contributor to a violent society. The following questions are explored: To what extent does the provision of education enhance ethnic dominance? Is the location of educational institutions a reflection of political bias and hence open to enhancing division in society? Is the competition brought about by examination in itself clear evidence of the violent nature of education in Africa?

---

6   According to Tony Jackson, as published by International Alert (2000), in Burundi, Tutsi leaders in government had made education the exclusive preserve of their particular social group, even excluding other Tutsis, by manipulating the allocation of resources. To an extent, the conflict may have been exacerbated by these educational inequalities.

Education, Ethnicity and Social Divisions

Education systems have been accused of being the root of conflicts such as inequality, ethnicity or gendered violence in society (Davies 2003). As Kenneth D. Bush (1996) noted, the structures and processes that appear to turn ethnic intolerance into unbridled violence are highly complex. A list of causal factors might include historical forces, economic tensions, bad governance, perceived threats to cultural identity and the formal, non-formal and informal educational processes. Ethnic exclusion based on "them versus us" is often considered a key contributor to ethnic conflict; this attitude is increasingly mobilized and politicized in contemporary political conflicts, often turning violent, as in the cases of South Sudan and the 2007-2008 post-election violence in Kenya.

In the case of Rwanda, Jill Salmon (2004) noted that before the 1994 genocide, education contributed to the social exclusion[7] of the majority Rwandans by benefiting the ruling elite and by propagating ethnic divisions. The schooling system was a political mechanism for propping up a status quo that was characterized by injustice and inequality. It intensified the ethnic divide between the Hutus and Tutsis so much that harmony was not possible.

In Kenya, as well as in other large parts of Africa, education is promoted as a cornerstone for development. Although education is supposed to be politically neutral, members of the ruling elite see it as an instrument of the state and want to stamp their authority in the sector. As noted by Leah Keriga and Abdalla Bujra (2009), the colonial education model was based on a system

of segregation. This approach resulted in separate educational systems for Europeans, Asians and Africans and perpetuated inequalities in accessing education. This segregation has continued to the present but in a different form. The emerging elite are now at the top, followed by the middle class and, finally, the poor, who still make up the majority of people in the public schooling system.

The introduction of free primary and secondary education in most parts of Africa has led to segregation, over-enrolment and compromised quality. In the case of Uganda, A. Mubatsi (2012) and René Vermeulen (2013) noted that the introduction of universal primary and secondary education has been marked by compromises in the quality of students produced. Surveys have shown that pupils from public schools offering free education cannot read or solve simple arithmetic problems. Free education has basically been left to parents of the poor. Writing about South Africa, Nic Spaull (2015) noted that despite 20 years of democratic rule, most black children continue to receive low-quality education, which condemns them to the underclass of South African society, where poverty and unemployment are the norm. He further opines that this substandard education does not develop the children's capabilities or expand their economic opportunities, but instead denies them dignified employment and undermines their own sense of self-worth. Low-quality education becomes a poverty trap from which it is impossible to escape (Van der Berg et al. 2011). Similar experiences have been reported in Tanzania, where, after primary school fees were scrapped in 2001, massive enrolment was experienced, followed by compromised quality since the growth was not accompanied by sufficient manpower and the necessary infrastructure (Ndoye 2008).

Spaull (2015) further notes that those parents in South Africa who can afford to pay fees and to send their children to well-functioning government or independent schools ensure that their children get access to the top part of the labour market. Those parents who cannot afford school fees, however, are excluded from these schools, often in informal ways.

---

7   Social exclusion involved stereotyping in textbooks and by teachers between Hutu and Tutsis. The textbooks of the German and Belgium colonial periods emphasized the physical differences, teaching prevailing racist doctrines by linking physical appearance and intellectual capacity. Such textbooks praised the intellectual capacities of the Tutsi and classified the Hutu as unintelligent, meek and suitable only for manual work.

As it currently stands, the dualistic South African educational system is not an engine of social mobility, but rather one of the key mechanisms through which an unequal society is reinforcing itself.[8]

Writing on Nigerian higher education, Romina Ifeoma Asiyai (2013) notes that several variables act as challenges to quality in higher education. These include inadequate funding, inadequate and poor quality of teaching staff, poor policy implementation, lack of resources, lack of information communication technology facilities, frequent labour disputes and university closures, lack of vibrant staff development programs, brain drain and poor leadership. All of the above is made worse by frequent strikes staged by students, faculty and teachers (Moja 2000). Regional disparities in enrolment exist between the southern zones (95 percent) and northern zones (19.9 percent), which make equity issues problematic and, therefore, increase the probability of regional tensions and conflicts between the Christian south and the Muslim north.

In the Kenyan context, several attempts have been instituted to reform the education system, including a special quota system that effectively bypassed deserving high scoring students for ill-equipped, low-scoring students to achieve ethnic balance, thereby favouring members of the ruling elite.[9] Schools themselves have been equipped in a manner that is regionally skewed, disadvantaging the majority and thereby creating ethnic tensions. The exclusionary practices of the ruling elite based on ethnic interests have continued to ensure they retain preferential treatment in access to resources and social amenities.

Worse still, the basic education received in local neighbourhood schools only enhances certain stereotypes that are of no help in fostering ethnic cohesion. Pupils are taught at very young ages to recognize the differences between themselves and other people in a way that does not create harmony. Over the years, students of development anthropology in Kenya have expressed their reservations regarding the stereotypes and ethnic baggage they carry with them to university. When asked what their major fears are in terms of ethnic relations, their responses have been alarming, ranging from ethnic superiority to outright absurd assertions of differences based on geography, cultural practices and political control.[10] These are the values that students get from the educational system, and then universities become the location of the actualization of these perceived differences. As a result, institutions of higher learning have of late become the centres of division and politics based on ethnic differences. Student elections have become too violent and a closer look at events reveals that ethnicity has taken a new dimension.[11]

The other key issue related to the ethnic divide is access to state resources. Many students complain that the state as presently structured is too sectarian and does not enhance ethnic cohesion. Those who do not belong to the communities of the top political elites see their own future as bleak and, for that reason, pity themselves and perceive their academic endeavours as being in vain.

---

8   These differences observed in educational opportunities and segregation in the job market could explain recent manifestations of xenophobia, as when local people acted violently against and expelled fellow non-South Africans.

9   Traditionally, there has been an assumption that some communities, for instance, the Luo, are intellectually more endowed; but these have been communities that are not part of the ruling elite. To ensure that the bright students from these communities are denied a chance to access the high-performing national schools, the quota system was introduced to balance the ethnic admission, thereby favouring the political elites instead of emphasizing quality.

10   This observation is based on personal experience of more than 15 years of university lectureship, with students who have always expressed biased ethnic stereotypes.

11   At the time of writing, a number of public universities were closed because of student unrest. The protests were all related to student elections and the ethnic nature and political support of those elections.

The introduction of both free primary education in 2003 and free secondary education in 2008 has had a drastic impact on the quality of education and has been characterized by ethnic punishment in various indirect forms. For example, teacher postings involve some elements of politics, and it is therefore not uncommon to find schools in certain regions having fewer teachers than before despite increased enrolment. This has compromised quality and created regional disparities.

Commenting on this situation, Kendra Dupuy (2008, 29) notes that, at the national level, education underpins the maintenance and reproduction of political, economic and social structures. In doing so, education can reinforce entrenched structural patterns and disparities, socially, economically and politically, be they constructive or destructive.

As earlier noted, education is a highly symbolic indicator of equity, linked to income-earning potential and an ability to lessen or perpetuate inequalities (Barakat, Karpinska and Paulson 2008). At the same time, a perception of inadequate educational service can become another grievance to exacerbate already fragile relationships. In a nutshell, education in Kenya, as in other countries in Africa, is slowly being recognized as an area of possible conflict, for which remedial measures are necessary to forestall such conflict. It should also be noted that secondary and tertiary education raises the political aspirations of student citizens in ways that might be destabilizing, especially in Kenya and other African societies in which democratic institutions are not well entrenched. If certain sectors of the society feel excluded, the education they receive can sharpen their grievances and shorten the fuse of what may be a time bomb.

Politics in the Distribution of Educational Institutions

Whereas institutions of education solidified a system of segregation during the colonial period, post-colonial governments simply created a new breed of "Europeans and Asians" to occupy the positions of privilege. As noted by Keriga and Bujra (2009) and the Central Bureau of Statistics (2007), regional inequalities have persisted, and regions that have never ascended to the apex of political leadership remain the poorest of the poor. The new schooling system has created high-cost schools, mostly private institutions that deliver quality education at the expense of the poor, who still attend crowded and congested public schools. Good schools have also been located in the neighbourhoods of the political elites. For example, Kiambu County has the highest number of traditional national schools, most of them high performing. Kiambu County also happens to be home to the first independent president, Mzee Jomo Kenyatta, whose son is the current president, Uhuru Kenyatta. At independence, the Kikuyu elite ensured that through their ethnic influence, the best academic institutions were all located in their district.

In response to this anomaly, the Kibaki administration elevated[12] several schools all over the country to national level. This politically motivated elevation was unfortunately not accompanied by a corresponding adequate allocation of resources to improve on the infrastructure, and so the performance of those elevated schools has remained dismal. Moreover, the competition to access the better-performing national schools has been very intense, mostly among the elites and the middle class coming from private academies. The existing inequality is thus exacerbated because students in the regions that have remained poor do not have the resources to pay the high fees for the private academies.

---

12 Elevation here means that the president promoted several schools to national status, not on merit, but simply by declaration, in order to make it look as if several districts and administrative units had their fair share of good schools.

Six universities[13] existed before President Kibaki took power; he has since increased them to 22, including nine constituent colleges, simply through presidential decrees and roadside pronouncements. The congestion in the universities caused by the double intake introduced in the 1990s has now become even worse. These 22 public universities are products of politics and their distribution is testimony to the politicized and skewed regional thinking of the elites. Of the 22 universities and their nine constituent colleges, most are in the central and eastern regions, President Kibaki's political backyard. A common problem with the new universities is that they are run as part of the tribal institutions. Both staff and students are divided along ethnic lines, which can lead to conflicts, such as, for instance, the recent staff turbulence at the University of Eldoret, where the local community felt that the leadership was not local enough. This unrest incited students along ethnic lines, ultimately resulting in student riots and unduly exposing the university to public ridicule. The Maasai Mara University has experienced similar disquiet, as has the Masinde Muliro University of Science and Technology, as well as Moi University, where the local political elites have insisted that one of their own must be installed as the vice chancellor.

This politically motivated upgrading of schools, colleges and universities in certain regions has far-reaching implications. It has localized universities and increased ethnic animosities. It has weakened universities by reducing them to ethnic enclaves, as opposed to centres of academic excellence. They have become institutions that protect local ethnic interests and, instead of embracing globalism, they have elevated the stereotypic forms of ethnic division. This regionalization of institutions deepens the economic divide and ensures that certain regions remain poor, further increasing inequality and elevating ethnic grievances against the state. In essence, instead of creating opportunities for all, the education system serves only certain citizens and subordinates the rest.

Quality of Education, Examinations and Conflict

There are gaps in the infrastructure and quality of education throughout most of Africa. The forms of education provided do not enhance the kind of cognitive skills that can foster innovation and promote technology diffusion. Eric A. Hanushek and Ludger Woessman (2008) demonstrated that cognitive skills have substantial and robust effects on economic growth. Students' cognitive skills are measured by reading, mathematics and science tests. The question is whether graduates of our school systems have had their cognitive skills sufficiently honed and sharpened.

Chinedu Ohanyido (2012) suggests, based on several examples, that we are obsessed with the numbers and not with quality in education. He further observes that there is a major gap between the quality of education and its application to real-life situations. Inventions and research outcomes that should form the basis of innovation and creativity for industries in Africa have not been sufficiently linked.

The Uganda National Council for Science and Technology (UNCST) (2012) noted that pupils in Uganda are taught mainly with the aim of passing the national Primary Leaving Examinations. The education system forces pupils to cram without being given opportunity for further inquiries. The report notes that the science curriculum is exam-based and devoid of activity-based learning and therefore does not stimulate interest and innovation. This problem is reinforced by the method of assessment, which rewards those who can regurgitate what they have

---

13　The six universities were the University of Nairobi (1970), Moi University (1984), Kenyatta University (1985), Egerton University (1987), Jomo Kenyatta University of Agriculture and Technology (1994) and Maseno University (2001).

memorized, instead of those who are innovative (UNCST 2012, 13). The report further remarks that teachers are limited by the curriculum because of the emphasis placed on its completion, rather than on how well students can apply and explain what they have learned. It is noted that in this context examinations serve not to reward achievement but to operate as a crude filtering device to remove from the ladder to the next level of education all but those who can master the art of passing examinations (Clegg et al. 2007).

Spaull (2015) observes that schools in South Africa are characterized by wasted learning time, incomplete coverage of the curriculum, weak subject and content knowledge among teachers, low cognitive demands placed on learners and exceedingly poor educational outcomes.

Reports of leaked exams in Tanzania have dealt a large blow to education quality efforts in that country, destroying trust among stakeholders and reducing satisfaction levels. This has been seen as impeding innovative thinking and academic excellence (Nyanje 2011).

Further, teaching in Tanzanian secondary schools has been criticized as ineffective in preparing competent individuals (Davidson 2006). The perception is that secondary school students finish school unprepared and unable to demonstrate competencies in work and life (Benson 2006) and, therefore, are likely to be a burden on their societies (Shahzad 2007). Teaching and learning in secondary schools are seen as producing temporary knowledge and skills useful only in answering examinations (Wedgwood 2006). In addition, teachers are accused of devoting less attention in their teaching to conceptual knowledge and focusing instead on procedural knowledge, which further leads to memorization of facts rather than conceptual meaning formation (Wedgwood 2007). As is the Kenyan educational system, the Tanzanian system is based on rote learning and has a correspondingly high potential for creating and fomenting conflict based on grievances.

The problem of cheating in exams is widespread. As Teboho Moja (2000) observes, in the Nigerian context, intense competition for access to the system has led to widespread cheating in examinations for the purpose of obtaining higher scores to improve chances of gaining admission to the next level of education.

Regarding the Kenyan system, Keriga and Bujra (2009) note that the 8.4.4 system of education in Kenya is by nature competitive and highly elitist. It has failed to engrain key values of morality and democracy because it focuses on academic achievement as an end in itself. It has been criticized for promoting a system of rote learning in which students study to pass by cramming their way through the educational curriculum. Mwalimu J. Shujaa (1995) observed that rote learning inhibits creativity and innovativeness, making learning a passive affair for students. He further noted that, in this context, students are taught that an education is a means to an end, a passport to a job; the studying to pass examinations has replaced the ethics of studying to develop a deep understanding and mastery of one's life and environment. In Shujaa's view, rote learning techniques produce individuals who cannot "think outside the box." Further damage is caused by the failure of the education system to provide adequate co-curriculum activities of the kind that are vital for mental, physical and talent development of pupils and students. Today, most pupils and students spend few hours engaging in play. Additionally, most schools substitute time that is meant for extra-curricular activities with extra studies and holiday lessons.

Since access to higher education is very competitive and determined by high scores in the high schools, students, parents and teachers are always in a cutthroat competition to excel. This has led to an increase in unorthodox practices epitomized by rote learning, exam irregularities and outright cheating in examinations. Students and teachers work extra hard to ensure that as many students as possible make it through the national examinations. Many students have been affected by an examination system characterized by leaks and anomalies. Examination results were cancelled for 5,100 candidates accused of cheating in the 2015 Kenya Certificate of Secondary Education (KCSE) exams. This was the highest number of disqualified students in the history of the national examinations (Aduda 2016). David Aduda observes that when the KCSE results were released in December 2015, 2,709 candidates had their results cancelled for cheating.

Regarding the 2015 national examinations, other than the confirmed cases of cheating, several sources confirmed the illegal sale of examination papers as early as two days before the exams date. An investigation by the *Daily Nation* revealed that Kiswahili and Geography papers were available before the exams on October 22, 2015 (Kasami 2015). The *Daily Nation* team apparently managed to buy copies of Mathematics Paper 1, which were sent to candidates on October 21, hours before the exams. The *Daily Nation* quoted a teacher in Vihiga County, who lamented the situation: "What is happening is disturbing. I have personally talked to my students and they have admitted that it is easy to get the examination questions in advance after paying KSh1,000" (Amadala and Kaluoch 2015).

Aduda (2016) also noted that in some schools, the cheating was organized and executed by teachers. The teachers who received the leaked questions organized sessions for the candidates to review the questions hours before the exams were taken. Several teachers were implicated in accusations involving the use of mobile phones in cheating. It was alleged that the teachers used their social networking group to leak the exams. Police officers in charge of storing the exams were also accused of distributing the exams through their WhatsApp group. Some university students were also implicated in the sharing of exams.

What is disturbing is that despite all the glaring evidence, the authorities maintained that exams were not leaked. The Kenya National Examinations Council (KNEC) director maintained that the papers and questions being circulated were fake and urged KCSE 2015 candidates to ignore what he called rumours. The KNEC chief executive officer was quoted as saying: "The Council is aware that fraudsters are lurking around engaging in various fraudulent activities such as printing, circulating and selling fake examination papers fully branded with KNEC information purported to be genuine examination papers" (Njagi and Wanzala 2015).

After the examinations, the council's investigation revealed that the main source of the leaked national examination papers was a teacher in Mandera County. The deputy principal of a school in Wargadud, near El Wak on the Kenya-Ethiopia border, confessed to investigators how he had planned to steal the exams since July 2015 with the collusion of police officers from the region. According to the confidential report, the teacher detailed how the exams were distributed to his students, who then forwarded them to their friends in Nairobi via mobile phones. Also involved in the scheme was a student at the Jomo Kenyatta University of Agriculture and Technology, who distributed the exams widely on behalf of teachers for monetary rewards (Namunane 2016).

It was reported in the *Daily Nation* (Mwinzi 2016) that the teacher approached a policeman in the area who linked him to the officer in charge of the armoury at the police station where exams would be stored. The three hatched a plot whereby, for KSh60,000[14] a week, one of the police officers would break the seals of exam packages and take photos of questions using an iPad before resealing the whole package using special glue. The teacher then approached the KCSE exams candidates, 115 in all, and asked each to pay KSh5,000 for the leaked papers. The headboy collected the money and handed it over to the teacher at the school who then passed it on to the deputy principal.

---

14   The exchange rate at the time of writing this chapter was KSh105 per US$1.

As well as distributing the exams to his students, the deputy principal sent them to colleagues in Nairobi, who in turn sent him KSh200,000.

The public reaction to the report was telling. In essence, it questioned the examination system and the damage done to the Kenyan education system. One professor commented that Kenyan graduates risked being locked out of the international job market. He said, "When you bring below average students to the university, it means we will churn out below average professionals into the job market. In the long run, we will have so many graduates who cannot practice what they have studied" (Otieno and Wanzala 2015).

Another academic commented, "Universities are supposed to train the best brains. Imagine a scenario where you admit a student to study medicine based on such results. This country is sitting on a time bomb and it is high time we moved first to redeem this society" (ibid.).

The Ministry of Education has recently implemented changes in how the national exams are handled. There have been new appointments. There are fears in most schools that the 2016 national exams at both the primary and secondary levels will be difficult since they will not be leaked. At the time of writing this chapter, more than 100 secondary schools have been set ablaze by students, in part because they fear the exams and believe that since the controls have been tightened they will fail.

Given this scenario, one wonders whether the kind of education being offered is not in itself violent because of its emphasis on examination. The violent strikes in the universities and the rate at which the students are unable to solve their problems through dialogue could be related to the way they qualified to join universities.

In recent times, lecturers as well as administrators in the universities have come to doubt the level of preparedness, both social and academic, of the students who are admitted. The incidences of excessive consumption of alcohol and other drugs,

the physical violence against each other and the level of destruction of university property through arson, vandalism and other criminal activities have been unparalleled in recent history. There has also been an increase in the number of students performing dismally in their coursework and requiring a high level of supplementary exams. The universities have also lost many students through unexplained deaths, suspicious accidents, suicide and outright recklessness, events that should not in any way be associated with institutions of higher learning.

The level of collusion in leaking exams reveals the involvement of several actors, among them the police, teachers, parents and secondary and university students. The questions that arise, then, are these: what do we take education to be? Do we still have values as a society or do we all believe that the end justifies the means? As parents, teachers and other responsible people, are we saying that money is everything and "bought" success in exams does no harm to the individual or to society at large? The conclusion drawn from this example is that the whole society requires review and deep reflection. Irrespective of the system, whether it be seven or eight years of primary education and four or more years of secondary and university education, or some modification thereof, education must foster development of the skills in literacy, numeracy, humanities and technologies that are necessary to negotiate economic self-sufficiency in the country. Education must also instill citizenship skills based on a realistic and thorough understanding of the political system, supporting citizenship and teaching democratic values. The system must reward mastery of content rather than glorify passing examinations for the sake of passing.

A country's education system must appreciate the diversity inherent in the country and ensure that its graduates are able to be self-sustaining. It must balance academic work with other physical exercises for the growth of the mind and soul. Education must not merely be a means to an end but, if possible, an end in itself. It must have the capacity to create opportunities and to bring out the best in each of its products: the students as well as the graduates of the system. We must inculcate a sense of responsibility and service to others. Our objectives should be greater than simply passing exams for the sake of furthering one's education. As the world increasingly becomes a global village, the system must be structured in such a way that students are exposed to various issues that will allow them to grow as global citizens.

The emphasis on exams and grades, and the notion of failing in exams as the end of a bright future, has done more harm than good; this attitude is in itself a violent creature of the system that must be reviewed. The African educational system should amend its methods of assessment methods. Assessment should be continuous and not limited to examination periods. Students should be rewarded for understanding the underlying concepts, as opposed to memorizing and repeating facts. The education system must empower individuals, engage them, connect them to the global village and allow them to be reflective.

Conclusion

While education undeniably has a pivotal role in contributing to non-violent behaviour in a society, the curriculum content and delivery modes more often than not are not politically neutral. The incumbent regimes tend to influence the tone of education, which, while praising the regime, plants roots for dissent among socially and politically marginalized groups. Students have to be taught the values of cooperation and tolerance of cultural differences to overcome the prejudicial stereotypes that opportunistic leaders routinely use for their own ends.

Education must be able to enhance peace by increasing life skill opportunities and ensuring that curriculum content promotes tolerance, justice and non-inflammatory language. To secure

the future for the coming generations of Kenyans, and Africans in general, education systems must prepare the next generation for a globalized, knowledge-based economy. African governments must depart from modes of teaching and learning that rely solely on didactic approaches that only demand regurgitation from students. Educating the next generation for a global economy demands that countries embrace new approaches that are consistent with contemporary views of epistemology and learning theories that treat knowledge as co-constructed by the student and the teacher or professor. Such approaches will demand that students learn analytical reasoning, critical thinking and problem-solving skills as well as engaging in reflective practice, innovation and entrepreneurship.

African leaders must realize that education can make or break the continent. It can either shape a peaceful future or entrench ethnicity, sectarianism and myopic elite interests at the expense of the majority, thereby increasing social and political fragility. A functioning mechanism for ensuring that education contributes to national as well as regional integration needs to be developed. Education systems must produce graduates for the global market. Parents must see their children as ambassadors of their country and of their continent. The future belongs to those who can see beyond passing exams for the sake of passing and can look forward to a continent that is at peace with itself. Only an education system that holds these values inherently and supports these values in the mode of education delivery can possibly guarantee peace now and in the future.

Works Cited

Aduda, David. 2016. "Leakage Has Been Getting Worse but Little Has Been Done to Check It." *Daily Nation*, March 25. www.nation.co.ke/news/KCSE-2015-leakage-was-worst-in-history-of-exam/1056-3132980-4cfh2w/index.html.

Agbor, Julius A. 2013. "Effects of Primary, Secondary and Tertiary Education on Conflict Intensity in Africa." Economic Research South Africa Working Paper No. 347.

Amadala, Benson and Maurice Kaluoch. 2015. "Sh1,000 and Mobile Phone Are All You Need to Get a Full Paper." *Daily Nation*, October 21. www.nation.co.ke/news/BENSON-AMADALA-MAURICE-KALUOCH/1056-2924594-format-xhtml-m7hibbz/index.html.

Asemoglu, Daron and James A. Robinson. 2010. "A Theory of Political Transitions." *American Economic Review* 91 (4): 938–963.

Asiyai, Romina Ifeoma. 2013. "Challenges of Quality in Higher Education in Nigeria in the 21st Century." *International Journal of Education Planning and Administration* 3 (2): 159–172.

Bates, Robert, Avner Greif and Smita Singh. 2007. "Organizing Violence." *Journal of Conflict Resolution* 46 (5): 599–628.

Barakat, Bilal, Zuki Karpinska and Julia Paulson. 2008. *Desk Study: Education and Fragility*. Oxford, UK: Conflict and Education Research Group.

Becker, Gary. 1996. *Accounting for Tastes*. Cambridge, MA: Harvard University Press.

Benson, John. 2006. "A Complete Education? Observation about the State of Primary Education in Tanzania in 2005." HakiElimu Working Paper No. 1.

Bush, Kenneth D. 1996. "Cracking Open the Ethnic Billiard Ball: Bringing in the Intra-group Dimensions of Ethnic Conflict Studies." Joan B. Kroc Institute for International Peace Studies, University of Notre Dame, Occasional Paper.

Bush, Kenneth D. and Diana Saltarelli, eds. 2000. *The Two Faces of Education in Ethnic Conflict: Towards a Peace-Building Approach to Education*. Florence, Italy: UNICEF Innocenti Research Centre.

Central Bureau of Statistics. 2007. *Basic Report on Well-being in Kenya*. Nairobi: Regal Press.

Connell, Robert W. 2000. "Arms and the Man: Using the New Research on Masculinity to Understand Violence and Promote Peace in the Contemporary World." In *Male Roles, Masculinities and Violence: A Culture of Peace Perspectives*, edited by Ingeborg Breines, Robert Connell and Ingrid Eide. Paris: UNESCO.

Clegg, Andrew, Wout Ottevanger, Jacob Bregman, Harriet Nannyonjo and Kasha Klosowska. 2007. "Uganda Secondary Education and Training: Curriculum Assessment and Examinations (CURRASE), Roadmap for Reform." Washington, DC: World Bank.

Davidson, Euan. 2006. "The Pivotal Role of Teacher Motivation in Tanzania." HakiElimu Working Paper No. 7.

Davies, Lynn. 2003. *Education and Conflict: Complexity and Chaos*. London: Routledge Falmer.

Dupuy, Kendra. 2008. *Education for Peace: Building Peace and Transforming Armed Conflict through Education Systems*. Oslo, Norway: Save the Children.

Francis, Andrew M. 2009. "The Human Capital Peace: Development and International Conflict." *Defence and Peace Economics* 20 (5): 395–411.

Galor, Oded and Omer Moav. 2004. "Das Human-Kapital: A Theory of the Demise of the Class Structure." Review of Economic Studies 73 (1): 85–117.

Hanushek, Eric A. and Ludger Woessman. 2008. "The Role of Cognitive Skills in Economic Development." *Journal of Economic Literature* 46 (3): 607–668.

Harber, Clive. 2004. *Schooling as Violence: How Schools Harm Pupils and Societies*. Abingdon, UK: Routledge.

Hirschleifer, Jack. 1995. "Anarchy and Its Breakdown." *Journal of Political Economy* 103 (1): 26–52.

International Committee of the Red Cross (ICRC). 1949. *Geneva Convention Relative to the Protection of Civilian Persons in Time of War (Fourth Geneva Convention)*. August 12, 75 U.N.T.S. 287. https://ihl-databases.icrc.org/ ihl/38 5ec082b509 e76c412567 39003e636d/67 56482d86146898c125641e004aa3c5.

Jackson, Tony. 2000. "Equal Access to Education: A Peace Imperative for Burundi." London, UK: International Alert. www.international-alert.org/publications/equal-access-education.

Kasami, Dickens. 2015. "KCSE 2015 Exam Papers Being Sold AtKSh 1,000." TUKO. www.tuko.co.ke/55581-how-kcse-2015-exam-papers-are-being-circulated-for-as-low-as-ksh-1000.html.

Keriga, Leah and Abdalla Bujra. 2009. "Social Policy Development and Governance in Kenya: An Evaluation and Profile of Education in Kenya." Nairobi: Development Policy Management Forum.

Moja, Teboho. 2000. "Nigeria Education Sector Analysis: An Analytical Synthesis of Performance and Main Issues." Washington, DC: World Bank.

Mubatsi. 2012. "Is Uganda Losing the Quality of Education Battle to Businessmen/women?" Learning Our Lesson on Africa. June 12. https://futurechallenges.org/local/is-uganda-losing-the-quality-of-education-battle-to-businessmenwomen/.

Mwinzi, Bernard. 2016. "Kenya: A Mandera Teacher Made 1.5 Million from Selling Leaked Exam." *Daily Nation*, March 29. www.allafrica.com/stories/201603290180.html.

Namunane, Bernard. 2016: "Kenya: KCSE Exam Leakage Was Countrywide Conspiracy." *Daily Nation*, March 29. www.allafrica.com/stories/201603290165.html.

Ndoye, Mamadou. 2008. "Education in Africa: Knowledge Makes the Difference." Washington, DC: World Bank.

Njagi, John and Ouma Wanzala. 2015. "Fears of KCSE Exam Leak as Teachers Seized." *Daily Nation*, October 21. www.nation.co.ke/news/5-teachers-seized-over-exams-leak/1056-2924590-xbawa/index.html.

Nyanje, Peter. 2011. "Cheating All the Way from Primary School." *The Citizen*. http://allafrica.com/stories/201112220035.html.

Ohanyido, Chinedu. 2012. "The Pivotal Role of Education in Africa's Development." *Chinedu Ohanyido* (blog), July 24. www.Globaleducationconference.com.

Otieno, Daniel and Ouma Wanzala. 2015. "Exam Leaks Put Kaimenyi on the Spot." *Daily Nation*, October 31. www.nation.co.ke/news/Exam-leaks-put-Kaimenyi-on-the-spot/1056-2936630-grop2vz/index.html.

Porter, James. 1999. *Reschooling and the Global Future*. Oxford, UK: Symposium Books.

Salmon, Jill. 2004. "Education and Its Contribution to Structural Violence in Rwanda." In *Education in Emergencies and Post-conflict Situations; Problems, Responses and Possibilities*, vol. 1, edited by Tammy Arnstein, Christine Pagen and Zeena Zakharia, 79–86. New York, NY: Society for International Education.

Shujaa, Mwalimu J. 1995. *Too Much Schooling, Too Little Education: A Paradox of Black Life in White Societies*. Trenton, NJ: Africa World Press.

Shahzad, Saqib. 2007. "A Study to Investigate the Quality of Education at Intermediate Level in Punjab." Doctoral thesis, University of Arid Agriculture, Rawalpindi, Pakistan.

Sifuna, Daniel N. 1998. "Crisis in the Public Universities in Kenya." In *Education Dilemmas: Debate and Diversity*, vol. 2, edited by Keith Watson, Sohan Mogdil and Celia Mogdil, 219–229. London: Cassell.

Smith, Alan, and Tony Vaux. 2003. "Education, Conflict and International Development." London: Department for International Development.

Smyth, Marie, Marie Therese Fay, Emily Brough and Jennifer Hamilton. 2004. "The Impact of Political Conflict on Children in Northern Ireland." Belfast: Institute for Conflict Research.

Sommers, Marc. 2005. "It Always Rains in the Same Place First": Geographic Favouritism in Rural Burundi. Woodrow Wilson International Centre for Scholars Africa Programme Issue Briefing No. 1.

Spaull, Nic. 2015. "Schooling in South Africa: How Low Quality Education Becomes a Poverty Trap." In *South African Child Gauge 2015*, edited by Ariane De Lannoy, Sharlene Swartz, Lori Lake and Charmaine Smith, 34–41. Cape Town: Children's Institute, University of Capetown.

UNCST. 2012. "The Quality of Science Education in Uganda." Kampala: UNCST Science and Technology Policy Coordination Division.

UNGA. 1948. *Universal Declaration of Human Rights*. December 10, GA Res 217 A (III). www.un.org/en/universal-declaration-human-rights/.

———. 1951. *Convention Relating to the Status of Refugees*. July 28, 189 UNTS 137. www.unhcr.org/3b66c2aa10.

———. 1959. *Declaration of the Rights of the Child*. November 20, A/RES/1386(XIV). www.ohchr.org/EN/Issues/Education/Training/Compilation/Pages/1DeclarationoftheRightsoftheChild(1959).aspx.

———. 1966. *International Covenant on Economic, Social and Cultural Rights*. December 16, 993 U.N.T.S. 3. www.ohchr.org/Documents/ProfessionalInterest/cescr.pdf.

———. 1979. *Convention on the Elimination of All Forms of Discrimination against Women*. December 18, 1249 UNTS 13. www.un.org/womenwatch/daw/cedaw/text/econvention.htm.

———. 1989. *Convention on the Rights of the Child*. November 20, 1577 U.N.T.S. 3. www.ohchr.org/Documents/ProfessionalInterest/crc.pdf.

UNESCO. 1960. *Convention against Discrimination in Education*. December 14. http://portal.unesco.org/en/ev.php-URL_ID=12949&URL_DO=DO_TOPIC&URL_SECTION=201.html.

———. 2000. *The Dakar Framework for Action*. Paris: UNESCO.

———. 2002. *EFA Global Monitoring Report: Education for All: Is the World on Track?* Paris: UNESCO.

Van der Berg, Servaas, Cobus Burger, Ronelle Burger, Mia de Vos, Gideon du Rand, Martin Gustafsson, Eldridge Moses, Debra Shepherd, Nicholas Spaull, Stephen Taylor, Hendrik van Broekhuizen and Dieter von Fintel. 2011. "Low Quality Education as a Poverty Trap." Stellenbosch, South Africa: University of Stellenbosch.

Vermeulcn, René. 2013. "The Quality of Public Primary Education in Rural Uganda: An Assessment Using a Capability Approach." Master's thesis, Utrecht University.

Walker-Keleher, Jessica. 2006. "Reconceptualizing the Relationship between Conflict and Education: The Case of Rwanda." *Praxis, The Fletcher Journal of Human Security* 21: 35–53.

Wedgwood, Ruth. 2006. "Education and Poverty Reduction in Tanzania." HakiElimu Working Paper Series No. 9.

———. 2007. "Education and Poverty Reduction in Tanzania." *International Journal of Educational Development* 27: 383–396.

World Bank. 2002. *Lifelong Learning in the Global Knowledge Economy. Challenges for Developing Countries*. Washington, DC: World Bank.

9

Trends in Urbanization and Migration in Africa: Implications for the Social Cohesion of African Societies

Mariama Awumbila

Urbanization is increasingly being acknowledged as one of the most defining issues of the twenty-first century. More than half of the world's population now live in towns and cities, and that figure is projected to rise to 75 percent by 2050 (UN Department of Economic and Social Affairs [UN DESA] Population Division 2014), with most of this urban growth concentrated in Africa and Asia. In the developing world, Africa has experienced the highest urban growth over the past two decades, at 3.5 percent per year, and this rate of growth is expected to hold into 2050. It is estimated that by 2025 more than half of Africa's population will live and work in urban centres, compared with 14.5 percent in 1950, 28 percent in 1980 and 34 percent in 1990 (UN-Habitat 2010). Migration is a significant contributor to urban growth and to the urbanization process, as people move in search of social and economic opportunity and away from environmental deterioration. However, the capacity of urban towns to plan for and cater to the needs of increasing numbers of migrants by providing employment, access to land and basic amenities is limited. This is leading governments, city authorities and host communities to largely negative policy positions on migration into urban areas.

This rapid urban growth presents opportunities as well as challenges. Africa's economic, social and environmental development will depend on how this growth is handled. Urbanization by itself is not a problem, as cities normally provide the engines for economic growth of countries and can greatly enhance people's well-being by offering potential access to a variety of resources, services and opportunities essential for people's welfare and resilience. When inadequately managed, however, rapid urbanization can actually result in conditions of exclusion, segregation and vulnerability for migrants as well as other socially disadvantaged groups in urban areas. These conditions can then increase threats of conflict, violence and insecurity and create a society devoid of social cohesion. Failure to integrate migrants can further lead to and accentuate tensions that ultimately manifest themselves in conflict (Hugo 2008). The proliferation and expansion of urban slums, which house mainly poor urban migrants, increase these potential conflicts. Specific vulnerable populations such as women, migrants and refugees bear the brunt of this lack of security, facing significant impacts on their livelihoods, health and access to basic services. Even though migration and migrants are central to the urbanization process and to the promotion of social capital and cohesion as a means of preventing and reducing urban violence and insecurity, little focus has been put on the interaction between urbanization, migration and social cohesion in Africa.

This chapter examines trends in urbanization and migration patterns in Africa and assesses their impacts on the social cohesion of African societies and their capacity to resist or recover from conflict. It takes the approach, as highlighted by the United Nations Economic Commission for Africa (UNECA) (2016), that social cohesion is not the absence of diversity but the management of it in a way that creates a sense of community, advancing the interests of all those involved. This chapter argues that if Africa is to harness its gains from urbanization, then migration and how it is governed should be at the front line of urban planning and sustainable development, which will promote not only migrant-inclusive urban governance, but also social cohesion among all the diverse urban populations.

Key Migration Trends in Africa

Before discussing key urbanization trends in Africa, it is important to discuss the context within which these trends have occurred. This section therefore provides a brief discussion of the key migration patterns and trends in Africa and how these have provided the context for rapid urbanization in Africa.

Africa has had a long history of population mobility, which is both dynamic and complex, and present-day migration trends are deeply rooted in historical antecedents. Migration has always played a central role in the livelihood and advancement strategies of both rural and urban populations. However, despite the lack of reliable data on African migration, there is evidence of an increase in the wave of migration on the continent and a diversification of migration destinations, actors and characteristics (Adepoju 2006; Awumbila et al. 2014). Recent destinations of African migrants have become more diverse and have included countries in the Far East, such as China and the Gulf States, as well as some north African countries, such as Libya, Egypt and Morocco, that have become major transit countries for migrants seeking to enter the European Union countries through irregular means. As a result, Africans are continuing to move out of the continent as both regular and irregular migrants.

Nevertheless, it is important to note that although the focus is often on African migration to Europe and North America, the bulk of migration takes place within the continent, as people circulate within Africa, looking for economic opportunities as their major reason for movements. Intra-regional mobility within Africa therefore remains the dominant form of mobility flows in Africa. For example, 84 percent of migration movements from west African countries in 2006 were directed toward another country in the region, and such intra-regional migration movements, estimated at 7.5 million persons, are estimated to be seven times greater than migration movements from west Africa to the rest of the world, including Europe and North America (Sahel and West Africa Club and Organisation for Economic Co-operation and Development [OECD] 2006). Similarly, a study on intra-regional labour mobility in the Economic Community of West African States (ECOWAS) region (Awumbila et al. 2014) observes that the majority of west African movements are largely intra-regional in nature and that much of this movement is critical for the livelihoods of many families and communities in west Africa. Therefore, intra-regional labour mobility can play a key role in facilitating poverty reduction and development in Africa.

Moreover, migration in Africa has always had an important cross-border component, partly reflecting the arbitrary nature of most national boundaries inherited from colonial administrations, partly drawing on the economic interdependence between ecological zones and partly encouraged by the creation of regional political and economic alliances in the 1960s and 1970s (McGranahan et al. 2009). People also increasingly move between regions. For example, in the past decade relatively substantial numbers of west African citizens have moved, largely to the cities of southern Africa. While it is very likely that these longer distance movements will grow in significance, more localized regional dynamics will remain crucial in shaping specific patterns of mobility. West Africa, in particular, has a long history of cross-border mobility linked to factors such as long-distance trade, the need for pastoralists to look for pasture in a drought-prone environment and the importance of smallholder plantation agriculture, which has traditionally attracted large numbers of migrant farmers. It is estimated that one-third of West Africans live outside their settlement of birth (Black et al. 2006; McGranahan et al. 2009). In southern Africa, the end of apartheid and the integration of South Africa within the Southern African Development Community region resulted in a major increase in cross-border and intra-regional mobility. High rates of rural and urban poverty and high levels

of unemployment as well as differential levels of social service provision have contributed to make mobility an increasingly important livelihood strategy, with South Africa remaining the preferred destination for many migrants, despite the perceived growing xenophobia (Human Sciences Research Council 2008). These examples demonstrate that cross-border migration is linked to urbanization and to urban problems and issues.

Additionally, although international migration has received more attention in recent debates on African migration streams, internal migration within individual African states is far more significant in terms of the numbers of people involved and perhaps even the quantum of remittances sent home and the poverty reduction potential of these (United Nations Development Programme [UNDP] 2009). Recent analysis of household survey data indicates that, for example, the total sum of internal remittances in Ghana — US$324 million — exceeds international remittances of US$283 million. The data also show that these internal remittances, which are mainly from poorer migrants, tend to reach a larger number of poor source families and, thus, have a more significant impact on poverty reduction (Castaldo, Deshingkar and McKay 2012). Therefore, internal migration can play an important role in poverty reduction and development and can allow poor people to access better opportunities in richer regions, despite occasional negative consequences.

Within internal movements, the importance of temporary and seasonal migration for multi-local households and diversified livelihoods is especially critical. Seasonal, circular and other forms of short-term mobility are especially important in Africa, as these are the migrants who, once they move to the city, are likely to be more vulnerable and in need of specific social protection policies. Temporary movement — often, but not necessarily always, on a seasonal basis — has long underpinned the diversification of income sources by rural households and, importantly enough, by urban households as well. Migration is a key element of income diversification. Research on rural-urban linkages in Mali, Nigeria and Tanzania found that about 50 percent of rural households interviewed had at least one migrant member and that remittances were a growing component of household budgets (Bah et al. 2003). In Ghana, a migration survey in five migration source regions of Ghana in 2013 and a follow-up survey in 2015 indicated that 65 percent of households had at least one migrant member in urban areas and that sending remittances home was a top priority for the majority of migrants (Awumbila et al. 2016). Thus both internal and seasonal migration, either as a response to local or national difficulties or as a way to access opportunities located elsewhere, has long been an integral part of labour markets and livelihoods across much of Africa. Indeed, it is an important livelihood strategy of both the poor as well as those who are better off.

Lastly, of these mobility flows within Africa, rural-to-urban migration remains a dominant migration stream. As people increasingly move to cities and towns in search of social and economic opportunities or as a result of environmental deterioration, migration has become a significant contributor to urbanization. Urban populations in Africa are expected to triple in the next 50 years, thus changing the profile throughout the region and challenging policy makers to harness urbanization for sustainable and inclusive growth.

Urbanization and Migration Linkages in Africa: Opportunities and Challenges for a Cohesive Society

Africa's urban transition is proceeding rapidly, with the accumulated relative growth rate of its cities now among the highest in the world. Although in absolute terms, Asian cities still remain the world's fastest growing, the global share of African urban dwellers is projected to rise from 11.3 percent in 2010 to 20.2 percent by 2050, with almost two-thirds of its population growth expected to occur in urban areas. Such intense demographic pressure in urban areas has been a justifiable source of concern for African governments and international observers for decades. The accelerating urban transition and the shift from rural to urban population majorities has been described as perhaps the most decisive phenomenon since independence in most African nations (Awumbila 2014).

Africa's economic, social and environmental development will depend on how this rapid urban growth is handled. Moving to cities can greatly enhance people's well-being. It can offer an escape from the impact of the hazards of a fragile rural livelihood and access to diverse employment opportunities and better health and education, all of which have the potential to reduce the poverty of the people moving as well as of those who stay behind. Cities also offer potential access to a variety of resources, services and opportunities that are essential for people's well-being and resilience. For most migrants, therefore, moving to a city is a sound decision that is likely to benefit their well-being and strengthen their resilience in facing adversity. However, when inadequately managed, migration can actually result in conditions of exclusion and vulnerability for the individuals who are moving, as well as for host communities. Migrants are often faced with legal, cultural and social barriers and obstacles to accessing formal housing, employment, education, health and other social services. These barriers may force them to live in conditions of exclusion, segregation and vulnerability.

The following discussion examines key issues in Africa's urbanization trajectory and highlights the challenges as well as opportunities it presents for promoting the social cohesion of African societies.

Concerns about Over-urbanization

Data from recent population censuses (Potts 2012) indicate that although Africa is not the world's fastest urbanizing region, what is true is that Africa's urban population has been growing at a historically unprecedented rate for decades (UN-Habitat 2014). Urbanization, defined as the increasing share of a population that is living in urban areas, can be attributed in general to natural population growth and net rural-to-urban migration and also to the progressive extensions of urban boundaries and creation of new urban centres. Human mobility and migration clearly play an important part in the urbanization process, as internal and international migrants gravitate to cities and urban areas (Tacoli, McGranahan and Satterthwaite 2014). Thus, urbanization and migration often go hand in hand. Migratory movements are shaping diverse forms of urban settlements. These range from large-sized global cities such as Tokyo and New York to large, informal settlements or slums where inhabitants struggle to meet the most basic of human needs. One such settlement is Kibera, the largest slum in Kenya, estimated to host 170,000 residents (Kenya National Bureau of Statistics [KNBS] 2010).[1] Another is Old Fadama, the largest slum in Ghana, estimated at about 80,000 residents in 2009 (Housing the Masses 2010).

Data projections indicate that African countries will continue to urbanize, with migration, particularly rural-to-urban migration, continuing to play an important role in the urbanization process (International Organization for Migration [IOM] 2015). Contemporary drivers of migration, such as environmental and climate change and their future impacts — in particular, their predicted debilitating impact on agriculture and rural livelihoods — and new natural resource

discoveries, such as oil and gas, in many African countries are likely to further trigger increased migration to urban centres. Together, these factors are likely to intensify mobility dynamics in Africa (Awumbila 2014). For example, the *Foresight: Migration and Global Environmental Change Final Project Report* (Government Office for Science 2011), which considered migration in the context of environmental change over the next 50 years, highlights among key conclusions that "the impact of environmental change on migration will increase in the future. In particular, environmental change may threaten people's livelihoods, and a traditional response is to migrate" (ibid., 9). Furthermore, recent discoveries of oil and gas deposits in some African countries, such as Ghana, Equatorial Guinea, Ethiopia, Sierra Leone, São Tomé and Príncipe, and Uganda, are attracting changes in migration inflows and presenting opportunities that could be harnessed for sustainable development if properly managed (Aryeetey and Asmah 2011).

Celia Tacoli, Gordon McGranahan and David Satterthwaite (2014) argue that although urbanization is primarily the result of migration, it is not just a simplistic result of rural-to-urban migration — in particular, if rural-urban migration is taken to mean long-term rural dwellers moving permanently to urban centres — but it is the net result of complex migratory movements between rural and urban areas, including circular migration back and forth. Second, urbanization involves both the net movement of people toward and into urban areas and the progressive extension of urban boundaries and the creation of new urban centres, which can also result from higher natural population growth in urban areas (ibid.).

Tacoli, McGranahan and Satterthwaite further argue that comparing Africa's levels of urbanization with those in other parts of the world can be misleading, as Africa's urban growth rates are especially high because of high overall population growth rates. Thus, although Africa's urbanization

1 Other sources suggest the total Kibera population may be 500,000 to well over 1,000,000, depending on which slums are included in the definition of Kibera.

rate is still a bit lower than Asia's, its population growth rate is considerably higher, resulting in a higher overall urban growth rate (ibid.). These findings indicate that Africa may still be in its early stages of urban transitions and do not necessarily imply that Africa's situation is exceptionally rapid (Montgomery 2008). In fact, concerns about over-urbanization in Africa are not borne out by the evidence (Tacoli, McGranahan and Satterthwaite 2014). Despite this, many African governments hold increasingly strong anti-urban sentiments. In 1996, 54 percent of African governments responding to a UN questionnaire said that they had or desired to have policies to reduce migration to urban agglomerations — a figure that rose to 78 percent in 2007 (UN DESA Population Division 2014). These anti-urban sentiments are mainly born out of the perception largely held by many African governments that the severe urban housing, infrastructure and service deficiencies and various forms of urban congestion often faced by rapidly growing African cities and towns are a result of migration. The blame for these shortfalls and problems is often put on rural-to-urban migrants. Rather than see the lack of proactive planning to accommodate rapid urban growth as the cause, many African governments develop policies intended to exclude migrants. Tacoli, McGranahan and Satterthwaite (2014, 11) argue that taking measures to inhibit migration is unlikely to be a good solution as it can easily cause severe hardship, not just for current and aspiring migrants but also for low-income urban populations generally. It can also cause violence and conflicts in urban areas, as witnessed in xenophobic attacks against migrants in South Africa and more recently in Côte d'Ivoire.

Assumptions that Rural-Urban Migration Increases Urban Poverty

As widely acknowledged, urbanization can provide opportunities for development, but it can also pose serious challenges in urban areas. Africa is the last continent to go through an urban transition, and it faces a challenging combination of high population growth and rapid urbanization. However, as noted by a number of authors (McGranahan et al. 2009; Tacoli, McGranahan and Satterthwaite 2014), Africa's urbanization rates are not historically or economically exceptional, and there is a danger that, in blaming urban problems on urbanization, important policy measures to improve the quality of urban development are being neglected. Gordon McGranahan, Diana Mitlin, David Satterthwaite, Cecilia Tacoli and Ivan Turok (2009), in particular, argue that attempts to stem the rural-urban migration are rarely successful and can make it harder for poor groups to escape poverty. Furthermore, if urban slums are misdiagnosed as symptoms of over-urbanization, when in fact they reflect excessive national poverty, it becomes harder to justify slum improvement. They further note that the fear that slum improvement will simply encourage more rural migrants to move to cities is commonly used by many African governments to justify the lack of provision of services in slum settlements as a means of discouraging rural-urban migration.

The long-held view that rural-urban migration is the principal cause of urban poverty has led many policy makers to favour solutions that try to resolve poverty in rural areas, while also attempting to prevent rural-urban migration, in the hope that this will prevent the transfer of poverty to cities. This perception by policy makers is currently being contested as misguided (Martine et al. 2008; Owusu 2008; Awumbila et al. 2014). Recent studies (Tacoli, McGranahan and Satterthwaite 2014; Awumbila 2014) argue that rural-to-urban migrants themselves benefit from relocation. Indeed, the increase in pressure on services and infrastructure associated with urban growth actually highlights the development gap that exists in most urban centres in African cities, which is caused not by migration, but by African city authorities' overall lack of forward planning for population growth and urbanization. It is the anti-urban attitudes of policy makers, who often view migration as a factor that exacerbates urban poverty and should be directly controlled, that need to be questioned.

In spite of the strong correlation between urbanization and economic growth, the majority of governments (80 percent of 185 countries reviewed), especially in low- and middle-income nations in Africa and Asia, had policies to lower rural-to-urban migration (UN DESA 2014). These policy makers tend to assume that most migrants "transfer" their poverty to urban contexts. This does not, however, recognize the complexity of such population movements. Migrants are not a homogeneous group; they have differentiated access to resources and institutions and differing capacities to undertake migration.

Studies (IOM 2015) further indicate that there is little evidence to suggest that migration drives up urban poverty. In fact, those moving to urban contexts in many developing countries are often relatively better off. For instance, in the Upper West region of Ghana, wealthy migrants were found to move more often to the urban centres of the south, including Accra, while the poor and illiterate migrated over shorter distances, usually to the rural parts of the Brong Ahafo region (Van der Geest 2011; IOM 2015). Poorer migrants tend to have more limited choices and, instead of migrating to urban areas, are more likely to seek work in other rural destinations. Moreover, recent studies highlight the economic benefits of migrating from rural to urban areas. A recent study among the poor migrants living and working in two urban informal settlements in Accra indicates that, despite living in a harsh environment with little social protection, an overwhelming majority of the migrants (88 percent) believed that their overall well-being had been enhanced by migrating to Accra (Awumbila, Owusu and Teye 2014). Deborah Potts (2008), in a study of rural-urban migrants in Harare, Zimbabwe, in 2001, similarly found that about 50 percent of respondents estimated that their standard of living had improved in comparison to the standard in their rural areas of origin.

Migration and Urban Informal Settlements

Rapid urban population growth in the context of poor economic performance in most African countries has created a "face" of poverty characterized by a significant proportion of urban populations living in overcrowded informal settlements, or slums. In many parts of Africa, in the past few decades, the rise of informal settlements has contributed to the physical growth of cities. The expansion of urban settlements that lack access to water, adequate sanitation, durable housing and sufficient living space has contributed to the growth of slums (UN-Habitat 2013). While the proportion of urban residents living in slum settlements in Africa declined from 70 percent to 62 percent between 1990 and 2010, the actual number of slum dwellers doubled from 103 million to 200 million over this period (UN Population Fund 2007; UN-Habitat 2013).

Recent studies indicate that migrants are disproportionately represented among the urban poor in these informal settlements (Hoang, Truong and Dinh 2013; Rigg, Nguyen and Luong 2014). For example, in Accra, Ghana, 92 percent of migrant households live in one slum, Old Fadama, without access to water within their residences. Water has to be purchased daily or drawn from nearby wells, and 94 percent of migrants in the same slum do not live in accommodations with toilet facilities (Awumbila, Owusu and Teye 2014). For many poor migrants, the first point of entry in a city is often an informal settlement or slum, such as Kibera in Nairobi or Old Fadama in Accra, and their first jobs are often in the informal sector. Despite the hardships of living in such conditions, migrants are able to find economic activity and opportunities to improve their current well-being and future prospects in these informal settlements (ibid.). Early migration models viewed urban informal sector employment as a temporary staging post for new migrants on their way to formal sector employment (Benergee 1983). But decades of experience in developing countries have shown that the informal sector has persisted and grown, and graduation to the formal sector has been elusive.

Informal Urban Economies and Migrant Livelihoods

African labour markets are characterized by high informality and a lack of adequate labour-market statistics for policy planning and decision making. In many African countries, more than 60 percent of the labour force works in the informal sector. For instance, a study of intra-regional labour flows in the ECOWAS region (Awumbila et al. 2014) showed that the formal sectors in Benin, Liberia, Mali, Gambia, Ghana, Guinea and Nigeria accounted for between only 3.9 percent and 25 percent of employment in these countries, respectively, with an increasing shift into the informal sector. Studies indicate that rural-urban migration has contributed to the dominance of informal employment in urban areas (Chen 2006).

Informal activities in many developing countries offer employment opportunities for millions of people beyond the formal economy, providing a main source of employment and income for a majority of the poor in urban centres and poor urban women, in particular. Thus, the informal sector has been described as "the big story in African cities." In Ghana's Old Fadama — considered Ghana's largest slum and inhabited mostly by migrants from the rural north — most of the residents earn their living from business transactions within the slum itself and mostly in the informal economy.

Livelihoods in the informal sector among the urban poor are insecure, wages are low and irregular, and work conditions are hostile. In Ghana, slums are booming with various forms of entrepreneurial businesses, mainly in the informal sector, which tends to be gendered (Awumbila et al. 2014). Migrant women work mainly as petty traders, food vendors, catering assistants, head porters, shop assistants and hairdressers.

Young girls from rural areas, particularly the northern regions, move to markets in the urban centres of Accra and Kumasi to serve as *kayayei* (female porters), who carry goods on their heads for a negotiated fee (Awumbila and Ardayfio-Schandorf 2008). Migrant men work as artisans, construction workers and *okada* (motorbike) operators and in the collection and sale of metal scraps, in particular, of old discarded computers, also known as the electronic or e-waste business. In Zimbabwe, local authorities often harass migrants working in the informal sector and demand unofficial payments before they can do any business (Awumbila 2014). Cross-border traders in some southern African countries have also complained of high and fluctuating duties, unwarranted confiscation of goods, long queues and physical harassment (ibid.).

Migration, Urban Violence and Migrants' Specific Vulnerabilities

Population movements are a key dynamic to the evolution of urban areas. They contribute to shaping the location, size, composition and characteristics of human communities, as well as the features of the environment. Clemens Greiner and Patrick Sakdapolrak (2012) note that migrating to another location modifies the migrants' exposure to hazards and access to resources that would help them anticipate, cope with and recover from stresses in the new environment. They also note that migration changes the risk patterns faced by urban dwellers in host communities. As people increasingly move into urban areas, cities and towns are increasingly becoming the main arena in which these risk dynamics unfold (ibid.). Depending on the circumstances in which migration takes place and how institutions manage migration, urban migration can have widely diverse effects on the vulnerability and resilience of migrants and host communities.

As noted already, rural-urban migration has traditionally offered people the opportunity to escape socio-economic and other pressures in their areas of origin and to diversify livelihoods. Migrating to cities can, however, result in increased vulnerability, especially if formal employment, decent housing and access to basic services needed for a decent life are lacking. This can force people into making trade-offs between meeting their immediate needs and achieving their long-term well-being and security (Cannon 2008; Gaillard et al. 2010). This may then create patterns of spatial segregation and marginalization, with people settling in informal or poorly planned areas where they face a number of natural and man-made hazards such as floods, disease and violence.

However, as pointed out by William Donner and Havidán Rodríguez (2008), urban mobility in itself does not necessarily lead to vulnerability. It is only when population pressures on urban labour, housing markets, health and education systems, and access to basic services and infrastructures are poorly managed that conditions of marginalization, exclusion, risk and potential conflict situations are produced (Kapur, Eswaran and Blum 2011). Although such marginalization in cities is not unique to migrants, migrants and, in particular, recent migrants, who tend to be disproportionately represented among the poor and vulnerable of urban populations in Africa, are generally more heavily affected (IOM 2015). Other weak social groups such as women, youth and the elderly are also badly affected (UNDP 2009). As discussed, poor urban migrants are likely to live in the cities' most marginal and least-safe locations, where the migrants are forced to make a living from informal income opportunities with little or no access to basic service provision.

Vulnerability can be particularly acute for specific migrant groups such as migrant women, who are more likely to work in low-paid, irregular, insecure and potentially exploitative jobs, often in the informal sector, and are exposed to diseases,

accidents, violence and abuse. This is highlighted in Ghana by the case of an increasing stream of young women and girls, some as young as 10 years old, who move from the rural north to cities in the south to work as headload porters in markets in the city (Awumbila and Ardayfio-Schandorf 2008). The exploitative conditions they work in reflect the minimal benefits of migration for women and girls in some situations.

Domestic service is the other major category of employment for poor migrant women in urban areas in Africa. In South Africa, in 2004, domestic service was the second-largest employment sector for black women, employing some 755,000 workers, a large proportion of whom were internal migrants from rural areas (Peberdy and Dinat 2005). Wages are low and, while accommodation provided by employers makes domestic service relatively attractive, especially for migrants, long working hours, potential abuse by employers and social isolation increase workers' vulnerability. Mariama Awumbila, Joseph Kofi Teye and Joseph Awetori Yaro (2016) found in a study of domestic workers in Ghana that migrant female domestic workers tended to work longer hours and with lower remuneration compared to migrant male domestic workers, and they had less agency in negotiating for better conditions of service and wages. These conditions push people into situations of limited social, financial and environmental security (UN-Habitat 2003). Despite this, urban areas also present potential opportunities, such as increased economic independence, better access to services and greater capacity to challenge rigid social and gender norms and values (IOM 2015). As the number of women migrating to cities in Africa has generally been growing in recent decades (Adepoju 2006), understanding the conditions of migrants in urban contexts and acknowledging gender as an important dimension of migrants' vulnerability in cities is key to reducing risks, vulnerability, segregation and lack of social cohesion in increasingly diverse cities (IOM 2015; Juzwiak, McGregor and Siegel 2014).

The linkages between migration dynamics, urbanization, violence and social cohesion have come into focus as urbanization has been on the increase. As Michael Collyer notes in the *World Migration Report 2015,* the city may be a refuge from violence but, as the world's population has become predominantly urban, the city has also become the site of more and more violent activity (IOM 2015, 78-79). Thus, the relationship between migration to cities and violence is not a straightforward one. Where rapid urbanization coincides with a significant rise in urban violence, migrants are often blamed. However, migrants are overrepresented among poor and marginalized groups who typically suffer the most serious consequences of violence, as they are much more likely to be victims of violence than perpetrators. Collyer (ibid.) further notes that urban migrants may experience violence in the form of direct and indirect threats to their lives, integrity and freedom of choice in three main ways: violence as a reason for moving to cities, violence as a reason for displacement within cities and violence as a factor worsening the living conditions of migrants in cities.

Published by the IOM, the *World Migration Report 2015* highlights, in particular, vulnerability to ill-health as a specific issue facing migrant populations in urban areas (IOM 2015). While opportunities for better health services are available in urban areas, migrants often have little choice but to live and work in unsafe conditions that result in exposure to infectious and non-communicable diseases, as well as accidents, violence and abuse, which in turn have an adverse effect on their mental and psychosocial well-being. The recent outbreak of Ebola in west Africa highlighted the critical role of high population mobility in the spread of the disease across porous borders and demonstrated how swiftly the virus spread once it reached urban settings and densely populated slums (World Health Organization 2015; IOM 2015).

Migrant-sensitive Urban Policies: Implications for a Socially Cohesive Society

This discussion acknowledges that Africa's increasing urbanization brings about potential opportunities for the poor in urban areas, but also new challenges in terms of conflict, violence, urban governance, citizen security and social cohesion, in particular. The *World Development Report 2011* (World Bank 2011) highlights the close relationship between violence, insecurity and poverty and further notes the significance of violence as a development problem. Social violence, including violence within the household, is also a significant problem, particularly for vulnerable youth and women living in marginalized urban environments. A report on eastern Africa notes that in six east African countries for which there is data, between one-third and one-half of all women report that they have suffered gender-based violence (UNECA 2016).

In many African cities, high urban poverty, especially among youth, has been identified as a major trigger of urban violence. In Lagos, Nigeria, one of Africa's largest cities, Jane Lumumba (2016, 38) identifies the sources of stress and fragility in Lagos as being linked to political struggles, the city's complex economic hierarchy and acute urban — in particular, youth — poverty. Lagos' large youth population is identified as contributing to urban conflicts as a result of high rates of unemployment and underemployment, especially among the more than 80 million Nigerian youth, leading to acute urban poverty that ultimately contributes to violence and unrest in the city. In this situation, migrants, especially new migrants to the city, are notably vulnerable. Over the past five years, Lagos has absorbed numerous migrants from northern Nigeria, either fleeing from Boko Haram terrorist activities or as "climate migrants." These new migrants end up in the bustling informal settlements of Lagos, living in extreme poverty, sometimes resorting to crime and suffering from social isolation because of religious and cultural differences. These have sometimes resulted in tension and conflicts as, for example, brought out by intense riots between the Muslim Hausa from the north and the Christian Yoruba in 2001.

Robert Muggah (2012) argues that policy makers across the security and development domains are facing an "urban dilemma," exemplified by the paradoxical effects of urbanization in the twenty-first century as a force for unparalleled development on the one hand and as a risk for insecurity among the urban poor on the other. Concerns have been expressed especially about the ways in which the urban poor are directly and indirectly implicated in violence and insecurity and about the wider consequences of violence in cities for national and regional stability and development more generally (ibid.). This state of affairs calls for the formulation of new, wide-ranging urban policies and strategies that promote societal unity and cohesion to prevent future conflicts and protect urban populations.

Although in recent years there has been an increase in the number of networking initiatives among city authorities, urban practitioners, civil society leaders, business development communities and migrant and diaspora groups to discuss urban integration issues and foster participative economic growth, many of such public and private sector initiatives do not take full account of migrants as key players in city development, growth, resilience and sustainability (IOM 2015). Migrants themselves can make significant and essential contributions to the economic, social and cultural development of their host countries and their communities back home. Yet often these contributions go unrecognized or are at best measured only in terms of the remittances the migrants manage to send back home. Although urban migrants may be part of the challenge, they can also be part of the solution. It is therefore important, as cities plan for and manage the challenges of population growth and migration into cities and increased socio-

cultural diversity, that migrants are included in the planning and management (IOM 2015).

These urban policies must include migrant-inclusive urban governance that provides realistic, affordable and local solutions such as housing, health, clean air, water and green spaces that are necessary for the social integration of immigrants and for local development (Collier and Venables 2013). Inclusive urban governance must also include partnerships with migrants that will not only accommodate the diverse interests of migrants — whether they are refugees or internal, international, labour or irregular migrants — but will also promote social cohesion by empowering migrants as actors to enhance their human and social potential for co-development in their cities of destination (IOM 2015; Muggah 2012).

To address the challenges of rapid urbanization, several African governments have in the past few years developed national urban policies to promote a more transformative, productive, inclusive and resilient urban development for the long term, with the support of the United Nations Settlement Programme (UN-Habitat 2014). This new generation of national urban policies guides the urbanization process by promoting more compact, socially inclusive, better connected and integrated cities and territories that foster sustainable urban development and are resilient to climate change (ibid.). Gordon McGranahan, Daniel Schensul and Gayatri Singh (2016) argue that within this framework, achieving inclusive cities can be a means of realizing human rights, including those of aspiring migrants and rural dwellers wanting to access urban markets, services and spaces. Indeed, they argue that the concept of the "right to the city" provides a specifically urban concept of inclusion as it focuses on a notion of a city co-produced through the labour, actions and daily exchanges of urban residents who have a right not only to inhabit the city but also to be the architects of urban transformations and to reshape the process of urbanization through engagement with the state.

In the past few years, within this inclusive city framework, some civil society organizations are also beginning to participate in the urban policy space in some countries in Africa. The Slum/ Shack Dwellers International (SDI), a network of federations of urban poor groups working in alliance with supporting non-governmental organizations (NGOs), provides an example of this approach, in which SDI's federations demand not just their rights, but offer to cooperate in their realization (ibid.). Their strategy, in effect, is to co-produce their own inclusion, developing a better relationship with and more influence over local authorities along the way. Mariama Awumbila (2014) discusses various initiatives by the urban poor for engaging with city authorities and for inclusive governance in Ghana. These include setting up the Ghana Federation of the Urban Poor (GHAFUP), a network of community savings groups in informal settlements and poor communities in Ghana, including four of Ghana's five largest urban areas: Accra, Kumasi, Ashaiman and Takoradi. The alliance was borne out of an eviction crisis that threatened over 30,000 residents of Old Fadama, the largest squatter settlement in Accra. GHAFUP is helping communities to make improvements through daily savings, local and international exchanges, community settlement profiles, and negotiating and building partnerships with local governments. Through these partnerships, GHAFUP is working with the People's Dialogue on Human Settlements, a community-based NGO established in 2003 to demonstrate community-led solutions to address urban poverty in Ghana and help communities to improve living conditions. These initiatives, among others, have the potential to bring about broader engagement of civil society and the urban poor and to ensure that policy makers and planners are hearing the voices and concerns of the urban poor and, thus, warranting inclusivity in urban development.

With an estimated one billion people living in slums and as many as 1.4 billion by 2020, a concerted focus on "upgrading" is one of the hallmarks of the late twentieth and early twenty-first century urban planning. Slum upgrade programs became increasingly common since the 1970s as a counter to more traditional strategies, such as razing slums and resettling populations. UN-Habitat (2014), for example, argues that the promotion of slum upgrading in informal settlements can stimulate transformations in urban safety and ultimately increase real and perceived security. It is worth noting, however, that the outcomes of slum upgrading are still highly contested, with some authors indicating varying socio-economic benefits for the urban poor (Muggah 2012). Examples of slum upgrade programs include the Kenya Slum Upgrading Program in Nairobi, Kenya, and the Douala Infrastructure Program, Cameroon, all launched by national and metropolitan governments to upgrade essential infrastructure, promote open public spaces, formalize land title and tenure, and improve housing. These programs are lauded for enhancing the conditions for local resilience and promoting social cohesion without focusing explicitly on urban violence (ibid.).

Finally, to promote social cohesion in a rapidly urbanizing Africa, challenged by the diversity of its cosmopolitan cities, it is important that local and city authorities play a key role in promoting social cohesion among the increasing multiple identities of the various migrant communities and citizens. This requires that urban governance promotes not only migrant inclusion, but also the sharing of common values while respecting cultural diversity. This will ensure the coexistence of people of different cultural, linguistic and religious backgrounds that might otherwise have led to conflicting value systems and competition for resources. Migrant inclusion also requires a connection between central migration policies, often set and managed by national governments, and local urban development plans and capacities, which are essential to migrant access to services, jobs and housing and are the responsibility of city administrations.

Some cities, notably in the developed world, are proactively developing their own plans for integration of migrants into urban communities, at least to the extent that they have the autonomy to do so. A good example in Africa is Morocco. As Morocco has evolved from a country of emigration to a country that is increasingly hosting Sub-Saharan Africans, its government has begun working on a new, more liberal immigration policy that is attentive to the basic rights of migrants and the provision of basic services to them. This includes the special regularization of certain categories of undocumented migrants. As of October 2014, the number of regularization requests had reached nearly 20,000, representing 103 countries. Nearly half of these requests have been approved (IOM 2015).

Despite the challenges of urbanization, which together with demographic pressures is putting a strain on scarce resources, leading to social pressure which further tests cohesion, studies have shown that many African countries and cities have shown resilience in the face of numerous challenges since the beginning of the twenty-first century (UNECA 2016; Lumumba 2016). Despite the challenges facing Lagos, for example, Lumumba (2016) notes that it has been able to build and achieve resilience through the capacity to adapt and reinvent itself. In eastern Africa, to strengthen social cohesion, some countries have taken explicit policy measures (UNECA 2016). For example, Kenya established the National Cohesion and Integration Commission in 2010, in response to the violence following the 2007 general elections. The mandate of the commission is to facilitate and promote equality of opportunity, good relations, harmony and peaceful coexistence between persons of different ethnic and racial backgrounds and to advise the government accordingly. It also addresses issues that pose threats to national cohesion, such as inequality, marginalization, insecure property rights, discrimination and poor governance. Many of these are directed at internal migrants in urban areas of Kenya. In the United Republic of Tanzania, Vision 2025 for Tanzania

mainland and Vision 2020 for Zanzibar both emphasize the importance of cultivating social cohesion and unity. To this end, the former proposes a number of measures, including working toward an inclusive education system and ensuring that the basic needs of all people are met. Analysts note that this is in line with earlier policies developed since independence (UNECA 2016; Barkan 2012).

Conclusions

That Africa is witnessing rapid urban growth, with migration — in particular, rural-urban migration — continuing to play an important role in the urbanization process, is not in question. It is argued, therefore, that, in an increasingly urbanized world, the development challenges of the twenty-first century will no longer be met in rural areas but in Africa's cities and towns. The growth of slums and informal settlements is an indicator that urban planning, management and governance have failed to address the challenges of urbanization for many African countries.

Among other potential advantages, urbanization provides the potential for new forms of social inclusion, including greater equality, access to services and opportunities, and engagement that reflects the diversity of cities. As this discussion has shown, urbanization can represent enormous opportunities for inclusive and sustainable development. Yet too often this is not the form of urban development. Inequality and exclusion abound, often then engendering violence, conflicts and insecurity, in particular, in areas where poor migrants are segregated. If Africa is to harness its gains from urbanization, then migration and how it is governed should be an issue at the front line of urban planning and sustainable development. As this chapter has shown, however, migration is largely omitted from the global debate on urbanization, and many city and local governments also do not include migration or migrants in their urban development planning and implementation.

The promotion of social capital and cohesion as a means of preventing and reducing urban violence has not until recently received much attention in Africa.

Whether African states can manage the urbanization trends in a way that promotes societal unity rather than division and how they harness the benefits of migration and rapid urbanization remains to be seen. As the *World Migration Report 2015* (IOM 2015) and the African Development Bank (2016) note, about two-thirds of the investments in African urban infrastructure to 2050 have yet to be made. Therefore, the scope is large for new, wide-ranging urban policies and strategies that will include migration governance to turn African cities and towns into engines of sustainable structural transformation. In 2016, the common African position on urban development and the emerging international New Urban Agenda offer opportunities to discuss options and start articulating those new urbanization policies that promote strategies for Africa's structural transformation. As noted by UN-Habitat, what is needed is sustainable urbanization that is inclusive and safe for all the diverse groups of urban populations, that promotes equity, welfare and shared prosperity, and that aims to leave no one behind.

Works Cited

Adepoju, Aderanti. 2006. *The Challenge of Labour Migration Flows between West Africa and the Maghreb*. Geneva, Switzerland: International Migration Programme, International Labour Office.

African Development Bank/OECD/UNDP. 2016. *African Economic Outlook 2016: Sustainable Cities and Structural Transformation*. Paris, France: OECD Publishing. www.afdb.org/fileadmin/uploads/afdb/Documents/Publications/AEO_2016_Report_Full_English.pdf.

Aryeetey, Ernest and E. Ekow Asmah. 2011. "Africa's New Oil Economies: Managing Expectations." In *Foresight Africa: The Continent's Greatest Challenges and Opportunities for 2011*, edited by Emmanuel Asmah, Ernest Aryeetey, Ezra Suruma, John Mukum Mbaku, John Mutenyo, John Page, Mwangi S. Kimenyi, Nelipher Moyo, Olumide Taiwo and Zenia A. Lewis, 22–24. Washington, DC: Africa Growth Initiative at Brookings.

Awumbila, Mariama. 2014. "Linkages between Urbanization, Rural-Urban Migration and Poverty, Outcomes in Africa." World Migration Report 2015 Background Paper. Geneva, Switzerland: IOM. www.iom.int/sites/default/files/our_work/ICP/MPR/WMR-2015-Background-Paper-MAwumbila.pdf

Awumbila, Mariama and Elizabeth Ardayfio-Schandorf. 2008. "Gendered Poverty, Migration and Livelihood Strategies of Female Porters in Accra, Ghana." *Norwegian Journal of Geography* 62: 171–179.

Awumbila, Mariama, Yaw Benneh, Joseph Kofi Teye and George Atiim. 2014. *Across Artificial Borders: An Assessment of Labour Migration in the ECOWAS Region*. Research Report 2014 ACP/OBS/2014/PUB05. Brussels, Belgium: African, Caribbean and Pacific Observatory on Migration.

Awumbila, Mariama, George Owusu and Joseph Kofi Teye. 2014. "Can Rural-Urban Migration into Slums Reduce Poverty? Evidence from Ghana." Migrating Out of Poverty Research Programme Consortium Working Paper No. 13. Brighton, UK: University of Sussex.

Awumbila, Mariama, Louis Boayke-Yiadom, Eva-Maria Egger, Julie Litchfield, Joseph Kofi Teye, and Collins Yeboah. 2016. "Gains and Losses from Internal Migration: Evidence from Migrant-Sending Households in Ghana." Migrating Out of Poverty Research Programme Consortium Working Paper No. 44. Brighton, UK: University of Sussex.

Awumbila, Mariama, Joseph Kofi Teye and Joseph Awetori Yaro. 2016. "Of Silent Maids, Skilled Gardeners and Careful Madams: Gendered Dynamics and Strategies of Migrant Domestic Workers in Accra, Ghana." Geojournal. doi:10.1007/s10708-016-9711-5.

Bah, Mahmoud, Salmana Cissé, Bitrina Diyamett, Gouro Diallo, Fred Lerise, David Okali, Enoch Okpara, Janice Olawoye and Cecilia Tacoli. 2003. "Changing Rural-Urban Linkages in Mali, Nigeria and Tanzania." Environment and Urbanization 15 (1): 13–24. www.ucl.ac.uk/dpu-projects/drivers_urb_change/urb_economy/pdf_Urban_Rural/IIED_Bah_Mali.pdf.

Barkan, Joel. 2012. "Ethnic Fractualization and the Propensity for Conflict in Uganda, Kenya and Tanzania." In On the Fault Lines: Managing Tensions and Divisions within Societies, edited by Jeffrey Herbst, Terence McNamee and Greg Mills. London, UK: Profile Books.

Benergee, Biswajit. 1983. "The Role of the Informal Sector in the Migration Process: A Test of Probabilistic Migration Models and Labour Market Segmentation for India." Oxford Economic Papers 35 (3): 399–422.

Black, Richard, Jonathon Crush, Sally Peberdy, Savina Ammassari, Lyndsay McLean-Hilker, Shannon Mouillesseaux, Claire Pooley and Rahda Rajkotia. 2006. "Migration and Development in Africa: An Overview." African Migration and Development Series No. 1. South African Migration Project. Cape Town, South Africa: Institute for Democracy in South Africa.

Cannon, Terry. 2008. "Vulnerability, 'Innocent' Disasters and the Imperative of Cultural Understanding." Disaster Prevention and Management 17 (3): 350–357.

Castaldo, Adriana, Priya Deshingkar and Andy McKay. 2012. "Internal Migration Remittances and Poverty." Migrating Out of Poverty Research Programme Consortium Working Paper No. 7. Brighton, UK: University of Sussex.

Chen, Martha. 2006. "Rethinking the Informal Economy: Linkages with the Formal Economy and the Formal Regulatory Environment, in Guha-Khasnobi." In Unlocking Human Potential: Concepts and Policies for Linking the Informal and Formal Sectors, edited by Basudeb Guha-Khasnobis, Ravi Kanbur and Elinor Ostrom. Oxford, UK: Oxford University Press.

Collier, Paul and Anthony J. Venables. 2013. "Housing and Urbanization in Africa: Unleashing a Formal Market Process." Centre for the Study of African Economies Working Paper Series No. 2013-01. Oxford, UK: University of Oxford. www.csae.ox.ac.uk/workingpapers/pdfs/csae-wps-2013-01.pdf.

Donner, William and Havidán Rodríguez. 2008. "Population Composition, Migration, and Inequality: The Influence of Demographic Changes on Disaster Risk and Vulnerability." Social Forces 87 (2): 1089–1114.

Gaillard, J. C., Ben Wisner, Djillali Benouar, Terry Cannon and Laurence Creton-Cazanave. 2010. "Alternatives for Sustained Disaster Risk Reduction." *Human Geography* 3 (1): 66–88. http://scholars.wlu.ca/cgi/viewcontent.cgi?article=1015&context=geog_faculty.

Government Office for Science. 2011. *Foresight: Migration and Global Environmental Change Final Project Report*. London, UK. www.gov.uk/government/uploads/system/uploads/attachment_data/file/287717/11-1116-migration-and-global-environmental-change.pdf.

Greiner, Clemens and Patrick Sakdapolrak. 2012. "Rural-Urban Migration, Agrarian Change, and the Environment in Kenya: A Critical Review of the Literature." *Population and Environment* 34 (4): 524–553. doi:10.1007/s11111-012-0178-0.

Hoang, Xuan Thanh, Tuan Anh Truong and Thi Thu Phuong Dinh. 2013. "Urban Poverty in Vietnam: A View from Complementary Assessments." International Institute for Environment and Development Working Paper. http://pubs.iied.org/ pdfs/10633IIED.pdf.

Housing the Masses. 2010. "Final Draft Report on Community-Led Numeration of Old Fadama Community, Accra, Ghana." Unpublished report. Accra, Ghana: Housing the Masses/Peoples' Dialogue.

Hugo, Graeme. 2008. *Migration, Development and Environment*. IOM Migration Research Series No. 35. Geneva, Switzerland: IOM. http://publications.iom.int/bookstore/free/MRS_35.pdf.

Human Sciences Research Council. 2008. "Citizenship, Violence and Xenophobia in South Africa: Perceptions from South African Communities." www.hsrc.ac.za/en/research-data/ktree-doc/6253.

IOM. 2015. *World Migration Report 2015: Migrants and Cities: New Partnerships to Manage Mobility*. Geneva, Switzerland: IOM. http://publications.iom.int/system/files/wmr2015_en.pdf.

Juzwiak, Teressa, Elaine McGregor and Melissa Siegel. 2014. *Migrant and Refugee Integration in Global Cities: The Role of Cities and Businesses*. The Hague: Hague Process on Refugees and Migration. http://thehagueprocess.org/wordpress/wp-content/uploads/2014/04/MigrantRefugeeIntegrationGlobalCities.pdf.

Kapur, Selim, Hari Eswaran and Winfried E.H. Blum, eds. 2011. *Sustainable Land Management: Learning from the Past for the Future*. Berlin, Germany: Springer.

KNBS. 2010. *Kenya 2009 Population and Housing Census*. KNBS. www.knbs.or.ke/index.php?option=com_phocadownload&view=category&download=584:volume-1c-population-distribution-by-age-sex-and-administrative-units&id=109:population-and-housing-census-2009&Itemid=599.

Lumumba, Jane. 2016. "Impossible Possibilities: The Fragility and Resilience of Lagos." In *Building Resilience in Cities under Stress*, edited by Francesco Mancini and Andrea Ó Súilleabháin. New York, NY: International Peace Institute.

Martine, George, Gordon McGranahan, Mark Montgomery and Rogelio Fernández-Castilla, eds. 2008. *The New Global Frontier: Urbanization, Poverty and Environment in the 21st Century*. London, UK: Earthscan.

McGranahan, Gordon, Diana Mitlin, David Satterthwaite, Cecilia Tacoli and Ivan Turok. 2009. "Africa's Urban Transition and the Role of Regional Collaboration." Human Settlements Working Paper Series No. 5. http://pubs.iied.org/pdfs/10571IIED.pdf.

McGranahan, Gordon, Daniel Schensul and Gayatri Singh. 2016. "Inclusive Urbanization: Can the 2030 Agenda Be Delivered without It?" *Environment and Urbanization*, February 22. doi:10.1177/0956247815627522.

Montgomery, Mark. 2008. "The Demography of the Urban Transition: What We Know and Don't Know." In *The New Global Frontier: Urbanization, Poverty and Environment in the 21st Century,* edited by George Martine, Gordon McGranahan, Mark Montgomery and Rogelio Fernández-Castilla, 17–36. London, UK: Earthscan.

Muggah, Robert. 2012. *Researching the Urban Dilemma: Urbanization, Poverty and Violence.* Ottawa, ON: International Development Research Centre. www.idrc.ca/sites/default/files/sp/Images/Researching-the-Urban-Dilemma-Baseline-study.pdf.

Owusu, George. 2008. "Indigenes' and Migrants' Access to Land in Peri-urban Areas of Accra, Ghana." *International Development Planning Review* 30 (2): 177–198.

Peberdy, Sally and Natalya Dinat. 2005. "Migration and Domestic Workers: Worlds of Work, Health and Mobility in Johannesburg." South African Migration Project Migration Policy Series No. 40.

Potts, Deborah. 2008. "Recent Trends in Rural-Urban and Urban-Rural Migration in Sub-Saharan Africa: The Empirical Evidence and Implications for Understanding Urban Livelihood Insecurity." Environment, Politics and Development Working Paper Series No. 6. London, UK: Department of Geography, King's College.

———. 2012. *Whatever Happened to Africa's Rapid Urbanization?* Counterpoint Series. London, UK: Africa Research Institute.

Rigg, Jonathan, Tuan Anh Nguyen and Huong Thi Thu Luong. 2014. "The Texture of Livelihoods: Migration and Making a Living in Hanoi." *The Journal of Development Studies* 50 (3): 368–382. doi: 10.1080/00220388.2013.858130.

Sahel and West Africa Club and OECD. 2006. *The Socio-Economic and Regional Context of West African Migrations.* Paris: Sahel and West Africa Club /OECD. www.oecd.org/migration/38481393.pdf.

Tacoli, Cecilia, Gordon McGranahan and David Satterthwaite. 2014. "Urbanization, Rural-Urban Migration and Urban Poverty." World Migration Report 2015 Background Paper. Geneva, Switzerland: IOM.

UN DESA Population Division. 2014. *World Urbanization Prospects: The 2014 Revision.* UN DESA. https://esa.un.org/unpd/wup/Publications/Files/WUP2014-Report.pdf.

UNDP. 2009. *Human Development Report 2009: Overcoming Barriers: Human Mobility and Development.* New York, NY: UNDP. http://hdr.undp.org/sites/default/files/reports/269/hdr_2009_en_complete.pdf.

UNECA. 2016. *Social Cohesion in Eastern Africa.* Addis Ababa, Ethiopia: UNECA Subregional Office for East Africa. www.uneca.org/sites/default/files/PublicationFiles/social_cohesion_in_eastern_africa_fin_eng.pdf.

UN-Habitat. 2003. *The Challenge of Slums. Global Report on Human Settlements 2003.* New York, NY: UN-Habitat. http://unhabitat.org/books/the-challenge-of-slums-global-report-on-human-settlements-2003/.

———. 2010. *State of African Cities 2010: Governance, Inequalities and Urban Land Markets.* Nairobi, Kenya: UN-Habitat. www.unhabitat.org/books/state-of-african-cities-2010-governance-inequalities-and-urban-land-markets-2/.

———. 2013. *State of the World's Cities 2012/2013: Prosperity of Cities.* New York, NY: Routledge. www.unhabitat.org/books/prosperity-of-cities-state-of-the-worlds-cities-20122013/.

———. 2014. *State of African Cities 2014: Re-imagining Sustainable Urban Transitions.* Nairobi, Kenya: UN-Habitat. www.unhabitat.ord/books/state-of-african-cities-2014-re-imagining-sustainable-urban-transitions/.

UN Population Fund. 2007. *State of World Population: Unleashing the Potential of Urban Growth*. UN Population Fund. www.unfpa.org/sites/default/files/pub-pdf/695_filename_sowp2007_eng.pdf.

Van der Geest, Kees. 2011. *The Dagara Farmer at Home and Away: Migration, Environment and Development in Ghana*. Leiden, Netherlands: African Studies Centre.

World Bank. 2011. *World Development Report 2011*. Washington, DC: World Bank.

World Health Organization. 2015. *Factors That Contributed to Undetected Spread of the Ebola Virus and Impeded Rapid Containment: One Year into the Ebola Epidemic*. www.who.int/csr/disease/ebola/oneyear-report/factors/en/.

Part Four
Inclusion and Exclusion in Conflict Environments

10

Inclusion in Peacemaking:
From Moral Claim to Political Fact

Alex de Waal

There is an international norm of inclusion in peace processes and political settlements. This is recent. Twenty years ago, the participation of unarmed political parties, civil society actors and women was only a moral principle and an aspiration, disputed by political elites and questioned by conflict mediators. Today, it has become a norm of international political practice, in the sense that people in conflict-affected countries demand inclusion, the international sponsors of peace processes seek it and protagonists in conflicts tactically call upon it, occasionally to good effect. Inclusion is not law. It is still contested, but its challengers are in retreat. This chapter examines what has occurred.

Inclusion in peacemaking encompasses all of the following: people may be directly represented in peace processes or participate in those processes and their outcomes in less direct ways; and their interests may be included through representatives

of groups or through public deliberation. There is no precise definition of inclusion: it is a family-resemblance concept, part normative and part empirical, sustained by an untheorized consensus of what it should be and the work it should do. The progress of the norm of inclusion can be seen in the participation of a widening group of political and civil groups in negotiating political settlements, the standard framing of peace agreements to provide for representative government and political liberalization and the hard work that advocates of exclusion need to do to justify their positions — with one or two signal exceptions, such as refusing to deal with groups labelled as terrorists.

The norm of inclusion is part of the broader normative penetration of peace processes and post-conflict peace building. Inclusion has gained recognition and political traction through a process of deliberative democracy (see Habermas

1997), with international organizations such as the United Nations and African Union (AU) playing a leading role in constituting a global "interpretative community" (Johnstone 2007; 2011). The norm of inclusion has been adopted partly through Habermasian processes of true reasoning and strategic argumentation in the public sphere. It has also been utilized selectively and opportunistically by political protagonists, but those politicians may find that they do not remain masters of a more inclusive process for long.

Inclusion is part of the global cascade of norms that has been gathering pace since World War II. Article 25(a) of the International Covenant on Civil and Political Rights (ICCPR) of 1966 specifies the right of every citizen "to take part in the conduct of public affairs, directly or through freely chosen representatives" (UN General Assembly 1966). The principle is also manifest in African documents, notably the African Charter on Democracy, Elections and Governance of 2007 (AU 2007). For 30 years, the ICCPR was applied neither to situations of armed conflict nor to countries emerging from war. Only recently has the principle enshrined in article 25 been considered relevant to peacemaking and post-conflict political settlements, and peacemakers tend to apply it flexibly, with a "light touch" (Saul 2014). Nonetheless the active participation of a wide range of political and civil actors in a country is now generally considered good for peace, and also a foundational component for a legitimate political settlement. It is also attracting the attention of scholars of international law (May 2012; The *Jus Post Bellum* Project 2012). *Lex pacificatoria* — the law of the peacemakers and, by extension, the discretion of the negotiators and mediators to fashion their own agreement — is being challenged by the *jus post bellum*, which consists in the formulation of much less flexible international norms and principles for peace (Bell 2008). Thus far, the claim for a law of peacemaking has been made by only a few legal scholars and is far from being recognized in practice, but the direction is evident.

The norm of inclusion has grown up alongside the historically novel embrace of peace as a norm (in both senses of the word), as opposed to previous epochs' acceptance of war as a normal state of affairs and celebration of martial virtues (Howard 2000). There is a clear parallel between inclusion and accountability for war crimes: both are becoming accepted norms, despite resistance from specific quarters and over particular applications of the principle.

The first part of this chapter examines the concentric circles of inclusion: armed belligerents (among them terrorists); unarmed political actors and civil society; weak and marginal groups; and women, and how they relate to diverse and changing logics of exclusion. The second part examines the tension between pragmatic efficacy in peacemaking (in which the principal belligerents make their peace) and the legitimacy of the agreement that results (a national political settlement). The chapter then turns to different approaches to inclusion in peace processes and political settlements and to how inclusion can be envisaged in a post-democratic era of turbulent political markets, in which some important pre-democratic political principles remain, notably that loyalty takes precedence over legitimacy. The fourth section looks at methodological issues with the study of inclusion in peacemaking, and the final part reflects on the process whereby the norm of inclusion has become a political fact in a changed terrain of peacemaking in which there is no longer a meaningful separation between conflict mediation and political processes.

The Concentric Circles of Inclusion

The inclusion of actors and interests in peace processes and political settlements can be envisaged as concentric circles. At the centre are the principal belligerents: the political-military leaders who determined the course of the war and who, in prior times, would have dictated the peace to the exclusion of all others. Typically, there are just two principal parties: government and the biggest or most politically influential anti-government group. They represent themselves at the negotiating table. Surrounding them are other belligerents who are less powerful and who would previously have had no option but to accept the peace terms of the principals or face a war waged against them. They may be represented or participate indirectly. Special cases among belligerents are groups designated as terrorists: governments usually refuse to talk to them, but engaging with them or their trusted intermediaries may ultimately be unavoidable. The third circle consists of civil political parties and other organized components of civil society. The fourth circle encompasses those who are politically marginalized or neglected, who would not be included were it not for special efforts by mediators. For these outer circles, inclusion may consist of participation in public discourse or recognition of their interests within that deliberative process. Much of the literature on inclusion is concerned with women: they are represented in all four circles, but the extent and significance of their inclusion as women increases in the outer circles.

Inclusion can also be analyzed using another, complementary, lens, namely the political logic of exclusion: who has been excluded from the political process and for what reason. In this respect, it is useful to distinguish between three different kinds of ethno-political exclusion. A constituency or category of people can be excluded for instrumental reasons (because it is possible to ignore them), strategic reasons (because it is necessary to keep them away from power) or normative reasons (their political role is antithetical to an exclusivist ideology) (Roessler 2016, 63–66). For the scholar, each different logic of exclusion may generate a different causal relationship between inclusion and outcome, creating methodological and analytical problems for comparative research projects. For the practitioner, political analysis of the basis for exclusion is required if an effort at inclusion is to succeed.

Armed Political Actors

The earliest discussions of inclusion in peacemaking focused on conflicts with multiple belligerents and the question of spoilers. The terms of analysis were pragmatic and game theoretic. An influential example is Stephen Stedman's (1997) theorization of spoilers. Note that the concept of a spoiler is meaningful only in the context of a normative peace process: outside such a process, actors are only pursuing their interests and not spoiling anything. (Note also that a spoiler that causes a peace process to slow down or incorporate others may be a contributor to a more inclusive and robust outcome [Newman and Richmond 2006].) Stedman's concern is that increasing the number of political actors commensurately decreases the space for a negotiated settlement: "In recent years, there appears to have been a shift toward including all politically relevant actors at the negotiating table, turning many civil war negotiations into something resembling a national conference on politics in the country.... If international actors are interested in achieving an end to violent conflict, this trend could prove counterproductive. Including additional parties in the negotiations leads to an even smaller bargaining range and decreases the incentives for the main combatants to share power" (Stedman 1997, 891).

Quantitative research subsequently found that the larger the number of different groups of belligerents, the longer the war. David Cunningham (2006) attributed this to multiple actors holding veto powers. He posited four mechanisms whereby increasing the number of political actors in a negotiation delayed reaching an agreement, namely, as follows: a smaller bargaining range of acceptable agreements on account of the multiplicity of actors; more acute information asymmetries among the parties; each actor having incentives to hold out to get the best deal as the last signer; and shifting alliances that could prevent the emergence of stable negotiating blocs. The third section of this chapter examines how the framework of a turbulent political marketplace provides an alternative explanation for the same phenomenon.

Neither Stedman nor Cunningham deals with the issue of secrecy or transparency in negotiations, but their analyses implicitly apply to this. The more that is known publicly about the negotiating process, the more the principals are beholden to their constituencies and others exerting political influence. As well, the problems that arise with multiple negotiating parties apply all the more. This reflects the practical insight of mediators that reaching an agreement is much more feasible when negotiations are conducted in secret between two parties. Indeed, very often in a formal and open negotiating process, the underlying political pact is hammered out informally by two principals meeting face to face, without advisers and note takers, let alone a third party. (Those who advocate for more inclusive peace processes must guard against the tendency for a broader process to have an inner, exclusive core.)

Pragmatic "real politics" (see Geuss 2008), therefore, counsels caution with respect to broader inclusion in peace processes, or at least inclusion within the inner track where the elite bargain is struck.

This approach is prevalent in African-led peacemaking. The paradigmatic cases of negotiated transitions to peace and democracy in Namibia, Mozambique and South Africa in the early 1990s have been highly influential in shaping subsequent mediation practices. While international scholars tend to stress the liberal peace elements of these settlements, African mediators have focused instead on the elite processes and bargains as the precondition for transformation. Power sharing lies at the heart of this perspective, which can be defined as establishing a unity government — typically labelled inclusive — and distributing senior executive positions among the leaders of the parties to the conflict. Usually, the incumbent stays in power ad interim, bringing his rivals into the cabinet. Nic Cheeseman perceptively notes that "the power-sharing model bore a close

resemblance to the distinctive combination of inclusion and restricted competition that had underpinned the stability of the one-party state in the 1970s, and so struck a chord with the political elite in many of the continent's gerontocracies" (Cheeseman 2011, 337).

The inclusion of multiple armed groups in a peace process and a peace settlement is particularly challenging. Where there is an established state with a dominant security sector (as in South Africa in 1990) or a victorious and well-organized liberation front (as in Ethiopia in 1991), inclusion in the security sector can follow the dictates of the political leadership, tempered by considerations of professionalism. Where these preconditions do not exist, the trajectory of the security sector is different, and inclusion is likely to entail multiple parallel armed groups persisting after a peace agreement is signed, irrespective of any paper commitments to an integrated national army. This issue will be examined in the section on political markets.

Groups Designated as Terrorists

Principle and reputation are also at work in the question of with whom it is permissible to talk. Commonly, armed groups labelled as terrorists are, by the fact of that designation, rendered beyond the pale, excluded on normative grounds. Colonial and racist governments regularly, even inevitably, ended up negotiating with groups that they formerly designated as terrorist, often signing agreements that brought the latter into government. Three conspicuous examples of talking to terrorists are Namibia, South Africa and Northern Ireland (Powell 2014). Africans are particularly aware of this historic reality, as evidenced by AU positions on the issue, including, for example, the outcome statement of the AU mediators' retreat in Windhoek, Namibia — a venue that was significant because many of the country's national leaders were convicted on terrorism charges in the 1960s (AU 2015).

A study for the Rand Corporation on "how terrorist groups end" (Jones and Libicki 2008) found that "transition to the political process is the most common reason that terrorist groups end (43 percent)."[1] This was related both to the government's strategy and to the terrorists' own political goals: the more extreme the goals, the less likely they were to engage seriously in a peace process. About one-quarter of these groups — and here the authors include groups such as Namibia's South-West African People's Organization (SWAPO) and South Africa's African National Congress (ANC) — achieved their political aims and ended up in power. Note that "political process" means negotiations between adversaries and not the process of trying to enforce the legitimacy of the government in power through state building. Police and (to a much lesser level) military action was effective to end small terrorist cells operating in strong states, such as Germany's Baader Meinhof Gang.

The alternative strategy of not talking to terrorists follows its own distinct logic. The relentless killing of the leaders of armed units does not, as a general rule, lead to a reduction in violence but rather to the spread and mutation of that violence (Cockburn 2015). Targeted assassination may diminish the coherence of a political-military organization, creating a fragmented hydra-like structure and making it more difficult to bring into a political process. This may be intended to reduce its capacity to inflict sophisticated terrorist actions and may indeed accomplish that goal, but it does not resolve the armed conflict. It also threatens to make society ungovernable: eliminating more experienced leaders passes leadership to younger, angrier and less controllable people. Having embarked upon targeted killing as

policy, the counterterrorist is required to keep it up indefinitely. The Israelis call this "mowing the grass" (Dicter and Byman 2006).

Terrorist groups are rarely defeated by military action: it is usually necessary to talk to them. To be precise, it is hard to identify any insurgent group that controlled territory, practised terrorism among its other military tactics and has been defeated by the imposition of state authority, with or without international coercion, to the exclusion of any political negotiations. For a negotiated settlement to be possible, a political partner is needed. This entails shifting the basis for exclusion from normative to strategic: the terrorist group is redefined as a political threat, rather than an existential threat. The British government could, at any time, have killed the leaders of the Irish Republican Army, just as the South Africans could have killed the leaders of the ANC or SWAPO. Their choice not to do so was retrospectively vindicated. Having advanced far down the track of debarring negotiation with violent Islamist extremists and instead killing their leaders one by one, the United States, Israel and other states fighting terrorism face a familiar challenge, albeit on a global scale that has no precedent, of how they could talk politics, at some point now or in the more distant future, with a largely decapitated enemy.

Unarmed Political Actors including Civil Society and Marginal Groups

The third circle of potential negotiating participants is unarmed actors: civilian political parties, civil society organizations and businesses. These are usually excluded on instrumental grounds: if the aim is ending fighting, they can safely be ignored. Anthony Wanis-St. John (2008) writes: "An emerging consensus on the role of civil society in peace processes generally underplays the difficulties of inclusion at the negotiating table while normatively advocating for grassroots

---

1   The authors did not define "end," but specify as follows: "The end year of a terrorist group was assigned based on the earliest evidence that the group no longer existed or that the group no longer used terrorism to achieve its goals" (Jones and Libicki 2008, 5).

participation in peacebuilding. This results from two opposing needs: the need to produce negotiations that include the minimum number of factions/participants required to get agreement, and the need to create the broadest possible support among the population and political parties for a peace process" (ibid., 4).

Mediators and negotiators have grappled with these challenges, seeking formulas to square the circle. In addition to direct representation in official negotiations, ways of bringing additional political groups into the process include the following: a formal but non-binding advisory role; a role as a semi-official technical resource for negotiating teams; through creating the space for talks; through mass mobilization for peace; through localized citizen-led peace agreements; and through Track Two dialogue as the foundation for official negotiation (Inclusive Security 2013). In the Livingstone Formula, the African Union has officially recognized the need to engage civil society in peace and security issues (AU 2008). The northeast African Intergovernmental Authority on Development (IGAD) adopted a similar principle in its 2005 Khartoum Declaration, but it has taken few, if any, steps to implement this commitment (IGAD 2007).

Inclusion has been divided into short-term and long-term inclusion, the latter referring also to outcome inclusion, which takes the form of representation within the political structures established by the agreement (Suazo 2013). Mediators hope that groups excluded from immediate participation in talks will be content with provisions for democratization. There are variants on this as well, beyond the standard provision of multi-party elections, including community dialogue and consultation, decentralization of governance structures and formal processes such as referendums (Paffenholz 2014b; 2015).

Unfortunately, there is a marked tendency for the negotiated distribution of posts in a transitional unity government to be submerged during an election, when patronage politics means that those

with the biggest amounts of money to dispense can consolidate their power bases and squeeze out smaller players. The outcome is that post-agreement elections often end up consolidating dominant parties in power — the opposite of the pluralization of political representation anticipated by mediators.

Conflict resolution models have been strongly influenced by the ethnic conflict model, which was influential in the 1990s (Lake and Rothchild 1996; Sisk 2006). As theories of armed conflict and political violence have moved on (Fearon and Laitin 2000; Kalyvas 2006; Tarrow 2007; de Waal 2015), mediation practices have been slower to adjust. Often, in fact, they have not changed at all — testament perhaps to the extraordinary dogged patience of the best mediators, who remain at the coal face for decades. A fine example of this is the role that Martti Ahtisaari and Chester Crocker played in Namibia (Merikallio and Ruokanen 2015; Vukovic 2015). Persistence and patience are essential, but in different ways, according to the nature of the conflict. For old-style frozen conflicts — such as Namibia in the 1980s, for which Crocker was the mediator and Ahtisaari retained the watching brief at the United Nations until he was able to implement the peace plan — sticking to the same script may be appropriate. For conflicts in constant flux — such as Sudan today — a core formula may remain unchanged, but the tactics of engagement may need to change frequently. Some of the possibilities are explored in the third section of this chapter, which is concerned with political markets.

The group-framed theory of conflict that underlies much conflict resolution means that a group with a territorial or ethnic base has a stronger claim on recognition in a peace process and its outcome than a group without any such base. This reflects not only the fact that territory and ethnicity tend to be the basis on which violence can readily be organized, but also the supposed robustness of the constituencies represented and the relative ease with which their numbers can be enumerated. As a result, ethnic minorities can often make claims to political representation in peace processes more effectively than they can organize within democratic politics.

The business sector is an important constituency, usually neglected in formal processes but commonly exerting enormous influence outside the meeting room. In the political market framework for conflict and peacemaking, one of the central elements driving politics, including peace, is political finance (de Waal 2015). There are instances in which national and international business people have, through the conditions on which they fund the belligerents' political budgets, been the determining factor in war or peace. The political settlement in Somaliland is a positive example of this (de Waal 2015, chapter 8; Phillips 2015). However, the inclusion of the business sector in peace processes and outcomes is largely neglected in the theoretical and policy literature. Approaches to corruption that regard unregulated financial transactions between business people and politicians as, ipso facto, corrupt fail to recognize that all systems require political financing. Approaches that instead place corruption within wider political economic frameworks provide a better lens for addressing this issue (Johnston 2014).

The Inclusion of Women

A particular focus of the study of inclusion in peace processes is the representation of women. The fact that wars are run by men means that classic formulas for peace negotiations are similarly male dominated. This is such a manifest injustice, in so many ways, that the clamour for women's participation in peace processes has been particularly vibrant and persuasive. In the current literature, inclusion often refers to women's participation. Approximately half the results of a Google search for "inclusion in peace processes" and its variants are specifically concerned with women's participation. Much of the detailed study

of civil society inclusion in peace processes has been done with an emphasis on women or as a by-product of concern for women's participation.

Detailed case studies of women's participation (Paffenholz 2014b; O'Reilly, Ó Súilleabháin and Paffenholz, 2015; Mazurana and Van Leuven 2016) suggest that this meant that a greater number of issues were brought to the table, including, especially, human security issues. Women were able to push for finalization of negotiations when momentum stalled; women were able to successfully advocate for context-specific women's rights and gender equality in agreements; and the agreement reached was more likely to be implemented. Across the board, where women have been active in peace processes, the processes and outcomes are reported to be better throughout. Is this because women are more committed to peace or because women are significant actors and their inclusion therefore strengthens the process? Either way, this finding challenges the pragmatic assumption of mediating behind closed doors among the principal belligerents and poses most starkly the question of whether there is a trade-off between (short-term) efficacy and (long-term) legitimacy in these processes.

Efficacy versus Legitimacy?

The question of efficacy in securing agreement between principal belligerents, and the legitimacy of a broader political settlement, is at the heart of the mediator's dilemma. The choices are not simple, as neither efficacy nor legitimacy are simple concepts, and each depends to some degree on the other. No contemporary peace deal can work without an element of legitimacy, among both domestic populations and the international community, while no draft of a peace agreement can be considered legitimate if it is simply rejected by the belligerents.

From a normative legal perspective, Christine Bell (2014) argues in favour of the flexibility of *lex pacificatoria* over the emergent rigidities of *jus post bellum*. From a mediator's perspective, Jean Arnault (2014) worries that the constraints on the international third-party mediator entailed by emergent international norms shrink the mediation space and reduce the prospect of national ownership, so that the prospect of negotiated settlements to difficult civil wars is imperilled not only by an international reluctance to negotiate with belligerents identified as militants and terrorists, but also "by well-meaning but ill-founded prescriptions for international legitimacy" (ibid., 25).

What each is arguing for is a greater degree of discretion, dependent on the circumstances, for mediators to seek appropriate paths toward goals that, if not identical, share many family resemblances. In a situation in which the principal belligerents are ready to chart a common approach to national questions (South Africa, Guatemala and Sudan briefly after 2005), a more classic narrow approach can work. In cases in which it is imperative to find a political settlement, but one or more of the main belligerents is absent from the table, an approach that includes as wide an array of national stakeholders as possible is more workable (Afghanistan in 2001, Burundi in the 1990s and Mali after 2012). We see the logic of "two-level games" at work, in which negotiators are bargaining both with one another and with their respective constituents (Putnam 1988). But whereas most analysis of two-level games focuses on the constraint that this places on the mediator, the game can also be observed as having the reverse logic, in which the constituents press a reluctant leader toward agreement.

Stedman's criticism of how peace talks become national conferences has been noted above. One case he specifically cited was Burundi. At the time of the broadly participatory and long-winded Arusha talks, the president of Burundi was Pierre Buyoya, who describes how the most important outcome of those talks was not the agreement itself, but the exercise in civic education. The politics of the country were conducted in and around the negotiating chamber. After engaging in this process, he said, Burundi's citizenry and civil society were no longer quiescent but were active participants in the country's public life (Buyoya personal communication to the author). Indeed, following the Arusha Peace and Reconciliation Agreement for Burundi of 2000, the country became paradigmatic for life after violence and a poster child for the success of an inclusive process (Uvin 2009; Twagiramungu 2016a). Buyoya had a political interest in broadening participation to civil society groups, as he feared the ethnically sexclusivist implications of a purely majoritarian system. However, today this achievement appears fragile. The test of Buyoya's hypothesis will be whether Burundian society is able to withstand the pressures for authoritarianism and conflict unleashed by President Pierre Nkurunziza's actions to remain in power beyond the two terms stipulated in the constitution.

The mediator's own legitimacy derives from his or her success, defined minimally as stopping war. Peacemaking is by definition attempted in hard cases in which there are bitter conflicts. The hardest of these hard cases are those in which action is demanded by international strategic priorities (Afghanistan, Somalia, Mali and Syria) or humanitarian concerns (Burundi and South Sudan). These may be cases in which the mediators arrive within days of the conflict erupting (as in South Sudan in 2013) and in which there can be no reasonable expectation that the belligerents are exhausted, or have exhausted their options, or even fully measured one another up, let alone achieved a "mutually hurting stalemate" or any other form of "ripeness" (see Zartman 2001). When there is no space for agreement among principal belligerents, anchoring the legitimacy of the process in wider participation becomes not only an ethical practice but also a mechanism for pressuring belligerents. Examples of this include Burundi in 2000 and Kenya in 2008.

Peace Processes and Political Settlements

Inclusion and legitimacy also lie at the centre of political settlements. The scholarship on political settlements originates with distinctly different policy questions from those of peace processes, which are focused more on state fragility and state building, democracy and development. Political scientists and economists have defined this field. Their central question is how a society transitions from conflict and fragility to an institutionalized state that can deliver development objectives. The microprocesses that may occur during such a transition are considered a secondary detail.

Mushtaq Khan (2010) provided a key conceptualization of political settlements as elite bargains that accommodate the power interests of key players, establishing equilibrium such that sustainable institutional arrangements for governance and development are possible. This draws upon scholarship concerned with the structural conditions that enable a transformation in the political system of a country from patrimonial to institutional politics (for example, Olson 1993; North, Wallis and Weingast 2009). Political settlements, peace agreements and elite pacts are not the same thing (Laws 2012), but they are related. Each political settlement has an elite bargain at its heart. In turn, any national peace process aims at an elite bargain, at least, as a necessary condition. While scholarship on conflict resolution tends to be animated by the demand to help the mediator, the study of political settlements is concerned with the structural conditions for political-economic equilibrium. But the two fields share a focus on the formal, institutional and long-term and binding commitments. Implicitly or explicitly, a peace agreement represents a political settlement, or a stage immediately prior to such a settlement.

The concept of an inclusive political settlement has been widely adopted by policy makers, including the Department for International Development (DFID) (2005; 2010) and the World Bank (2011). While acknowledging the need for an elite bargain, leading international development institutions regard broader societal inclusion in a political settlement as a positive thing that makes for a more durable settlement (Evans 2012; Rocha Menocal 2015). Such a settlement purportedly underpins a transition from conflict or fragility to stability and growth (Ghani and Lockhart 2007).

These formulations fall short of strict adherence to the norms of liberal democracy and encompass the developmental patrimonialism of authoritarian countries, such as Ethiopia and Rwanda, that pursue strategies of broad-based economic growth (Kelsall 2013). These framings take account of centralized monarchical systems, such as Oman, and political stability founded on deals among political financiers, such as Somaliland (Phillips 2015). The World Bank's (2011) *World Development Report 2011* squares the circle by speaking of "inclusive enough" settlements.

The creation of the g7+ group of fragile states,[2] as part of the New Deal for Engagement in Fragile States, and consequent peace- and state-building goals (PSGs), represents an attempt to broaden inclusion in two respects (g7+ 2012; Organization for Economic Cooperation and Development [OECD] 2012). First, it brings the governments of fragile and conflict-affected states into the process of defining the goals and strategies for paths out of fragility and conflict. This is intended to move away from the template-based approach that was inherent in the prior, donor-driven agenda. Second, the PSGs explicitly emphasize societal inclusion (Hearn 2015). However, in many respects, the g7+ agenda appears to represent the domestication of those donor templates within fragile country policies, rather than a substantively different alternative. The g7+ governments are all

---

2 The g7+ (now numbering 20 fragile states) should not be confused with the G7 (Group of Seven advanced economies).

dependent on donor funds and, for some of them at least, references to inclusion of civil society groups are window dressing.

The notions of a peace agreement and a political settlement share another element: concern with a critical juncture or key moment of transition. These are events or periods of significant societal change that can produce distinct legacies (Berins Collier and Collier 1991), or "moments of flux when the rules of the game are being contested and rearticulated," providing an opportunity for "a transition from one equilibrium to another" (Rocha Menocal 2015, 27). This conceptualization assumes that societies are ordinarily in some kind of steady state, either functional or dysfunctional, and that the challenge is to engineer a historic shift to a new steady state that can provide sustainable democracy, development and an end to internal armed conflict.

However, critics note that most experiences of peacemaking and democratization have not led to these outcomes (Putzel and DiJohn 2012). The ideal type of a peace agreement or political settlement is a definitive and irreversible transition, giving rise to a new stable political system. There are indeed some cases that approximate this, such as several countries in southern Africa and central America in the early 1990s, but two decades on from those transitions, they now appear as a historically-specific experience (immediately following the end of the Cold War) that is hard to emulate. More characteristic today are protracted peace processes without a clear end and political settlements that are continually up for renegotiation. As we begin to loosen our grip on the idea of a fixed settlement or equilibrium and to abandon the notion that peace processes and peace outcomes are distinct, we can recognize instead that all the phenomena of concern can be classed as political processes.

The peace-building agenda has grappled with bridging the gap between ending war and building sustainably peaceful politics. The UN Secretary-General's report *No Exit Without Strategy* (UN Security Council 2001) refers to "participatory governance" and "legitimate and broad-based institutions" (ibid., paragraph 10) as requirements for this. As in other UN documents, the principle is asserted rather than demonstrated. Scholars have explored this further. Michael Doyle and Nicholas Sambanis (2006) use the term "participatory peace." Recognizing that full participatory politics are likely to be out of reach in a post-conflict country, but that the limited "sovereign" or "negative peace" of stopping war is insufficient for a sustainable peace, they instead write of "positive" or "participatory peace" as "a self-sustaining conflict resolution mechanism — the promise that future disputes will be negotiated, resolved according to constitutionally agreed procedures" (ibid., 18). The definition of participatory peace does not specify inclusion — but the choice of words is indicative. Others have elaborated on this insight, moving beyond the liberal templates to focus instead on the political processes that sustain a transition to (at best) democracy and (at least) peace. Michael Barnett (2006, 89) writes of "republican peace building" based on "deliberation, constitutionalism, and representation" and Ian Johnstone (2011, 146) of peace building as a deliberative process.

Transactional Loyalties in the Political Marketplace

Inclusion in a political marketplace can mean one of two different things. It can mean wider participation in fairer transactions of loyalty, or it can mean engagement in a public sphere that transforms the political marketplace into a legitimate state. Exclusion in a political marketplace is commonly instrumental and occasionally strategic — people are excluded because they do not have clout, and leaders are sometimes excluded because of the threat they might pose if they were brought into a power-sharing arrangement.

The historian and anthropologist Jane Guyer (2004) makes the point that perpetual uncertainty and disequilibrium are the historic norm for many societies and that we must challenge our "intellectual homing instinct" toward equilibrium, systematicity and slow directional change (ibid., 129). Alex de Waal (2014) characterizes this as "turbulence": the character of a political system that is unpredictable from one moment to the next, but retains a recognizable structure over a longer period of time (ibid., 17). The challenge of political leaders is not to steer the ship of state to a distant shore (state building, sustainable development or some such goal) but rather to remain afloat in a stormy sea (see Jackson and Rosberg 1982, 18).

This refocusing can be combined with other insights into the nature of governance, violence and politics in countries on the global margins. The study of fragile states has moved toward recognizing that non-formal political systems can work and that other forms of governance are dominant in many parts of the world. Some authors prefer the term "hybrid political orders" (Boege, Brown and Clements, 2009); others are more precise in identifying "neo-patrimonial" systems (Bratton and Van der Walle 1997). A strand of scholarship particularly strong in Africa identifies "little traditions" of governance, with strong continuities from pre-colonial times, which are manifest in the subversion of formal institutional governance to fit with enduring patronage politics and idioms of legitimacy (Schatzberg 2001; Bayart 2009). This scholarship is unanimous in challenging the implicit teleology of the institutional transition framework that underpins most of the political settlements literature.

The unpredictable, contingent and informal (non-institutional) nature of power and politics and the dominant role played by global finance come together in the concept of post-democracy (Crouch 2004). The idea that political life in developed countries is increasingly determined by the influence of major corporations has its counterpart in the concept of the political marketplace in the global margins, where we see political funds deployed to rent loyalties and political services (de Waal 2015). The implication of this analysis is that no political order is in fact settled and that political life behaves more as a turbulent market, driven by the laws of supply and demand, than as the orderly conduct of political life in accord with laws and institutions. The key concepts to understanding how such a system works are the political budget (the funds used for political purposes by any political actor), the price of loyalty (determined by market forces), the key regulatory constraints on the market (barriers to entry, means of communication and fora for dispute resolution) and the political business models and skills of the main actors. Meanwhile, the formal institutions and rules that are the concern of Western policy makers (including mediators) are subordinate to the transactional real politics of trading power and material benefits. War and peace are a continuum and forms of violence are ever-present options for political elites.

The remainder of this section is able only to sketch out what it might mean to take the political marketplace framework and apply it to conflict resolution and the challenge of inclusion.

At the outset, it must be recognized that a peace agreement, rather than being the agreed draft of a national constitution or a relational agreement that binds the parties together to work toward a common future, should be seen instead as a transactional bargain in a marketplace, good for only as long as those particular conditions in the market are present. It follows that any commitment to an institutional formula for inclusion is subject to the political interests of the key actors in the political market. For example, elections are likely to become exercises in competitive clientelism. If an institution that is functioning in a rule-bound manner is spotted, it will be found to be protected by a particular configuration of political market factors, and its bubble of integrity will be at risk of being popped when that configuration changes. Insofar as an institution continues to behave consistently when the political circumstances have changed adversely, it is not because the political actors are sticking to the rules, but because institutional habits are persisting for the time being.

The triumph of tactical factional politicking over institutionalization is particularly significant in the case of the security sector because it is so central to the possession and exercise of power. The inclusion of multiple belligerents in a peace agreement faces its toughest challenge with security arrangements, and, specifically, with the integration of combatants into a unified national security sector, along with the reform of that sector. There is a growing body of technical expertise on security sector reform that in the African context derives strongly from the southern African experience. However, these templates do not transfer readily to other contexts, in which national militaries are highly politicized with very close ties to the executive. Attempts to build unified security sectors in Somalia, South Sudan and Sudan have been total failures because the political demand for these measures has not existed (Gebrehiwot 2016; Detzner 2016). In practice, inclusion in security arrangements may also mean the continued existence of two or more parallel armies within a country.

In Sudan's 2005 Comprehensive Peace Agreement, two armies were formally recognized. The Sudan People's Liberation Army (SPLA), former rebels, reported to the head of state only in name. Within the autonomous region of southern Sudan, the SPLA was the army, and, between 2006 and 2011, southern Sudan's President Salva Kiir followed a policy of paying militia commanders to be part of an ostensibly unified SPLA, resulting in a bloated security sector that was united for only so long as the interests of the individual commanders were aligned. President Kiir spoke of a "big tent," but this was inclusion in the sense of incorporation into a single patronage network. When they were not aligned, the army split apart and civil war followed (de Waal 2014). In Chad, the national army has similarly become a mechanism for inclusive patronage, but not an effective fighting force: it is the General Directorate of Security Services for National Institutions, a de facto presidential guard personally loyal to President Idriss Déby, recruited from carefully selected groups, that serves as the effective fighting force (Debos 2016).

In a political marketplace, inclusion can be conceptualized in two ways. First, there is inclusion that works with the grain of the system. This takes the form of a more inclusive political marketplace, in which a wider range of people has greater power to set the terms of their loyalties to the regime. The second, alternative, form of inclusion — discussed below — seeks to transform the political market into a rule-bound, institutionalized public sphere.

Inclusion without transformation maintains the political marketplace, which follows a readily understandable logic based on money, competition, regulatory power and political business skills and practices. As in commercial markets, the forces of competition can drive them in one of two opposite directions. One is toward a proliferation of small firms, with low barriers to entry and exit for entrepreneurs and a free and equitable flow of market information. The other is toward a few major near monopolies, with high barriers to entry and exit, with major asymmetries in access to information and with the dominant corporations able to shape the market in their own interests. Some systems, such as the Chadian political marketplace outlined above, contain elements of both.

Understanding how a political market functions demands analyzing political financiers: those who fund politics (such as national and international businesses and security operators with dark budgets). Influencing a political marketplace means engaging with these people. On that basis, the strategic question is this: what kind of political marketplace do we want to see? The danger is that the efforts to dismantle an authoritarian or closed system will lead not to democracy, but to a deregulated and violent political marketplace, as has been seen in Libya and Syria following the Arab Spring. Or the efforts to consolidate a central authority that can deliver security and development will lead to a highly exclusive political system, as has been seen in Chad and Rwanda.

All the key actors in a political market must follow the same basic precepts of securing funds, paying for political services and allegiances and keeping options open given the pervasive uncertainty. This applies, *mutatis mutandis*, to armed actors such as militia leaders, political parties, traditional leaders, religious leaders and civil society organizations (CSOs). With CSOs, it is common for international donors to worry that their favoured organizations are, or are becoming, elitist, urban, monetized and with political aspirations. Some may even be covertly militarized. These characteristics make donors uneasy, as they seem contrary to the spirit of civil society. They are nonetheless a means for expanding political participation. An active civil society lowers the barriers to entry to the political marketplace and compels the key political business managers to respond to CSOs' demands, at least rhetorically.

International support for a centralized security sector tends to have the opposite outcome. Security cooperation for counterterrorism has been ably utilized by numerous political leaders to secure their positions and to generate a less inclusive political business structure. Development cooperation assistance for a central government can have similar impacts, though in the post–Cold War era this is rarely an explicit rationale for aid, and donors are aware of the unintended consequences of their assistance.

Peacekeeping operations and their interaction with the local armed units on the ground in their areas of operation pose particular challenges for inclusion. Peacekeepers typically operate under a status of forces agreement with a central government, but need to deal on a day-to-day basis with those actually in control of localities. An extreme case is Somalia, in which each of the African troop contributors has separately sponsored and trained a contingent of the Somali National Army drawn from the clans of that specific sector. The national army exists only in name (Yohannes and Gebreegziabher 2016). This is an inclusive militarized political market, but it is also a recipe for armed conflict should the peacekeepers withdraw.

People who live in political marketplace countries invariably understand the dynamics of their political marketplace well, although they tend to lack the vocabulary with which to describe their everyday experience of political life and are constantly required to dress their complaints, claims and aspirations in the conventional language of democracy and state building. If taken literally, this discourse is simply irrelevant to the realities they face, or else a disguise for other political business strategies better suited to those realities. However, the aspirational language of citizenship and inclusion opens up another channel for political change, namely, Habermas' notion of deliberative democracy.

The second, alternative, form of inclusion is more ambitious: it seeks to transform the political market into a rule-bound, institutionalized public sphere. The goal is that personalized loyalties should be superseded by public legitimacy: there should be a functional state in which all citizens are represented and a public sphere in which all can participate. Current international policies toward post-conflict countries tends to promote both state building and political liberalization, without a clear understanding of how the two could be made to work together.

The different types of political transaction in a deregulated or competitive political marketplace, a monopolistic political business and an institutional state match the three kinds of political communication identified by Habermas.

In a deregulated political marketplace, political communication is transactional bargaining over personal loyalty or specific political services on the basis of immediate interests. In a monopolistic political market, there is short-term transactional bargaining but also negotiation aimed at a relational contract or long-term political business partnership. This matches Habermas' "strategic argumentation." This is what is seen in authoritarian clientelistic countries. An institutionalized political system with an open public sphere characterized by civility and mutuality can be a forum for all kinds of political communication, including strategic argumentation and true reasoning.

The first policy implication that follows is that public fora for the sustained discussion of all matters of public interest should be a priority. The second implication is — crucially — that the mechanics of the political marketplace itself should be a main agenda item. Political finance and the price of loyalty should be matters for structured public debate. National and international business people and aid donors should be part of the discussion. The security sector should also be on the agenda. Solutions to the twin problems of military authoritarianism and a fragmented security sector may be remote, but they can only be brought closer by involving a wide array of people in the discussion.

Methodological Issues

In a chapter such as this, it is standard to address methodological issues first, before turning to findings and analysis. In this case, the order is reversed. The reason is that the study of the life history of a political norm is so closely bound with the historical particularities of how it arose within political practice and theorization that the empirical study of the topic tends to follow behind practitioners' accounts and lawyers' elaboration. That is how it transpired in the case of inclusion in peace processes: practice and norms came first, empirical social science second.

This section seeks to show that the empirical investigation into inclusion and peace agreements is severely constrained by the data available. It is not only that the data quality is poor, with many demonstrable errors, but also the nature of the data determines what can and cannot be investigated and concluded. This section gives two examples, one illustrating the poor quality of primary data on peace processes, and the second making the same point with regard to conflict, before examining an exemplary case of a quantitative empirical study of inclusion in peace processes.

According to a briefing paper by Inclusive Security (2013), the Darfur peace process of 2004–2006 presents "an innovative case of civil society inclusion, particularly focused on women" (ibid., 4). The paper makes reference to the Gender Expert Support Team of 15 Darfurian women who "had semi-official status and were not part of any one entity but consulted for the delegates, the AU mediation team, and other partners" (ibid.). I was a member of the mediation team and, along with other colleagues, can testify that this is at best an extremely optimistic reading of the inclusion of women, which was (despite the efforts of the chief mediator) between minimal and non-existent. Another paper makes the claim that "in the Darfur negotiations of 2009, representatives of militarized Arab groups were deliberately included in the negotiation" (Paffenholz 2014a, 15). This is also a considerable exaggeration, not least because there were no substantive negotiations at that time. In their place was a somewhat farcical process of bringing civil society groups and other stakeholders to the mediation venue in Doha, Qatar, but the groups' presence appeared to be window dressing, as they were obliged to applaud a document written by an expert team that they had not had the opportunity to read beforehand. This case is therefore better seen as an exemplar of how a performance of participation obscures an exclusive inner process.

The researchers who cite these snippets are struggling with the fact that peace processes are very poorly documented. When a peace process succeeds, mediators or participants may publish their own memoirs. These are useful but inevitably subjective. Any record of the actual proceedings remains locked away. When peace processes fail, usually no documentation at all is made public; sometimes, this is because it is not clear that the processes have failed, the parties and mediator hope that there is a chance of continuing, and they do not want to jeopardize a possible future resumption. Moreover, participants are acutely aware of the thin line between what counts as success or failure and the way that a particular episode can quickly shift from one category to the other. What counts as success is highly contextual and often can be interpreted only within the actors' anticipation of multiple possible trajectories. Hence, datasets on mediation consist of data points that are either very summary, very subjective or both. Until there are far better data for peace processes, based on much more detailed accounts of what actually happened, quantitative research will remain seriously handicapped.

A second area in which data are seriously deficient is defining what counts as conflict. The leading armed conflict database, the Uppsala Conflict Database Project (UCDP) is widely used, but contains some significant shortcomings for the purposes of identifying who are the significant political actors. The UCDP uses battlefield deaths as its threshold for defining a conflict and codes the great majority of African conflicts as internal, with a smaller number coded as internationalized internal based on the deployment of foreign troops. Note that this is a combat dataset, not a political dataset, and should be used for political analysis with caution. The dyad captured in the UCDP data is parties in lethal combat, not parties in armed political dispute. This becomes particularly problematic where political actors engage in armed conflicts covertly or by using proxies. Thus, experts who are familiar with the facts of cross-border military actions by national armies (most of which are disguised or not publicized) and the realities of political support (including arms, logistics, training, intelligence and funds) for rebels by neighbouring

states would code substantially more of Africa's internal conflicts as politically internationalized (Twagiramungu 2016b). Neighbouring states may be principal protagonists.

These observations put the question of the mediation of internal conflicts in Africa in a new light. What needs to be addressed is how to conceptualize the roles of neighbouring governments that are covertly involved directly, or are sponsors of armed groups in a conflict-affected country, but that are also involved in the peace process. Are they to be treated as belligerents, mediators or both? Thus, the question of inclusion needs to be broadened to include another circle, namely the (secret or disguised) neighbouring state belligerents. And not all of the interstate or transnational armed conflict is conducted by governments: so-called non-state actors are also actively engaged in these activities.

The upgrading of basic data points on armed conflicts is, therefore, also an absolute necessity in order for the quality of quantitative scholarly analysis to reach a standard at which it can speak sensibly to policy makers.

Researchers have nonetheless made sterling efforts to draw robust conclusions from these data. Let me examine an important case, directly relevant to the focus of this paper on inclusion in peace processes. This is the study by Desirée Nilsson (2012) on the inclusion of civil society in peace processes and its impacts. She finds civil society involvement in about one-third of peace accords since the end of the Cold War. Taking account of all the usual confounding variables and selection effects, she finds a clear positive correlation between civil society inclusion, the success of peace processes and the robustness of the peace agreements reached (measured by the inverse of the probability of return to conflict). This is, of course, correlation, not cause, though attention to other possible competing causes makes the claimed causal relationship much more plausible. Nilsson does not claim that inclusion is the major determinant of these outcomes, only that it is a statistically significant factor. (Other key factors include the power-sharing provisions of an agreement, number of warring parties, the intensity of the conflict and the presence of peacekeeping forces.) She finds no indication of the negative impacts that would have been predicted by Stedman or Cunningham.

Nilsson is fully transparent with her methods and suitably cautious in expressing her findings. A brief examination of her method underscores the problem examined above, namely, the enormous problem of finding accurate data points.

As with almost every other scholar, she relies on the UCDP dataset for identifying conflicts and conflict actors. As noted, this is problematic. In the absence of good granular data for the nature and extent of civil society participation, Nilsson is obliged to use a proxy: "Civil society actors are considered to be included in a peace agreement when they, based on the text of the peace agreement, are given a role in drafting the agreement, or the accord stipulates that they are to participate in the subsequent peace process" (ibid., 252).

This does not capture the multiple types of engagement revealed in qualitative studies. It is arguably less a measure of actual participation than of the participants' deference to the norm of inclusion in the drafting of their final text.

Nilsson's conclusion is that "the inclusion of civil society in peace accords can serve to enhance legitimacy of the peace process, which, in turn, would likely enhance the prospects for peace" (ibid., 259). However, as the next section explores, this conclusion is normative and conceptual first, and empirical second.

Conclusion: From Moral Aspiration to Political Fact

The key term linking inclusion and peace outcomes in Nilsson's conclusion is legitimacy. She does not measure legitimacy, but rather infers it. Her conclusion is a fine example of how an aspirational norm can become a political reality, how a moral claim moves toward becoming positive law (it has not yet arrived and may, of course, never do so). This becomes evident by examining what is actually meant by the terms "inclusion" and "legitimacy."

The inclusion of people requires that they participate meaningfully in a political process or are satisfied that their interests are represented in political deliberation. Legitimacy is famously hard to define. However, all liberal political theories identify governmental legitimacy with the voluntary consent of the governed, which — in the contemporary world — is a product of inclusion in this sense. Thus, insofar as inclusion is said to cause legitimacy, there is a risk of making a circular argument.

This near-tautology is not, however, a trivial finding. Let us refer back to the caveat in the definition of legitimacy: legitimacy through inclusion is a feature of the contemporary world. It was not always thus: in previous centuries, legitimacy could be gained by might, charisma or religious status. One thing that has changed is that instrumental exclusion is now contrary to the norm, implying that the salient forms of exclusion today are strategic and normative. Also, in subaltern concepts of political legitimacy (such as those in hybrid political orders), there are alternative sources of legitimacy. Lastly, there are contours and limits to inclusion, which can be explored by investigating who is excluded and why. The interesting and non-trivial fact is that inclusion has become nearly synonymous with legitimacy. The democratic and consultative variant of legitimacy has prevailed over the others: it is now hegemonic. Politicians who oppose inclusion must nonetheless pay lip service to it, the tribute that political vice pays to the dominant norm.

In a purely transactional political marketplace, there is no public realm, no pure reasoning and, indeed, no public as such. Norms would therefore have no traction. There are, fortunately, no such perfect marketplaces devoid of any public sphere. The demand for individual rights and public goods arises both from people and from international public discourse.

In the context of peace negotiations, the hegemony of the inclusivity norm simply overrides the tensions between efficacy and legitimacy that have so preoccupied practitioners of mediation. One reason for this is the international norm escalator — the general adoption and uptake of principles of human rights and democracy (Pinker 2011). This does not make empirical research redundant, but instead requires the reformulation of research questions, making them more granular. For example: is it the case that instrumental exclusion is now diminishing, and strategic and normative exclusion are taking new forms? And, if so, what challenges do these pose?

A second reason is the changed circumstances of peace negotiations; mediators are intervening in conflicts in which the principal belligerents are unready to make peace, and the mediators, therefore, need to find other sources of leverage, including broadening participation in peace talks. Peace processes have become seamless with wider political processes, involving both the conflict-affected societies and international engagement with those societies. With the political process as the organizing framework, the perspective can shift from no-longer-tenable distinctions between process and outcome, between negotiation and settlement, and, indeed, in many circumstances, between conflict and post-conflict. Inclusive political processes can become a forum for public deliberative democracy. When these have been tried, for example, in the national conventions of many francophone African countries in the early 1990s, in the conferences that established peace and order in Somaliland, in the Burundi talks in Arusha or in the public consultations of the African Union High Level Panel on Darfur in 2009, the results have exceeded expectations.

Rather than being posed in competition to one another, efficacy and legitimacy should instead be seen in a synergistic relationship. Both are hegemonic norms, both are constituted by historical conjuncture and, most of the time, they overlap or reinforce each other. On other occasions, they are in tension. Both are changing and contested, but there is — at least, in the historical present — a clear direction to that change: efficacy and inclusion are drawing together. The norm of inclusion has become a political reality that has its own impacts. Inclusion is now unavoidable. One challenge is for scholars: to focus on the granularity of inclusion and unpick the ways in which different reasons and strategies for inclusivity operate. Another challenge is for practitioners: how best to turn a general political fact into the real politics of a workable peace. This agenda can be advanced in the difficult cases of political marketplace countries by a process of inclusive deliberative democracy, in which the agenda for public debate includes the functioning of the political marketplace in the country concerned.

Author's Note

This chapter has benefited from comments and contributions from Pamela Aall, Bridget Conley-Zilkic, Sophia Dawkins, Sarah Detzner, Mulugeta Gebrehiwot, Sarah Nouwen and Ian Johnstone.

Works Cited

AU. 2007. *African Charter on Democracy, Elections and Governance.* January 30.

———. 2008. "Conclusions on a Mechanism for Interaction between the Peace and Security Council and Civil Society Organizations in the Promotion of Peace, Security and Stability in Africa." Addis Ababa, Ethiopia: AU.

———. 2015. "Silencing the Guns: Terrorism, Mediation and Non-state Armed Groups: A report on the proceedings of the Sixth African Union High-level Retreat of Special Envoys and Mediators on the Promotion of Peace, Security and Stability in Africa, held on 21-22 October 2015 in Windhoek, Namibia." AU Commission.

Arnault, Jean. 2014. "Legitimacy and Peace Processes: International Norms and Local Realities." *Accord* 25: 21–25.

Barnett, Michael. 2006. "Building a Republican Peace: Stabilizing States after War." *International Security* 30 (4): 87–112.

Bayart, Jean-François. 2009. *The State in Africa: The Politics of the Belly.* London, UK: Polity.

Bell, Christine. 2008. *On the Law of Peace: Peace Agreements and the Lex Pacificatoria.* Oxford, UK: Oxford University Press.

———. 2014. "Of Jus Post Bellum and Lex Pacificatoria: What's in a Name?" In *Jus Post Bellum: Mapping the Normative Foundations*, edited by Carsten Stahn, Jennifer Easterday and Jens Iverson, 181–206. Oxford, UK: Oxford University Press.

Berins Collier, Ruth and David Collier. 1991. *Shaping the Political Arena: Critical Junctures, the Labor Movement, and Regime Dynamics in Latin America.* Notre Dame, IN: University of Notre Dame Press.

Boege, Volker, Anne Brown and Kevin Clements. 2009. "Hybrid Political Orders, Not Fragile States." *Peace Review* 21 (1): 13–21.

Bratton, Michael and Nicolas van de Walle. 1997. *Democratic Experiments in Africa: Regime Transitions in Comparative Perspective.* Cambridge, UK: Cambridge University Press.

Cheeseman, Nic. 2011. "The Internal Dynamics of Power-sharing in Africa." *Democratization* 18 (2): 336–65.

Cockburn, Andrew. 2015. *Kill Chain: The Rise of the High-Tech Assassins.* New York, NY: Henry Holt & Co.

Crouch, Colin. 2004. *Post-Democracy.* Cambridge, UK: Polity.

Cunningham, David. 2006. "Veto Players and Civil War Duration." *American Journal of Political Science* 50 (4): 875–892.

Debos, Marielle. 2016. *Living by the Gun in Chad: Combatants, Impunity and State Formation.* London, UK: Zed Books.

Detzner, Sarah. 2016. *The Evolution of Post-conflict Security Sector Reform in Africa.* World Peace Foundation, African Peace Missions Program.

de Waal, Alex. 2014. "When Kleptocracy Becomes Insolvent: The Brute Causes of the Civil War in South Sudan." *African Affairs* 113 (452): 347–369.

———. 2015. *The Real Politics of the Horn of Africa: Money, War and the Business of Power.* Cambridge, UK: Polity.

DFID. 2005. *Reducing Poverty by Tackling Exclusion.* London, UK: DFID.

———. 2010. *Building Peaceful States and Societies: A DFID Practice Paper.* London, UK: DFID.

Dicter, Avi and Daniel Byman. 2006. "Israel's Lessons for Fighting Terrorists and Their Implications for the United States." Saban Centre for Middle East Policy at the Brookings Institution Analysis Paper No. 8.

Doyle, Michael and Nicholas Sambanis. 2006. *Making War and Building Peace.* Princeton, NJ: Princeton University Press.

Evans, William. 2012. "A Review of the Evidence Informing DFID's 'Building Peaceful States and Societies: A DFID Practice Paper.'" London, UK: DFID.

Fearon, James D. and David D. Laitin. 2000. "Violence and the Social Construction of Ethnic Identity." *International Organization* 54 (4): 845–877.

g7+. 2012. "Introducing the g7+: Goodbye Conflict, Welcome Development." http://g7plus.org/sites/default/files/resources/Intoduction-of-g7%2B-Brochure.pdf.

Gebrehiwot, Mulugeta. 2016. "The Ethiopian Post-Transition SSR Experience: Building a National Army from a Revolutionary Democratic Army." World Peace Foundation, African Peace Missions Program.

Geuss, Raymond, 2008. *Philosophy and Real Politics*. Princeton, NJ: Princeton University Press.

Ghani, Ashraf and Clare Lockhart. 2007. "Writing the History of the Future: Securing Stability through Peace Agreements." *Journal of Intervention and State-building* 1 (3): 275–306.

Guyer, Jane. 2004. *Marginal Gains: Monetary Transactions in Atlantic Africa*. Chicago, IL: University of Chicago Press.

Habermas, Jürgen. 1997. *Between Facts and Norms: Contributions to a Discourse Theory of Law and Democracy*. Translated by William Rehg. Cambridge, UK: Polity.

Hearn, Sarah. 2015. "Independent Review of the New Deal for Engagement in Fragile States." New York, NY: New York University Center on International Cooperation.

Hickey, Samuel. 2013. "Thinking about the Politics of Inclusive Development: Towards a Relational Approach." Effective States and Inclusive Development Research Centre Working Paper No. 1.

Howard, Michael. 2000. *The Invention of Peace: Reflections on War and International Order*. New Haven, CT: Yale University Press.

IGAD. 2007. *Towards the IGAD Peace and Security Strategy: The Khartoum Launching Conference*, 1-3 October 2005. Djibouti: IGAD.

Inclusive Security. 2013. "Nine Models for Inclusion of Civil Society in Peace Processes." Washington, DC: Inclusive Security.

Jackson, Robert and Carl Rosberg. 1982. *Personal Rule in Black Africa: Prince, Autocrat, Prophet, Tyrant*. Berkeley, CA: University of California Press.

Johnston, Michael. 2014. *Corruption, Contention and Reform: The Power of Deep Democratization*. Cambridge, UK: Cambridge University Press.

Johnstone, Ian. 2007. "Consolidating Peace: Priorities and Deliberative Processes." *Annual Review of Global Peace Operations* 2007: 13–28.

———. 2011. *The Power of Deliberation: International Law, Politics and Organizations*. New York, NY: Oxford University Press.

Jones, Seth and Martin Libicki. 2008. *How Terrorists Groups End: Lessons for Countering al Qa'ida*. Washington, DC: Rand Corporation.

The *Jus Post Bellum* Project. 2012. *Jus — Post — Bellum: Mapping the Normative Foundations, 31 May – 1 June 2012 Conference Report*. Leiden, Netherlands: Grotius Centre for International Legal Studies.

Kalyvas, Stathis. 2006. *The Logic of Violence in Civil War*. Cambridge, UK: Cambridge University Press.

Kelsall, Tim. 2013. *Business, Politics and the State in Africa: Challenging Orthodoxies on Growth and Transformation*. London, UK: Zed Books.

Khan, Mushtaq. 2010. "Political Settlements and the Governance of Growth-enhancing Institutions." London, UK: DFID.

Lake, David and Donald Rothchild. 1996. "Containing Fear: The Origins and Management of Ethnic Conflict." *International Organization* 21 (2): 41–75.

Laws, Edward. 2012. "Political Settlements, Elite Pacts and Governments of National Unity — A Conceptual Study." University of Birmingham Developmental Leadership Programme Concept Brief No. 1.

May, Larry. 2012. *After War Ends: A Philosophical Perspective.* Cambridge, UK: Cambridge University Press.

Mazurana, Dyan and Dallin Van Leuven. 2016. "Protection of Civilians from Sexual and Gender-Based Violence (SGBV): Insights for African Union Peace Missions." Somerville, MA: World Peace Foundation.

Merikallio, Katri and Tapani Ruokanen. 2015. *The Mediator: A Biography of Martti Ahtisaari.* Translated from the Finnish by David Mitchell and Pamela Kaskinen. London, UK: Hurst Publishers.

Newman, Edward and Oliver Richmond. 2006. "Peace-building and Spoilers." *Conflict, Security and Development* 6 (1): 101–110.

Nilsson, Desirée. 2012. "Anchoring the Peace: Civil Society Actors in Peace Accords and Durable Peace." *International Interactions* 38 (2): 243–266.

North, Douglass, John Joseph Wallis and Barry R. Weingast. 2009. *Violence and Social Orders: A Conceptual Framework for Interpreting Recorded Human History.* Cambridge, UK: Cambridge University Press.

OECD. 2012. "Building Blocks to Prosperity: The Peacebuilding and Statebuilding goals (PSGs)." Paris, France: OECD.

Olson, Mancur. 1993. "Dictatorship, Democracy and Development." *American Political Science Review* 97 (3): 567–576.

O'Reilly, Marie, Andrea Ó Súilleabháin and Thania Paffenholz. 2015. *Reimagining Peacemaking: Women's Roles in Peace Processes.* New York, NY: International Peace Institute.

Paffenholz, Thania. 2014a. "Civil Society and Peace Negotiations: Beyond the Inclusion-Exclusion Dichotomy." *Negotiation Journal,* January: 69–91.

———. 2014b. "Mediation Practice Series, June 2014, Broadening Participation in Peace Processes: Dilemmas and Options for Mediators." Geneva, Switzerland: Centre for Humanitarian Dialogue.

———. 2015. "Inclusivity in Peace Processes." UN University, Centre for Policy Research Briefing Paper for the UN High-Level Review Panel.

Phillips, Sarah. 2015. "Two Remarkable Transitions: Lessons from Oman and Somaliland." University of Birmingham, Developmental Leadership Program. www.dlprog.org/opinions/two-remarkable-transitions-lessons-from-oman-and-somaliland.php.

Pinker, Steven. 2011. *The Better Angels of Our Nature: Why Violence has Declined.* New York, NY: Penguin Books.

Powell, Jonathan. 2014. *Talking to Terrorists: How to End Armed Conflicts.* Oxford, UK: Bodley Head.

Putnam, Robert D. 1988. "Diplomacy and Domestic Politics: The Logic of Two-level Games." *International Organization* 42 (3): 427–460.

Putzel, James and Jonathan DiJohn. 2012. *Meeting the Challenges of Crisis States.* London, UK: Crisis States Research Centre at the London School of Economics and Political Science.

Rocha Menocal, A. 2015. "Political Settlements and the Politics of Inclusion." University of Birmingham, Developmental Leadership Program State of the Art Paper No. 7.

Roessler, Philip. 2016. *Ethnic Politics and State Power in Africa: The Logic of the Coup-Civil War Trap*. Cambridge, UK: Cambridge University Press.

Saul, Matthew. 2014. "Creating Popular Governments in Post-Conflict Situations: The Role of International Law." In *Jus Post Bellum: Mapping the Normative Foundations*, edited by Carsten Stahn, Jennifer Easterday and Jens Iverson, 447–466. Oxford, UK: Oxford University Press.

Schatzberg, Michael. 2001. *Political Legitimacy in Middle Africa: Father, Family, Food*. Bloomington, IN: Indiana University Press.

Sisk, Timothy. 2006. *Power-sharing and International Mediation in Ethnic Conflicts*. Washington, DC: Carnegie Corporation.

Stedman, Stephen J. 1997. "Spoiler Problems in Peace Processes." *International Security* 22 (2): 5–53.

Suazo, Adan E. 2013. "Tools of Change: Long-term Inclusion in Peace Processes." *Praxis: The Fletcher Journal of Human Security* 28: 5–27.

Tarrow, Sidney. 2007. "Inside Insurgencies: Politics and Violence in an Age of Civil War." *Perspectives on Politics* 5 (3): 587–699.

Twagiramungu, Noel. 2016a. "Burundi: The Anatomy of Mass Violence Endgames." In *How Mass Atrocities End: Case Studies from Guatemala, Burundi, Indonesia, the Sudans, Bosnia-Hercegovina and Iraq*, edited by Bridget Conley-Zilkic, 56–82. Cambridge, UK: Cambridge University Press.

———. 2016b. "Transnational Armed Politics in Africa: A Synthesis Report." World Peace Foundation, African Peace Missions Program.

UN General Assembly. 1966. *International Covenant on Civil and Political Rights*. December 16, 999 UNTS 171.

UN Security Council. 2001. *No Exit without Strategy: Security Council Decision-making and the Closure or Transition of Peacekeeping Operations*. Report of the UN Secretary-General to the Security Council. April 20, S/2001/394.

Uvin, Peter. 2009. *Life after Violence: A People's Story of Burundi*. London, UK: Zed Books.

Vukovic, Sinisa. 2015. *International Multiparty Mediation and Conflict Management: Challenges of Cooperation and Coordination*. Abingdon-on-Thames, UK: Routledge.

Wanis-St. John, Anthony. 2008. "Peace Processes, Secret Negotiations and Civil Society: Dynamics of Inclusion and Exclusion." *International Negotiation* 13: 1–9.

World Bank. 2011. *World Development Report 2011: Conflict, Security and Development*. Washington, DC: World Bank.

Yohannes, Dawit and Daniel Gebreegziabher. 2016. "AMISOM: Charting a New Course for AU Peace Missions." World Peace Foundation Summary Paper No. 6 from the Program on African Peace Missions.

Zartman, I William. 2001. "The Timing of Peace Initiatives: Hurting Stalemates and Ripe Moments." *Global Review of Ethnopolitics* 1 (1): 8–18.

11

What Is the Role of Civil Society in Confronting Africa's Political and Security Challenges?

Gilles Olakunlé Yabi

The role of civil society in conflict prevention and resolution in Africa is widely recognized, with numerous examples cited each year (CIVICUS 2015). Since the beginning of the 1990s, the armed conflicts and violent political crises that have destabilized numerous countries of central and west Africa have triggered the emergence of civil societies with more or less clearly defined contours and with highly variable degrees of organization and independence from political organizations.

In certain cases, civil society organizations have directly participated in peace negotiations alongside political and military parties to the conflict (Wairimu Nderitu 2016). In others, such organizations have spoken out at key junctures to demand that political actors and armed groups consider the general interest of the civilian populations who have suffered the most from the normalization of violence and the collapse of states and economies.

These mobilizations have taken many different forms from country to country and have helped shape the political, economic and social evolution of Sub-Saharan Africa over the last 20 years. Based on an analysis of the major political, security and social dynamics at play in several African countries, this chapter shows that the degree to which a given context is conducive to the construction of a strong, practical and independent civil society is closely linked to the history of the country, the vigour of its economic, social and cultural transformations, and the influence of international actors.

This chapter will offer a somewhat personal perspective on the challenge of creating spaces in which African civil societies can aspire to effect change commensurate with the demands of the populations they serve. It invites international partners to adopt a nuanced and realistic vision of African civil society as a mirror of the diversity of multicultural African countries and societies, rather than acting as if capacity building for civil society were antithetical to the consolidation of state legitimacy and efficacy. Strategies and methods for offering international support to civil societies in countries governed by authoritarian regimes must be particularly subtle; efforts must be made not to weaken the legitimacy of internal actors working for change on behalf of their national communities.

Civil Society in the New African States

Most of the armed conflicts and other situations of insecurity occurring on the African continent are tied to political crises taking place in the upper echelons of power. These crises have generally taken shape during periods of flux, as various forces wrangled to bring about regime change or defend the regime in power.

Violence and threats would seem to be among the most effective tactics for gaining or holding on to political power and thereby controlling important economic resources (Gilpin 2016; Fomunyoh 2016; Reno 2016).

The insecurity prevailing in many regions of the continent is due in large part to conflicts between political figures, whose supporters often fall into rival camps based on their common membership in an ethnic, regional or, more rarely, religious group. This layering of politics atop ethnic or regional allegiances transforms power struggles between figures with narrow, perfectly identifiable interests into national conflicts pitting large factions against each other (Olonisakin 2016). The resulting dynamic has jeopardized the peace and cohesion

of societies in Kenya (2007), Côte d'Ivoire (2010-2011), Central African Republic (2013–2015), South Sudan (2014-2015) and Burundi (2015-2016). Outbreaks or threats of violence before, during and after elections confirm the political nature of many conflicts (Bekoe 2012).

To understand the violent conflicts raging in Africa, one must identify the central actors involved, their personal interests, the interests of the groups who rely on them and on whom they rely, their strategies and tactics and the political, economic, social and cultural context in which they are deployed. Violent conflicts and major crises erupt when actors and groups with conflicting interests are able to mobilize the human, political and financial resources necessary to stage armed confrontations in local or national contexts, or even in regional and international contexts where circumstances are conducive. While the moves made by the actors and the timing of the events leading to a breach of the peace may be highly circumstantial, the context is inevitably the result of structural factors and a specific history.

What African countries share most clearly is the recent and unfinished nature of their political, economic, social and cultural institutions. It may seem tedious and pointless to harp on the fledgling nature of autonomous African states within their current borders and the peculiar historical conditions that gave birth to these states. Yet, these historical facts are essential to understanding the dynamics of peace and conflict throughout the continent. Building legitimate, organized states that can guarantee the security and gain the confidence of the people living in the geographical area under their responsibilities is by far the most vital challenge facing the continent. Africa's political systems are not yet stabilized; its societies, with their immense cultural diversity, have had great difficulty adopting a common vision of the principles and values on which to build political organizations that all subgroups of the population can perceive as legitimate (Bates 2008; Olonisakin 2016).

The fragile institutional setting for these struggles over power, land and natural resources — some of them brutal, others less so — is the same setting in which the actors and organizations of civil society operate. This civil society is, in fact, indefinable, given the great variety of its leaders' motivations, its modes of organization, its methods and its degree of reliance on local political actors or foreign donors, Western or otherwise (Srinivasan 2016; Wairimu Nderitu 2016). Just as the historical circumstances attending the formation of African states have influenced their political trajectories for six decades, these circumstances have also given rise to notable variations in the observable characteristics of civil societies from one country to another (Bayart 1986).

African civil societies include organized groups of actors who have, in many cases, played decisive roles in the political struggles and major developments taking place in their countries since the end of the colonial era and the early years of independence. Prominent among these groups are the labour unions, formed at a time when public administrations were becoming the employer of choice for elites emerging from the colonial educational system. The unions and their umbrella organizations played an active part in political and social movements in the era of independence, and many leaders of newly independent states got their start in the union movement before leading political parties (Fall 2006). Due to its particular genesis, this largely urban sector of civil society, dominated to a great extent by the bureaucratic class, remains close to political power in the literal sense of the word. Along with the political elites, it forms the substance of the post-colonial states.

The proximity of unions to the political sphere has manifested itself at times as an objective alliance with the powers that be, at other times, as a conflict with governments over remuneration and, at still other times, as vigorous opposition to regimes deemed authoritarian or incapable of governing satisfactorily. Elsewhere on the continent, the labour movements retained significant influence over authorities who, though perhaps unable to deliver an exceptional performance in terms of governance, at least, managed to keep the public service running and preserve social stability in the cities. Public service strikes are a much greater concern to governments than are opposition demonstrations. In French-speaking west Africa, for example, perennial teachers' strikes have, in general, succeeded in exacting significant concessions from governments. In Guinea, a series of general strikes declared by the trade union federations led to popular protests in 2006-2007 against the excesses and incompetence of the regime of the late President Lansana Conté.

While the unions and other professional organizations have extended their influence beyond the public sector, actors and groups deriving their strength from traditional legitimacy continue to wield powerful influence over rural populations and over social classes less supportive of the dominant elites. One thinks of the vastly differing political forms taken by traditional chiefdoms from one country to another — and even within a single country — or of the majority religious authorities in each country, which still exert decisive influence over the minds, behaviour and representations of good social and political organizations and, thus, over the activities of many people (Bayart 1986; International Crisis Group 2013).

Youth and women's organizations have likewise structured themselves as active components of civil society in many countries in order to convey specific demands to the authorities or, conversely, to act as mouthpieces for government policy to the public at large. In every country ruled now or in the past by single-party or quasi-single-party systems, women's and youth organizations — whether fully integrated into the party apparatus or not — have been integral to the mechanisms whereby governments held on to power. Before the tide of political and economic liberalization swept over Africa, with the emergence of an international civil society bolstered by outside financing, local civil societies generally enjoyed very limited room in which to act independently of the political sphere.

In the 1990s, civil society organizations, often under the banner of non-governmental organizations (NGOs), underwent rapid growth in a climate in which state power was sapped by serious budget crises and heavy reliance on international or bilateral financial aid (Lewis 2002; Thiriot 2002). Budgetary crises, along with stabilization and structural adjustment programs overseen by the International Monetary Fund and the World Bank, considerably reduced the capacity of states and political authorities to control and regulate the public arena. The result was that individual initiatives came to be geared toward the founding of NGOs in domains of activity left to their own devices by the state.

The Spectacular Rise of NGOs

With the democratization process encouraged by Western powers and wealthy international organizations came increasing economic interest on the part of certain African elites in the establishment and operation of local civil society organizations. It was a period of widespread dissatisfaction with states being accused of having failed to deliver on their promises of public security, let alone economic and social development. After the fall of the Berlin Wall, the dominant international ideology harboured a dim view of what African governments could contribute to improving the welfare of society.

Two strong trends emerged: the promotion of private sector development as an alternative to the economic role of the state; and the promotion of a new sector of activity revolving around NGOs in fields as varied as health, education, access to water, rural development, women's empowerment, human rights and democracy. The role of elite leadership and the public service would be handed off to entrepreneurs in a position to create wealth and employment within the framework of

liberalized economies and also to citizens who, no longer under the thumb of authoritarian or overly intrusive governments, could organize themselves to produce public goods independently of the state.

What actually happened was that a portion of the political class members migrated into civil society, pursuing their economic survival by adapting to the new economic and political circumstances. After all, a person seen to be investing in the creation of civil society organizations that work for the people of a given locality can, by this means, effectively acquire a positive public image, which can then be converted into political influence at the local or national level. Moreover, the trend toward periodic multi-party elections gave impetus to the creation of a civil society inhabited by figures motivated by political self-interest, rather than selfless service.

The formally democratic political context that is now the norm in Sub-Saharan Africa has also fostered the emergence and entrenchment of civil society organizations dedicated to citizenship education, awareness raising around electoral issues, prevention of election-related violence and independent observation and monitoring of the electoral process (CIVICUS 2015). The spread of democracies governed by four- or five-year electoral timetables has thus led to new spheres of activity for civil society actors. The importance placed by Africa's traditional economic partners (the former colonial powers, the European Union and the United States) on "free and transparent" elections as the ultimate benchmark of a healthy democracy has resulted in substantial external funding of electoral processes.

Civil society organizations have found their place among the recipients of these resources and have used them to conduct a wide array of election-related activities. One, in particular, is the practice of election observation by coalitions of civil society organizations working side by side with African or international observer missions (from the African Union, the Economic Community of West African States or the European Union).

While the experience has been a mixed success and the capacities, independence and determination of these civil society elements vary greatly between countries, these initiatives have often been crucial to reining in electoral irregularities and preventing or halting post-election violence (Bekoe 2012; Wairimu Nderitu 2016).

This, unfortunately, was not the recent experience in Côte d'Ivoire. The efforts of civil society in that country were insufficient to prevent the descent of a tense presidential election into a predictable armed conflict, in large part because many civil society actors were themselves politicized, partisan or too poorly organized and equipped to influence the political figures battling for power. In highly polarized political contexts, and especially where politicians base much of their electoral strategy on the manipulation of ethnic, regional and religious identities, civil society is often drawn into the fray.

In Guinea (from 2006 to 2010), civil society — spearheaded by trade union federations and a coalition of NGOs, working alongside a portion of the political class — played a crucial role in the mass mobilization for change. This coalition was unable to prevent a military junta from taking power in December 2008, but nonetheless managed to thwart the junta's ambitions and create the conditions for the election of a civilian president in December 2010. Even so, the major actors of Guinean civil society could not shake the popular suspicion of being in cahoots with one or another of the actors or political parties, which are, in turn, generally associated with the country's major ethnocultural groups (with Mandinka, Fula and Susu being the most dominant).

With each electoral contest, tensions within Guinean society have been revived; the political rivalry has systematically been perceived as a rivalry between the communities with which the president and his main opponent identify. Although officially non-partisan, many civil society figures were tainted with the suspicion of acting in the interests of the political parties associated with their own ethnic groups.

In its broadest sense, civil society encompasses the vast majority of a country's population. Its primary function is as a mirror of a national community in all its diversity, embodying both its unifying factors and its divisions and conflicts. It does not, by nature, harbour values or visions vastly different from those of political society. However, civil society is simultaneously a source for the emergence of new actors, visions and values that can drive political and societal change and transform their country.

Civil Society in the Arab Revolutions and the Sub-Saharan Popular Movements

In 2011-2012, a new wind was blowing across African civil societies, particularly in north, west and central Africa. Originating in Tunisia, the movement known as the Arab Spring provoked unexpected changes in that country and, later, in Egypt and Libya. This wave also had political and social repercussions in Morocco and Algeria, where it forced the authorities to stave off popular unrest, and possibly their own downfall, by announcing reforms. The fall of long-entrenched regimes in Tunisia, Egypt and Libya touched off a period of great uncertainty in these countries. This was followed by a delicate but successful transition in Tunisia, a return to authoritarian rule in Egypt and the collapse of the state in Libya. This mixed record in no way detracts from the importance of what civil society accomplished in its mobilization against these repressive and authoritarian regimes.

For the most part, the Arab revolutions were precipitated by loosely organized movements of young people communicating through social media and sparking unprecedented demonstrations in their countries. What occurred on this occasion was to some extent the birth of a new component of active civil society, channelling the social and economic demands of unemployed youth, who feel marginalized and abandoned by their leaders. Before long, the protest movements had rallied large swaths of society against the arrogance of leaders who, after at least three decades in power, were seen as tyrannical, corrupt, incompetent and, above all, incapable of offering their countries anything new after so many years of nearly unchecked power.

The civil societies emerging in Tunisia, Egypt and Libya were also the products of the specific political, economic and social history of each country. Libyan civil society, which had known only the system instituted by and revolving around Muammar Gadhafi, could hardly be a carbon copy of Tunisian civil society, which had been active and had enjoyed a limited amount of freedom since the early years of independence under Habib Bourguiba. Egyptian civil society, also a reflection of the wider Egyptian society, inevitably bore the marks of the political and economic system established by the powerful military and of long-established resistance movements on the model of the Muslim Brotherhood.

In fact, the Arab Spring also rallied political organizations to the cause of opposing the regimes. Since movements basing their political discourse on religion were generally better organized, and because their charity work had made them more visible to the urban working classes, not to mention more credible in their opposition to the powers that be, they played a role in the ouster of these regimes, thus positioning themselves to capitalize on the outcome. In Tunisia and Egypt, the elections that followed transitional periods were won by Islamist parties. However, these parties were subsequently weakened in Egypt through a campaign of military repression waged against the Muslim Brotherhood and in Tunisia — a very different context — through compromises reached with the other political and social forces.

This detour through the north African events of 2011–2013 serves as a reminder that the forms taken by African civil societies, and their influence on political and security developments in their countries and regions, cannot be analyzed independently of specific historical contexts or of alliances, oppositions, divides, sympathies and complementarities between actors of civil and political society. Moreover, the aftermath of the Arab revolutions reflects the ideological and political diversity of civil society in each country and shows that it would be a mistake to exclude people, networks or organizations from the scope of civil society because they do not hold "progressive" political views. Religious movements of every variety constitute influential components of African civil societies, even when, as in north Africa, the boundaries separating them from political organizations are hazy.

New popular movements spearheaded by youth have also emerged in west Africa, representing a wind of renewal blowing through regimented, technocratic civil societies (Branch and Mampilly 2015). The popular uprising that led to the fall of President Blaise Compaoré on October 31, 2014, sent out a shock wave felt as far away as central Africa, where power rarely changes hands democratically. The revolution in Ouagadougou showed that the struggle of regimes to retain power remains a recurring trigger of tensions and violence in many of Africa's formal democracies. Hundreds of thousands of Burkinabé protestors changed the course of their country's history when they forced their president of 27 years to step down and go into exile. His government was on the verge of passing legislation that would have allowed him to stand for a third term in the last quarter of 2015.

The youth of Burkina Faso sent a powerful message to political leaders who change constitutional provisions at will to suit their own interests. Numerous media stories reported the reactions of west and central African leaders to the events surrounding the fall of a peer regarded as unshakable (Moussaoui 2014; Frère 2015). Throughout the continent, even in countries with markedly authoritarian regimes, the victorious popular movement of Burkina Faso spurred on those who struggle for the credible democratization of their countries and believe that constitutionally mandated transfers of power are essential.

An important factor in the successful mobilization was the level of cohesion in Burkinabé society; it was this factor — in part, a holdover from the political and revolutionary culture built during the idealistic reign of President Thomas Sankara (from 1983 to 1987) — that created the conditions for mass collective action transcending ethnic, regional, religious and social divides. But movements made up of young civil society idealists were not solely responsible for what transpired: also important in making the uprising one to be reckoned with was the defection of highly influential political figures from the Compaoré regime, in protest over the president's attempt to stay in power by amending the constitution yet again.

That is, the Burkinabé demonstrators could never have achieved critical mass if such a wide variety of influential actors from political and civil society had not managed to agree on a specific common goal: rejection of the attempt to abolish presidential term limits as the power grab it was. But neither was it enough to agree on this goal. It was also necessary to stir a sizable proportion of the youthful urban population to action. Such a mobilization demands strategy, tactics, planning, resources, rapid response capability, adaptability and the determination to see the effort through — in short, it demands a sustained effort. The success of the "people's democratic insurrection," as the Burkinabé called it, was that of a demand for change, no doubt, but also that of an organized movement.

In Burundi, the Democratic Republic of the Congo and the Republic of the Congo, the political tensions of 2015-2016 were likewise linked to attempts by their respective presidents to stay in power by amending or circumventing constitutional term limits. In Burundi, the violence produced a large number of casualties and the crisis dragged on into 2016, with the president succeeding in his bid to hold on to power. The peculiar history of each of these central African countries has weighed as heavily in the balance as have local and external pressures for observance of democratic principles and human rights.

In several central African countries possessing strategic natural resources or a tradition of violent repression, or both, it is very difficult for a youthful and committed civil society to mobilize against decades-old regimes. But, here too, where governments with an authoritarian bent strive to close down public spaces through violence or the threat of it, demographic pressures seem unstoppable in the medium term; the masses of young people seeking change are bound to make their desires felt. Still, there is no guarantee that future mobilizations will give rise to new regimes and political systems without an interregnum of violent crisis.

Civil Societies Grappling with Threats to Peace and Security

In west Africa, 2012 was the year when Mali lapsed into a grave political and security crisis involving a combination of Tuareg separatist rebellion, territorial conquest by self-styled jihadist groups and major political crisis provoked by a *coup d'état*. The Malian crisis, when broken down into its various dimensions, is characterized by internal and external factors intertwined with immediate, recent and long-standing circumstances.

The analysis sheds light on factors deriving from the bankrupt administration of civilian and military public affairs, resulting in the persistence of problems of coexistence between certain communities and their recalcitrance to centralized political administration. Added to this is the penetration of Malian society by extremist religious ideologies and transnational organized crime, including trafficking in drugs, human beings, cigarettes and weapons (Lacher 2012; Sidibé 2012). In 2011, the aftermath of the war in Libya, home to many Tuareg combatants of Malian origin, appears to have played a significant role in precipitating or accelerating the new separatist rebellion in the north.

The fact that this crisis occurred in a west African country that had regularly held elections that had been deemed acceptable for two decades — a country praised as a model of African democracy — was particularly significant. In reality, this perception of the Malian political system had always been overly flattering: election results had often been contested as fraudulent, while democratization had gone hand in hand with an increasingly visible monopolization of political positions, opportunities and economic resources by a small circle of civilian and military elites (Wing 2013). But since numerous African countries had followed political trajectories marked by resistance to authoritarian power, violence and even armed conflict in the 1990s and 2000s, the criteria used by Western countries for considering a country to be an African model were not particularly exacting.

For these reasons, Mali enjoyed a lasting image of democracy that translated into sizable foreign aid flows from Western donor countries. The aid was allocated to a great many economic and social development projects, some of them in the northern part of the country, where a long Tuareg rebellion and recurring episodes of violence were already part of the landscape. The aid also fostered the emergence of a huge economic sector composed of NGOs (Thiriot 2002). In Mali, as elsewhere, civil society cannot be described as a cohesive, structured group of actors sharing a common vision of the role they should play, the kinds of relations they should carry on with political formations, the areas of activity on which they should focus, the population segments they should put a priority on helping or the type of relations to be maintained with foreign donors.

Instead, civil society organizations emerged and proliferated spontaneously, thanks to the initiatives of men and women driven by a multitude of interests, their ambitions differing greatly as a function of access to resources. In an overwhelmingly Muslim country deeply rooted in tradition, a portion of the new civil society naturally organized around the promotion of Islam; it moved into sectors of society such as education, through the Koranic schools. Like civil society organizations funded by Western donors, those associated with the Muslim community also succeeded in mobilizing foreign resources, especially from the Gulf countries, Libya and, more broadly, from the Muslims around the world. This segment of civil society showed its political strength and influence over Malian society when it fiercely opposed a draft reform of the family code, attracting thousands to stadium rallies in support of its position. The government and the Parliament were forced to backtrack.

All these things — Malian civil society's vitality in diversity, the considerable flows of foreign resources that enabled hundreds of NGOs to operate in every region of the country with the putative goal of improving societal well-being and social cohesion and the long-standing practice of formal democracy — did not prevent it from undergoing the profound crisis from which it has yet to emerge at the time of writing. The Malian experience shows, among other things, that democratization must not be confused with state consolidation and the strengthening of cohesion in a multicultural society. Democratization, when reduced to its routine electoral dimension, in no way guarantees progress toward these two other essential goals. Malian democracy has become tolerant of all manner of corruption, which has extended into the military and security realms and rendered the state vulnerable to multiple external and internal threats.

The crisis in Mali, which rapidly spread throughout the entire Sahel region, pointed up the extreme difficulties many African countries have had in finding workable institutional arrangements with which all ethnic communities can identify — in building a national community without requiring its population subgroups to give up their cultural identities. This raises the whole question of the political management of diversity in African countries (Deng 2008). National democratization, even when it coincides with decentralization and hence local-level democratization, as occurred in Mali, has not provided a fully satisfactory answer to this question. It might even be argued that it has brought about a sharp swing back toward political mobilization along ethnic, clan or tribal dividing lines, with ensuing local episodes of intercommunity violence.

The recent proliferation of terrorist attacks in east Africa, west Africa and the Sahel has added a new dimension to existing forms of violence and insecurity (Institute for Economics and Peace 2015). The apparently religious motivations of the most dangerous African terrorist groups (Al-Shabaab, Boko Haram and al-Qaeda in the Islamic Maghreb) and their capacity to recruit hundreds or thousands of young combatants have led observers to worry about the radicalization of youth.

In every region of the continent, the lag between demographic growth and socio-economic progress appears to offer terrorist groups a huge pool of disaffected individuals from which to recruit. In reality, socio-economic pressures and state fragility make young people vulnerable to recruitment into all sectors of the emerging criminal economy, with the process being aided by the increasing mobility of goods, persons and ideologies (Lacher 2012; Sidibé 2012)

Africa Needs Committed, Creative and Pragmatic Components of Civil Society

For African states, the establishment of complex security mechanisms to fight organized crime and the corruption of state institutions with which it is associated remains a huge challenge. While fears of terrorist extremism are legitimate, other forms of violence involving rural youth deserve more attention than they have been given. In most of west Africa and the Sahel, simmering tensions between herders and farmers frequently

degenerate into episodes of deadly violence. Casualties have increased due to the substitution of modern weapons of war — now much easier to obtain thanks to their low cost across all of Africa — for traditional arms. Competition for rare natural resources, with land still the most valuable among them, is exacerbated by ethnic and religious differences in a context in which the state is non-existent or its presence is barely felt.

There remains an immense amount of work to be done in Africa to adopt the institutional arrangements best suited to producing states that are democratic, effective and efficient at protecting peace, security and societal well-being. Beyond what has happened to states, African societies, in their enormous diversity, show signs of having been weakened by the brutal confrontation of their ways of life, economic systems and social and political structures with powerful and globalized economic, geopolitical, cultural actors. In this context, opportunities are highly limited for African countries to autonomously devise and put in place the political, economic and social institutions necessary to respond to present and projected basic needs. Civil societies in every region of the continent can make a useful contribution by helping to generate new ideas that can give meaning, coherence and depth to positive African economic dynamics.

In countries long mired in armed conflict, where state structures are as fragile as anywhere on the continent, it is understandable that many civil society organizations are concentrating their efforts on intercommunity and interfaith dialogue, local-level reconciliation programs, victim assistance programs and so on (CIVICUS 2015). Yet, the idea that civil society could canton itself within the realm of peace building or conflict prevention and resolution is out of step with the evolution of African realities. These organizations are no doubt doing essential grassroots work in volatile and dangerous security environments. But if there is no parallel group of societal actors getting together to discuss the political conditions necessary to break cycles of instability and violence, civil society will remain confined to the role of a palliative care provider.

In these countries, there is very little space for the development of a civil society capable of putting pressure on the dominant political and economic actors, and this is where international support can make a difference. Such support must, however, be measured, tailored to needs and focused on institutional and material assistance to people working and innovating to bring about profound changes in their society.

In the many African countries that have not experienced civil war and violent crisis on a recurring basis, the outlook for peace is, and will continue to be, closely tied to progress on the stabilization of political institutions tailored to the diversity of their respective societies and to the imperative of rendering states more useful to their citizens, hence more legitimate in their eyes. Peace prospects will also be tied to the growth, economic diversification and job creation prospects held out to populations with large youth segments. Finally, they will be tied to the capacity of states, and all social institutions, to identify and rein in the most negative consequences of external influences, particularly those ensuing from the activities of transnational criminal networks, which nurture corruption locally.

African Civil Societies and State Consolidation

Paradoxically, the primary responsibility of African civil society leaders should be to occupy the political field, in the primary sense of the term "political"; that is, they must force the governing elites to revamp the operation of states so that the public can get an accounting of how the country's power and resources are being administered. This responsibility goes beyond what organizations working for human rights, democracy and good governance are already doing. African countries need to develop a critical mass of people who do not consider civil society merely a sector offering attractive career opportunities, but rather a vocation, a commitment to their national community. This critical mass of citizens need not and probably will not be reducible to a group of formally structured NGOs whose energies are taken up by activities for which donors demand short-term results.

New and future African civil societies must contain — alongside the diverse pursuits, motivations and resources already in existence — a category of persons who understand the political, economic, social and cultural issues crucial to the future of their respective countries: people who think outside the box, create fora for public debate, question the choices their governments make, challenge failing institutions and shake up the established order. The question of the proper relationship between civil society, the political class and the state (in the sense of the sum total of public institutions) must be raised. The widely held belief that civil society actors should keep separate from political actors, on the one hand, and state structures, on the other, leads to a paradoxical situation in which civil society organizations become a refuge for qualified, socially committed individuals while public institutions are drained of human resources.

More than ever, African countries need to engage in the painstaking work of building states that are both democratic and capable of instilling trust. To achieve this, they must be populated by political actors who care about the public interest along with public officials competent in all key areas of public action. International support for the emergence and strengthening of civil societies in African countries will not serve the abiding objectives of peace, security, and economic and social progress if it has the perverse side effect of hindering the consolidation of political and administrative institutions.

African countries, like countries on every continent, need balance among the different drivers of societal change that are political actors, economic actors and civil society actors. In reality, all citizens simultaneously belong to all three groups, in proportions that vary over time. To build strong civil societies in Africa, the relatively positive economic outlook for the continent must go hand in hand with the creation of country-level spaces, in every region of Africa, that are dedicated to preserving the most vital interests of society for current and future generations.

Works Cited

Bates, Robert H. 2008. *When Things Fell Apart: State Failure in Late-Century Africa.* Cambridge, UK: Cambridge University Press.

Bayart, Jean-François. 1986. "Civil Society in Africa." In *Political Domination in Africa: Reflections on the Limits of Power,* edited by Patrick Chabal, 109–25. Cambridge, UK: Cambridge University Press.

Bekoe, Dorina. 2012. *Voting in Fear: Electoral Violence in Sub-Saharan Africa.* Washington, DC: United States Institute of Peace Press.

Branch, Adam and Zachariah Mampilly. 2015. *Africa Uprising: Popular Protest and Political Change.* London, UK: Zed Books.

CIVICUS. 2015. *State of Civil Society Report 2015.* Johannesberg, ZA: CIVICUS: World Alliance for Citizen Participation. http://civicus.org/images/StateOfCivilSocietyFullReport2015.pdf.

Deng, Francis. 2008. *Identity, Diversity, and Constitutionalism in Africa.* Washington, DC: United States Institute of Peace Press.

Fall, Babacar. 2006. "Le Mouvement syndical en Afrique occidentale francophone: de la tutelle des centrales métropolitaines à celle des partis nationaux uniques, ou La Difficile quête d'une personnalité (1900–1968)." *Matériaux pour l'histoire de notre temps* 4 (84): 49–58. www.cairn.info/revue-materiaux-pour-l-histoire-de-notre-temps-2006-4-page-49.htm.

Fomunyoh, Christopher. 2016. "Crises of Political Legitimacy." In *Minding the Gap: African Conflict Management in a Time of Change,* edited by Pamela Aall and Chester A. Crocker, 33–48. Waterloo, ON: CIGI.

Frère, Marie-Soleil. 2015. "Pourquoi ce qui se passe au Burkina Faso concerne toute l'Afrique et le monde." *Le Soir,* September 24. www.lesoir.be/998368/article/debats/cartes-blanches/2015-09-24/pourquoi-ce-qui-se-passe-au-burkina-faso-concerne-toute-l-afrique-et-monde.

Gilpin, Raymond. 2016. "Understanding the Nature and Origins of Violent Conflict in Africa." In *Minding the Gap: African Conflict Management in a Time of Change*, edited by Pamela Aall and Chester A. Crocker, 21–32. Waterloo, ON: CIGI.

Institute for Economics and Peace. 2015. *Global Terrorism Index 2015: Measuring and Understanding the Impact of Terrorism.* http://economicsandpeace.org/wp-content/uploads/2015/11/Global-Terrorism-Index-2015.pdf.

International Crisis Group. 2013. "Burkina Faso: With or Without Compaoré, Times of Uncertainty." Africa Report No. 205. Dakar, Senegal, and Brussels, Belgium: International Crisis Group.

Lacher, Wolfram. 2012. *Organized Crime and Conflict in the Sahel-Sahara Region.* Washington, DC: Carnegie Endowment for International Peace.

Lewis, David. 2002. "Civil Society in African Contexts: Reflections on the Usefulness of a Concept." *Development and Change* 33 (4): 569–86.

Moussaoui, Rosa. 2014. "Burkina Faso: la leçon de Ouagadougou ébranle les présidents à vie." *L'Humanité*, November 3. www.humanite.fr/burkina-faso-la-lecon-de-ouagadougou-ebranle-les-presidents-vie-556464.

Olonisakin, 'Funmi. 2016. "Crises of War-to-Peace Transition and Civil War Recurrences." In *Minding the Gap: African Conflict Management in a Time of Change*, edited by Pamela Aall and Chester A. Crocker, 49–64. Waterloo, ON: CIGI.

Ould Mohamedou, Mohammad-Mahmoud. "Religious Extremism, Insurgent Violence and the Transformation of the New African Security Landscape." In *Minding the Gap: African Conflict Management in a Time of Change*, edited by Pamela Aall and Chester A. Crocker, 79–90. Waterloo, ON: CIGI.

Reno, William. 2016. "The Dimensions of the Future of Conflict in Africa." In *Minding the Gap: African Conflict Management in a Time of Change*, edited by Pamela Aall and Chester A. Crocker, 65–78. Waterloo, ON: CIGI.

Sidibé, Kalilou. 2012. "Criminal Networks and Conflict Resolution Mechanisms in Northern Mali." *IDS Bulletin* 43 (4): 74–88.

Srinivasan, Sharath. 2016. "Civil Society as Counter-power: Rethinking International Support Toward Tackling Conflict And Fostering Non-violent Politics in Africa." In *Minding the Gap: African Conflict Management in a Time of Change*, edited by Pamela Aall and Chester A. Crocker, 295–309. Waterloo, ON: CIGI.

Thiriot, Céline. 2002. "Role de la société civile dans la transition et la consolidation démocratique en Afrique: éléments de réflexion à partir du cas du Mali." *Revue internationale de politique comparée* 2 (9), 277–95. www.cairn.info/revue-internationale-de-politique-comparee-2002-2-page-277.htm.

Wairimu Nderitu, Alice. 2016. "African Peace Building: Civil Society Roles in Conflict." In *Minding the Gap: African Conflict Management in a Time of Change*, edited by Pamela Aall and Chester A. Crocker, 219–37. Waterloo, ON: CIGI.

Wing, Susanna. 2013. *Mali's Precarious Democracy and the Causes of Conflict.* Washington, DC: United States Institute of Peace Press.

12

Do Private Sector Activities Support Peace or Conflict in Fragile States?

Callisto Madavo

"Peace and development remain inextricably linked — one feeding on the other, enabling the other and securing the other. The renunciation of violence as a means of gaining and holding power is only the beginning. Then must follow a renewed commitment to national development founded on sober, sound and uncorrupted economic policies."
— Kofi Annan

Introduction and Definitions

The question that this chapter tries to address is whether private economic activities generally support and prolong conflict, or whether such private economic activities on the whole can contribute positively to recovery, reconstruction, increased stability and security and to economic growth that is sustained and inclusive. This chapter focuses on the latter question, on the assumption that the negative activities can be tackled through strict regulations and laws (this requires both capacity and strong governance, which is often weak at the country level) and through international cooperation and collective action where political will has been lacking. However, the enforcement of both laws and regulations is key to stemming such negative activities. In many African countries, even stable ones, this is still a work in progress, and international efforts to pass and enforce appropriate laws can be highly political. Nevertheless, for completeness, the chapter will provide a quick summary of these negative aspects both in African countries and internationally. While the ostensibly international outlook of private sector activities on the continent conjures images of multinational corporations arranging corrupt deals with incumbent governments to exploit state resources, this chapter's approach primarily focuses on the potential private sector contribution of funding, support and technical assistance.

Before outlining the sections of the chapter, it is important to define what is meant by private sector activity and to identify the principal actors behind those activities. Consistently with Paul Collier and Ritva Reinikka (2001), this chapter defines private sector economic activities as those carried out by households (subsistence and smallholder agriculture, informal sector products and their resulting trade), domestic firms (trade and usually light manufacturing), commercial farms (including tropical crop plantations) and foreign direct investment (FDI) channelled through international multinational corporations. In this regard, the African diaspora has begun to play an important role in both the investment and transfer of funds for consumption, school fees and so on (Beyene 2015). We therefore regard the diaspora funding as part of the private sector activities.

While lasting reconstruction will always require local ownership and government leadership, partnerships will be essential for successful implementation. Partnerships between the government, the people and other domestic non-state actors, such as non-governmental organizations (NGOs), community-based organizations (CBOs), business firms and foreign investors, as well as international civil society communities and donors, are critical. The external actors' roles are not those of owners and drivers of the process but of supporters and advisers.

The role of state-owned enterprises (SOEs) in reviving the economy and providing critical services, especially in the early phases of recovery, is acknowledged, but SOEs are an essential part of the public sector that should be reformed to make them more efficient and effective. As recovery gains footing and speed along the recovery continuum, deepening and sustaining it will require the kind of institutional reforms, deregulation and liberalization that allows incentives to enter the private sector, public-private partnerships and other modalities for providing services rather than entrenching SOE monopolies (Mills 2014).

Civil society activities can strengthen and support economic activities that are essential for recovery; this includes the role of CBOs, local NGOs, business fora and associations. Most often, if not always, international NGOs play important roles in providing funding and advisory services for community-based activities that build capacity, resilience and meaningful participation in local and provincial governance. This can also repair the links between citizens and governments and, therefore, deepen legitimacy, economic diversification and productivity.

This understanding of resistance and recovery places economic recovery and inclusive economic growth in a much larger context. Conflict destroys economies and hollows the state, key institutions and social cohesion within the rural communities in which most Africans live. The result is often widespread fragility in affected states and regions and a weakness to absorb and resist the impacts and shocks of change. Meaningful and sustainable post-conflict recovery must address the underlying issue of fragility — defined not in terms of a group of states or subregions, but rather as a phenomenon in which a country's state institutions and political and economic processes are too weak to resist shocks from conflict, violence and other crises, such as Ebola in west Africa and the recurrent droughts that are now occurring in the Horn of Africa and other parts of Africa (High Level Panel on Fragile States 2014; Organization for Economic Cooperation and Development [OECD] 2015).

The point of departure, therefore, is that economic activity driven for the most part by private sector actors as defined above is essential for economic recovery and must be accompanied by programs that address fragility through building resilient states, institutions and societies. Otherwise, economic recovery will neither develop deep roots nor endure. Resilience is essential for meaningful, stable and inclusive economic progress. Full recovery from conflict is a challenge lasting as long as 10 years (Collier and Hoffler 2002) and often best managed in phases.

Therefore, the chapter will proceed as follows. First, it will provide a quick review of private sector activity as a contributor to conflict. Second, it will deal with the first phase of the recovery continuum, which essentially covers the "standing up" of the economy. Third, it will cover the second phase of the recovery. This phase not only capitalizes upon the dynamic of a reviving economy but also looks further to a vision of accelerating and deepening inclusive economic growth and seizes opportunities to treat the challenges of jobs, poverty and inequality with increased economic diversification and productivity. Implementation is typically a major issue in the realization of recovery strategies. This will be an important part of the chapter, as it touches on the roles of the government, the domestic private sector and other non-state actors, and the potential contribution by the diaspora, foreign capital and donors. Particular attention will be paid to the importance of partnerships for the implementation phase of the government recovery plan.

Just as conflict often spills over borders into subregions, successful economic reconstruction and growth requires liberal trade and coordination across borders and carefully managed and equitable engagement with the global economy. The chapter will deal with the regional dimension because it is important for private sector market activities and for linkages to the global economy in terms of having a voice in global investment and in terms of fairness, transparency, accountability and effective learning in trade regimes across countries (Transition Support Group 2016).

The chapter will then look at the experience during the 1980s and 1990s of two countries that made relatively successful economic transitions from conflict (Uganda and Rwanda) and of two countries (Liberia and Sierra Leone) that had made good recovery progress in the first decade of this century, before the Ebola crisis in 2014-2015, and are starting again on the path of recovery from Ebola by using what they had learned before (Madavo 2015/2016).

The concluding section will offer key messages about the potential contribution of private sector activities to economic recovery and the steps necessary to build and grow upon resilience.

The Negative Externalities of Some Private Sector Activity

As indicated above, private sector activities have much to contribute positively to post-conflict reconstruction and development; nevertheless, there are ways in which the private sector can also cause, exacerbate and prolong conflict (Peschka 2011). First, private sector activities can be accompanied by both horizontal and vertical inequality that can create a source of grievance. This is especially so when economic activities and opportunities in resource-rich areas, as well as urban agglomeration, leave behind rural and isolated areas. Generally, income distribution, as measured by the Gini coefficient, is worse in Africa than elsewhere and more so in conflict and post-conflict countries. This means that there is substantial capture of the fruits of growth and wealth by the elites. Recent efforts by African governments to implement more economically inclusive policies have yet to make a big difference. In addition, experiments with conditional social safety net policies and grants along the lines of Brazil's *Bolsa Familia* are at pilot stages, and it remains unclear how well they will work to reduce inequality and poverty in an African context (World Bank 2015b).

Second, the poor management of natural resource wealth (land, crop plantations, forests, minerals, oil and gas) has been a primary source of conflict. While there have been recent outcries by civil society about land grabbing, illegal logging and so on, these issues will not be covered here. Minerals, oil and gas, in particular, have been especially problematic along the value chain: extraction, marketing and revenue sharing, and use (Transition Support Group 2016). With respect to extraction, much concern has been raised about the terms and conditions — the degree to which contracts, concessions and leases are comprehensive, transparent and fair. This chapter considers contracts comprehensive in terms of the extent to which they go beyond revenues and cover issues such as environmental protection, labour standards and corporate social responsibility. This chapter considers contracts transparent in terms of the extent to which public information is available on terms and conditions. This chapter considers contracts to be fair if they include equitable sharing of benefits with the countries and communities from which resources are being taken. The grievance, resentment and conflict around oil extraction from the Niger Delta of Nigeria is a good example for the potential negative externalities surrounding contract negotiation (Asuni 2009).

Third, problems have arisen from the weak financial management of and investment policies for sudden and huge windfall revenue: "Dutch disease" and the neglect of priorities in investments in infrastructure, agriculture, education, health and technology. No less concerning are increasingly frequent media reports of the corruption, patronage and abuse of human rights that are compromising governance in many resource-rich countries on the continent (McFerson 2009). On the eve of the anticorruption summit, David Cameron was not hesitant to tell the Queen that Nigeria was one of the most corrupt countries in the world (Mance and Fick 2016).

Finally, conflict and fragility create a political vacuum in which laws and regulations are poorly or hardly enforced and international norms and values no longer apply. We have seen in these fragile situations the emergence of criminal non-state actors involved in drug trafficking and pirate activities, including stealing oil on the west African coast, hijacking ships in the Gulf of Aden and poaching ivory in most of the subregions of Africa. These cartels and networks, while not a part of the legitimate private sector as it is known, are nonetheless economic activities beyond the control of the state (OECD 2015).

A panel organized by the United Nations Economic Commission for Africa (UNECA) focuses specifically on the hugely damaging effects of illicit financial flows (IFFs) in fostering corruption, heightening inequality and draining the progress of development on the continent (High Level Panel on Illicit Financial Flows from Africa 2015). Africa, as a whole, is a net loser in transcontinental capital flows: more money leaves the continent in IFFs than enters through FDI and foreign aid flows combined (Spanjers and Foss 2015). The very financial system of anonymous shell companies and tax havens that permits these flows also undergirds various forms of transnational crime. Whether in the contexts of phenomena such as Congolese coltan, Sudanese gold, Tanzanian ivory, ransom for Somali pirates, Angolan crude or run-of-the-mill grand-scale government kickbacks, the opacity of this system of exchange is drowning the continent (and the world) with opportunities for corruption and crime — and diverting money from the people most in need. There is no doubt that this complex web of IFFs and transnational crime represents a development drain in Africa and further entrenches already corrupt rulers and fragile states. The amount of money leaving African states through these illicit networks is astounding when compared with government spending. A June 2015 report by Global Financial Integrity found the outsized impact these flows had on African countries from 2008 to 2012: Ethiopia's IFFs were 1,355 percent of the FDI flowing into the country. Zambia's IFFs were equal to 24.1 percent of total trade, and Rwanda's IFFs were equal to 51.7 percent of the government's total tax revenue. Those in Liberia equalled 257.4 percent of its total tax revenue, and Togo's IFFs were equal to 76.3 percent of its GDP (ibid.).

While responsibility for actions to contain and minimize some of these activities primarily lies with African national and regional authorities on whose territories the actions are occurring, it is obvious that these issues should be of concern to international stakeholders as a whole. Multi-stakeholder initiatives such as the Kimberley Process, Publish What You Pay and the Extractive Industries Transparency Initiative have been underway for some time. No matter what the case is, the coordination of external countries is critical. For example, it is all very well for China to ban ivory imports for one year, but without coordinated action with countries such as Vietnam, this will not take the world very far in dealing with this problem. This is one issue for which the West could make a serious difference, and for which only the West has the power to address, due to the nature of these activities as a collective action problem. Shared public registries of beneficial ownership could be implemented, tax loopholes sewn shut and corporate regulation increased. Illicit finance enables massive leakage of productive revenue from recipient countries. It is a drain on the progress of economic development. A failure on the part of the international community and bilateral donors to craft a policy framework mitigating its negative externalities seems a missed opportunity to further aid countries in need.

Clearly, this discussion of the negative externalities of private sector actors in Sub-Saharan Africa is in no way limited to the experience of post-conflict states. Instead, it is a symptom of fragility and a lack of civil society and good institutional development, both of which are necessary to build a vibrant business community across the continent.

Phases of Recovery

Immediately Following Conflict (First Phase)

The first phase of recovery takes place immediately after the conflict or disaster in question. Much of the literature focuses on this immediate period as one defined by the propping up of a society and its economy. The necessary task at this stage of emerging from the conflict revolves around an understanding of restoring the country's economy to a level equivalent to that before the conflict. Throughout this emergency phase, the domestic government must be the first and critical actor in restoring the vitals of an economy through ensuring basic levels of security, minimum stability and the return to pre-conflict levels of basic infrastructure, energy, security, stability and light manufacturing.

While the international community usually plays an important role in this emergency stage in terms of funding and technical assistance, the domestic government remains the critical factor in determining the success of an emergency revival. In the case of post-conflict reconstruction, only the domestic government itself can shape the vision and direction of recovery, especially in returning to the minimum business environment necessary to revive economic activity.

The first action by government after a conflict is ensuring the return of basic levels of security. This step will lay the groundwork so that, no matter what type of peace process takes place later, various socio-economic groups in the country will feel included and invested in a sustainable peace. As this chapter will explain later, the steps taken to increase social inclusion will decrease state fragility; this is an essential foundation to genuine economic recovery. We cannot expect the economy to function or people to resume daily life without an improved sense of security. People cannot be concerned about dying if the economy is to move in the direction of productivity. Measures to reinstate a basic sense of security — physically, psychologically and socially — should be the first priority of the government, with a strong emphasis on inclusivity (Stewart 2004).[1] The ongoing turmoil in South Sudan illustrates

---

1   This citation was suggested by the editors of this volume.

well the importance of a broadly based political settlement by both the leaders and the people.

During the conflict in question, and especially in cases of a drawn-out conflict, critical infrastructure is often destroyed or eroded. In the immediate post-conflict space, domestic governments face an inundation of policy and investment priorities and limited funds. A 2004 World Bank social development paper examined the bank's Private Participation in Infrastructure database and found that while the governments of "countries emerging from a conflict urgently need to provide access to basic infrastructure services for their populations…[t]hey lack adequate public revenues" to do so (Schwartz, Hahn and Bannon 2004). Furthermore, the fragile condition of the country's infrastructure in the immediate post-conflict space remains a block that continually restricts economic activity and trade.

For these reasons, a productive government plan to swiftly stand up the economy must include measures that contribute to the revival of the most fundamental unit of an economy: households. The measures in question must include immediate support for both rural and urban households that generate money primarily through the agricultural and informal sectors, respectively. However, with the obvious destruction of the processes of government and economy following a conflict, the government, while it is the primary and coordinating actor, will likely require the help of international community support in the form of funding and advisory expertise from the international financial institutions (IFIs), bilaterals, NGOs and think tanks. An equally concerted effort should be made by the government to entice back any FDI lost due to the conflict, in an effort to pump resources and capital back into the system. In general, new FDI is not depended on as one of the first sources of funding for recovery, but its necessity in the medium and long term is recognized.

Reconstruction and Development and Shaping of the Government Vision (Second Phase)

Once the economy is revived, the next step is to create both a long-term vision as well as intermediate strategies, typically covering periods of five years, and action plans covering even shorter periods, all moving toward the achievement of the long-term vision. Long-term visions normally cover periods of 15 to 20 years and have been prepared in post-conflict countries, as well as other more stable countries. While some of the visions and strategies have not always been well implemented, they can provide a broad shared vision and direction of the country's ambitions over the long view. Countries such as Ghana and Rwanda are good examples of how this can be done. Both Liberia and Sierra Leone made commendable efforts in this direction before and after the Ebola crisis. The visions and policies — and the action plans embedded in them — set objectives and programs to provide security and stability, strong inclusive growth and institutional and societal resilience.

A strong prime mover and organizer is critical in creating both the vision and the medium-term strategy and action plans; this can only be performed by government. In some countries, the process of formulating these frameworks has been participative through extensive consultative mechanisms that embrace domestic stakeholders (private sector, local civil society and communities) and also bring inputs and knowledge from external partners such as the diaspora and foreign investors, as well as donors. As they are inclusive, these frameworks have tended to work better. The diaspora has participated through remittance funds and advisory services on the ground, contributing to funding of households and community in a way that greatly impacts poverty and providing foreign exchange to governments, most of which goes to support consumption. The private sector has provided funding, technical knowledge and advocacy for reforms to let the markets work through deregulation and liberalization. Donors and international organizations such as the African Development Bank (AFDB), the World Bank, European Union institutions, and key bilateral agencies (the Department for International Development [DFID], the United States Agency for International Development [USAID] and so on) and some parts of the UN system have also contributed in terms of funding, experience and knowledge that added value to vision, strategy and implementation. Similarly, there is openness to collaboration and dialogue among countries of the greater south through mechanisms such as the "new deal" dialogue (International Dialogue for Peacebuilding and Statebuilding [International Dialogue] n.d.).

The New Deal for Engagement in Fragile States grew out of the international movement to improve aid effectiveness in developing countries. Important milestones were the Paris Declaration in 2005 and the Accra Third High Level Forum on Aid Effectiveness in 2008 (OECD 2005/2008) and, finally, the High Level Meeting in Seoul in 2011 at which development partners and fragile post-conflict g7+ states endorsed the New Deal for Engagement in Fragile States. The phrase "g7+ states" refers to a group of fragile post-conflict states that cooperated to develop a framework in which aid partners should engage with the special circumstances of fragile states with the assistance of the Overseas Development Institute in the United Kingdom. This new deal is supported by an international dialogue that includes the fragile states themselves but has also been signed by 40 other partners, including virtually all the Western countries involved in development.

The new deal spells out the objectives and principles of engagement and ownership and the focus on legitimate politics, security, justice and building inclusive economies to remain sensitive to issues of fragility and recovery. It is special because, while it includes the influence of international financing institutions and traditional

aid partners, it was initiated by the fragile states themselves, which brought in the other partners for the purpose of technical advice and assistance. To start implementation, a number of countries were chosen as pilots, and both Liberia and Sierra Leone were among them. The deal, therefore, influenced the formation of recovery strategies in these countries before Ebola. For example, a reading of Sierra Leone's poverty reduction strategies and subsequent recovery plans shows that they reflect the new deal influence, as do those for Liberia, such as the Agenda for Transformation (Liberia 2008). Interestingly, the new deal approach began to influence the strategies of the major donor partners, such as the DFID, USAID, the World Bank and the AFDB, as seen in their strategies for supporting post-Ebola recovery, for example. This influenced not only the financing institutions but also the progressive side of the bilateral donors (USAID, DFID) and, in that sense, has provided an overall framework for any dialogue on the issues that these post-conflict and fragile states face as they try to recover and normalize (Hughes et al. 2014).

Visions in post-conflict countries and others normally articulate wide-ranging and ambitious agendas for a country's development and transformation over a 15- to 20-year period. The ambition of most is to develop their economies to a middle-income status in which the provision of services, inequality and poverty are being addressed through inclusive growth. Recent examples of post-conflict vision and strategies are those of Liberia before Ebola, such as the Lift Liberia Poverty Reduction Strategy and the Agenda for Transformation (Liberia 2008). Similarly, before Ebola, Sierra Leone made good progress in this regard, as illustrated in documents such as the Poverty Reduction Strategy of 2005 (Sierra Leone 2005). These two countries have also used past experience to put in place post-Ebola strategies that have been used by many international agencies as a basis of support, such as the joint strategy of the World Bank and the AFDB, which outlined the funding and assistance post-Ebola (AFDB/ World Bank 2015). While post-conflict economic activity and transformation are important drivers of economic growth and social development, it is important to stress that economic activities depend in no small part on other non-economic pillars of recovery, namely peace, security, the rule of law and the rebuilding of key institutions, human development and skills, as well as political and economic governance reform.

The country's vision and sequential strategic plans will have to recognize and acknowledge that accelerated inclusive growth in the medium term will largely be driven by the private sector, both domestic and foreign. The government's role will be to create a stable, secure, supportive and attractive investment climate. This is important not only for foreign investment but also for an open, competitive domestic sector that welcomes and grows domestic entrepreneurs.

Some areas that will be essential for sustainable economic progress during the many phases of recovery and that will allow the private sector to play its role include the following: maintaining stability, peace, security and the rule of law; welcoming and promoting the private sector (domestic and foreign) as powerful agents for accelerating growth; implementing liberal and pro-market policies in terms of macroeconomic and fiscal management to support private sector growth; prioritizing public investments in hard infrastructure, including power and transport, as well as "soft infrastructure," such as customs and regulations to facilitate trade; public and private investing in the provision and delivery of services; paying particular attention to human resource development; and ensuring a recovery strategy that includes provision to raise production and productivity, especially in agriculture, in which, typically, 70 percent of Africans make their livelihoods. Other strategies fall into areas including input financing, training and extension, managing natural resource wealth so that it contributes to the long-term vision of the

recovery, improving political space and focusing on economic governance with financial management systems to ensure the transparent collection and expenditure of government revenues.

While the list above may seem vague, it is impossible to narrow down the priorities to form a post-conflict recovery blueprint, however helpful that may be. We do not find the one-size-fits-all plan for recovery to be realistic, since the strategy of recovery in a specific country depends on the historical and social context of the conflict in question, the style of the ruling government and the goals and fears of its people. One of the primary determinants of a successful recovery plan is its acute configuration to fit the context of the country in question.

Partners for Governments in Implementing Plans (Implementation Phase)

Households

In order to mobilize an economic recovery, the government must orient its vision around the smallest unit of economic activity — the household. It is no accident that we place households at the forefront of tools for achieving the government's vision; the success or failure of reforms must be crafted from this perspective. By understanding the incentive structures and economic changes taking place at the household level, the government can measure and implement pro-poor policies and, therefore, promote more comprehensive and sustainable growth.

Tools such as household surveys, especially when conducted repeatedly over the course of the implementation phase, provide the government with insight and an opportunity to adapt policies based on the evolution of poverty, income and expenditures. They enable a view into the actual mechanisms taking place in a country or subregion in which macro government policies and the provision of public services transform into changes in livelihood for the average citizen.

Furthermore, by acting as a close monitor of the evolving poverty of a populace, the government can address more aptly the root causes of the recent conflict that relate to poverty or inequality in economic access.

During an extended conflict, political instability or an economic collapse, the rural poor sections of a population typically "retreat into self-sufficient agriculture" (Larson and Deininger 2001, 177). Over the initial implementation phase of the vision, the ideal pattern the government should aim to find at the household level includes a gradual move away from subsistence production and toward market-based activity, the profits of which are then reinvested in the household, producing higher yield and improved livelihoods. Because postwar reconstruction takes even longer at the household level, "post-war reconstruction policy should re-capitalise household endowments and stimulate rural markets as part of a broadly based program of rural development" (Brück 2001, 2). This transformation is economic in nature, but takes place at the household level as a decision of risk. For that reason, the return to household productivity involves issues of internal and societal peace and the issue of perceptions of peace, which will be discussed to a greater extent later in this section. Generally speaking, a good figure gleaned from household surveys that can indicate changes in economic household welfare is household private consumption per capita (Appleton 2001, 87). If the growth created by the government plan is appropriately and equally affecting the broad-based citizenry, then one should find commensurate growth between the national accounts and the average increase in per capita household consumption (ibid.).

In hopes not only of recovery but also of creating "fresh growth" and diversification at the household level, the rural agricultural sector is key in impacting the lives of many countries' poor (ibid., 113). To further encourage the expansion of household consumption, the government can increase rural access to credit and to electricity,

water and sanitation. It can expand education, improve the provision of public services and address inefficient or problematic land rights legislation or implementation. Steps taken by the government in the immediate standing-up phase of the recovery, such as a restoration of infrastructure, should cut transaction costs for rural households as they bring their crops to market. In the same way, government or private sector efforts to share pricing information between markets would also decrease the transaction costs of households involved in informal, non-export agricultural activities. All of these measures contribute to an increased sense of economic stability and the slow increase of risk-taking at the household level. With increased and more reliable profits, households can be expected to reinvest those earnings in increased farming technology, such as fertilizer or livestock-fuelled techniques, both of which increase yields and go on to fund non-agricultural microenterprises (Deininger and Okidi 2001, 126).

Domestic Firms

In the same way that private consumption provides a helpful measure of changes in household welfare, changes in investment for domestic firms indicate growth. Vijaya Ramachandran, Alan H. Gelb and Manju Shah (2009) used enterprise surveys across Sub-Saharan African to understand the limits firms perceive to their own growth. In order of significance, these perceived limitations to growth in domestic investment include a lack of infrastructure, particularly of reliable sources of electricity; ethnically segmented or minority-dominated business sectors; lack of national or regional transport infrastructure; utility costs; lack of access to credit; and the cost of bribery payments (ibid.). Ritva Reinikka and Jakob Svensson (2001, 220) found similar constraints for future growth, cited in a 1994 Ugandan enterprise survey: firms cited high utility prices and poor services, high taxes, interest rates, corruption, tax administration, access to finance and high transport costs as the main barriers to the expansion of their businesses. Because the key measure this chapter recommends is domestic enterprise investment, issues regarding expensive capital goods (due to expensive and inefficient transport), wasted spending of infrastructure (for supplementary power generation) and corruption costs (for firms that invest more, employ more workers, operate in the formal sector and are trade oriented) are of particular concern (ibid., 227).

In response to macroeconomic reforms and deregulation by the government, we should see domestic firms adjust by taking more financial risks in expanding enterprises, mostly through domestic reinvestment. In addition to these macroeconomic efforts, the government must pay close attention to crafting innovative ways to unburden the process of doing business in that country (World Bank 2016a). Tax reform leads to increased levels of domestic investment, and export tax reform increases the incentives for firms to export with more diversity of products and at a larger volume.

It goes without saying that government efforts to liberalize must include fairly developed anticorruption and anti-bribery stipulations if economic recovery is the goal. Jakob Svensson (2001, 319) finds that "bribery slows firm growth... far more than taxation does," effectively reducing not only profit, but also, more significantly in the scope of this chapter, the amount of money available to reinvest in the domestic economy. Furthermore, because the increase or decrease of bribe payments is typically based not on a fixed rate but on the ability of the firm in question to pay, bribery is an indirect disincentive for the growth of enterprises in volume or diversity of products (ibid., 334). Generally speaking, the incentives and conditions that move households (or micro, small and medium enterprises, in other words) to increase their economic activity are the same that motivate medium-sized domestic actors (usually in light manufacturing and consumer-facing service enterprises) and large-scale operations (including domestic and foreign multinational corporations and foreign investment). The same factors remain in play for actors at different levels of the economic continuum; the difference emerges in the importance of certain factors or constraints over others for certain groups.

In a post-conflict situation in which multiple aspects of society have been weakened or destroyed, the government finds itself awash with competing needs but, of course, must focus on the highest priorities. While all of the categories explained above are important, the prioritization of some is more crucial in order to stimulate domestic business in African states in a post-conflict situation. These include addressing immediate security concerns so the economy can begin its path to normalcy, reconstructing infrastructure in a way that facilitates trade in goods and services, and investing time and resources in creating a reliable energy supply for small-scale domestic manufacturing (Ramachandran, Gelb and Shah 2009). All of these processes require management by strong governmental institutions, which must be built as quickly as feasible.

Foreign Firms

Foreign firms and FDI have been crucial in past cases of post-conflict economic recovery. While foreign firms and FDI doubtless provide much-needed capital in a cash-starved system, they do not represent a silver bullet solution. Foreign money can only help the system in a measure commensurate to its prior quality. We envision the role for foreign investment in terms of contributions to infrastructure investment, skills, training and technology transfer. In the immediate standing-up phase of the recovery, the government should have already restored any FDI lost to the recent conflict. Generally speaking, non-commercial risks such as political instability threaten to ward off potential investors — not those already engaged in the country (ibid., 87-88). The government should continue to nurture relationships with those foreign partners who already had operations in the country pre-conflict and continue recruitment of new FDI as long as these efforts support and help to grow domestic private sector development. Foreign firms are not key drivers in the earlier phases of recovery, but are, instead, key supporters of the vision, as the growth of a vibrant domestic recovery will require domestic actors to play an increasingly central role.

IFIs and Foreign Bilateral Donors

In the past 20 years, the international development community has provided strong support for post-conflict recovery and inclusive economic growth. First, the community's contribution in the form of expanding and deepening our understanding of the phenomenon of conflict and its companion, fragility, has been acknowledged. Understanding the drivers of conflict and fragility has enabled countries to put together strategies for recovery and building resilience of institutions and societies. The international development community has facilitated consultation mechanisms for dialogue and the sharing of experience and knowledge as seen in the new deal dialogue on engaging with fragile states and many international conferences and fora on this subject. The international donors have also provided the bulk of funding for the initial phase of recovery and reconstruction. The IFIs (the World Bank and the AFDB), the EU Commission, the UN system and key bilaterals, such as USAID, the DFID, the Africa Development Fund and the Japan International Cooperation Agency, and interesting newcomers to the donor group, including China, India, Brazil and Turkey, who are expanding their engagement with Africa, have also made contributions to post-conflict recovery (Paczynska 2011). However, the funding from donors tends to decline about five years after the conflict, requiring a shift to domestic resource mobilization (Collier and Hoffler 2002). This is not wholly deliberate on their part, but is instead a natural reaction in a situation of constant international crises and decreasing attention in developed countries. As the conflict in question grows farther away, its priority lessens, especially if conditions are perceived to be improving as new conflicts arise elsewhere. The urgency and attention given to the conflict in the immediate period declines over time, and support from donor countries and institutions diminishes along with it.

Key bilaterals have also been active in funding analytical work that adds to knowledge and in building partnerships. For example, the major donors, together with the g7+ fragile states, were instrumental in the creation of the new deal and its 2011 dialogue forum in Seoul. Some of these bilateral agencies have been able to tap into the capacity of prominent think tanks, such as the Centre for Global Development in Washington, DC, and the Overseas Development Institute in the United Kingdom, thus raising awareness and funding support among aid constituencies in the countries of the north on the issues of fragility and conflict in Africa.

Donors and IFIs have traditionally provided technical assistance for policy formulation and implementation. Because of the push for country ownership and systems that fit the purpose, African countries have been asking for experts who understand local circumstances. Some donors have become more creative and flexible in funding advisory services. Some countries have been given the space to draw on their diaspora or other African countries and think tanks that have capacity and expertise, such as in Ghana, Kenya and South Africa. The use of this African experience has made a huge difference without compromising country ownership.

Although taken together the contribution by donors in technical assistance over the years has improved, issues remain that need to be tackled, going forward. One is alignment with country strategy and systems and nurturing the respect for country ownership. Second, a much stronger effort is needed to help build state institutions that make economic policies and deliver services, while promoting private sector, think tank or community participation in providing services, where appropriate. Third is the role of relevant conditionality (what, when and how) in encouraging program ownership, flexibility and adjustment to ensure that post-conflict recovery proceeds quickly. Historically, the role of conditionality and its evolution has been controversial. Up to the end of the 1970s, it covered mostly technical and financial issues of project implementation. This changed in the 1980s and early 1990s, under structural adjustment, when conditionality covered policy and institutions and, subsequently, governance. The design of conditions was often stylized and rigid and did not take into account local contexts. Part of the reason the adjustment programs failed, at least in Africa, was the lack of ownership, flexibility and fitness for local conditions. The design of content flexibility in post-conflict states has made progress but needs to be deepened. As the network of prominent actors and funders widens in the development and recovery assistance available to states in Sub-Saharan Africa, competition between them may, in fact, lessen the nature and number of conditionalities to the advantage of the recipient countries. In any case, there continue to be lingering questions about the effectiveness of development through conditionality.

Civil Society

Last, but not least, in its role as the primary managing actor in the economic recovery, the government must not overlook the role of civil society in helping communities to grow from below. It may seem unusual at first blush to include a section on civil society in a chapter on the private sector effects in post-conflict recovery, but it should not. If the primary concern is with changing the economic incentives for and motivating the activity of household units, perceptions of societal trust and cohesion created by strengthened civil society *do* matter.

At this fundamental household level, especially in more rural-based societies on the continent, one's social and economic situations are completely intertwined, as economic activity takes place predominantly at the community level. The economic modes of different household units are conceptualized as part and parcel of one's immediate social perceptions. Marginal household decisions to increase economic output or activity depend on individual beliefs that increasing economic activity is the best decision for the household at that time. Certainly, we cannot expect one member of the household to begin a new marginal economic activity or small enterprise if a feeling of panic or distrust permeates the society, or if a sustained peace between different groups feels strained. In essence, if we operate with the household incentive model at the forefront of our recovery plan, which it must be to widen the scope of recovery to the comprehensive society, people will not make risky decisions to increase economic activity or increase consumption where there is a lack of confidence and permanence in the society immediately around them.

In this indirect way, civil society acts as the yeast that facilitates the growth of private sector activities from the bottom up, from the household level. Although the government must maintain its leading role in this process, as it has throughout all stages of the recovery, the best thing a government can do in this case is to allow space for civil society to grow without limitation. A government that wholly controls a civil society will have the opposite effect of what we seek and will mostly work toward limiting the political voices of all levels of a community, as will be explored further in the examples of Rwanda and Uganda later in this chapter. The appropriate role for the government at this critical juncture is to provide support where it can, but overall to allow civil society to flourish and consolidate in a way that best voices the political, economic and social interests of the society as a whole.

In a place where civil society was either limited before the conflict in question or destroyed during it, steps may be necessary to solidify a foundation. In some cases we have seen, organized international peace and reconciliation commissions, led by outstanding and recognized nationals with support from the international community, have achieved initial success. Trust-building exercises at the local level, such as those that took place in Rwanda (gacaca) and Sierra Leone, were crucial in remaking and strengthening the relationships between individuals and households that lay the groundwork for economic activity and exchange in those countries. The trust-building actions that ease the anxieties of civil society, whether internationally or locally organized, are critical in contributing toward a sustainable reconciliation.

Enabling the voices of the average citizen through this political breathing room via a strengthened civil society creates a crucial dynamic between citizen and state: a public and political discussion with autonomy from the state. Political autonomy creates space for economic autonomy from the state, which is a necessary factor in a vibrant economy. Enhanced political processes that "increasingly include competitive (if ideologically indistinct) parties, widespread popular participation in the electoral process, and free and fair elections…[p]rovide new opportunities for citizens to hold state actors accountable, including in the form of better service delivery" (Taylor 2012, 62-63). In another way, "democracy, in short, allows the market to expand, in economic as well as social terms…. Political liberalization, like the economic changes that generally occurred in parallel, augurs positively for business in Africa" (ibid., 63).

The reformulation of this relationship between the state and its people, while initiated by the central government, is ultimately a task of devolution of power to the community and household level. The government consciously relinquishes power to the local level, building the very capacity for resilience we intend to foster. An example of this type of opening up of political space took place when Kenya reformed its constitution in 2010. The new constitution, in addition to strengthening the role of human rights and the separation of powers, included provisions to largely devolve power from the national level to newly created county governments with their own county assemblies and county executives (Akech 2010,

23). These steps were taken to counter feelings of political marginalization of certain groups by the central government, and they effectively increased civil society, integrated marginalized voices and increased access to service provision at the local level. But, as we have observed elsewhere, the devil is in the implementation; it is too early to say whether and how well Kenya's experiment will work.

The best interests of both general citizens and communities at a household level, as well as economic activity from the micro to multinational, are served by creating this space that is autonomous from the state. Steps taken to foster political voices will also serve to support those private sector activities that we find imperative for genuine and sustainable economic recovery. Leonardo R. Arriola (2013) takes the argument a step further, positing that the solution to the problems of unequal economic access and state capture of the economy can be solved with the formation of a multi-ethnic opposition coalition. Arriola understands that since the two main sources of capital in many Sub-Saharan African states are state-captured assets and non-state private sector firms, an autonomous private sector is the main route through which legitimate opposition politics can take place and force a relationship of accountability on the incumbent regime (ibid., 19). Taylor (2012, 68) finds that "poverty alleviation is perhaps most directly linked to the fostering of growth and jobs through private sector development initiatives, wherein individual (and community) empowerment will emerge through the encouragement of small- and medium-scale enterprises."

Case Studies: Older Cases

Now we will turn to the cases of Rwanda and Uganda, where strong leaders created visions that produced remarkable recoveries in terms of both macroeconomic stability and post-conflict reconstruction and of economic growth in the 1990s and 2000s.

Rwanda

Rwanda represents a post-conflict recovery marked by remarkable economic growth that rested on the Asian model of a developmental state leading the formation of a competitive advantage. Further, Rwanda achieved increases in certain indicators measured by the International Monetary Fund, including issues of gender and poverty. With the help of the World Bank's International Development Association, Rwanda solidified its fragile economic base following the 1994 genocide with programs including massive infrastructure strengthening, more comprehensive education of the citizenry and strong macroeconomic measures (International Development Association 2009). Large-scale efforts of privatization of state-owned operations and projects in the agricultural sector stabilized the domestic need for employment, especially at the household level. The government developed a strong private sector development program, focused on an export promotion strategy for its competitive agricultural and natural resource products, and streamlined processes to facilitate foreign business development, including an export processing zone (ibid., 5-6). Decentralization efforts and privatization enabled pro-poor initiatives at the local level, which led to increases in household income and greatly increased Rwanda's social indicators in education and health (ibid., 6). Paul Kagame's technocratic leadership has created robust economic growth, which is to be celebrated by both African countries and the international development community. For many outsiders, including Tony Blair, Rwanda has become an economic star in Africa. Rwanda's visionary leadership and strong strategy represent an important model; however, post-conflict reconciliation and political participation should be given a stronger emphasis. The story of the Rwandan recovery would be incomplete without mention of foreign assistance; Rwanda recovered with the help of huge amounts of private and public foreign aid and now faces the difficult task of evolving past that dependence. All in all, this is a developmental state model that promotes, rather than strangles, the market economy.

Uganda

Following decades of conflict and economic strife, Uganda began on a path of recovery under the strong leadership of Yoweri Museveni, who came to power in 1986. This recovery, seen as one of the most ambitious cases of economic liberalization in an African state, also consisted of massive government-led efforts for both economic recovery and poverty reduction. This dual mandate of restoring internal security after the decades of conflict and of laying the groundwork for economic growth and subsequent poverty reduction presented a challenge that could only be properly navigated with a strong government vision. The vision focused on changing the predatory tax regime to one that provided crucial services to citizens and increased foreign investment, including an anticorruption action plan that helped in both efforts and a more transparent information dissemination about government spending that held civil servants accountable (Svensson 2001; Reinikka 2001).

Uganda undertook massive financial reform programs, "especially in the areas of fiscal policy, exchange rate reforms, trade policy, and the use of debt relief to enhance public expenditure on basic social services" (Tumusiime-Mutebile 2001, xviii). This economic reform was experienced at the household level as a move from agricultural subsistence to market-based economic activity. Government efforts surrounding initiatives to increase agricultural productivity, especially for smallholder farmers, and increased market access motivated this change at the household level (Henstridge and Kasekende 2001). Growth in the poorest segments of the society reduced inequality and further contributed to the internal peace of the country. For larger enterprises, measures for internal peace were crucial to recommence operations and to entice foreign investment (ibid.).

The cases of Rwanda and Uganda illustrate that although much economic growth and recovery can take place in a manner that improves the lives of citizens in some ways, recoveries of this nature remain stillborn in the area of political and social reconciliation. Because a limited political space cannot be a forever-sustainable method, these recoveries may be confronting the boundaries of their effectiveness, a confrontation that could lead to a recovery trap. To realize fully the dynamism and innovation intended for each recovery, a political opening up, not only at the centre but also at the community level, must take place to address the political aspects of the reconciliation and free participation that might boost the recovery to the next level.

More Recent Case Studies

This section focuses on the experiences of Liberia and Sierra Leone as more recent and continuing cases. Their very encouraging progress in reconstruction and recovery in the first decade of the twenty-first century was still being consolidated when Ebola hit in 2014 — creating what is called elsewhere the "double tragedy": both the conflict plus the Ebola shock (Madavo 2015/2016). But our concern is with how these countries handled the post-conflict period from 2002 and 2003 to 2014, before the outbreak of the Ebola virus. During that decade, both countries had built strong participatory visions and strategies for transforming their economies and institutions. They had strong support from their international partners. Economies grew by between six to 11 percent in Liberia and Sierra Leone (World Bank 2015a; 2016b).

Sierra Leone

In the case of Sierra Leone, we see a government vision focused on liberal economic policies, but also on governance, political participation and reconciliation, incorporating society and committees. For comparison, the processes in Uganda and Rwanda, however successful, did not adequately consult varied groups in society, and, if not rectified, could weaken the sustainability of the recoveries in these countries. The government tried to create a broad-based consensus on the reconstruction and recovery strategy, allowing its

citizens to participate in order to build broad-based ownership of the vision, strategies and action plan's theory. However, in spite of the progress made in the decade spanning from 2004 to 2014, the country's institutions and economic and political processes were still fragile and not resilient enough to resist and manage the Ebola shock. Happily, the decade of experience with reconstruction has provided lessons that Sierra Leone is applying to the post-Ebola recovery programs and strategies.

Liberia

The peace agreement signed at the end of the Liberian war in 2005 featured virtually all major stakeholders, internal and external. In order to address the challenges of peace consolidation on taking office in 2005, President Sirleaf recognized that first she had to make a tangible impact on the lives of millions of disillusioned Liberians. The administration worked closely with donors, civil society and the Liberian diaspora to develop the Interim Poverty Reduction Strategy (iPRS), which was eventually upgraded to the Poverty Reduction Strategy (PRS) in 2008 (Liberia 2008). The iPRS was comprehensive in targeting multiple aspects of the reconstruction agenda, including national security, economic growth, infrastructure and investment, and social services delivery. In order to better align the reconstruction agenda with the actual needs of the country, the government undertook thorough stakeholder participation, including public consultations and working groups (Cubitt 2011, 36–38). A critical aspect of this process was that each county in Liberia was given the opportunity to customize its own PRS based on local conditions (United Nations Development Program 2010, 46).

The Two Countries

Overall, both Liberia and Sierra Leone put together tangible plans involving their people and local and external partners to kick-start growth after their respective civil wars. Their governments had the support of the international community with substantial funding to rebuild infrastructure and state capacity. Effective leadership in both countries by Sirleaf and Ernest Bai Koroma was crucial to coordinating implementation with donors, multilateral institutions and the private sector. The new deal program, a major framework for both countries' reconstruction plans, ensured that all actors were on the same page and that the governments would have substantial ownership over development strategy. As a result, both countries showed remarkable promise in the decade of post-conflict reconstruction; growth was among the highest in the world and government capacity was substantially improving and consolidating.

However, the extent of the damage caused by civil war meant that a decade of growth and institutional consolidation would not be enough (compared to about 20 years in the older countries) — the two states were still highly fragile on the eve of the Ebola outbreak. Institutional capacity was still weak and infrastructure, especially in health care and delivery of social services, had remained a work in progress. Consequently, in spite of the progress made, Liberia and Sierra Leone remained vulnerable to exogenous shocks, a legacy of their fragility. This circumscribed measurable success in the areas of economy, political participation and transparency in both countries in the last decade. The measure of a successful recovery is not determined by the improvement of certain metrics alone; a truly successful recovery creates a state and society of resilience that can regenerate after exogenous shocks. These cases are an unfinished lesson in the process of post-conflict recovery. But these states are continuing their recovery within a politically and economically open system, however fragile.

Conclusion

Experience from Sub-Saharan Africa and elsewhere (Timor-Leste) tells us that a recovery from conflict with depth and sustainability is possible. Such recovery is neither linear nor quick;

it often takes at least five years or more to be embedded in local conditions and owned by the country and its people. There are no blueprints or shortcuts. Nonetheless, there are a number of factors that must be present to provide an environment for progress. First, as South Sudan shows, is the importance of peace, durable political settlements, security and stability. Here, country leadership is key. While both regional players (the African Union and the regional economic communities) and the United Nations have provided mediation and post-conflict peacekeeping, this has not worked in situations where leaders were weak and more interested in power than the development of their people. Second, where durable settlements are in place, strong leadership (broadly defined) at home is needed to spearhead a participative and well-developed recovery vision; the government must be the initial driving force, especially in the early phases of recovery, without monopolizing the state. Third is the importance of standing up and expanding the economy. The state would provide the infrastructure and other services (education, health, water and so on) that are needed to revive and sustain production and productivity. This requires sound macroeconomic policies creating regulation and incentives that stimulate the private sector activities from the household level upward. Fourth is the importance of remaining open to the economies of the subregions and the world through trade and investment. Fifth is the importance of implementation. Effective implementation often divides the good visions from the successful recoveries. This often requires the mobilization of a partnership that includes all relevant actors, domestic and international. Finally, and no less important, is the need to invest in building the capacity of state and non-state institutions that deliver political, economic and social services. Such capacity and resilience will enable countries to absorb shocks and manage changes, such as conflict, violence and epidemics. Literature in the recent years has called the latter building resilience in fragile states.

Assuming the above factors are met and are moving forward, institutional and economic recovery are possible, as shown in the brief cases presented above. This raises interesting questions. What should successful recovery look like? Is strong, inclusive economic growth without a political opening up adequate?

Although this is not the primary focus of this chapter, the contention is that if post-conflict economic recovery is to happen with any degree of depth and sustainability, it needs to be accompanied by a parallel political opening up, however gradual. In addition, political transitions are a critical issue, and one of the government's most critical roles in bringing about lasting post-conflict recovery is in passing on power at the right time within entrenched rules such as the constitution. In a system with a limited political space, government accountability is necessarily precarious, and the issues both between groups and between the people and the government threaten to re-erupt into the troubles that precipitated the initial conflict. Focus must be given to maintaining political openness and due process in countries such as those in both the old and new cases.

All in all, despite remarkable performance on economic and social indicators, the incumbent governments of Rwanda and Uganda operate relatively autocratic political systems, marked also by underlying situations of closed social space. The newer cases of Sierra Leone and Liberia show that, however struggling and incomplete their recoveries may be, progress toward sustainable recovery can take place within a framework of political rights and participation. While the recoveries in the more recent cases in Sierra Leone and Liberia may not have shown as impressive rates of growth as the older cases, in terms of economic and social indicators, these states have nevertheless tried to push reconstruction within the framework of democratic institutions and traditions. Whether this can be called a successful post-conflict recovery depends on how we define success. These cases have shown that a post-conflict

recovery that includes sizable economic growth may not allow for political space and societal reconciliation, while a post-conflict recovery that involves political openness and due process may not be characterized by sizable economic growth. If we define a successful post-conflict recovery as one that has depth and is sustainable, the challenge for the future will be to determine whether that can encompass both sizable economic growth and a framework of strong political rights, peace, security and stability.

Acknowledgement

The author would like to give special acknowledgement to his research assistant, Sophie Sweeney Haggerty, Georgetown class of 2016, for her excellent support and contributions to this chapter.

Works Cited

AFDB/World Bank. 2015. "Joint African Development Bank World Bank Support for Post Ebola Economic Recovery in the Mano River Union Member Countries and Guinea-Bissau: AFDB-WB Shared Vision and Support Strategies." Draft shared with the author by the AFDB.

Akech, Migai. 2010. *Institutional Reform in the New Constitution of Kenya*. October. www.ictj.org/sites/default/files/ICTJ-Kenya-Institutional-Reform-2010-English.pdf.

Appleton, Simon. 2001. "Changes in Poverty and Inequality." In *Uganda's Recovery: The Role of Farms, Firms, and Government*, edited by Ritva Reinikka and Paul Collier, 83–122. Washington, DC: World Bank.

Arriola, Leonardo R. 2013. *Multiethnic Coalitions in Africa: Business Financing of Opposition Election Campaigns*. Cambridge, UK: Cambridge University Press.

Asuni, Judith Burdin. 2009. "Understanding the Armed Groups of the Niger Delta." Council on Foreign Relations Working Paper. www.cfr.org/nigeria/understanding-armed-groups-niger-delta/p20146.

Beyene, Hailay Gebretinsae. 2015. "Are African Diasporas Development Partners, Peacemakers or Spoilers? The Case of Ethiopia, Kenya and Nigeria." *Diaspora Studies* 8 (2): 145–161.

Brück, Tilman. 2001. "Coping with Peace: Postwar Household Strategies in Northern Mozambique." Master's thesis, University of Oxford. http://citeseerx.ist.psu.edu/viewdoc/download?doi=10.1.1.201.4041&rep=rep1&type=pdf.

Collier, Paul and Anke Hoeffler. 2002. "World Bank Policy Research Working Paper 2902: Aid, Policy, and Growth in Post-Conflict Societies." Policy Research Working Paper No. 2902. doi:10.1596/1813-9450-2902.

Collier, Paul and Ritva Reinikka. 2001. "Introduction." In *Uganda's Recovery: The Role of Farms, Firms, and Government*, edited by Ritva Reinikka and Paul Collier, 1–11. Washington, DC: World Bank.

Cubitt, Christine. 2011. *Local and Global Dynamics of Peacebuilding: Post-conflict Reconstruction in Sierra Leone*. New York, NY: Routledge.

Deininger, Klaus and John Okidi. 2001. "Rural Households: Incomes, Productivity, and Nonfarm Enterprises." In *Uganda's Recovery: The Role of Farms, Firms, and Government*, edited by Ritva Reinikka and Paul Collier, 123–75. Washington, DC: World Bank.

Henstridge, Mark and Louis Kasekende. 2001. "Exchange Reforms, Stabilization, and Fiscal Management." In *Uganda's Recovery: The Role of Farms, Firms, and Government*, edited by Ritva Reinikka and Paul Collier, 49–80. Washington, DC: World Bank.

High Level Panel on Fragile States. 2014. *Ending Conflict & Building Peace in Africa: A Call to Action*. Tunis: AFDB.

High Level Panel on Illicit Financial Flows from Africa. 2015. "Illicit Financial Flows." Report for the Joint African Union Commission/UNECA, January 26. www.uneca.org/sites/default/files/PublicationFiles/iff_main_report_26feb_en.pdf.

Hughes, Jacob, Ted Hooley, Siafa Hage and George Ingram. 2014. "Implementing the New Deal for Fragile States." Global Economy and Development Report No. 2014–02. Washington, DC: Brookings Institution.

International Development Association. 2009. "Rwanda: From Post-Conflict Reconstruction to Development." International Development Association at Work news release, August. http://siteresources.worldbank.org/IDA/Resources/ida-Rwanda-10-02-09.pdf.

International Dialogue. n.d. "A New Deal for Engagement in Fragile States." www.pbsbdialogue.org/media/filer_public/07/69/07692de0-3557-494e-918e-18df00e9ef73/the_new_deal.pdf.

Larson, Donald and Klaus Deininger. 2001. "Crop Markets and Household Participation." In *Uganda's Recovery: The Role of Farms, Firms, and Government*, edited by Ritva Reinikka and Paul Collier, 177–204. Washington, DC: World Bank.

Liberia. 2008. "Poverty Reduction Strategy Paper." International Monetary Fund Country Report No. 08/219. www.imf.org/external/pubs/ft/scr/2008/cr08219.pdf.

Madavo, Callisto. 2015/2016. "The Double Tragedy in MRU: Reconstruction after Conflict and Ebola." Paper prepared for AFDB.

Mance, Henry and Maggie Fick. 2016. "Cameron Calls Nigeria and Afghanistan 'Fantastically Corrupt.'" *Financial Times*, May 10. www.ft.com/content/69e196e2-16c9-11e6-9d98-00386a18e39d.

McFerson, Hazel M. 2009. "Governance and Hyper-corruption in Resource-rich African Countries." *Third World Quarterly* 30 (8): 1529–47. doi:10.1080/01436590903279257.

Mills, Greg. 2014. *Why States Recover: Changing Walking Societies into Winning Nations — from Afghanistan to Zimbabwe*. London, UK: Hurst.

OECD. 2005/2008. *The Paris Declaration on Aid Effectiveness and the Accra Agenda for Action*. www.oecd.org/dac/effectiveness/34428351.pdf.

———. 2015. *States of Fragility 2015: Meeting Post–2015 Ambitions*. Paris, France: OECD Publishing. doi:http://dx.doi.org/10.1787/9789264227699-en.

Paczynska, Agnieszka. 2011. "Emerging Donors and Post-Conflict Reconstruction." *Global Studies Review* 70 (3). www.globality-gmu.net/archives/2712.

Peschka, Mary Porter. 2011. "The Role of Private Sector in Fragile and Conflict and Fragile States." World Bank World Development Report 2011 Background Paper.

Ramachandran, Vijaya, Alan H. Gelb and Manju Shah. 2009. *Africa's Private Sector: What's Wrong with the Business Environment and What to Do about It*. Washington, DC: Center for Global Development.

Reinikka, Ritva and Jakob Svensson. 2001. "Confronting Competition: Investment, Profit, and Risk." In *Uganda's Recovery: The Role of Farms, Firms, and Government*, edited by Ritva Reinikka and Paul Collier, 207–34. Washington, DC: World Bank.

Reinikka, Ritva. 2001. "Recovery in Service Delivery: Evidence from Schools and Health Centers." In *Uganda's Recovery: The Role of Farms, Firms, and Government*, edited by Ritva Reinikka and Paul Collier, 343–70. Washington, DC: World Bank.

Schwartz, Jordan, Shelly Hahn and Ian Bannon. 2004. "The Private Sector's Role in the Provision of Infrastructure in Post-Conflict Countries: Patterns and Policy Options." The World Bank Social Development Papers: Conflict Prevention and Reconstruction Report No. 16. Washington, DC: World Bank.

Sierra Leone. 2005. "Poverty Reduction Strategy Paper." International Monetary Fund Country Report No. 05/191. www.imf.org/external/pubs/ft/scr/2005/cr05191.pdf.

Spanjers, Joseph and Hakon Frede Foss. 2015. "Illicit Financial Flows and Development Indices: 2008–2012." *Global Financial Integrity* (blog), January 3. www.gfintegrity.org/report/illicit-financial-flows-and-development-indices-2008-2012/.

Stewart, Frances. 2004. "Development and Security." Centre for Research on Inequality, Human Security and Ethnicity Working Paper No. 3. Oxford, UK: University of Oxford. www3.qeh.ox.ac.uk/pdf/crisewps/workingpaper3.pdf.

Svensson, Jakob. 2001. "The Cost of Doing Business: Firms' Experience with Corruption." In *Uganda's Recovery: The Role of Farms, Firms, and Government*, edited by Ritva Reinikka and Paul Collier, 319–41. Washington, DC: World Bank.

Taylor, Scott D. 2012. *Globalization and the Cultures of Business in Africa: From Patrimonialism to Profit*. Bloomington, IN: Indiana University Press.

Transition Support Group. 2016. *From Fragility to Resilience: Managing Natural Resources in Fragile Situations in Africa*. Abidjan, Côte d'Ivoire: AFDB.

Tumusiime-Mutebile, Emmanuel. 2001. "Foreword." In *Uganda's Recovery: The Role of Farms, Firms, and Government*, edited by Ritva Reinikka and Paul Collier, xiii–xv. Washington, DC: World Bank.

United Nations Development Program. 2010. "Leadership and Change in Post-Conflict States: A Case Study of Liberia." Global Event Working Paper.

World Bank. 2015a. "Sierra Leone Overview." *The World Bank*, October 5, August 1. www.worldbank.org/en/country/sierraleone/overview.

———. 2015b. *The State of Social Safety Nets 2015*. Washington, DC: World Bank.

———. 2016a. *Doing Business 2016: Measuring Regulatory Quality and Efficiency*. Washington, DC: World Bank. doi:10.1596/978-1-4648-0667-4.

———. 2016b. "Liberia Overview." *The World Bank*, April 9, August 1. www.worldbank.org/en/country/liberia/overview.

13

Women and Conflict: Roles in Conflict Mitigation and Resolution in Africa

Akinyi Roselyn Walender

Conflict tears the fabric of society apart. For many, families are torn apart and life as they know it ceases to exist. Women and young boys and girls are often particularly affected, and the long-term effects can be very devastating. Many families find themselves displaced and exiled within or outside their home borders, where they are subjected to fear, violence, hunger and disease. Whenever women are involved in war and in emergencies, there is significant impact on traditional gender roles and, in fact, the social structure of the society involved is effectively significantly altered.

When the men are away engaging in warfare, women find themselves with no choice but to assume the role of supporting and protecting their families, taking on full responsibility as head of the household with no support system for themselves and their children, who also stop being children and take on adult roles. Women have never been merely passive victims of conflict. They are stakeholders in their communities in more ways than one; they are mothers, sisters, wives, friends and daughters. The important roles they play in the social, political and economic events may sometimes lead to conflict.

Women also play a role in local peace processes that may lead to de-escalation of conflict. Thus, women must not be treated as innocent bystanders or victims of conflict, because they very rarely are. Unfortunately, the roles and efforts women undertake during times of crisis often go unnoticed, in part because of social norms and the restricted opportunities accorded to women in the public and political spaces to engage in governance structures. Women are relegated to the lower ranks with numerous roadblocks placed on their paths, so many that the very notion of gathering the strength to vie for a position of leadership becomes an act of sheer bravery. Yet, giving up is not and cannot be an option.

This chapter seeks to examine women and conflict, and the roles women play in conflict mitigation and resolution in Africa. It will examine how women organize themselves to respond to crises and the challenges and opportunities that accrue to them in leadership and decision-making spaces.

Collectiveness and Collaboration

In terms of a coping mechanism, the African philosophy of *ubuntu* — "I am because we are" — provides strength for women, in the recognition that nobody survives on their own: the burden is far too big and heavy to contemplate.

Women often employ various coping mechanisms to ensure their families and communities survive during conflict and crises. Circumstances lead them to gravitate naturally into organizing in the African spirit of *ubuntu*, which emphasizes collectiveness, solidarity, mutual support and the acknowledgement that caring for one another is the essence of humanity. When women organize themselves to respond to the crisis facing their communities, they take on roles that are traditionally ascribed to men. Women organizing themselves is not a new phenomenon in many global communities. In Africa, women come together to start community projects through various fora. For example, through mother unions in the church, they support one another when their children are getting married and for funerals and at farming and harvest times. In Kenya, women organize around informal cooperatives called *chamas*. As a *chama*, they pool their resources to meet one person's needs and continue to provide resources to one another until every member of the cooperative has been served. Or they may form a *chama* for investment purposes. When a crisis occurs, these forms of organizing become even more critical for a community's well-being and survival.

South Sudan is a country that has undergone numerous crises, including a civil war that lasted for decades and continuing conflict, even after independence, famine and flooding. The county has been in a perpetual humanitarian emergency mode for decades. Thousands of people have become refugees in neighbouring countries and even more are internally displaced. Gender roles are clearly differentiated by unequal power relations between men and women, with women relegated to subservient roles and positions in society. The civil war changed this power imbalance, at least for the period of the war when women became heads of households. At the height of the civil war, before South Sudan gained independence from Sudan, many communities in the areas liberated by the Sudanese People's Liberation Army were highly insecure with very limited access to basic services. Even though they were in the liberated areas, they lived in fear of being bombed by the Khartoum government, which frequently dropped bombs from Russian-made Antonov cargo planes on the unsuspecting civilian population. Women became responsible for the overall survival of their families — a vital support network for the military — and visionary male and female leaders emerged to organize them into community-based associations.

The Tonj Area Women's Association (TAWA) is a classic example of a community-based organization headed by a person with vision, determination and energy. TAWA was founded by Mary Nyibol, a soft-spoken Dinka woman who received much respect from her peers. She was the organization's greatest source of energy. Through TAWA, the women members, who were living under very difficult conditions, collaborated to alleviate their situation and promote opportunities for fellow women to improve their lives and to support each other. They started off with small projects, such as a tea shop, and small-scale credit for farming inputs, and eventually got involved in cattle trading. When the famine started in 1998, it was no surprise that these women, who understood their community needs so well and were already highly organized, would be the ones to take on the responsibility to run a feeding centre. They kept their community and neighbours alive for more than six months before the international community arrived. Mary Nyibol and the countless other women who continue to mobilize their fellow women, energizing them to respond to numerous unimaginable crises, are quite simply exceptional.

With support in the form of small grants, the members of TAWA went on to implement several projects for their community. These included a primary school, for which members learned how to sew and made a small profit selling uniforms; a grinding mill for their immediate community and neighbours; and, the most interesting project, cross-border trade in cattle. With their proceeds from the grinding mill and selling uniforms, they bought cattle, which some of the women, accompanied by a few young men, walked from Tonj to northern Uganda, an approximately three-week journey. Then, armed with the proceeds from cattle sales, they bought spare parts for the grinding mill, materials for uniforms, books for the school, and other commodities the community required such as soap, salt and cooking oil for a local shop they were operating. The members of TAWA understood what their community needed and, in their simple, unsophisticated, yet visionary, way, did everything in their power to meet these needs.

The TAWA example also illustrates how conflict and crises challenge traditional structures at the household level. As women take charge at the community level, they become part of the peace building and negotiation mechanisms; many too begin to venture into the political space. Evidence shows, however, that once a crisis is over, women are not accorded equal opportunities to use their experiences in nation building.

Participation and Leadership of Women

"The belief that public life and leadership positions should be reserved for men remains widespread, and women vying for leadership positions have difficulty winning the trust of voters" (Bubenzer and Stern 2011, citing Abwunza 1997).

Patriarchal practices that perpetuate the view that women are subservient to men's authority persist widely, as does the belief that public life and, accordingly, leadership positions are the privilege of men. To address gender inequality and the empowerment of women, women's participation in decision making at all levels must be encouraged and ensured. Women continue to struggle to make their voices heard; increasingly, they are marginalized and sidelined.

"Political life is organized for male norms and values, and in many cases even for male lifestyles. In politics, you are looked at as an intruder because they think that politics is not in the space of women, and you feel lonely because of being few in numbers" (Sarah Nyanath Elijah interview, quoted in Bubenzer and Stern 2011).

Women continue to face numerous barriers to leadership and participation because governance structures remain male dominated; this makes it very difficult for women to engage. In political circles, the purpose of any consultation with women is rarely to truly represent their views, but more to court them for their votes.

"Yet, it often happens that when women make it to the public sphere, they have been selected because they are women who cannot rise, confront, or challenge the issues at the negotiation table, or they are included without due consideration for caliber, knowledge, and capacity to represent the constituencies and issues relevant to their communities" (Walender 2016).

Selection criteria are often obscure. As one South Sudanese woman stated, "It is true there are women leaders in most states, but most of them have been placed in those positions to add cosmetic value. We are still not aware of what criteria were used to make these women leaders" (quoted in Chimbi 2009).

The practice of political parties making token appointments is a major impediment to actual women's leadership. The practice is prevalent especially where there is no political will and when an affirmative action law is passed without clear provisions for its implementation. In some cases, civil society groups or external forces, such as charitable donors, may push and advocate for a gender balance in political leadership spaces and or peace processes. Political parties have been known, however, to nominate women who are not qualified to assume these positions and as such have very limited chances of influencing agendas.

The appointment of women as tokens in positions of leadership is also demonstrated in other ways by political parties supporting only those women whom they can control and who are related to them in some way or other.

These women tend to have some affiliation to their nominators. They cannot raise their voices or go against the party line or their benefactors; their role is simply to fill the numbers and add to votes. Unfortunately, too, these nominations get carried out without any consultations with wider society through the ballot, other women or civil society. Token appointments are especially prevalent in peace processes. For example, in the various Sudan and South Sudan peace processes, either there were no women represented at all or those who were appointed were deemed not to represent the voices of women at the negotiation table. In some instances, although many women were capable of articulating the needs of their communities, they could not even gain access to the negotiators to present their positions and demands for inclusion in the settlements.

Women are concerned about the quality of leaders who can make a difference and not the quantity who cannot deliver. One woman in South Sudan stated the problem thus: "We know there is an under representation of women in leadership, what we need to do is learn how to better strategies [sic] by marshalling strength in support of the most promising candidates.... How about women as equal stakeholders of society? Are we also not entitled to participate in making decisions that determine our future as a nation? Wouldn't it be better to have fewer women leaders who can

deliver, rather than more who are there to make the leadership class look good in terms of being more gender representative?" (quoted in Gathigah 2010).

If consultations with civil society in search of qualified and able women were undertaken, and women's organizations were involved, there would be many names of women who were known for their deeds and actions and were capable of filling leadership positions. The practice of tokenism ultimately does women a great disservice. It edges women out of leadership positions because it denies women who have merit, passion and vision the opportunities to serve their communities and country. Furthermore, it erodes any recognition that women are equal stakeholders in society and are entitled to participate in making decisions that determine their future and that of their nation and their children.

Women have made it clear that they are change agents, and want to bring changes in their lives and their communities. Yet there persists the recognition that unless women put themselves out to vie for leadership positions and engage in decision making, the status quo will not change. Some of the key challenges women face, and this is by no means an exhaustive list, are as follow. There is the notion and expectation of having to get permission from husbands and family to engage in politics; societal perceptions of women engaged in the political sphere are terrible and very often detrimental to women's reputations. Female political aspirants are subject to verbal abuse and find their reputations tarnished; some are physically and sexually assaulted, and their families are threatened. In extreme cases, some women have been assaulted and raped and others have lost their lives. Election violence against women is manifested in various forms and degrees and in some countries is almost inevitable.

Financial challenges greatly hamper women's quest for political space. It costs money to participate in politics, and many women cannot afford the costs nor do they have the personal wealth to fund their campaigns. Often women do not have resources; a woman's resources are family resources, which means that she does not have any authority over them because men control the resources. For example, land title deeds or house deeds may not be in a woman's name, making it difficult for her to use these properties as collateral for financial resources to campaign for political office. Political campaigns are extremely expensive; when men and women use personal resources for campaigns, they risk plunging their families into debt and poverty, especially if the campaign is not successful and there is no income. While men tend to have access to finances and support from political parties and cronies, the men do not hesitate to augment these funds with family resources. Most of the time, the men squander their family's security and future to fund their election campaigns. Women do not have this kind of access at any level.

Once women are in office, the situation does not get any easier. Whether nominated or elected, women still face various serious challenges in navigating the male-dominated political systems and structures. Very often women are not immediately empowered in their positions to effect changes. Few women have the political leadership skills and experience or, especially in a post-conflict environment, the formal political education that would enable them to quickly manoeuvre the complicated political systems and effectively carry out their mandates. In conversation with the author, female cabinet member in the South Sudan government revealed that the women in the cabinet were often not included in making decisions, because important discussions and decision making took place late at night and outside the office. Women in leadership positions often face many dilemmas due to societal expectations that conflict with their roles. While the women have to rush home at the end of the day to assume their domestic roles, they cannot join their male counterparts in meetings convened after work; these meetings may run late into the night and take place either at bars or restaurants or even at one of their male colleague's houses where the men sit to discuss and their wives prepare and serve food for the guest. Here, the men discuss official matters and take decisions; because the female legislators may not attend these late-night meetings, they only hear of the decisions taken after the fact, and, by then, they they have no opportunity to contribute their views. This effectively excludes women from decision-making tables.

Most African cultures frown on women staying out late at night, whether they are married or single. Women who join their political colleagues would be labelled prostitutes by society and even by the very colleagues with whom they were meeting, and their husbands or partners would be ridiculed for not being able to "control" their wives. If women choose to engage, they risk their reputations being tarnished, and their marriages and relationships breaking.

Cultural taboos are linked to women's exclusion from public space; the experiences expressed by women at the grassroots level also play out at all other levels of society. A number of women said that their husbands did not want them to participate in public meetings because "a woman who always joins the company of men will fall in love with other people's husbands" (Porter, Smyth and Sweetman 1999, 72).

Ways to Support Women in their Quest to Represent their Views in Society

To create a conducive environment for women to engage in decision making and leadership, and thus represent the needs of the whole society, it is imperative, first, to acknowledge the factors that hinder their effective participation in the political and decision-making space. Mechanisms to address these factors should be put in place to enable more women to come forward and claim this space.

Among the practical interventions could be identifying, targeting and encouraging women who have the right knowledge, skills, capacities, capability and passion to step forward for nominations and appointments into leadership and managerial positions. These women would need to be supported financially and morally by other women and by men too. One way to achieve this is by establishing a system that allows for senior women leaders who have been in politics for a long time, including those who have served in senior managerial and board positions, to mentor those entering the leadership space. The senior leaders could share experiences of best practices, pitfalls to avoid and how to engage effectively. In instances where there is no formal system in place, women should strive to reach out and support other women in leadership roles. Women should also not shy away from seeking mentorship from men who champion gender equality. The ensuing benefits will be reaped by society at large. Once in leadership positions, women need support to ensure they achieve key goals. Forming strategic alliances and networks both inside and outside with women's groups and allies is key, and crucial for their lobbying and influence. Women leaders need to keep abreast of critical issues affecting their constituencies and understand how they would like to be represented. Women leaders need to understand the political environment they are engaging in; forging alliances with both men and women is critical to their success.

Further, improving women's access to education at all levels is crucial to ensuring leadership and participation. A lack of education has led to women being excluded from processes that are deemed complex and technical, and also limits their ability to understand and interpret key documents, policies and strategies.

What Next?

Women's contributions to society cannot be underestimated. Interventions are much more effective when women's perspectives are taken into account. In all conflict environments, evidence shows that crises have often significantly and radically challenged gender roles, generally for the better when women assume non-traditional roles and greater independence.

Yet because of persisting injustice and inequality, equal access to opportunities and resources continues to be elusive. Women have not been able to participate equally in the decision-making processes that determine their lives and their society's direction and future. Excluding women in decision making has political, social and economic consequences for society. It deprives nations of an all-important resource for the growth and development of current and future generations.

Works Cited

Abwunza, Judith. 1997. *Women's Voices, Women's Power: Dialogue of Resistance from East Africa.* Peterborough, ON: Broadview Press.

Bubenzer, Friederike and Orly Stern, eds. 2011. *Hope, Pain & Patience: The Lives of Women in South Sudan.* Aukland Park, South Africa: Fanale. www.orlystern.com/wp-content/uploads/2016/08/Hope-Pain-and-Patience.pdf.

Chimbi, Joyce. 2009. "Women Ready to Take their Place." *IPS News*, 24 June. http://www.ipsnews.net/2009/06/politics-south-sudan-women-ready-to-take-their-place/.

de Wet, Johann C. 2010. *The Art of Persuasive Communication: A Process.* Clairmont, South Africa: Juta.

Gathigah, Miriam. 2010. "South Sudan: Women's Eyes on the Political Prize." *IPS News*, 7 January. http://ipsnews.net/news.asp?idnews=49907.

Kitcher, Ingrid. 2013. *Challenges to Security, Livelihoods and Gender Justice in South Sudan.* Oxford, UK: Oxfam GB. www.oxfam.org/sites/www.oxfam.org/files/rr-challenges-security-livelihoods-gender-south-sudan-130313-en.pdf.

Porter, Fenella, Ines A. Smyth and Caroline Sweetman, eds. 1999. *Gender Works: Oxfam Experience in Policy and Practice.* Oxford, UK: Oxfam GB.

van Reisen, Mirjam, ed. 2015. *Women's Leadership in Peace-building: Conflict, Community and Care.* Trenton, NJ: Africa World Press.

Walender, Akinyi R. 2016. "Engendering Responses to Complex Emergencies: Lessons from South Sudan." *Prism: Women, Peace & Inclusive Security* 6 (1): 154–163. http://cco.ndu.edu/Publications/PRISM/PRISM-volume-6-no1/Article/684585/engendering-responses-to-complex-emergencies-lessons-from-south-sudan/.

14

The Outcast Majority and Postwar Development: Youth Exclusion and the Pressure for Success

Marc Sommers

Youth and the Status Quo

Across today's developing world, unprecedentedly large youth populations are evident alongside a second predominant phenomenon: the profound and persistent exclusion of youth. Rare is the case where national governments, or their international development partners, introduce a viable solution to address these dual challenges. Much too often, colossal cohorts of youthful citizens are considered security threats, to be counteracted with a mix of state repression and employment programs for a tiny fraction of the youth population. The approach is unintentionally counterproductive and heavily gendered. It is also often based on assumptions drawn from suspect evidence. The popular conception of demographic youth bulge populations as threats to social cohesion and

stability is unfounded. Most female and male youth, it turns out, are peaceful, including in times of war.

This chapter explains why the approach to youth exclusion is not working, and what can be done to transform it. The chapter draws mainly from the case of war and postwar Africa, where the distance between youth and governments and international development agencies tends to be pronounced, and where inaccurate stereotypes about young people pervade.

The changes that are required necessarily move governments and international development agencies out of their comfort zone. The reason is simple: the extensive exclusion of youth underscores how the status quo does not work. The proposed solutions of governments and development agencies promise to be inadequate or misguided, largely because their target group — excluded youth majorities — usually has no say in the initiatives that governments and agencies implement. The state violence that occurs concurrently with this lack of voice merely fuels the disconnect.

The chapter concludes with a series of proposed remedies, mainly focused on the international development actors, that promise to address youth exclusion by enhancing inclusiveness, relevance and receptivity in the development response. The chapter draws from the findings, analysis and reform framework of my book, *The Outcast Majority: War, Development, and Youth in Africa* (Sommers 2015).

Peaceful Youth?

Why are most youth peaceful? The exact reverse has been a much more common perception: that youth (male youth, in particular) are threats to their own societies. The starting point for this assertion begins with youth bulge demographics, a trend that has become a dominant force in recent decades in the developing world. By 2006, 86 percent of all youth (1.3 billion) were in developing countries (World Bank 2006, 4). The rate of youth in developing countries has slowed but is still rising: 90 percent of the world's youth will be in developing countries by 2025 (Zeus 2010, 7). The youngest overall population on the planet lies in Sub-Saharan Africa, which "will remain the youngest region in the world in the decades to come" (Filmer and Fox 2014, 26).

A "youth bulge" is thought to exist when an unusually large proportion of the adult population is constituted of youth. One published source asserts that the youth bulge threshold arrives when youth comprise more than 40 percent of all adults in a population (Cincotta, Engelman and Anastasion 2003, 43). Current approaches to youth challenges during and after wars routinely emphasize the potential of male youth to promote instability and violence. Some commentators have emphasized the correlation between populations

with youth bulge demographics and the likelihood of violence or social disturbance (Goldstone 2002; Mesquida and Weiner 1999; Urdal 2004; Zakaria 2001). Related to this assertion is the idea that many male youth are apt to rebel violently when given the chance (Cincotta, Engelman and Anastasion 2003; Collier, Hoeffler and Rohner 2006; Kaplan 2000), in particular, those in countries with strong urbanization levels (Goldstone 2010). Quantitative correlations have been highlighted, in short, to propose that when unusually large numbers of male youth are around, societies can become dangerously unstable and political conflict can result.

Further research has questioned this assertion. Among the key issues is that many youth bulge countries have never had major conflicts while others have emerged from conflict and never returned to it (as in Sub-Saharan Africa: Sommers 2011). In addition, when wars do take place, "only a minority of young men participate in conflicts" (Barker and Ricardo 2006, 181). Furthermore, large youth populations in cities have been found to moderate, not increase, the risk of social disturbance (Urdal and Hoelscher 2009). Recent research also has challenged the idea that male youth are the "protagonists of virtually all violent political action as well as political extremism with a potential to threaten democracy" (Weber 2013, 335). In contrast, researchers have uncovered a direct relationship between youth bulge populations and state repression. The research highlights a tendency for states to apply proactive force toward youth-dominated populations, as by restricting rights or instigating arrests, disappearances and violence (Nordås and Davenport 2013). Finally, questions have also been raised about the touted connection between youth unemployment and violent unrest (Cramer 2010; Izzi 2013; Walton 2010). Drivers of youth violence have been found to be tied more directly to issues of poor governance and exclusion than to unemployment (Mercy Corps 2015).

In the end, the tantalizing data on the perceived danger of "too many young men with not enough to do" (Cincotta, Engelman and Anastasion 2003, 44) largely surfaces when members of the target group — male youth/young men — are not interviewed. Overwhelmingly, the data that supports the "youth bulge and instability thesis" is quantitative.[1] Qualitative interviews with male (and female) youth could reveal how and why most youth resist engagement in violence, even when they live with inequality, state violence routinely directed against many of them, significant social and cultural constraints, and poverty. Nearly all youth experiencing all of this and more — and with no reasonable expectation of support or recognition coming their way from government or international actors — nonetheless regularly resist contributing to violence or conflict. Exactly why most youth resist engagement in violence — despite the prospect of exclusion and failed adulthood, as shortly will be explained — remains under examined. Fortunately, evidence highlighting the role of youth as agents for positive change is beginning to emerge (for example, Ankomah 2005; Ensor 2013; Law, Sonn and Mackenzie 2014).

War and the Sea of Exclusion

Given the substantial attention paid to youth by so many researchers, governments and development professionals, the absence of an agreed-upon definition for youth is remarkable. The broad trend is to define youth by a simple age range. Richard P. Cincotta, Robert Engelman and Daniele Anastasion (2003, 43), for example, define youth (or young adults) as people between ages 15 and 29. However, the United Nations typically employs a 15-to-24 age range (UNESCO n.d.), while the United States Agency for International Development (USAID) uses ages 10 to 29 (2012, 4). For a great many African governments, the youth category extends from age 14 or 15 up to age 35 (as in Sierra Leone, Rwanda and many

others). No common definition for youth exists for the multitude of international institutions and governments that are concerned with them.

Cultural definitions of youth in Africa connect directly to a pervasive form of youth exclusion. Being a youth often is considered a stage of life between childhood and adulthood. The process has less to do with age than with gaining recognition as a man or woman. But in most (if not all) African countries, it is nearly impossible for most youth to attain womanhood or manhood. Male youth in Rwanda, for example, must build a house before getting married and becoming a parent. Yet, most cannot get off square one: completing a house is impossible for nearly everyone.

Three dimensions of the tragic situation in Rwanda are particularly notable:

- First, many male youth in rural Rwanda drop out of school to work. While the pay tends to be low, one primary purpose is to save money to build a house. Yet extensive field interviews with youth in Rwanda made it clear that male youth suspected they would never complete their houses. A common comment from male youth was that they had no choice — cultural expectations forced many of them to try to build a house. In such a situation, failed manhood is practically guaranteed.

- Second, Rwandan government villagization policies have made the house construction task substantially more difficult. State mandates for where all new houses must be built (in collective *imidugudu* villages) and their size (a government official surmised that the state requirement for house size was six times what an ordinary male youth could afford to build [Sommers 2012, 128]) were considerable obstacles.[2]

---

1   The literature on the youth and instability thesis has been reviewed by the author at length in prior works (Sommers 2015; 2011; 2007; 2006).

2   The *imidugudu* villages and their impact on Rwandan youth are described thus: "There is a government regulation that directly and negatively affected youth efforts to construct houses: the national policy mandating that all new houses in rural areas should be built in community housing areas known as *imidugudu*" (Sommers 2012, 25).

• The third notable dimension concerns how a female youth secures socially accepted womanhood. In Rwanda and very far beyond, female youth cannot gain social recognition as women if they do not marry (and then have children). But if male youth cannot secure the necessary pre-marriage requirements, then neither male nor female youth can marry.

While Rwanda is on the cusp of having almost an entire generation of youth who are failed adults (Sommers 2012, 193),[3] the failed adulthood trend reportedly is pervasive across all of Africa. As Alcinda Honwana (2012, 165) notes, "Youth are the majority of Africa's population, but they have been pushed to the margins of their societies and live in a limbo between childhood and adulthood." Even African youth who eventually attain adulthood may not be safe: Irit Eguavoen (2010, 268) finds that in Africa "there is growing empirical evidence that the social status of adulthood may be reversed if the individual falls back into poverty, which means that young adults are socially delegated back to youth status and, as a direct consequence, denied full adult rights, again resulting in low social status and limited access to resources and political decision making."

The cultural exclusion of African youth (and the resulting social identification as a failed man or failed woman) is routinely overlooked by governments and international institutions. A second pervasive yet regularly sidestepped form of exclusion is systemic. State laws, policies and regulations, together with traditional practices, can prevent most female and male youth from gaining access to valuable assets such as land. In addition, education systems across Africa (and elsewhere) are structured to exclude most young people from attending secondary school. One relative success of the UN Millennium Development Goals (MDGs) has been Target Two: expanding access to primary school. Even war-affected countries in Africa have managed to secure high levels of primary school attendance.[4]

But across much of Africa, limited proportions of youth attend secondary school. A UNICEF survey, for example, reports that the average net attendance rate for secondary school in the Sub-Saharan African region (in 2009–2015) was 38 percent. More than half of the 43 countries in the survey (53.5 percent) had average rates that were less than a third of all secondary-school-age youth. Some war-affected countries had exceptionally low rates, in particular, Somalia (5 percent) and South Sudan (8 percent), as well as Angola (19 percent), Burundi (17 percent), Central African Republic (18 percent), Chad (17 percent), Côte d'Ivoire (27 percent), Eritrea (22 percent), Ethiopia (15 percent), Liberia (26 percent), Mali (27 percent), Mozambique (24 percent), Rwanda (23 percent) and Uganda (20 percent). It is worth noting that much larger proportions of youth in a small handful of Sub-Saharan African nations affected by conflict attend secondary school: the Democratic Republic of Congo (DRC) (48 percent), Namibia (60 percent) and Sierra Leone

---

3   The youth situation described here is detailed in the author's *Stuck: Rwandan Youth and the Struggle for Adulthood* (University of Georgia Press, 2012). A proposed remedy to Rwanda's crippling adulthood mandates is as follows: "Local and national conversations about how youth gain acceptance as men and women promises to initiate a reconsideration of adulthood mandates" (Sommers 2012, 236–37). Such discussions also are required in other nations where youth struggle to gain acceptance as adults.

4   The African Development Bank describes the situation: "Most countries in Africa have achieved universal primary enrolment, with rates above 90 per cent. As a result, the continent as a whole is expected to achieve Goal 2 [of the MDGs]. Low completion and high grade repetition remain a challenge, however. Indeed, one in three pupils enrolled in a primary school will drop out. Reasons include late entry, poverty, poor quality of education and a lack of awareness of the importance of schools. Some 30 per cent of students with six years of schooling cannot read a sentence, and girls are more likely to drop out than boys" (African Development Bank n.d.).

(45 percent). Despite these promising exceptions, nearly two in three secondary-school-age youth in Sub-Saharan African are not in secondary school (UNICEF 2016).

Most African youth know that their prospects for social acceptance and conventional success are exceedingly low. Securing adulthood is often even more difficult than gaining access to (and then graduating from) secondary school. The chances of gaining access to vocational school or a youth program of any kind also are slim. The following irony thus serves as the starting point for understanding African youth: while youth are demographically dominant, most see themselves as members of an outcast minority.[5]

The awareness and reality of youth as outliers in their own societies was a pronounced trend in my field research in 15 war-affected African nations. It also has been noted by others about African youth. Eguavoen (2010), for example, introduces the concept of "adults without adult status" to describe the extended effort that is required to gain social recognition as an adult in Africa. He defines his concept as "individuals who have not succeeded in establishing themselves socially as adults by getting married, finding their own household and/or being able to take economic care of themselves and dependents." He also warns that "[t]he group of people who fail to become social adults because of poverty is constantly growing in number, as well as in age" (ibid., 268). Mats Utas (2005b) highlights the plight of male urban youth in Liberia to underscore how African youth can be trapped in a situation from which seemingly they cannot escape: "Due to economic crisis and increasing dependence on the central state in the 1980s an ever-growing number of young people in urban and semi-urban environments were excluded even from the possibilities of becoming adults. Possibilities to participate in the wage economy diminished and education ceased having

any importance. With this crisis looming, many young men lost even the possibility to establish themselves as adults, by building a house, or getting married — even though they continued to become fathers, of children for whom they could not provide" (ibid., 150).

The situation often is similarly dim for female youth. Research has found that in many African countries the ability of female youth to gain social recognition as a woman "depends on having a man or male youth to marry" (Sommers 2015, 77). Since frequently there are few male youth able to get married, many female youth cannot escape a future as a failed woman. The tragedies of failed manhood and womanhood are intimately and directly linked.

The inability to escape life on the edge of society is infused in accounts of the lives of both male and female youth in war and postwar Africa. The humiliating prospect of living as a failed adult pushes some female and male youth to join (or accept life in) military groups. Utas underscores how life as a soldier for former Liberian military leader and president Charles Taylor allowed youth to do things they otherwise could not achieve. He describes how male Liberian soldiers would wash their cars in beer, "a beverage most could not even afford to drink prior to the war — and that they could drive a car until it ran out of gasoline and then just dump it for another one. Likewise, the young girlfriends [also affiliated with Taylor's army] got hold of commodities that they had only dreamt of before" (Utas 2005a, 66).

Yet, failing to access a secondary school education and gain social recognition as an adult man or woman, much less secure stable employment, has created other difficulties as well. A significant field research finding in war-affected African countries such as Burundi, Rwanda and Sierra Leone is the presence of large numbers of unmarried mothers among the female youth population. This outcome is partly a result of a simple fact noted above: often there appears to be no one for many female youth to marry, since male youth struggle and frequently

---

5   This irony marks the starting point for analysis, noted in Sommers (2015, 3).

fail to secure the prerequisites of marriage. In the meantime, female youth may have relations with male youth or older men that result in offspring. Some enter into informal, live-in arrangements with the father of their child or children. But if the father cannot support his new family, he may leave. Unmarried motherhood and the resultant children constitute a profound yet largely overlooked youth phenomenon.[6]

Female youth also may be victimized by sexual violence during and after wars. The prevalence of sexual violence in war zones is thought to increase significantly if forced recruitment into military forces is prevalent (Cohen 2009, 21). That said, Dara Kay Cohen's research also found that "levels of sexual violence in one-third of the wars in Sub-Saharan Africa were low" (ibid., 9). Where sexual violence is prevalent, one of its most tragic consequences is how it can undermine adjustment into postwar life for girls and female youth. Susan Shepler (2010) dramatizes the difficulties that some girls and female youth faced in postwar Sierra Leone. She observed that "in many cases it is easier for a boy to be accepted after amputating the hands of villagers than it is for a girl to be accepted after being the victim of rape" (ibid., 97).

Girls and female youth who were associated with military groups during wars tend to face particular difficulties in postwar Africa. One review of former girl combatants in Angola, Mozambique and northern Uganda found that, following their return to civilian life, they encountered "profound invisibility and seemingly unrelenting victimisation...during and following armed conflict" (Denov 2008, 831). In eastern DRC, the level of social stigmatization for "girls formerly associated with armed forces and groups" was found to be so severe that "some of the girls see returning to [their former armed group] as an alternative to staying at home and [enduring] discrimination and insults" (Tonheim 2012, 287, 289). The findings are not,

however, uniformly dispiriting. One field study of former women and girl combatants in northern Uganda found that, following their return to their homes, "social acceptance [of them] is high, many women and girls are psychologically resilient, and there is little evidence of aggression and violence" against them (Annan et al. 2011, 879).

A second irony about youth and war frames the frustrations that youth face after surfacing from the crucible of war. It is this: the military commanders who exploit children and youth during times of war (by abducting and exploiting them, often in extreme ways) frequently are the same ones who recognize their remarkable talents, resilience and sheer tenacity. Boys and girls fighting in militias fight on the front lines, may serve as combat commanders and perform dangerous, high-risk surveillance behind enemy lines. While many may become victims and perpetrators of extreme sexual violence, they also may be forced to develop skills as caregivers. Sometimes they must rely on ingenuity simply to survive in hostile environments, often without shelter or much food. These youngsters, in addition to being abused in the extreme by their commanders, nonetheless demonstrate courage, shrewdness, smarts, toughness, imagination and resourcefulness. Military commanders (including notorious warlords such as Liberia's Charles Taylor) recognize and make use of the diverse abilities of child and youth soldiers. War zones, despite their traumatic and debilitating dimensions, also can provide young people with opportunities for self-discovery. It is a sad fact of contemporary war that, perhaps more than any other group of adults, warlords and other military commanders recognize the talents and unsinkable nature of youngsters in their midst.

Development Pressures and Tendencies

According to some observers, governments and the international development enterprise seem to have hit their stride in recent years. The United Nations

---

6   The situation and plight of unmarried mothers is examined at length by the author in two books: Sommers 2012 and Sommers 2015.

Development Programme (UNDP), for instance, has proclaimed that "all groups and regions" in the Global South "have seen notable improvement" in all features of UNDP's Human Development Index (HDI).[7] UNDP adds that "the South has risen at an unprecedented speed and scale" (UNDP 2013, 1). As for Sub-Saharan Africa, the UNDP predicts that "[b]y 2050, aggregate HDI could rise 52%" (ibid., 5). Similarly upbeat descriptions of Africa's current and future situations have surfaced elsewhere (see, for example, One 2013 and Radelet 2010). Things seem to be going great.

An increasingly common trademark of institutions and experts trumpeting dramatic success in international development is their overwhelming reliance on quantitative data. A second tendency in many publications describing Africa's positive transformation is that they emerge from institutions likely to benefit from pronouncements about such achievements. It is difficult not to imagine some degree of self-interest in the proclamations of progress from donor and implementing agencies. While such publications spotlight types of progress for Africa, it also is evident that little of this success has cascaded down to many members of its burgeoning youth population. Qualitative studies of African youth, including those affected by conflict, tend to tell a very different story. See, to name just a few examples, Christopher Maclay and Alpaslan Özerdem (2010) on Liberia, Desiree Lwambo (2011) and Koen Vlassenroot and Frank Van Acker (2001) on eastern DRC, Sommers (2012) on Rwanda, Danny Hoffman (2011) on Sierra Leone and Liberia, Henrik Vigh (2006) on Guinea-Bissau, Mike McGovern (2011) on Côte d'Ivoire, and Honwana (2012) on the entire continent. Too many African youth, the collective research suggests, appear to be in freefall.

Interviews with 28 officials from donor and non-governmental organizations, as well as youth, development and evaluation experts, support this general assessment of the gap between youth and development practice.[8] There were numerous findings arising from these interviews. Two will be shared here. The first highlighted the narrow nature of development perspectives. The officials and experts who were interviewed stressed how development institutions (as well as governments) tend to think in terms of sectors (also known as silos or stovepipes) such as health, education, agriculture, water and sanitation, economic development and governance. The sectoral prism for examining development challenges is narrow. As one donor official explained, "We have fragmented, siloed, sector-based programs" (Sommers 2015, 155). The sectoral stovepipes tend to predetermine what agencies will do and where they will invest their funds. The orientation runs the risk of cultivating unintended disjunctures with everyday realities. For example, while wars have been found to fuel youth movement into cities and informal sectors, international development work often focuses on the opposite: agriculture and the formal economy. Such decisions may not be driven by information on the ground as much as by what sector-dominated organizations decide to do.

A second orientation emerges from pressure on donor and implementing agencies to succeed. It is a striking and extraordinary expectation, as it implies that just about everything agencies invest in must work. The attitude is exemplified by the Canadian government's Aid Effectiveness Agenda, which "delivers results and demonstrates value for every dollar invested in international development" (Canadian International Development Agency 2012, 1). The orientation on successful investment dovetails with an extraordinary fixation in the international development world on things you can

---

7   UNDP describes the Human Development Index as "a composite measure of indicators along three dimensions: life expectancy, educational attainment and command over the resources needed for a decent living" (UNDP 2013, 1).

8   The remainder of this section draws from chapter four of *The Outcast Majority: War, Development, and Youth in Africa* (Sommers 2015, 154–75).

count to demonstrate achievement. The fixation often is referred to as "numbers" or "metrics." Often it boils down to the concept of "indicators." An evaluation expert defined indicators as "signs of change" that are quantifiable (Sommers 2015, 158): the numbers of people an initiative trained, for example, or how many people participated in a program.

The interview data indicated that pressure on donor agencies to demonstrate the success of a program *from the first quarter* of a youth program puts unusual pressure on implementing agencies. Privately, implementing agency officials related that, to respond to high expectations of success, they may be forced to pluck well-adjusted (and mostly male) youth to be participants of a youth program, since such youth have a better chance of engendering program success. Many donor officials who were interviewed reported that they were aware of this strategy. As one related, "Those youth in the greatest need are not often reached. Programs focus on elite youth because they're easier to get" (ibid., 164).

In other words, a youth program producing upbeat indicators and touted by donors and implementers as successful could, in fact, do just the opposite by promoting inequality; undermining efforts to address youth poverty or exclusion; and demonstrating (in cases where the elite youth in programs are connected directly to influential government officials) support for unpopular, and perhaps nepotistic and corrupt governments. In addition, research with youth who are desperate for assistance but routinely are left out of such programs revealed an issue that program evaluations rarely examine: the impact of youth programs on those who cannot get into them. It is entirely conceivable that youth programs marked as successful (thanks to their positive indicators) simultaneously may promote rage or fatalism among youth left out of such programs. This particularly may be the case for initiatives in which elite and favoured youth are participants while

members of the outcast youth majority are, once again, left out and overlooked. Taken together, the findings suggest that international development work, in general, is currently not oriented to address the priorities of excluded youth.

A Framework for Reform

International development work is largely ineffective and inefficient in reaching marginalized youth, including war-affected African youth, who are among those most in need of acceptance and support. The development status quo is not working for most youth. It is unlikely that the current approach can succeed. Development techniques and approaches tend to reach tiny proportions of young people (many of whom may be elites) with initiatives that often are not informed by the priorities of outcast youth majorities.

What follows are some ideas from the detailed framework featured in *The Outcast Majority* (ibid., 187–200) for collectively supporting a process to reverse this trend and tap into the reserve of tenacity, ingenuity and diverse skills that youth in war and postwar Africa, and elsewhere, have to offer. Here is a sampling of ideas from the framework:

- *Place excluded female and male youth at the centre of development work.* If colossal populations of young people (in Sub-Saharan Africa and well beyond) dominate developing country populations, and most of them endure systemic, cultural and other forms of exclusion, then focusing on their priorities and reversing the factors that exclude most young people should rest at the centre of development work.

- *Conduct sound assessment research of the priorities and circumstances of marginalized youth.* The starting point for development work should be what excluded youth majorities require — not what governments and development institutions are prepared to provide. The research should have two purposes. First, it should uncover both the priorities of prominent subgroups of marginalized youth majorities (rural and urban, male and female, and so on) and the main causes of youth exclusion. Second, it should propose detailed policy and programming responses, with roles for governments and development actors, that address youth priorities and counteract the primary factors that exclude young people.

High-quality, trust-based, mainly qualitative research methods rest at the core of this endeavour, as they promise to draw out and empower youth to share their views and detail the situations they face. Accordingly, the tendency to rely on focus group interviews for information on youth should be reconsidered. Focus groups tend to be structured and hierarchical settings that are prone to promoting the views only of those who speak (quite often, educated elites). Interviewing youth in peer groups, which are unstructured, informal gatherings of young people with similar backgrounds, is recommended. After conducting research with young people for more than two decades, I have found that youth in peer groups are much more likely to speak openly, honestly and frankly about their lives.

- *Rebalance policy and program work.* The development world seems to be awash with sophisticated programs that ultimately reach small numbers of people. Even a large youth development program may reach, at best, 0.001 percent of all youth in a country. This orientation toward programs for the few must change. The proposed initial research of marginalized youth lives (detailed above) promises to reveal the primary forces (that is, policies, practices and players) that are marginalizing youth and collapsing their options for stability and advancement.

There may be policies that keep youth out of secondary and vocational school, make them vulnerable to exploitation in informal economies, severely limit youth access to land, marriage, credit, housing and adulthood, and deny them protection from predatory state actors (such as members of the police, intelligence or military).

Working to reverse such policies and practices, and to limit the abuses of actors who exploit young people, should become a top priority for international development actors. Advocating to reverse forces that exclude youth is especially important in countries where it is too dangerous for citizens to do so. The case of Rwanda, detailed earlier, is instructive. Youth and government officials alike highlighted the profound and negative impact of the government's villagization policies (Sommers 2012). In countries such as Rwanda, where not even government officials dare question sacrosanct policies, international actors must advocate against policies and practices that debilitate and marginalize youth majorities.

Programs for youth should, in turn, draw from youth assessments (again, noted above) to target particular subsets of excluded youth populations strategically and in line with their priorities. But development actors should keep in mind that policy and practice reform has the potential to reach exponentially more youth lives than nearly all programs. This work should become central to development practice.

- *Cultivate learning environments for policy and program work.* Pressures to demonstrate success may drive international donors and implementers toward practices that have little or nothing to do with reversing youth exclusion. Instead, the context for success may be internal, driven by institutional expectations and procedures. Such an environment is not conducive to learning how to reach youth majorities on the margins. Having the freedom to make and learn from mistakes is.

A key component of learning how to reach and support excluded youth populations — through effective advocacy and targeted programming — is to institute high-quality, independent evaluation research that pinpoints promising as well as challenging results (and, yes, failures). Such an environment rarely is allowed to exist, much less thrive: research for *The Outcast Majority* revealed how donor and implementing agency officials often have an exceptionally low regard for the quality of their own evaluations. As one donor official recalled about evaluations produced under his watch, most were "just whitewashing. As I look back on the M&E [monitoring and evaluation] of programs I was involved with, it was pathetic" (Sommers 2015, 174). All evaluations should investigate the impact of programs on those who cannot access them. Evaluators also should cease employing biased terms such as "beneficiary" until positive program impact has been established.

Prevailing trends in international development work call for significant improvements in how development is envisioned, implemented and assessed. Most fortunately, concern about the need to respond to huge youth populations — in war-affected contexts and in developing countries more broadly — is on the rise. Significantly, the tendency for most youth to support peace also is beginning to be recognized: the new United Nations Security Council Declaration 2250 on Youth, Peace and Security[9] effectively turns the tables on perceptions of youth, especially male youth, as promoters of violence and instability. Instead, it highlights their real and potential roles as contributors to peace building (United Nations Meetings Coverage and Press Releases 2015). Declaration 2250 underscores the need to position youth, excluded youth majorities, in particular, at the centre of how peace building and development action is defined and practised.

9   www.youth4peace.info/UNSCR2250_ Introduction.

Works Cited

African Development Bank Group. n.d. "Goal 2: Achieve Universal Primary Education." www.afdb.org/en/topics-and-sectors/topics/millennium-development-goals-mdgs/goal-2-achieve-universal-primary-education/.

Ankomah, Baffour. 2005. "Mano River Youth: From Warriors to Peace Builders." *New African* 437: 40–43.

Annan, Jeannie, Christopher Blattman, Dyan Mazurana and Kristopher Carlson. 2011. "Civil War, Reintegration, and Gender in Northern Uganda." *Journal of Conflict Resolution* 55 (6): 877–908.

Canadian International Development Agency. 2012. *Development for Results 2010-2011: At the Heart of Canada's Efforts for a Better World*. Gatineau, Quebec. http://reliefweb.int/sites/reliefweb.int/files/resources/d4r-2010-2011-eng.pdf.

Barker, Gary T. and Christine Ricardo. 2006. "Young Men and the Construction of Masculinity in Sub-Saharan Africa: Implications for HIV/AIDS, Conflict, and Violence." In *The Other Half of Gender: Men's Issues in Development*, edited by Ian Bannon and Maria C. Correia, 159–193. Washington, DC: World Bank.

Cincotta, Richard P., Robert Engelman and Daniele Anastasion. 2003. *The Security Demographic: Population and Civil Conflict after the Cold War*. Washington, DC: Population Action International.

Cohen, Dara Kay. 2009. "The Causes of Sexual Violence by Insurgents during Civil War: Cross-National Evidence (1980–1999)." Unpublished manuscript.

Collier, Paul, Anke Hoeffler and Dominic Rohner. 2006. "Beyond Greed and Grievance: Feasibility and Civil War." CSAE Working Paper Series No. 2006-10. Oxford, UK: Centre for the Study of African Economies, University of Oxford.

Cramer, Christopher. 2010. "Unemployment and Participation in Violence." World Development Report 2011: Background Paper, November 16. Washington, DC: World Bank. https://openknowledge.worldbank.org/bitstream/handle/10986/9247/WDR2011_0022.pdf?sequence=1.

Denov, Myriam S. 2008. "Girl Soldiers and Human Rights: Lessons from Angola, Mozambique, Sierra Leone and Northern Uganda." *International Journal of Human Rights* 12 (5): 813–36.

Eguavoen, Irit. 2010. "Lawbreakers and Livelihood Makers: Youth-Specific Poverty and Ambiguous Livelihood Strategies in Africa." *Vulnerable Children and Youth Studies* 5 (3): 268–73.

Ensor, Marisa O. 2013. "Youth, Climate Change, and Peace in South Sudan." *Peace Review* 25 (4): 526–33.

Filmer, Deon and Louise Fox. 2014. *Youth Employment in Sub-Saharan Africa*. Africa Development Series. Washington, DC: World Bank.

Goldstone, Jack A. 2002. "Population and Security: How Demographic Change Can Lead to Violent Conflict." *Columbia Journal of International Affairs* 56: 245–63.

———. 2010. "The New Population Bomb: The Four Megatrends that Will Change the World." *Foreign Affairs*, January/February. www.foreignaffairs.com/print/65877.

Hoffman, Danny. 2011. *The War Machines: Young Men and Violence in Sierra Leone and Liberia*. Durham, NC: Duke University Press.

Honwana, Alcinda. 2012. *The Time of Youth: Work, Social Change, and Politics in Africa*. Sterling, VA: Kumarian Press.

Izzi, Valeria. 2013. "Just Keeping Them Busy? Youth Employment Projects as a Peacebuilding Tool." *International Development Planning Review* 35 (2): 103–117.

Kaplan, Robert D. 2000. "The Coming Anarchy: How Scarcity, Crime, Overpopulation, Tribalism, and Disease Are Destroying the Social Fabric of the Planet." In *The Coming Anarchy: Shattering the Dreams of the Post Cold War*. New York, NY: Random House. Originally published February 1994 in *The Atlantic Monthly*.

Law, Siew Fang, Christopher Sonn and Cynthia Mackenzie. 2014. "Situating Peace in the Globalized Era: Perspectives of Youth Peace-Builders in Laos." *Peace and Conflict: Journal of Peace Psychology* 20 (2): 109–23.

Lwambo, Desiree. 2011. *"Before the War, I Was a Man": Men and Masculinities in Eastern DR Congo*. Goma, DRC: Heal Africa. www.healafrica. org/wp-content/uploads/2011/10/men-and-masculinities-in-eastern-dr-congo.pdf.

Maclay, Christopher and Alpaslan Özerdem. 2010. "'Use' Them or 'Lose' Them: Engaging Liberia's Disconnected Youth through Socio-political Integration." *International Peacekeeping* 17 (3): 343–60.

McGovern, Mike. 2011. *Making War in Côte d'Ivoire*. Chicago, IL: University of Chicago Press.

Mercy Corps. 2015. *Youth & Consequences: Unemployment, Injustice and Violence*. www. mercycorps.org/research-resources/youth-consequences-unemployment-injustice-and-violence.

Mesquida, Christian G. and Neil I. Wiener. 1999. "Male Age Composition and Severity of Conflicts." *Politics and the Life Sciences* 18 (2): 181–89.

Nordås, Ragnhild and Christian Davenport. 2013. "Fight the Youth: Youth Bulges and State Repression." *American Journal of Political Science* 57 (4): 926–40.

One. 2013. "Summit in Sight: The G8 and Africa from Gleneagles to Lough Erne." Policy Brief, February 28. http://one.org. s3.amazonaws.com/pdfs/summit_in_sight_report_en.pdf.

Radelet, Steven. 2010. *Emerging Africa: How 17 Countries Are Leading the Way*. Washington, DC: Center for Global Development.

Shepler, Susan. 2010. "Post-war Trajectories for Girls Associated with the Fighting Forces in Sierra Leone." In *Gender, War, and Militarism: Feminist Perspectives*, edited by Laura Sjoberg and Sandra Via. Santa Barbara, CA: Praeger.

Sommers, Marc. 2006. "Fearing Africa's Young Men: Male Youth, Conflict, Urbanization and the Case of Rwanda." In *The Other Half of Gender: Men's Issues in Development*, edited by Ian Bannon and Maria Correia, 137–58. Washington, DC: World Bank.

———. 2007. "Embracing the Margins: Working with Youth amid War and Insecurity." In *Too Poor for Peace? Poverty, Conflict and Security in the 21st Century*, edited by Lael Brainard and Derek Chollet. Washington, DC: Brookings Institution.

———. 2011. "Governance, Security and Culture: Assessing Africa's Youth Bulge." *International Journal of Conflict and Violence* 5 (2): 292–303.

———. 2012. *Stuck: Rwandan Youth and the Struggle for Adulthood*. Studies in Security and International Affairs Series. Athens, GA: University of Georgia Press, in association with United States Institute of Peace Press, Washington, DC.

———. 2015. *The Outcast Majority: War, Development, and Youth in Africa*. Athens, GA: University of Georgia Press.

Tonheim, Milfrid. 2012. "'Who Will Comfort Me?' Stigmatization of Girls Formerly Associated with Armed Forces and Groups in Eastern Congo." *International Journal of Human Rights* 16 (2): 287–97.

UNDP. 2013. *Human Development Report 2013: The Rise of the South: Human Progress in a Diverse World*. New York. http://hdr.undp. org/en/2013-report.

UNESCO. n.d. "Learning to Live Together: What Do We Mean by 'Youth'?" www.unesco.org/new/en/social-and-human-sciences/themes/youth/youth-definition/.

UNICEF. 2016. "Data on Secondary Education: Net Attendance Rates: UNICEF Data: Monitoring the Situation of Children and Women." Updated September 2016. http://data.unicef.org/education/secondary.html.

United Nations Meetings Coverage and Press Releases. 2015. "Security Council, Unanimously Adopting Resolution 2250 (2015), Urges Member States to Increase Representation of Youth in Decision-Making at All Levels." Meetings coverage, December 9. www.un.org/press/en/2015/sc12149.doc.htm.

USAID. 2012. *Youth in Development Policy: Realizing the Demographic Opportunity.* October. Washington, DC: USAID. www.usaid.gov/policy/youth.

Urdal, Henrik. 2004. "The Devil in the Demographics: The Effect of Youth Bulges on Domestic Armed Conflict, 1950–2000." Social Development Papers, Conflict Prevention and Reconstruction Paper No. 14. Washington, DC: World Bank.

Urdal, Henrik and Kristian Hoelscher. 2009. "Urban Youth Bulges and Social Disorder: An Empirical Study of Asian and Sub-Saharan African Cities." Policy Research Working Paper No. 5110. Washington, DC: World Bank.

Utas, Mats. 2005a. "Agency of Victims: Young Women in the Liberian Civil War." In *Makers and Breakers: Children and Youth in Postcolonial Africa*, edited by Alcinda Honwana and Filip de Boeck, 53–80. Trenton, NJ: Africa World Press.

———. 2005b. "Building a Future? The Reintegration & Remarginalization of Youth in Liberia." In *No Peace, No War: An Anthropology of Contemporary Armed Conflicts,* edited by Paul Richards, 137–54. Athens, GA: Ohio University Press, and James Currey Ltd.

Vigh, Henrik. 2006. *Navigating Terrains of War: Youth and Soldiering in Guinea-Bissau.* New York: Berghahn Books.

Vlassenroot, Koen and Frank Van Acker. 2001. "War as Exit from Exclusion? The Formation of Mayi-Mayi Militias in Eastern Congo." *Afrika Focus* 17 (1-2): 51–77.

Walton, Oliver. 2010. "Youth, Armed Violence and Job Creation Programs: A Rapid Mapping Study." Governance and Social Development Resource Center Research Paper, September. University of Birmingham and Norsk Ressurssenter for Fredsbygging. www.gsdrc.org/docs/open/EIRS11.pdf.

Weber, Hannes. 2013. "Demography and Democracy: The Impact of Youth Cohort Size on Democratic Stability in the World." *Democratization* 20 (2): 335–57.

World Bank. 2006. *World Development Report 2007: Development and the Next Generation.* Washington, DC: World Bank.

Zakaria, Fareed. 2001. "The Roots of Rage." *Newsweek* 138 (16): 14–33.

Zeus, Barbara. 2010. "Whole People, Holistic Approaches: Cross-Sectoral Action and Learning. Framing Paper 3, INEE 2010 Policy Roundtable, An Enabling Right: Education for Youth Affected by Crisis." Inter-Agency Network for Education in Emergencies (INEE). www.ineesite.org/en/inee-events/policy-roundtable_10.

Part Five
Strengthening Resilience and Social Cohesion

15

Relying on One's Self: Traditional Methods of Conflict Management

I William Zartman

Africa lives under two conflicting traditions. It is popularly known as the land of palaver, where disputes are handled judiciously by reconciliation after open discussion, not as the peaceful kingdom but the peaceable kingdom. On the other hand, it is known historically as a place where conflict between and within entities, in particular over chieftainship succession, provided an excuse for colonial intervention to install an era of peace, replacing intra-African conflict with intercolonial wars. As is often the case with competing images, both are correct, but the first bears some examination and updating, in an effort to improve conflict reduction in the twenty-first century in Africa and, if lessons transfer, elsewhere as well. What have been traditional methods of settling conflict, and are they still alive? Under what conditions have they worked, what are their limits, and how can they be expanded? Although Africa is a collection of societies, these societies are generally similar enough in their indigenous conflict management values and practices for a general discussion to be pertinent and for some more specific statements to be broadly applicable (Lundy and Adjei 2015, 6).

There is, however, a contradiction in reviving traditional peacemaking practices. The purpose and basis of traditional conflict management in Africa is to restore the parties to normal social relations and to restore the tissue of society. The resilience in the face of risks of conflict onset or recurrence is the resilience of society that enables it to bounce back and restore its established functions. Thus, traditional African conflict management is basically conservative, aimed at absorbing the changes and challenges inherent in new events. It is not peaceful change; it is peaceful restoration. That is an admirable goal in many types of conflict situations, but it falls short when the conflict comes from basic alternations in the relations of the elements. Intergenerational conflicts, conflicts over changing sizes of ethnic groups and the emergence of drug-trafficking warlords, among others, are conflicts in which putting the pieces back together again may simply no longer be possible: they just do not fit. In other situations, the spirit of traditional methods may be applicable to the situation of change, even if traditional practices are no longer directly appropriate. It will be useful to keep these limitations in mind, as well as the conditions for exceptions.

Indigenous Conflict Management — Reconciliation

Conflict was as pervasive among Africans as among any groups of human beings anywhere and involved all levels of social interaction. Domestic quarrels, theft and murder (from wives to goods to cattle), boundary disputes, authority contests and inter-entity relations, including wars, form the ladder of conflict, often involving several types at the same time. The common element in the way these disputes have been handled through traditional justice is reconciliation. All procedures are related to this goal, which means that truth in disputes is less important than relations, and punishment is restorative rather than retributive. Much is made of these characteristics, but one must watch the wording: fact-finding is important, but truth is not paramount; punishment is involved, but restoration *is* paramount. These distinctions are often missed in broader treatments of practices.

The focus on reconciliation derives from a particular notion of conflict management. The purpose is to erase the infraction or the conflict and restore the status quo ante, seen as the proper functioning of social relations. It is thus a backward-looking exercise, based on the notion that the status quo was one of appropriate relations. The action is to eliminate a culture of impunity by making retributive punishment unnecessary, since the anti-social action has been removed or resolved, rather

than using punishment to deter future breaches of relations. As a result, it is premised on the permanence of the status quo and is not designed to handle change; new conditions must find their place in present relations. At the same time, this approach emphasizes norms, the basic element in conflict prevention, by establishing accepted practices and consensual limitations of behaviour (Zartman 2015).

These elements undergird specific approaches to particular levels of conflict. Domestic quarrels provide a microcosm of restorative methods. The conflict is submitted to a council of the entire family in which testimonies from the parties directly involved and all others having something to do with the situation are aired. Once the situation is fully discussed, a decision representing a broad consensus is formulated by one or more elders. The goal is to resolve the dispute without finding fault (or by finding countervailing and cancelling faults) and to reconcile the parties and reintegrate them into the family, which then supportively closes ranks around them "as a mother hen gathers her chicks." (Ohwovoriole 2011; Phillips 2011; Uwazie 2000; Deng 2000, 98). Group context and consensus, reconciliation and reinsertion, and resolution by integration are the highlighted characteristics. Although such family quarrels are at the lowest level of the ladder of disputes, the characteristics of their management will be found at all higher levels.

Theft and murder are more serious breaches of conduct, against — not within — society or against individuals. Again, the goal is reconciliation between damaged and damaging parties and reintegration of the errant member back into society.

> "[T]he overriding concern of the [Buems'] normative order is to sustain social harmony in the social system. The philosophical foundation of this worldview is encapsulated in the phrase *kanye ndu nowi*, 'the ingredients of harmony'…translate[d]…into practical

reality through the imposition of 'intrinsic sanctions,' the subtle but persuasive means by which members of the community are molded into complying with the rules of social control — the moral code, the normative order, and the belief and value systems. Intrinsic sanctions are both positive (the psychic rewards that people receive when they conform to the approved mode of behavior) and negative (the feeling of moral discomfort that the people experience when they default.)" (Fred-Mensah 2000, 35; also Nukunya 1992, 81; Radcliffe-Brown 1952, 205; Gluckman 1965, 202–07).

When an infraction such as a theft or murder takes place, intrinsic sanctions have proven ineffective, but they still condition the community's response. Although decisions are taken at a higher level by chiefs and their councils, they place the infraction in a holistic context of community welfare and not just within the limits of the infraction (Uwazie 2000). The chiefs or other appointed figures can also serve as mediators to sew society back together again (Udofia 2011). Regulatory societies, somewhat like fraternal lodges, serve a broad range of functions in maintaining social customs and appropriate behaviours, including initiation into civic behaviour, but they can also act as mediators and decision fora in cases of conflict within the ethnic group (Kah 2011); where such institutions do not exist, the elders can set up their own training sessions in proper behaviour and resolution practices. Restoration and compensation are used, again, to reconstruct the torn social fabric and put society back together again. Appropriate compensations are often pre-established for losses of life and property (a cow, a service and so on), designed to undo the action, symbolically, if restoration to life is not possible, rather than to punish for it (Evans-Pritchard 1940). Amnesty is also possible, under appropriate conditions (Eselebor 2015, 243–45). But the infractor is not just an object; admission and atonement must accompany the societal mending.

If not, the mending is accomplished by removing the offensive actor, by ostracism — a harsh action in a world where there are only communities and no free space in between them (Fred-Mensah 2000, 35).

African social philosophies from *kanye ndu nowi* in west Africa to *ubuntu* in southern Africa (discussed below) have undergirded systems of conflict management that stand in deep contrast to Western notions of retributive justice and punishment, in which crime tends to be considered as an incident to be judged by legal standards that allocate sentences according to the severity of the offence (Cobban 2000). If there is a social implication for the Western process, it is to not "let 'em get away with it." There is another Western procedure into which African traditional practices might seem to fit, and that is alternative dispute resolution (ADR), in which outcomes are subject to negotiation rather than to judgment (Danso and Osei-Tutu 2015, 121, 125; Asogwa 2015, 143–44). Anthropologists have claimed that justice is less well served by ADR, in which power between lawyers comes into play, rather than a judge's or jury's verdict (Nader 1989). However, it may be that the similar procedures can work to bring together their different philosophical bases (Kolawole and Kolawole 2015, 269–78).

Boundary disputes are a frequent occurrence in a world made up of communities abutting each other, as noted. Land is the platter for society, and its use and ownership are the warp and woof of the social tissue. Whether the land involves transhumant rights, seasonal grazing versus farming, tribal versus squatter rights, indigenous versus settler rights or *Lebensraum* versus sacred sites, the issue always ends up as a boundary matter, as well as a matter of occupancy within the boundaries (Aluaigba 2011; Boone 2014). Boundary disputes can take place within the community, as well as between communities, and conflict resolution procedures differ greatly between the two. They can also be both, such as when an ethnic group has been split by a modern state boundary, leaving two communities instead of one in sovereignty terms, but the two reflect the same traditional structures and practices, often commonly held. Intracommunity land disputes resemble matters of theft and murder in the way they are handled.

Intercommunity boundary disputes involve two communities, each with its structures and procedures; on each side, there will be a council of elders and leaders contacting each other. Typically, the reconciliation spirit translates into a beginning with adoption of confidence-building measures (CBMs) and even confidence- and security-building measures to calm the land before actual negotiations begin (Ndi 2011; Mbagwu 2015). The two communities can undergo training to deal with subsequent border disputes through their regulatory societies and, in their discussions, make tangible concessions in order to strengthen their relationship together. If direct conciliatory processes do not succeed, the disputing parties may invoke a mediator; an elderly sage, possibly from a neighbouring community; a paramount chief or even an arbitrator, who not merely reconciles but adjudicates (*du nku* in Benin; *ajwad* in Sudan) (Kouassi 2000; Deng 2000).

These procedures may produce a substantive result allocating land to one side or the other or reaffirming previous boundaries. Here, the spirit may be reconciliation and restoration of good relations between claimants, but the actual result tends toward allocation of land, possibly with compensation through whatever usage or payment arrangements may be devised — a good negotiation procedure. Trade-offs between ownership and usufruct may be invoked. Propriety over the land may be reaffirmed or established, but, in exchange, the owner allows the other party passage, as to a sacred shrine or spot in the other's territory, or exploitation, as in the extraction of farmed or mined goods (Ndi 2011, 42; Danso and Osei-Tutu 2015, 126). Nonetheless, lest it appear that these procedures will always arrive at a chummy result, there is always war, announced,

declared and then fought wholeheartedly (Masina 2000, 175). War is always a strong manager of conflict, and the threat of war is an important aid to negotiation.

Authority conflicts were probably the least successfully reconciled by traditional conflict management because they represented a breakdown of the system in its own terms (Fonkem 2015, 315). Most of the time (a quantity difficult to count), the tribal structure was durable and resistant to challenge, but when it broke down, the system for managing the conflict itself had broken down; authority disputes mark the limits of the system (and incidentally mark the limits of the modern, colonially installed legal system and its post-independence successor as well). As in any political structure, there were rules and mechanisms for succession (even where, as in the modern independence period, the procedure for succession was strongman takeover), but there were bound to be exceptions to and unclarities in the rules. In modern practices, elections are the ultimate procedure for resolving authority conflict, and so they were in traditional African conflict management, but the rules of the procedures were more open to challenge. As usual, the conflict went to community councils, consensual mediators, higher authorities and then alliances within and among communities. But succession conflicts split councils, divide authorities and roil alliances, until what is left is war.

Resolution by these devices allowed for little compromise: someone had to be chief. Even when one candidate or incumbent passed away, usually a definitive resolving mechanism, the conflict could continue or be renewed over the succession (Zartman and Nuameh 2005). The Dagbon (Dagomba) chieftainship conflict in northern Ghana has lasted over two centuries with creative persistence (Danso and Osei-Tutu 2015; Brewoo and Abdallah 2015; Nuameh 2000; Ahorsu and Gebe 2011). One device that permits an innovative solution is withdrawal of a faction into a new territory and establishment as a new community (Fred-Mensah 2000, 39; Wilson-Fall 2000, 61; Kouassi 2000, 73). African history is full of stories of the putative ruler who migrated like a queen bee with all her suite to set up a new kinship group in a new land. Walking away is an established conflict management mechanism and, in notable African cases, is a motor of history. In present-day Africa, there is not much free land to walk away to, but the Ishaak and Dir clans did walk away from Somalia to resurrect Somaliland, and the Eritreans ran away from Ethiopia to restore an old kinship community. The first was done with little violence and was not internationally recognized; the second was carried out with much violence followed by recognition, for whatever lesson one might want to draw.

Intercommunity relations involve the highest level of conflict, taking place between unrelated ethnic groups or larger multi-community entities. The substance of such disputes can involve some of the issues already discussed, including boundaries, withdrawal and even domestic quarrels (for example, in cross-tribal marriages). These conflicts did end in war on occasion, but, characteristically, efforts were made to retain good, neighbourly relations (including specifically cross-tribal marriages, still practised) (Kouassi 2000). At all levels, the occurrence of conflicts is considered normal in proportion to the intimacy and frequency of the contacts. "Close though the tongue is to the teeth, they sometimes clash" for the Yoruba; "Conflict is inevitable between two close friends" (Ajibade 2015, 222, 225); "Today's enemies were yesterday's friends and should not forget the good days together before" for the Nweh in Cameroon (Fonkem 2015, 317).

The reference in the proverbs is to the large list of intercommunity conflicts that are not considered existential for the parties, who, rather, seek to overcome their differences in a way that will preserve the entities involved and reconcile them so that their integrity is preserved and they can resume their normal relations. By the same token, procedures to manage conflict at the intercommunity level have the same characteristics as intracommunity management. Elders in council, full hearings, restitution, appeals to principles of harmony, rituals of reconciliation and establishment of kinship are principal, traditional ingredients of conflict management, even at the "highest" level of separateness (Mbagwu 2015, 63). If it sounds too good to be true, it must be noted that these practices were established on the job over centuries and were maintained by repeated usage. As with any human activity, they broke down often enough to be human, but worked consistently enough to be maintained and institutionalized.

However, it should be noted that many of the actual practices are standard conflict management devices in all societies. Hearings before councils of elders, efforts to reconcile narratives, search for win-win solutions, mediation among parties and even the hotly debated topic of restorative versus retributive justice (Anstey and Rosoux, forthcoming) are all characteristics of contemporary peacemaking. These practices are typical to Africa, just as they are to other societies, having evolved through human experience. It is, rather, in the two basic African elements of reconciliation and community that the difference lies.[1]

Indigenous Conflict Management — Community

The one element that is common to all levels of conflict and the procedures for their management is the basic component of community. This element is capital in the traditional African experience in that it provides a distinctive normative construct and socio-political condition as a base for practical methods of handling conflict (Anderson 1983;

---

1   To call these elements refers to the subject of this chapter, not to any claim that other cultures do not share a similar approach in their own ways (King-Irani 2000; Abu-Nimer 2000; Faure 2000).

Cobban 2000). Pre-modern African life and hence its conflict management techniques were posited on the existence of a kinship community that defined social relations. A person's existence was conceived of in terms of the community: I am because we are (*umuntu ngumuntu mgabantu* in Nguni [South Africa]), the constructed opposite of the Western individualist notion of "We are because I am" (although the relation between the two could be constructively debated) or *cogito ergo sum*, the most individualistic statement that contains no reference to community at all. The syllogism is encapsulated in the Bantu term of *ubuntu*, "that one can be a person only through others. It is only in the spirit of *ubuntu*, with its emphasis of working together, that problems can be solved" (Masina 2000, 170–71; Mbagwu 2015, 59). Or there is *kanye ndu nowi* for the Buems.

Community can come in many sizes contained in the notion of an extended family — from a small, related group to a tribe — but one in which beliefs and values and kinship relations are shared. The senior figures and family councils and the decisions, integration, exclusion, confidence building and all other measures that seem so exemplary only have meaning, legitimacy and effectiveness within a given community; when the community is riven, as in authority conflicts, the referent conditions of conflict management are weakened along with it. Tongue and teeth have a mouth to keep them working together, and, without the mouth, they are merely meat and dentures. "Kinship manages conflict" (Lundy and Adjei 2015, 4).

Kinship relations can be imagined and mythologized as long as they provide a credible reference to legitimize behaviour. Kinship is indeed the essence of community, and, in strict genealogical terms, African kinship provides only imagined communities because real ancestry is from long ago (Anderson 1983); the original ancestor is far enough away and his descendants intermarried enough to be only mythologically related. But that only reinforces the cognitive element that legitimizes the management of conflict. Conflict is bad only to the extent that it hurts the community; if not, we could live with it, as we live with drought.

Yet there are two limitations on the provision of even imagined-kinship communities, referring to content and context. Community practices contain specific contents that are hard to perpetuate and replicate. Indigenous methods involve folklore, proverbs, rituals, songs, symbolic practices, atonement and forgiveness, ancestors, age grades, oaths, ceremonies, regulatory societies, fetishes and magic that play many roles in the management of conflict, including convocation, validation and solutions themselves (Mbagwu 2015; Masina 2000; Houtondji 1997). Perhaps the most important indigenous ingredient is time, the pace of the process; as an African friend remarked, "one thing we have a lot of in Africa is time." These are the cobwebs that hold the community and its practices together, and the community is only as solid as they are. It has taken a long time to put such elements in place, and, although they are resistant, they are hard to replace if destroyed. This leads to the limitation of context.

Modernization has damaged the community. It began with colonization and the introduction of competing legal and conflict management systems, but also with the introduction of different belief systems — notably Christianity and Islam — that competed with the mythology of the kinship groups. Beyond these forces of formal competition with traditional practices and beliefs came less direct challenges to the structure of the community. Wage labour, migration, schooling — including school graduates and school leavers — science and indeed conflict itself have weakened the eminence of chiefs, dispersed the availability of councils, upset the importance of rituals, ruptured the assurance of identities, undermined the authority of mythologies and left the community a wraith of its former self. Possibly worse yet, when some of its elements remained, they were taken over by the conditions of modernization that had destroyed their content. When conciliators sought to involve traditional elders in rebuilding state and society in Somalia, they found that the elders observed that power comes out of a gun and so merely followed the warlords whose dominance they were supposed to counterbalance (Menkhaus 2000). When the customary system holds the authority and identity in a society, its conciliatory adjudication can be effective. But when that authority is challenged and identity dispersed or, more, ignored, power is on a different level and elders can only follow.

This means that indigenous conflict management has lost not only its capabilities but also its enabling meaning. Atonement and reinsertion mean nothing if there is no community tissue to re-mend. Win-win solutions with other communities have no mutual referents if the social structures are dispersed. Curiously perhaps, in an age of democratization, if the collective element of community has been subverted by modernization, its authoritarian element has been reinforced, even over democratization. Throughout colonial times and afterward, tribal lands, the "corporately held endowment of a descent-based community," have been under a chiefly jurisdiction "in allocating access to farmland and in adjudicating land-related disputes arising over boundaries, inheritance, and transactions" (Boone 2014, 35-36, 37–51). Less curiously, therefore, the chief's authority over land issues made him the prime organizer for the parties in election times; the chief, like any good party boss, became the authoritarian base not only of community identity but also of democratization. Boone (2014) terms this authority and its land tenure regimes "neocustomary"; the community becomes dependent on the chief rather than the reverse.

Contemporary Conflict Management — Revival

Yet indigenous conflict management practices are not dead, and, where they are in disuse, an analytical argument can be made for their revival. A number of elements support these observations.

If the traditional imagined-kinship community is weakened by modernization, the counter could be its succession by a modern imagined-kinship community. The African political project is to create a nation-state to encompass and modernize the component traditional nations or ethnic groups of the country. In some cases, they come with a nationally accepted founding father, such as Leopold Sedar Senghor in Senegal and Nelson Mandela in South Africa; few of the other fathers of their countries have become the subject of consensual idolization, which does take time and charisma. The traditional community was manageably small, but it is harder to instill a notion — even a myth — of kinship in a national community of millions. Making a nation-state out of a state of many traditional nations has proven beyond the current capability of most African polities, and even a much-vaunted nation-state such as Somalia fell apart into its segments when the common enemy — Ethiopia — itself fell into turmoil.

Despite the encroachments and vulnerabilities invoked above, modern versions of traditional communities have shown a good deal of resilience and persistence in a number of areas.[2] They fill functional social and political, as well as identity, needs, particularly when they involve stable rural populations. In some areas of activity, most importantly in land ownership matters, the state is forced to take traditional practices into account. Land and border issues are perennial matters of conflict and time-honoured measures have been established to handle them. Governments recognize the functional utility of customary authorities (and are obliged to admit their identity importance in democratic politics). That recognition is a necessary condition for the

---

2   A few years ago in Ghana, the author visited the chief of a tribe who was in a ceremonial setting and wearing traditional dress, and who also happened to have been the head of the economics department in a major New England university, but had come to fill his duty when called. The situation is not unique.

useful functioning of neocustomary communities. Where local communities can keep domestic quarrels within the purview of extended family conflict management, it is best for the state to leave them there and not see them escalate to the courts. Longevity has given such measures great authority; newly imposed measures themselves are a source of conflict.

In most of Africa, neocustomary authorities allocate land, and individuals are theoretically able to take their decisions to a higher level, in courts or in politics (Boone 2014). Where such modern procedures can be held in check, the danger of land issues reaching the national level is minimized; where they are not, land issues can become the source of insurrection and civil war, as in Sudan and South Sudan, eastern Congo and Sierra Leone (Autesserre 2010; Peters 2011; Haaland 1969; Reno 2007, 2011). However, the neocustomary is customary more in form than in practice. The chief acts as a judicial authority, rather than as the agent of a participating community, adjudicating rather than reconciling (Aluaigba 2011). The community is there in name more than in function, riven by the disturbances of modernism mentioned. The elders work for the state, if only by delegation of reinforcing authority, and so lose respect (Kah 2015). In electoral and democratizing regimes, the customary chief's usefulness in delivering votes allows him to claim greater unimpeded jurisdiction in local disputes, if only to reinforce his authority over the community in electoral times. Every silver lining has its cloud, however: such newfound usefulness can also undermine the impartiality and standing of the chief (Osaghae 2000; Kah 2011).

In a second area of conflict, intrapersonal disputes, neocustomary practices are still followed but tend to run afoul of modernity, both in their functioning and in their effects. Councils and chiefs, with a large measure of public and stakeholder participation, often work well to manage disputes from marriage to murder in which conflict analysis, atonement and reconciliation are more important

than punishment and where time is deployed as an adjunct to these values, which are closeted in the manners of another era. But here, traditional practice runs into problems. Within its exercise, which often depends on use of rituals, sacrifices and oaths, and appeals to ancestors, modern religion weakens such effects and prevents parts of the community from participating. Once the conflict has been handled traditionally, civil authorities come in to apply modern law, which seeks punishment, eschews reconciliation, establishes guilt, punishes oathing and renders judgment, nullifying and contradicting the customary process and result (Adesina 2015a). Or, as some complain, the state — possibly in an effort to bridge the gap — institutes a commission of inquiry, which then finds its own facts and files its report, without further incidence, or with political manipulation from the outside.

In these situations, observers and practitioners of neocustomary conflict resolution plead for recognition and for space. Many types of interpersonal conflicts can be handled traditionally, without meeting the modern requirements of decisional justice, but building wider conflict management as conciliatory justice. When indigenous mechanisms are allowed space and time to run their courses, there is an opportunity for a more satisfying and stable result. Recognized, these practices would return to wider acceptance and participation and would contribute to dealing with conflict at its base, avoiding dangers of escalation to higher instances and wider involvement.

In some places, countries have ventured into modernizing traditional practice by appointing their own peace committees, modelled on customary practice but extended, enlarged, formalized and modernized in various other ways. The committees tend to receive complaints that they lack experience and long-standing roots, but they do perpetuate community control over peacemaking. Commentators frequently call for training, so that the participation that characterized past practices can return. Similarly, well-meaning Western conflict management experts have, on occasion, sought funding to provide resources for wider use of traditional practices (for example, for the *idiawit*, or independent elders, who perform inter-tribal mediation in Sudan), which, at the same time, subjects the supported activities to Western donors' requirements of accountability and success (Chauzal 2015). Even more noteworthy have been President Umaru Yar' Adua's amnesty program for the Niger Delta in 2009 and the Economic Community of West African States (ECOWAS) Conflict Prevention Framework, inaugurated in 2008, which incorporate traditional methods and practices.

Such experiences, both positive and negative, have been recorded in the Tiv area of north central Nigeria (Aluaigba 2011), in the Cross Rivers region of Nigeria and Cameroon (Kah 2011), in western Cameroon (Ndi 2011), in Kenya (Boone 2012), in Côte d'Ivoire and Zimbabwe (Boone and Kriger 2010), in Wajir in Kenya (International Crisis Group 2015), in Abyie in Sudan, for the moment, (Deng 1986; Deng and Zartman 2002), in Nigeria (Odoziobodo and Didiugwu 2015) and in west African states' conflicts in general (Bolaji 2011), among others.

Finally, in much of Africa, the biggest domestic threat is burgeoning jihadi gangsterism that feeds on other problems, such as unemployment, corruption and spiritual vacuity. Although Islam is now well rooted in over half of the continent, it is often cited as a foreign religion that has helped destroy the affective basis of the community — its *assabiya* (solidarity), to borrow an Arabic term. Where community spirit and organization have nonetheless persisted, the dangers of takeover by radical Islam are reduced; where they have not, there is room for community reconstruction, even for incorporating a more customary form of Islam as a firebreak against radicalism. There are large areas of Somalia where communities have held together and not fallen victim to Al-Shabaab;

Tuareg solidarity in some places held its own against al-Qaeda in the Arab Maghreb (AQIM) or Ansar Dine in Mali and Niger; and the *turuq* (Sufi sects) have made Senegal remarkably impervious to AQIM and other radical encroachment.

Conclusion

Traditional conflict management has been the active ingredient of whatever harmony existed in pre-colonial African relations, and it has continued to some extent under debilitating circumstances into the present time. Difficulties of content and context have weakened beliefs and practice, yet for large parts of the African population, they remain. In many situations, notably conflicts of land use and ownership and in interpersonal disputes, they have often proven their worth; chiefly authority is frequently more compelling and acceptable than modern judicial and legal proceedings, although it runs up against the positivism of modern law. African experts complain not about the irrelevance of their heritage but about the interference of new norms and practices — about the run to pastors, priests and imams for counsel and advice and the refuge in civil or criminal law and even politics — for judgments and justifications.

There is an obvious response to the contradictory logic of this situation: instead of completing the modernization process by crowding out the customary practices that work, give them space and respect. Using customary practices and venues can help indigenous systems work for themselves, rather than taxing the government with conflicts often more impervious to legal methods of judgment than to traditional measures of reconciliation. In the process, use of traditional councils will help return the councils to practice and relevance, while insulating government from local disputes that can rise to overthrow state systems if untended at the local level through local methods. Co-opting traditional venues and enrolling their practices actively in a modern context is another option, but care must be taken not to tame the neocustomary role with modern demands and thus delegitimize it. This is the practice accorded to the post of chieftain, which has found new usefulness by being incorporated into contemporary politics. A third option is to build new institutions of civil society that adopt customary values and the best of the customary methods, notably the participation of stakeholders and the search for conciliation to erase conflict.

There is certainly room for a translation of neocustomary conflict management methods to the highest level of international disputes. The event is doubtless rare, but the spirit needs to and can be cultivated. It takes a de Gaulle and Adenauer to launch, personally as well as nationally, a real reconciliation after a history of conflict (Rosoux 2001); de Klerk and Mandela did it nationally, even if not personally (Sisk 1995). Yet the spirit of reconciliation participation, time and building an overarching sense of community are necessary elements in peacemaking, if conflict is to be not only managed but truly resolved and transformed. On the other hand, it is hard to imagine Afwerki and Meles in east Africa, Mohammed VI and Bouteflika in North Africa, or Salva Kiir and Riek Machar in South Sudan seeking personal as well as national reconciliations, despite all the *ubuntu* that might be pumped into the process. Like all ideals, it remains a real and guiding inspiration, but not a *sine qua non*, in Africa any more than elsewhere.

The conclusion of another study on the subject is relevant for its various emphases: "indigenous conflict management approaches are now only useful in addressing local, communal, intra- and intergroup conflicts.... A rigorous mechanism has yet to be developed...to extend the efficacy of indigenous systems to large-scale international crises in the region" (Benjamin and Adebayo 2015, 327). If the local, communal and intra- and inter-group efficacy of traditional methods are recognized and strengthened, a great contribution has already been registered. Large-scale international crises themselves are doubtless beyond the reach of traditional methods without exceptional leadership, but that should not tarnish their lower-level activity. And such activity, when successful and expended, can provide a major contribution to preventing conflicts from escalating to larger crises. On the continental level, it is a pertinent challenge for the African Union to hold the ideal of reconciliation and peaceful, accommodative resolution of conflicts before the eyes of its members, so that the African Union can meet its own cultural standards and serve as a model for other regional organizations (Deng and Zartman 2002).

Works Cited

Abu-Nimer, Mohammed. 2000. "Contrasts in Conflict Management in Cleveland and Palestine." In *Traditional Cures for Modern Conflicts: African Conflict "Medicine,"* edited by I William Zartman. Boulder, CO: Lynne Rienner Publishers.

Adebayo, Akanmu, Brandon Lundy, Jesse Benjamin and Joseph Adjei, eds. 2015. *Indigenous Conflict Management Strategies in West Africa.* Lanham, MD: Lexington Books.

Adesina, Olutayo. 2015a. "Conflicts in Africa." In *Indigenous Conflict Management Strategies in West Africa*, edited by Akanmu Adebayo et al. Lanham, MD: Lexington Books.

———. 2015b. "Ilepa among the Yoruba of Western Nigeria." In *Indigenous Conflict Management Strategies in West Africa*, edited by Akanmu Adebayo et al. Lanham, MD: Lexington Books.

Adjei, Joseph. 2015. "The Role of the Chieftaincy Institution in Ensuring Peace in Ghana." In *Indigenous Conflict Management Strategies in West Africa*, edited by Akanmu Adebayo et al. Lanham, MD: Lexington Books.

Ahorsu, Ken and B. Y. Gebe. 2011. *Government and Security in Ghana: The Dagbon Chieftaincy Crisis.* Stockholm: Stockholm International Peace Research Institute.

Ajibade, Olusola. 2015. "Sparks of Resistance, Flames of Change." In *Indigenous Conflict Management Strategies in West Africa*, edited by Akanmu Adebayo et al. Lanham, MD: Lexington Books.

Aluaigba, Moses. 2011. "Exploiting the Tiv Traditional Methods of Conflict Resolution in North Central Nigeria." *African Conflict and Peacebuilding Review* 1 (2): 74–103.

Anderson, Benedict. 1983. *Imagined Communities: Reflections on the Origins and Spread of Nationalism.* London, UK: Verso.

Anstey, Mark and Valerie Rosoux, eds. Forthcoming. *Reconciliation and Negotiation.*

Asogwa, Felix Chinwe. 2015. "Women's Involvement in Indigenous Conflict Management." In *Indigenous Conflict Management Strategies in West Africa*, edited by Akanmu Adebayo et al. Lanham, MD: Lexington Books.

Autesserre, Severine. 2010. *The Trouble with the Congo.* Cambridge, UK: Cambridge University Press.

Benjamin, Jesse and Akanmu Adebayo. 2015. "Conclusion: Implications of Epistemic Diversity for Conflict Management in West Africa and the World." In *Indigenous Conflict Management Strategies in West Africa*, edited by Akanmu Adebayo et al. Lanham, MD: Lexington Books.

Bolaji, Kehinde. 2011. "The ECOWAS Conflict Prevention Framework." *African Conflict and Peacebuilding Review* 1 (2): 183–204.

Boone, Catherine. 2012. "Land Conflict and Distributive Politics in Kenya." *African Studies Review* 55 (1): 75–105.

———. 2014. *Property and Political Order in Africa.* Cambridge, UK: Cambridge University Press.

Boone, Catherine and Norma Kriger. 2010. "Multiparty Elections and Land Patronage." *Commonwealth and Comparative Politics* 48 (3): 178–202.

Brewoo, Sherwaa and Mustapha Abdallah. 2015. "Exploring Indigenous Mechanisms for Peacemaking in West Africa." In *Indigenous Conflict Management Strategies in West Africa*, edited by Akanmu Adebayo et al. Lanham, MD: Lexington Books.

Chauzal, Gregory. 2015. "Fix the Unfixable." Clingendael Conflict Research Unit Policy Brief. The Hague: Netherlands Institute of International Relations.

Cobban, Helena. 2000. *The Moral Architecture of World Peace.* Charlottesville, VA: University of Virginia Press.

Danso, Sarah Okaebea and Joana Ama Osei-Tutu. 2015. "Homegrown Crises, Homegrown Solutions? The Efficacy of Indigenous Conflict Resolution/Management Approaches in Ghana." In *Indigenous Conflict Management Strategies in West Africa*, edited by Akanmu Adebayo et al. Lanham, MD: Lexington Books.

Deng, Francis M. 1986. *The Man Called Deng Majok*. New Haven, CT: Yale University Press.

———. 2000. "Reaching Out: A Dinka Principle of Conflict Management." In *Traditional Cures for Modern Conflicts: African Conflict "Medicine,"* edited by I William Zartman. Boulder, CO: Lynne Rienner Publishers.

Deng, Francis M. and I William Zartman. 2002. *A Strategic Vision of Africa*. Washington, DC: Brookings Institution Press.

Eselebor, Willie Aziegbe. 2015. "The Challenges of Conflict Transformation." In *Indigenous Conflict Management Strategies in West Africa*, edited by Akanmu Adebayo et al. Lanham, MD: Lexington Books.

Evans-Pritchard, E. E. 1940. *The Nuer: A Description of the Modes of Livelihood and Political Institutions of a Nilotic People*. London, UK: Oxford University Press.

Faure, Guy Olivier. 2000. *"Traditional Conflict Management in Africa and China."* In *Traditional Cures for Modern Conflicts: African Conflict "Medicine,"* edited by I William Zartman. Boulder, CO: Lynne Rienner Publishers.

Fonkem, Achankeng. 2015. *"Bekem* in Peacemaking in Nweh Society." In *Indigenous Conflict Management Strategies in West Africa*, edited by Akanmu Adebayo et al. Lanham, MD: Lexington Books.

Fred-Mensah, Ben. 2000. "Bases of Traditional Conflict Management Among the Buems." In *Traditional Cures for Modern Conflicts: African Conflict "Medicine,"* edited by I William Zartman. Boulder, CO: Lynne Rienner Publishers.

Gluckman, Max. 1965. *Politics and Ritual in Tribal Society*. New Brunswick, NJ, and London, UK: AldineTransaction.

Haaland, Gunner. 1969. "Economic Determinants in Ethnic Processes." In *Ethnic Groups and Boundaries*, edited by Frederik Barth. Boston, MA: Little, Brown & Co.

Houtondji, Paulin, ed. 1997. *Endogenous Knowledge*. Dakar: Council for the Development of Social Science Research in Africa.

International Crisis Group. 2015. "A Dying Breed of Peacemakers in Kenya's North East." *In Pursuit of Peace* (blog), November 19. http://blog.crisisgroup.org/africa/kenya/2015/11/19/a-dying-breed-of-peacemakers-in-kenyas-north-east/.

Kah, Henry Kam. 2011. "Regulatory Societies, Peacebuilding and Maintenance in the Cross Rivers Regions of Nigeria and Cameroon." *African Conflict and Peacebuilding Review* 1 (2): 50–73.

———. 2015. "Beitonghekeh: People's Power and Conflict Resolution in Cameroon." In *Indigenous Conflict Management Strategies in West Africa*, edited by Akanmu Adebayo et al. Lanham, MD: Lexington Books.

King-Irani, L. E. 2000. "Rituals of Forgiveness and Processes of Empowerment in Lebanon." In *Traditional Cures for Modern Conflicts: African Conflict "Medicine,"* edited by I William Zartman. Boulder, CO: Lynne Rienner Publishers.

Kolawole, Clement and Toluwalope Kolawole. 2015. "Alternative Dispute Resolution Strategies." In *Indigenous Conflict Management Strategies in West Africa*, edited by Akanmu Adebayo et al. Lanham, MD: Lexington Books.

Kouassi, Edmond Kwam. 2000. "West Coast Diplomacy among the Akan and their Neighbors." In *Traditional Cures for Modern Conflicts: African Conflict "Medicine,"* edited by I William Zartman. Boulder, CO: Lynne Rienner Publishers.

Lundy, Brandon and Joseph Adjei. 2015. "Reconciliation and Conflict Management in West Africa through Cultural Traditions." In *Indigenous Conflict Management Strategies in West Africa*, edited by Akanmu Adebayo et al. Lanham, MD: Lexington Books.

Masina, Nomande. 2000. "Khosa Practices of Ubuntu for South Africa." In *Traditional Cures for Modern Conflicts: African Conflict "Medicine,"* edited by I William Zartman. Boulder, CO: Lynne Rienner Publishers.

Mbagwu, Joan. 2015. "Border Disputes in Africa and Traditional Approaches for Resolving Them." In *Indigenous Conflict Management Strategies in West Africa*, edited by Akanmu Adebayo et al. Lanham, MD: Lexington Books.

Menkhaus, Ken. 2000. "Traditional Conflict Management in Contemporary Somalia." In *Traditional Cures for Modern Conflicts: African Conflict "Medicine,"* edited by I William Zartman. Boulder, CO: Lynne Rienner Publishers.

Nader, Laura. 1989. "Disputing without the Force of Law." *Yale Law Journal* 88 (5): 998–1021.

Ndi, Tanto Richard. 2011. "Land Stakeholder Empowerment in the Bagam/Bamenyam Conflict in Cameroon." *African Conflict and Peacebuilding Review* 1 (2): 34–49.

Nuameh, Kwaku. 2000. "Legitimacy in Dispute Mediation." Ph.D. dissertation, The Johns Hopkins University.

Nukunya, G. K. 1992. *Tradition and Change in Ghana*. Accra: Ghana Universities Press.

Odoziobodo, Severus Ifeanyi and Ifeanyi Didiugwu. 2015. "From Militancy to Amnesty." In *Indigenous Conflict Management Strategies in West Africa*, edited by Akanmu Adebayo et al. Lanham, MD: Lexington Books.

Ohwovoriole, Felicia. 2011. "Peacemaking and Proverbs in Urhobo and Yoruba Marital Conflict, Part 1." *African Conflict and Peacebuilding Review* 1 (2): 122–35.

Osaghae, Eghosa. 2000. "Applying Traditional Methods to Modern Conflict." In *Traditional Cures for Modern Conflicts: African Conflict "Medicine,"* edited by I William Zartman. Boulder, CO: Lynne Rienner Publishers.

Peters, Krijn. 2011. *War and the Crisis of Youth in Sierra Leone*. Cambridge, UK: Cambridge University Press.

Phillips, Oluwaseun. 2011. "Peacemaking and Proverbs in Urhobo and Yoruba Marital Conflict, Part 2." *African Conflict and Peacebuilding Review* 1 (2): 136–52.

Radcliffe-Brown, A. R. 1952. *Structure and Function in Primitive Society*. London, UK: Cohen & West.

Reno, William. 2007. "Patronage Politics and the Behavior of Armed Groups." *Civil War* 9 (4): 324–42.

———. 2011. *Warfare in Independent Africa: New Approaches to African History*. Cambridge, UK: Cambridge University Press.

Rosoux, Valerie. 2001. *Les usages de la mémoire dans les relations internationales*. Brussels, Belgium: Bruylant.

Sisk, Timothy. 1995. *Democratization in South Africa*. Princeton, NJ: Princeton University Press.

Udofia, David. 2011. "Peacebuilding Mechanisms in Akwa Ibom State Oil-Bearing Communities in Nigeria." *African Conflict and Peacebuilding Review* 1 (2): 104–19.

Uwazie, Ernest. 2000. "Social Relations and Peacekeeping among the Igbo." In *Traditional Cures for Modern Conflicts: African Conflict "Medicine,"* edited by I William Zartman. Boulder, CO: Lynne Rienner Publishers.

Wilson-Fall, Wendy. 2000. "Conflict Resolution and Prevention among the Fulbe." In *Traditional Cures for Modern Conflicts: African Conflict "Medicine,"* edited by I William Zartman. Boulder, CO: Lynne Rienner Publishers.

Zartman, I William, ed. 2000. *Traditional Cures for Modern Conflicts: African Conflict "Medicine."* Boulder, CO: Lynne Rienner Publishers.

———. 2011. "Peacemaking in West Africa." *African Conflict and Peacebuilding Review* 1 (2): 1–5.

———. 2015. *Preventing Deadly Conflict.* Cambridge, UK: Polity.

Zartman, I William and Kwaku Nuameh. 2005. "The Ndougou Dispute." Washington, DC: Africa Studies, The Johns Hopkins University-School of Advanced International Studies.

16

Religion, Society and Conflict

Alexander Thurston

Religious violence in contemporary Africa affects millions of people and can shape local and national politics. Religious violence frequently involves the two dominant religions in Africa, Christianity and Islam, but violence can also involve African traditional religions.[1] Such violence can be inter-religious — for example, pitting Christians and Muslims against one another in places such as Nigeria's Middle Belt. Such violence can also be intra-religious, sometimes taking the form of clashes between co-religionists over sectarian differences. Violent groups with a religious dimension sometimes prey on civilians, including civilians of the same faith, or become involved in clashes with the state. This chapter treats both inter-religious and intra-religious violence, especially, because some violence that is widely framed in the international media

as inter-religious is, in fact, largely intra-religious — the majority of those victimized by Nigeria's Boko Haram, for example, have been Muslim civilians, but that conflict is frequently presented as a Muslim-Christian war.

Religion is never the sole factor in provoking violence, and religion's role can shift during a conflict. Some conflicts include a religious dimension from the beginning. Religious identities and vocabularies have been central to Nigeria's Boko Haram and Somalia's Al-Shabaab since those movements were founded in the early 2000s.[2] Other conflicts begin as struggles in which religious identities are secondary, but the trajectory of the violence activates and politicizes those identities. In the Central African Republic (CAR), the majority Muslim Séléka militia did not present itself as Islamic during its rebellion in 2012. Over time, however, religious identification became a

---

1   One example is the Ombatse group of Nigeria's Nasarawa State, which made headlines for its clashes with security forces in 2013. See Okoli and Uhembe (2014).

2   On Boko Haram, see *Journal of Religion in Africa* (2012) and Thurston (2016b). On Al-Shabaab, see Hansen (2013).

central axis of the conflict, activating pre-existing tensions over ethnicity, economic resources and politics.[3] Starting in 2013, predominately Christian "anti-Balaka" groups began to turn on the CAR's Muslim population (and to prey on some non-Muslim civilians) in retaliation against Séléka. Today, religious tensions are a powerful part of the CAR's politics and society.

These examples call attention to the need for analytical care. Master frameworks for generalizing about religious violence in Africa — the idea of an "arc of instability" running from Algeria to Somalia (Sanders and Lau 2012; Guterres 2012) or the notion that countries along the "tenth parallel" are uniquely prone to Muslim-Christian clashes (Griswold 2010) — have limited applicability once one examines the intricacies of conflict at the local level. Similarly, the idea that Middle Eastern influences have radicalized African Muslims has been exaggerated.[4] When outsiders contribute significantly to religious tensions, it is often in localities where communities are already divided along political, economic, ethnic or religious lines. Leaving aside these flawed master narratives, this chapter treats religious violence as a deeply local and context-specific phenomenon.

As religious violence in Africa attracts more attention, a multi-vocal conversation about solutions has developed. The violent responses to conflict are well known and widely implemented: heavy-handed crackdowns by African security forces (often generating the unintended consequence of exacerbating conflict),[5] air strikes

against jihadist camps and commanders,[6] manhunts for rebel leaders[7] and collective punishment of ethno-religious communities.[8] In addition to violent measures, many African governments have pursued a strategy of strategic silence, hoping that repression will neutralize perpetrators of violence and that silence will lead victims to drop their grievances against perpetrators or the state.

Leaving these violent solutions aside, this chapter concentrates on non-violent conflict resolution strategies, especially those generated by actors within religious communities. The chapter argues that enduring solutions to violent conflict in Africa will have to take into account the continent's changing religious landscape, rather than attempting to turn back time. With that in mind, the chapter first surveys changes in the structure of religious authority, especially the tendency toward fragmentation — the splintering of communities and the increase in the number of voices seeking to speak for each religion. Emphasizing fragmentation does not mean that African religious communities formerly had a golden age of religious unity, or that there are no unifying figures today. This emphasis does mean, however, that population growth, new media and various forms of liberalization have brought more voices than ever before into the religious arena.

The chapter further argues that three of the most prominent strategies for resolving religious conflict in Africa are often either rigidly top-down or insufficiently scalable. These strategies are the

3   For an analysis of how these dynamics operated at the local level, see Kilembe (2015).

4   For an example of this type of argument, see Trofimov (2016). For my effort to offer a more nuanced perspective on how Middle Eastern influences can intersect with local politics and intra-religious tensions, see Thurston (2016a).

5   For an example concerning Nigeria, see Human Rights Watch (2012). For an example concerning Ethiopia's 2006–2009 occupation of Somalia, see Human Rights Watch (2008).

6   In recent years, the main African theatres of fatal air strikes against jihadists have been Somalia and Libya, but aerial surveillance missions have also become a key part of counterterror campaigns in the Sahel and Nigeria.

7   The main example here is the manhunt for leaders of the Uganda-born Lord's Resistance Army, especially its top commander Joseph Kony. See Arieff, Blanchard and Husted (2015).

8   For a Kenyan example, see Amnesty International (2014). Greater historical background on collective punishment of ethnic Somalis in Kenya can be found in Whittaker (2015).

following: entrenching conservative religious authorities; facilitating interfaith dialogue; and pursuing countering violent extremism (CVE) initiatives. After reviewing the shortcomings of these strategies, the chapter then argues that fragmentation can yield possibilities for conflict resolution even as it simultaneously exacerbates some conflicts. Enduring solutions to religious violence should grapple with, rather than seek to reverse, the fragmentation of religious authority. Interfaith dialogue and CVE initiatives, meanwhile, should be pursued with the understanding that ending violence must involve political solutions and messy compromises; absent a workable political solution, "bringing everyone to the table" or "teaching the youth not to hate" are insufficient measures for ending or preventing violence.

Changing Structures of Religious Authority in Africa

The past two centuries have brought massive changes to the religious makeup of African societies. The two dominant religions in Sub-Saharan Africa today, Christianity and Islam, only attracted massive followings across Africa in the twentieth century. Christianity has been present in north Africa since the first century and in Sub-Saharan Africa since approximately the fourth century (in Ethiopia). Starting in the fifteenth century, European (and later North American) missionary activities brought sustained contact between European Christians and African peoples, especially in coastal regions. Yet in 1900, only an estimated nine percent of Sub-Saharan Africa's population was Christian, whereas 62.9 percent of the population was Christian by 2010. Islam, meanwhile, arrived in Sub-Saharan Africa (also Ethiopia) during the life of the Prophet Muhammad, and Muslims conquered north Africa during the seventh and early eighth centuries. Over a millennium ago, Muslim traders and scholars became a consistent presence in the Sahel and along the coast of east Africa. But in 1900, only

14 percent of Sub-Saharan Africa's population was Muslim, compared with over 30 percent by 2010. By 2050, Sub-Saharan Africa may be 58.5 percent Christian and 35 percent Muslim. The growth in Christianity and Islam has come at the expense of traditional or indigenous religions, whose share of the population plunged from an estimated 76 percent in 1900 to as low as 3.3 percent in 2010.[9]

Colonialism was the decisive factor in the massive spread of Christianity and Islam. European colonial powers and their missionary allies actively sought to spread Christianity in many areas, but they also unwittingly sparked mass conversion to Islam in some territories. Sometimes, colonialism inadvertently spread Islam from the top down by empowering Muslim rulers as intermediaries with formerly non-Muslim or partly Muslim peoples, although such strategies could also engender long-lasting bitterness among those who resisted conversion (Ochonu 2014). Sometimes, Islam spread from the bottom up, as colonialism introduced new forms of mobility — freeing slaves, conscripting people into labour or military service, fuelling urbanization and commerce, sparking emigrations and creating peaceful conditions that allowed preachers and scholars to circulate more freely (Peterson 2011). Meanwhile, colonized peoples' Christianity quickly began to escape the control of colonial authorities and missionaries. Independent African churches flourished by the early twentieth century, sometimes generating indigenous revival movements that reached large numbers of Africans.[10]

At independence, African countries often boasted significant intra-Muslim and intra-Christian diversity. Certain forms of both religions were highly influential in Africa, however. Within Islam, Sufism — a Sunni mystical tradition often structured around hierarchical orders or brotherhoods — was

---

9   For figures from 1900, see Pew Forum on Religion and Public Life (2010, i). For figures from 2010 and projected figures for 2050, see Pew Research Center (2015).

10   For a Nigerian example, see Peel (1968).

responsible for much of the spread of Islam in Africa. Within Christianity, Roman Catholicism and mainline Protestant churches were the choice of many African elites. From the 1960s through the 1990s, partnerships between political and religious elites translated into substantial top-down control over religious life in many countries. In Niger, for example, the Islamic Association of Niger — run by Sufi Muslims — had a major role in regulating mosques and managing state-society relations under military rule from 1974 to 1991 and retained some influence afterwards (Elischer 2015). Intra-religious and inter-religious clashes occurred during the early post-colonial period, but single-party states, their security forces and their religious allies could sometimes repress or prevent such conflicts with relative ease. Rebellions in this period, moreover, often used left wing, nationalist or secular rhetoric, rather than religious identification. The religious violence that did exceed authorities' capacity to manage, however, foreshadowed later trends; in northern Nigeria, the "Maitatsine" riots of a fringe Muslim group in the early 1980s revealed a dangerous confluence of forces: uncontrolled urban sprawl and inequality, political authorities' timidity in confronting radical preachers, lack of coordination between security agencies and the rising anxiety of established religious leaders about their growing inability to command respect, especially among urban youth.[11]

The advent of liberalization in the 1980s and 1990s introduced lasting changes — and persistent fragmentation — into the religious life of Sub-Saharan Africa. Liberalization occurred in the political sphere, with many African countries holding competitive multi-party elections during the 1990s. Liberalization extended to the media and civic spheres, giving religious actors new opportunities to found newspapers, appear on radio and television and create associations and organizations (Otayek and Soares 2007). Some movements were well poised to thrive in this environment; in 1990s Ghana, Pentecostal Christianity benefited not only from deregulation of the media, but also from the liberalization of the economy: "With its emphasis on the capacity of the Holy Spirit to induce personal change, enable ruptures and ever new beginnings, effect miracles, follow and protect born-again Christians wherever they went, and bring about health and wealth, Pentecostalism articulated a strain of Christianity that fit exceptionally well into the new climate of millennial capitalism" (Meyer 2015, 8-9). Meanwhile, Muslim preaching movements that had been clandestine and unofficial in the 1980s, such as southern Mali's non-violent Ançar-Dine (not to be confused with northern Mali's jihadist Ansar Dine organization), became more visible and assertive in the 1990s (Ançar-Dine France 2013).[12] Old alliances between single-party regimes and key religious elites could no longer manage the religious field with the same degree of control: many single-party regimes gave way to elected ones, and religious elites faced an unprecedented degree of competition, making many partnerships either less effective than before, prone to greater resistance or outright impossible.

Especially since the 1990s, a fragmentation of religious authority has thus occurred in many African religious communities, Christian and Muslim alike.[13] In Ethiopia, once the unshakable bastion of the Ethiopian Orthodox Church, new religious movements have been transforming the landscape, especially since the fall of the Marxist Derg regime in 1991. Pentecostal churches now attract as much as one-fifth of Ethiopia's population (Anderson 2013, 126), and the country's Prime Minister Hailemariam Desalegn (who took office

---

11 These concerns emerge clearly in two Nigerian government reports from this period: Federal Government of Nigeria (1981) and Borno State of Nigeria (1982). For secondary literature on Maitatsine, see Lubeck (1985) and Hiskett (1987).

12 For context about liberalization in 1990s Mali, see Brenner (2001, chapter 8).

13 On the idea of a "fragmentation of sacred authority" across the Muslim world, see Eickelman and Piscatori (1996).

in 2012) is a Pentecostal elder. Meanwhile, as much as one-third of Ethiopia's population is now Muslim. The Muslim community has resisted the state's efforts to control Islam from the top down: in 2012-2013, massive protests broke out over the state's closure of certain mosques and Muslim schools, as well as the state's decision to stack the Ethiopian Islamic Affairs Supreme Council with members of a quietist Muslim movement known as Al-Ahbash. Even as the state attempted to blame the protests on "extremism" (Østebø 2012), the protests revealed the difficulties that even one of Africa's most powerful single-party regimes presently faced in controlling its religious field.

The fragmentation of religious authority has intersected with, and been accelerated by, the changing demographics of Africa, particularly the continent's youth bulge. As of 2014, half of Sub-Saharan Africa's population was under the age of 25, and "each year between 2015 and 2035, there will be half a million more 15-year-olds than the year before" (Filmer and Fox 2014, 2). Within many religious communities, the growing numbers of youth can add to the strains affecting "gerontocracies" — that is, power structures dominated by old people, usually old men. For youth, the concerns of old men can seem increasingly remote from the burdens that youth face in negotiating difficult economies, turbulent politics, decisions about marriage and sex and other challenges.

Many new religious voices explicitly position themselves as youth movements, and others attract significant youth constituencies. Commentators sometimes depict this development as inherently dangerous, assuming that youth movements are prone to radicalization and violence, but many youth-based religious constituencies in Africa are largely peaceful. In Gambia, for example, the transnational Muslim missionary movement Tabligh Jama'at has particular appeal for youth, allowing them to assert a new form of religiosity focused on "personal virtue, a renewed moral order, frugality, and greater social equality (both between

the younger and older generations, and between men and women)" (Janson 2013, 14). Such youth-based piety movements can represent a formidable challenge to the status quo, reshaping social relationships in everyday life.

The rise of new religious voices, driven by fragmentation or youth, or both, has profoundly changed structures of power in Africa. This does not mean that older and more established religious communities have been sidelined. As Benjamin Soares points out, Western scholars' focus on the new and the exotic in African religiosity, especially Pentecostalism, can distract attention from the continued importance of Catholics and mainline Protestants (Soares 2014, 28). Within the study of Islam in Africa, scholars have rightly pointed out that Salafis, "Wahhabis" and other reformists have commanded a disproportionate amount of attention. This trend can give the misleading impression that Sufi Muslims and classical models of Islamic practice and learning are dying out. In fact, Sufism remains a vibrant force in Africa, and many African Muslims continue to seek knowledge through classical institutions such as the traditional Qur'an school (Ware 2008). Yet much is changing. Although similarities between Pentecostals and Salafis are often exaggerated, the two movements share at least one similarity: both are more decentralized and less hierarchical than their co-religionist rivals. Individual leaders may act as unifying figures for these movements, and powerful associations can unite some Pentecostals or Salafis under their umbrellas, but neither movement has a structure equivalent to the Catholic or Anglican churches or to Sufi orders.

Amid substantial continuity and change in the structures of religious authority in Africa, the challenge is to understand how various religious movements — old and new, conservative and radical, and pro– and anti–status quo — are competing, cooperating and coexisting. Among other trends, some new movements have leveraged their massive, enthusiastic followings to gain pronounced institutional and political influence.

In Nigeria, Pentecostals held the presidency of the Christian Association of Nigeria from 2010 to 2015 and now hold the vice presidency of the country itself. Indeed, shortly after being elected to his post in 2015, Vice President Yemi Osinbajo said that he was merely "on loan" to the federal government of Nigeria. "I am still the pastor-in-charge of Province 48 in Lagos and my wife remains wife of the pastor-in-charge," he explained. "The most important part of our lives is that we are God's children; there is nothing more important than that" (Bamgboye and Azu 2015). In some countries, one finds that established religious authorities have navigated the challenges of post-coloniality with a great degree of success; in others, one finds new voices gaining the upper hand. In Senegal, most politicians continue to seek the advice and support of Sufi sheiks;[14] but in neighbouring Mali, Salafis have acquired influence in electoral politics and street-level activism, acting as one major pressure group on successive governments (*Le Monde* 2013).

In assessing the effects of religious fragmentation, what should command attention is not just who wins or loses in competitions for religious influence, but also how intense the competitions are, and what forms they take. The most dangerous forms of religious fragmentation and competition occur in environments already gripped by crisis: intense political anger, unresponsive authorities, prior histories of unresolved conflict, economic crisis or pervasive feelings of spiritual insecurity. For example, when one traces the genealogy of Nigeria's Boko Haram, a history of fragmentation amid wider social crisis stands out as one factor in generating conflict. In the early 2000s, Boko Haram broke away from a non-violent network of quasi-independent Salafi Muslim preachers in Nigeria (Thurston 2016a), a network that had itself broken away from the mass movement Izala

in the 1990s.[15] Religious fragmentation helped to radicalize Boko Haram, as its founders sought to distinguish their movement in a crowded religious marketplace (*Journal of Religion in Africa* 2012). Fragmentation also isolated the movement once its one-time mentors and allies began deserting it in the mid-2000s. This fragmentation was dangerous because it occurred in a broader context: other factors that contributed to Boko Haram's rise include poverty, regional disparities within Nigeria, legacies of inter-religious conflict and impunity for violence and contentious politics at the local and national levels (Thurston, forthcoming).

Sometimes the most dangerous radicalization occurs among jihadists themselves. At the global level, the fallout of fragmentation is visible in the ferocious competition between al-Qaeda and the Islamic State since 2013: in Syria, Libya and elsewhere, an array of jihadists now compete for territory, influence and attention. Sometimes, this competition leads to an increase in the level and brutality of violence. In Africa, the proliferation of fragments and offshoots of al-Qaeda in the Islamic Maghreb (AQIM) has heightened the unpredictability and geographical scope of that group's violence, especially since the collapse of a proto-state that AQIM and its allies briefly controlled in northern Mali in 2012-2013. Since that time, factional commanders have staged attacks from eastern Algeria to southern Côte d'Ivoire. The fragmentation within AQIM has left even the best-informed observers struggling to understand the motivations for such attacks and the multi-causal roots of west Africa's current susceptibility to jihadist violence.[16] Sometimes, authorities are left to sift through multiple claims of responsibility from multiple AQIM affiliates and splinter groups.

---

14   Even to the extent that some Senegalese intellectuals expressed concerns about "the republic on its knees" when President Abdoulaye Wade prostrated himself before the Mouridiyya order's top sheik after he won the presidency in 2000. See Carayol (2012).

15   Izala is the nickname of Jama'at Izalat al-Bid'a wa-Iqamat al-Sunna, "The Society for the Removal of Heretical Innovation and the Establishment of the Prophet's Model." For two major studies of Izala, see Kane (2003) and Amara (2011).

16   Daniel Eizenga and Leonardo Villalón (2016) grapple with these complexities in their piece.

Three Prominent Non-violent Conflict Resolution Strategies

Faced with the challenges of jihadism on the one hand and localized, inter-communal violence on the other, the international community has seized upon three main non-violent strategies for resolving and preventing religious conflict in Africa: entrenching conservative religious authorities, pursuing interfaith dialogue and implementing programs for CVE. CVE programs variously seek to prevent radicalization, especially of youth, and to de-radicalize members of violent groups. CVE is meant to offer a non-violent complement to violent counterterrorism measures such as drone strikes.

African governments and religious leaders have also pursued these strategies — sometimes as self-generated responses to conflict, but sometimes as a form of opportunism and even tokenism that responds to incentives and pressures generated by the international community. Authoritarian African regimes have learned that branding domestic dissent "terrorism" can be an effective way of deflecting international criticism, and a variety of regimes, including elected ones, have proclaimed "soft approaches," even as they continue to pursue heavy-handed military responses to conflict.[17] In the absence of pressure from the West to adopt CVE and other non-violent programs, it seems that many African states would prefer primarily repressive strategies.

Entrenching Religious Authority

In terms of entrenching conservative religious authority, many voices are keen to have African and Western governments strengthen or partner with communities such as Sufi orders. This thinking fits

with global trends, as Western powers search the globe for moderate Muslims to participate in the softer aspects of the war on terror (Rabasa et al. 2007). In Africa, some thinkers see Sufis as the ideal partners for African governments and Western powers, arguing that Sufis are well positioned to manage social change and rebut radicals' theological arguments (Hill 2010). This strategy is, in historical perspective, well worn: colonialism in Muslim Africa often rested partly on authorities' cooperation with hereditary Muslim rulers and those Sufi orders that accommodated colonial rule (Robinson 2000), even as colonial regimes designated certain other Sufis politically dangerous (Reynolds 2001; Umar 2006, chapter 1). Today, proposals to partner with Sufis likely overestimate the potential for such communities to control the religious field in their countries. In Nigeria, Sufi sheiks worked vigorously to rebut Salafi arguments in the 1970s and 1980s, when the Salafi movement first began to loudly proclaim anti-Sufi sentiments and to organize at the mass level. Sufis also used their institutional control over mosques and their influence over politicians to help deny Salafis some access to mosques, schools and media (Loimeier 1997; Kane 2003). Sufis' opposition to Salafism helped Sufis to retain massive influence in Nigeria, but today the Salafi movement in Nigeria is larger and more influential than it was in the 1970s.

Perhaps with greater government backing or Western support, Sufis in Africa could reshape the religious landscape there. But proposals to entrench a conservative status quo also downplay the risks that established religious authorities take by aligning too closely with governments. In Senegal, a country often hailed as a model of religious tolerance founded on Sufism, senior Sufi sheiks have been reluctant to endorse presidential candidates since 1988, when young Sufi voters clearly rejected one senior sheik's command to vote for the incumbent. The backlash against senior sheiks helped opened the door to some intra-Sufi competition for political influence, especially among younger sheiks (Villalon 1995, 197-198). But even the younger Senegalese sheiks who have

---

17 This was the approach of Nigerian National Security Advisor Sambo Dasuki (who served from 2012 to 2015), who announced a new soft approach toward Boko Haram in 2014, even as the Goodluck Jonathan administration's actual approach remained overwhelmingly militarized and heavy-handed. See *Premium Times* (2014).

thrown themselves into politics have often ended up discredited — or out of favour once the political winds change. Sheik Bethio Thioune, a relatively minor figure in the Mouridiyya Sufi order, was an ally of President Abdoulaye Wade (who served from 2000 to 2012). Once Wade left office in 2012, Thioune found himself vulnerable, especially after several disciples died at one of his homes under mysterious circumstances. Since 2012, Thioune has been in and out of jail (Thurston 2012).

For Christian leaders, too, there are risks in tying their fortunes to those of governments and politicians. Churches, especially mainline churches, were often at the forefront of democratization movements in the 1990s, sometimes becoming key sites of opposition activity when single-party regimes blocked other channels of dissent; many African parishioners expected their leaders to give voice to popular discontent, rather than to act as props of unpopular regimes (Gifford 1995). In contrast, Pentecostals and Evangelicals have often been close to political incumbents in recent decades. In Nigeria, there was even something of a Pentecostal presidency under the born-again Christian Olusegun Obasanjo (who served from 1999 to 2007). Obasanjo surrounded himself with Christian pastors and publicly devout advisers, and he cultivated an atmosphere of Christian prayer and worship in the presidential villa (Obadare 2006). The "rump of the theocratic class" that had supported Obasanjo later gravitated toward the next Christian president of Nigeria, Goodluck Jonathan (who served from 2010 to 2015). In the contentious election of 2015, however, some of the country's most prominent Pentecostals either abstained from endorsing Jonathan or even hedged their bets. Nigeria's most influential Pentecostal pastor, Enoch Adeboye of the Redeemed Christian Church of God, not only declined to make an endorsement (even though he had "ostentatiously" blessed Jonathan in 2010) (Obadare 2015), but also, presumably, consented to the decision of one of his pastors, Yemi Osinbajo, to become the running mate of Jonathan's rival, Muhammadu Buhari. As Pentecostal pastors gained wealth and power across Africa, moreover, they simultaneously became targets of more scrutiny by some governments: South Africa's Commission for the Promotion and Protection of Cultural, Religious and Linguistic Communities has initiated inquiries into major churches' finances, investigating figures such as the Nigerian mega-pastor Chris Oyakhilome.

Conflict resolution and prevention strategies that rely on prominent religious authorities, then, are vulnerable to the same forces that can affect those authorities: shifting political winds, financial scandals and splits between leaders and constituencies. Within religious communities, as in any community, power can run in multiple directions. If religious leaders had unilateral authority to either incite or prevent violence by their followers, then patterns of religious violence in Africa would look significantly different. Religious leaders sometimes find themselves reacting to the demands and feelings of their followers, in which case leaders may remain silent or even go along with pressures to support violence and conflict. None of this is meant to say that religious leaders cannot or should not be key planks of conflict resolution efforts — rather, all actors should keep in mind that strategies overly focused on top-down conceptualizations of religious power will likely stumble.

Interfaith Dialogue

In the interfaith domain, models of conflict resolution are often either top-down, as with the broader reliance on established religious authorities as described above, or the models centre on a kind of tokenism. The international media and Western governments are quick to seize upon stories of change makers, such as Nigeria's *The Imam and the Pastor* (FLT Films 2009), or the CAR's Interfaith Peace Platform. The heroism of interfaith actors operating in conflict zones is undeniable, but international praise for their efforts can obscure troubling trends. First, it is difficult to assess interfaith groups' impact on the ground; well-publicized fora and reconciliation ceremonies do not always translate into a decrease in violence or tension. Interfaith groups may also lack roots in the communities they claim to represent, limiting their ability to talk to potential spoilers of peace settlements. Second, interfaith actors' work may be undermined by factors beyond their control — government policy, security forces' human rights abuses, youth unemployment, underfunded post-conflict reconstruction initiatives and so forth. Third, and related, the political recommendations of interfaith actors may go ignored. In the CAR, the Interfaith Peace Platform was honoured with the 2015 Sergio Vieira de Mello Award, from an organization whose eminent persons include former heads of state, cabinet ministers and senior diplomats (Sergio Vieira de Mello Foundation). At the awards ceremony, the platform's leaders stated that, in their view, disarmament should precede elections in the CAR (Chonghaile 2015). Their view lost out; the international community was happy to give the platform awards, but was unwilling to compromise on an accelerated timetable for elections, which ultimately concluded in March 2016. At worst, interfaith actors can become political props for domestic and foreign governments, useful for photo ops and for preaching a depoliticized tolerance, but given no voice in real politics.

When successful interfaith or ecumenical conflict resolution occurs, religious leaders' efforts can take years. Amid Mozambique's 1976–1992 civil war, the Mozambican Christian Council spent its first five years of existence (the council was founded in 1982) calling for a national dialogue before the ruling Mozambique Liberation Front (FRELIMO) regime heeded its counsel. The council spent 1988 and 1989 carefully preparing for dialogue, seeking meetings with the rebel Mozambican National Resistance (RENAMO) group, and acting as an intermediary between FRELIMO and RENAMO. The two factions did not meet directly until July 1990. Mozambican churches remained deeply involved in the peace talks through the signing of the General Peace Agreement in 1992 — the end of the civil war and the culmination of a decade of involvement by the churches (Sengulane and Gonçalves 1998). The Mozambican example stands as a reminder that governments are naïve if they expect quick breakthroughs simply by bringing everyone to the table.

CVE Programs

With CVE, the problem of tokenism is even worse. Initiatives such as prison dialogues and de-radicalization programs often involve very small numbers of imprisoned jihadists. Nigeria's de-radicalization program for Boko Haram members was serving a mere 43 prisoners as of autumn 2015 (Anyadike 2015), and the program's head was abruptly fired in October of that year, suggesting that the new administration of President Muhammadu Buhari gave little weight to non-military responses to Boko Haram. Outside prisons, CVE programs often focus on feel-good initiatives that also involve relatively small numbers of people, especially sports programs for youth. As with certain kinds of interfaith initiatives, these depoliticized CVE programs can give the impression — deliberately or not — that policy makers believe violence results simply from extremist ideologies or from a lack of productive activities for youth, rather than from deep political, socio-economic and religious crises. Getting Muslim and Christian youth together to play soccer is not only difficult to scale up, it also provides a weak theory of change about resolving religious conflict in situations in which there is no broader context of policy change.

A final problem with dominant CVE approaches is conceptual: the term is simply too broad. CVE now encompasses a range of development activities, governance initiatives and feel-good programs. This breadth has a distorting effect, especially in terms of what counts and does not count as legitimate forms of politics. As the International Crisis Group warns, "Re-hatting as CVE activities to address 'root causes,' particularly those related to states' basic obligations to citizens — like education, employment or services to marginalised communities — may prove short-sighted," especially when CVE efforts involve "delegitimising political grievances and stigmatising communities as potential extremists" (International Crisis Group 2016). Defining CVE too broadly could even make conflict resolution more difficult. If CVE is defined narrowly as the effort to combat violent ideologies and highly exclusivist world views, rather than as a broad project of social development, it is more likely to avoid the pitfalls that the International Crisis Group mentions.

Possibilities Emerging from Religious Fragmentation

As discussed above, the risks and costs of religious fragmentation are significant. The conflict resolution possibilities stemming from religious fragmentation are less obvious. Given that fragmentation seems to be a fact of religious life in the twenty-first century, however, such possibilities are worth considering.

First, an increasingly diverse religious landscape can, under the right circumstances, nurture a kind of cosmopolitanism and tolerance. Indeed, forms of bottom-up interfaith interaction may be more enduring and far-reaching in their effects than top-down interfaith dialogue among leaders. Some of the most celebrated examples of everyday inter-religious coexistence in Africa, such as the largely positive relations between Christians and Muslims in majority-Yoruba southwestern Nigeria, reflect decades of interaction between ordinary people in relatively stable political environments, rather than top-down efforts to promote interfaith dialogue. African governments and the international community would do well to study examples of such cosmopolitanism, in order to draw lessons that might aid in conflict resolution elsewhere.

Second, religious diversity can help to marginalize uncompromising radicals. Indeed, the most effective denunciations of radicals often come from those theologically closest to them, but whose political outlooks differ. In northern Nigeria, Boko Haram seems most threatened and angered when it faces public condemnations from Salafis who are not jihadis. Such condemnations have come at a cost — Nigeria's mainstream Salafis have become targets of Boko Haram's violence (Thurston 2015). The condemnations also may not directly peel away or de-radicalize members of Boko Haram. But if Boko Haram fears the words of its theological cousins, it is because the mainstream Salafis likely convince various fence-sitters and potential recruits not to join the jihadists. When and if the Boko Haram crisis ends, some of the most consequential religious conversations in northern Nigeria may be those that occur quietly, out of the government's earshot, in Salafi mosques and discussion circles.

For this reason, the International Crisis Group is right to warn governments to "disaggregate not conflate" when dealing with religious activists (International Crisis Group 2016, iii); governments may not always be able to enlist the help of non-violent Salafis or other theological conservatives, but by distinguishing among activists, governments can avoid antagonizing innocent people or hampering productive intra-faith dialogues. Even intra-jihadi competition can have an upside: if intra-jihadi fragmentation has made AQIM and its offshoots more unpredictable, it could also make some of those offshoots more susceptible to disruption, co-optation or even moderation. For the international community, one implication of this picture is that diplomats, aid workers and non-governmental organizations would do well to cultivate broader links within Africa's diverse religious landscapes, rather than relying on familiar intermediaries.

Third, religious fragmentation and competition give religious leaders an incentive to respect popular sentiments, which can translate into an effort to try to hold political authorities more accountable. Despite the exorbitant wealth and financial scandals that often surround Pentecostal preachers (and not only in Africa), new religious movements' emphasis on personal morality can provide a vehicle for political demands, especially in terms of anticorruption. Some Pentecostals may find that "the domestication of Pentecostal moralism, focusing attention on sexuality, marriage, and family, has enabled the prosperous to live piously even as they loot the state and society" (Smith 2006, 214). Yet Pentecostal leaders who either disappoint congregations' moral expectations or depoliticize them may create openings for other, more outspoken, pastors to gain followings by criticizing politicians.

Similar tensions, and openings, exist in African Muslim communities. The banker and Islamic intellectual Sanusi Lamido Sanusi, who served as governor of the Central Bank of Nigeria from 2009 to 2014, was dismissed after suggesting that the administration of then-president Goodluck Jonathan had allowed billions of dollars to go missing from the accounts of the Nigerian National Petroleum Corporation. After his firing, and with a considerable bit of luck, Sanusi soon found his feet as the new emir of Kano, one of the most powerful hereditary Muslim offices in Nigeria. As emir, Sanusi continued his criticisms of the Jonathan administration, and continued to give public statements and interviews about economic and social policy matters once Buhari took office. Sanusi's background is unique, but his tenure as emir will be a test case for how a new generation of hereditary Muslim leaders in Africa, born after independence, will proceed. Such leaders face pressures to balance the weight of tradition and decorum, on the one hand, with the demands of a turbulent political environment on the other. Figures like Sanusi also grapple with the realities of religious competition: the growing diversity of Muslim religious activism in Kano complicates the task of being an emir for the entire state and adds to the pressure to deny religious rivals a chance to outflank him on political issues. For international diplomats and policy makers, religious leaders who dissent non-violently can represent key interlocutors; even if such leaders anger the political authorities, their efforts can help to channel popular discontent into a productive form of protest politics.

Conclusion

Fragmentation is changing the structure of religious authority and the nature of inter- and intra-religious life in Africa. Fragmentation creates problems, especially when religious actors advocate radicalism and violence to distinguish themselves in crowded religious marketplaces. Yet fragmentation also creates possibilities for greater cosmopolitanism, more effective denunciations of radicals and productive competition, leading to more accountable leadership in both religion and politics.

At present, some of the dominant approaches to resolving religious conflict do not sufficiently account for the challenges posed by fragmentation. Approaches that centre on entrenching conservative religious authorities ignore the brittleness of some authorities' power, as well as the risks that such authorities take when they align closely with governments. Approaches that emphasize interfaith dialogue sometimes concentrate too much on top-down, quick fix initiatives whose ground-level impact is unclear or on token efforts that are divorced from politics. Finally, CVE efforts can suffer from a similar lack of scalability and a lack of sufficient attention to politics. Grappling more thoroughly with the reality and consequences of fragmentation offers a way to strengthen conflict resolution approaches.

Works Cited

Amara, Ramzi Ben. 2011. "The Izala Movement in Nigeria: Its Split, Relationship to Sufis and Perception of Sharia Re-Implementation," Ph.D. dissertation, University of Bayreuth.

Amnesty International. 2014. "Somalis Are Scapegoats in Kenya's Counter-Terror Crackdown," May 27. www.amnesty.org/en/documents/AFR52/003/2014/en/.

Ançar-Dine France. 2013. "Bibliographie de Chérif Ousmane Madane HAIDARA." www.ancardine.com/ancardine/index.php?option=com_content&view=article&id=1:vie-et-enseignement-de-cherif-ousmane-madane-haidara&Itemid=102&showall=1&limitstart=.

Anderson, Allan Heaton. 2013. *An Introduction to Pentecostalism: Global Charismatic Christianity*. Cambridge, UK: Cambridge University Press.

Anyadike, Obi. 2015. "Road to Redemption? Unmaking Nigeria's Boko Haram." *IRIN*, October 1. http://newirin.irinnews.org/boko-haram-road-to-redemption/.

Arieff, Alexis, Lauren Ploch Blanchard and Tomas Husted. 2015. *The Lord's Resistance Army: The U.S. Response*. Washington, DC: Congressional Research Service.

Bamgboye, Adelanwa and John Chuks Azu. 2015. "Osinbajo: I'm on Loan to FG." *Daily Trust*, June 11. www.dailytrust.com.ng/daily/index.php/news-menu/news/56941-osinbajo-i-m-on-loan-to-fg.

Borno State of Nigeria. 1982. *Government White Papers on the Report of the Commission of Inquiry into the Religious Disturbances in Bulum-Kutu Area of Maiduguri Between the 26th-29th October, 1982*. Maiduguri: Borno State Government.

Brenner, Louis. 2001. *Controlling Knowledge: Religion, Power, and Schooling in a West African Society*. Bloomington, IN: Indiana University Press.

Carayol, Rémi. 2012. "Sénégal: marabout power ou l'influence des confréries." *Jeune Afrique*, March 6. www.jeuneafrique.com/142651/politique/s-n-gal-marabout-power-ou-l-influence-des-confr-ries/.

Chonghaile, Clár Ní. 2015. "Central African Republic Still a Powder Keg, Warn Clerics Awarded Peace Prize." *The Guardian*, August 21. www.theguardian.com/global-development/2015/aug/21/central-african-republic-powder-keg-sergio-vieira-de-mello-prize-interfaith-peace-platform.

Eickelman, Dale and James Piscatori. 1996. *Muslim Politics*. Princeton, NJ: Princeton University Press.

Eizenga, Daniel and Leonardo Villalon. 2016. "Taking Stock of Burkina Faso's Democracy After al-Qaeda Attack." *Washington Post, Monkey Cage* (blog), January 21. www.washingtonpost.com/news/monkey-cage/wp/2016/01/21/taking-stock-of-burkina-fasos-democracy-after-al-qaeda-attack/.

Elischer, Sebastian. 2015. "Autocratic Legacies and State Management of Islamic Activism in Niger." *African Affairs* 114 (457): 577–597.

Federal Government of Nigeria. 1981. *Report of the Kano Disturbances Tribunal of Inquiry*.

Filmer, Deon and Louise Fox. 2014. *Youth Employment in Sub-Saharan Africa*. Washington, DC: World Bank.

FLT Films. 2009. *The Imam and the Pastor*. United States Institute of Peace. www.fltfilms.org.uk/imam.html.

Gifford, Paul. 1995. "Introduction: Democratisation and the Churches." In *The Christian Churches and the Democratisation of Africa*, edited by Paul Gifford, 1–13. Leiden: Brill.

Griswold, Eliza. 2010. *The Tenth Parallel: Dispatches from the Fault Line Between Christianity and Islam*. New York, NY: Farrar, Straus and Giroux.

Guterres, Antonio. 2012. "Why Mali Matters." *The New York Times*, September 4. www.nytimes.com/2012/09/05/opinion/why-mali-matters.html.

Hansen, Stig Jarle. 2013. *Al-Shabaab in Somalia: The History and Ideology of a Militant Islamist Group*. Oxford, UK: Oxford University Press.

Hill, Jonathan N. C. 2010. *Sufism in Northern Nigeria: Force for Counter-Radicalization?* Strategic Studies Institute. www.strategicstudiesinstitute.army.mil/pdffiles/pub989.pdf.

Hiskett, Mervyn. 1987. "The Maitatsine Riots in Kano, 1980: An Assessment." *Journal of Religion in Africa* 17 (3): 209–223.

Human Rights Watch. 2008. "'So Much to Fear': War Crimes and the Devastation of Somalia." December. www.hrw.org/sites/default/files/reports/somalia1208web.pdf.

———. 2012. "Spiraling Violence: Boko Haram Attacks and Security Force Abuses in Nigeria." October. www.hrw.org/sites/default/files/reports/nigeria1012webwcover_0.pdf.

International Crisis Group. 2016. "Exploiting Disorder: Al-Qaeda and the Islamic State." March 14. www.crisisgroup.org/~/media/Files/exploiting-disorder-al-qaeda-and-the-islamic-state.pdf.

Janson, Marloes. 2013. *Islam, Youth and Modernity in the Gambia: The Tablighi Jama'at*. Cambridge, UK: Cambridge University Press.

Journal of Religion in Africa. 2012. "The Popular Discourses of Salafi Radicalism and Counter-Radicalism in Nigeria: A Case Study of Boko Haram." *Journal of Religion in Africa* 42: 118–144.

Kane, Ousmane. 2003. *Muslim Modernity in Postcolonial Nigeria: A Study of the Society for the Removal of Innovation and Reinstatement of Tradition*. Leiden, Netherlands: Brill.

Kilembe, Faouzi. 2015. "Local Dynamics in the Pk5 District of Bangui." In *Making Sense of the Central African Republic*, edited by Tatiana Carayannis and Louisa Lombard, 76–101. London, UK: Zed Books.

Loimeier, Roman. 1997. *Islamic Reform and Political Change in Northern Nigeria*. Evanston, IL: Northwestern University Press.

Lubeck, Paul. 1985. "Islamic Protest under Semi-Industrial Capitalism: 'Yan Tatsine Explained." *Africa* 55 (4): 369–389.

Meyer, Birgit. 2015. *Sensational Movies: Video, Vision, and Christianity in Ghana*. Berkeley, CA: University of California Press.

Le Monde. 2013. "Au Mali, les wahhabites de Sabati veulent peser sur la présidentielle." *Le Monde*, July 27. www.lemonde.fr/afrique/article/2013/07/27/au-mali-les-wahhabites-de-sabati-veulent-peser-sur-la-presidentielle_3454516_3212.html.

Obadare, Ebenezer. 2006. "Pentecostal Presidency? The Lagos-Ibadan 'Theocratic Class' & the Muslim 'Other'." *Review of African Political Economy* 33 (110): 665–678.

———. 2015. "Electoral Theologies: Pentecostal Pastors and the 2015 Presidential Election in Nigeria." *Africa at LSE* (blog), December 16. http://blogs.lse.ac.uk/africaatlse/2015/12/16/electoral-theologies-pentecostal-pastors-and-the-2015-presidential-election-in-nigeria/.

Ochonu, Moses. 2014. *Colonialism by Proxy: Hausa Imperial Agents and Middle Belt Consciousness in Nigeria*. Bloomington, IN: Indiana University Press.

Okoli, Al Chukwuma and Ahar Clement Uhembe. 2014. "Of Cult and Power: A Political Phenomenology of the Ombatse Cult in Nasarawa, Nigeria." *International Journal of Liberal Arts and Social Science* 2 (7): 13–20.

Østebø, Terje. 2012. "Salafism, State-Politics, and the Question of 'Extremism' in Ethiopia." *Comparative Islamic Studies* 8 (1-2): 165–184.

Otayek, René and Benjamin Soares. 2007. "Introduction: Islam and Muslim Politics in Africa." In *Islam and Muslim Politics in Africa*, edited by Benjamin Soares and René Otayek, 1–24. New York, NY: Palgrave Macmillan.

Peel, J. D. Y. 1968. *Aladura: A Religious Movement Among the Yoruba*. Oxford, UK: Oxford University Press.

Peterson, Brian J. 2011. *Islamization from Below: The Making of Muslim Communities in Rural French Sudan, 1880–1960*. New Haven, CT and London, UK: Yale University Press.

Pew Forum on Religion and Public Life. 2010. *Tolerance and Tension: Islam and Christianity in Sub-Saharan Africa*. www.pewforum. org/files/2010/04/sub-saharan-africa-full-report.pdf.

Pew Research Center. 2015. "Size and Projected Growth of Major Religious Groups in Sub-Saharan Africa, 2010-2050." www. pewforum.org/2015/04/02/sub-saharan-africa/163-3/.

Premium Times. 2014. "Boko Haram: Nigeria Rolls Out Soft Approach to Counter-Terrorism." *Premium Times*, March 20. www.premiumtimesng.com/news/157111-boko-haram-nigeria-rolls-soft-approach-counter-terrorism.html.

Rabasa, Angel, Cheryl Benard, Lowell Schwartz and Peter Sickle. 2007. "Building Moderate Muslim Networks." Rand Corporation. www.rand.org/content/dam/rand/pubs/monographs/2007/RAND_MG574.pdf.

Reynolds, Jonathan T. 2001. "Good and Bad Muslims: Islam and Indirect Rule in Northern Nigeria." *International Journal of African Historical Studies* 34 (3): 601–618.

Robinson, David. 2000. *Paths of Accommodation: Muslim Societies and French Colonial Authorities in Senegal and Mauritania, 1880–1920*. Athens, OH: Ohio University Press.

Sanders, Angela and Sam Lau. 2012. *Al Qaeda and the African Arc of Instability*. Brussels, Belgium: NATO Civil-Military Fusion Centre.

Sengulane, Dínis and Jaime Pedro Gonçalves. 1998. "A Calling for Peace: Christian Leaders and the Quest for Reconciliation in Mozambique." *Accord* 3: 26–33. www.c-r. org/downloads/Accord%2003_4A%20calling%20for%20peace_1998_ENG.pdf.

Sergio Vieira de Mello Foundation. "Structure of the Foundation." www.sergiovdmfoundation. org/the-foundation/structure/.

Smith, Daniel Jordan. 2006. *A Culture of Corruption: Everyday Deception and Popular Discontent in Nigeria*. Princeton, NJ: Princeton University Press.

Soares, Benjamin. 2014. "The Historiography of Islam in West Africa: An Anthropologist's View." *Journal of African History* 55 (1): 27–36.

Thurston, Alexander. 2012. "Senegal: The Affair of Sheikh Bethio Thioune." *Sahel Blog* (blog), May 2. https://sahelblog.wordpress. com/2012/05/02/senegal-the-affair-of-sheikh-bethio-thioune/.

———. 2015. "Nigeria's Mainstream Salafis Between Boko Haram and the State," *Islamic Africa* 6 (1-2): 109–134.

———. 2016a. *Salafism in Nigeria: Islam, Preaching and Politics*. Cambridge, MA: Cambridge University Press.

———. 2016b. "'The Disease Is Unbelief': Boko Haram's Religious and Political Worldview." Brookings Institution Project on U.S. Relations with the Islamic World, Analysis Paper No. 22. www.brookings.edu/~/media/research/files/papers/2016/01/boko-haram-ideology-thurston/brookings-analysis-paper_alex-thurston_final_web.pdf.

———. Forthcoming. *Boko Haram: Jihadism in Nigeria and the Lake Chad Basin.* Princeton, NJ: Princeton University Press.

Trofimov, Yaroslav. 2016. "Jihad Comes to Africa." *Wall Street Journal,* February 5. www.wsj.com/articles/jihad-comes-to-africa-1454693025.

Umar, Muhammad Sani. 2006. *Islam and Colonialism: Intellectual Responses of Muslims of Northern Nigeria to British Colonial Rule.* Leiden, Netherlands: Brill.

Villalon, Leonardo. 1995. *Islamic Society and State Power in Senegal: Disciples and Citizens in Fatick.* Cambridge, UK: Cambridge University Press.

Ware, Rudolph III. 2008. "Review of *Islam, histoire, et modernité en Côte d'Ivoire* by Marie Miran." *International Journal of African Historical Studies* 41 (1): 135–137.

Whittaker, Hannah. 2015. "Legacies of Empire: State Violence and Collective Punishment in Kenya's North Eastern Province, c. 1963–Present." *Journal of Imperial and Commonwealth History* 43 (4): 641–657.

17

Radio, Social Media and Language as an Agent in Conflict: A Case Study of Dandal Kura Radio International in the Lake Chad Basin

David Smith and Stephanie Wolters

"The single biggest problem in Nigeria is corruption, with impunity being the Ph.D. in this discipline."[1]

Countering violent extremism (CVE) is one of the hottest topics in the development business. In the Lake Chad basin, CVE is about defeating Boko Haram. What gets less attention, however, is why groups such as Boko Haram exist. Without addressing the root cause of the problem, attempts to bring stability and, ultimately, progress to the region are likely to be in vain.

There is a homegrown remedy that is as old as the first settlements that were established in the Sahel — dialogue. Dialogue is a tool that is now used for almost every peacekeeping operation in Africa. Radio remains the most widespread and accessible media in Africa. Radio dramatically increased the footprint for spreading information, and the advent of the cellphone turned the radio into an instrument for dialogue. The United Nations Department of Peacekeeping Operations has had a series of hits and misses with radio services it has set up at its various African missions. These range from a low point in Rwanda in the mid-1990s, with a radio service that had limited success, to the high point of Radio Okapi in the Democratic Republic of Congo (DRC), which

---

1   Faruk Dalhatu (managing director of Dandal Kura Radio International [DKRI], Maiduguri, Nigeria) speaking to the author on the challenges facing his country, May 2016.

has received accolades from far and wide for the role it continues to play in helping to stabilize the country, and to others somewhere in between, including services in Liberia, Côte d'Ivoire, Sierra Leone and the Central African Republic.

The idea behind peacekeeping radio is to provide a link between the local population and the international efforts to stabilize the region concerned. The radio provides a voice for the mission, as well as a window for both sides to see, understand and comment on what is and is not working. Perhaps most importantly, peacekeeping radio helps create a space for dialogue between civilians and the military component of the mission. The military component is the part that is usually misunderstood and tends to inspire fear in those who have lived through the horrors of militia operations in their communities and do not necessarily understand that the Blue Berets of the United Nations moving through their villages are there to help.

Slowly, but surely, the African Union (AU) is following in the footsteps of the United Nations and is adding a radio component to its peace and security operations. The AU-mandated Multinational Joint Task Force tasked with stabilizing the Lake Chad region is in the process of implementing radio in its communication strategy.

This chapter examines how this is done. What is the appropriate technology necessary for reaching and engaging with an isolated and far-flung population that has been traumatized for years by Boko Haram, as well as by their own security forces and local administrators? How is new technology, notably social media, the Internet and smart phones, changing the way both the good guys and the bad guys get their message across? And what lessons have been learned that can be applied to this new peacekeeping operation in order to avoid some of the pitfalls of previous efforts?

Radio in the Lake Chad Region

The crisis in the Lake Chad region started long before the world knew of the existence of Boko Haram. One of the principle reasons northeastern Nigeria, northern Cameroon, southeastern Niger and northwestern Chad are in a state of crisis today is that they have been ignored to a large extent by those in power in their respective capitals. The disconnect is so extensive that there are few on any sides of the borders between these states who expect anything from elected officials.

Service delivery protests, so common at the other end of the continent in South Africa, are a rare occurence. In the countries bordering Lake Chad, there is a general assumption that government simply does not deliver. It is assumed, often correctly, that any money available for development stands a good chance of going into the pockets of the politicians, rather than into road building or education.

With an almost total disconnect between government and the general population, it is hardly surprising that people take the law into their own hands, sometimes by taking part in insurgent actions. There is an element of frustration and desperation that drives people to groups such as Boko Haram, Al-Shabaab, Ansar Dine, al-Qaeda in the Islamic Maghreb (AQIM) and others.[2] Addressing the root causes of this frustration and desperation can take the wind from the sails of these insurgencies, but doing so requires a commitment to change, as well as an effective means of engaging with people on the ground.

Radio Works

There are not as many secrets in Africa as one might expect on a continent with poor infrastructure and

---

2   Boko Haram in the Lake Chad area, Al-Shabaab in Somalia, Ansar Dine in Mali and AQIM in Algeria.

many challenges regarding cross-border travel. This is true in relatively stable areas, as well as in fragile states and zones of conflict. News does generally manage to reach the most-out-of-the-way places, the back of beyond, where a motor vehicle may not have passed in years, if ever. The fact that millions of Africans are illiterate and may never purchase a newspaper during their lifetimes or see their homes connected to a functioning electricity grid to provide them with a view of the world through television does not mean they will not find out that their president has changed the constitution in order to stay in power or that a war in the Middle East is prompting thousands of refugees to look for security elsewhere.

How do they know these things? Radio. In Africa, radio is king. Roughly 90 percent of adults in most African countries own a radio receiver (Myers 2008), and these receivers tend to have a shortwave band, providing listeners with access to international broadcasters, in particular, to the British Broadcasting Corporation (BBC), Radio-France Internationale (RFI), Deutsche Welle (DW) and the Voice of America (VOA).

These international broadcasters offer a service many state broadcasters on the continent do not offer — news and current affairs programs with content that may be critical of the people in power. Most of this content tends to be offered in European languages, with a few exceptions, notably Hausa and Kiswahili, two of Africa's most spoken languages. There are others; however, the area this chapter focuses on, the Lake Chad region, is an overwhelmingly Kanuri-speaking area. Until recently, no international broadcaster included Kanuri in its broadcast-language lineup. No commercial or state broadcaster in the region uses Kanuri as its dominant broadcast language.[3]

There are a number of reasons for this dearth of Kanuri content, some budgetary and others political. International broadcasters have been cutting both language services and shortwave broadcasts over the past few years due to budget cuts.[4] In the four countries in which significant Kanuri-speaking populations are found — Nigeria, Niger, Cameroon and Chad — the language is spoken by a minority of the population within the larger context of the country as a whole. The most spoken language in Nigeria is Hausa, and this is especially the case in the north of the country. In the parts of the country where Kanuri is spoken, government broadcasters tend to provide much more airtime for content in English and Hausa. In Niger, the mix tends to be French and Hausa, while in Cameroon and Chad, it is French, as well as English in the former and Arabic in the latter.

But whatever the language of broadcast, the news tends to get through, not only because most people in even the most remote regions of the continent have radio receivers, but also because most Africans speak several languages, including the dominant language of their region, even if that language is not their mother tongue. It is for this reason that the Hausa, Kiswahili, Arabic, French, English, Somali and Kinyarwandan services of international broadcasters have such large listenerships.[5]

It is this availability of credible news targeting the continent using shortwave, FM and partnerships with local stations that allows the news to get through to the fishers on the shores of Lake

---

3   Borno State Radio, based in the northeastern Nigerian city of Maiduguri, uses Kanuri as a minority language in some of its programming, reaching an audience restricted to the area close to the city covered by an FM transmitter.

4   The BBC has had as many as 73 separate language services; however, it is now down to 29. RFI is currently broadcasting in 15 languages, down from 33 several years ago.

5   Hausa has an estimated 50 million speakers in Africa; up to 150 million speak Kiswahili. In both cases, the languages serve as a lingua franca for millions who possess another mother tongue. (*Slate Afrique* 2011; Humboldt-Universität zu Berlin n.d.).

Chad and countless others living far from the closest tarred road in this far-flung region. This area, like thousands of others, has little in the way of a formal economy or a government-built infrastructure, but the people have radio, and they have cellphones.

Radio is there during the good times and the bad. It is there to stir emotion and prompt people to hate each other to the point at which they are willing to slaughter their neighbours. But radio is also there to convince people that dialogue is better than violence.

Radio signals do not respect borders, especially if those signals are broadcast from a shortwave transmitter, old-school technology that has been mothballed in most parts of the world, but still plays a vital role in many of Africa's conflict zones and fragile states. There is not one square centimetre of Africa that does not receive a radio signal. That signal may not be local, but it will be there, providing a link to the outside world.

Increasingly, remote areas are also being covered by cellphone signals. The cellphone has not only given people in conflict zones and fragile states the ability to access even more information from beyond their isolated regions, but it has also created a link with the radio, making it possible to receive information and to transmit content back to the broadcaster. This makes radio a recipient of information as well as a diffuser.

New and less expensive technology that allows people to communicate more easily, to have access to vital information that could be life-saving and to hold power to account is certainly a positive development, but a disclaimer must be inserted. In fragile states, the technology infrastructure is usually fragile as well. There are vast stretches of land across the continent, especially in the Sahel and, more particularly, in the Lake Chad area, where FM networks have yet to be established, where cellphone relay towers have yet to provide a network connection to the entire population and,

perhaps more importantly, where an electricity grid has yet to be installed. FM transmitters rely on a source of electricity, either a generator or a connection to an electricity grid. They also require security. Throughout much of the Lake Chad area, reliable access to electricity is not available, and the risk of insurgents destroying the transmitter is high. FM allows listeners in an area much smaller than a shortwave footprint to hear a higher quality audio signal. In much of the Sahel region, listeners are accustomed to listening to the inferior quality of shortwave simply because the infrastructure allowing the establishment of an FM network is not there.

Fragile states with fragile communications infrastructure tend to be ruled by a political elite with an aversion to free access to information. When state authorities in these and similar states feel threatened, access to communications is usually one of the first casualties.

At election time, when votes are counted, when the president is on the move or when anti-government protestors take to the streets, short message service (SMS) texting, social media and Internet services are often suspended. These are the times when the ability to communicate quickly and freely is usually most vital. This problem is particularly acute in central Africa. In Gabon, SMS services were shut down and Internet connections severely disabled from the time when the election results were announced in August 2016 until well into the following month.

While voting was taking place in the presidential elections in Chad in April 2016, SMS services were suspended; during anti-government protests in the DRC in 2015, Internet services were suspended; while violence occurred in the Central African Republic in 2014, SMS services were suspended — the list goes on. Part of the problem lies in the ownership of cellphone networks; senior ruling party members, especially members of the presidential family, frequently have important stakes in these networks.

When a threat is perceived from the electorate, those in power are able to shut off the cellphone networks.

A similar fate often befalls international broadcasters reaching their listeners through local FM relays. When there is civil unrest, or when reports become too critical of those in power, it is not uncommon for the transmitters of the RFI, the BBC or other broadcasters to be shut down.[6]

When electronic communications are either shut down or tampered with in any way, access to credible information is severely handicapped, especially outside of urban areas. Newspapers that circulate in capital cities are, for the most part, not available in rural areas. This includes virtually the entire Lake Chad region. Even if newspapers were available, there is not enough disposable income available to the average person to buy a copy. This, combined with high illiteracy rates and lack of distribution channels for newspapers, adds to the vital nature of information by radio.

Independent radio, both community-based and commercial, is flourishing in some of the region's countries, but not in the region, itself. The commercial stations of Nigeria, Chad, Cameroon and Niger are found where the advertising money is — capital cities and important economic centres.

Opposition politics tends to thrive in the urban, more economically prosperous areas. Support for the ruling parties tends to come from rural, less-informed regions. Obtaining permission to broadcast a non-government voice in the area of the insurgency is a difficult challenge. The establishment of an internationally mandated peacekeeping operation provides a window of opportunity.

Dandal Kuri Radio International — A Kanuri Voice for the Lake Chad Region

It is not surprising that the Lake Chad basin is a conflict zone. Four fragile states — Nigeria, Niger, Chad and Cameroon — share lakefront footage; to the north is Libya, and to the south is the Central African Republic. Boko Haram or not, this is one of our planet's least stable regions.

Instability is not new here. For more than 600 years, the Kanem-Borno Empire has been a fault line between movements south from the Arabian Peninsula and Black Africa, south of the Sahara. Islam first moved south of the Sahel through the Lake Chad basin. Clashes with the Christian and animist areas south of the lake were inevitable. Clashes with other Muslims, notably those settling further west in what is today northwestern Nigeria, especially in the Sokoto area, were also inevitable. This was particularly so once the founder of the Sokoto caliphate Usman Dan Fodio moved east early in the nineteenth century to extend his influence.[7] This transition zone, part of the Sahel, has, especially in post-colonial times, been ignored to a large extent by the political elites in the distant capitals of each country.

Infrastructure development in the Lake Chad basin lags behind other parts of Chad, Cameroon, Niger and Nigeria. There are fewer roads, fewer schools, fewer health facilities and fewer job opportunities than there are in N'Djamena, Niamey, Yaoundé and Abuja (European Commission n.d.).

The region was ripe for the emergence of an insurgent group such as Boko Haram. Apart from the obvious disaffection and frustration with central authority and the dearth of options for improving

---

6   The shutting down of FM transmitters belonging to international broadcasters occurs on occasion in Burundi, Rwanda, Chad, the DRC and elsewhere when these stations broadcast reports of anti-government protests or stay-aways.

7   The Fulani War, during which Usman Dan Fodio became a political as well as a religious leader, challenged the perceived supremacy of the Kanem-Borno Empire to the east, in what is today the Lake Chad basin.

dismal living standards, there is a tie that binds across the international borders. That tie is language, and Boko Haram takes advantage of it. The dominant language along the shore of Lake Chad is Kanuri. It was through the Kanuri-speaking population of this region that Islam first moved south into this part of the continent (Usman 1983). Boko Haram uses this as the core of its narrative that the people of the Lake Chad area represent an original and pure form of the Muslim faith. Whether Boko Haram, referring to itself as the Islamic State of West Africa, has any rightful claim to being devout is another matter. What Boko Haram does do is take advantage of the relative vacuum that exists regarding any other pan-Kanuri narrative.

Boko Haram uses social media to punch above its weight. Campaigns using YouTube, Twitter and Facebook allow this group to send its message far beyond its primary target area to a global audience. The relatively disorganized and uncoordinated responses from the four countries that are victims of Boko Haram attacks have tended to thwart efforts to defeat them.

This is not to say that Boko Haram's followers or its targets are active social media users. For the most part, they are not. Boko Haram's social media campaign targets authorities and decision makers, from the local government level right up to the United Nations. The perceived inability of the Nigerian government to combat Boko Haram during the previous Goodluck Jonathan administration prompted others, including neighbouring states, regional organizations and the wider international community, to consider ways and means of bypassing Abuja to address the crisis.

Evidence coming out of court cases in Nigeria post-Jonathan indicate that there was a high level of corruption among senior members of the government and military that prevented the army from effectively combatting Boko Haram (Tukur 2016; *Sahara Reporters* 2016).

The election of Muhammadu Buhari in 2015 as Nigeria's new president has changed the dynamics in the field (Usman 2016). The army is receiving new

supplies and diplomatic relations between Abuja and its neighbours have improved, providing hope that a regional peacekeeping effort, the Multinational Joint Task Force (MNJTF), just might be able to remove Boko Haram.

The MNJTF, however, faces an uphill battle. Regional security forces sometimes act, unwittingly, as recruiting agents for Boko Haram because of their heavy-handed tactics in dealing with the local population. Through a combination of fear, poor discipline and lack of proper equipment, the Nigerian army has, on occasion, used violence, sometimes lethal, against civilians after suffering casualties resulting from Boko Haram attacks.[8]

Shortly after coming to power, President Buhari's first international trip took him to Niamey and N'Djamena for talks with his Nigerian and Chadian counterparts, Mahamadou Issoufou and Idriss Déby. The talks centred on coordinated efforts to defeat Boko Haram, coordination that did not appear to have been a priority during the previous Nigerian administration.

The MNJTF, headed by a Nigerian major general, Lamidi Adeosun, as well as the regional economic community within which it is housed, the Lake Chad Basin Commission, which is also headed by a Nigerian, Sanusi Imran Abdullahi, are based in N'Djamena. The idea behind this joint force is good, but it is missing a key element — the ability to communicate directly with the people concerned, in their own language.[9]

The force consists of troops from Nigeria, Niger, Chad, Cameroon and Benin. Deployment has been

---

8   Within the Lake Chad area, the Nigerian army operates exclusively on Nigerian territory while the MNJTF, including Nigerian soldiers, operates in parts of Cameroon, Niger and Chad.

9   The AU Commission's Peace and Security Council recognizes the importance of relevant communications strategies within its peacekeeping mission. At the AU mission in Somalia, a new strategy was tried in which an outside contractor was hired to set up a Somali-language radio station with links to the mission.

slow, due to logistical and financial constraints; however, there is a presence on the ground in Chad, Cameroon and Niger.

Among the soldiers within the force are few who speak Kanuri and even fewer who have adequate training on how to communicate effectively with the people who live in their area of operation. There is a general fear of people in uniform who carry guns, even if their intentions are noble. A big part of the process of winning hearts and minds is the ability to clearly communicate intentions, and these intentions must be followed up by actions indicating that the intention is to create conditions for a better life.

Militarily, the 2015 offensive by the Nigerian army in the northeast of the country helped liberate territory from Boko Haram, but, as a consequence, attacks across the borders in Chad, Niger and Cameroon increased, adding urgency to the need to rapidly deploy the regional force.

Early that same year, an internationally funded Kanuri-language radio station began broadcasting on shortwave from Kano, in northern Nigeria. The station, Dandal Kura Radio International (DKRI), covers the entire Lake Chad area using old analog technology — or shortwave — which is the technology that is appropriate for the target audience.[10] DKRI's frequencies are close to those of the BBC's Hausa service, making it easy for Kanuri speakers to stumble across the station while looking for the service they usually follow on their manually tuned radios.[11]

DKRI's unique value is language. There are an estimated 10 million Kanuri speakers in the Lake

Chad area, and DKRI is their only dedicated radio station. More importantly, it provides factual information and varied perspectives that counter Boko Haram's propaganda.

Since May 2016, DKRI has been operating out of new studios in Maiduguri, the capital of Nigeria's Borno State. Until recently, Maiduguri had been one of Boko Haram's primary zones of influence. An improving security situation in the city has allowed the radio, as well as several humanitarian agencies, to operate from there.

Maiduguri and Borno State, like most of the area bordering Lake Chad, were isolated at the best of times. The University of Maiduguri had a reputation as one of the better centres of higher learning in Nigeria, attracting students not only from the entire country but also from neighbouring states as well. Despite the university's remaining open throughout the insurgency, the number of outsiders willing to relocate to Maiduguri for studies, or virtually any other activity, is small. As long as Boko Haram continues to operate in the region, restoring confidence and rebuilding a positive reputation will be difficult.

The isolation of the region has been a major factor in the perpetuation of the crisis. Put simply, if there were not so many places to hide, where access is difficult, the belligerents would have a much tougher time gaining a foothold. The lack of infrastructure throughout the Lake Chad area means borders are porous, allowing Boko Haram to move at will with little risk of ground pursuit by military vehicles. The thousands of islands formed by the dropping water levels in Lake Chad provide effective cover for Boko Haram when in retreat mode.

Isolation does not, however, mean that communication is not possible.

Social media, in concert with cellphones, has changed the landscape. Facebook and WhatsApp have given people the ability to communicate directly with each other and with the radio. They allow people to engage effectively in real

---

10   The most listened-to radio stations in the region are international services broadcasting on shortwave, notably the Hausa-language services of the BBC, DW, VOA and RFI. Inexpensive analog shortwave radios are readily available in virtually all local markets, and a majority of the local population has access to the daily programs provided by these services.

11   A majority of Kanuri speakers also speak Hausa as a second language. These same Kanuri speakers listen to international broadcasts in Hausa simply because, until DKRI went on air, there were no Kanuri alternatives.

time on issues affecting their security. The most common listener engagement is through SMS. Smart phones are still the exception to the rule in the region. Most of the phones in circulation are, however, able to send texts. Roughly 300 texts are arriving at DKRI each month from people who want their voices to be heard. The most common threads involve calls to government officials to make good on promises that were made during election campaigns. Road repairs, electricity supply, support for agriculture and comments on security feature prominently. DKRI is still in its implementation phase, making it too early to gauge how government will react in the medium to long term. The fact, however, that the voiceless now have a voice is already a step in the right direction, acting as a means to empower an extremely frustrated population.

Perhaps more importantly, it has created an effective means of providing content to the radio, which can then be used to reach the entire region through the use of a single shortwave transmitter. Using the most basic smart phones, correspondents in northeastern Nigeria, southeastern Niger, northern Cameroon and northwestern Chad are able to record and send interviews and photographs via WhatsApp back to the Maiduguri studios.

The people who comprise Boko Haram are, for the most part, ethnic Kanuri from within the Lake Chad area (Baca 2015). Finding a way to reintegrate them into the society from which they originate, difficult as it certainly is, is a means of ensuring that the insurgents do not regroup elsewhere and continue to launch attacks. Reintegration may take a long time and be difficult; however, reintegration requires finding ways of convincing belligerents to return to the fold. There has to be a credible voice to do this — a voice that not only delivers a message but also listens as well. This is a key role for DKRI to play: to provide food for thought, to be a venue for discussion and to be a platform for exploring potential compromises and negotiated settlements.

Before DKRI was established, the prevalent Kanuri narrative about insecurity in the region was the one determined by Boko Haram. Now there is competition, and Boko Haram is listening. Listeners claiming to belong to Boko Haram send text messages to the station on occasion disagreeing with items they have heard in the news bulletins. As is the case with radio in other zones of conflict, if it is popular, even the belligerents will want to be part of it. The authors of this chapter firmly believe that engaging with belligerents through dialogue has a more positive long-term effect than engaging with them through military action.

Structurally, the model for DKRI as a regional broadcaster is based on the model used when the authors of this chapter established Radio Okapi in the DRC. The hugely successful Radio Okapi network was built on a foundation of providing a voice to all the belligerents.[12] In 2001, when the UN mission was established and the DRC was divided into three zones ruled by the Kabila government and rival rebel armies, breaking down the front line and reuniting the country was a priority for the international community and, in particular, for those funding the efforts of what was quickly to become the biggest and most expensive peacekeeping mission in UN history.

Radio became one of the United Nation's most effective tools in achieving that goal. Radio Okapi was launched on February 25, 2002, the very day that the Inter-Congolese Dialogue was launched at Sun City, in South Africa. The timing was not a coincidence.

The former president of Botswana, Quett Masire, was a facilitator for the Inter-Congolese Dialogue; it was his job to get the various factions around

---

12 The head of the United Nation's peacekeeping mission to the DRC (the United Nations Organization Stabilization Mission in the DRC [MONUSCO]), Amos Namanga Ngongo, said that Radio Okapi had electronically dismantled the front line in a conflict that is often referred to as Africa's first world war.

the negotiating table and to get them to agree on a new political dispensation. MONUSCO's head of radio, David Smith (co-author of this chapter), convinced Masire to coincide the start of the talks with the launch of Radio Okapi. Radio studios opened simultaneously in Kinshasa, Goma and Kisangani.[13] Gbadolite, the MLC's headquarters, followed shortly thereafter in order to assure all factions that no side was being favoured over another. Most importantly, the launch in these three cities in conjunction with the live coverage of the Sun City talks gave the Congolese population access and insight into the peace talks.

Radio Okapi's broadcasts proved so popular that rebel leaders vied for time to get their points across to their constituencies.[14] The United Nation's radio station was, at the time, the only means of reaching Congolese in all parts of the divided country. The state broadcaster, Radio-Télévision nationale congolaise (RTNC), was the voice of those in power in each of the political enclaves until the country was reunited and RTNC became the voice of the Kabila administration.

And therein lies one of the strongest arguments for independent radio services during a time of insurgency — credibility. There are few, if any, government broadcasters on the continent that have an outstanding record when it comes to objectivity and the provision of diverse opinions. Public broadcasters are public in name only and tend rather to be state organs. Even South Africa's national broadcaster, the South African Broadcasting Corporation (SABC), is gradually becoming little more than the voice of the ruling party after having been feted during the Mandela era as Africa's most promising public broadcaster.[15] In the four countries in the Lake Chad area where Boko Haram is active, state radio is, without exception, the voice of the ruling party. In societies where the population's level of trust and confidence in those in power tends to be extremely low, even positive messages broadcast via the state broadcaster are received with skepticism.

One of DKRI's greatest strengths is its ability to help fill the credibility gap. As long as listeners believe that the content on DKRI is about, for and by the people of the region, it will be taken seriously. There is ample evidence of this from social media sites, as well as from SMS messages sent to the station. A US government survey conducted during the first quarter of 2016 found that 74 percent of respondents in Borno State listen to DKRI regularly and 90 percent of them had a positive opinion of it.[16]

Language is one of the principal ways to garner a devoted listenership.[17] If DKRI did not broadcast in Kanuri, and rather chose Hausa, it would not have the ability to create a community of listeners throughout the Lake Chad area.

As long as the radio is perceived as having the interests of its listeners at heart, it will be possible to maintain credibility. This is what sets it apart from the state broadcaster and from the many commercial stations, which can often be vehicles

---

13 Kinshasa was the seat of the Kabila administration, Goma was the headquarters of the Rally for Congolese Democracy (RCD) and Kisangani was the headquarters of the RCD-Kisangani-Movement for Liberation, which was in an on-off alliance with the Movement for the Liberation of the Congo (MLC).

14 RCD leader Azarias Ruberwa summoned Radio Okapi's director to his room during the Sun City talks to complain about not getting enough airtime, a complaint dealt with by dispatching a journalist to interview him.

15 See www.bdlive.co.za/opinion/columnists/2016/05/30/how-motsoeneng-has-subverted-the-news.

16 Country-wide Nigeria survey conducted by the United States Africa Command (AFRICOM) determining political tendencies, affiliations and expectations, including five questions focusing on DKRI and its perceptions among listeners in northeast Nigeria.

17 According to the same AFRICOM survey, the main reason people listen to DKRI is because it is in their own language.

for political interests. Until the ruling elites are able to convince the electorate that they intend to serve, rather than loot, the state, any media outlet the elites are perceived to be influencing is unlikely to be taken seriously. Similar precautions must be taken regarding sources of funding. Belligerents can turn listeners against media outlets if they successfully convince them that content is manipulated or dictated by foreign governments. Even if there is no outside influence, suggestions to the contrary can be harmful and difficult, if not impossible, to repair.

Maintaining credibility among the listenership is a priority and requires constant vigilance. The use of local voices as presenters of all programs and as the interviewers in all current affairs content helps to ensure that the target audience identifies with the station and accepts it as a credible voice within the community.

For all of the credibility that international services such as the BBC, RFI and DW may enjoy, the fact that they are based not only outside the region but also on another continent prevents them from having an intimate, community-type relationship with their target audience. In any case, the target audience of these broadcasters is considerably wider than that of the Lake Chad basin, making it more difficult for them to narrowcast to a more specific and segmented audience.

DKRI's long-term strategy is to put in place a radio network similar to Radio Okapi, with one central operation and several smaller regional studios. DKRI's network hub is now in Maiduguri, while regional studios and FM transmitters covering the main areas of instability in Cameroon, Chad, Niger and Nigeria are gradually being added. As the MNJTF develops its forward facilities throughout the Lake Chad area, there is the possibility of co-locating radio facilities within their compounds at Mora in Cameroon, Diffa in Niger, Baga Sola in Chad and Baga in Nigeria as well as at the MNJTF or Lake Chad Basin Commission headquarters in N'Djamena. This is along the lines of how Radio Okapi co-locates at MONUSCO facilities throughout the DRC.

Studios located throughout the region will serve the dual purpose of broadcasting content specifically targeting a smaller region, in relevant languages, as well as gathering and generating local content that will be broadcast locally and through the network studios in Maiduguri. The plan is for Maiduguri to broadcast 24 hours a day, while the regional studios break away twice a day, for an hour in the morning and an hour in the early evening, with local content that targets their immediate surroundings.

Co-locating regional studios at MNJTF forward bases provides the added benefit of not only having access to intelligence the forces gather in the field, but also, perhaps more importantly, helping to manage the communications relationship the military has with the civilian population. Lasting stability depends upon the creation of a relationship of trust. Currently, the relationship is fragile at best and antagonistic at worst, laced with a strong element of fear. This relationship needs to be managed between both the Nigerian military operating on its own territory, as well as with the MNJTF operating in the neighbouring states.

A challenge at every peacekeeping radio operation is to convince the military element that it is in their interest to share information with the wider civilian population and that information-sharing is a two-way street and an excellent means of defusing tension between soldiers and civilians. In co-author David Smith's experience as a senior public information official in numerous UN peacekeeping missions, military personnel often feel that the best information is no information, especially when interacting with the public.

Whatever the lifespan of the military effort in the Lake Chad area is, it will come to an end. In general, peacekeeping missions end before all the elements are in place to maintain stability and move toward growth and progress. This is usually because the political appetite for keeping a peacekeeping operation has waned, as has the funding. One way to help ensure that there is a watchdog and escape valve for dissent in the region is by keeping the radio on the air. With such a large potential audience in the Kanuri-speaking world, the possibility of transitioning DKRI from a donor-funded operation to a commercial service is strong.

Such a large pool of listeners should be attractive to potential advertisers and sponsors. At the very least, cellphone networks, soap and other household product manufacturers, as well as distributors of certain basic commercial foodstuffs, can reach a captive market that has few other means of receiving advertising. Humanitarian and development agencies are likely to continue operating long after the last MNJTF contingents pack up their equipment. They will be around to sponsor programs devoted to health, education, agriculture and other capacity-building content that aims to restore stability by providing tools that help people to recover dignity. This is a long-term plan. Moving the Lake Chad area from instability to progress is not a quick fix and requires extended support from outside sources to make it happen.

One of the results of an increased efficiency within the Nigerian army at removing Boko Haram from territory it holds, in Borno State, in particular, is an increased number of insurgent attacks in neighbouring northern Cameroon, where the Cameroonian army has been less successful in repelling attacks. This reality underlines the need to extend any media campaign targeting areas affected by Boko Haram wherever and whenever necessary. A certain amount of flexibility must be built into any media service airing in a shifting theatre of operations.[18]

DKRI is a work in progress. A growing relationship with the MNJTF could prove to be a new way of bringing peacekeepers and civilians in conflict zones closer together and better able to work toward the common goals of peace and stability. Forging a successful relationship between a professional radio service and an AU-mandated peacekeeping mission can create a symbiosis that can be replicated when and where the need arises. To a large extent, DKRI is the test case. At the United Nations, there is a trend (one that has yet to take hold firmly) to consider finding ways to keep peacekeeping radio stations operating once the mission mandate has come to an end. For long-term sustainability, solutions beyond the usual reliance on the international donor community need to be found. Exploring the commercial route is one way to do this. With the immense popularity of radio in almost all corners of this continent, and the immense reach it has, following the commerical path would appear to be a good option.

DKRI is an experiment in cross-border and cross-institution cooperation.

The project is pioneering in its outlook — DKRI is the first Africa-based international cross-border radio network. It can only succeed with buy-in from the African Union, the Lake Chad Basin Commission and the governments of the host countries: Nigeria, Chad, Cameroon and Niger. Such buy-in is an enormous exercise of good faith among entities that are often antagonistic among each other and, more importantly, are not the strongest proponents of freedom of expression.

Apart from maintaining permission to remain on the air in each of the four participating countries, maintaining credibility is probably the next greatest challenge. All peacekeeping radio services, without exception, endure efforts to influence, manipulate and control content from host agencies, whether the United Nations or the African Union, from funders and from local politicians, as well as warlords. Firm but diplomatically talented management is required to maintain editorial control on an objective and relevant path. Credibility is hard won and easily lost. Few state broadcasters on the continent have enjoyed credibility. Once an information service is viewed as "His Master's Voice," there is little that can be done to change this view among the listenership.

---

18 Radio Okapi opens and closes radio studios in the DRC's hinterland as need dictates. For example, studios in Kananga have closed following the arrival of a relatively stable political climate in Kasai-Central province, while next door, in Mbuji-Mayi, a studio was added when stability in Kasai-Oriental province deteriorated.

The risk of losing permission to broadcast locally on FM will always be present. Solid support from the African Union as well as the United Nations, as is the case with Radio Okapi in the DRC, would provide some insurance. When, inevitably, a government minister hears content he or she disagrees with, any conflict that may ensue must be managed carefully. Providing a platform for opposing viewpoints is usually a good way to defuse such situations. Fortunately, shortwave broadcasts are not affected should any threat be made to stop FM transmission. The option of jamming a shortwave broadcast is both expensive and politically dangerous, given that the peace effort in the region involves multiple countries.

Conclusion

There is no one-size-fits-all format for using media in zones of conflict. Language, format, technology and even time of broadcast vary from radio to radio and target audience to target audience. Credibility is vital. It is tough to get and easy to lose, and then it is even more difficult to restore. The international community is behind the financing of most media projects, especially radio, in conflict zones. A radio station identified as the voice of the funder or a particular political faction, rather than as the voice of the community concerned, is not likely to succeed. The US government's VOA international radio service has faced this conundrum for decades. No matter how well produced and objective some of their programs may be, there is often an element of doubt among listeners about the editorial line and the message being relayed.[19]

19   During the apartheid days in South Africa, South Africans turned to shortwave to find reports about their country that had not been produced by the state broadcaster, the SABC. The African National Congress' Radio Freedom was one source of information, as was the BBC's Africa service. VOA was popular for music programs; however, at the top of the hour, it was common for listeners to retune to the BBC for the news.

Credibility and ownership are generated by local content that is produced and presented by locals in languages that are spoken by the communities that are bearing the brunt of the conflict: Kanuri in the Lake Chad region, Sango in the Central African Republic and Kiswahili in the eastern DRC. The United Nations has often made the mistake of using English and French as the primary language of communication with local audiences in the zones where its peacekeeping operations are located. While these unarguably important languages have their place, they tend to reach elites rather than the masses who will communicate in the country's vernacular languages.

Language should not be exclusive. Mistakes have been made in the past with radios at peacekeeping missions broadcasting in languages not understood by people in the target audience. While it is not possible or even effective to broadcast in all the languages of a target area, compromises and choices must be made. Broadcasting in too many languages can also have a detrimental effect. Hundreds of languages are spoken in the area covered by the DKRI transmitters. Should the radio cater to all of them? Of course not. Adding languages to the broadcast day also alienates the listener who does not understand a particular language. The primary target audience must be identified — in the case of DKRI, it is Kanuri — and served as well as possible. In more general terms, an important point to take into consideration is ensuring that the main belligerent groups operating in the area are catered to when language choices are made. If the belligerents do not understand the message, they are not likely to be drawn into the peace process.

DKRI's use of Kanuri is a guarantee that Boko Haram is listening. This is clear because they have made telephone and SMS contact with the station. Given that the dominant language of Boko Haram is Kanuri, it is also a safe assumption that, as the only Kanuri-language broadcaster in the region, DKRI is reaching this audience.

Understanding the potential of language to effect change is vital. At the time of writing, it is too early to effectively predict how DKRI will influence members of Boko Haram, but lessons can be learned from experiences at other broadcasters in conflict zones. Language played, and continues to play, an important role in understanding the success of Radio Okapi. From almost the first day of broadcast, the one official and four national languages of the DRC were used for daily broadcasts.[20] The intentional use of all of these languages served to indicate that no matter what forces were attempting to divide the country, Radio Okapi was a station for all Congolese, no matter what side of the front line they happened to find themselves on.[21]

The choice of language can also be controversial. Radio Okapi introduced Kinyarwanda-language content targeting Rwandan Hutu rebels operating in eastern Congo. The program, Gutahuka, was produced in collaboration with the UN mission's Department of Disarmament, Demobilization, Repatriation, Reintegration and Resettlement as part of an effort to convince the rebels to disarm and return home. Gutahuka was extremely unpopular with Congolese listeners when it first aired. There was widespread anger at hearing Kinyarwanda, the language of the occupying force in the east. Over a period of weeks, through numerous information programs in relevant languages, and involving discussions with listeners, Gutahuka was accepted as not only a necessary program but also a desirable one because of its stated purpose of attempting to convince Rwandans to leave the DRC.

As language has created a link between Radio Okapi and belligerents in the DRC, a similar result is hoped for in the Lake Chad area. While it is virtually certain in the short to medium term that Boko Haram will publicly denounce efforts of DKRI, Boko Haram is made up of individuals, who are listening and forming their own opinions. These individuals are, predominantly, part of the Kanuri community. Whether or not they like or agree with what DKRI is saying, at least, it is in a language they understand. The message gets through.

Of course, no matter how effective any message is, it must reach its target audience. The use of appropriate technology is vital. In places where the rate of illiteracy is high, where access to electricity is low and income levels are at or below the poverty line, radio is the most efficient and economical means of engaging with the target audience. Shortwave works as a means of transmission in places where the target area is vast, there is poor infrastructure and there is a high risk of sabotage to any FM installation. Shortwave is also an effective alternative for reaching an audience where local authorities may not allow the establishment of transmission facilities on their territory. One caveat is that a target audience that does not have a tradition of listening to shortwave is not likely to begin using this technology for the first time during a crisis. The use of other types of appropriate technology, such as satellite transmission, needs to be considered. Today, unless there is a culture of shortwave listening in any given society, chances are that shortwave radios are no longer available in the local markets. In the Lake Chad region, they are sold almost everywhere.

Radio stations operating in conflict zones should, wherever possible, operate in partnership with local peacekeeping efforts, whether they are regional or part of a larger entity, such as the African Union or the United Nations. The reasons for this are twofold: first, to provide a relatively safe and secure environment for locating a radio

---

20 French, Lingala and Kiswahili were used from the first day of broadcast. The third and fourth national languages, Tshiluba and Kikongo, were added several months later. The addition of Kikongo brought numerous comments from listeners that Radio Okapi had finally become a national broadcaster.

21 One of the first radio jingles to air on Radio Okapi was "100% Congolais."

studio and an FM transmitter, creating both local reach for program content and a pole for collecting local, relevant information for rebroadcast; and, second, to create a link between the peacekeepers and the local community by providing a space for the two sides to engage in discussion and debate and to voice concerns.[22]

Social media has been credited with fuelling revolutions and helping to topple governments, especially during the Arab Spring. The effectiveness of Facebook, Twitter and other Internet-based services must be taken with a strong pinch of salt in many of Africa's conflict or potential conflict zones. The most important factor to take note of is who owns the means of electronic communications. In other words, social media is not a foolproof means of ensuring that information circulates when traditional media outlets are either shut down or viewed to be neither free nor fair.

In all four countries bordering Lake Chad, the means of conveying information electronically, whether through radio, television or cellphone networks, is, to a large extent, in the hands of government or, more precisely, the ruling party. Users of social media are at the mercy of those who can switch off the networks or control access to studio microphones. Reporters Without Borders' World Press Freedom Index ranks three of the four countries concerned extremely poorly, with only Niger managing an acceptable ranking of 52 out of 180.[23]

The success of Radio Okapi in the DRC has prompted even the state broadcaster, RTNC, to improve its output. A hoped-for outcome of the DKRI presence in the Lake Chad region is the improvement of standards among state and other broadcasters. Success tends to breed imitation.

There will come a time when either television, smart phones with fast Internet connections or some yet-to-be-invented technology is widely available throughout the continent, facilitating the rapid flow of relevant information to where it is needed. In most of the Lake Chad basin and well beyond this region, that time is not close at hand.

---

22 An often recurring theme among listeners calling in to peacekeeping radio stations concerns confusion or misunderstanding of the military mandate of the peacekeeping mission. Prior to the deployment of peacekeepers in conflict zones, the relationship between civilians and military usually involves a strong element of fear, often on both sides. It takes a considerable effort involving relevant communication skills to convince civilians, especially in isolated areas, that soldiers wearing, for example, the blue UN helmet are there to protect them and not to perpetuate the insurgency.

23 Reporters Without Borders ranks Niger at 52 out of 180, Nigeria at 116, Cameroon at 126 and Chad at 127 in its 2016 World Press Freedom Index (Reporters Without Borders 2016).

Works Cited

Baca, Michael. 2015. "Boko Haram and the Kanuri Factor." *African Arguments*, February 16. http://africanarguments.org/2015/02/16/boko-haram-and-the-kanuri-factor-by-michael-baca/.

European Commission. n.d. "Sahel and Lake Chad Window of the EU Emergency Trust Fund Overview." http://ec.europa.eu/europeaid/regions/africa/eu-emergency-trust-fund/sahel-region-and-lake-chad-area_en.

Humboldt-Universität zu Berlin. n.d. "The Hausa Language." www.iaaw.hu-berlin.de/en/africa/linguistik-und-sprachen/african-languages/hausa.

Myers, Mary. 2008. "Radio and Development in Africa: A Concept Paper." International Development Research Centre of Canada. www.amarc.org/documents/manuals/12481943581Radio_and_Development_in_Africa,_a_concept_paper.pdf.

Reporters Without Borders. 2016. "2016 World Press Freedom Index." https://rsf.org/en/ranking.

Sahara Reporters. 2016. "How Femi Fani-Kayode Used Fronts To Receive Funds From Ex-NSA Dasuki's Arms Purchase Funds." *Sahara Reporters*, January 8. http://saharareporters.com/2016/01/08/how-femi-fani-kayode-used-fronts-receive-funds-ex-nsa-dasuki%E2%80%99s-arms-purchase-funds.

Slate Afrique. 2011. "Le kiswahili, un joyau linguistique." *Slate Afrique*, May 21. www.slateafrique.com/1693/kiswahili-joyau-linguistique.

Tukur, Sani. 2016. "Ex-Borno Gov. Sheriff, Accused of Boko Haram Ties, Emerges PDP Chairman." *Premium Times*, February 16. www.premiumtimesng.com/news/headlines/198527-breaking-ex-borno-gov-sheriff-accused-boko-haram-ties-emerges-pdp-chairman.html.

Usman, Talatu. 2016. "Boko Haram Not Holding any Nigerian Territory — Buhari." *Premium Times*, February 11. www.premiumtimesng.com/news/top-news/198316-boko-haram-not-holding-nigerian-territory-buhari.html.

Usman, Yusufu Bala. 1983. *Studies in the History of Pre-colonial Borno*. Borno State, Nigeria: Northern Nigeria Publishing Company.

18

Building a Common Vision of the State: The Role of National Dialogues

Elizabeth Murray and Susan Stigant

National dialogues have attracted significant attention over the past five years as a tool for countries emerging from conflict or navigating political transitions. As "national dialogue" has claimed its place in the lexicon of policy makers and the tool kit of mediators and practitioners, there is good reason for skepticism and further research. Debates continue about whether and how this approach can contribute to preventing, managing and resolving violent conflict. There is increasing agreement about the value of inclusive processes to analyze the drivers of conflict and bring about consensus on ways to address these issues meaningfully. As national dialogues occur with more regularity, there is also a growing body of knowledge on the design and implementation options. On the other hand, the adoption of a single phrase, national dialogue, to describe processes that differ widely in composition, objective, scope and implementation has complicated the study and analysis of their successes and failures. As national dialogue has become a buzz phrase in the international community, this has also resulted in the concept being appropriated by some political leaders seeking to placate their citizens and the international community without any true intent to allow for an inclusive, meaningful and transformative discussion.

An entire book could be devoted to a debate about the typology and definition of a national dialogue. For the purposes of this chapter, we focus on processes that are convened to address a broad set of issues or problems (that is, not dialogues on single issues); that operate outside of the permanent institutions of governance, such as the Parliament, and under their own rules and procedures; and that have buy-in from a coalition of key stakeholders who are sufficiently inclusive to address the agreed issues and are positioned to implement the recommendations that emerge from the dialogue.

Roots of Contemporary National Dialogues

The idea and practice of a national dialogue process is not new. It has historical precedent in the formation of the modern state, including the US Constitutional Convention and the French National Convention. Two centuries later, in the early 1990s, a series of national conferences in francophone West Africa became the mechanism for pro-democracy forces in the region to institutionalize new systems of governance. The first and most well known of these was the Benin national conference, during which the participants proclaimed the conference sovereign and made a host of sweeping changes, including agreeing upon a timeline for multi-party elections, selecting an interim prime minister and removing many of the president's powers. In "The National Conference Phenomenon in Francophone Africa," Pearl T. Robinson (1994) documents the spread of these processes throughout the region and traces their heritage to the Estates General process in France in 1789, which had been widely discussed in francophone Africa in the late 1980s on its 200th anniversary. During the 18 months following the Benin national conference, opposition political forces successfully lobbied for national conferences in Gabon, Congo, Mali, Togo, Niger and Zaire. The results of these were mixed, but the phenomenon of employing national conferences in times of political upheaval had been established.

Although the national conferences in Africa in the early 1990s have more directly influenced the current and recent national dialogues in the region, processes elsewhere in the world in the 1980s and 1990s demonstrate a broader emergence of national dialogues during this time frame. In Poland, the round table talks in 1989 between the Communist government and the Solidarity movement were a first step in the country's democratization process. The round table talks were closed-door negotiations but were inclusive of social and political forces that represented the interests of significant parts of the population. In Central America, the Guatemalan Grand National Dialogue was stipulated by the Esquipulas II peace process of 1987 that ended the region's civil wars. The dialogue process was initiated in 1989 and was directed by the National Reconciliation Commission, which had been created through the peace process and was led by a prominent Catholic bishop. With its 84 delegates representing 47 organizations and 15 thematic commissions, the Grand National Dialogue was poised to debate and form proposals on many of the issues that had contributed to the civil war. When the human rights commission presented its findings, several delegates were kidnapped and tortured, and the process was suspended shortly thereafter.

National Dialogue: A Singular Name for a Set of Varied Processes

National dialogues are time-bound processes with a beginning and an end. They are designed with the objective of providing space for a conversation that is not possible to convene within a country's existing institutions. At the conclusion of the national dialogue proceedings, the resulting recommendations are placed in the charge of permanent institutions, advanced through constitutional reform or passed to a follow-up committee that will monitor progress toward implementation.

The relationship of national dialogues to permanent institutions of governance and to constitutional reform varies greatly depending on political context and the nature of the dialogue. In Tunisia, the national dialogue had a direct linkage to the deadlocked National Constituent Assembly (NCA): the national dialogue drew its membership explicitly from the political parties represented in the NCA and was tasked with, among other responsibilities, agreeing upon a draft constitution and reverting the draft to the NCA for its approval. In the Central African Republic

(CAR), the transitional government named the preparatory and oversight committees for the national dialogue (Bangui Forum). Senegal, as discussed below, was a rare exception in that the national dialogue (*Assises Nationales*) operated entirely outside of the formal institutions of governance.

National dialogues can be roughly categorized according to their relationships with permanent institutions: national dialogues that feed directly into constitution-making processes (such as in Tunisia and in Yemen before the resurgence of conflict disrupted the conclusion of the dialogue and follow-up); national dialogues that do not feed directly into constitution making but have the blessing of or formal linkages to government (CAR); and national dialogues that operate outside of the government (Senegal). It is also possible to categorize national dialogues according to the level of international support they receive: heavy (Yemen, CAR); moderate (Kenya); or minimal (Senegal, Tunisia).

More difficult is devising a typology of national dialogues according to their objectives. Possible objectives are numerous: from breaking political deadlock to deepening a peace process; initiating national reconciliation; issuing a challenge to the status quo in governance; and even validating — some might say rubber-stamping — a decision that has already been made at the executive level. This is just a sampling. Some national dialogues have more than one formal objective and, in nearly all, different stakeholders have differing perceptions about the desired outcome of the dialogue.

The Centrality of Political Will

Political will is perhaps the most critical ingredient in determining the success of a national dialogue process. Those who have previously been excluded from government, decision making or other aspects of political and social life have to make a calculation about whether those in power are truly committed to a genuine discussion. At the same time, those in power must make a constant assessment of whether to push forward, even if some opposition groups refuse to join, and whether there are sufficient guarantees for their role in the post-dialogue dispensation. For everyone, there is a constant assessment of whether there is commitment to implement the agreements emerging from the dialogue. In the early phases, the selection of the chairperson, the structures for the dialogue preparations and concrete actions to provide a context that is conducive for dialogue are important to watch. In later phases, opening of space for informal processes and tangible mechanisms for implementation should be monitored.

The chairperson of the national dialogue plays a pivotal role. He or she manages the agenda, leads the meetings and is responsible for ensuring that decisions are made according to the agreed rules. Therefore, the selection of a neutral — or, at least, balanced — chairperson is an important signal. In Senegal, Amadou-Mahtar M'Bow, who had served as the head of the United Nations Educational, Scientific and Cultural Organization and was considered to be neutral in national politics, set the tone for the Assises Nationales. By contrast, the Government of Sudan's decision for President Omar al-Bashir to chair their national dialogue weakened appeals for political and armed opposition to join.

The composition of committees empowered to prepare for the national dialogue provides an early opportunity to signal the degree of political will. Preparatory committees are typically charged with developing criteria for the selection of participants, setting the agenda, establishing a secretariat, drafting a budget, fundraising, preparing rules and procedures for the dialogue, and managing a range of logistical aspects. While some of these tasks are mundane, they provide important opportunities to signal inclusion and to build relationships among key groups. And some of these tasks are critical to defining who will be at the table and how decisions will be made.

Similarly, confidence-building measures in the lead-up to the formal dialogue process can begin to signal the shift from promises to action. The Yemen National Dialogue Preparatory Committee consulted with key groups outside the government and recommended 20 points for action before the National Dialogue Conference was convened. These points included compensation for damages resulting from the arbitrary closure of a newspaper and prompt establishment of an independent, impartial committee that met international standards to investigate all human rights violations in the 2011 youth-led uprising. In Sudan, the government's call for participation was undermined by documented cases of closure of newspapers, detention of civil society and limits on basic rights and freedoms.

As the preparations for dialogue progress, the opening of political space for public participation and complementary dialogue processes bodes well for the success of the national dialogue. Track 1.5 or Track Two processes convened by civil society, the private sector or religious-led organizations extend the dialogue beyond the elite. The emergence of these common spaces also demonstrates that there has been an authentic opening, not just a continuation of business as usual within the walls of a large convention centre or hotel where the dialogue is taking place. Over Kenya's constitutional process, discussion about core political decisions, including the structure of the state, land reform and anti-corruption, took place in every community. This information was compiled and shared with those negotiating the text. As importantly, though, it signaled that these were issues for all Kenyans. During Sudan's national dialogue, the debate among the delegates was vibrant, open and contentious. However, those outside the walls of the dialogue venue could not hold a meeting with more than four people without permission from the National Intelligence and Security Services. As well, discussions in newspapers and civil society forums

on national identity, the role of religion and the economy were forcefully shut down.

Finally, defining a clear and practical mechanism for implementation is an essential indicator of political will and success. Few national dialogues have managed to have the degree of decision-making authority enjoyed by the Benin national conference in the 1990s. In fact, most have suffered from lack of clarity about whether the decisions of the national dialogue will be binding and, if so, who is responsible for their implementation. From the CAR to Sudan, final reports that detail thousands of resolutions create an impossible task for any future government. In some cases, the absence of detailed reports on public consultations and input or deliberations of committees means that the complexities behind a decision (or lack of agreement) may be glossed over in future legislation or policy. A clear set of priorities for action, including a timeline, a responsible body and mechanisms for oversight by civil society can signal political will for implementation. Political will thus matters at every step of the process: as the dialogue is designed; as it is carried out; and as the dialogue recommendations are implemented by the permanent institutions of government.

When national-level leaders do not have a genuine desire to champion an inclusive and open process, national dialogues can sputter and fail to launch or can proceed as essentially an act of political theatre. Such national dialogues can exacerbate conflict and undermine progress. As national dialogue has captured the imagination of diplomats, negotiators and peace builders, there is a growing tendency for presidents to attempt to use a national dialogue as an endorsement or as political cover for an unpopular or an unconstitutional decision. In 2016, Democratic Republic of the Congo (DRC) President Joseph Kabila devoted extensive political capital to selling the idea of a national dialogue that would justify the postponement of elections and, thus, the lengthening of his term. The political opposition and public responded with widespread protests within the DRC. Kabila's attempt to use a national dialogue to further cement his grip on power is not unique. As we seek to better understand the circumstances in which national dialogue can be an effective tool for political transition and conflict resolution, we must guard against inadvertently empowering those leaders who only desire to use dialogue to further their own interests.

The political will of the most senior government leaders matters immensely. Indeed, it is often they who have the influence and the authority to determine whether a national dialogue will meaningfully include all stakeholder groups, especially those that have traditionally been excluded. At the same time, it is not just the political will of the government that is important. The political will of armed and unarmed opposition and civil society — or the absence thereof — can also influence the trajectory of a dialogue. In Tunisia, the political will of the National Dialogue Quartet (the Quartet), the civil society coalition that convened and facilitated the dialogue, brought the process into existence. In Senegal, the willingness of civil society to join the political opposition lent the Assises Nationales an air of credibility that it might not have otherwise had. In the CAR, the political will of armed groups vis-à-vis the Bangui Forum has vacillated during the process — they were, at times, willing participants and, at other moments, they edged toward being spoilers. Although the armed groups allowed the pre-dialogue popular consultations to take place in most sub-prefectures, they disrupted the consultations in a few prefectures. The majority of armed groups were willing to participate in the Bangui Forum itself and in side negotiations that resulted in a disarmament, demobilization and reintegration (DDR) agreement. Shortly after the agreement was signed, however, many of the armed groups disavowed it.

Diverse Objectives and Contexts: The Cases of the CAR, Senegal and Tunisia

As discussed above, national dialogues have been convened in diverse contexts and to accomplish varied objectives. In the national conferences in West Africa in the early 1990s, economic crises and consequent unpopular structural reforms led pro-democracy forces to demand inclusive dialogue processes to renegotiate key elements of the state. Over the past decade, national dialogues have been convened to break political deadlock, to deepen peace agreements and provide for the inclusion of conflict-affected populations, to address drivers of low intensity or latent conflict and to prepare for or complement constitution-making processes. National dialogues are more likely to be successful when the objectives are clearly defined and when their structure and level of inclusivity are appropriate to the stated objectives. A defined implementation plan prior to the start of the dialogue is also important for ensuring that the agreed-upon outcomes from the dialogue are realized through law, policy or other institutional mechanisms.

The 2014-2015 national dialogue process in the CAR was convened at a time of deep crisis; violence between Séléka and anti-Balaka armed elements had continued even after the inauguration of a transitional government in January 2014.[1] The national dialogue process was conceptualized in three stages: a permanent ceasefire agreement between armed groups and the government;

---

1   Séléka, a coalition of primarily Muslim armed groups, took control of Bangui and staged a coup in March 2013. Their leader, Michel Djotodia, was installed as president, but he was unable to stop Séléka forces from carrying out continued abuse of civilians. The primarily Christian anti-Balaka self-defence groups organized in response and have also carried out abuses against civilians.

public consultations across the country; and a week-long inclusive national forum. Although the ceasefire agreement signed in Brazzaville in July 2014 was violated almost immediately, these negotiations did provide the momentum for the public consultations and the Bangui Forum that would follow.

The international community played a prominent role in the CAR national dialogue process. The Economic Community of Central African States convened the mediation in Brazzaville and initially worked alongside the national authorities on the preparations for the popular consultations and the Bangui Forum. In September 2014, the United Nations Multidimensional Integrated Stabilization Mission in the Central African Republic (MINUSCA) peacekeeping mission arrived in country and subsequently adopted a leading role in the preparations by convening a preparatory meeting in Bangui in November 2014.[2] Shortly thereafter, transitional President Catherine Samba-Panza named a preparatory committee that would be responsible for implementing public consultations and using the resulting data to prepare for the Bangui Forum. With methodological assistance from the United Nations Development Program and logistical support from MINUSCA, the preparatory committee succeeded in holding popular consultations in all 16 prefectures (although armed groups blocked consultations in some

sub-prefectures) between January and March 2015. The opportunity to participate in popular consultations was widely celebrated by CAR citizens, who had no such opportunity in previous national dialogues in 2003 and 2008.

The preparatory committee, and the technical organizational committee that was subsequently named to replace it, used the comments from the popular consultations as the basis for the agenda for the Bangui Forum. The popular consultation data was also used to draft reports related to the four thematic commissions of the Bangui Forum: peace and security; justice and reconciliation; governance; and socio-economic development. The technical organizational committee was responsible for determining participant quotas for each stakeholder group. (Representatives to the Bangui Forum from each of the 16 prefectures were selected from the participants in the popular consultations.) Ultimately, the number of participants who arrived was far higher than the 600 that were officially expected. Although the Bangui Forum's organizing entities were aware of the presence of dozens of delegates that had not been officially authorized to attend, they decided not to turn anyone away given the tense political climate and high risk of violence in the CAR.

With an estimated 200 to 300 participants in each of the concurrent thematic commissions, there was not sufficient time for in-depth conversations. The preparatory committee and technical organizational committee had prepared reports for each of the four themes in advance, and these served as the basis for conversation within the commissions. Each delegate was afforded only approximately three minutes to offer his or her contribution. During the final plenary session, the Republican Pact for Peace, National Reconciliation and Reconstruction was read aloud to delegates and approved by consensus. The pact listed key principles for the future of the country, including a call to postpone elections to allow for a more realistic timeline, the proposed recognition of Muslim holy days as public holidays, the

---

2   MINUSCA was created by the Security Council through UN Resolution S/RES/2149. The mission operates under Chapter VII and was instructed to focus initially on the following tasks: protection of civilians; support for the implementation of the transition process, including efforts in favour of the extension of state authority and preservation of territorial integrity; facilitation of the immediate, full, safe and unhindered delivery of humanitarian assistance; protection of the United Nations; promotion and protection of human rights; support for national and international justice and the rule of law; and Disarmament, Demobilization, Reintegration and Repatriation (MINUSCA n.d.).

creation of a special court for war crimes, and a truth and reconciliation process.

On the sidelines of the larger Bangui Forum, MINUSCA brokered an agreement between the government and 10 major armed groups on their DDR.[3] This was negotiated in a much smaller forum, with key representatives of armed groups and the government. The decision to tackle this issue in a parallel setting — as opposed to the larger forum — was strategically sound in that it allowed for in-depth negotiations between a smaller number of key stakeholders without the distraction and deadlock that could come with a larger group. On the opposite end of the spectrum, the extremely high number of participants in the Bangui Forum also represented an appropriate degree of inclusivity for the task at hand. Although time constraints meant that participants could only offer short contributions, it was reportedly a cathartic experience for citizens to share their views in a national forum. While the Bangui Forum and the DDR agreement negotiations were appropriately inclusive, the implementation of the Republican Pact for Peace, National Reconciliation and Reconstruction has been extremely slow, owing to the change of administration and persistent inaction on the part of the Bangui Forum follow-up committee (*comité de suivi*).

The Bangui Forum was a holistic national visioning exercise for a country that has been beleaguered by conflict for much of its history. Senegal's most recent national dialogue, the Assises Nationales of 2008-2009, emerged in a markedly distinct context. Known as a model of stability within West Africa, Senegal underwent a period of increased political polarization in the months preceding the 2007 presidential elections, when

President Abdoulaye Wade and his administration engaged in repression to ensure that he would win the elections. The Senegalese political opposition, largely united under the Front Siggil Senegal, boycotted the 2007 elections in protest, effectively locking themselves out of national-level politics. They subsequently issued a statement in July 2007 declaring that Senegal was facing a major ethnical, moral, political and economic crisis and proposed a national-level dialogue to address this crisis. Cognizant that the dialogue would be perceived as biased if it did not include a broader coalition of organizations, they began outreach to request that civil society participate. Several of Senegal's leading civil society organizations agreed to participate, but only if the parties agreed that the dialogue would be chaired by civil society in order to avoid perceptions of bias. The Assises Nationales formally commenced in June 2009.

Senegal's Assises Nationales were a paragon of inclusivity and participation. All Senegalese citizens were invited to attend the plenary sessions and the thematic committee meetings of their choosing. A dedicated communication committee within the Assises Nationales worked to disseminate the schedule of meetings to the public. In spite of this open invitation, the majority of participants in the national-level conversations were Senegalese elite, either prominent stakeholders with a specific interest in a given theme or experts that were recruited to provide technical expertise. Most Senegalese citizens elected to participate in local consultations that were held in each department in Senegal and in three diaspora communities. These were organized by local-level structures created by the national organizing committee. The general reports from each set of departmental dialogues and local consultations were then fed into the final comprehensive report.

The Assises Nationales' broad inclusivity and comprehensive public participation opportunities are a credit to its organizers, but they also reflect circumstances unique to Senegal. President Wade and his administration refused to attend the Assises

---

3   One armed group, the Democratic Front of the CAR, did not sign. Following the signing of the agreement, there was also discord between the political representatives who had signed and some of the groups' military commanders (*IRIN News* 2015).

Nationales and employed intimidation to dissuade citizens from participating. This largely backfired, but given perceptions among the ruling party that the Assises Nationales were aimed at regime change, it was critically important that the process be as open as possible to dispel suspicions of bias. Moreover, although Senegal was experiencing a period of greater interparty polarization and government-led repression, the country was still at peace, save for a low-level secessionist conflict in the Casamance region. The relative stability and absence of armed conflict was thus a luxury that allowed the Assises Nationales to successfully create local committees in each department and to extend ample public participation opportunities.[4]

Senegal's Assises Nationales concluded in May 2009, nearly a year after they had begun. The exercise was a comprehensive reflection on Senegal's first 50 years post-independence, current challenges and ways in which citizens at all levels of society could make positive changes to benefit Senegal's future. The Charter for Democratic Governance was approved at the final plenary session, and it included a general call for the reestablishment of institutions rooted in Senegalese tradition, as well as specific recommendations to shorten the presidential term, strengthen judicial independence and form institutions to combat corruption. The Charter for Democratic Governance was adopted as a central pillar of opposition campaigns in the 2012 presidential elections, and Macky Sall was elected to the presidency after promising to implement reforms recommended by the Assises Nationales. Although a successful referendum in March 2016 shortened the presidential term and paved the way for several other reforms, many in Senegal are disenchanted with Sall's slowness to adopt the recommendations that he so heartily endorsed during his campaign.

The Senegalese and the CAR national dialogues included large numbers of participants who divided into thematic committees to make recommendations on a broad set of topics. Tunisia's 2014 national dialogue, with four specific objectives and a participant group comprised of political elites, was a marked contrast to these broader processes. When Tunisia descended into a dangerous political deadlock during the first half of 2013, the Quartet of prominent civil society organizations persuaded leaders to agree to an elite-centred national dialogue comprised of two representatives of each political party that was represented in the NCA. The dialogue had four specific objectives: to select a caretaker president; to finalize a draft constitution and return it to the NCA for approval; to create an electoral management body; and to set a timetable for presidential and parliamentary elections.

Members of the national dialogue accomplished the four tasks in nine months, likely motivated by the dramatic unravelling of the Arab Spring in Egypt and the significant pressure brought to bear by the largest Quartet member, the Tunisian General Labour Union (UGTT).[5] Among non-elite Tunisian citizens, the dialogue has left mixed impressions, with some Tunisians believing that the dialogue's results were predetermined and that it was essentially a bargain among the country's most powerful political forces (M'rad 2015, 80-81). Tunisia's national dialogue did not allow for a broad-based, inclusive conversation on the issues facing the country, but it did facilitate the passing of a new constitution and enable progress toward the 2014 elections. The leverage and legitimacy of the Quartet that facilitated the dialogue were instrumental to its success, as was the political will of Tunisian elites to reach agreement and thus avert a descent into further crisis.

---

4   Senegal has 44 departments, which are its regional units of governance, similar to states, districts or prefectures.

5   UGTT leaders threatened a general strike if Tunisia's main political leaders would not agree to participate in the national dialogue. With over 500,000 members, a UGTT strike could have paralyzed the national economy.

A Role for the International Community?

International partners must be judicious in their diplomatic, logistical and financial support for national dialogues. International support for national dialogues that are intended to temporarily placate critics or buy more time in power is detrimental as it delays real change and risks enabling autocratic leaders. Moving to a national dialogue too early — before there are clear representatives, minimum confidence-building measures in place or basic security and freedoms for citizens to participate directly or indirectly — is equally risky. In such circumstances, a national dialogue is likely to replicate existing power dynamics and leave people disillusioned about the idea of any future national dialogue. In these cases, the international community should consider support for informal, preparatory activities that could set the stage for a more credible national dialogue. The international community can also outline benchmarks for progress toward confidence building and reaching an environment that is ripe for an inclusive process.

Even if a context is ripe, international organizations and bilateral donors must take care to protect national ownership while guarding against the endorsement of processes that are not backed by a true desire for open dialogue. When dialogues are rooted in a genuine national impetus, donor countries and international organizations can support them with process or technical expertise. As national dialogues have become more prevalent, donors should also consider the possibility of supporting peer learning in which participants or organizers from a recent national dialogue share their expertise with representatives from countries that are considering or planning their own national dialogue.

On the logistical side, donors may assist with transportation for participants or for those conducting public consultations, as was the case when the UN peacekeeping mission provided transportation for public consultation teams traveling to the CAR's prefectures. Donors can support accommodations for participants traveling to attend the national dialogue from outlying regions.

It may also prove useful for budget experts or international financial organizations to offer expertise on the estimated cost of reforms that may be proposed through a national dialogue. Such expertise, offered at the right time, could ensure that conversations remain within the realm of the feasible.

Furthermore, dialogue participants from under-represented groups may find themselves less prepared for a national-level forum than their counterparts from the traditional elite. Donors can help to prepare delegates through training and by providing a forum for facilitated dialogues in cases where it behooves a certain group to agree on a collective position prior to the dialogue's inception. Where possible, this can be undertaken through grants to local non-governmental organizations, which may be better positioned to undertake this capacity building with dialogue participants.

In some cases, national leaders and other stakeholders may prefer that the international community remain entirely uninvolved. This was the case with Senegal's Assises Nationales, in which Senegalese themselves undertook all of the preparation, fundraising, logistics and provision of thematic expertise. The organizers believed that the outcomes of the dialogue would be better accepted if the process remained entirely Senegalese. This concern was particularly salient in light of President Wade's refusal to attend the dialogue and his intimidation of prospective participants. Several foreign governments had expressed interest in supporting the dialogue, but the organizers declined this offer.

Following the conclusion of the dialogue, the organizers did accept support from Open Society West Africa for the final phase of compiling the comprehensive report. This critical follow-up phase, including documenting outcomes and working within national institutions to ensure that outcomes are implemented, often falls by the wayside as more pressing priorities emerge. Donors can provide valuable assistance here, through the provision of technical expertise, diplomatic pressure or financial aid to support the realization of priorities articulated through the national dialogue.

National Dialogues: Tools for Preventing and Resolving Violent Conflict?

While national dialogues have the potential to broaden inclusion, establish new decision-making processes and break deadlocks on difficult problems, they are not a panacea. Within the national dialogue itself, recent experiences in the CAR, Yemen and Tunisia demonstrate the myriad of decisions that must be negotiated at each step, the political will required and the challenge of responding to complex and shifting conflict dynamics. These experiences also underline that including a national dialogue in a peace agreement tells us little about the shape, purpose or potential of such a process.

National dialogues can be misused by leaders seeking to cement their own grips on power. And even where intentions are relatively pure, a national dialogue can distract from the daily business of governance or from important transitional processes. This is particularly detrimental in less developed countries or in countries emerging from conflict, where large proportions of the population may lack food, shelter, medical care, education and other basic needs. In these circumstances, such as in the context of the May 2015 Bangui Forum, it is important to weigh the pros and cons of holding a time- and cost-intensive process amid so many other pressing needs.

A final cautionary note relates to what is generally the reason for holding national dialogues in the first place: the existing institutions of governance are unable or unwilling to convene an inclusive conversation on the roots of the conflict. Since national dialogues arise from a shortcoming of governance, the fundamental — if fuzzy — measure of their success is whether they succeed in addressing that shortcoming. In other words, a country that holds national dialogues on a regular basis is not succeeding in addressing the drivers of conflict and the failures of existing institutions that make the dialogue necessary. Such is the case in the CAR, where the government has convened three separate national dialogue processes in less than 15 years. Countries contemplating national dialogue and the international community must take care not to encourage a national dialogue when more practical solutions are available.

Many continue to refer to South Africa's successful transition as a model for the continent. Some have even argued that South Africa makes the case for national dialogue. However, the national dialogues that took place during South Africa's transition included a complex set of related strands. The multi-party negotiation process provided a forum for the political negotiations based on an agreement reached through years of closed-door discussions. The constitution drafting provided a mechanism for discussion about the fundamental structures and identify of the state — both through the constituent assembly and through the complementary education and consultation led by civil society. The National Peace Accord created national, regional and local structures that drew on volunteers to monitor conflict, address issues of justice and mediate local conflicts. The Truth and Reconciliation Commission served as a platform to develop a shared narrative about the country's history — and future.

If anything, South Africa serves as a reminder that the problems that drive violent conflict in Africa are complex, and the processes to move beyond conflict require more than a singular approach. A national dialogue may be a piece of that puzzle, but absent other elements, it is unlikely to succeed.

Works Cited

IRIN. 2015. "Briefing: Can New Pact Bring Peace to the CAR?" *IRIN*, May 15. www.irinnews.org/analysis/2015/05/15/ briefing-can-new-pact-bring-peace-car.

MINUSCA. n.d. "MINUSCA Mandate." www.un.org/en/peacekeeping/missions/ minusca/mandate.shtml.

M'Rad, Hatem. 2015. *National Dialogue in Tunisia*. Tunis, Tunisia: Nirvana.

Robinson, Pearl T. 1994. "The National Conference Phenomenon in Francophone Africa." *The National Conference Phenomenon in West Africa* 36 (4): 575–610.

19

Building Resilience to Conflict: The Case of West Africa

Alexandre Marc, Neelam Verjee and Stephen Mogaka

The short post-independence history of west Africa has been marred by a number of highly destabilizing conflicts. These conflicts, which have ranged from large-scale civil wars to long-running episodes of simmering violence, conferred a certain notoriety upon the subregion, which briefly became known for its association with blood diamonds and child soldiers. Among the conflicts that have wracked the subregion since the 1960s are the Biafran War in Nigeria, the civil wars in the Mano River basin that devastated Sierra Leone and Liberia and, to a lesser degree, the conflict in Côte d'Ivoire.

In recent years, a new wave of violence and conflict in the subregion and the rise of violent extremism have raised concerns that a fresh generation of emerging threats could undermine the subregion's development and cost it hard-won economic gains. Episodes of conflict and violence in Nigeria and the Lake Chad basin, as well as

instability in the Sahel, which has had particular ramifications for Mali, have shown that violent extremism has succeeded in exploiting historical grievances to establish a solid footing in the subregion. Meanwhile, the insidious threats of drug trafficking and maritime piracy have made inroads into west Africa and have contributed to locking some countries, such as, for instance, Guinea-Bissau, into fragility traps.

Notwithstanding this reputation for bloody conflict, an examination of the subregion's post-colonial history reveals that west Africa has, in fact, been less affected by conflict and violence than other regions in Africa. It has suffered fewer fatalities from conflicts over the last 60 years than have the other subregions on the continent. Despite its various political and governance challenges, west Africa has also recorded fewer conflict events in its post-independence history than have Africa's other subregions, as it largely escaped the Cold War–related conflicts that destabilized countries in other parts of the continent.

Despite the recent violence in the Sahel and Nigeria, as well as the impact of the devastating Ebola epidemic, which highlighted the long-term consequences of conflict and violence on the social and institutional fabric of a country, west Africa has made important progress in the reduction of fragility and conflict over the last decade. The region is home to some of Africa's most stable countries, such as Senegal and Ghana, and has witnessed successful transitions from war to peace in Sierra Leone, Liberia and Côte d'Ivoire. It has also made tremendous progress toward the democratization of political processes and in endorsing systems of political alternation and power-sharing, marking a major break with other subregions on the continent. The region therefore offers lessons in post-conflict recovery and reconstruction that can be useful for countries around the world in similar situations. As such, it is a subregion that can offer some important lessons in terms of experiences in resilience.

This chapter will look into how resilience has played out in west Africa. Resilience here is termed in a way that differs somewhat from the original usage of the word, defined as "the ability to return to the original situation before a shock happens." For the purposes of this chapter, we use the term to express "a return to a peaceful situation in a sustainable way." This is in keeping with recent peace-building literature, wherein resilience is seen as the ability to uphold positive or sustainable peace (Menkhaus 2013). As such, resilience takes the form of societal transformation, involving a process through which the drivers of conflict are addressed (Interpeace 2016).

Framed in this way, resilience does not mean reverting to the pre-conflict situation. In most cases, conflict has stemmed from unaddressed grievances, most often coupled with the weakening of institutions — especially political, justice and security institutions. A return to peace will require addressing grievances and strengthening these institutions. In consequence, if peace is to be sustainable, there needs to be more than a simple return to the pre-conflict situation. A condition of peace necessitates that grievances are addressed, that political agreements are renegotiated and that there is the beginning of reform of security and justice institutions. Therefore, in the case of situations of conflict and violence, resilience implies the ability of the system to be reformed and changed, rather than the ability to return to a pre-conflict situation.

Resilience can be fostered and bolstered in several key ways. Among the factors of resilience that play a role in facilitating the return to a peaceful situation in a sustainable way are greater inclusiveness of political systems and alternation in power, a diverse and vocal civil society, civic institutions that can channel opinion and dissent and act as a safety valve of sorts, and strong institutions that can mediate conflict. Other factors include addressing the reform of security and justice institutions, as well as a clear demonstration of effort on the part of governments to address socio-economic factors of fragility, such as subregional inequalities.

This chapter will be divided into five sections. The first section will look at the conflict dynamics and the centrality of institutions in resilience; the second section will examine the transformation of political systems and opening up more inclusive processes, including the role of regional organizations, such as the Economic Community of West African States (ECOWAS), as well as that of civil society organizations; the third section will investigate resilience in the context of addressing regional imbalances; the fourth section will look at how the process to reform the justice and security apparatus has contributed to resilience; and the final section will cover unfinished business that has the potential to erode resilience.

Conflict Dynamics in West Africa and the Centrality of Institutions in Resilience

The nature of the violence in west Africa has significantly altered in the period since independence. The subregion was largely spared the wars for independence that dominated elsewhere on the continent. Furthermore, the countries of the subcontinent established peaceful relations among themselves; the vast majority of armed conflicts in west Africa were intrastate as opposed to between states. Since the 1960s, west Africa has recorded five large-scale civil wars and at least seven other conflicts of a lesser magnitude, with more localized unrest (M'Cormack 2011), in addition to a significant number of military coups. The Biafran War (1967–1970), which cost up to two million lives (Oloyede 2009), was the subregion's first large-scale civil war. The other major civil wars, which took place following the end of the Cold War, were the two phases of the Liberian civil war (from 1989 to 1996 and then again from 1999 to 2003), as well as the civil war in Sierra Leone (1991–2002), Guinea-Bissau (1998-1999) and, finally, Côte d'Ivoire (from 2002 to 2007 and then again in 2010 and 2011).

Two years after the end of the crisis in Côte d'Ivoire, northern Mali was rocked by a Tuareg-led insurgency. The insurgents were joined by extremist groups composed of fighters from several countries. Attempts by these groups to move southward were stymied by a French-led military intervention. Nigeria has also experienced a significant insurgency involving the Boko Haram extremist group, which has cost over 11,000 lives to date and dealt a major blow to development outcomes in the country's northeast. In recent years, the insurgency has spilled over into the border areas of Chad, Niger and Cameroon. Nigeria has begun working with its neighbours to jointly confront the challenge.

The incidence of civil war in west Africa dramatically dropped off after the beginning of the new millennium, in line with trends across Sub-Saharan Africa during the same period (Straus 2012). Liberia, Sierra Leone and Guinea-Bissau all entered a post-conflict phase and successfully conducted multi-party elections. As well, after a brief relapse in 2010 following its elections, Côte d'Ivoire has once again returned to stability. This trend represents a milestone in the political stabilization of the region, even as emerging threats and alternative forms of political violence, such as tensions linked to elections, have come to replace large-scale conflicts and civil wars.

Most conflicts in west Africa have been triggered by drivers that have not only combined to ignite conflict but have also conspired to drag these conflicts out for an exceptionally long time. As across the rest of the continent, perceptions of group-based exclusion have been particularly strong in the subregion. Even where new dynamics have emerged to play a role, such as the rise in violent extremism and trafficking, a sense of group-based exclusion remains central to existing conflicts. It is also clear that the political dimensions of conflict and, in particular, the inclusion or exclusion of elites from various socio-cultural groups, has played a key role in conflicts in the subregion since independence.

The trend toward a reduction in battle deaths is in part a consequence of the move toward democratization and multi-party elections, which has provided opportunities for greater power-sharing and political alternation. It has also come about as a result of the stabilizing influence of regional mechanisms for dispute resolution and conflict prevention and management. These mechanisms include those developed by ECOWAS, which helped to bring the civil wars of the Mano River basin to a close.

Fragility and conflict are products of the inability of institutions to contain and manage internal and external stresses. In some cases, the intensity of the stresses is such that even strong institutions are unable to contain them; in other cases, it is the institutions themselves that are weak and ineffective. In the latter scenario, even low-intensity stresses create instability and violence that can spin out of control. Across west Africa, stresses that increase the risk of conflict stem largely from structural and global factors. These include the fast-growing youth population; increasing movement of populations within countries and across borders; increasing inequalities and rapidly evolving regional disparities within countries; the rapid development of the extractive industry, with huge investments into the sector; and the explosion of various forms of trafficking and criminal activities, especially involving narcotics.

Institutions are central to resilience at all levels. It is very difficult to externally support changes in institutions as dynamic socio-cultural adaptation is central to what makes an institution change. A key factor that seems essential to making institutions strong and effective is the way in which they reflect and incorporate various social norms (Marc et al. 2012). How institutions interact with one another, and the quality of these interactions, is also important, especially in dealing with conflicts (ibid.). Strong institutions shape social groups' norms and behaviours and frame the collective behaviour of members: they can either foster cohesion or lead to further fragmentation.

Institutions constantly need to adapt to make sure they are in sync with the social needs, norms and demands of the individuals who comprise a society. When social structures change quickly and norms are transformed rapidly, institutions are usually faced with issues of legitimacy and efficiency. The rapid pace at which societies in Africa are changing is putting enormous strain on its institutions, pushing them to transform rapidly, but also risks rendering them illegitimate and ineffective. Relations between various types of institutions are particularly problematic, especially those between state institutions (which try to answer a society's global needs) and customary institutions (which dominate at the local level and deal locally with a variety of social needs).

The centrality of institutions in mediating conflict was witnessed during the September 2015 military coup in Burkina Faso, following the detention of the transitional President Kafando and Prime Minister Zida by members of the presidential guard. The presidential guard had been created by the former President Blaise Compaoré and had played a central role in upholding his regime before he was ousted via popular protest in October 2014. Although the initial intervention by ECOWAS and Presidents Sall of Senegal and Yayi of Benin helped to restore civilian rule, subsequent tensions between the military and the presidential guard threatened to tip the country back into crisis. This time, however, it was a traditional king, the Mogho Naba, who was key to brokering the return of civilian rule, demonstrating that resilience can be the function of different processes and institutions (Bjarnesen and Lanzano 2015).

In acknowledgement of the role that traditional institutions play in conflict management, countries such as Ghana have incorporated such institutions into their national conflict management mechanisms. Although these institutions encourage resource sharing while promoting intra-group solidarity, a number of them are also highly exclusionary on the basis of gender and age. An optimal approach would therefore be to harness the capabilities of these institutions while including other groups within society in the process (Murithi 2006).

The Transformation of Political Systems and the Opening Up of More Inclusive Political Processes

West Africa has made important progress in conflict resolution since the end of the conflicts in the Mano River basin countries. In large part, this is due to greater inclusiveness of the political systems. Alternation in power has acted as a crucial safety valve, as most recently evidenced in the political changes in Burkina Faso and

Guinea-Bissau, as well as in the peaceful elections in Senegal, Nigeria and Côte d'Ivoire. Research shows that excluding societal groups from access to power can act as a major source of conflict (Vogt 2007). Excluding specific groups can also dilute the legitimacy of institutions and weaken them (Bujones et al. 2013). Although a few highly undemocratic systems remain, such as in Gambia and Togo, these are in the minority.

The closed nature of politics in west Africa has historically contributed to the incidence of coups and conflicts. Military coups continuously challenged the stranglehold that dictators and "Big Man" presidents kept on the state in the decades following independence. West Africa experienced nearly three times as many military coups (both successful and unsuccessful) in the decades after 1960 as any other subregion on the continent.

Increased democratization, combined with security sector reform (SSR) and regional and continental norms, has contributed to a significant decline in military coups. In 1985, 11 of the 16 countries in the region were under military rule (Omotola 2011). Today, this situation has been nearly entirely reversed. Gambia and Nigeria are the only countries in the region to be led by presidents with backgrounds in the military, and, indeed, Nigeria's President Buhari is a retired major general who was elected to office in 2015 via democratic process.

Democratic consolidation has been accompanied by an increase in measures aimed at political accommodation across the subregion, amid the widespread adoption of policies to encourage power-sharing among elites. In several countries, elite bargaining has resulted in prominent political parties sharing the positions of president and deputy president between geographical divisions, such as the north and the south. Elite bargaining has also led to the principle of rotation of the presidency and other senior positions across different regions. In some countries where

institutionalized arrangements are absent, the centrality of political accommodation to stability is acknowledged in the existence of mechanisms that give elites from marginalized regions prominent positions in government.

Since the 1990s, several countries in the region have undergone democratic consolidation, which has helped to foster greater stability. Competition for power has found expression via the ballot box as opposed to the battlefield, as formal and legal institutions trump the use of force as a channel for dissent and expression. The progression of democracy and inclusive politics has taken place at both national and regional levels, and has been underpinned by norms. The transition to democracy was supported by the role of civil society, an increase in citizen mobilization and the buildup of external pressure. In turn, the increasing number of fledgling democracies helped to shore up support for democratic norms at the regional level and provided incentives for the political leadership to establish a regional framework for democratic norms under ECOWAS (Hartmann and Striebinger 2015). It is notable that the move toward more inclusive political systems and political alternation is largely the product of national and regional actors and processes, rather than of an external agenda imposed by donors and development agencies. This trend owes its progression in part to the influence of regional organizations, as well as to the role played by civil society and civic organizations.

Despite the progress made in terms of political stabilization, there have been occasional setbacks, such as the 2012 military coup in Mali, the 2015 putsch in Burkina Faso and, more recently, the 2016 dismissal of the government of Guinea-Bissau. In the case of the latter, the country had been in the throes of a protracted political crisis since August 2015. The calm brought to Guinea-Bissau by the restoration of constitutional order in 2014 with the election of José Mário Vaz as president came to an abrupt end when the president dismissed his prime minister. A new government was formed in October 2015 but that too was dismissed in May 2016, with the ministries placed under the control of the security forces. The refusal of members of the government to vacate the presidential palace triggered a crisis, which was only resolved through ECOWAS-mediated talks. However, the Parliament is locked in an ongoing stalemate amid political disagreements over some of the president's appointments. ECOWAS played a pivotal role throughout this period in the way of mediation and via its peacekeeping mission, the ECOWAS mission in Guinea-Bissau (ECOMIB) — which in turn has been cited as a deterrent to potential putchists (International Crisis Group 2015). News that ECOMIB would pull out in June 2017 has raised fresh fears over instability ahead of planned elections in 2019.

Setbacks notwithstanding, the overall picture in west Africa remains one of progress and the consolidation of democratic and inclusive politics. Between 2015 and 2016, democratic and peaceful political transitions took place in Nigeria, Benin and Burkina Faso. While challenges also linger around the incidence of military coups, significant progress has likewise been made, as demonstrated in Nigeria and Ghana, which were the regional trendsetters in terms of coups. Both countries have transitioned to civilian rule as a result of domestic factors, with Ghana heralded as a model for successful democratic transition following several peaceful handovers of power.

The two countries that have bucked the regional trend of democratic consolidation are Togo and Gambia. Prompted by pro-democracy demonstrations in the early 1990s, Togo hosted a national conference and, in 1992, introduced a new constitution that dramatically curtailed the president's powers. However, the democratic experiment turned out to be short-lived as President Gnassingbé Eyadéma deployed the military against the incipient democratic institutions. Following his death in 2005 after nearly four decades in office, the military rapidly named his son Faure Gnassingbé as his successor. Under pressure from ECOWAS and the international community (Ebeku 2005; Kohnert 2015), the administration held hasty elections, and these too resulted in a win for Faure Gnassingbé. In recent years, civil society and other actors have agitated for the reintroduction of presidential term limits.

Gambia is one of four countries on the continent that had maintained a democratic system even before the end of the Cold War. This met with a premature end in July 1994 as several junior military officers, including the current president, Yahya Jammeh, overthrew the democratic regime of Dawda Jawara (Loum 2002). The country has since held four presidential elections, with all four coming under heavy criticism from observers for various irregularities and state-sponsored violence. Indeed, ECOWAS refused to dispatch observers in 2011 on the grounds that the elections would not be free and fair (*BBC News* 2011). In response to protests against President Jammeh — the most recent of which took place in April 2016 — the government detained both citizens and political leaders.

Today, all sitting presidents in west Africa have either been elected to their posts via multi-party elections or have been confirmed to their positions in the same way, even in cases in which the outcome of elections has been highly contested (Musah 2009). This reflects the gradual "institutionalization of power" (Posner and Young 2007) whereby political transitions are taking place via elections (Omotola 2011). However, new forms of violence and disorder have emerged following the dismantling of authoritarian structures, as the "partially reformed state" has proven to be substantially weakened (Young 2004).

The move toward democratization has seen an accompanying increase in electoral violence across the subregion. Nigeria, Côte d'Ivoire, Togo, Burkina Faso and Sierra Leone have all experienced varying degrees of turmoil and political violence before, during or after elections. The deadliest incidence of election-related violence was witnessed in Côte d'Ivoire in 2010 when an estimated 3,000 people were killed in political violence in the wake of the elections (International Crisis Group 2011). Given the high stakes of the outcome, political rivals came to view elections as a zero-sum game, with control of the state equating to very strong control over the economy and associated trappings, often for private gain (Souaré 2010, 6).

Challenges posed by democratization have been exacerbated at times by the nature of the electoral system. The winner-take-all system has been described as "an obstacle to democracy in Africa's highly ethnicized politics" (Mesfin 2008, 3) and does not adequately express the will of the voter. In some countries, as in the case of Guinea, elections have led to the ethnicization of politics and hardening of ethnic identities. The countries in the region have recognized the challenge posed by election-related violence and, in 2011, they agreed on the Praia Declaration on Elections and Stability in West Africa.

The Role of ECOWAS and Regional Mechanisms

The regional organization ECOWAS has provided an arena for the development of norms that underpin resilience and, as such, has helped to strengthen domestic efforts toward promoting resilience in west Africa. ECOWAS has become more effective in part due to the increased inclusivity of the politics of its member states. Nevertheless, it is significant that, as an economic organization, it has chosen to place such great emphasis on conflict prevention, particularly on the political underpinnings of conflicts.

ECOWAS has been credited with playing an outsize role in conflict management in west Africa (Adetula 2015; International Crisis Group 2016). Its first attempt at conflict management came when it deployed peacekeepers to Liberia and Sierra Leone, in a bid to end hostilities. These early interventions were crucial for the stabilization

of the Mano River basin region (International Crisis Group 2016). Furthermore, they provided ECOWAS with valuable lessons that helped to strengthen subsequent interventions and establish normative frameworks by which to underpin resilience (Adetula 2015).

The Liberia and Sierra Leone interventions led to a fundamental rethink of the role and mandate of ECOWAS. The organization adopted a new treaty in 1993, which was followed in 1999 by the adoption of the Mechanism for Conflict Prevention, Management, Resolution, Peacekeeping and Security — simply known as the "Mechanism." In its provisions, the Mechanism emphasized that economic development cannot be separated from domestic policies, the implications of which had been seen to spill over into neighbouring countries. As such, ECOWAS abandoned the principle of non-intervention and embraced the concept of human security (Adetula 2015; International Crisis Group 2016), giving the organization a stronger foundation from which to address the crises afflicting the subregion. Indeed, the emphasis on state sovereignty in the Southern African Development Community protocol is in part a cause of the organization's limited efficacy in mediating crises (Adetula 2015).

The Mechanism created a foundation for subsequent norms in the form of protocols and other agreements. It recognized the threat posed by cross-border security challenges such as transnational crime and the proliferation of small arms. The 2001 Protocol on Democracy and Good Governance, which is supplementary to the 1999 Mechanism, contains a clear provision against unconstitutional changes in government. Acknowledging the long-standing threat posed by military rule, the protocol also contains provisions emphasizing the supremacy of democratically elected civilian leaders over the armed forces and a ban on military involvement in politics. In 2008, the regional body launched the ECOWAS Conflict Prevention Framework, which provides a broad framework for improving governance.

ECOWAS became an important vehicle for norm-setting in part as a result of the trend toward democratization and the push to institutionalize inclusive politics. As the countries of the subregion embraced democracy, leaders sought to strengthen adherence to this form of political system in order to safeguard their national democratic institutions. Over time and as part of this process, ECOWAS became an important enabler of norms that strengthen resilience.

In comparison to other regional bodies on the continent, ECOWAS has adopted a proactive approach to resolving crises. The weakness of regional bodies in east Africa and the Horn of Africa has meant that they are unable to intervene effectively in the protracted crises in South Sudan and Burundi. There is greater political will in west Africa to resolve conflicts and not allow them to fester. ECOWAS has also demonstrated its ability to work with the African Union, the United Nations and other international actors to bring a rapid end to conflict and political turmoil.

ECOWAS has fiercely guarded its role as gatekeeper to international interventions in West Africa. This has helped to ensure the timely resolution of conflicts in a number of cases, such as, for instance, the 2010-2011 crisis in Côte d'Ivoire. ECOWAS endorsed the victory of Alassane Ouattara in the presidential elections, opposing attempts by his rival Laurent Gbagbo to circumvent the will of the people. In the process, ECOWAS set the tone for the responses of actors such as the African Union, putting paid to arguments by some within the African Union for a power-sharing deal that might have exacerbated the crisis. The robust position taken by ECOWAS was likely key to convincing China and Russia to support a common UN position on the crisis (Williams 2015).

The regional hegemon Nigeria has played a pivotal role in conflict resolution in west Africa. It has spent a significant amount of its resources on various interventions, notably in Liberia, Sierra Leone and, most recently, Guinea-Bissau. Its role

has not been without controversy, however, with differences in opinion also emerging between anglophone and francophone countries during the initial interventions in Liberia and Sierra Leone (Odigbo, Udaw and Igwe 2014). This aside, the countries of the subregion have displayed high levels of cooperation. Nigeria's role in stabilizing the region has been complemented by the efforts of "enclave powerbrokers," or countries that took the lead in resolving conflicts within their immediate neighbourhood. For instance, Guinea played an important role in mediation and peace initiatives in the Mano River basin region, while Côte d'Ivoire has historically played an important role in peace initiatives in francophone west Africa. Burkina Faso has been an important powerbroker since 2003 and was deeply involved in the crises in Côte d'Ivoire, Togo and Mali. These examples help to underscore the importance of cooperation in a region where stability is not solely dependent on a single hegemon, but relies on smaller countries expending their resources toward regional peace and stability (Musah 2009).

In contrast to other regions on the continent, the countries in west Africa, under the aegis of ECOWAS, have confronted the challenge of term elongation and the removal of term limits. Across east and central Africa, removing term limits has stoked political instability and violence, in some cases even spilling over borders. Several attempts at term elongation in west Africa have been soundly defeated, including in Nigeria, Niger and Burkina Faso. Robust provisions in the constitutions of the majority of countries in the subregion stipulate executive term limits. In 2015, a proposal was tabled at an ECOWAS summit for a regional ban on the removal of term limits. This was rejected, however, reportedly under pressure from Gambia and Togo, countries that have not instituted constitutionally mandated term limits (Trithart 2016).

This rejection notwithstanding, such initiatives underscore the robustness of democratic norms in west Africa. Where term limits are viewed as a domestic matter across much of the continent or a "normative no-man's land in Africa's foreign policy" (Hengari 2015, 3), there is growing evidence that they are treated as a regional and collective concern in west Africa. In particular, civil society organizations have played a central role in lobbying for a regional agreement on term limits amid the recognition that conflict and political crises can destabilize the entire subregion. Recent developments in Senegal and Benin have also bucked trends seen elsewhere on the continent. In Senegal, the president proposed and supported a referendum that cut presidential terms from seven years to five, while in Benin, debunking reports that he would amend the constitution and run for a third term, former President Yayi left office at the end of his second term. His successor, President Patrice Talon, announced his support for an amendment to the constitution that would decrease limits from two terms to a single term. There is optimism that these positive examples may influence trends across the continent (Trithart 2016).

Despite its successes, ECOWAS continues to face multiple challenges ranging from stretched finances, which have been blamed on delays by member countries in remitting levies, to logistical and other challenges associated with deploying troops to manage conflicts, as underscored by the Malian crisis.

Civil Society and Civic Organizations

The development of civic organizations has been a defining feature of the last two decades in Africa. Although still imperfect in terms of representation, these organizations have played a major role in fostering more inclusive debate and addressing grievances. In west Africa, civil society organizations have helped to promote the resilience agenda — a role that has been recognized and institutionalized at the regional level.

Civil society actors emerged as vocal actors in the early 1990s during the push for democratization.

Student groups, religious groups and professional organizations were at the vanguard of the transition to democratic rule. Over the last decade, civil society actors have once again championed democracy. This time, the resistance has been against those leaders seeking to amend the constitution and alter term limits. Pressure from civil society and civic organizations has helped to strengthen the bargaining position of political elites opposed to such amendments. In Nigeria, civil society actors so effectively mobilized public opinion against President Olusegun Obasanjo's reported intention to run for a third term that senators ultimately opposed the mooted amendment (Kew and Oshikoya 2014; Posner and Young 2007). In Burkina Faso, the youth-led grassroots movement Le Balai Citoyen was central to the campaign against extending presidential term limits.

The conflicts in Liberia and Sierra Leone marked a turning point for the role of civil society in fostering resilience. Civil society organizations mediated between the warring parties while channelling the views of the public. Coalitions of women's groups were especially critical for ending conflict and reestablishing peace. The Women for Liberia Mass Action for Peace played a role in the peace agreement of 2003 (Ekyor 2008), while the establishment of the Mano River Women's Peace Network in 2000 marked a new level of engagement for women in regional peace initiatives and is credited with contributing to the prevention of a recurrence of conflict between Sierra Leone, Liberia and Guinea.

In terms of building community resilience, civil society actors have been key to uniting communities from different ethnic and religious backgrounds. Significant progress has been made in interfaith dialogue in countries such as Sierra Leone, Senegal, Liberia and Gambia. Among the first to intervene in the conflict in Liberia were faith-based groups, such as the Interfaith Mediation Committee, which held talks with the conflict parties and made recommendations that formed part of the ECOWAS peace plan (Atuobi 2010). In 1995, a coalition of civil society groups formed the National Coordinating Committee for Peace with the objective of bringing the combatants to the negotiating table. Civil society also played a role in the August 1995 Bintumani Conference, which set elections for 1996. The Inter-Religious Council of Sierra Leone is credited with preventing religious schisms from emerging during the civil conflict, as it became an important vehicle for confidence-building measures between the government and the rebels (Pham 2004).

The exclusion of civil society groups from the peace processes during the first civil war in Liberia and at the beginning of the negotiations in Sierra Leone meant that the focus of mediation was largely on the armed groups. As a consequence, peace agreements reflected only the interests of combatants (such as Sierra Leone's 1999 Lome Accord). Intense lobbying by civil society organizations, amid dawning realization of their roles as important stakeholders, led to their inclusion in the Accra peace talks in 2003. Civil society groups were subsequently also included in the power-sharing agreement that emerged from the talks, a fitting acknowledgement of their role in safeguarding peace (Fayemi 2004).

ECOWAS has broken ground on the continent in terms of its recognition of the role of civil society and civic organizations in conflict resolution and through its move to formalize collaboration between the regional body and civil society actors. In turn, civil society actors have played a key role in shaping the position of ECOWAS on issues including that of executive term limits. By inputting timely and accurate information from the West Africa Network for Peacebuilding, civil society has strengthened the regional Early Warning and Response Network (Adetula 2015; International Crisis Group 2016).

Addressing Regional Imbalances and Lagging Regions

Strong subregional differentiation is a key characteristic of many countries in west Africa. This differentiation is the product of geographical and historical dynamics that have strongly influenced present-day tensions and conflicts. The coastal regions have historically been much more productive in terms of agriculture than the inland regions, while also receiving the lion's share of investments in infrastructure, in particular, in terms of transport and urbanization. Even in counties without a coastline, such as Mali, Niger and Burkina Faso, there exists a strong north-south divide that is linked to modes of production and culture, with the southern zone being more amenable to agriculture and the northern zone favouring pastoralism while being intricately linked to trans-Saharan trading routes.

Historically, the Sahel was the site of large empires that had developed and flourished in the region since the Middle Ages. The Sahel is also better connected due to the extensive trading system that criss-crosses the Sahara and has helped to foster strongly connected cultural zones, including, for instance, the Mandingo region, which stretches from the fringes of the Sahara to occupy the northern parts of most of the coastal region. This zone has become progressively Islamized since the twelfth century. The combination of the geographic differences that favour the southern and western areas of the subregion and the impact of climate change, as well as colonial and post-colonial neglect, is at the root of strong subregional differentiations.

These differentiations have been very present in the history of conflict in west Africa. A number of conflicts have come about directly as a result of the deep-seated, historical grievances of various communities at the subregional level. The most notable include conflicts and episodes of violence in Nigeria and Côte d'Ivoire, as well as violence in Mali and Niger. The pronounced north-south divide in Côte d'Ivoire and, in particular, the long-standing marginalization of northern elites and communities was a key driver of the conflict there. For several decades, the north had experienced significant social and economic inequalities, but this had been successfully managed by President Félix Houphouet-Boigny through a combination of high economic growth and inclusive policies. Conflict erupted in the late 1990s following the death of Houphouet-Boigny, as political elites moved away from accommodation and toward the exclusion of northern elites. As such, conflict came about through the combination of social and economic inequalities and political marginalization (Langer 2005). Likewise, the Boko Haram crisis in Nigeria has in part been blamed on social and economic inequality in the north, which has dovetailed with a sense of political disenfranchisement among some northern political elites in the wake of the 1999 transition to civilian rule (Olojo 2013; Hoffmann 2014).

However, it is important to emphasize that while the existence of horizontal inequalities — severe inequalities between culturally formed groups (Stewart 2000) — and regional imbalances raises the risk of conflict, they are not an automatic trigger. Other factors must be present for this risk to manifest in violent conflict, while the manner in which inequalities are managed can decrease their salience as a driver of violence and conflict. Several countries in west Africa have demonstrated significant commitment to addressing regional imbalances. Ghana and Niger have both found highly effective ways of managing these conflict drivers and have demonstrated the efficacy of efforts to reduce regional imbalances through a strong focus on political inclusion.

Ghana has moderated the destabilizing effect of the "serious" developmental and ethno-regional divide between its north and the south by implementing a range of politically inclusive measures and policies (Langer and Stewart 2014). The country has made "substantial progress" over the last 15 years in improving the socio-economic situation in the north as well as in the south, even though the divide is still noteworthy (ibid.). Confronted by major ethno-regional tensions and mobilization at independence, Ghana's first president, Kwame Nkrumah, moved to promote national integration and build a regionally and ethnically inclusive cabinet (ibid.). His efforts have to some degree been institutionalized, both formally, in the constitution, and informally (ibid.), with the president usually hailing from the south or the east and the vice president from the north. Additionally, measures such as economic redistribution to the deprived northern regions and the inclusion of northern elites in key political institutions, as introduced by successive Ghanaian regimes, helped to minimize the destabilizing potential of the north-south cleavage (ibid.).

Ghana has also institutionalized efforts to address horizontal inequalities by anchoring development plans within major planning strategies (African Development Bank 2015). The Ghana Shared Growth Development Agenda prioritized the tackling of regional imbalances in development via specific interventions. The country also established the Savannah Accelerated Development Program, which is geared toward the particular development challenges of the historically marginalized north. Other west African countries that have adopted development strategies to address regional imbalance and mitigate its salience as a conflict driver include Mali, where the Accelerated Development Programme for the Northern Regions has been held up by corruption and inefficiencies, as well as Benin, which boasts an official, national spatial development plan, including major infrastructural development in order to better connect the country (ibid.).

Niger has also made great progress of late in bridging its internal schisms, as it has taken important steps to address the marginalization of its Tuareg population. The government has promoted a policy of decentralization as part of its national development strategy. Despite challenges (ibid.), the creation of institutions at the local level has expanded the political elite and has seen a number of former Tuareg leaders, including former combatants, take office at mayoral and other levels (International Crisis Group 2013). Backed by donor support, the government has also implemented programs that aim to improve livelihoods in the marginalized north of the country. Furthermore, it has granted a percentage of royalties from oil and other minerals to local communities, many of which have historically been marginalized. These measures are expected to benefit Diffa, in particular, as the country's least developed region (African Development Bank 2015).

Other countries in the subregion have also launched cross-border initiatives to improve the livelihoods of communities in border and lagging regions. One example of such an initiative is the Senegal River Basin Development Authority, which incorporates Senegal, Guinea, Mali and Mauritania, and offers a framework under which the countries can share the Senegal River. Another example is the regional park between Niger, Burkina Faso and Benin, which has been credited with boosting economic activity and improving livelihoods of local communities (ibid.).

Despite the imperative for such measures, as well as the heightened sense of inclusion engendered by such policies, efforts to address regional imbalances and foster resilience are still at risk of elite capture. In some cases, such arrangements have resulted in development policies that favour regions with significant political influence at the national level, at the expense of marginalized regions. In Ghana, for instance, education budgets have in the recent past benefited parts of the south more than the historically deprived north, in direct reflection of the outsize influence wielded by southern elites (Abdulai and Hickey 2014). In other cases, attempts to address regional imbalances through a concerted effort to establish an inclusive government, such as has been seen in Nigeria, Niger and Ghana, have led to charges that powerful elites appoint individuals with no real power to senior positions and, in the process, undermine the basis of inclusion.

Reforming the Security and Justice Apparatus

Over two decades after the end of the Cold War, the countries of west Africa have largely undergone a process of democratization. They have made significant strides in transforming their civil-military relations and in improving the quality of their security and justice sectors. Historically, the security sector across the region was poorly managed and, as such, acted as a major cause of instability, in particular, through the prevalence of military coups. Although many countries have since reformed their civil-military relations, the imbalance remains in some, such as Togo, Guinea-Bissau, Gambia, Mauritania, Niger and, more recently, Mali (Houngnikpo 2012; Bryden and Chappuis 2015).

Despite ongoing challenges, the countries of west Africa appear to have made more progress in the reform of justice and security institutions than have the continent's other subregions. Although security and justice institutions are a very important area in which to build resilience, the effective and comprehensive reform of these institutions very much depends on the pre-existence of a more inclusive political system. The establishment of democratic and inclusive political systems creates an enabling environment for the reform of security and justice sectors. Nevertheless, democratization does not automatically translate to effective SSR (Bryden, N'Diaye and Olonisakin 2005).

Along with the embrace of democratic politics, which has to some degree girded reforms, the donor community has played an important role in SSR since the mid-1990s, especially in post-conflict countries, as seen in the comprehensive and long-term involvement of the United Kingdom in Sierra Leone. Regional frameworks and collective security mechanisms to address threats in west Africa have also been central to the reform effort. Although such arrangements have been in place since the late 1970s and early 1980s, they only took effect in the 1990s during the region's civil wars.

ECOWAS has also played an increasingly important role in SSR in terms of both norm-setting and as a lead actor. In Guinea-Bissau, for instance, the organization established a pension system, a move viewed as a critical ingredient for the peaceful retirement of security personnel (Uzoechina 2014). Recurring bouts of instability in Guinea-Bissau, along with the complex nature of politics in the country and the legacy of conflict, undermined attempts at reform and saw the donor-driven SSR program grind to a halt. ECOWAS restarted the process in 2012 as part of a managed transition in the wake of a military coup. The relative success of this effort, including some progress in the thorny area of establishing the pension fund (International Crisis Group 2015), helped the country to rebuild relationships with key donors (International Crisis Group 2016). The regional body has also been credited with creating an enabling environment for the removal of spoilers from office, such as General Antonio Indjai, the former head of the armed forces.

ECOWAS is currently developing a regional strategy on SSR for west Africa. It has set up regional centres for military training, which also serve as a conduit for diffusing norms concerning stable civil-military relations to the militaries of the member countries. In this way, there has been a push toward greater regional input and ownership over SSR. The establishment of the Supplementary Act on the Code of Conduct for the Armed Forces and Security Services of ECOWAS 2011 has represented a defining moment for the region in terms of the setting of norms. The code promotes democratic governance with regard to the security sector and increases the professionalization of the armed forces, while seeking to deter unconstitutional changes in government (Uzoechina 2014).

While reforms of the security sector and of institutions in recent years have helped to correct civil-military relations, further adaptation is necessary to counter emerging challenges that have the potential to destabilize tracts of the subregion. To be effective, SSR requires strong political commitments and an overhaul of governance that can only come through internal processes, as demonstrated by Senegal, Nigeria and Ghana. Improvements in accountability, the rule of law and the security sector need to be coordinated. Once the political commitment is in place, technical support and financing can play a critical role — but there is no substitute for political commitment. In this sense, peer pressure and the framework provided by regional mechanisms are essential. This is a truly critical factor for the future stability of west Africa.

An Unfinished Business

Although the subregion has made tremendous strides in bolstering resilience, there are still areas in which limited progress has been made, despite their centrality for conflict. Conflict drivers such as land have received insufficient attention and, as such, the land issue in west Africa remains a potential source of instability. An increased focus on the management of land and on addressing grievances linked to land access is necessary to lessen its salience as a driver of conflict. These include a greater focus on improving land titling systems; refining regulations that govern the use of community land; managing the use of land between pastoralist and agricultural communities; managing and improving grazing lands; and enhancing policies on land acquisition in urban areas, or areas where extractive development or large-scale agriculture programs are hosted.

The exponential increase in the number of youth entering the market each year, with expectations for improved livelihoods, is another formidable challenge for stability. The surge in economic growth has failed to create sufficient unskilled and semi-skilled jobs to meet the demand of west Africa's labour market. Many young people do not have the possibility of improving their livelihoods or finding their places in the new societies. This situation will not necessarily result in conflict, but it is likely to lead to an increase in grievances, across not only west Africa but also the whole continent. It is only through the accelerated development of informal activity and livelihood options that such levels of demand can be satisfied.

Part of the solution to the issue of youth livelihoods lies in internal migration, both within states and within the subregion. Improvements in the management of migrants is therefore an additional urgent priority in west Africa. West Africa hosts a large number of forcibly displaced people in the Sahel and in the Mano River basin region, as well as around conflict zones in northern Nigeria and Mali. A protracted situation of forced displacement contributes to grievances and generates vortices of instability while creating challenges for service delivery and poverty reduction.

The handling of emerging global threats is a further cause for concern, in particular, regarding trafficking and violent extremism. Preventing violent extremism does not always require development interventions that are very different from those for conflict prevention. When it takes on the dimensions of an insurrection, violent extremism is usually based on historic grievances. With regard to emerging global threats, it is essential to deploy holistic approaches that focus on development and governance, as purely security-oriented responses are insufficient.

Emerging security threats in west Africa in the form of trafficking, piracy and terrorism have boosted the case for further reform and improvement of security sectors. A key obstacle is the insufficient connection between support for overall state building and for SSR. SSR needs to go hand in hand with the improvement of justice and the rule of law, particularly because most security threats today emanate from within countries' borders and from their citizens. Reform of formal justice systems is necessary but largely insufficient. Conflict management mechanisms, with the involvement of local authorities, civil societies and communities, are essential in the medium term, at the least, to manage justice issues in most countries.

Conclusion

West Africa's path toward increased resilience to conflict has largely been achieved through progress in the political realm. The subregion has made progress on more inclusive political systems and has fostered a much stronger respect for political alternation — even though the process has not always been linear and has been punctuated by a series of political crises. Of note is the fact that this evolution has been primarily driven by domestic and regional factors, rather than by the influence of external actors. The regional organization ECOWAS has played an especially important role in facilitating the momentum of democratization in the region and in pushing for respect for democratic processes. The championing of democracy by ECOWAS is regarded as a major factor in preventing a return to the conflicts of the 1990s.

While the increase in political inclusion goes a long way toward explaining west Africa's resilience with regards to conflict, progress has also been made in a number of other important developmental areas, in particular, in trying to address some of the strong perceptions regarding subregional inequalities. How to deal with the "lagging" parts of the country has been a recurring and major challenge for many of the subregion's countries. Where resilience has been at its strongest is also where governments have demonstrated clear efforts in attempting to address subregional inequalities.

Finally, as clearly demonstrated in the World Development Report of 2011 (World Bank 2011) on conflict, security and development, addressing the reform of security and justice is also critical in order to advance toward resilience. Despite difficulties, it is clear that some progress has been made in this area. Crucially, there is general agreement across the region that improving both the competence and accountability of security forces is essential.

Works Cited

Abdulai, Abdul-Gafaru and Sam Hickey. 2014. "Rethinking the Politics of Development in Africa? How the 'Political Settlement' Shapes Resource Allocation in Ghana." Effective States and Inclusive Development Working Paper No. 38. www.effective-states.org/wp-content/uploads/working_papers/final-pdfs/esid_wp_38_abdulai_hickey.pdf.

Adetula, Victor. 2015. *African Conflicts, Development and Regional Organizations in the Post-Cold War International System.* Uppsala, Sweden: Nordic Africa Institute. www.pcr.uu.se/digitalAssets/65/65805_1camp-8.pdf.

African Development Bank. 2015. *Regional Development and Spatial Inclusion: The African Economic Outlook.* African Development Bank.

Alaga, Ecoma. 2011. "Gender and Security Policy in West Africa." Friedrich-Ebert-Stiftung Working Paper. http://library.fes.de/pdf-files/bueros/nigeria/08162.pdf.

Albrecht, Peter Alexander. 2010. "Transforming Internal Security in Sierra Leone: Sierra Leone Police and Broader Justice Sector Reform." Danish Institute for International Studies Report No. 7. www.dcism.dk/graphics/Publications/Reports2010/RP2010-07_transforming_Sierra_Leone_web.pdf.

Arthur, Peter. 2010. "ECOWAS and Regional Peacekeeping Integration in West Africa: Lessons for the Future." *Africa Today* 57 (2): 3–24.

Atuobi, Samuel. 2010. "State-Civil Society Interface in Liberia's Post-Conflict Peacebuilding." Kofi Annan International Peacekeeping Training Centre Occasional Paper No. 30. www.kaiptc.org/Publications/Occasional-Papers/Documents/Occasional-Paper-30-Atuobi.aspx.

Barka, Habiba Ben and Mthuli Ncube. 2012. "Political Fragility in Africa: Are Military Coups d'Etat a Never-Ending Phenomenon?" African Development Bank. www.afdb.org/fileadmin/uploads/afdb/Documents/Publications/Economic%20Brief%20-%20Political%20Fragility%20in%20Africa%20Are%20Military%20Coups%20d%E2%80%99Etat%20a%20Never%20Ending%20Phenomenon.pdf.

BBC News. 2011. "Gambia: Ecowas Observers Boycott 'Unfair Poll.'" *BBC News*, November 23. www.bbc.com/news/world-africa-15851706.

Bendix, Daniel and Ruth Stanley. 2008. "Security Sector Reform in Africa: The Promise and the Practice of a New Donor Approach." African Centre for the Constructive Resolution of Disputes Occasional Paper Series. www.gsdrc.org/go/display&type=Document&id=4977.

Bjarnesen, Jasper and Christiano Lanzano. 2015. *Burkina Faso's One-week Coup and its Implications for Free and Fair Elections.* Uppsala, Sweden: Nordic Africa Institute.

Brown, David. 1982. "Who Are the Tribalists? Social Pluralism and Political Ideology in Ghana." *African Affairs* 81: 37–69.

Bryden, Alan and Fairlie Chappuis. 2015. *Learning from West African Experiences in Security Sector Governance.* London, UK: Ubiquity Press. doi: https://doi.org/10.5334/bau.

Bryden, Alan, Boubacar N'Diaye and 'Funmi Olonisakin. 2005. "Security Sector Governance in West Africa: Turning Principles to Practice." Geneva Centre for the Democratic Control of Armed Forces Policy Paper No. 8.

Bujones, Alejandra Kubitschek, Katrin Jaskiewicz, Lauren Linakis and Michael McGirr. 2013. *A Framework for Analyzing Resilience In Fragile and Conflict-Affected Situations.* United States Agency for International Development Final Report. https://sipa.columbia.edu/sites/default/files/USAID%20Final%20Report.pdf.

Cederman, Lars-Erik, Nils B. Weidmann and Kristian SkredeGleditsch.2011."Horizontal Inequalities and Ethnonationalist Civil War: A Global Comparison." *American Political Science Review* 105 (3): 478–95.

Cederman, Lars-Erik, Kristian Skrede Gleditsch and Halvard Buhaug. 2013. *Inequality, Grievances, and Civil War.* New York, NY: Cambridge University Press.

Cook, Nicolas. 2011. "Côte d'Ivoire's Post-Election Crisis." Washington, DC: Congressional Research Service.

Coulibaly, Massa and Michael Bratton. 2013. "Crisis in Mali: Ambivalent Popular Attitudes on the Way Forward." *Stability: International Journal of Security & Development* 2 (2): 1–10.

Deutsche Welle. 2016. "Guinea-Bissau's President Dissolves Government, Fires Prime Minister." *Deutsche Welle,* May 12. www.dw.com/en/guinea-bissaus-president-dissolves-government-fires-prime-minister/a-19252630.

Ebeku, Kaniye. 2005. *The Succession of Faure Gnassingbe to the Togolese Presidency: An International Law Perspective.* Uppsala, Sweden: Nordic Africa Institute. www.diva-portal.org/smash/get/diva2:240415/FULLTEXT02.pdf.

Ekiyor, Thelma. 2008. "The Role of Civil Society in Conflict Prevention: West African Experiences." *United Nations Institute for Disarmament Research, Disarmament Forum: The Complex Dynamics of Small Arms in West Africa* 4: 27–34. www.gsdrc.org/document-library/the-role-of-civil-society-in-conflict-prevention-west-african-experiences/.

Fayemi, J. 'Kayode. 2004. "Governing Insecurity in Post-Conflict States: The Case of Sierra Leone and Liberia." In *Reform and Reconstruction of the Security Sector,* edited by Alan Bryden and Heiner Hänggi, 179–206. Münster, Germany: LIT. www.apcof.org/files/5175_8.pdf.

Godwin, Ashlee and Cathy Haenlein. 2013. "Security-Sector Reform in Sierra Leone: The UK Assistance Mission in Transition." *RUSI Journal* 158 (6). https://www.rusi.org/publications/journal/ref:A52B036B3C82F9/#.VCLw3_mSywc.

Hartmann, Christof and Kai Striebinger. 2015. "Writing the Script? ECOWAS' Military Intervention Mechanism." In *Governance Transfer by Regional Organizations,* edited by Tanja A. Börzel and Vera van Hüllen, 68–83. Basingstoke, UK: Palgrave Macmillan.

Hengari, Alfredo Tjiurimo. 2015. "Presidential Term Limits: A New African Foreign Policy Challenge." South African Institute of International Affairs Policy Briefing No. 138. www.saiia.org.za/policy-briefings/849-presidential-term-limits-a-new-african-foreign-policy-challenge/file.

Hoffmann, Leena Koni. 2014. "Who Speaks for the North? Politics and Influence in Northern Nigeria." Chatham House, The Royal Institute of International Affairs Research Paper. https://www.chathamhouse.org/sites/files/chathamhouse/field/field_docu ment/201 40703NorthernNigeriaHoffmann.pdf.

Houngnikpo, Mathurin C. 2012. "Africa's Militaries: A Missing Link in Democratic Transitions." Africa Center for Strategic Studies, Africa Security Brief No. 17. http://ndupress.ndu.edu/Portals/68/Documents/archives/asb/ASB-17.pdf.

International Crisis Group. 2011. "A Critical Period for Ensuring Stability in Côte d'Ivoire." Africa Report No. 76. www.crisisgroup.org/africa/west-africa/c%C3%B4te-divoire/critical-period-ensuring-stability-cote-d-ivoire.

———. 2013. "Niger: Another Weak Link in the Sahel?" Africa Report No. 208. www.crisisgroup.org/africa/west-africa/niger/niger-another-weak-link-sahel.

———. 2015. "Security Sector Reform in Guinea-Bissau: An Opportunity Not to Be Missed." Africa Briefing No. 109. www.crisisgroup.org/africa/west-africa/guinea-bissau/security-sector-reform-guinea-bissau-opportunity-not-be-missed.

———. 2016. "Implementing Peace and Security Architecture (III): West Africa." Africa Report No. 234. www.crisisgroup.org/en/regions/africa/west-africa/234-implementing-peace-and-security-architecture-iii-west-africa.aspx.

Interpeace. 2016. *Assessing Resilience for Peace: A Guidance Note*. Geneva, Switzerland: Interpeace. www.interpeace.org/wp-content/uploads/2016/06/2016-FAR-Guidace-note-Assesing-Resilience-for-Peace-v7.pdf.

Kew, Darren and Modupe Oshikoya. 2014. "Escape from Tyranny: Civil Society and Democratic Struggles in Africa." In *The Handbook of Civil Society in Africa*, edited by Ebenezer Obadare, 7–23. New York, NY: Springer.

Kohnert, Dirk. 2015. "Togo: Recent Political and Economic Development." Munich Personal RePEc Archive Paper No. 63411. https://mpra.ub.uni-muenchen.de/63411/8/MPRA_paper_63411.pdf.

Langer, Arnim. 2005. "Horizontal Inequalities and Violent Group Mobilisation in Côte d'Ivoire." *Oxford Development Studies* 33 (1): 25–45.

Langer, Arnim and Frances Stewart. 2014. "Regional Imbalances, Horizontal Inequalities and Violent Conflicts: Insights from Four West African Countries." World Bank, Fragility, Conflict and Violence Group Paper.

Leininger, Julia. 2014. *A Strong Norm for Democratic Governance in Africa*. Stockholm, Sweden: International Institute for Democracy and Electoral Assistance. https://www.die-gdi.de/uploads/media/Leininger_2014_A-Strong-Norm-for-Democratic-Governance-in-Africa.pdf.

Loum, Momodou. 2002. "Bad Governance and Democratic Failure: A Look at Gambia's 1994 Coup." *Civil Wars* 5 (1): 145–174. www.tandfonline.com/doi/abs/10.1080/13698240208402498#.VzX2x_l97IU.

Marc, Alexandre, Alys Willman, Ghazia Aslam, Michelle Rebosio and Kanishka Balasuriya. 2012. *Societal Dynamics and Fragility: Engaging Societies in Responding to Fragile Situations*. Washington, DC: World Bank. https://openknowledge.worldbank.org/handle/10986/12222.

Marshall, Monty G. 2005. "Conflict Trends in Africa, 1946–2004: A Macro-Comparative Perspective." Report prepared for the Africa Conflict Prevention Pool. www.systemicpeace.org/africa/AfricaConflictTrendsMGM2005us.pdf.

M'Cormack, Freida. 2011. "Conflict Dynamics in West Africa." University of Birmingham Governance and Social Development Resource Centre Helpdesk Research Report.

Menkhaus, Ken. 2013. "Making Sense of Resilience in Peacebuilding Contexts: Approaches, Applications, Implications." The Geneva Peacebuilding Platform Paper No. 6. www.gpplatform.ch/sites/default/files/PP%2006%20-%20Resilience%20to%20Transformation%20-%20Jan.%202013.pdf.

Mesfin, Berouk. 2008. "Democracy, Elections & Political Parties: A Conceptual Overview with Special Emphasis on Africa." Institute for Security Studies Paper No. 166. https://issafrica.s3.amazonaws.com/site/uploads/Paper166.pdf.

Murithi, Tim. 2006. "African Approaches to Building Peace and Social Solidarity." *African Journal on Conflict Resolution* 6 (2): 9–34.

Musah, Abdel-Fatau. 2009. "West Africa: Governance and Security in a Changing Region." International Peace Institute, Africa Program Working Paper Series.

Odigbo, Jude, Joseph Effiong Udaw and Adaona Frank Igwe. 2014. "Regional Hegemony and Leadership Space in Africa: Assessing Nigeria's Prospects and Challenges." *Review of History and Political Science* 2 (1): 89–105.

Ogude, Helen. 2012. *Coups in West Africa: A Reflection of Deficiencies in Africa's Electoral Democracies?* Consultancy Africa Intelligence.

Olojo, Akinola. 2013. "Nigeria's Troubled North: Interrogating the Drivers of Public Support for Boko Haram." International Centre for Counter-terrorism Research Paper. www.icct.nl/download/file/ICCT-Olojo-Nigerias-Troubled-North-October-2013.pdf.

Oloyede, Olajide. 2009. "Biafra in the Present: Trauma of a Loss." *African Sociological Review* 13 (1): 2–25.

Omotola, Shola. 2011. "Unconstitutional Changes of Government in Africa: What Implications for Democratic Consolidation?" Nordiska Afrikainstitutet Discussion Paper No. 70. http://nai.diva-portal.org/smash/get/diva2:478511/FULLTEXT01.pdf.

Pham, J. Peter. 2004. "A Nation Long Forlorn: Liberia's Journey from Civil War Toward Civil Society." *International Journal of Not-for-Profit Law* 7 (1). www.icnl.org/research/journal/vol6iss4/art_1.htm.

Posner, Daniel and Daniel Young. 2007. "The Institutionalization of Political Power in Africa." *Journal of Democracy* 18 (3): 125–137.

Pritchett, Lant and Frauke de Weijer. 2010. *Fragile States: Stuck in a Capability Trap.* World Bank World Development Report Background Paper.

Souaré, Issaka K. 2010. "A Critical Assessment of Security Challenges in West Africa." Institute of Security Studies Situation Report.

Striebinger, Kai. 2010. *Sleeping Beauty — Explaining the Legalization of Democracy Standards in the Economic Community of West African States (ECOWAS).* Köln, Germany. www.uni-koeln.de/phil-fak/afrikanistik/kant/data/Striebinger-KANT3.pdf.

Stewart, Frances. 2000. "Horizontal Inequalities: A Neglected Dimension of Development." Queen Elizabeth House, University of Oxford, Working Paper No. 81.

———, ed. 2008. *Horizontal Inequalities and Conflict: Understanding Group Violence in Multiethnic Societies.* Basingstoke, UK: Palgrave Macmillan.

Straus, Scott. 2012. "Wars Do End! Changing Patterns of Political Violence in Sub-Saharan Africa." *African Affairs* 111 (443): 179–201.

Trithart, Albert. 2016. "Mixed Results as Term Limits Put to the Vote on Africa's 'Super Sunday.'" *International Peace Institute Global Observatory*, March 28. https://theglobalobservatory.org/2016/03/third-term-africa-elections-benin-congo-niger/.

Uzoechina, Okey. 2014. "Security Sector Reform and Governance Processes in West Africa: From Concepts to Reality." Geneva Centre for the Democratic Control of Armed Forces Policy Paper No. 35. www.dcaf.ch/Publications/Security-Sector-Reform-and-Governance-Processes-in-West-Africa-From-Concepts-to-Reality.

Vogt, Manuel. 2007. "Ethnic Exclusion and Ethno-Nationalist Conflicts: How the Struggle over Access to the State Can Escalate: A Quantitative and Qualitative Analysis of West Africa." National Centre of Competence in Research: Challenges to Democracy in the 21st Century Working Paper No. 18. www.nccr-democracy.uzh.ch/publications/workingpaper/pdf/WP18.pdf.

Williams, Paul. 2015. "Regional Arrangements and the Use of Force." In *Managing Conflict in a World Adrift*, edited by Chester A. Crocker, Fen Osler Hampson and Pamela Aall, 331–344. Waterloo, ON: CIGI.

World Bank. 2011. *World Development Report 2011 : Conflict, Security, and Development*. World Bank. https://openknowledge. worldbank.org/handle/10986/4389.

World Politics Review. 2013. "Global Insider: Security Sector Reform Stalling in Côte d'Ivoire." www.worldpoliticsreview.com/ trend-lines/12959/global-insider-security-sector-reform-stalling-in-cote-d-ivoire.

Young, Crawford. 2004. "The End of the Post-colonial State in Africa? Reflections on Changing African Political Dynamics." *African Affairs* 103 (410): 23–49.

Zounmenou, David. 2008. "Managing Post-War Liberia: An Update." Institute for Security Studies Situation Report. www.issafrica. org/publications/situation-reports/ situation-report-managing-post-war-liberia-an-update-david-zounmenou.

20

A Practitioner's View

Princeton N. Lyman

In reading this book, I find myself, as a sometimes scholar and sometimes practitioner, impressed but also overwhelmed. There is no doubt that out of this work has come a much richer understanding of both the sources of conflict and the possible sources of resilience on which both scholars and practitioners can draw. But what this extraordinary output of scholarship might also do is leave the practitioner, the mediator, overwhelmed. Is it possible, after absorbing all the aspects that drive conflict — the underlying and the immediate — and the countering forces of resilience with their own contradictions and limitations, to come up with a methodology of conflict prevention or resolution?

Vasu Gounden, founder and director of ACCORD, a major conflict mediation organization, has warned that the pressures on African society are greater now than ever before. Africa, he said, faces a dangerous time: "For the first time in the history of humanity we face the convergence of factors that threaten our very existence. Exponential population growth, rapid urbanization, climate change, and a global financial crisis, are all converging at the same time…a phenomenon unprecedented in the history of humanity, presenting us with huge complexity. For developing countries like ours, this will exacerbate poverty, unemployment and inequality" (Gounden 2016).

The chapters in this volume, while seeking out sources of resilience, provide no less a warning. Eghosa Osaghae catalogues quite dramatically the many forces that are today driving conflicts and making them more difficult to overcome:

> Issues of contested citizenship, resource inequalities, uneven development and political exclusion and marginalization, which have been accentuated by shocks of resource boom and doom, upsurge in global terrorism and conflicts, violent electoral politics and the like, have been crucial factors in this regard….

To these must be added the policy and governance failures of the weak state, which made it unable to cope with the admittedly unusual, unconventional, and new forms of conflict, of which Boko Haram, Niger Delta minorities militancy, and the ethnic riots of the Fulani herdsman were prototypical. The guerilla, terrorist and militant strategies employed by the warring groups — the sophisticated firearms, kidnapping, robbery, rape, suicide bombing, unprecedented scales of killing and destruction, clandestine operations and large areas attacked, and cross-boundary mobility, which was fuelled by forces of globalization, made the conflicts difficult to engage. (See chapter 4 of this volume.)

With this breathtaking list, the background noise — if you will — of environmental and global economic factors and the more immediate, but no less difficult, factors of land, ethnic, political and religious competition, what are the factors the mediator — or indeed anyone committed to conflict prevention — should address or focus on? For practitioners, it is important to understand which forces are operating that might turn grievances and low-level conflict into something much more serious. A greater understanding of underlying causes and pressures is certainly of value and helps one to avoid going down wrong tracks. But, armed with that knowledge, where to focus? How deep into societal issues should the mediator seek to go when confronting impending or ongoing conflict? Moreover, many of these forces are beyond the purview or, at least, the mandate, of the mediator. The timelines for action surely do not coincide. How does one then incorporate all this into a methodology for conflict prevention or resolution?

One approach, in keeping with the subject matter of this volume, is to examine the countries facing all these same forces and factors that have not been engulfed in conflict. Zambia is a good

example. Zambia has a history of poor governance; persistent poverty, despite rich natural resources; a large, urbanized population with high levels of unemployment; and strong political rivalries, but it has not experienced civil war or widespread internal conflict. Zambia came dangerously close to significant violence during the 2016 election, but the situation remains calm, even if tense. Can we learn from Zambia what the danger points, the tripwires of violence, that should be watched and addressed might be? As well, what are the sources of resilience?

This is not a full discourse on Zambia, but Zambia illustrates the interplay between immediate institutional strength and underlying conditions that are ominous. There is no doubt that the political and societal institutions that have contained violence held sway in Zambia, but it turns out that Zambia ranks among the highest countries in the world in rates of gender-based violence (GBV) (*QFM Zambia* 2016; CSIS n.d.).[1] If our experience — which is borne out in some of the studies in this volume and elsewhere — is instructive, any wide-scale violence erupting in Zambia could thus well result in shocking levels of rape and other GBV, as has been seen in the Democratic Republic of the Congo (DRC), South Sudan and Nigeria. There are no deep societal traditions that would thwart it. But where to start on preventing this in Zambia if political tensions once again rise to dangerous levels? Would it be to focus on the leaders, to dissuade them from provoking violence and from unleashing these underlying predilections? Or would it be to focus on the cultural sources of GBV and build resilience against them in society such that, if politically stoked violence does break out, it does not, at least, sink to that level of viciousness? There are, of course, programs under way in Zambia to

---

1   Lest one think Zambia is exceptional in this regard, a study of rural youth in South Sudan found that one in three — including women — felt violence was justified if a spouse refused sex or did household chores poorly (Mercy Corps 2014).

address the GBV problem, but their success may well take years. In a time of potential crisis in Zambia, the practitioner has to act. If he or she gets it wrong, the consequences can be great.

There are two other examples that illustrate this set of choices. In South Africa, during the transition period, the threat of civil war and terrible levels of violence was quite real. The threat was of violence not between whites and blacks, as many had predicted, but between the supporters of Nelson Mandela's African National Congress (ANC) and Mangosuthu Buthelezi's Inkatha. The violence was concentrated in the province of Kwa-Zulu Natal, but took place also in the surrounding area of Johannesburg. Thousands of lives were lost. The attacks in the villages of Kwa-Zulu Natal, usually in the dead of night, were vicious, and civilians were the primary targets and victims. The attacks seemed meaningless in their cruelty but were, in fact, part of a political struggle. In the midst of this period, as the situation seemed to crater on the edge on the verge of civil war, Rian Malan, in his book *My Traitor's Heart,* delved into the foundations of this violence (Malan 1991). He found that the divisions among villages and between ethnic subgroups had deep roots in issues of cattle and land, long-past historical grievances and the desperation of the poverty that had been aggravated by the practices of apartheid. Some of these divisions went as far back as the British occupation of the province in the nineteenth century (ibid., 339–409). Obviously, there were deep and complex historical cleavages in that society that were being mobilized in the contemporary struggle.

How relevant was all that to the immediate crisis? That history was helpful to me, then the US ambassador to South Africa, in arguing against the insertion of a UN peacekeeping force, as advocated by Archbishop Tutu and others. I could not see how a foreign force could possibly operate knowledgeably in that environment. However, as for resolving the violence, was this historical and cultural ethos the heart of the conflict, or was it simply a tactical manifestation of the contending parties? Did one need to delve into those historical and indigenous cleavages to address this conflict? Or was it more relevant to address the political forces' aggravation of these differences for their own purposes and to urge the leadership to come to its senses?

This conflict was, in fact, being stoked as much by the South African government as by the ANC and Inkatha. It was fairly well known that the South African security personnel were secretly training and equipping Inkatha forces. Nelson Mandela told me some years later that he had discovered that the number two man in the ANC chapter in the province had also been a South African *agent provocateur,* which explains the radical and violence-prone policies of that ANC chapter during this period.

I was convinced then — and am today — that if Buthelezi had not, at the very last moment, acceded to the election and the interim constitution and the ANC had not reciprocated in a behind-the-scenes election deal, giving Inkatha electoral victory in that province, South Africa might well have begun its democratic independence, as Zimbabwe had, with a vicious, ethnically tinged civil war that would have marked the country ever after.

What is relevant here, however, is that once the political leadership had settled their rivalry, the violence ended. It ended so completely that people were surprised. What happened to all those underlying cleavages? What about the Xhosa-Zulu rivalries, centred on hostels of Zulu workers, that had made the environs of Johannesburg no-go zones in the run-up to the election? All of that disappeared overnight as well. Maybe we were lucky in focusing on the political leadership and its ability and willingness to reach political compromises. But political compromise was also the most accessible entry point for international activity and was a means far more suited to our capacity than sorting through the historical and ethnic mysteries of Kwa-Zulu Natal, which, in fact, proved to be beside the point of this conflict. Those underlying rivalries — those historic cleavages and the political rivalries — continue but are now expressed through the political process.

However, let me turn to a more complex and less satisfying situation: South Sudan. Just two years after achieving independence, the country descended into civil war between the government and the forces of the recently deposed vice president. The scope of violence — horrific mutilations, rape and murder — that has taken place in this civil war is beyond comprehension. It is hard to read the descriptions. The African Union commissioned a study of the war and, in particular, of these human rights violations: a Commission of Inquiry (COI), chaired by former Nigerian President Olusegun Obasanjo. The COI painstakingly analyzed the weaknesses of the institutions that should have prevented the war — the party, Parliament, judiciary, security forces and various levels of government — and found all of them wanting. The COI report took the international community, especially those heavily involved in the Comprehensive Peace Agreement (CPA) of 2005 that brought about South Sudan's independence, to task for their failure to foresee these weaknesses and the prospect of violence and to take more steps to prevent it (African Union 2014, 37-38). There is some justice in that conclusion, but the question here is which among these factors were those that could have been best addressed in the run-up to this terrible conflict?

Prior to the outbreak of the civil war in 2013, the Institute of Peace and Security Studies at the University of Addis Ababa had mapped some 900 low-level conflicts already under way in South Sudan. The conflicts were over land, cattle, kidnappings, borders and ethnic rivalries. Land issues were acute at the state and local level; cattle rustling was traditional but had become more deadly and politically linked in modern times. When the leaders of South Sudan turned on each other and launched the civil war in

2013, they mobilized supporters, drawing on all these traditional rivalries and adding motives of vengeance and pure desire for loot and resources. They ran roughshod over the institutions that should have put the brakes on their ambition.

In these circumstances, the COI charge is too easy a conclusion. In practice, it would have impossible for the leaders of the CPA to address all these factors as conditions for South Sudan independence. Independence was, by at least 2010, indispensable to prevent a return to the war between Sudan and South Sudan that had already taken two million lives. These problems, moreover, would require decades of improved governance, rule of law and committed democratic leadership. This was the dilemma the international community faced, the imperative of self-determination to end the north-south civil war and the need (and the hope) to address South Sudan's serious shortcomings over time. Even addressing the more immediate source of unrest — the vast corruption arising out of oil revenues and the misuses of security forces as sources of patronage and ethnic division — would have required putting South Sudan under some degree of international oversight, for which there was no appetite among either the Western or the African countries involved.

However, let us not let the international community off too easily. It was possible early enough in its independence to see the readiness of South Sudan's leaders to stir ethnic conflict, commit major human rights violations and act out of greed and power-seeking, rather than to pay any serious attention to development. All of this was clear in the two years before the outbreak of civil war, for example, in the attacks on the Murle in Jonglei state and similar ethnic attacks elsewhere, in the intimidation and assassination of journalists and in other acts of authoritarianism. In those years, perhaps, steps could have been taken to stop these practices before they grew beyond outside influence or control. There is no time here to answer why such efforts did not take place, at least, at an intensity that would have mattered. But they did not, and that, surely, was a failure.[2]

Where does this leave us? The South Africa example, so encouraging, nevertheless gives no sure clues as to conflicts elsewhere. In South Africa, the leaders, as they approached the precipice, stopped before going over — before plunging the country into the kind of civil war that would have left many scars and changed it forever. Leaders, there, mattered. However, in South Sudan, the leaders not only did not stop but almost purposefully hurled the country over that precipice, willing to tear the country asunder in pursuit of their political aims. It is too late now to address all the underlying matters that these leaders exploited in stoking hatred and violence or to rely on traditional sources of resilience — tribal leaders, churches and women's groups — which have, in any case, been easily overwhelmed by the forces of violence. Zambia is a case that is made for prevention, especially because the sources of societal resilience may well be antithetical to containing the worst forms of violence should such break out. But changing those traditional attitudes is, at best, a long-term process.

The conclusion one can reach, drawing on the experience of conflicts in South Sudan, Nigeria, the Central African Republic (CAR) and in the DRC, is that in the threats of conflicts that may erupt elsewhere on the continent, the prospects are not just of violence, but also of the widespread use of rape, murder and other dehumanizing acts of terror. It is harder today to harness such conflicts with traditional peacemaking strategies, and harder to keep them from being exploited by power-hungry leaders. We may be able, in a few cases, to bring leaders to the table to stop this, but Mandelas, Buthelezis and De Klerks are rare finds today.

---

2   For a fuller analysis of the peace agreement, its outcome and issues of responsibility, see Lyman (2016).

What is the precise role of conflict resolution in this milieu? How does the practice acknowledge forces over which it has no control — forces of climate change, globalization, population, competition for land and resources, unemployment and poor education — that are well beyond its mandate and that, very often, roll over traditional forms of resilience and resistance? What tools does the practitioner use in these circumstances? Others should be working on these underlying factors, but practitioners of conflict prevention and resolution cannot wait until they are addressed.

Indeed, if, as Gounden suggests, the various forces acting on Africa are of such magnitude and simultaneity that tensions in Africa are only to become greater, then we need to ask whether we need not only knowledge of these factors but also, perhaps, new methods of prevention or resolution, new ways to build walls against the undercurrents of potentially vicious forms of violence that such tensions may release.

I am particularly disturbed — horrified — by the brutishness, the viciousness, of some of today's violence. I have described it in relation to South Sudan above. It is truly sickening and suggests that the worst demons in our collective psyche are being unleashed. We see it, too, elsewhere in Africa and, of course, with ISIS and others in the Middle East and South Asia. Much of the worst is GBV, the source of which lives deep within many societies, and that is a caution against counting too much on traditional sources of resilience.

In this vein, I hark back to a meeting I had many years ago with the late Prime Minister Meles of Ethiopia. This was long before my role in Sudan and South Sudan, many years earlier. I was leading a team to Ethiopia to evaluate the progress against HIV/AIDS. In our meeting, I called attention to the practice, particularly in southern Ethiopia, of kidnapping women and sexually assaulting them in order to force them into marriage. It was so common and accepted that the governor of the province had acquired his bride that way. Meles replied that it was indeed deplorable, but asked why the women did not rise up to object. "It would not happen in [my home province] Tigre," he claimed, "because women there would not stand for it but [would] organize to stop it." Spoken by a true revolutionary.

However, there is some value in his comment. I am a strong supporter and great admirer of the Institute of Inclusive Security and Vital Voices, and of the wonderful work they and many other organizations do on behalf of women in peace. But there are only a few instances in which women have had a real impact on stemming conflict and surely too few in preventing the worse forms of GBV in such conflicts. The Sudan and South Sudan women's groups are marvellous, and they do wonderful work on behalf of peace. But, in truth, as we can see in the current conflict in South Sudan, their impact is marginal, as is that of much of civil society.

Perhaps we need to think differently about resilience and, in particular, the role of civil society. When it comes to GBV, women are often fighting both their traditional culture and the leaders of armies. Even responsible traditional and local leaders with well-established methods of conflict abatement are overrun today by the "guys with the guns." Turning to them for answers may be a fool's errand.[3]

Instead, maybe we need to cultivate the philosophy, the strategy and the practices of non-violent civil disobedience. It is a methodology and practice that Gandhi and Martin Luther King Jr. understood well. It was not simply civil disobedience or demonstrations for their own sake. Rather, non-violent civil disobedience involved a sophisticated understanding of one's societies and which vulnerabilities can be exploited by those who are not armed, but who may be able and willing to be mobilized. It is inherently risky. It means putting bodies on the line. It dares opponents to do their worst, knowing that the worst could galvanize more public opinion and create more moral pressure on oppressors. It was daring, risky and often costly, but ultimately successful in India, in the United States and, indeed, in more situations than are generally recognized. Maria Stephan and others have long argued for more attention to this form of resistance:

> [R]esearch shows that societies that experience major nonviolent campaigns, including those that fail…are almost 10 times more likely to democratize and avoid civil war than those that experience armed campaigns. Successes, like that of the Tunisian National Dialogue Quartet, which was awarded the Nobel Peace Prize this past October, can be used as guides for converting upheaval to positive change.

So why doesn't this symbiosis of nonviolent resistance, which involves escalating conflict nonviolently, and peace building, which involves de-escalating conflict, occur more often? One reason is that populations challenging their governments make the foreign donors that most often support peace-building techniques more than a little nervous. After all, movements and their outcomes are unpredictable, as was seen with the 2011 Arab Spring. Confrontational activity can sometimes lead to violence. Nonviolent direct action, furthermore, often happens outside of normal institutions and processes that donors are more familiar with (Stephan 2016).

---

3 A telling example comes from the CAR, in a report by a US Institute of Peace staff member: "The Sultan in NE CAR is unique and occupies an important role, both historically and in the present day. The Sultan is viewed as the most respected person in the town, but under the current situation, he feels he cannot protect citizens and doesn't have the ability to deal with bandits and uncontrolled fighters. In the same town, the prefect was beaten and wounded by rebels and 'obliged' to leave town."

I would certainly agree that the risks for such movements are great in many contemporary situations. However, maybe, nevertheless, some of the resilience we need to help build has to be bolder, more dramatic, more risky and more forceful. Breaking through against the increasingly vicious practices of violence may well take much more than we are willing to contemplate. Perhaps we are relying too much on traditional methods, both within indigenous cultures and in our cultural norms of teaching tolerance and conflict resolution skills. Maybe resilience needs to be something much greater than what we have been discussing so far, something that has to be built in the face of deeply embedded opposition and the larger forces that are pressing down on societies in ways over which we will have even less control in the immediate future.

Works Cited

African Union. 2014. *Final Report of the African Union Commission of Inquiry on South Sudan.* https://paanluelwel2011.files.wordpress.com/2015/10/final-report-full-report.pdf.

CSIS, Global Health Policy Center. n.d. *It's Time to Listen: Young Women and HIV/AIDS in Zambia.* www.csis.org/programs/global-health-policy-center/hivaids/it%E2%80%99s-time-listen-young-women-and-hivaids-zambia-0.

Gounden, Vasu. 2016. Keynote address on receiving an honorary doctorate of social sciences at the University of KwaZulu-Natal graduation, Durban, South Africa, April 11.

Lyman, Princeton N. 2016. "Sudan and South Sudan: The Tragic Denouement of the Comprehensive Peace Agreement." In *Africa in World Politics,* 6th ed., edited by John W. Harbeson and Donald Rothchild. Boulder, CO: Westview Press.

Mercy Corps. 2014. *South Sudan Through Youth's Eyes.* https://www.mercycorps.org/research-resources/south-sudan-through-youths-eyes.

Malan, Rian. 1991. *My Traitor's Heart.* London: Vintage.

QFM Zambia. 2016. "Zambia Ranks 20th among Countries with High GBV cases." *QFM Zambia,* September 23. www.qfmzambia.com/2015/09/23/zambia-ranks-20th-among-countries-with-high-gbv-cases/.

Stephan, Maria J. 2016. "The Peacebuilder's Field Guide to Protest Movements." January 22. www.usip.org/publications/2016/01/22/the-peacebuilder-s-field-guide-protest-movements.

Part Six
Conclusion

21

Can State and Society Be Woven Together?

Chester A. Crocker and Pamela Aall

This book ends as it began, with a call to broaden conflict management in Africa beyond the political and military spheres that so often dominate policy making and implementation. Conflict is a highly complex phenomenon and in responding to it, we often identify specific points on which to apply leverage — government leaders, rebel chiefs, heads of militaries, militias and other armed groups, and others who have a direct effect on the conflict's outcome. These are indeed the critical elements to engage in reaching a political settlement, but they exist in a wider social setting that will help to implement or undermine their agreements. Understanding the role that this social environment plays allows peacemakers — whether from within the conflict or outside of it — to design a more sustainable peace.

That said, the book also ends with a strong focus on the state and the need for strong, responsive state institutions. As we examined ways in which the social environment can help in the prevention or resolution of conflict, the arrow landed again and again on that grey area, which is the borderland between state and society. In both specific suggestions — for instance, to reform educational curricula to prepare students for a rapidly changing world — and the general recommendations, the authors of this book highlighted the importance of government engagement in building a healthy state-society relationship by providing responsive governance, making space for civil society, encouraging different (and at times difficult) points of view, and allowing a diversity of ideas, peoples and cultures to exist side by side.

It is no doubt that this task is enormous, even in relatively peaceful countries and regions. Building a strong state-society relationship in turbulent settings or after wrenching confrontations is made even more difficult in situations where civil war threatens to break out or – as so often happens – to break out again. And yet, this state-society relationship is the key to a future in which disputes can be handled through negotiation and legal means, and conflicting points of view and objectives can be managed without resort to violence.

The Challenge

State-Society Gaps

We begin with the familiar observation that there is a weak social compact between state and society in many African states. This should not be surprising. Most of the region's states were defined geographically by European cartographers at the start of the colonial period. The modern African state system had external origins and is only gradually being Africanized, albeit on more or less the identical territorial basis it began with six decades ago. Less than 20 percent of Africa's states achieved statehood following rebellion or armed insurgency; in the others, independence flowed from negotiated transitions and peaceful transfers of authority from colonial officials to African political elites. To be sure, most of the new leaders were democratically elected, but the political and juridical basis for those elections seldom reflected a broad-based process of indigenous constitution-making. The constitutions and legal systems were of largely European origin. Through these mechanisms, colonial rulers transferred power to African successors.

In addition to these factors, the historical context of Africa's re-entry into the international system played a role in reinforcing the state-society gap. Cold War geopolitics in the first post-independence decades tended to favour African incumbents, and frequently assured they would receive significant assistance from external powers seeking to build diplomatic ties with the new states. This situation reinforced an external orientation in African politics in which Cold War reference

points and former colonial relationships assured that national governments often enjoyed only a limited sense of connection to their own societies. The African state system has gradually developed a stronger indigenous quality only in the last 25 years or so.

Another source of the state-society disconnect is the reality that the state is only one focus of individuals' allegiances. This pattern is by no means unique to Africa, but Africa's states are among the world's newest, and it can hardly be surprising that Africans define themselves in terms of multiple affiliations and allegiances. In addition to being citizens of a state, they may be residents of a region with a long pedigree — for example, the Ogaden, Darfur, the Niger Delta — and members of an ethnic or religious group, a sect or a tribe. Sometimes, these ties bind more strongly than those to the state and its national political institutions.

For these and other reasons, the state-society gap lies at the heart of the problems faced by many states. Governments that rely on foreign counterparts and foreign investment in natural resources for a major portion of their budgets may not enjoy (or know how to develop) effective linkages to their own societies. In their different ways, Pierre Englebert, Mathurin Houngnikpo, Eghosa E. Osaghae, Charles Olungah, and Arnim Langer and Leila Demarest each speak to the challenge of building national identities and the risk that political elites and social groups will capture the state for narrower, self-interested purposes that weaken social cohesion.

The Centrality and Ambiguity of Inclusion

Inclusion is a component of successful conflict management that is much discussed, but difficult to achieve. Assuming that it wants to do so, how does a well-meaning political leadership group become more inclusive? A number of African states have faced pressures to decentralize their political decision-making systems and to share or delegate authority from the centre to provincial or local levels. The jury is still out on the cases of Nigeria and Kenya, where significant devolution has had major fiscal and governance consequences. Large countries such as the Democratic Republic of Congo, Ethiopia and Mozambique are especially likely to experience pressures against centralized authoritarian or one-party governance (whether accompanied by a veneer of elections or not).

A basic problem is whom to include. The challenge has several dimensions. Non-official institutions and social groups, including civil society, will have their own ideas. If the national government does all the defining, the exercise will not be perceived to be legitimate. Yet governments are expected to govern and make decisions after consulting relevant stakeholders. Gilles Yabi argues that a relatively responsive government is necessary for civil society to lobby effectively for changes to laws; likewise, a competent state apparatus is needed to provide governance continuity when civil society successfully presses for regime change and genuine elections. Ideally, African nations will benefit when civil society respects the state's role (as well as the other way around); rather than one-sided advocacy, it should strive to create a space for debate in order to legitimize tolerance of multiple views in society.

Well-meaning political leaders will need to consider the possible answers to these questions. Should the priority be to achieve inclusion of diverse elites, of ethnic and confessional constituencies, of a sample of grass roots opinion leaders? Should inclusion be an ongoing process or a single event? For example, is it more effective to negotiate a power-sharing pact among key groups (however defined) or is there possible merit in a periodic "national dialogue" to address issues that risk triggering conflict? The chapters by Gilles Yabi, Susan Stigant and Elizabeth Murray, David Smith and Stephanie Wolters point in different ways to a variety of techniques that can be deployed to build inclusivity and to reach those voices that may not be well represented at the political centre. The chapter on west Africa by Alexandre Marc, Neelam Nizan Verjee and Stephen Mogaka discusses inclusion at

both the national and regional levels, and argues that this region has made important strides toward building social cohesion since the end of the conflicts experienced in the 1990s and early 2000s. On the other hand, it may not always be possible to manage or control political conflict. Rather, it may be necessary to accept some measure of conflict fluidity and mobility in which actors and groups operate in a dynamic "political marketplace" where violence and political tools operate side by side, to use Alex de Waal's striking conception.

Building an inclusive political system also raises the question of what levels of society to include and how to assure that local communities as well as groups operating at the national level can get their voices heard. I William Zartman notes that traditional authorities may offer better informed and connected governance, provided they are not simply interested in decentralized self-enrichment and that they operate within the rule of modern or customary law. The chapter by Callisto Madavo suggests that the private sector, through its economic activities, offers another powerful venue to contribute directly to peace and stability, especially in societies recovering from conflict. Allan Ngari and Raeesah Cachalia point out that legal norms are an integral part of the discussion about inclusivity since they affect every aspect of economic and personal life and can help to sew a peaceful social fabric. However, a critical question arises over whether the individual or the group takes precedence in the normative hierarchy.

Still another dimension of the inclusion question relates to demographic cohorts, as explored in the chapters by Marc Sommers, Akinyi Walender and Mariama Awumbila. African women, youth and migrants from rural to urban areas (including migrant women) all face issues of exclusion that can have an impact on conflict and governance. Misguided policies at the national level along with cultural constraints facing these social groups combine to increase exclusion and create seeds of future trouble.

Resilience Gone Wrong

The ideal attributes of a society resilient to conflict, according to Lauren Van Metre (2014), feature social solidarity and cohesion, a sense of fairness and equity, and an ability to participate in decision making. This proposition obliges us to recognize several sobering features of current conditions. First, some social groups and institutions with the potential to weave a cohesive fabric may, in practice, have less benign goals. In some cases, as Pierre Englebert, Mathurin Houngnikpo and Charles Owuor Olungah remind us, their goals may be limited to manipulating or capturing the formal political institutions. Moreover, proposals and policies to strengthen the state may exacerbate the risks of particularistic capture by powerful coercive actors, adding to societal stress and undermining solidarity. Much depends, as discussed below, on the nature and vitality of the society's political institutions.

Second, we have wrestled in this project with the varied meanings of resilience in the context of African conflict management. The core of the problem is the relative emphasis to be placed on social and political stability on the one hand, and on the ability to solve problems and bring about needed change on the other. The dilemma is not confined to Africa; it is universal. But African societies are exposed to severe pressures, while governments must operate in an environment of high social demands and limited resources and capacity to meet them. All too often, the political reflex of weak or fragile regimes facing such pressures is to "circle the wagons" instead of calling for a "town hall" meeting or an *indaba*. This reflex points toward authoritarian policies that may produce a type of temporary resilience of the regime, but also leads to shaky political stability, declining cohesion and eventual regime brittleness.

The third point revolves around terrorism. The risk of terrorism used to be associated with desert wastelands or remote regions where government presence is weak. But vulnerability has moved to cities such as Abidjan, Ouagadougou, Bamako and Nairobi. When violent actors such as terrorist movements seek not only to challenge the state but also to replace it, we should not be surprised when incumbent regimes fight back and, in some cases, exploit the challenge in order to crack down on anyone they can accuse of links to extremists. Nor is it surprising if such regimes succeed in recruiting external partners to join the fray. In the short-term, these may be the obvious alternatives, even though these scenarios appear more likely to produce a narrowing base of support for the regime and to add more targets for extremist recruitment.

Some regimes seem resilient because of their staying power, but actually have a narrow base of support founded on exclusionary policies. The regime in this case co-opts the state and dissolves civil society. When a seemingly brittle regime reaches the end of its life, it becomes clear that the state and the regime have become indistinguishable from each other. The state-society gap is a regime-society gap, while the state withers and its institutions become hollow shells that serve mainly to extract rents. This kind of false resilience leads to state decay and social alienation, strengthening a few and oppressing many.

The Elusive Nature of Social Cohesion

A sense that the national government serves all citizens equally is also important to building social cohesion. The reality is that most African states are far from realizing this objective. A survey conducted by GlobeScan for the Centre for International Governance Innovation (CIGI) in April 2016 asked respondents in Ghana, Kenya, Nigeria, Senegal and South Africa, to rate the performance of their national governments in a number of issue areas including addressing terrorism, out-migration, climate change, poverty, corruption, disease and "responding to the need of our population." (CIGI-GlobeScan 2016). Answers varied by country, but as the chart below indicates, respondents in Ghana, Kenya and South Africa gave their governments relatively low marks across the board, whereas respondents in Nigeria and Senegal gave higher marks to their governments in addressing terrorism, fighting corruption, and reducing disease (see Table 1). In all countries, interviewees thought their governments were doing a better job in fighting terrorism than reducing poverty or responding to the needs of the population (the exception was in Ghana where government performance on terrorism and serving population needs received the same relatively low score).

However, when asked about which of these issues concerned them most on a personal basis, poverty outranked terrorism in every country except Kenya, and corruption was at the top of the list in every country apart from Senegal (see Table 2). The survey also indicated regional differences within countries on these issues, pointing to the situations in which certain parts of individual countries felt more marginalized and disaffected. Despite the fact that these governments range from middling to high in the Freedom House rankings of democracies, the survey highlights a gap between state and society on some of the most important popular issues (Freedom House 2016).

Table 1: Government Performance By Country, in Percentages

	Ghana	Kenya	Nigeria	Senegal	South Africa
Average Performance	32	30	42	38	35
Addressing terrorism	35	37	56	62	36
Avoiding migration	28	34	39	32	32
Addressing climate change	31	45	35	38	40
Reducing poverty	28	20	24	40	32
Addressing corruption	27	12	54	40	27
Reducing disease	39	40	56	67	47
Responding to the needs of the population	35	24	27	41	32

Data source: CIGI-Globescan (2016).

Table 2: Personal Concern with Each Global Issue, in Percentages

	Ghana	Kenya	Nigeria	Senegal	South Africa
Terrorism	88	96	96	76	76
Emigration	77	64	79	64	73
Climate change	89	80	89	61	83
Poverty	91	95	98	92	95
Corruption	94	96	98	82	96
Disease	91	95	95	87	93

Data source: CIGI-Globescan (2016).

Social cohesion arises often in states with a mostly homogeneous population, as was the case with the Nordic countries until relatively recently. This cohesion shapes the political culture and has made it possible to identify a "Nordic model" of social democracy based on a political system that incorporates consultation and consensus. Social cohesion in Africa will look different. African countries are generally characterized by diversity rather than homogeneity, by different tribes, clans, ethnic groups and religious communities. Social cohesion may have to draw on common narratives and their interpretations, imaginary communities (in Benedict Anderson's words) constructed to help form a sense of allegiance to an idea or body outside of one's own group (Anderson 2006). A critical factor in building social cohesion is developing a sense of common goals and objectives about social and political issues that touch the broader population — how people relate to each other and to their government; participation in public policy; decisions around the use of natural resource revenues (especially in countries that hold natural resources to be the property of the state rather than private individuals or companies); responses to droughts, floods or famine; the effects of a massive economic upheaval; the sanctity of the constitution; relations with "the other," and similarly weighty issues.

Developing a sense of social cohesiveness over these issues takes time, but it also takes a willingness on the part of individuals and groups to engage in the process. In a multicultural setting, that sense of cohesion might come from norms and beliefs that are embraced by most of the inhabitants, such as in Canada. An embrace of local democracy and neutrality have bound together the three language groups in Switzerland for more than 200 years. A commitment to "democracy, development, self-reliance and unity" in Botswana has guided relatively peaceful relations in that country for over 50 years (Masire 2016). Another means of producing a sense of cohesion is through sports, the arts and other activities that bring people together. Nelson Mandela understood well the power of using sports in constructing a national identity when he appeared at the 1995 Rugby World Cup in the jersey of the Springboks national rugby team, which had been a symbol of the white minority's favourite sport in apartheid South Africa.

It is clear that in order to bridge the divides identified above and build more equitable societies, it is necessary to engage both state and wider social environment. How can states and societies work together to build social cohesion, and increase a sense of fairness and inclusiveness in decision making? And what can the international community do to help? The following observations may serve to start the process.

The Response

If African decision makers wish to strengthen the conflict management capacity in their institutions, they should focus on three main areas: supporting social cohesion, encouraging fairness and promoting political inclusion. These suggestions come out of the thoughtful essays included in this book and are offered in full recognition of the complexity of the task. It is easy to recommend and much harder to realize. These remarks are not aimed at one particular audience, but are offered to all persons engaged in trying to help societies successfully to cope with the risks of conflict onset and recurrence — civil society members, traditional and social group leaders, local and national authorities, and international funders and practitioners.

The Importance of Leadership

Good leadership in both official circles and in civil society is critical to building strong relationships within and between the two sectors. Leadership in government — national and local — has to recognize the potential that broader social groups and institutions (including civil society) bring to the table. For instance, these social entities can help to give a government or specific policies legitimacy, provide a conduit for communication between the government and the people, and become a rich source of new approaches to old problems. Civil society needs to know how to reflect its community's concerns, to help authorities that are genuine in their objectives to address those concerns, and to call to account those that are not. Official authorities need to make room for civil society, and civil society needs to know how to act as a bridge between authorities and the people.

Princeton Lyman emphasizes in his chapter the key role that leaders can play in averting disaster and acting to strengthen the social fabric, giving an opportunity for the right sort of political institutions to take root. He notes the telling contrast between South Africa (where leaders stopped before plunging the country into civil war in the midst of the historic transition to majority rule) and South Sudan (where leaders were "willing to tear the country asunder in pursuit of their political aims" just a few years after independence).

The Importance of Fact-based Analysis

A critical aspect of good leadership is the ability to ask questions and listen to the answers, to analyze information well and develop policy around a strong understanding of the consequences. Marc Sommers' chapter discusses Rwanda's policy of "villagization" — instituted with the purpose of providing better services to a previously far-flung population — which has had the unintended consequences of locking young men out of the housing market. Mariama Awumbila notes that government assumptions that urban migration leads to increased unemployment and crime-filled neighbourhoods instead of a richer urban environments have produced anti-migration policies discouraging free movement of labour. Assumptions that women can only play a victim's role in conflict rather than being active contributors have excluded from peace processes half of the population whose participation is vital if peace is to last. The kind of research that upends these assumptions could come from government itself or from civil society, but the best resource is the network of African universities that conduct rigorous research on a regular basis. Making room to reach out to these institutions is always difficult for busy practitioners, but the contribution they can make to good policy is well worth the effort.

The Need for Communication and Feedback

As the Susan Stigant and Elizabeth Murray chapter indicated, national dialogues provide opportunities for authorities to consult with large swaths of the population and for citizenry to articulate and form coalitions around issues. While their success must be measured by how much public opinion affects official policy, the process of consultation, of a sense of give and take with the authorities, is also important. However, they are large, expensive processes that are most appropriate for discussion about the biggest issues — the nature of the state and where it is going. On the other hand, polling exercises and surveys can give a sense of public opinion on smaller issues and the barriers to conducting these surveys have been reduced in the era of social media. At the local level, dialogue processes can provide a means to surface issues and, as importantly, to build relations among disparate communities. And opening the space for radio programming on the same themes in different languages can also help to build a common understanding of issues of concern across society.

The Search for Inclusion and Cohesion

The requirements for a strong social environment for peace — one that brings significant assets to conflict management — may vary from place to place, but a common element is a stress on the participation of many peoples, groups and institutions in activities ranging from social occasions to official business. In recent decades, inclusion has been recognized as a critical element for effective governance, social and economic development, and peacemaking, but how to achieve inclusion remains elusive.

As this book has emphasized, a few institutions play outsized roles in setting social attitudes. Outside of the home, the education system is the most important mechanism for transmitting understanding, culture and social attitudes from one generation to the next. Increasing access to educational opportunity is a high priority for many countries, but this policy in Kenya did not necessarily result in a more equitable educational system. There are more institutions but at a cost to quality, and the new institutions — captured as they are by different ethnic groups — serve to exclude some groups as they expand opportunity for others. Not being able to access education adds to the alienation of the youth. Recognizing the importance of civic education, of expanding access to secondary education, and of preparing students well for future employment are important components. So is the deliberate search for a common understanding of history, for literatures and arts that recognize diversity while bringing out the universal nature of the experience, and for curriculum that is not one-sided or prejudicial toward other groups,

The justice system, including courts and policing practices, also plays a vital role in determining whether inhabitants feel that they are getting equitable treatment under the law and in comparison with their peers. A sense of equal status under the law is a critical component of a healthy society that resolves disputes peacefully. The rule of law also applies to the complex issue of enabling rural Africans to obtain titles to their land, protecting them from abuse by powerful interests and serving as a basis for grassroots dispute settlement. However, trust in the law — the law-making apparatus, the courts, prosecutors and judges — as well as confidence that political leaders will respect basic laws should be bolstered. Strengthening legal institutions is vital to supporting a rule-of-law culture. In so doing, taking specific measures to help prevent and resolve conflict — equal (or at least fair) access to justice and development of transitional justice legislation to handle past grievances — can help to build a sense of social belonging. Incorporation of human security norms into policing as part of a nation-wide effort to reform the security sector in post-conflict settings can also help to build trust in the law as an instrument of fairness as well as justice.

A long-term route to political and economic success has been comprehensively documented by Daron Acemoglu and James Robinson (2012) in their study of why nations fail or succeed. In this view, nations fail because of "extractive economic and political institutions" that do not provide incentives for growth and stability. They succeed when there are political conditions that permit a broad coalition to impose "pluralist political institutions" and "limits and restraints" on ruling elites. Thus, resilience of both state and society may hinge in the end on the rule of law replacing the rule of men. This rarely happens as a result of gradual tinkering with reformist agendas. Often, the development of inclusive institutions involves struggles that enable political and societal actors to check the domination of entrenched rulers and to broaden participation in policy decisions. Such turning points occur in specific historical circumstances that arise in a society's development. This point is well illustrated in the excerpted remarks of former Botswana President Ketumile Masire. Unfortunately, as Alex de Waal points out, there are *other* circumstances where formal institutions and official rules are "subordinate to the transactional 'real politics' of

trading power and material benefits." In this kind of "political marketplace," politics is essentially about elite competition to capture the state and extract resources for the benefit of a ruling group. This poses hard choices, but also opportunities for other political and social groups — embrace or avoid the marketplace or find ways to confront it.

Exclusion Has Consequences

An outcome of a marketplace approach to politics is the strong possibility that one or several groups will be excluded from the process. Nearly every country in the world faces challenges around the exclusion of some subsection of society. Exclusion does not always come from deliberate intentions to cut people out of the social process. It can be the result of an economic downturn or policies that have unintended consequences, for instance, the "villagization" policies that put the price of houses out of reach of young people just starting their working life. However, the cost of excluding youth from the status and benefits of adulthood denies a whole generation the opportunity to participate as constructive members of society. Excluding women from political participation prevents half of the population from contributing to public policy. Excluding members of minority groups from social, political and economic spheres fuels resentment and resistance to the legitimacy of local and national authorities.

Gathering power around central authorities tends to result in exclusion, if only because it is difficult for central governments to represent all voices and all groups. Ceding power to local authorities would help to increase this representation; however, it is also difficult for national governments to devolve responsibility to the local level. The rise of divergent points of view in society, whether in civil society or in other associational groups is also often viewed as a challenge to authority. Where state institutions are unable to assert and maintain effective central authority, the result may only guarantee a political free-for-all in which no one is able to establish institutions of governance.

And yet, as several authors in this book point out, devolution of power and diversity of points of engagement can improve communication, legitimacy and impact rather than undercut them. Alex Thurston observes that social fragmentation, rather than threatening the state, "creates possibilities for greater cosmopolitanism, more effective denunciations of radicals and productive competition leading to more accountable leadership in both religion and politics". Others have suggested that having several systems to achieve the same goals — for instance, elders practising conflict management alongside courts — creates a redundancy that promotes resilience in many cases (Sagarin 2015). A society organized around exclusion will not be able to develop healthily redundant systems that can support each other in times of crisis.

Building on Structures and Institutions That Work

An important element of promoting resilience is to build on structures and institutions that work. These are structures and institutions that are capable of delivering the services that society needs without negative consequences in terms of access, rights or security. In some instances, this may mean strengthening institutions that already exist, or getting some state institutions (for example, central banks, courts, public service commissions, electoral commissions) beyond the direct control of the regime. It may also mean making space for civil society and community-based activities. These structures that work exist at all levels. Akinyi Walender relates the story of the spontaneous organizing of women to set up a feeding centre during the 1998 humanitarian crisis in what is now South Sudan. I William Zartman highlights the potential of traditional systems of conflict management to resolve local level conflict, particularly in the area of land disputes. Alex de Waal agrees, reminding the reader that "[t]he study of 'fragile states' has moved towards recognizing that non-formal political systems can 'work.'" And in their discussion of

the growth of resilience in west Africa, Alexandre Marc, Neelam Nizar Verjee and Stephen Mogaka note the particular contribution of the Economic Community of West African States in reinforcing democratic norms. Where institutions and structures do not work properly and only serve the interests of a narrow elite, there is a need for basic political change, as in some of the cases discussed by Mathurin Houngnikpo, and Charles Owuor Olungah. Equally important is identifying existing institutions and structures that do work (or have worked in the past) and can provide a strong base for increasing resilience and conflict management capacity.

Implications for Africa's Partners

While these themes are most relevant for African audiences, they also have implications for Africa's partners. Most important is to support efforts within and among African countries to build resilience and support efforts to build more cohesive, inclusive and flexible societies. Being effective partners in these circumstances may mean changing the way that outside partners function, particularly in the area of funding. Donor agencies are often required to develop relatively short-term programming with outcomes that can be evaluated and monitored. This may help to determine the efficiency of the donor agency, but it does not necessarily provide the kind of long-term collaboration that societies need in order to bring formerly excluded individuals and groups into civil and political spheres. Equally, a focus on efficiency might prevent support for the types of redundant systems that foster resiliency. Changing these approaches to programming is not an insurmountable hurdle for donor agencies. Rather, it is a matter of adapting ongoing programs and projects so that they focus on building resilient societies as well as economic development, effective governance and national security. As the above discussion makes clear, external partners should carefully assess the diverse conditions of governance in specific African countries in order to weigh basic choices about engagement, disengagement and strengthening institutions that work.

A place to start is to dig deeper into the communities affected by international activities. For decades, the principal interlocutors of international partners were governments, with the rest of society well hidden from sight behind officialdom. In the last two decades, ties between international non-governmental organizations and local civil society actors have been greatly strengthened in almost all countries on the continent, and a number of foreign governments and international institutions have followed suit in reaching beyond governments. However, the international community outreach is often limited to local institutions that have mastered the Western approach to funding (Srinivasan 2016). Other institutions — some of which represent more closely local concerns and attitudes — remain out of reach. Connecting beyond the usual partners will help international actors to understand better the social environment of their interlocutors. International partners also need to recognize the divisive potential of their own programming and focus instead on projects that strengthen social cohesion — supporting unifying leadership and activities that are meaningful to local communities.

The process of weaving a fabric of peace on a continent of 54 countries is complicated. The process takes time and engages vast and diverse populations. Outsiders can suggest models and help locate strong, resilient threads. But the creation of this tapestry will be Africa's own and the texture, colour and design will reflect African experience, desires and vision.

The Journey of Botswana: Where we come from, where we are, who we are and where we are heading

Excerpt from a lecture by Sir Ketumile Masire, former president of Botswana, to the Botswana International University of Science and Technology, June 28, 2016.*

[W]hen I saw that I was asked to speak about the journey of Botswana — where we come from, where we are, who we are and where we are heading — I wondered, where does one begin? It struck me as a topic that could fill several books.... But, on further reflection, I thought I might rather try to dig a bit deeper by focusing on some of the long-standing, shared qualities that have defined who we are as a nation.

Certainly, one of our strengths as a nation has been our ability of the last five decades to uphold our unity in diversity through our practices of consultation and consensus building, buttressed by tolerance and mutual respect. Other social values that have propelled our progress would include our prudence and, at least in the past, collective commitment to self-reliance.... I believe that the democracy and good governance we enjoy today has to a great extent been grounded in our own social norms, rather than in foreign ideology.

In this context, while the 81 years of British overrule that ended in 1966 was an important, indeed transformative, episode in our history, it was clearly not the beginning of our story. Archaeologists have shown that for at least two millennia the territory of Botswana, along with the rest of Southern Africa, has been a place of continuous settlement and interaction among people of various cultures and economic livelihoods. Such findings confirm the fact that our contemporary communities are the heirs of an ancient indigenous cultural cluster, which has given rise to its own enduring values.

Over the centuries, what we now know as Botswana has been, as it remains, the home of people of different languages and ethnic traditions living, more often than not, in harmony with each other and the land they share. Lest my words appear overly romantic, let me acknowledge that, as with virtually any part of the world, the social orders that have evolved in Botswana were not without inequality, exploitation and, on occasion, even violent conflict. But the best evidence is that such conflict among local communities was of a relatively modest scale. The mid-nineteenth century was characterised in Botswana, as elsewhere in the region, as a period of turbulence. Yet even during this epoch, the general pattern was for various local communities to join together in the face of external threats from, for example, the Amandebele and Boers.

I rather make the point that the ideal, and challenges, of realising unity in diversity is not new to us. It has been an aspect of our pre-colonial, as well as post-colonial, sovereignty. Modern Botswana's 50th anniversary is thus an opportunity for us to once more take stock of our diverse identity by asking ourselves who we are and wish to be as a collective? We have certainly come a long way since 1966. But this is [only] relevant to the extent that it may guide us toward further progress.

Any state's path of development is marked by continuity and change. The collective wisdom of any political or social order, therefore, lies in its ability to strike an appropriate, that is to say prudent, balance between that which can and should be changed and that which is preserved. Such prudent sentiment is reflective of traits that have and will continue to guide us as we build upon the legacy of our forebears.

In this dynamic era of globalization, driven as it is by rapid technological transformation, no society or social aspect can be isolated from change. An evolutionary state must, therefore, have the capacity to respond to the shifting needs and legitimate expectations of its own citizens. At the same time, it should be appreciated that the underlying values that hold together any community are often quite resilient.

Around the world, globalization has not led to anything like a homogenization of outlook. For the foreseeable future, we shall continue to live in a multicultural world. As elsewhere, Botswana will continue to progress within a framework of its own evolving values and perspectives.... In 1970, [Botswana's first president] Seretse Khama observed in an address at the Dag Hammarskjold Centre in Sweden:

> "We in Botswana have chosen to develop our own guiding principles and describe them in terms readily comprehensible to our people. And these principles, rooted in our culture and traditions, are now being tested in practice [such as Kgotla].[1] Although we have chosen to develop our own ideology, our nationalism and our non-alignment will not be permitted to degenerate into narrow chauvinism and isolation. Rather we seek to identify ourselves with what is positive and humane in all national ideologies. We recognize certain fundamental values and hold them to be universal."

Any country's success is, in part, a reflection of its willingness to accept and adapt, but also reject, external influences as appropriate. In our own case, we have been fortunate over the years to have benefited from the metaphysical, as well as material, contributions of development. This was facilitated by the fact that they shared our basic aspirations. To once more quote our first president, this time from a statement he made in Denmark just two days later: "We are aware of our limitations but we are not without aspirations. Our principle aspiration is to make a contribution to the victory of democracy, dignity and self-determination throughout South Africa. This ambition must be fulfilled by the only means available to us — the development of Botswana as a viable non-racial democracy whose unity and independence is based on social and economic justice for its people, regardless of race, colour or tribe." What Seretse, back in 1970, described as the four pillars of our national ideal of Kagisano remained as the guiding principles of our Vision 2016: democracy, development, self-reliance and unity....[2]

It has been often said that a lack of internal social coherence has been a common weakness of many of Africa's post-colonial states. This is generally attributed to the challenges of managing ethnic and/or regional competition over the nation's largess, resulting, in popular parlance, in the so-called curse of tribalism.

It has also been alleged that Botswana's peculiar progress has been paralleled by a relatively high degree of internal cohesion. To the extent that this latter assumption holds true, and I believe to the greater extent it does, why is this then the case?

One explanation that can be dismissed is that our lack of severe intercommunal conflict is a reflection of social homogeneity. As I have observed, Botswana has for many centuries been the common home of various ethnolinguistic groups. Another misconception, albeit one with an element of truth, is that our success can simply be ascribed to our mineral wealth. While our progress over the past five decades has, heretofore, indeed been largely financed by the exploitation of minerals, more especially diamonds, this alone certainly did not get us to where we are today. Indeed, the prevailing literature on natural resource development in recent years has tended to emphasize the notion that their exploitation can be as much an economic and social curse as a boon.

Just as the various ethnic identities found in modern Botswana have a long history of living and interacting with one another, so too have they shared certain common values, including a basic belief in government of and by the people. This has been and remains true at the local, traditional leadership level, as well as with our more modern state structures. We thus may view ourselves not only as a mature democracy in light of our uninterrupted record of multi-party politics. We can also believe that we are an indigenous democracy in the context of a deeply embedded political culture that values consultation and mutual respect….

No matter how venerable, political and social value systems cannot exist in isolation of material conditions. Given the extent of Botswana's poverty 50 years ago, when we were rated as one of the five least developed countries in the world, what beside our democratic nature has ensured that our natural wealth became a boon, rather than a burden? I believe that the answer lies in our decision at independence to reaffirm the principle that the natural resources of Botswana are our common heritage. For this reason, their ownership is legally vested with the state irrespective of who owns the land upon which they are found.

As was the case with our traditional authorities in the past, the modern state is further understood to be acting as the steward for the citizenry not only of today but also of tomorrow. This basic principle is equally true in the context of the minerals under our ground, our wildlife, and our communal and state lands. The above is consistent with a common understanding, found among virtually all of our indigenous communities, that nature can never be owned. It is also a pragmatic appreciation of the fact that as long as we are a developing country, dependent on finite natural resources, it will be necessary to ensure that they continue to be of direct benefit to all our citizens, rather than just those few who by a chance of birthplace or geography find themselves sitting on a particular deposit.

It was our underlying unity, combined with the grace of God, which shielded us throughout the turbulent years of our region's liberation struggles. Let us also take pride in the fact that when our neighbours resisted violent and racist minorities, our nation remained at the frontline of their struggle. Their struggle was, indeed, our struggle…. Over the years, this has tested our forebears', as well as our own, ability to strike an appropriate balance between that which can and should be changed and that which ought to be preserved. This is true in the realms of both cultural and natural heritage.

The sustained economic progress we have registered over the past 50 years, prudence in the use of our nation's resources and our determination to remain a peaceful, united and proud nation are all among the many reasons why we deserve to celebrate…. Let us further recognize that the challenges we face moving forward will continue to require combined efforts and collective sacrifice. We should be mindful of the fact that, regardless of the development strides we have made, we are still very much a developing society, located within a still marginalized continent.

If we are to attain the levels of development that we aspire to, we also need to resuscitate our national principle of self-reliance. Like many elders, I am concerned that we seem to be losing our grip on the time-tested spirit of self-reliance. While I am aware that many of our fellow citizens were born when our fortunes had enormously improved, I need to remind the nation that it was only through the spirit of self-help and hard work that our poverty-stricken country survived the worst phases of its existence. The role of government should, therefore, be to empower its citizens to succeed in today's increasingly competitive world, not to protect them from it.

Works Cited

Acemoglu, Daron and James A. Robinson. 2012. *Why Nations Fail: The Origins of Power, Prosperity, and Poverty.* New York, NY: Random House (Crown).

Anderson, Benedict. 2006. *Imagined Communities: Reflections on the Origin and Spread of Nationalism.* Revised edition. Verso Books.

CIGI-GlobeScan. 2016. *A Changing Tide in Africa: Conflict, Corruption & Economic Opportunity.* A five-country public opinion survey. www.cigionline.org/africa-poll-2016.

Freedom House. 2016. *Anxious Dictators, Wavering Democracies: Global Freedom under Pressure.* Freedom in the World 2016. https://freedomhouse.org/sites/default/files/FH_FITW_Report_2016.pdf.

Masire, Ketumile. 2016. "The Journey of Botswana, Where We Come From; Where We Are, Who We Are, and Where Are We Heading." Lecture delivered at Botswana International University of Science and Technology. June 29. www.facebook.com/Botswana.Government/posts/1030059667076691:0.

Sagarin, Rafe. 2015. "Learning from the Octopus: What Nature Can Tell Us about Adapting to a Changing World." In *Managing Conflict in a World Adrift,* edited by Chester A. Crocker, Fen Osler Hampson and Pamela Aall. Washington, DC: US Institute of Peace Press.

Srinivasan, Sharath. 2016. "Civil Society as Counter-Power: Rethinking International Support Toward Tackling Conflict and Fostering Non-Violent Politics in Africa." In *Minding the Gap: African Conflict Management in a Time of Change,* edited by Pamela Aall and Chester A. Crocker. Waterloo, ON: CIGI.

Van Metre, Lauren. 2014. "Resilience as a Peacebuilding Practice: To Realism from Idealism." US Institute of Peace Insights. Washington, DC. www.usip.org/insights-newsletter/resilience-peacebuilding-practice-realism-idealism.

Contributors

Pamela Aall is a senior fellow with CIGI's Global Security & Politics Program, leading the African Regional Conflict Management project. She is also a senior adviser for conflict prevention and management at the United States Institute of Peace (USIP), where she was founding provost of the USIP's Academy for International Conflict Management and Peacebuilding. She is on the advisory council of the European Institute of Peace, and serves on the boards of Women in International Security and the International Peace and Security Institute.

Kofi Annan is the founding chair of the Kofi Annan Foundation, a Nobel Peace Prize laureate (2001), and was the seventh Secretary-General of the United Nations (1997–2006). With the support of his Foundation, Kofi Annan mobilizes political will to overcome threats to peace, development and human rights.

Mariama Awumbila is associate professor at the Department of Geography and Resource Development and, until August 2013, was also the founding director of the Centre for Migration Studies, both at the University of Ghana. She has undertaken extensive research and published in the areas of migration, livelihoods and development; intra-regional labour migration in West Africa; and gender and development in Africa, among others. Mariama recently facilitated the Ghana government toward the development of Ghana's national migration policy. She currently serves on several professional and national governing boards.

Chester A. Crocker is a distinguished fellow at CIGI. He is the James R. Schlesinger Professor of Strategic Studies at Georgetown University's Walsh School of Foreign Service, and serves on the board of its Institute for the Study of Diplomacy. A former assistant secretary of state for African affairs (1981–1989), he served as chairman of the board of USIP (1992–2004) and is a founding member of the Global Leadership Foundation. With Fen Osler Hampson and Pamela Aall, he has edited and authored a number of books on conflict management and mediation.

Raeesah Cassim Cachalia is a South Africa-based researcher who has worked within government as well as in civil society. Her areas of interest include conflict, violent extremism and human rights, with an emphasis on the Middle East and north Africa. Raeesah holds a B.A. in law (international relations) and an LL.B. from the University of Pretoria and is currently pursuing her LL.M. (human rights law) at the University of South Africa. Raeesah's most recent published works focus on youth radicalization and violent extremism in Africa.

Leila Demarest is a Ph.D. fellow at the Centre for Research on Peace and Development at the University of Leuven (KU Leuven). She is in the final stages of her Ph.D., which focuses on social movements and (violent) protest dynamics in Sub-Saharan Africa. Leila has extensive field research experience in Senegal and Nigeria and has published both qualitative and quantitative papers on the subject of her Ph.D. research.

Alex de Waal is executive director of the World Peace Foundation and research professor at the Fletcher School of Law and Diplomacy, Tufts University. He is considered one of the foremost experts on Sudan and the Horn of Africa. His scholarly work and practice has also probed humanitarian crisis and response, human rights, HIV/AIDS and governance in Africa, and conflict and peace building. Alex has served as an adviser to the African Union for mediation efforts in Sudan and has published several books, including, most recently, *The Real Politics of the Horn of Africa: Money, War and the Business of Power* (Polity 2015). He was on the list of *Foreign Policy*'s 100 most influential public intellectuals in 2008 and *Atlantic Monthly*'s 27 "brave thinkers" in 2009.

Pierre Englebert is the H. Russell Smith Professor of International Relations and professor of African politics at Pomona College. His research focuses on the political economy of African states, with an emphasis on Central and West francophone Africa. His most recent books include *Inside*

African Politics (with Kevin Dunn, 2013) and *Africa: Unity, Sovereignty and Sorrow* (2009). He is a member of the editorial boards of *African Affairs* and the *Journal of Modern African Studies*.

Mathurin C. Houngnikpo is an independent scholar on security sector reform and civil-military relations in Africa. Until July 2013, he was the academic chair of civil-military relations at the Africa Center for Strategic Studies. In that capacity, Mathurin oversaw curriculum and program development in the area of civil-military relations, focusing on Africa's military history, democratic control of the security sector and issues of strategic thinking, accountability, transparency and good governance. His publications include *L'Afrique au Futur Conditionnel* (2011); *Guarding the Guardians: Civil-Military Relations and Democratic Governance in Africa* (2010); and *Economic Integration and Development in Africa* (with H. Kyambalesa, 2006). He holds a doctorate in political science from the University of Paris VIII and a Ph.D. in international studies from the University of Denver.

Arnim Langer is the director of the Centre for Research on Peace and Development and associate professor of international relations and chair holder of the UNESCO Chair in Building Sustainable Peace at the University of Leuven (KU Leuven). He is also a research associate at the Oxford Department of International Development at the University of Oxford in the United Kingdom and an honorary research fellow at the University of Western Australia in Perth, Australia. His research focuses on the causes and consequences of conflict, post-conflict reconstruction, sustainable peace building, the dynamics of horizontal inequalities, and group behaviour and identity formation processes.

Princeton N. Lyman is senior adviser to the president of the USIP. His career with the US government included positions as deputy assistant secretary of state for African affairs, US ambassador to Nigeria, director of the refugee bureau, US ambassador to South Africa, assistant secretary of state for international organization affairs and presidential special envoy for Sudan and South Sudan. He is a board member of the National Endowment for Democracy and co-chair of the Carter Center's Africa-China-United States Consultation for Peace. He has a Ph.D. in political science from Harvard University and has published books and articles on US foreign policy, African affairs, economic development, HIV/AIDS, UN reform, peacekeeping and conflict resolution.

Callisto Madavo is a visiting professor in the African Studies Program at Georgetown University. He held several senior level positions in the World Bank, including as the regional vice president and vice president for the Africa region and country director for the East Asia and East Africa regions, as well as division chief of the Pakistan programs department. Most recently, he served as a special adviser to the president of the World Bank. Callisto was in charge of a myriad of World Bank-supported activities in 47 Sub-Saharan African countries including Kenya, Ethiopia, Uganda, Somalia and Sudan. The main activities focused on economic growth and poverty reduction, and promotion of good governance. Other activities included private sector development, post-conflict programs and social sector development.

Alexandre Marc is the chief specialist for the Fragility, Conflict and Violence Group at the World Bank. He was the cluster leader for the Social Cohesion and Violence Prevention team within the Social Development Department of the World Bank from 2009 to 2012. Alexandre joined the World Bank in 1988 in the Africa Region and, from 1999 to 2005, was sector manager for social development in the Europe and central Asia region. In addition to his World Bank experience, Alexandre was director of the Roma Education Fund from 2006 to 2007 and

a visiting fellow, in 2005, at the Centre d'Etude des Relations Internationales in Paris. Alexandre holds a doctorate in political science from the Paris Institute of Political Studies (Sciences Po). His most recent publications are *The Challenge of Stability and Security in West Africa* (2015), *Societal Dynamics and Fragility: Engaging Societies in Responding to Fragile Situations* (2012) and *Violence in the City: Understanding and Supporting Community Responses to Urban Violence* (2010).

Stephen Mogaka is a consultant with the Fragility, Conflict and Violence Group of the World Bank. He is a Kenyan national and political scientist with a bachelor's degree in political science from the University of Delhi in India and a master's degree in political science from the University of Nairobi in Kenya. Stephen's areas of expertise and interest include identity politics in Africa, security sector reform, civil-military relations, democratization, and terrorism and counterterrorism. He is a co-author of *The Challenge of Stability and Security in West Africa* (2015) and *Power, Conflict, and Justice in Africa: An Uncertain March in Global Africa* (forthcoming).

Elizabeth Murray is a senior program officer for the USIP's Africa program, where she has overseen programming and research on the CAR, Uganda and Sudan. She also leads USIP's research on emerging conflicts in Africa and co-chairs USIP's national dialogue working group, which is developing case studies and thematic research to explore when and how national dialogue can be an effective tool for conflict management and peace building. Elizabeth first joined USIP to work on the institute's grant making in Colombia, and she also authored a chapter on Honduras in USIP's recent edited volume *Electing Peace: Violence Prevention and Impact at the Polls*.

Donald Anthony Mwiturubani was a senior researcher in the environmental security program of the Institute for Security Studies' Nairobi office and a formal lecturer of geography at the University of Dar es Salaam, Tanzania. He holds a B.A. in land-use planning and environmental studies, an M.A. in geography and environmental studies and a master of research and Ph.D. in water resources management.

Allan Ngari is a senior researcher in the Transnational Threats and International Crimes Division at the Institute for Security Studies. He holds a bachelor of law (hons.) from the University of Nairobi, Kenya, and a master's in international criminal law (cum laude) from Stellenbosch University, South Africa. Allan is an advocate of the High Court of Kenya with experience in civil litigation, conveyancing, commercial law and international criminal law and procedure. He has 10 years of experience working in transitional justice, particularly with accountability processes and participatory and reparative rights of victims of armed conflict and affected communities. His professional and academic interests lie in the international criminal justice system and, specifically, its impact on and correlation with domestic criminal justice systems. Allan previously worked as a project leader for the Kenya and International Justice Desk at the Institute for Justice and Reconciliation, Cape Town, South Africa, and the Chambers of the International Criminal Tribunal for Rwanda in Arusha, Tanzania.

Charles Owuor Olungah is a senior research fellow and director of the Institute of Anthropology, Gender and African Studies, University of Nairobi. He holds a B.A. in anthropology from the University of Nairobi, a master of philosophy in social anthropology and the community from the University of Cambridge, a postgraduate diploma in research methodology from the University of Copenhagen and a Ph.D. in anthropology from the University of Nairobi. His research interests are in the areas of reproductive health, violence and conflict

resolution, development anthropology, democracy and political participation. Charles has consulted for various organizations locally, regionally and internationally in areas of reproductive health, gender and political participation, gender violence and conflict resolution.

Eghosa E. Osaghae is a tenured professor of comparative politics at the University of Ibadan and is currently vice chancellor of Igbinedion University Okada, Nigeria. He was the Emeka Anyoaku Chair of Commonwealth Studies at the University of London in 2013/2014 and delivered the chair's inaugural lecture, "A State of Our Own: Second Independence, Federalism and the Decolonization of the State in Africa," in April 2014. Eghosa is leader of the Programme on Ethnic and Federal Studies at the University of Ibadan and also served as director of the university's Centre for Peace and Conflict Studies in 2004. He has published extensively on ethnicity, federalism, state politics and governance in books and journals. Eghosa served as chair of the panel on quality assurance assessment, United Nations Economic Commission for Africa, 2011-2012, and, as a consultant to the African Development Bank's country mission to Zambia, he produced the country's governance profile in 2002.

Simon Palamar is a research fellow in the Global Security & Politics program at CIGI. His research interests and expertise include arms control, non-proliferation and disarmament, mediation and negotiation, armed conflict, and empirical research methods. He holds a Ph.D. from Carleton University's Norman Paterson School of International Affairs.

David Smith is the founding director of Okapi Consulting in Johannesburg, which specializes in media in conflict zones and fragile states. David's media projects have included Radio Okapi in the DRC, Dandal Kura Radio International in the Lake Chad region and Radio MINURCA (now Radio Ndeke Luka) in the CAR. A pop-up TV station, 1st TV Zimbabwe, took to the air less than two weeks after Okapi Consulting received a request to provide a platform for all points of view in the 2013 presidential elections. While working in conflict zones, David writes about books by local authors in an occasional column called Book Safari in the *Mail & Guardian*. He is currently working on his Ph.D. at the University of Johannesburg, jointly through the South African Research Chair in African Diplomacy and Foreign Policy, as well as with the Department of Anthropology and Development Studies.

Marc Sommers is an internationally recognized youth, conflict, peace building, gender and development expert. An anthropologist, Africanist and educationalist, he has provided technical advice and carried out research, assessment and evaluation work for donor and UN agencies, NGOs and policy institutes in 21 war-affected countries. Marc's books include *The Outcast Majority: War, Development, and Youth in Africa*, which received honourable mention for the 2016 Senior Book Prize; *Stuck: Rwandan Youth and the Struggle for Adulthood*, which received honourable mention for the 2013 Bethwell A. Ogot Book Prize; and *Fear in Bongoland: Burundi Refugees in Urban Tanzania*, which received the 2003 Margaret Mead Award. Marc taught for many years at the Fletcher School, Tufts University, and has had fellowships at the Woodrow Wilson International Center for Scholars and the USIP. He is a visiting researcher with the African Studies Center, Boston University, and a member of the UN Advisory Group of Experts for the Progress Study on Youth, Peace and Security.

Susan Stigant is the director of Africa Programs at the USIP, where she oversees programming in South Sudan, Nigeria, Sudan, the CAR, the DRC, Tanzania and Kenya and with the African Union. Susan's thematic focus is on the design and implementation of inclusive constitutional reform and national dialogue processes. She advises government officials and civil society actors on inclusive processes in Sudan, South Sudan, Libya, Somalia and elsewhere. Susan also serves as co-chair of USIP's national dialogue working group. Prior to joining USIP, she managed constitutional development, citizen engagement and election observation programs with the National Democratic Institute (NDI). From 2005 to 2011, Susan served as program director with NDI in South Sudan, where she supported the implementation of the peace agreement. She also worked with the Forum of Federations on comparative federalism and with the research unit of the Western Cape Provincial Parliament in South Africa.

Alexander Thurston is visiting assistant professor of African studies at Georgetown University. He has conducted field research in Senegal, Nigeria and Morocco. In 2013-2014, Alexander was an international affairs fellow with the Council on Foreign Relations. His first book, *Salafism in Nigeria: Islam, Preaching and Politics*, was published by Cambridge University Press in 2016.

Neelam Verjee has worked for the Fragility, Conflict and Violence Group of the World Bank since December 2013. She is a former journalist and has written extensively for the print media, including as a business reporter and features writer for *The Times* in London, England, from 2002 to 2007 and as a features writer for *Mint* in Mumbai, India, from 2007 to 2009, where she covered Bollywood. She has contributed to *Quartz*, an online publication of Atlantic Media. Previously, Verjee worked as program manager at Sisi Ni Amani, a Kenya-based NGO that developed technology as a tool for peace building, and for the World Policy Institute in New York. She has a master's degree in public administration from the School of International and Public Affairs at Columbia University and a bachelor of science degree in social policy and government from the London School of Economics. She is a co-author of *The Challenge of Stability and Security in West Africa* (World Bank 2015).

Akinyi Roselyn Walender is an expert in women, peace and security; women's economic and political empowerment; gender justice; and international development management. As country director in South Sudan and director of Women Leadership for Peace and Security in The Hague, Akinyi worked with women and civil society organizations in Afghanistan, Palestine, Colombia, Guatemala, the Democratic Republic of Congo, Burundi, northeast India and elsewhere. She has extensive experience in post-conflict reconstruction; facilitating multi-stakeholder processes at national, regional and international levels; and partnership development. Akinyi has a B.A. in sociology and political science from the University of Ghana (Legon) and a postgraduate diploma in governance and political transformation from the University of Free State Bloemfontein, South Africa.

Stephanie Wolters is the head of the Peace and Security Research program at the Institute for Security Studies (ISS). Her research focuses on political and conflict dynamics in the Great Lakes region, elites and political change, and the crisis in Zimbabwe. Prior to joining ISS, Stephanie conducted conflict analysis for the International Finance Corporation's Conflict Affected States in Africa program, focusing on the private sector and conflict across Africa, and she was the political economy focal point for the World Bank team's Country Economic Memorandum in the Democratic Republic of Congo. Stephanie has worked in over 30 African countries as a researcher and journalist for the BBC, Reuters, the Economist Intelligence Unit, Swisspeace, the Institute for War and Peace Reporting and others. She was the *Mail & Guardian's* Africa editor from 2006 to 2009 and the editor in chief of Radio Okapi from 2001 to 2003. She has published widely on conflict dynamics in Africa and led numerous media projects, including First TV,

Zimbabwe's first independent television station. Stephanie holds an M.A. in African Studies from the Johns Hopkins University, School of Advanced International Studies.

Gilles Olakounlé Yabi, a political analyst and economist, spent seven years as senior political analyst and later as project director for the West Africa Project of the International Crisis Group, a think tank dedicated to conflict prevention and resolution. Holding a Ph.D. in economics from the University of Clermont-Ferrand in France, Gilles also worked as a journalist for the weekly magazine *Jeune Afrique*. After leaving International Crisis Group in November 2013, Gilles has been working as an independent consultant in the fields of conflict analysis, security and political governance in west Africa. He also publishes articles and editorials on his blog: *Le Blog de Gilles Yabi*. In December 2014, he created WATHI, a participative and multidisciplinary citizen-focused think tank on west African crucial issues.

I William Zartman is the Jacob Blaustein Distinguished Professor Emeritus at the Nitze School of Advanced International Studies of The Johns Hopkins University in Washington, DC, and member of the Steering Committee of the Processes of International Negotiation Program at Clingendael, Netherlands. He has been a distinguished fellow of the USIP, and of the Woodrow Wilson Center for International Scholars, Olin Professor at the US Naval Academy, Elie Halévy Professor at Sciences Po in Paris, and holder of the Bernheim Chair at the Free University of Brussels, and received a lifetime achievement award from the International Association for Conflict Management, as well as distinguished career awards from CIGI and the Peace Section of the International Studies Association. He was also president of the Tangier American Legation Institute for Moroccan Studies, founding president of the American Institute for Maghrib Studies and president of the

Middle East Studies Association. His doctorate is from Yale (1956) and his honorary doctorate from Louvain (1997).

He is the author and editor of such books as *Preventing Deadly Conflict* (2015); *Arab Spring: Negotiating in the Shadow of the Intifadat* (2016); *The Global Power of Talk* (2012, with Fen Osler Hampson); *Negotiation and Conflict Management: Essays on Theory and Practice* (2010); *International Cooperation: The Extents and Limits of Multilateralism* (2010); *Engaging Extremists: Trade-offs, Timing and Diplomacy* (2010); *Negotiating with Terrorists: Strategy, Tactics, and Politics* (2006); *Cowardly Lions: Missed Opportunities to Prevent Deadly Conflict and State Collapse* (2005); *Rethinking the Economics of War: The Intersection of Need, Creed and Greed* (2005); *Escalation and Negotiation in International Conflicts* (2005); and *Ripe for Resolution* (1989).

Index

A